# Communications in Computer and Information Science 2950

Series Editors

**Rationale**

The CCIS series is devoted to the publication of proceedings of computer science conferences. Its aim is to efficiently disseminate original research results in informatics in printed and electronic form. While the focus is on publication of peer-reviewed full papers presenting mature work, inclusion of reviewed short papers reporting on work in progress is welcome, too. Besides globally relevant meetings with internationally representative program committees guaranteeing a strict peer-reviewing and paper selection process, conferences run by societies or of high regional or national relevance are also considered for publication.

**Topics**

The topical scope of CCIS spans the entire spectrum of informatics ranging from foundational topics in the theory of computing to information and communications science and technology and a broad variety of interdisciplinary application fields.

**Information for Volume Editors and Authors**

Publication in CCIS is free of charge. No royalties are paid, however, we offer registered conference participants temporary free access to the online version of the conference proceedings on SpringerLink (http://link.springer.com) by means of an http referrer from the conference website and/or a number of complimentary printed copies, as specified in the official acceptance email of the event.

CCIS proceedings can be published in time for distribution at conferences or as post-proceedings, and delivered in the form of printed books and/or electronically as USBs and/or e-content licenses for accessing proceedings at SpringerLink. Furthermore, CCIS proceedings are included in the CCIS electronic book series hosted in the SpringerLink digital library at http://link.springer.com/bookseries/7899. Conferences publishing in CCIS are allowed to use our online conference service (Meteor) for managing the whole proceedings lifecycle (from submission and reviewing to preparing for publication) free of charge.

**Publication process**

The language of publication is exclusively English. Authors publishing in CCIS have to sign the Springer CCIS copyright transfer form, however, they are free to use their material published in CCIS for substantially changed, more elaborate subsequent publications elsewhere. For the preparation of the camera-ready papers/files, authors have to strictly adhere to the Springer CCIS Authors' Instructions and are strongly encouraged to use the CCIS LaTeX style files or templates.

**Abstracting/Indexing**

CCIS is abstracted/indexed in DBLP, Google Scholar, EI-Compendex, Mathematical Reviews, SCImago, Scopus. CCIS volumes are also submitted for the inclusion in ISI Proceedings.

**How to start**

To start the evaluation of your proposal for inclusion in the CCIS series, please send an e-mail to ccis@springer.com

Tai Tan Mai · Allie Ly-Duyen Tran · Lily Zhang ·
Luca Rossetto · Hyowon Lee · Gerard Marks ·
Liting Zhou · Alice Dajung Jung · Ellen Rushe ·
Tomas Ward · Cathal Gurrin
Editors

# Artificial Intelligence and Cognitive Science

## 33rd Irish Conference, AICS 2025
## Dublin, Ireland, December 1–2, 2025
## Revised Selected Papers

Springer

*Editors*
Tai Tan Mai
Dublin City University
Dublin, Ireland

Lily Zhang
Dublin City University
Dublin, Ireland

Hyowon Lee
Dublin City University
Dublin, Ireland

Liting Zhou
Dublin City University
Dublin, Ireland

Ellen Rushe
Dublin City University
Dublin, Ireland

Cathal Gurrin
Dublin City University
Dublin, Ireland

Allie Ly-Duyen Tran
Dublin City University
Dublin, Ireland

Luca Rossetto
Dublin City University
Dublin, Ireland

Gerard Marks
Dublin City University
Dublin, Ireland

Alice Dajung Jung
Dublin City University
Dublin, Ireland

Tomas Ward
Dublin City University
Dublin, Ireland

ISSN 1865-0929 ISSN 1865-0937 (electronic)
Communications in Computer and Information Science
ISBN 978-3-032-25808-3 ISBN 978-3-032-25809-0 (eBook)
https://doi.org/10.1007/978-3-032-25809-0



This Springer imprint is published by the registered company Springer Nature Switzerland AG
The registered company address is: Gewerbestrasse 11, 6330 Cham, Switzerland

# Preface

The 33rd International Conference on Artificial Intelligence and Cognitive Science (AICS 2025) was held in Dublin, Ireland, on December 1–2, 2025. The conference was hosted by Dublin City University (DCU) in collaboration with the Artificial Intelligence Association of Ireland (AIAI). AICS is the premier forum for the presentation and discussion of advances in artificial intelligence and cognitive science, bringing together researchers from academia, industry, and the public sector. Over the years, the conference has fostered a vibrant community around AI research and its applications, while providing a venue for both established researchers and early-career scholars to exchange ideas and present new findings.

AICS 2025 featured contributions on a wide range of topics in artificial intelligence and cognitive science. The accepted papers in this volume cover themes such as applications of AI, machine learning and deep learning methods, dataset construction and analysis, AI for social good, AI ethics and responsible AI, cognitive science and learning theory, and semantic web technologies. These contributions reflect both theoretical advances and practical applications of AI technologies in different domains.

The conference attracted strong international interest. In total, 122 submissions were received across all tracks, including 89 submissions to the Full Paper Track, 32 to the Student Paper Track, and one demonstration submission. Following a rigorous peer-review process, 33 papers were accepted for publication in the main proceedings, corresponding to an acceptance rate of approximately 36% within the track (26% overall). This volume includes 32 full papers and one demonstration paper.

In addition, 24 submissions from the Full Paper Track were accepted for publication as companion proceedings papers, which were published separately as a companion volume on Zenodo. The Student Paper Track received 32 submissions, of which 19 papers were accepted for publication in the companion proceedings.

All submissions underwent a double-blind peer-review process. Each paper was reviewed by at least three members of the Programme Committee, with many papers receiving four or five independent reviews. The Chairs of the Programme Committee carefully managed the review process to ensure fairness and quality. Conflicts of interest were handled through the conference management system by preventing reviewers from evaluating submissions from their own institutions or collaborators. Papers co-authored by committee members were handled independently to maintain the integrity of the evaluation process.

In addition to the technical paper sessions, AICS 2025 featured two invited keynote talks from leading researchers and industry practitioners. Mattia Fumagalli (Etsy) delivered the keynote "Generative AI in E-commerce: Applications and Challenges", presenting real-world applications of multimodal large language models in e-commerce, including content moderation, recommendation systems, and seller–buyer interaction tools. His talk highlighted how generative AI can drive both operational efficiency and improved user experience, while addressing challenges such as cold-start problems and policy compliance.

Mahnaz Arvaneh (University of Sheffield) presented the keynote "Using AI to Move Neurotechnology Out of the Lab", focusing on how artificial intelligence can enable practical, real-world deployment of brain–computer interfaces and rehabilitation technologies. Her presentation explored approaches such as transfer learning and generative models to reduce calibration effort and improve system reliability, ultimately supporting more accessible and user-centred neurotechnology in clinical and home environments.

The conference programme also featured several associated events that broadened the scope of the conference. A tutorial on "Introduction to Image Processing", delivered by Suzanne Little (Dublin City University) and provided through the CRT-AI programme introduced participants to the fundamentals of computer vision and image processing. The tutorial covered core concepts such as digital image representation, feature extraction, and basic neural network models for image classification using Google Colab notebooks. In addition, the AI in Medical Imaging Workshop, organised by the ADAPT Research Centre, brought together researchers, clinicians, and industry representatives to introduce current research, discuss real-world challenges, and explore opportunities for collaboration in medical imaging and MedTech.

The organisers would like to express their sincere gratitude to the members of the Program Committee and reviewers, whose careful evaluations and constructive feedback ensured the high quality of the technical programme. We also thank the authors for submitting their work and for contributing to the success of the conference. Finally, we acknowledge the support of Dublin City University, the Artificial Intelligence Association of Ireland, and the wider AI research community for their continued support of the AICS conference series.

We hope that the contributions collected in this volume will stimulate further research and collaboration within the AI and cognitive science communities.

December 2025

Tai Tan Mai
Allie Ly-Duyen Tran
Lily Zhang
Luca Rossetto
Hyowon Lee
Gerard Marks
Liting Zhou
Alice Dajung Jung
Ellen Rushe
Tomas Ward
Cathal Gurrin

# Organization

## General Chairs

| | |
|---|---|
| Cathal Gurrin | Dublin City University, Ireland |
| Tomas Ward | Dublin City University, Ireland |
| Ellen Rushe | Dublin City University, Ireland |

## Technical Program Committee Chairs

| | |
|---|---|
| Tai Tan Mai | Dublin City University, Ireland |
| Allie Ly-Duyen Tran | Dublin City University, Ireland |
| Lily Zhang | Dublin City University, Ireland |

## Program Coordinator

| | |
|---|---|
| Luca Rossetto | Dublin City University, Ireland |

## Track Chairs

| | |
|---|---|
| Hyowon Lee | Dublin City University, Ireland |
| Gerard Marks | Dublin City University, Ireland |
| Liting Zhou | Dublin City University, Ireland |

## Program Operations

| | |
|---|---|
| Alice Dajung Jung | Dublin City University, Ireland |

## Program Committee

| | |
|---|---|
| Kolawole Adebayo | ADAPT Centre, Maynooth University, Ireland |
| Kashif Ahmad | Munster Technological University, Cork, Ireland |
| Mansoor Ahmed | Maynooth University, Ireland |
| Naushad Alam | Dublin City University, Ireland |

| | |
|---|---|
| Deng Li | Lappeenranta-Lahti University of Technology, Finland |
| Jiaxi Li | University of Surrey, UK |
| Shuyan Li | Queen's University Belfast, UK |
| Tai Tan Mai | Dublin City University, Ireland |
| Brian Mac Namee | University College Dublin, Ireland |
| Mahsa Mahdinejad | Trinity College Dublin, Ireland |
| Gerard Marks | Dublin City University, Ireland |
| John P. McCrae | University of Galway, Ireland |
| Ian McLoughlin | Atlantic Technological University, Ireland |
| Aidan Meade | Technological University Dublin, Ireland |
| Jean Mélou | FittingBox / IRIT, France |
| Vasileios Mezaris | CERTH, Greece |
| Paul Moran | Atlantic Technological University Letterkenny, Ireland |
| Aidan Murphy | University College Dublin, Ireland |
| An Nguyen | ADAPT, Dublin City University, Ireland |
| Matthias Nickles | University of Galway, Ireland |
| Tu Ninh Van | Optum, Ireland |
| Diarmuid O'Donoghue | Maynooth University, Ireland |
| Ruairi O'Reilly | Munster Technological University, Ireland |
| Colm O'Riordan | University of Galway, Ireland |
| Arjun Pakrashi | University College Dublin, Ireland |
| Giovanni Patanè | University of Catania, Italy |
| Tho Quan | Ho Chi Minh City University of Technology, Vietnam |
| Debbie Rankin | Ulster University, UK |
| Daniel Riordan | Munster Technological University, Ireland |
| Lucas Rizzo | Technological University Dublin, Ireland |
| Luca Rossetto | Dublin City University, Ireland |
| Florian Ruosch | FPR Consulting, Switzerland |
| Ellen Rushe | Dublin City University, Ireland |
| Debora Russo | University of Naples Federico II, Italy |
| Jordi Sabater-Mir | IIIA-CSIC, Spain |
| Klaus Schöffmann | Klagenfurt University, Austria |
| Bianca Schoen-Phelan | Technological University Dublin, Ireland |
| Heiko Schuldt | University of Basel, Switzerland |
| Niladri Sett | SRM University AP, India |
| Davoud Shariat Panah | University College Dublin, Ireland |
| Yueming Sun | Durham University, UK |
| Kata Szita | Dublin City University, Ireland |
| Joshua Tobin | PayPal, Ireland |

| | |
|---|---|
| Mohammed Amine Togou | Dublin City University, Ireland |
| Allie Tran | Dublin City University, Ireland |
| Quang-Linh Tran | Dublin City University, Ireland |
| Neil Vaughan | University of Exeter, UK |
| Nestor Velasco Bermeo | Experient, USA |
| Sowmya Vijayakumar | Technological University of the Shannon, Ireland |
| Trong Sinh Vu | Banking Academy of Vietnam, Vietnam |
| Hui-Yin Wu | Inria, France |
| Lin Wu | University of Glasgow, UK |
| Liang Xu | Dublin City University, Ireland |
| Songpei Xu | University of Glasgow, UK |
| Ziyang Yan | University of Trento, Italy |
| Xhemal Zenuni | South East European University, North Macedonia |
| Xiao Zhang | University of Groningen, The Netherlands |
| Rongzhen Zhao | Aalto University, Finland |
| Xinran Zheng | University College London, UK |
| Liting Zhou | Dublin City University, Ireland |
| Tianxing Zhou | University College London, UK |
| Xuemei Zhou | CWI & TU Delft, The Netherlands |

## Additional Reviewers

Dung Dao
Thao-Nhu Nguyen
Anastasiia Potyagalova
Mai Boi Quach
Le Lai
Bao Le
Khoi Pham

# Contents

# Architecture-Dependent Synthetic Data Strategies for Leukemia Diagnosis with Explainable Deep Learning

Ibrahim Malik[1](✉) and Bharat Agarwal[2]

[1] School of Computing, National College of Ireland, Dublin D01 K6W2, Ireland
malikib@tcd.ie

[2] Dublin City University, Dublin, Ireland
bharat.agarwal@insight-centre.org

**Abstract.** Deep learning for leukemia diagnosis via blood smear microscopy faces data scarcity and interpretability challenges. We demonstrate that optimal synthetic data generation is architecture-dependent: evaluating three GAN variants (DCGAN, WGAN, cGAN) across CNN, Vision Transformer, and Hybrid CNN-ViT architectures on the C-NMC dataset reveals distinct preferences. CNNs achieve best performance with cGAN augmentation (71% accuracy), ViTs excel with WGAN data (74% accuracy, 0.50 sensitivity), while Hybrid models achieve highest accuracy (80%) but only with DCGAN, exhibiting extreme sensitivity to GAN choice with 33% accuracy variation.

For clinical screenings that require prioritizing the reduction of false negatives, ViT-WGAN provides the best performance-robustness trade-off at a sensitivity improvement of 167% (0.187→0.500). Multi-method XAI validation using Grad-CAM, SHAP, and LIME on identical test images confirms convergent attention towards clinically relevant morphological features, including cell boundaries and nuclear irregularities. This challenges conventional single-GAN-for-all approaches, demonstrating synthetic data strategies must be co-designed with target architectures for medical AI deployment.

**Keywords:** Leukemia Diagnosis · GANs · Vision Transformers · Explainable AI · Medical AI

## 1 Introduction

Leukemia detection using microscopic examination of blood smears remains challenging due to inter-observer variability among pathologists [13, 18, 21], with diagnostic concordance rates ranging from 65–85% for some leukemia subtypes. Precise and early detection is critical for patient prognosis and treatment planning [4, 24], driving interest in AI-assisted diagnostic systems.

Deep learning methods, especially CNNs and ViTs, have demonstrated exceptional results in various medical imaging tasks [20, 21]. However, two major obstacles have prevented their clinical adoption: (a) limited availability of blood-smear


T. T. Mai et al. (Eds.): AICS 2025, CCIS 2950, pp. 1–14, 2026.
https://doi.org/10.1007/978-3-032-25809-0_1

data with proper annotation, coupled with class imbalance between samples, and (b) lack of model interpretability, given that black-box model predictions may undermine clinician confidence in decisions. GANs alleviate data-related issues by generating synthetic images with high quality, while XAI provides model interpretability by visualizing model decision-making processes.

This work integrates GAN-based augmentation with multiple architectures (CNN, ViT, Hybrid) and multi-method XAI to achieve diagnostic accuracy with clinical interpretability. We systematically evaluate how GAN variants interact with specific architectures—addressing a gap where existing medical AI assumes uniform synthetic data strategies.

**Research Question:** How do different GAN-based synthetic data generation methods interact with specific neural network architectures (CNNs vs. Vision Transformers vs. Hybrid models) in medical image classification, and what implications does this have for clinical deployment?

**Key contributions:**

1. Demonstration that optimal GAN variants are architecture-dependent
2. Systematic comparison of 3 GAN architectures (DCGAN, WGAN, cGAN) for medical image synthesis, evaluated on both image quality metrics and downstream classification performance across architectures
3. Multi-method XAI convergent validation (Grad-CAM, SHAP, LIME) confirming models learn clinically relevant morphological features rather than spurious correlations

Section 2 surveys related work, Sect. 3 describes our methodology, Sect. 4 presents results/discussion, and Sect. 5 concludes with future directions.

## 2 Related Work

### 2.1 Deep Learning in Leukemia Detection

CNNs have driven early leukemic cell classification based on blood smear images. An accuracy of 94% was claimed by Giammarco et al. [10] for CNN ensembles based on CAM explanations. Vision Transformers employ self-attention mechanisms for global views. A high accuracy of 99.96% was attained by Nunna et al. [17] using ViT-CNN fusion. ViT advantages for explanation were explored by Almenwer et al. [1]. Hybrid CNN-ViT architectures integrate global and local views. An accuracy of 99% was attained by Raghaw et al. [20] by introducing the CoTCoNet model along with an increase in computational cost. Previous research has not investigated how different synthetic data generation methods interact with specific architecture designs—a gap our research aims to fill.

### 2.2 Generative AI and Synthetic Data

Data sparsity and class imbalance are pervasive challenges in medical imaging, with class imbalance hampering outlier detection and negatively affecting classification performance [7,12]. GANs have demonstrated ability to generate realistic images of blood cells, data augmentation of training sets, and improving model performance [3,7]. Traditional GANs are afflicted by mode collapse, which reduces dataset diversity [11]. 3 GAN variants address these weaknesses in different manners. DCGANs employ convolutional layers for higher-resolutions of medical images, and accuracy rises from 96.2% to 98.94% when using leukocyte images produced by DCGAN as per Raghaw et al. [20]. WGANs stabilize training through Earth Mover's distance optimization with more varied outputs for leukemia subtypes [6,22], though with increased computation [5]. Conditional GANs support class-specific generation with precise control of balancing classes.

Recent advances in diffusion probabilistic models (DDPMs, Stable Diffusion) have shown promise for high-fidelity medical image synthesis [14,16]. Diffusion models offer advantages in stability and quality [16], however, require substantially higher computational cost (10–100× training/inference times) that limits clinical feasibility compared to GANs [14]. We focus on GAN variants due to their established efficiency, extensive validation in medical imaging, and practical deployment considerations for resource-constrained clinical settings.

With benefits, clinical AI systems pose ethical issues like potential data breach and diagnostic accountability in the event that models based on simulated data make errors [3,5]. Notably, prior work failed to extensively contrast performance of these GAN variants over different neural architectures, our main contribution uncovering architecture-sensitive GAN performance.

### 2.3 Explainable AI in Medical Diagnostics

Model interpretability is a precondition for clinical AI adoption, as black-box predictions erode clinician trust despite high accuracy [6]. 3 key XAI approaches address this challenge with different strengths and limitations. Grad-CAM generates visual heatmaps of decision-relevant regions. Giammarco et al. [10] used Grad-CAM for blood smear interpretation, building clinician trust by revealing morphological features driving misclassifications. However, reliance on spatial feature maps limits application to transformer architectures [8]. SHAP provides model-agnostic global feature importance through Shapley values. Inturu et al. [11] applied SHAP on CNN-ViT leukemia diagnosis, showing key diagnostic factors. Although offering fine attributions, SHAP's computational cost limits clinical deployment for high-dimensional medical images. LIME offers faster local explanations through input perturbation and surrogate model fitting, applicable to any architecture. However, Deshpande et al. [6] demonstrated the existence of instability problems in producing diverse explanations for similar blood cell samples—unwanted for diagnostic consistency.

Current studies typically apply single XAI methods post-hoc [1,10,20,22], which often provide misleading information about model behavior with poor fidelity to actual decision-making processes [9,23]. Single-method approaches suffer from methodological blind spots: Grad-CAM may highlight spurious correlations, SHAP's approximations achieve only 30–40% fidelity in medical imaging [23], and LIME exhibits instability across similar inputs. Without convergent validation across multiple XAI methods, clinical stakeholders cannot distinguish genuine learned features from method-specific artifacts. Our multi-method XAI approach addresses this gap by validating clinical relevance through convergence across Grad-CAM, SHAP, and LIME, providing stronger evidence of morphologically relevant feature learning than single-method analysis.

### 2.4 Research Gaps

Despite advances in AI-driven leukemia identification, critical gaps prevent clinical adoption. Data scarcity and class imbalance remain pervasive [7,12], with public datasets lacking stain protocol diversity [11]. While GANs address this through synthetic generation, prior work applies uniform augmentation strategies without investigating architecture-dependent effectiveness. Additionally, XAI approaches that are single-method suffer from poor fidelity and methodological blind spots [9,23], limiting clinical trust. Generalizability of models also remains with limited—architectures performing well on controlled datasets experience degraded performance under clinical distributional shifts [20].

Our study addresses these gaps by: (1) comparing GAN-based augmentation across 3 architectures (CNN, ViT, Hybrid), revealing architecture-dependent optimal strategies with CNNs achieving best performance with cGAN data while ViTs benefit from WGAN's structural diversity; and (2) validating clinical feature learning through convergent multi-method XAI analysis. This challenges assumptions of universal augmentation strategies and establishes architecture-aware data generation as critical for medical AI development.

## 3 Methodology

### 3.1 Dataset and Preprocessing

We used the C-NMC leukemia dataset containing high-resolution blood smear images of pediatric patients with expert labels. Images were resized to $224 \times 224$ pixels and scaled to $[0, 1]$ range. Standard augmentations (random horizontal/vertical flipping, rotation 0–360°, zoom ±15%) were selected to simulate natural variations in microscopy imaging without introducing morphologically unrealistic transformations that could compromise structure interpretation.

**Dataset Structure and Class Distribution:** The dataset was divided into training and validation sets, with the distribution as shown in Table 1.

In the dataset, the cancer cell is outnumbered by normal cell images by 2.15:1 in the training samples. This can pose as a problem in terms of biasing the classes during classification: when creating the model to classify normal cells, sensitivity will be low because of biased classes. To counter these problems, 3,883 normal cell images were created using the GAN variant.

We evaluate generated images using Fréchet Inception Distance (FID) and Structural Similarity Index Measure (SSIM). FID measures distributional similarity between real and synthetic images using Inception network features, with

**Table 1.** Dataset Class Distribution and Synthetic Data Generation Strategy.

| Class | Training Set | Validation Set |
|---|---|---|
| Normal Cells | 3,389 | 648 |
| Cancer Cells | 7,272 | 1,219 |
| Synthetic (Generated) | 3,883 | - |

lower values indicating higher quality (range: 0–$\infty$). SSIM quantifies perceptual similarity at the pixel level (range: 0–1, higher is better). This combination assesses both statistical fidelity (FID) and perceptual quality (SSIM), addressing limitations of single-metric evaluation [2, 7, 10]. For classification evaluation, we report accuracy, F1-score, AUC-ROC, sensitivity, and precision, prioritizing sensitivity given clinical importance of minimizing false negatives in screening.

**Training Pipeline:** Our experimental pipeline follows a sequential approach: **Stage 1 - GAN Training:** Each GAN variant (DCGAN, WGAN, cGAN) was trained independently on the training set to generate synthetic cell images. **Stage 2 - Classification Training:** Synthetic images were combined with real training data to create augmented datasets. Deep learning architectures were then trained separately on each augmented dataset. Models were validated on held-out validation set. **Stage 3 - XAI Analysis:** After classification model training, XAI methods (Grad-CAM, SHAP, LIME) were applied post-hoc to interpret trained model predictions on test images.

## 3.2 Model Architectures

**Generative Adversarial Networks:** We employed 3 GANs for synthetic data generation. Deep Convolutional GAN (DCGANs) [19] use convolutional architectures for stable image generation. The generator uses dense-to-7×7 projection and transposed convolutions upsampling to 224 × 224, while training used 225 epochs, batch size 32, with Adam optimizers (generator lr = 0.0001, discriminator lr = 0.0002). Wasserstein GAN (WGANs) [2] uses Earth-Mover distance for improved training stability and mode collapse avoidance. Gradient penalty ($\lambda$gp = 10) was used to enforce Lipschitz constraints with training 200 epochs, 5:1 critic-to-generator update ratio and Adam optimization (lr = 0.0001). Conditional GAN (cGANs) [15] enables class-specific generation by conditioning on class-specific binary labels. Generator noise input is combined with one-hot labels, and discriminator input is image and labels. Training used 250 epochs with class-specific Adam optimization rates.

All variants used TensorFlow/Keras with tf.GradientTape for alternating updates [25], following standard hyperparameters from original papers.

**Convolutional Neural Network (CNN) Architecture:** The CNN performs binary classification with 3 hierarchical feature extraction convolutional blocks.

Each employs 3×3 kernels (32, 64, 128 filters respectively) with ReLU activation and "same" padding, followed by 2×2 max-pooling for spatial downsampling.

After final pooling, features are flattened and processed through BatchNormalization, a Dense layer (128 units, ReLU), Dropout (0.5), and sigmoid output. Training is using binary cross-entropy loss and Adam optimizer (lr = 0.0001) with normal augmentation (rotations ±20°, shifts ±10%, zoom ±10%).

**Vision Transformers (ViTs):** Vision Transformers segment images into patches and employ self-attention for global context. Input images (224×224×3) are split into 16×16 patches (196 total), linearly embedded to 256 dimensions with a learnable [CLS] token and positional embeddings. We employ 4 encoder layers with multi-head self-attention (4 heads, d_k=64) and feed-forward networks (hidden sizes [512, 256]) with GELU activation. The final [CLS] token is fed to an MLP classifier for binary classification. Training used categorical cross-entropy loss, Adam optimizer $lr = 10^{-4}$, batch size 32, with standard augmentation.

**Hybrid CNN–ViT Architecture:** Hybrid combines CNN local feature extraction with ViT global context modeling. The former uses 4 convolutional blocks (32, 64, 128, 256 filters) with global average pooling output of 256-dimensional features. The latter processes CNN feature maps (rather than raw pixels), sampling 16×16 patches (9 total) through 6 Transformer blocks. Both branches output 256-dimensional representations added element-wise. The fused features pass through MLP classifier (512→256 units, GELU) with sigmoid output. Training used binary cross-entropy loss and Adam optimization $lr = 10^{-4}$ (Fig. 1).

**Fig. 1.** Hybrid CNN-ViT Architecture.

**Explainable AI (XAI) Integration:** We employ convergent validation across 3 complementary XAI methods rather than single-method post-hoc analysis (suffers from poor fidelity and method-specific artifacts) [9,23]. Grad-CAM, SHAP, and LIME independently highlight similar morphological features on identical test images, providing stronger evidence of clinically relevant feature learning.

**Grad-CAM** localizes regions using gradient computations of class score maps, emphasizing regions critical to decision making. **SHAP** assigns importance values to predictions using Shapley values, emphasizing regions that highlight abnormal cell clustering. **LIME** uses Local Interpretable Model-agnostic

Explanation, localizing regions critical for decision making using the top 5 superpixels to emphasize medically critical regions.

# 4 Results

## 4.1 GAN-Based Synthetic Data Generation

We evaluated 3 GAN variants for synthetic generation using quantitative image quality metrics and visual inspection. Table 2 presents comparative results, with Fig. 2 showing representative synthetic samples alongside a real normal cell.

**Table 2.** Quantitative Metrics for GAN-Generated Blood-Smear Images

| Model | FID | $IS_{mean}$ | $IS_{std}$ | SSIM |
|---|---|---|---|---|
| DCGAN | 1.2745 | 1.000 | 0.000 | 0.8604 |
| WGAN | 2.9208 | 1.000 | 0.000 | 0.8685 |
| cGAN | 1.1897 | 1.000 | 0.000 | 0.8869 |

**Image Quality Metrics:** cGAN achieved best overall quality with lowest FID (1.1897) and highest SSIM (0.8869), followed by DCGAN (FID: 1.2745, SSIM: 0.8604) and WGAN (FID: 2.9208, SSIM: 0.8685). WGAN's FID was 2.5× higher than cGAN, indicating greater distributional divergence from real images. All models achieved IS of 1.0, reflecting limited applicability of ImageNet-trained Inception features to microscopy images as cellular structures are expected to exhibit low inter-sample variability.

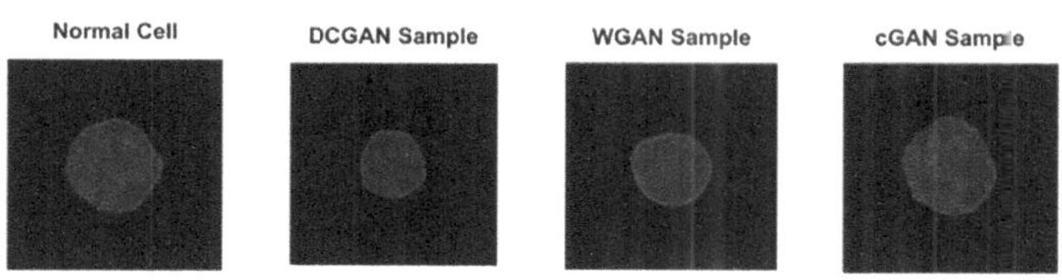


**Fig. 2.** Representative Synthetic Cell Images.

**Visual Quality Assessment:** Figure 2 reflects different generation characteristics. cGAN provides sharp cell boundaries with high-fidelity morphological detail and is similar to the reference normal cell. DCGAN produces structurally sound cells with moderate detail preservation. WGAN results show softer boundaries and a loss of fine-grained detail, which is consistent with its higher FID score. However, WGAN's training stability in terms of consistent convergence across runs implies advantages beyond pixel-level fidelity. Critically, these quality metrics do not predict downstream performance—as demonstrated in Sect. 4.2, architecture-specific responses to synthetic data quality diverge substantially from conventional quality-performance assumptions.

## 4.2 Architecture-Specific Classification Performance

**Baseline Performance Without Augmentation:** Table 3 presents baseline results on the unbalanced dataset without GAN augmentation. All architectures achieved similar moderate accuracy (0.69–0.70), but exhibited critically low sensitivity: CNN (0.194) and ViT (0.186) correctly identified fewer than 20% of leukemia cases. This severe false-negative rate reflects class imbalance bias, where models default to predicting the majority class. Hybrid architecture exhibited higher baseline sensitivity (0.508) but with reduced precision (0.57), suggesting different learning dynamics that warrant GAN-specific optimization.

**Table 3.** Baseline Performance on Unbalanced Dataset without GAN Augmentation

| Architecture | Accuracy | F1-Score | AUC | Sensitivity | Precision |
|---|---|---|---|---|---|
| CNN | 0.70 | 0.60 | 0.59 | 0.194 | 0.71 |
| ViT | 0.70 | 0.55 | 0.58 | 0.186 | 0.72 |
| Hybrid | 0.69 | 0.54 | 0.72 | 0.508 | 0.57 |

**Architecture-Dependent GAN Performance:** Table 4 reveals that optimal GAN variants are architecture-dependent, with performance varying substantially based on architecture-GAN pairing.

**Table 4.** Architecture-Specific GAN Performance

| Architecture | GAN | Accuracy | F1-Score | AUC | Sensitivity | Precision |
|---|---|---|---|---|---|---|
| CNN | DCGAN | 0.68 | 0.61 | 0.56 | 0.15 | 0.68 |
| CNN | WGAN | 0.70 | 0.63 | 0.58 | 0.21 | 0.72 |
| CNN | cGAN* | 0.71 | 0.65 | 0.60 | 0.27 | 0.72 |
| ViT | DCGAN | 0.68 | 0.67 | 0.63 | 0.48 | 0.67 |
| ViT | WGAN* | 0.74 | 0.73† | 0.68 | 0.50 | 0.73 |
| ViT | cGAN | 0.70 | 0.69 | 0.65 | 0.48 | 0.69 |
| Hybrid | DCGAN* | 0.80† | 0.69 | 0.85† | 0.63† | 0.76† |
| Hybrid | WGAN | 0.55 | 0.56 | 0.56 | 0.50 | 0.58 |
| Hybrid | cGAN | 0.47 | 0.47 | 0.51 | 0.62 | 0.55 |

* indicates best-performing GAN for that architecture.

† indicates overall best performance per metric.

*CNN Performance:* CNNs demonstrate predictable correlation between image quality and classification performance. Performance improves progressively with synthetic image fidelity: DCGAN (0.68 accuracy, 0.15 sensitivity), WGAN (0.70 accuracy, 0.21 sensitivity), and cGAN (0.71 accuracy, 0.27 sensitivity). The best-performing cGAN configuration aligns with its superior image quality metrics (FID: 1.1897, SSIM: 0.8869), suggesting CNNs benefit from pixel-level synthetic fidelity due to their spatial inductive bias and hierarchical feature learning. CNN-cGAN achieved 39% sensitivity improvement over baseline (0.194→0.27).

*ViT Performance:* Vision Transformers exhibit architecture-dependent GAN preferences that contradict image quality metrics. Despite WGAN producing lowest-quality images (FID: 2.9208—2.5× higher than cGAN), ViT-WGAN achieved best performance: 0.74 accuracy, 0.73 F1-score, 0.68 AUC, and 0.50 sensitivity. This represents a 169% sensitivity improvement over baseline (0.186→0.50), critical for reducing false negatives in clinical screening. ViT-cGAN underperformed (0.70 accuracy, 0.48 sensitivity) despite cGAN's superior image quality, suggesting ViTs leverage WGAN's training stability and structural diversity rather than pixel-perfect fidelity. This finding demonstrates that global self-attention mechanisms can transcend local synthetic artifacts that impair CNNs.

*Hybrid Architecture Performance:* The hybrid CNN-ViT models demonstrate extreme GAN-sensitivity with a 33-percentage-point accuracy range of 0.47–0.80, which constitutes the most dramatic result of our work. Hybrid-DCGAN achieved the overall highest performance: 0.80 accuracy, 0.85 AUC, 0.63 sensitivity, outperforming standalone architectures. However, performance collapses catastrophically with other GANs: WGAN yields 0.55 accuracy and cGAN 0.47 accuracy. This instability likely arises from competition between the optimization objectives of the convolutional spatial hierarchies, which favor cGAN, and attention mechanisms, which favor WGAN. DCGAN strikes a balance between them that allows hybrid training; any deviations cause the convergence to break. The sensitivity improvement of 24% (0.508→0.63) is well offset by the extreme GAN-sensitivity that raises clinical concerns on reliability.

### 4.3 Multi-method XAI Convergent Validation

To validate models learn clinically relevant features rather than spurious correlations, we applied 3 XAI methods (Grad-CAM, SHAP, LIME) to identical test images. Convergent attention patterns across methods provide stronger evidence of clinical interpretability than single-method analysis, addressing methodological blind spots inherent to individual XAI techniques [9,23].

**Leukemia Cell:** Figure 3 shows XAI analysis of a leukemia cell with high model confidence (0.998). All methods converge on cell boundary regions as primary diagnostic features. Grad-CAM generates strong activation heatmap (red/yellow

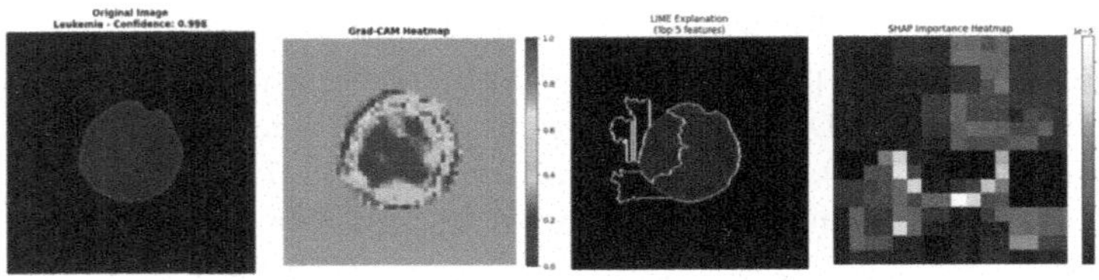


**Fig. 3.** XAI Convergent Validation on Leukemic Cell.

regions) concentrated at cell periphery, forming a characteristic "donut" pattern with high boundary activation and low interior activation. LIME identifies top-5 superpixels (yellow outlines) concentrated at cell boundaries, spatially overlapping with Grad-CAM's high-activation zones despite using fundamentally different methodology. SHAP assigns highest feature importance (red/white regions) to boundary areas, matching Grad-CAM's pattern despite using Shapley value decomposition rather than gradients. This convergent boundary focus aligns with clinical diagnostic patterns: hematologists examine cell membrane irregularities, nuclear-cytoplasmic ratio abnormalities, and chromatin patterns—manifest at cell boundaries [13,21].

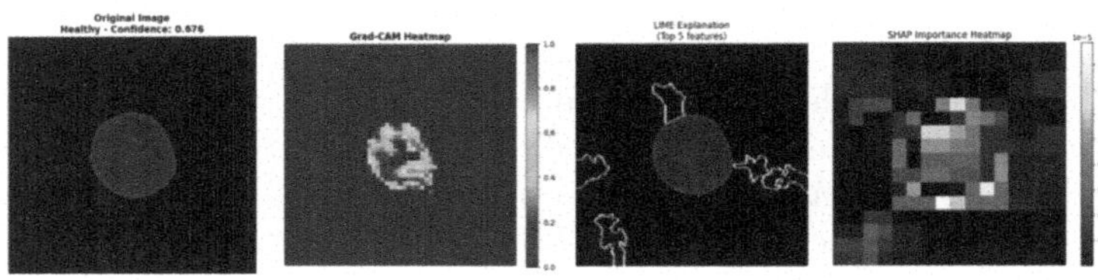


**Fig. 4.** XAI Convergent Validation on Healthy Cell.

**Healthy Cell:** Figure 4 shows XAI analysis of a healthy cell classified with moderate confidence (0.676). Unlike leukemia, all methods exhibit diffuse, low-intensity activation patterns. Grad-CAM produces predominantly blue (low activation) heatmap with small scattered activation regions. Notably absent is strong boundary activation observed in leukemia cells. LIME highlights scattered superpixels distributed across cell and periphery, contrasting with the concentrated boundary focus in leukemia cells. SHAP shows moderate, distributed importance without strong localization, with lower values than the leukemia case. The convergent absence of strong activation validates clinical expectations: healthy cells exhibit regular morphology without the nuclear irregularities, cytoplasmic changes, or membrane abnormalities that characterize leukemia [13].

**Interpretability Validation:** Multi-method XAI convergence strengthens clinical interpretability through agreement across gradient-based (Grad-CAM), perturbation based (LIME), and game-theoretic (SHAP) methods that provide stronger evidence than single-method analysis, mitigating method-specific artifacts [23]. Boundary-focused attention for leukemia cells matches pathologist diagnostic patterns [13, 21]. Diffuse patterns for healthy cells correctly reflect diagnosis by absence of pathology. Moreover, higher confidence for leukemia cells with strong convergent features versus moderate confidence for healthy cells with diffuse patterns demonstrates appropriate uncertainty quantification.

### 4.4 Discussion

**Medical AI Development and Clinical Deployment:** Architecture-dependent GAN performance challenges practices where developers select single generators based on image quality and apply uniformly. Our results show this is suboptimal: CNNs benefit from cGAN's pixel fidelity, ViTs leverage WGAN's structural diversity despite 2.5× worse FID, and Hybrid models exhibit 33% accuracy variation. These indicate that GANs should be matched to architectures based on inductive biases - convolutional hierarchies need pixel fidelity, while self-attention mechanisms leverage training stability.

The sensitivity improvement to 169% (0.186→0.50) addresses false-negative reduction, crucial for screening. However, sensitivity still remains low (0.50) compared with clinical threshold (>0.90) and would require multi-institutional validation and regulatory approval before deployment. Highest performance achieved by Hybrid-DCGAN of 0.80 exhibits extreme GAN-sensitivity; therefore, rigorous pipeline validation is required. ViT-WGAN provides more consistent performance with 0.74 accuracy, having already demonstrated robustness, and thus is suitable for applications where reliability outweighs marginal accuracy gains.

Hybrid CNN-ViT underperformance reflects conflicting optimization objectives: CNNs optimize for pixel patterns, favored by cGAN, while attention mechanisms would rather optimize for structural relationships, favored by WGAN. DCGAN's approach allows hybrid training, though deviations from that are disruptive for convergence. This calls for reevaluation in regard to assumptions that architectural complexity is a guarantee for improvements, and points out that practitioners should prioritize well-tuned standalone architectures.

**Limitations:** Limitations include single-institution C-NMC data, moderate absolute performance (accuracy range 0.47–0.80), absence of XAI validation by pathologist, and untested generalization of diffusion models. Main directions for further research include multi-institutional validation, comparison of diffusion models, multi-class leukemia subtyping, prospective clinical trials, and integration into foundation model. These findings position architecture-aware synthetic data generation as a crucial element in medical AI burdened with data scarcity.

## 5 Conclusion

This work shows optimal data generation for medical image classification is architecture-dependent and so challenges uniform augmentation strategies. CNNs perform best with cGAN at 0.71 accuracy, while ViTs perform best with WGAN despite low image quality, with 0.74 accuracy and 0.50 sensitivity. Hybrid models show high GAN-sensitivity, up to 33%. Synthetic data strategies should be codesigned with the target architectures instead of independently optimized.

The ViT-WGAN sensitivity enhancement of 169% implies a reduction in number of false negatives despite moderate absolute performance. Convergent validation by different methods in XAI (Grad-CAM, SHAP, LIME) proves models learn clinically relevant morphological features: boundary irregularities in leukemia cells and diffuse patterns in healthy cells, an approach that provides better evidence for interpretability than using a single method.

Future work should proceed with multi-institutional validation, diffusion model comparison, prospective clinical trials, and integration of foundation models toward privacy-preserving systems. This study positions architecture-aware synthetic data generation as an essential bedrock for the development of medical AI, whose implications will go beyond into areas other than leukemia diagnosis to a whole range of clinical applications suffering from data scarcity.

## References

1. Almenwer, S.: Early Detection of Pleuropulmonary Blastoma Using Vision Transformers Models. Proquest dissertations & theses, Bowie State University (2024)
2. Arjovsky, M., Chintala, S., Bottou, L.: Wasserstein generative adversarial networks. In: Proceedings of the 34th International Conference on Machine Learning (ICML), pp. 214–223. PMLR (2017)
3. Bansal, V., Jain, A., Kaur Walia, N.: Diabetic retinopathy detection through generative ai techniques: A review. Results Opt. **16**, 100700 (2024). https://doi.org/10.1016/j.rio.2024.100700, https://www.sciencedirect.com/science/article/pii/S266695012400097X
4. Bio, M.: Life expectancy for acute lymphoblastic leukemia (2025). https://massivebio.com/life-expectancy-for-acute-lymphoblastic-leukemia/. Accessed 12 Nov 2025
5. Chataut, S., Bhatta, S., Dahal, B., Ojha, G., Subedi, B., Bastakoti, B.: Advancements and applications of generative ai in healthcare. Eur. J. Theor. Appl. Sci. **2**(6), 1–5 (2024). https://doi.org/10.59324/ejtas.2024.2(6).xx
6. Deshpande, N.M., Gite, S., Pradhan, B.: Unlocking the Potential: Machine Learning and Deep Learning in Leukemia Diagnosis with Explainable AI, pp. 201–258. Springer, Cham (2024). https://doi.org/10.1007/978-3-031-68602-3_12
7. Gao, L., Zhang, L., Liu, C., Wu, S.: Handling imbalanced medical image data: a deep-learning-based one-class classification approach. Artif. Intell. Med. **108**, 101935 (2020). https://doi.org/10.1016/j.artmed.2020.101935
8. Genovese, A., Piuri, V., Scotti, F.: A decision support system for acute lymphoblastic leukemia detection based on explainable artificial intelligence. Image Vis. Comput. **151**, 105298 (2024). https://doi.org/10.1016/j.imavis.2024.105298, https://www.sciencedirect.com/science/article/pii/S0262885624004037

9. Ghassemi, M., Oakden-Rayner, L., Beam, A.L.: The false hope of current approaches to explainable artificial intelligence in health care. Lancet Digital Health **3**(11), e745–e750 (2021). https://doi.org/10.1016/S2589-7500(21)00208-9
10. Giammarco, M.D., et al.: Reliable leukemia diagnosis and localization through explainable deep learning. In: 2024 Fifth International Conference on Intelligent Data Science Technologies and Applications (IDSTA), pp. 68–75 (2024). https://doi.org/10.1109/IDSTA62194.2024.10746935
11. Inturu, C., Cirigiri, S., Sankar, H.: Advanced deep learning for white blood cell classification: A hybrid and interpretable approach. Int. Res. J. Modernization Eng. Technol. Sci. (2024). https://doi.org/10.56726/IRJMETS64525
12. Johnson, J.M., Khoshgoftaar, T.M.: Survey on deep learning with class imbalance. Journal of Big Data **6**(1), 1–54 (2019). https://doi.org/10.1186/s40537-019-0192-5
13. Kasim, S., et al.: Multiclass leukemia cell classification using hybrid deep learning and machine learning with CNN-based feature extraction. Sci. Rep. **15**(1), 23782 (2025). https://doi.org/10.1038/s41598-025-05585-x
14. Khader, F., et al.: Denoising diffusion probabilistic models for 3d medical image generation. Sci. Rep. **13**(1), 7303 (2023). https://doi.org/10.1038/s41598-023-34341-2
15. Mirza, M., Osindero, S.: Conditional generative adversarial nets. arXiv preprint arXiv:1411.1784 (2014). https://arxiv.org/abs/1411.1784
16. al Nomaan Nafi, A., Hossain, M.A., Rifat, R.H., Zaman, M.M.U., Ahsan, M.M., Raman, S.: Diffusion-based approaches in medical image generation and analysis (2024). https://arxiv.org/abs/2412.16860
17. Nunna, H.K., Altable, A., Gundala, P., Rangarajan, P.K.: Vista: vision transformer-attention enhanced CNN ensemble for optimized classification of acute lymphoblastic leukemia benign and progressive malignant stages. Int. J. Inf. Technol. (2024). https://doi.org/10.1007/s41870-024-02126-z
18. Park, S., Park, Y.H., Huh, J., Baik, S.M., Park, D.J.: Deep learning model for differentiating acute myeloid and lymphoblastic leukemia in peripheral blood cell images via myeloblast and lymphoblast classification. Digital Health **10**, 20552076241258080 (2024). https://doi.org/10.1177/20552076241258079, eCollection 2024 Jan-Dec
19. Radford, A., Metz, L., Chintala, S.: Unsupervised representation learning with deep convolutional generative adversarial networks. arXiv preprint arXiv:1511.06434 (2016). https://arxiv.org/abs/1511.06434
20. Raghaw, C.S., Sharma, A., Bansal, S., Rehman, M.Z.U., Kumar, N.: Cotconet: an optimized coupled transformer-convolutional network with an adaptive graph reconstruction for leukemia detection. Comput. Biol. Med. **179**, 108821 (2024). https://doi.org/10.1016/j.compbiomed.2024.108821, https://www.sciencedirect.com/science/article/pii/S0010482524009065
21. Rastogi, P., Khanna, K., Singh, V.: Leufeatx: Deep learning-based feature extractor for the diagnosis of acute leukemia from microscopic images of peripheral blood smear. Comput. Biol. Med. **142**, 105236 (2022). https://doi.org/10.1016/j.compbiomed.2022.105236, https://www.sciencedirect.com/science/article/pii/S0010482522000282
22. Ravindran, U., Gunavathi, C.: Deep learning assisted cancer disease prediction from gene expression data using wt-gan. BMC Med. Inform. Decis. Mak. **24**(1), 311 (2024). https://doi.org/10.1186/s12911-024-02712-y

23. Singh, Y., et al.: Beyond post hoc explanations: A comprehensive framework for accountable ai in medical imaging through transparency, interpretability, and explainability. Bioengineering **12**(8) (2025). https://doi.org/10.3390/bioengineering12080879, https://www.mdpi.com/2306-5354/12/8/879
24. Society, A.C.: Early detection, diagnosis, and prognosis of childhood leukemia (2025), https://www.cancer.org/cancer/types/leukemia-in-children/detection-diagnosis-staging.html. Accessed 12 Nov 2025
25. TensorFlow: Deep convolutional generative adversarial network (dcgan). https://www.tensorflow.org/tutorials/generative/dcgan (2024), tensorFlow Tutorial

# AI-Generated Images: What Humans and Machines See When They Look at the Same Image

Silvia Poletti(✉), Justin Ilyes, Marcel Hasenbalg, David Fischinger, and Martin Boyer

Austrian Institute of Technology, Vienna, Austria
{silvia.poletti,justin.ilyes.fl,marcel.hasenbalg,david.fischinger,martin.boyer}@ait.ac.at

**Abstract.** The misuse of generative AI in online disinformation campaigns highlights the urgent need for transparent and explainable detection systems. In this work, we investigate how detectors for AI-generated images can be more effective in providing human-understandable explanations for their predictions. To this end, we develop a suite of detectors with various architectures and fine-tuning strategies, trained on our large-scale photorealistic fake image dataset, AIText2Image, and assess their performance on state-of-the-art text-to-image AI generators. We integrate 16 different explainable AI (XAI) methods into our detection framework, and the visual explanations are comprehensively refined and evaluated through a novel approach that prioritizes human understanding of AI-generated images, using both textual and visual responses collected from a survey of 100 participants. This framework offers insights into visual-language cues in fake image detection and into the clarity of XAI methods from a human perspective, measuring the alignment of XAI outputs with human preferences.

**Keywords:** XAI · Explainability · Human-understanding · Transfer learning · AI detection · AI-generated images · Computer vision · Fake news

## 1 Introduction

Photographs were once trusted as reliable evidence due to the technical difficulty of realistic manipulation, but today generative AI models allow to easily create fake images directly from a simple text prompt. The misuse of generative AI can influence democratic elections through fake news and defame individuals with deepfakes, causing significant societal disruptions. Notably, humans show limited ability to detect image tampering [32], and governments worldwide are currently developing laws and regulations to mitigate the negative impact of synthetic media on society, for example with the AI Act by EU. However, given the widespread accessibility of generative AI, legal frameworks alone cannot


T. T. Mai et al. (Eds.): AICS 2025, CCIS 2950, pp. 15–27, 2026.
https://doi.org/10.1007/978-3-032-25809-0_2

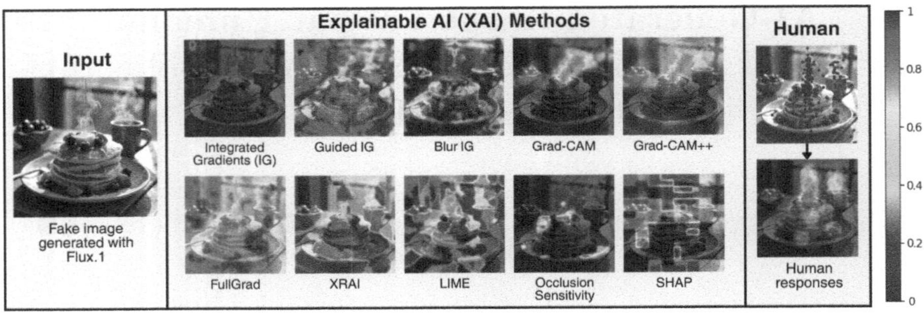


**Fig. 1.** Overview of visual explanations of the XAI methods when applied to the same AI detection model, and the visual explanation based on the survey's human responses. To reduce redundancy, XAI methods yielding visually comparable results are omitted.

prevent its harmful use, and technological safeguards such as AI-generated image detectors (hereafter referred to as AI detectors) must be developed in parallel. Since detectors typically output only a confidence score as prediction, they offer limited transparency of the decision-making process. Explainable AI (XAI) is then essential to clarify how and why a model classifies an image as fake.

To address the under-explored area of explainability in AI-generated image detection, this study makes the following contributions. We introduce AIText2Image, a large-scale dataset of photorealistic AI-generated images from modern text-to-image AI generators, and train detection models with multiple fine-tuning strategies, achieving robust accuracy in detecting outputs from modern text-to-image generators. We integrate 16 XAI methods into our framework, proposing a novel categorization based on the methods' visual features and prioritizing human preferences in their evaluation. To this aim, we investigate the alignment between image regions highlighted in the visual explanations and those indicated by 100 human participants in a user study. Importantly, participants are not merely asked to rate given explanations, but to provide their own. An illustrative example is in Fig. 1. Finally, we further analyze textual explanations in the context of multi-modal detection and explainability.

## 2 Related Work

As AI image generation advances, discerning real from synthetic images is proven to grow increasingly difficult [14]. According to Lu et al. [25], humans can correctly classify only 61% of images as real or synthetic, while state-of-the-art AI detectors largely surpass this performance, and therefore should serve as a tool to support human judgment. While prior studies have largely focused on humans' ability to detect AI-generated images, our work is the first to rigorously investigate through a user study how humans interpret and understand model predictions and reasoning, using widely adopted XAI techniques.

Model reasoning in fake image classification concerns different cues. Semantic-based detectors focus on physical inconsistencies or abnormalities [4], while spatial-based detectors consider the image domain and examine edges, textures or gradients [13, 24, 48]. Alternative approaches shift from the image domain and classify vector embeddings [33, 40] or expose the AI generator-specific fingerprints in the image's frequency domain [2, 27, 44], especially for detecting Generative Adversarial Networks (GANs) [45, 49]. This work focuses on human-understandable complex cues, thus mainly semantic and spatial, and does not consider AI generators leaving clearly detectable fingerprints, as this could bias the AI detectors to focus only on these low-level artifacts.

Bird and Lotfi [3] address the black box problem using the XAI method Grad-CAM [39], showing that only local patches of the image are considered to predict synthetic images. Our study further investigates which local image's areas are relevant for AI detection and extends beyond a single type of XAI method by integrating 16 different techniques and further analyzes the overlap between the obtained saliency maps and human expectations. Notably, research on human-AI collaboration has recently gained traction. Liu et al. [22] introduced HAG-XAI, a human attention–guided method that uses eye-tracking data to align saliency maps with human perception. However, fine-tuning well-established, pre-trained image classification models remains the overall simplest, while effective approach for detecting AI-generated images, as more complex architectures typically provide only limited improvements in accuracy and generalization [49]. In particular, Zhu et al. [49] and Dogoulis et al. [7] demonstrated ResNet-50 and CLIP-ViT backbones can achieve state-of-the-art results for the task.

## 3 Detection of AI-Generated Images

We examine two key aspects of explainability in AI detection models. First, **model architecture**: we assess explainability of convolutional layers in Convolutional Neural Networks (CNN) and self-attention layers in Visual Transformers (ViTs), using widely adopted backbone models to minimize the impact of specific model design choices and derive more universal XAI properties. Second, **fine-tuning strategy**: we start from models pre-trained on ImageNet [6] and implement four transfer learning approaches, each differing in the number of model's retrained layers.

**CNN Backbone.** We consider ResNet-50 [15] and distinguish ResNet50[fc] in which only the last fully connected layer is retrained, ResNet50[fc+l4] in which the fourth CNN block is additionally retrained, and then ResNet50[fc+l4+l3] in which all layers from the third CNN block onward are retrained.

**ViT Backbone.** We use ViT-B-16 [8] and retrain all model's parameters.

A total of 162k images from Microsoft COCO were used as natural samples during training, depicting objects in a realistic, cluttered environment and offering more complex scenarios than other datasets primarily intended for image classification. The **AIText2Image** training dataset includes 209k fake images from modern text-to-image AI generators that are among the most accessible, well-established, and widely used. Images are generated with engineered prompts covering a combination of subjects, locations, objects, image attributes and backgrounds. The generators are reported in Table 1 under the Train cluster, and the diversity of their output quality is essential to train detectors to be robust enough to variations of generative models.

**Table 1.** F1-scores of detection models across 13 image subsets. The number of images in each subset and the type of data (R for real and F for fake) is reported. All AI detectors are trained under the same early-stopping regime.

| | Microsoft COCO [21] | Midjourney 5.2 [28] | SDXL 0.9 [36] | SDXL 1.0 [36] | DALL-E 2 [34] | ImageNet100 [6] | Pascal-VOC2012 [11] | OpenImages-v7 [18] | Flux.1 [19] | Adobe Firefly [1] | Midjourney 5&6 [28,29] | DALL-E 3 [35] | GLIDE [31] | |
|---|---|---|---|---|---|---|---|---|---|---|---|---|---|---|
| | **Train** | | | | | **Evaluation** | | | | | | | | |
| | 162k | 132k | 17k | 52k | 9k | 10k | 10k | 10k | 6.5k | 1.1k | 7.5k | 1.2k | 1k | |
| | R | F | F | F | F | R | R | R | F | F | F | F | F | |
| **AI detectors** | **F1-score** | | | | | | | | | | | | | **Avg.** |
| ResNet50[fc] | 97.2 | 97.3 | 99.5 | 99.4 | 89.1 | 87.1 | 82.5 | 96.4 | 98.2 | 92.2 | **96.7** | **98.1** | 84.9 | 93.8 |
| ResNet50[fc+l4] | 99.7 | **99.8** | 99.8 | **100** | 97.1 | 97.0 | 92.4 | 99.4 | **98.8** | **96.4** | 87.4 | 92.1 | 86.2 | 95.9 |
| ResNet50[fc+l4+l3] | **99.8** | 99.4 | 99.5 | 99.8 | 93.7 | **99.2** | **96.6** | **99.6** | 95.8 | 79.0 | 89.5 | 96.2 | 74.8 | 94.1 |
| ViT-B-16 | 99.2 | 99.6 | **99.9** | 99.9 | **98.2** | 94.2 | 89.6 | 97.5 | 94.9 | 86.9 | 93.8 | 97.0 | **89.9** | 94.7 |

# 4 Model Explainability

We focus on 16 explainable AI (XAI) methods for image classification, which provide local visual explanations by highlighting parts of the input image that are relevant for the classifier's prediction. If an image correctly classified as fake, these explanations reveal the visual cues that the AI detector associates with synthetic content. We only consider post-hoc methods that preserve the classifier's performance and avoid model retraining [23].

Given an AI detector and an RGB input image $\mathbf{I} \in [0, 255]^{w \times h \times 3}$, an XAI method produces an output matrix $\mathbf{M} \in \mathbb{R}^{w \times h}$ in which higher values indicate greater importance of the corresponding input pixels for the AI detector's prediction. $\mathbf{M}' \in [0, 1]^{w \times h}$ is the normalized matrix and is referred to as XAI mask. Depending on the specific XAI method, the normalization requires one or more of the following operations: k-Means clustering, Gaussian kernel smoothing with Gaussian blur, Min-Max Scaling and Percentile scaling.

**Min-Max Scaling:**

$$\mathbf{M}' = \frac{\mathbf{M} - \min(\mathbf{M})}{\max(\mathbf{M}) - \min(\mathbf{M})}. \tag{1}$$

**Percentile Scaling:**

$$M'_{ij} = p_{ij} \quad such\ that \quad M_{ij} = Q_{p_{ij}}(\mathbf{M}) \quad \forall 1 \leq i \leq w,\ 1 \leq j \leq h \qquad (2)$$

where $0 \leq p_{ij} \leq 100$ and $Q_p$ is the $p$-th percentile operation.

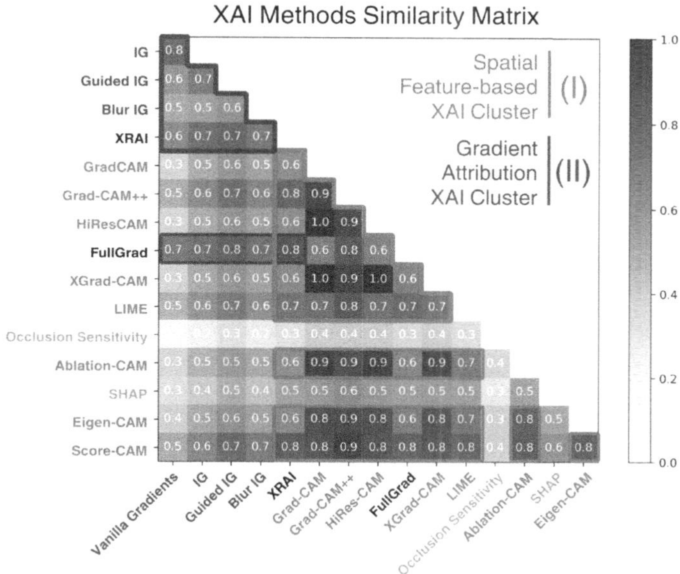


**Fig. 2.** XAI methods comparison based on the cosine similarity scores between pairs of XAI masks generated by different methods applied to the same AI detector, ResNet50[fc+l4]. Results for other detectors are comparable. The plot shows average scores computed over 100 images from AIText2Image, evenly distributed across the AI generators.

Liu et al. [22] categorize XAI methods solely based on their functioning, distinguishing between gradient-based methods using the classifier's gradients to compute feature importance, and perturbation-based methods evaluating changes in the model's output by altering the input features. Instead, we propose a novel categorization based on visual intra-similarity, indicating common discriminative features in the image domain (Fig. 2):

I. **Spatial Feature-based XAI Cluster**: Class Activation Mapping (CAM) XAI methods, namely Grad-CAM [39], Grad-CAM++ [5], HiResCAM [9], XGrad-CAM [12], Ablation-CAM [37], Eigen-CAM [30], Score-CAM [43] and FullGrad [41], exhibit scores consistently above or close to 0.8. LIME [38] also show a good similarity with CAM methods, since both capture spatial patterns: CAM captures them from the model's layers while LIME from the input image via segmentation.

II. **Gradient Attribution XAI Cluster**: Gradient-based XAI methods such as Vanilla Gradients [10], Integrated Gradients [42] (IG) and its variants, Guided IG [17] and Blur IG [46], have significant similarity. FullGrad is also similar to the three IG methods, as it is designed to capture gradient-based contributions across the network.

XRAI [16] belongs to both clusters, as it builds upon IG while also integrating spatial information through a gradient-based attention mechanism. In contrast, SHAP [26] and Occlusion Sensitivity [47] (OS) produce distinctly different XAI masks from the other methods, one featuring rectangular regions and the other sparse, scattered activation regions (see Fig. 1).

## 5 Human Study

Human perception of artifacts in AI-generated images is under-explored in literature. To address this, we use responses from a human survey to answer two key questions: *What visual cues do humans most associate with AI generation? How consistent are these with popular XAI Methods?* We submitted a survey to 100 candidates, required to be between 18 and 50 years old, and to be familiar with the internet and social media. Participants were shown fake images and asked to provide 1) a **visual response**, by indicating one or two points in the image they believed had traces of AI generation, and 2) a **textual response**, by writing a textual explanation for their choice. The survey instructions clarified that AI generation traces can be anything perceived as artificial, from textures or visual inconsistencies to elements that seem out of place in the image scene context. The survey includes 52 fake images from DALL-E 2, SDXL 1.0, Midjourney 5&6, and Flux.1, presenting diverse quality in terms of visual artifacts.

The experiments employ an image labeling system. Label **CONTEXT** (*Context is informative*) is assigned when AI generation can be inferred from contextual cues, such as floating objects defying gravity. The absence of this label implies that the image can be identified as AI-generated based solely on visual artifacts. Label **ENV** (*Visible environment*) indicates a discernible background, while its absence suggests an anonymous or heavily blurred background. Other labels are **ANIMAL** (*Visible animals*), **HUMAN** (*Human subject*), **HANDS** (*Visible hands*), **VIP** (*VIP subject*) assigned to images depicting recognizable individuals, **SOLO** (*Single human subject*), and **PORTRAIT** (*Human portrait*).

### 5.1 Analysis of Survey Visual Responses

For each survey image, a so-called human mask $\mathbf{H} \in [0,1]^{w \times h}$ is computed, as a result of the contributions of all the visual responses (i.e. points selected in the image) given by the participants for a picture $\mathbf{I} \in [0,255]^{w \times h \times 3}$. The mask is generated by increasing the matrix value by a constant factor $c > 0$ in a circular area of radius $R > 0$ centered around each point. Then, the mask is normalized

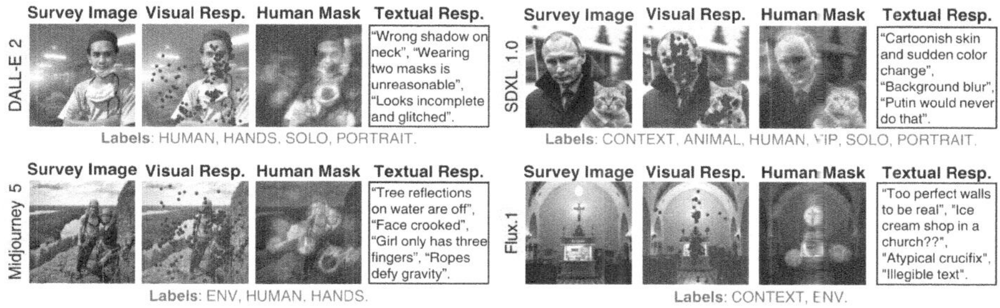


**Fig. 3.** Survey image examples from four different generators along with the participants' visual responses and corresponding human masks and assigned image labels. Due to space limitations, only a few textual responses are shown.

and the values are further skewed of a factor $\alpha > 0$ using exponential scaling. Examples of human masks are reported in Fig. 3 and Fig. 4.

Each XAI method $m_k$ provides a mask $\mathbf{M}_k \in [0,1]^{w \times h}$ of the input, representing the importance attributed to the image regions by the detector. The best-performing method $m_{k^*}$ should produce an XAI mask having highest similarity to the human mask, therefore providing the most human-understandable visual explanation. The faithfulness of the XAI methods, that is how accurately the explanations reflect the AI detector's decision-making process, has already been thoroughly established in the original publications of the methods. On the other hand, in this work our focus is specifically on human-centered plausibility – how well an explanation aligns with what humans perceive as meaningful.

Considering the cosine similarity $\mathcal{S}$, the optimal index $k^*$ and the highest similarity score $s^*$ are defined as:

$$k^* = \arg\max_k \mathcal{S}(\mathbf{H}, \mathbf{M}_k), \quad s^* = \max_k \mathcal{S}(\mathbf{H}, \mathbf{M}_k). \tag{3}$$

As shown in Fig. 4, the AI detectors clearly demonstrate varying compatibility with XAI methods. The highest similarity occurs in images without human subjects (**HUMAN(-)**), as they tend to absorb human attention, leading to human masks overall different from XAI masks. High similarity values are also obtained for Midjourney pictures, which present the highest level of realism in the dataset. In contrast, DALL-E 2 images lead to an overall lower similarity, indicating that for lower-quality outputs, as those produced by DALL-E 2, the most noticeable artifacts perceived by humans differ substantially from those detected by the models.

Figure 5 reports the changes in the fraction of survey responses where certain items were selected. For example, the human attention on the background decreases (i.e. the fraction of selected points in the background decreases) as it gets anonymous or heavily blurred (**ENV(-)**) or when a human subject is present (**HUMAN(+)**). The presence of a famous person (**VIP(+)**) moves the focus towards the human subject and, specifically, to their face. This happens also when there is only one human subject (**SOLO(+)**) present in the picture. When a human subject is selected (69.7% of the times), face and hands are the primary focus points, as they account for overall 62.3% of the selected items.

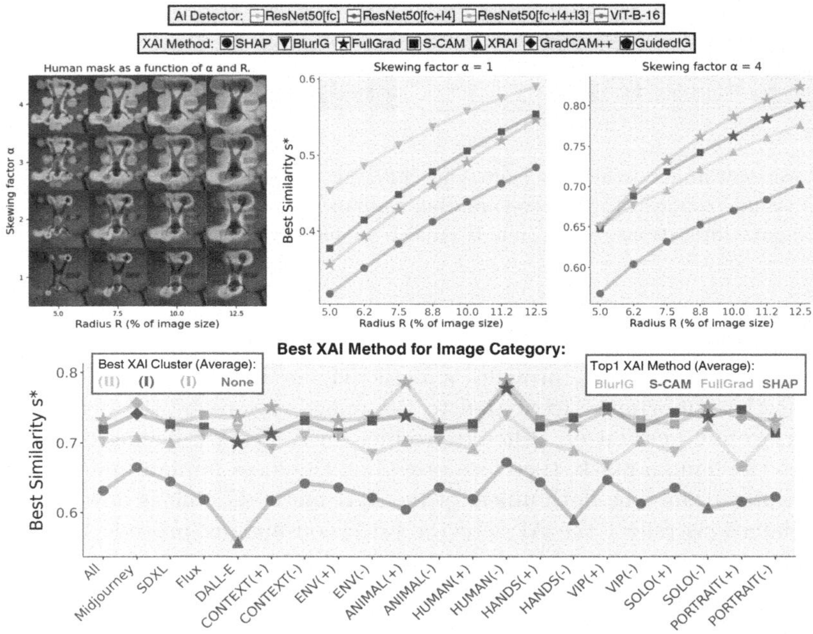


**Fig. 4.** First row: XAI methods achieving average optimal similarity $s^*$ across all the survey images for different AI detectors, evaluated for varying values of $R$ and $\alpha$ in the human mask. Second row: Best XAI methods by image category, for a fixed $R$ equal to 8.8% of the image size, and $\alpha = 3$, which are the values providing less bias towards the preference of one XAI method to another.

### 5.2 Analysis of Survey Textual Responses

There are two categories of survey textual responses: those referring to the image's visual quality and those reasoning about the realism of the image's content. The first includes the responses of people noticing (i) errors in the perspective, lights, and reflections; (ii) visual inconsistencies, as incomplete shapes or sudden color changes; (iii) errors in the texture, resolution, color and details; (iv) unnatural blurred background; (v) distortions and visual blend of multiple items. The second category is related to (vi) errors in shape, appearance and anatomy; (vii) lacking of imperfections; (viii) absence of physics; (ix) atypical content; (x) items presented in a novel, implausible design; (xi) atypical behavior

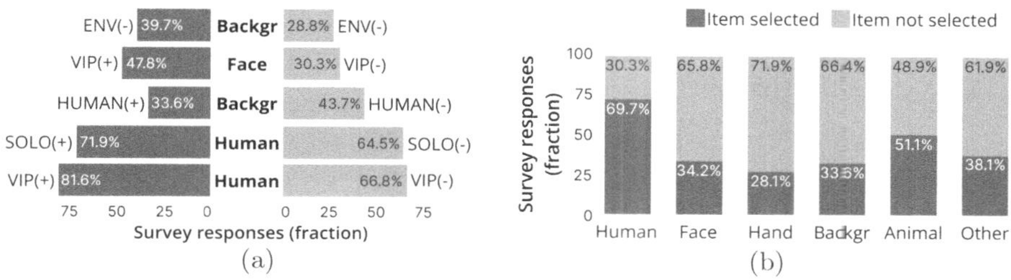


**Fig. 5.** (a) Each row represents a subset of images containing a specific item (Human, Face, or Background). Horizontal bars indicate the fraction of human responses selecting the corresponding item as indicator of AI traces, comparing two opposite image categories, e.g. **SOLO(+)** vs. **SOLO(-)**. (b) Only images with human subjects are considered. Blue bars indicate the human responses selecting a specific item, when present in the image. Note that each response is made of two clicks on the image, potentially indicating more than one item.

for well-known people; (xii) presence of non-sense writing and illegible characters (Table 2).

For each text category $C$, a text-based human mask $\mathbf{H}_C$ is generated as described in Sect. 5.1, but considering only the participants' visual responses that are accompanied by a textual response falling within $C$ (See Fig. 6).

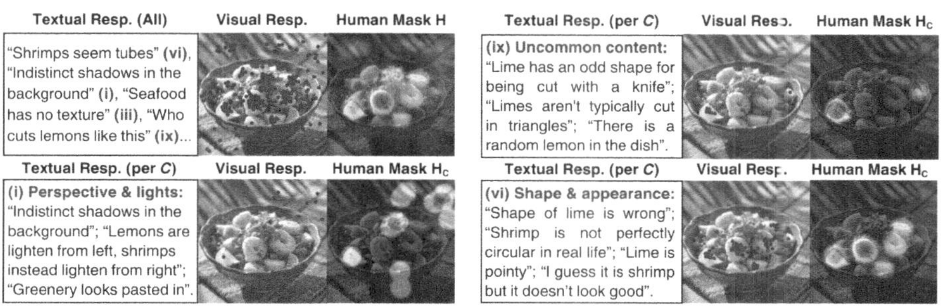


**Fig. 6.** Example of text-based human masks $\mathbf{H}_C$ for different text categories $C$, indicated in blue. Again, $R$ is equal to 8.8% of the image size, and $\alpha = 3$.

XAI methods achieve a significantly lower overall similarity to text-based human masks than Fig. 4, suggesting AI detectors rely on a cohesive combination of low-level image features rather than isolating singular, complex semantic concepts. As a result, training multi-modal AI detectors with textual explanations presents significant challenges, as the explanations are unlikely to align with human expectations given the functioning of current AI detection strategies. This finding supports the evaluation study of Large Multi-modal Models (LLMs) for AI detection proposed by Li et al. [20], stressing the importance of

**Table 2.** Best average cosine similarity score between XAI masks and text-based human masks achieved across all XAI methods and AI detectors.

| Text category | Sim. Score |
|---|---|
| (i) Perspective & lights | 0.29 |
| (ii) Inconsistency | 0.25 |
| (iii) Texture & details | 0.38 |
| (iv) Background | 0.18 |
| (v) Distortion & blend | 0.32 |
| Visual quality (All) | 0.47 |

| Text category | Sim. Score |
|---|---|
| (vi) Shape & appearance | 0.38 |
| (vii) Synthetic perfection | 0.26 |
| (viii) Absence of physics | 0.25 |
| (ix) Uncommon content | 0.37 |
| (x) Unknown design | 0.24 |
| (xi) VIP subject | 0.43 |
| (xii) Non-sense text | 0.22 |
| Realism of content (All) | 0.46 |

incorporating more human-interpretable forensic elements in visual-language AI detection.

## 6 Conclusion

This work comprehensively evaluates 16 XAI methods for AI-generated image detection models, categorizing them by visual features and assessing them across detectors with varying architectures and training strategies. A novel survey-based evaluation, collecting both visual and textual responses from human participants, highlights significant alignment between human preferences and specific combinations of XAI methods and AI detectors, for certain image categories. The study reveals patterns and cues needed to enhance interpretability, which future scientific work should consider when developing explainable AI detectors.

**Acknowledgments.** This work was supported by the GADMO 2.0 project, co-funded by the European Union's Digital Europe Programme (DIGITAL) and the Austrian Research Promotion Agency (FFG), under grant agreement No. 101083573, and by the defame Fakes project, funded by the Austrian security research programme KIRAS of the Federal Ministry of Finance (BMF).

**Disclosure of Interests.** The authors have no competing interests to declare that are relevant to the content of this article.

## References


1. Adobe: Adobe firefly text to image (2024). https://firefly.adobe.com. Accessed: 2025-01-16
2. Bammey, Q.: Synthbuster: Towards detection of diffusion model generated images. IEEE Open J. Signal Process. (2023)
3. Bird, J.J., Lotfi, A.: Cifake: Image classification and explainable identification of AI-generated synthetic images. IEEE Access (2024)
4. Borji, A.: Qualitative failures of image generation models and their application in detecting deepfakes. Image Vis. Comput. **137**, 104771 (2023)
5. Chattopadhay, A., Sarkar, A., Howlader, P., Balasubramanian, V.N.: Grad-cam++: Generalized gradient-based visual explanations for deep convolutional networks. In: 2018 IEEE Winter Conference on Applications of Computer Vision (WACV), pp. 839–847. IEEE (2018)
6. Deng, J., Dong, W., Socher, R., Li, L.J., Li, K., Fei-Fei, L.: Imagenet: a large-scale hierarchical image database. In: 2009 IEEE Conference on Computer Vision and Pattern Recognition, pp. 248–255 (2009). https://doi.org/10.1109/CVPR.2009.5206848
7. Dogoulis, P., Kordopatis-Zilos, G., Kompatsiaris, I., Papadopoulos, S.: Improving synthetically generated image detection in cross-concept settings. In: Proceedings of the 2nd ACM International Workshop on Multimedia AI against Disinformation, pp. 28–35 (2023)
8. Dosovitskiy, A., et al.: An image is worth 16x16 words: Transformers for image recognition at scale (2021). https://arxiv.org/abs/2010.11929
9. Draelos, R.L., Carin, L.: Use hirescam instead of grad-cam for faithful explanations of convolutional neural networks (2021). https://arxiv.org/abs/2011.08891
10. Erhan, D., Bengio, Y., Courville, A., Vincent, P.: Visualizing higher-layer features of a deep network. Univ. Montreal **1341**(3), 1 (2009)
11. Everingham, M., Van Gool, L., Williams, C.K.I., Winn, J., Zisserman, A.: The PASCAL Visual Object Classes Challenge 2012 (VOC2012) Results. http://www.pascal-network.org/challenges/VOC/voc2012/workshop/index.html (2015)
12. Fu, R., Hu, Q., Dong, X., Guo, Y., Gao, Y., Li, B.: Axiom-based grad-cam: Towards accurate visualization and explanation of CNNs (2020). https://arxiv.org/abs/2008.02312
13. Guarnera, L., Giudice, O., Battiato, S.: Level Up the Deepfake Detection: A Method to Effectively Discriminate Images Generated by GAN Architectures and Diffusion Models. In: Arai, K. (ed.) Intelligent Systems and Applications, vol. 1067, pp. 615–625. Springer Nature Switzerland, Cham (2024). series Title: Lecture Notes in Networks and Systems
14. Ha, A.Y.J., et al.: Organic or Diffused: Can We Distinguish Human Art from AI-generated Images? (2024). http://arxiv.org/abs/2402.03214, arXiv:2402.03214
15. He, K., Zhang, X., Ren, S., Sun, J.: Deep residual learning for image recognition (2015). https://arxiv.org/abs/1512.03385
16. Kapishnikov, A., Bolukbasi, T., Viégas, F., Terry, M.: Xrai: Better attributions through regions (2019). https://arxiv.org/abs/1906.02825
17. Kapishnikov, A., Venugopalan, S., Avci, B., Wedin, B., Terry, M., Bolukbasi, T.: Guided integrated gradients: An adaptive path method for removing noise (2021). https://arxiv.org/abs/2106.09788

18. Kuznetsova, A., Rom, H., Alldrin, N., Uijlings, J., Krasin, I., Pont-Tuset, J., Kamali, S., Popov, S., Malloci, M., Kolesnikov, A., Duerig, T., Ferrari, V.: The Open Images Dataset V4. Int. J. Comput. Vision **128**(7), 1956–1981 (2020). https://doi.org/10.1007/s11263-020-01316-z
19. Labs, B.F.: Flux (2024). https://github.com/black-forest-labs/flux
20. Li, Yet al.: Fakebench: Probing explainable fake image detection via large multimodal models (2024). https://arxiv.org/abs/2404.13306
21. Lin, T.-Y., Maire, M., Belongie, S., Hays, J., Perona, P., Ramanan, D., Dollár, P., Zitnick, C.L.: Microsoft COCO: Common Objects in Context. In: Fleet, D., Pajdla, T., Schiele, B., Tuytelaars, T. (eds.) ECCV 2014. LNCS, vol. 8693, pp. 740–755. Springer, Cham (2014). https://doi.org/10.1007/978-3-319-10602-1_48
22. Liu, G., Zhang, J., Chan, A.B., Hsiao, J.H.: Human attention guided explainable artificial intelligence for computer vision models. Neural Netw. **177**, 106392 (2024). https://doi.org/10.1016/j.neunet.2024.106392, https://www.sciencedirect.com/science/article/pii/S0893608024003162
23. Longo, L., et al.: Explainable artificial intelligence (xai) 2.0: A manifesto of open challenges and interdisciplinary research directions. Information Fusion **106**, 102301 (2024).https://doi.org/10.1016/j.inffus.2024.102301, https://www.sciencedirect.com/science/article/pii/S1566253524000794
24. Lorenz, P., Durall, R.L., Keuper, J.: Detecting images generated by deep diffusion models using their local intrinsic dimensionality. In: Proceedings of the IEEE/CVF International Conference on Computer Vision, pp. 448–459 (2023)
25. Lu, Z., Huang, D., Bai, L., Qu, J., Wu, C., Liu, X., Ouyang, W.: Seeing is not always believing: Benchmarking human and model perception of ai-generated images (2023). https://arxiv.org/abs/2304.13023
26. Lundberg, S.M., Lee, S.I.: A unified approach to interpreting model predictions. In: Guyon, I., Luxburg, U.V., Bengio, S., Wallach, H., Fergus, R., Vishwanathan, S., Garnett, R. (eds.) Advances in Neural Information Processing Systems. vol. 30. Curran Associates, Inc. (2017)
27. Ma, R., Duan, J., Kong, F., Shi, X., Xu, K.: Exposing the Fake: Effective Diffusion-Generated Images Detection (2023). http://arxiv.org/abs/2307.06272, arXiv:2307.06272
28. Midjourney: Midjourney 5.2 (2024). https://docs.midjourney.com/docs/model-version-5. Accessed 16 Jan 2025
29. Midjourney: Midjourney 6.1 (2024). https://docs.midjourney.com/docs/models. Accessed 16 Jan 2025
30. Muhammad, M.B., Yeasin, M.: Eigen-cam: Class activation map using principal components. In: 2020 International Joint Conference on Neural Networks (IJCNN), pp. 1–7. IEEE (2020)
31. Nichol, A., et al.: Glide: Towards photorealistic image generation and editing with text-guided diffusion models (2022). https://arxiv.org/abs/2112.10741
32. Nightingale, S.J., Wade, K.A., Watson, D.G.: Can people identify original and manipulated photos of real-world scenes? Cognitive Research: Principles and Implications **2**(1), 1–21 (2017). https://doi.org/10.1186/s41235-017-0067-2
33. Ojha, U., Li, Y., Lee, Y.J.: Towards Universal Fake Image Detectors that Generalize Across Generative Models. In: Proceedings of the IEEE/CVF Conference on Computer Vision and Pattern Recognition, pp. 24480–24489 (2023)
34. OpenAI: Dall-e 2: Generating images from text (2022). https://openai.com/index/dall-e-2. Accessed 16 Jan 2025
35. OpenAI: Dall-e 3: Generating images from text (2023). https://openai.com/index/dall-e-3. Accessed 16 Jan 2025

36. Podell, D., et al.: Sdxl: Improving latent diffusion models for high-resolution image synthesis. arXiv preprint arXiv:2307.01952 (2023). https://arxiv.org/abs/2307.01952
37. Ramaswamy, H.G., et al.: Ablation-cam: Visual explanations for deep convolutional network via gradient-free localization. In: Proceedings of the IEEE/CVF Winter Conference on Applications of Computer Vision, pp. 983–991 (2020)
38. Ribeiro, M.T., Singh, S., Guestrin, C.: "Why should i trust you?" explaining the predictions of any classifier. In: Proceedings of the 22nd ACM SIGKDD International Conference on Knowledge Discovery and Data Mining, pp. 1135–1144 (2016)
39. Selvaraju, R.R., Cogswell, M., Das, A., Vedantam, R., Parikh, D., Batra, D.: Grad-cam: visual explanations from deep networks via gradient-based localization. Int. J. Comput. Vision **128**, 336–359 (2020)
40. Sha, Z., Li, Z., Yu, N., Zhang, Y.: DE-FAKE: detection and attribution of fake images generated by text-to-image generation models. In: Proceedings of the 2023 ACM SIGSAC Conference on Computer and Communications Security. pp. 3418–3432. CCS '23, Association for Computing Machinery, New York, NY, USA (2023). https://doi.org/10.1145/3576915.3616588
41. Srinivas, S., Fleuret, F.: Full-gradient representation for neural network visualization (2019). https://arxiv.org/abs/1905.00780
42. Sundararajan, M., Taly, A., Yan, Q.: Axiomatic attribution for deep networks (2017). https://arxiv.org/abs/1703.01365
43. Wang, H., et al.: Score-cam: Score-weighted visual explanations for convolutional neural networks. In: Proceedings of the IEEE/CVF Conference on Computer Vision and Pattern Recognition Workshops, pp. 24–25 (2020)
44. Wang, Z., et al.: DIRE for Diffusion-Generated Image Detection. In: Proceedings of the IEEE/CVF International Conference on Computer Vision, pp. 22445–22455 (2023)
45. Wolter, M., Blanke, F., Heese, R., Garcke, J.: Wavelet-packets for deepfake image analysis and detection. Mach. Learn. **111**(11), 4295–4327 (2022). https://doi.org/10.1007/s10994-022-06225-5, https://link.springer.com/10.1007/s10994-022-06225-5
46. Xu, S., Venugopalan, S., Sundararajan, M.: Attribution in scale and space (2020). https://arxiv.org/abs/2004.03383
47. Zeiler, M.: Visualizing and understanding convolutional networks. In: European conference on computer vision/arXiv. vol. 1311 (2014)
48. Zhong, N., Xu, Y., Li, S., Qian, Z., Zhang, X.: PatchCraft: Exploring Texture Patch for Efficient AI-generated Image Detection (2024). http://arxiv.org/abs/2311.12397, arXiv:2311.12397
49. Zhu, M., et al.: Genimage: A million-scale benchmark for detecting ai-generated image. Adv. Neural Inf. Process. Syst. **36** (2024)

# Toward Trustworthy Policy Discovery: A Multilingual Hybrid RAG Approach Applied to EU and UK Peatland Restoration

Muhammad Yasar Khan(✉), Niall O'Brolchain, Al Margaret Waskow, Saeed Hamood Alsamhi, Waqas Shoukat, Fergus O'Donoghue, and Yifan Wang

Insight Research Ireland Centre for Data Analytics, Data Science Institute, University of Galway, Galway, Ireland
{muhammadyasar.khan,niall.obrolchain,margaret.waskow,saeed.alsamhi, muhammad.shoukat,fergusefe.odonoghue,wangyifan}@universityofgalway.ie

**Abstract.** Retrieval-Augmented Generation (RAG) enhances large language models (LLMs) by grounding answers in retrieved evidence; however, standard pipelines struggle in domains such as environmental policy, where documents are lengthy, multilingual, and frequently updated. Key provisions such as numeric targets, dates, and legal clauses are easily missed or inconsistently cited. We introduce PeatRAG, a multilingual hybrid RAG framework that combines Best-Match 25 (BM25) with dense multilingual embeddings and metadata filtering, and augments retrieval with a curated Fact Repository. A lightweight query parser detects fact-seeking intents and injects authoritative, versioned facts with provenance into the prompt, improving attribution and factual stability. We evaluate PeatRAG on 405 EU and UK peatland policy documents in 21 languages. Compared to strong baselines, PeatRAG achieves higher factual faithfulness (+0.09), context precision (+0.11), and citation precision on RAGAs benchmarks. These results demonstrate that fact injection and provenance-aware retrieval can increase trustworthiness in multilingual, high-stakes policy QA.

**Keywords:** Retrieval-Augmented Generation · Fact Injection · Hybrid Retrieval · Multilingual NLP · Environmental Governance

## 1 Introduction

Policy question answering in public governance requires exact numbers, dates, clauses, and clear provenance that remain stable across document versions [15]. Real corpora are long and mixed format, and decisive statements are often tucked into titles, recitals, annexes, and cross-references. Standard RAG pipelines can surface related passages yet still miss the definitive clause or cite broadly rather than precisely, which undermines trust when users seek concrete facts [18].


T. T. Mai et al. (Eds.): AICS 2025, CCIS 2950, pp. 28–37, 2026.
https://doi.org/10.1007/978-3-032-25809-0_3

Across Europe and the UK, the peatland restoration policy spans the European Union and member-state instruments, producing a patchwork of lengthy PDFs in many languages and jurisdictions [9,11]. A single query about conservation targets may require evidence from an EU regulation and several national strategies. Conventional monolingual or centrally indexed methods struggle to assemble such evidence into a precise, well-attributed answer.

Retrieval-Augmented Generation (RAG) provides a foundation by integrating retrieval with generation to reduce hallucinations and link answers to evidence [4,7,17]. However, in this domain, naive fragmentation and ranking often fail to surface the exact clause, handle multilingual alignment, or respect document versioning, leaving the grounding brittle for fact-seeking questions [5]. This gap motivates a design that can recognize when a query seeks a specific fact and then reliably elevate that fact with clear attribution.

We address these limitations with *PeatRAG*, a multilingual hybrid RAG framework that couples BM25 [12,13] and dense multilingual embeddings with metadata-aware filtering, along with a curated Fact Repository with versioning, confidence, and provenance. The query parser detects fact-seeking intents and prioritizes aligned facts during retrieval and re-ranking. Facts are injected as structured context into the LLM prompt alongside top passages, yielding clearer attribution and fewer inconsistent values.

To assess impact, we evaluate *PeatRAG* on a corpus of 405 policy documents annotated by governance level, category, country, language, and keywords. Using the Retrieval Augmented Generation Assessment (RAGAs) suite [3] together with blinded human judgments, *PeatRAG* achieves higher factual faithfulness, better answer and context relevance, and fewer erroneous substitutions than a strong baseline RAG. These results support the claim that fact-aware retrieval and prompting improve stability and trustworthiness. Our contributions are:

- **Fact-injected hybrid RAG:** We combine BM25 and multilingual dense retrieval with metadata-aware filtering, and inject structured facts with provenance and versioning into the prompt.
- **Curated Fact Repository:** We design a schema and lightweight REST APIs for fact authoring, validation, synchronization, and version control across jurisdictions.
- **Evaluation protocol:** We adapt RAGAs with multilingual and query-type ablations, and introduce citation precision as a measure of whether cited evidence matches the gold standard.

## 2 Related Work

A growing body of work seeks to make retrieval-augmented generation (RAG) reliable in high-stakes domains by clarifying what 'trustworthy' should mean and how to measure it. A recent survey frames trustworthiness in six dimensions: factuality, robustness, fairness, transparency, accountability, and privacy, and argues for stronger retrieval methods, better data curation, explicit knowledge attribution, and comprehensive benchmarks reflecting real-world complexity [18]. This lens motivates systems that not only retrieve relevant passages, but also expose provenance and control the influence of noisy context.

Complementing this perspective, robustness-focused evaluations show that RAG can degrade accuracy when the retrieved context is misleading. The RAGUARD benchmark shows significant drops compared to zero-context baselines when models are presented with conflicting or deceptive evidence; the risk increases as more documents are retrieved, underscoring the need for filtering and sufficiency checks rather than a 'more-is-better' retrieval approach [16]. These findings highlight failure modes, over-trusting retrieved text or misinterpreting it, which any practical pipeline must mitigate.

A recent survey of GraphRAG [6] highlights several issues that are directly relevant to our motivation for a curated fact layer. First, graph construction and retrieval are highly domain-specific: relations, encoders, and even useful traversal strategies differ across domains, so 'one-size-fits-all' designs rarely transfer well. This diversity makes query processing brittle, since errors in entity linking or relation extraction can cascade through traversal and degrade results.

A closely related line of work is RFPG [1], which studies factually aware RAG for low-resource Arabic QA. The authors couple a fact-checking-oriented retriever with tailored prompts and report strong gains in answer accuracy and source precision on a small hadith dataset, demonstrating that injecting factual constraints into retrieval and prompting improves faithfulness. Unlike our setting, RFPG is monolingual, task-specific, and does not maintain a versioned external fact store with provenance or metadata about governance level and jurisdiction, nor does it target long legal PDFs. Our fact-injection layer and multilingual hybrid retrieval therefore, complement RFPG by addressing policy-scale documents and multilingual curation while keeping the same core motivation of reducing hallucinations through structured factual signals.

Together, these strands motivate our focus on fact-aware retrieval and generation: adopt trustworthiness criteria and attribution from the survey, guard against misleading context as shown in robustness studies, and remain compatible with structured retrieval ideas from GraphRAG while prioritizing precise, verifiable facts for domains where small numeric or legal errors carry outsized consequences.

## 3 The PeatRAG Model

*Goal and setting* Given a user query $q$, a corpus of policy text chunks $\mathcal{D}$ with metadata, and a curated fact set $\mathcal{F}$, *PeatRAG* returns an answer grounded in $\mathcal{D} \cup \mathcal{F}$ with explicit citations. The model is optimized for factual stability on numeric targets and dates while preserving coverage for open policy questions.

### 3.1 System Overview

*PeatRAG* has five stages: (i) corpus ingestion and indexing, (ii) structured fact repository, (iii) query parsing and intent detection, (iv) hybrid retrieval and fact alignment, and (v) fact injection with grounded generation and verification. Figure 1 shows the data flow.

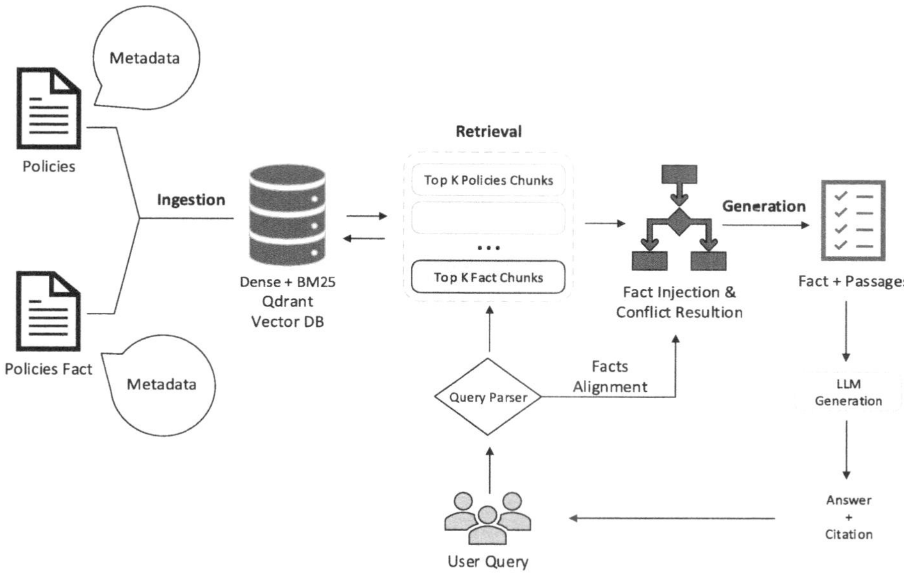


**Fig. 1.** PeatRAG Architecture Diagram.

### 3.2 Corpus Ingestion and Indexing

Policy PDFs are parsed and segmented into overlapping chunks (window 500 chars, overlap 50). Each chunk is embedded with a multilingual sentence encoder into a 768-dimensional vector and stored in a vector store with text and metadata (country, language, governance level, category, policy id). Tokenized text is cached for BM25. Metadata is normalized at ingestion and query time.

### 3.3 Structured Fact Repository

Each fact $f \in \mathcal{F}$ stores: *entity*, *predicate* (e.g., `target`, `publication_year`, `publisher`, `limit`, `location`, `value`), *value* (text or numeric), optional *unit* and *qualifier*, *jurisdiction* and *language*, *governance level*, linked *policy id* and *source document*, *version date*, flags for *current* or superseded, *confidence* and *priority*, keyword tags, and optional translations. A compact *index text* concatenates salient fields for retrieval. Facts live in their own collection with embeddings and can be filtered by metadata.

### 3.4 Query Parsing and Intent Detection

A lightweight classifier decides if $q$ is fact-seeking and predicts a target predicate $\hat{p}(q)$. It combines rule features for numbers, dates, and units with a linear head over a sentence embedding trained on synthetic templates and curated examples. The parser also extracts a small keyword set $K_q$ for alignment with fact metadata.

### 3.5 Hybrid Retrieval and Fact Alignment

We retrieve document chunks $d \in \mathcal{D}$ using a hybrid score

$$s(d \mid q) = \alpha \cdot \cos\big(\phi(q), \phi(d)\big) + \beta \cdot \mathrm{BM25}(q, d),$$

and keep candidates with $s(d \mid q) \geq \tau_d$ before deduplicating by policy and selecting the top $k$. Here, $\tau_d$ is a minimum relevance threshold used to filter low-scoring passages; we tune it on a small validation set to balance precision and recall.

For fact lookup, each fact $f \in \mathcal{F}$ receives an alignment score

$$a(f \mid q) = \lambda \cdot \cos\big(\psi(q), \psi(f)\big) + \mu \cdot J(K_q, K_f) + \nu \cdot \mathbf{1}\big[\hat{p}(q) = \mathrm{predicate}(f)\big],$$

where $J$ is the Jaccard similarity between keyword sets and the indicator encourages predicate agreement. The weighting parameters $(\alpha, \beta, \lambda, \mu, \nu)$ are selected through simple validation-based tuning to achieve the best retrieval and alignment accuracy. If the query is fact seeking, or if $\max_f a(f \mid q)$ exceeds a threshold, the top $m$ aligned facts are injected.

### 3.6 Fact Injection, Conflict Resolution, and Grounded Generation

We compile an *Authoritative Facts* block with identifiers, values, units, jurisdiction, and source names. If multiple facts disagree, we apply a deterministic rule: prefer facts marked *current*, then newer *version date*, then higher *confidence*, then higher *priority*, then higher $a(f \mid q)$. The prompt contains: (1) an instruction to ground all numbers and dates only in provided facts or passages and to cite every claim, (2) the fact block, if any, and (3) the top $k$ passages labeled by policy name and source filename. A local LLM is generated at low temperature. A post hoc scanner checks that a cited passage or injected fact supports numeric and temporal spans in the draft. Unsupported spans trigger constrained regeneration. The final answer includes inline citations to chunk or fact identifiers and a source list.

### 3.7 Design Choices

**Separate Collections.** Facts and passages are indexed independently, which allows different filters and scoring and reduces cross-contamination from noisy text. **Parser gating.** Intent gating avoids injecting irrelevant facts for descriptive questions. **Provenance first.** Every injected fact carries source identity and version, which improves transparency and simplifies audits. **Multilingual handling.** Dense retrieval covers cross-language matching while BM25 anchors terminology in the target language. **Efficiency.** Normalized metadata narrows the search space and allows early filtering in both indices.

## 4 Experimental Setup

**Dataset Collection.** The policy dataset was assembled from the *Peatland Policy Portal* (https://peatlandpolicyportal.eu/), part of the EU Life Multi-Peat project. The portal aggregates peatland-related policy documents, project boundaries, and map data across Europe and the UK. For our experiments, we selected the curated policy PDFs and their metadata on geography, governance level, and language. This domain provides a challenging testbed because policies are long, multilingual, and contain version-sensitive numeric targets.

**Corpus.** We use 405 peatland policy PDFs from the EU and the UK across 21 languages. Documents are labeled with country, language, governance level, category, and keywords.

**Models and Index.** We use paraphrase multilingual mpnet base v2 for embeddings [14], Qdrant for vector search [10], BM25 for lexical scoring, and a local Mistral class model for generation. Chunk window is 500 with 50 overlap. Retrieval keeps $k$=12 passages by hybrid score threshold $\tau_d$=0.3. Fact retrieval keeps up to $m$=4 aligned facts.

**Queries.** We evaluate 80 fact-oriented questions drawn from policy analysis tasks covering targets, dates, publishers, locations, and purpose statements. Queries are balanced across governance levels and languages.

**Baselines.** Dense only, BM25 only, Hybrid without facts, Hybrid with facts but no intent gating, and PeatRAG full.

**Metrics.** RAGAs faithfulness, answer relevance, context relevance, context precision, and context recall. We also report citation precision as the fraction of cited spans that match the evidence spans.

**FastAPI System.** We implement the retrieval pipeline as a FastAPI [8] application that manages PDF uploads, indexing, and querying. When a user uploads a policy document, the system extracts the text using PyPDF, splits it into 500-token overlapping chunks, and generates dense embeddings using the multilingual MPNet model. These vectors are stored in Qdrant, while the raw chunks are simultaneously indexed with BM25 for lexical search. Metadata such as country, language, and governance level is normalized at ingestion to support clean filtering during retrieval. At query time, the API applies any filters provided, retrieves top-scoring passages using a hybrid dense–BM25 score, and returns them as context for answer generation. Additional endpoints support index reloading, record normalization, deletion, and memory monitoring, allowing the entire system to run offline and consistently across experiments.

**LLM Model (Mistral via Ollama).** For generating answers, we use a locally hosted Mistral model running through Ollama. The FastAPI service sends the retrieved passages and the user's question to the model in a structured prompt that emphasizes accuracy and context grounding. The model is instructed to answer only from the provided snippets, avoid speculation, and use a clean academic tone. We keep the temperature low to maintain stability and reproducibility across runs. Hosting the model locally ensures fast response times and avoids dependency on external APIs, allowing the RAG evaluation to operate fully offline.

## 5 Results

Table 1 reports mean scores. PeatRAG improves faithfulness by 0.09 and context precision by 0.11 over Hybrid without facts. Answer relevance and context relevance also rise. The variant with facts but no intent gating helps but underperforms PeatRAG, which suggests useful routing by the parser.

**Table 1.** RAGAs metrics on 80 policy questions. Best in bold.

| Method | Faithfulness | Ans Rel | Ctx Rel | Ctx Prec |
|---|---|---|---|---|
| BM25 only | 0.61 | 0.68 | 0.66 | 0.49 |
| Dense only | 0.64 | 0.70 | 0.68 | 0.52 |
| Hybrid no facts | 0.69 | 0.75 | 0.72 | 0.58 |
| Hybrid facts no gating | 0.73 | 0.77 | 0.75 | 0.62 |
| **PeatRAG full** | **0.78** | **0.82** | **0.79** | **0.69** |

Table 2 breaks down gains by question type and gives representative examples and observed impact. The largest gains appear on numeric targets and dates where the fact layer supplies versioned and jurisdiction-scoped values. Location questions show smaller but consistent gains through metadata filters and aligned passages. Purpose and definition questions benefit less from facts and more from hybrid retrieval.

*Qualitative Example.* For a query about the publication year of an action plan, the hybrid baseline retrieved long prefaces and cited a summary page which led to an off-by-one error. PeatRAG injected a fact with version date and publisher, then retrieved the plan cover page. The answer reported the correct year with a citation to the header and the fact identifier.

**Table 2.** Question types, counts, and impact. $\Delta$ Faith is the faithfulness delta over Hybrid no facts. Cit Prec is citation precision.

| Type | #Qs | $\Delta$ Faith | Cit Prec | Example and impact |
|---|---|---|---|---|
| Targets numeric | 22 | +0.12 | +0.15 | Q: national restoration area by 2030. Baseline mixed EU and national targets. PeatRAG picks the national clause and cites the exact article. |
| Dates effective | 18 | +0.11 | +0.12 | Q: year the action plan was published. Baseline cited a press page. PeatRAG cites the plan header and correct year. |
| Publisher | 10 | +0.09 | +0.10 | Q: who published the plan. PeatRAG uses the fact store entry with provenance and confirms in the header. |
| Location | 12 | +0.06 | +0.08 | Q: does Cyprus have peatland and name. Filters plus facts avoid unrelated wetlands. |
| Purpose definition | 18 | +0.04 | +0.05 | Q: purpose of ENMAK 2030. Retrieval dominates and facts provide minor guidance. |

## 6 Discussion and Limits

The fact layer provides crisp anchors for numeric and temporal queries and reduces ambiguity when multiple jurisdictions overlap. This improves precision but also introduces dependencies: fact quality, completeness, and version management directly affect performance. Manual or semi-automated curation remains a bottleneck, and the approach is most effective when domains contain a stable set of high-value facts (e.g., policy targets, publication years). For broader or open-ended queries, hybrid retrieval and metadata filtering remain the main drivers of performance, and fact injection has a smaller effect. Although our evaluation shows significant gains on 80 balanced queries, future work should expand the testbed, report variance across annotators, and apply the method to other domains to confirm generality. Scalability to new settings may require automated fact extraction pipelines and community-maintained repositories. Future extensions include neural re-rankers, confidence-calibrated answer formatting, and semi-automated fact authoring tools to reduce curation costs.

In addition, PeatRAG naturally supports several transparency obligations outlined in Article 13 of the EU AI Act [2], which stresses traceability, documentation, and the ability to explain how an AI system produces outputs. Because PeatRAG maintains versioned facts with explicit provenance and associates every generated claim with a cited passage or fact identifier, users can inspect precisely which sources contributed to an answer. The separation between retrieved passages and injected facts further clarifies their respective roles in shaping the output, enabling more transparent and auditable behaviour. While not a full compliance solution, PeatRAG illustrates how fact-aware RAG architectures can operationalize key transparency principles in real policy-facing applications.

## 7 Conclusion

We presented PeatRAG, a fact-injected hybrid RAG framework for multilingual policy question answering. By combining intent-aware fact alignment with metadata-filtered hybrid retrieval, PeatRAG delivers answers that are better grounded, more faithful to source documents, and more transparent in their provenance. Our experiments on EU and UK peatland policies demonstrate consistent gains in factual stability, citation precision, and context quality compared to strong hybrid baselines. The approach remains simple to integrate into existing RAG stacks and directly supports emerging transparency expectations, such as those specified in the EU AI Act. Looking forward, PeatRAG provides a foundation for trustworthy, auditable policy QA systems and opens avenues for extending fact injection and provenance-aware retrieval to broader domains in environmental governance and public decision making.

**Acknowledgment.** This research is supported by the EU LIFE Multi Peat Project ID LIFE20 CCM/DE/001802 and funded by Research Ireland as part of Grant Number SFI/12/RC/2289_P2 Insight_2, the Insight Research Ireland Centre for Data Analytics.

## References

1. Alshammary, M., Uddin, M.N., Khan, L.: Rfpg: Question-answering from low-resource language (Arabic) texts using factually aware rag. In: 2024 IEEE 10th International Conference on Collaboration and Internet Computing (CIC), pp. 107–116. IEEE (2024)
2. Edwards, L.: The eu ai act: a summary of its significance and scope. Artif. Intell. (the EU AI Act) **1**, 25 (2021)
3. Es, S., James, J., Anke, L.E., Schockaert, S.: Ragas: Automated evaluation of retrieval augmented generation. In: Proceedings of the 18th Conference of the European Chapter of the Association for Computational Linguistics: System Demonstrations, pp. 150–158 (2024)
4. Gao, Y., et al.: Retrieval-augmented generation for large language models: a survey. arXiv preprint arXiv:2312.10997 (2023)
5. Hadi, M.U., et al.: Large language models: a comprehensive survey of its applications, challenges, limitations, and future prospects. Authorea Preprints **1**(3), 1–26 (2023)
6. Han, H., et al.: Retrieval-augmented generation with graphs (graphrag). arXiv preprint arXiv:2501.00309 (2024)
7. Lewis, P., et al.: Retrieval-augmented generation for knowledge-intensive NLP tasks. Adv. Neural. Inf. Process. Syst. **33**, 9459–9474 (2020)
8. Lubanovic, B.: FastAPI. Inc, O'Reilly Media (2023)
9. Nordbeck, R., Hogl, K., Schaller, L.: The integration of peatlands into the EU common agricultural policy: Recent progress and remaining challenges. Environ. Sci. Policy **169**, 104077 (2025)

10. Ockerman, S., et al.: Exploring distributed vector databases performance on hpc platforms: a study with qdrant. In: Proceedings of the SC'25 Workshops of the International Conference for High Performance Computing, Networking, Storage and Analysis, pp. 575–581 (2025)
11. Patel, N., Ievina, B., Kažmēre, D., Feofilovs, M., Kamenders, A. Romagnoli, F.: Towards resilient peatlands: Integrating ecosystem-based strategies, policy frameworks, and management approaches for sustainable transformation. Sustainability **17**(8), 3419 (2025)
12. Ranaldi, L., Haddow, B., Birch, A.: Multilingual retrieval-augmented generation for knowledge-intensive task. arXiv preprint arXiv:2504.03616 (2025)
13. Robertson, S., Zaragoza, H., et al.: The probabilistic relevance framework: Bm25 and beyond. Found. Trends® Inf. Retrieval **3**(4), 333–389 (2009)
14. Song, K., Tan, X., Qin, T., Lu, J., Liu, T.Y.: Mpnet: masked and permuted pre-training for language understanding. Adv. Neural. Inf. Process. Syst. **33**, 16857–16867 (2020)
15. Yun, L., Yun, S., Xue, H.: Improving citizen-government interactions with generative artificial intelligence: novel human-computer interaction strategies for policy understanding through large language models. PLoS ONE **19**(12), e0311410 (2024)
16. Zeng, L., Gupta, R., Motwani, D., Yang, D., Zhang, Y.: Worse than zero-shot? a fact-checking dataset for evaluating the robustness of rag against misleading retrievals. arXiv preprint arXiv:2502.16101 (2025)
17. Zhao, W.X., et al.: A survey of large language models. arXiv preprint arXiv:2303.18223 (2023)
18. Zhou, Y., et al.: Trustworthiness in retrieval-augmented generation systems: A survey. arXiv preprint arXiv:2409.10102 (2024)

# Towards Generating More Interpretable Counterfactuals via Concept Vectors: A Preliminary Study on Chest X-Rays

Bulat Maksudov[1(✉)], Kathleen M. Curran[2], and Alessandra Mileo[1]

[1] School of Computing, Dublin City University, Dublin, Ireland
bulat.maksudov2@mail.dcu.ie

[2] School of Medicine, University College Dublin, Dublin, Ireland

**Abstract.** An essential step in deploying medical imaging models in real-world settings is ensuring that these models align with established clinical knowledge and produce outputs that are interpretable by clinicians. Recent research has demonstrated that the latent spaces of pre-trained models contain directions corresponding to high-level concepts. In this work, we focus on mapping clinical concepts into the latent space of generative models to identify corresponding Concept Activation Vectors (CAVs). Using a simple reconstruction autoencoder, we show that user-defined concepts can be linked to image-level features without requiring explicit training on class labels. We demonstrate that the concepts extracted using CAVs are stable across datasets. This indicates that in principle they can be used to generate visual explanations that highlight clinically relevant features. Our method produces counterfactual explanations by traversing the latent space in the direction of concept vector, allowing for the exaggeration or curtailment of specific clinical features. Our preliminary study on chest X-ray data shows that while the method performs well for larger pathologies such as cardiomegaly, challenges remain for smaller pathologies like atelectasis due to limitations in reconstruction fidelity and feature localization. Our investigation, although preliminary, demonstrates potential for producing interpretable, concept-based explanations in medical imaging, which is a key step towards improving trust in AI-driven diagnostics and foster adoption. Despite the approach does not beat the baseline in its current form, we believe that finding clinically relevant concepts in the latent space of pre-trained models provides a pathway for generating visual explanations that align with clinical knowledge. We envision taking this approach further by improving the underlying generative model and going beyond single vector by modeling concept subspace as a distribution.

**Keywords:** Interpretability · Concept Activation Vectors (CAVs) · Autoencoders · Counterfactual Explanations · Visual Explanations · Explainable AI (XAI) · Feature Attribution


T. T. Mai et al. (Eds.): AICS 2025, CCIS 2950, pp. 38–48, 2026.
https://doi.org/10.1007/978-3-032-25809-0_4

# 1 Introduction

Interpretability and explainability are important aspects for the adoption of deep learning models, particularly in the healthcare domain. In medical imaging, model predictions are directly related to patient treatment and outcomes, so the ability to understand and trust a model's predictions is not just a technical challenge, but a clinical necessity. Although recent models achieve clinician-level performance on disease classification and localization, their "black-box" nature limits widespread adoption into hospital workflows. Clinicians are often reluctant to rely on models whose decision-making processes they cannot interpret or validate against their own expertise. This lack of trust poses a significant barrier to the integration of AI into routine medical practice.

Several methods have been introduced to make the model predictions more interpretable. One such approach is to generate saliency maps using backpropagation-based methods such as GradCAM [11]. However, recent work has shown that some of these methods are not indicative of semantically significant features [12] or simply correspond to edge detection models [1].

Another recent direction is to generate explanations by traversing the latent space of generative models. For example [2] introduce the method to traverse latent space of specifically pre-trained GANs. [4] propose a method that uses a simple autoencoder to transform the latent representation of a specific input image, exaggerating or curtailing the features used for prediction. This method decouples the generative and classification models, so that the generative model trained without prior knowledge of clinical concepts is driven by the classification model gradient. Building on this, we explore Concept Activation Vectors (CAVs) as another way to integrate clinical knowledge into latent space traversal methods. CAVs, originally introduced by [8], allow us to define directions in the latent space that correspond to user-defined concepts, enabling the generation of visual explanations that highlight clinically relevant features. Importantly, the autoencoder itself is trained without explicit knowledge of these concepts and concept information is introduced only via CAVs.

In this work, we present a first attempt at applying latent space traversal with CAVs to generate visual explanations that are both interpretable and clinically meaningful. We validate the basic principles of our approach, showing that concept vectors can capture meaningful information about target concepts and that these vectors exhibit stability across different datasets. The contributions of this paper are as follows:

- We demonstrate that user-defined concepts can be mapped to image-level features using the latent space of a generative model, even when the model is trained without explicit knowledge of these concepts.
- We propose a method for generating visual explanations by traversing the latent space with CAVs
- We show that concept vectors generated from different datasets exhibit similarity and stability, suggesting that they capture consistent and generalizable information about the target concepts.

## 2 Related Work

The use of latent space traversal for interpretability has been explored in medical imaging. Atad et al. [2] generated counterfactual explanations by manipulating latent directions in a trained model, while Cohen et al. [4] proposed Latent Shift, a method using autoencoders to transform latent representations for feature manipulation in chest X-rays. Diffusion-based approaches to counterfactual generation, such as those introduced by [3], leverage denoising models guided by classifier gradients to generate counterfactual images. Unlike linear latent space traversal methods, latent diffusion models allow for non-linear trajectories in the latent space, enabling more complex and high-quality image generation. However, these methods are inherently more complex, and their guidance process is less interpretable compared to linear traversals.

Concept Activation Vectors (CAVs), introduced by Kim et al. [8], have been widely used to interpret classification models by measuring the influence of user-defined concepts on model predictions.. Recent work in large language models (LLMs) has also explored similar ideas, such as In-Context Vectors (ICVs) [9], which steer model behavior by shifting latent representations based on demonstration examples. These methods highlight the broader applicability of concept-based explanations across different domains.

Building on these advances, our work extends the idea of latent space traversal by showing that prior knowledge about the visual representation of concepts can be discovered directly in the latent space of a reconstruction autoencoder, without requiring explicit training using class information. By leveraging CAVs, we map user-defined concepts to meaningful directions in the latent space, enabling the generation of visual explanations that highlight clinically relevant features. This approach not only simplifies the process of generating interpretable explanations but also aligns with recent developments in latent space manipulation, underscoring the potential of concept-based explanations as a unifying framework for interpretability.

## 3 Methodology

Our method uses two stage approach to generating visual counterfactuals. A detailed overview is provided in Fig. 1.

*CAV Generation.* Firstly, we construct Concept Activation Vectors in the latent space of an autoencoder model, using linear classifier.

*CAV-Guided Traversal and Counterfactual Generation.* Using CAVs we generate exaggerated and curtailed latent samples by adding and subtracting CAV respectively. After that, we decode new samples and subtract them to produce visual counterfactual.

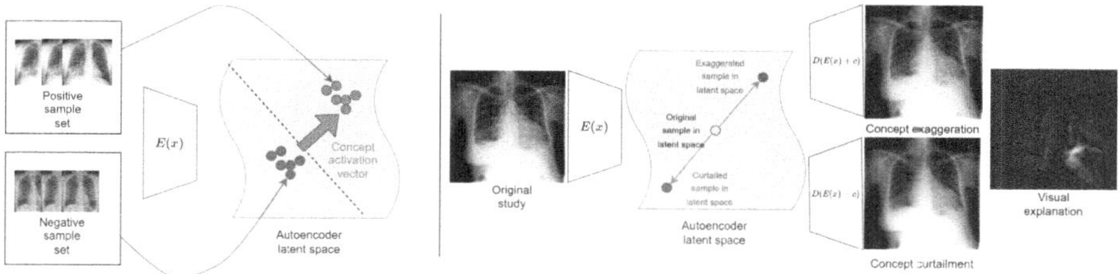


**Fig. 1.** Overview of our method: (a) Construction of Concept Activation Vector in the latent space of autoencoder using linear classifier (b) Generation of explanations by traversing the latent space using CAV. Visual explanation is constructed by pixelwise subtracting exaggerated and curtailed samples.

### 3.1 Concept Vector Generation

We generate concept vectors using the Concept Activation Vector (CAV) algorithm proposed by [8], which trains a linear classifier in the embedding space to identify directions corresponding to user-defined concepts. Given a set of positive concept samples $P_c$ and a negative set $N$, we train a linear classifier in the flattened embedding space of the autoencoder model. This work, we use class labels as proxies for the concepts. Specifically, given a set of positive concept samples $P_c$(studies labeled with the target class, e.g., "Cardiomegaly") and a negative set $N$ (studies without the target class label), the classifier learns to separate the two groups in the latent space. The decision boundary of this classifier defines a hyperplane, and the vector orthogonal to this hyperplane represents the direction in the latent space that best captures the target concept. This orthogonal vector is referred to as the Concept Activation Vector (CAV).

An overview of concept vector generation is provided in Fig. 1.a.

### 3.2 Visual Explanations

To generate visual explanations we follow the methodology of [4]. A sample is encoded into the latent space of the autoencoder model, and then we generate feature exaggeration and curtail it by adding and subtracting the concept vector from the embedding and generating reconstruction for it. An example of the resulting explanation is provided in Fig. 2.

To generate 2D attribution we compute the maximum absolute difference between traversed reconstructions and the original image. An example of the resulting 2D successful and failed attribution maps is shown in Appendix B, Fig. 3 and Fig. 4 respectively. An overview of visual explanation generation is provided in Fig. 1.b.

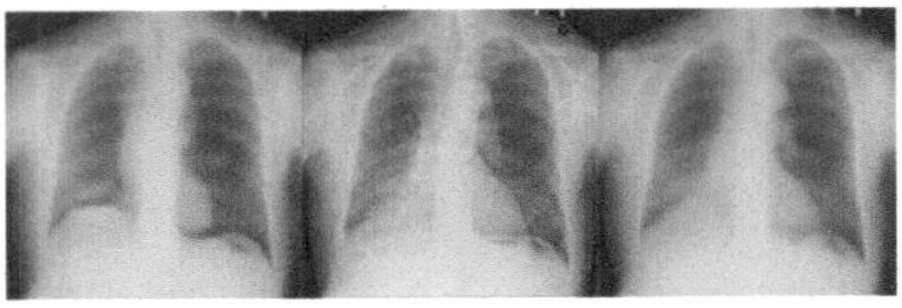

**Fig. 2.** Visual representation of feature manipulation for the "Cardiomegaly" concept. By traversing the latent space of the autoencoder, we add or subtract the concept vector from the image embedding to generate reconstructions that exaggerate or curtail cardiomegaly-related features. From left to right: (a) Feature curtail, reducing the heart area; (b) Original chest X-ray; (c) Feature exaggeration, enhancing cardiomegaly-related features.

## 4 Evaluation

### 4.1 Experiments

To establish that concept vectors meaningfully contain information about target concepts we conduct two main experiments:

- Measure the similarity of concept vectors in inter and intra dataset setting
- assess the quality of generated explanations and their correspondence to expected visual features of the concept

*Stability of Concept Vectors.* To assess the stability of concept vectors we performed three sets of experiments. Firstly, we compute the similarity of concept vectors with random vectors. This serves as a basic sanity check, confirming that the generated vectors capture meaningful information about the concept rather than random noise. Secondly, we evaluate inter-dataset similarity by computing the cosine similarity of concept vectors generated from different batches of the dataset. Lastly, we evaluate the intra-dataset similarity of concept vectors, which shows that concept direction captures relevant information, rather than dataset-specific properties.

To measure the alignment of concept vectors, we use cosine similarity, which captures the angular relationship between vectors in high-dimensional space, independent of their magnitude. This metric is particularly well-suited for our setting because we are interested in the direction of the concept vectors in the latent space rather than their absolute values. A cosine similarity close to 1 indicates that the vectors are pointing in the same direction, while a value close to 0 suggests no alignment. By using cosine similarity, we can quantify the consistency of concept vectors across datasets and batches, providing a robust measure of their stability and generalizability.

*Evaluating Quality of Visual Explanations.* To assess quantitative metrics of visual explanations we first generate 2D attribution maps by computing the absolute difference between exaggerated counterfactual and original images. We then follow the evaluation protocol described in [4] to compute Intersection over Union (IoU) between attribution maps and bounding boxes of the target concept. In our case, Intersection over Union provides a measure, with a value between 0 and 1, of similarity between ground truth segmentation mask and visual explanation, with higher similarity resulting in larger IoU values

### 4.2 Experimental Setup

*CAV Generation.* For the concept vectors calculation we construct batches with 500 samples, 250 of which contain the target concept and 250 are negative.

*Visual Explanations.* We use pre-trained autoencoder models from torchxrayvision [5]. The step_size of 10 is used for latent space traversal. We generate explanations using 4 sets of concept vectors for each dataset and then average those vectors and evaluate attribution quality for the averaged vector.

### 4.3 Datasets

For the experiments, we utilize two Chest X-ray datasets: NIH [13] and CheXpert [7]. We limit the number of pathologies that are examined to 5, namely "Cardiomegaly", "Mass", "Nodule", "Atelectasis" and "Effusion". For concept vector generalization experiments we consider pathologies from this list that are present in the CheXpert dataset, namely "Cardiomegaly", "Atelectasis", and "Effusion". The detailed number of samples for each dataset, as well as the subset of samples for which mask annotations were available, are present in Appendix A, Table 5.

*NIH* [13]. This dataset comprises 108,948 frontal view X-ray images of 32,717 unique patients with the text-mined eight disease image labels, from the associated radiological reports using natural language processing.

*CheXpert* [7]. It contains 224,316 chest radiographs of 65,240 patients. It is labeled by automatically extracting 14 pathologies from radiological reports. Additionally, a validation set of 200 images was labeled by 3 board-certified radiologists and 500 test images were annotated by consensus of 5 board-certified radiologists.

## 5 Results and Discussion

### 5.1 Generalization of Concept Vectors

The mean and std of concept vectors similarity is provided in Table 1. Based on our experimental data we observe the following:

First, concept vectors are distinct from random vectors, with cosine similarity scores close to 0 for random comparisons. This confirms that the generated vectors capture meaningful information about the target concepts rather than random noise.

**Table 1.** Similarity matrix of concept vectors for "Atelectasis," comparing intra-dataset, inter-dataset, and random vector similarities. Concept vectors are distinct from random vectors, and averaging improves alignment across datasets, demonstrating stability and robustness in capturing clinical concepts.

| | NIH | CheXpert | NIH mean | CheXpert mean |
|---|---|---|---|---|
| NIH | $0.2651 \pm 0.2447$ | $0.1011 \pm 0.0757$ | $0.5146 \pm 0.0668$ | $0.2116 \pm 0.0674$ |
| CheXpert | $0.1011 \pm 0.0757$ | $0.2178 \pm 0.2582$ | $0.1966 \pm 0.0726$ | $0.4666 \pm 0.0558$ |
| NIH mean | $0.5146 \pm 0.0668$ | $0.1966 \pm 0.0726$ | $0.9734 \pm 0.0088$ | $0.4060 \pm 0.0183$ |
| CheXpert mean | $0.2116 \pm 0.0674$ | $0.4666 \pm 0.0558$ | $0.4060 \pm 0.0183$ | $0.9655 \pm 0.0114$ |
| Random vector | $-0.0006 \pm 0.0323$ | $0.0010 \pm 0.0321$ | $-0.0205 \pm 0.0266$ | $-0.018 \pm 0.0326$ |

Second, concept vectors exhibit positive alignment both within and across datasets. For example, the cosine similarity between NIH-mean and CheXpert-mean concept vectors is 0.4060, which is significantly higher than the similarity with random vectors. This indicates that the vectors are pointing in a similar direction in the latent space, despite being derived from different datasets with distinct characteristics and labeling protocols. While the similarity is not perfect (which would be unrealistic given the inherent variability between datasets), the positive alignment supports the claim that concept vectors generalize across datasets.

Finally, high intra-dataset similarity scores demonstrate that the concept vectors are stable and consistent within each dataset. We believe that in high-dimensional latent space even the smallest observed value (0.1011 for NIH to CheXpert similarity) is very high and highlights feasibility of our approach. The similarity is further improved by taking an average of several concept vectors (e.g., 0.9734 for NIH-mean and 0.9655 for CheXpert-mean).

### 5.2 Visual Explanations

The evaluation of visual explanations is shown in Tables 2, 3. We observe that our method performs worse than latent shift in terms of IoU with the difference being more prominent on smaller pathologies, such as atelectasis or nodule. For larger pathologies, such as cardiomegaly, this difference is less significant. In smaller pathologies, we often observe no meaningful shift in feature exaggeration, which is shown in Appendix B, Fig. 4. We speculate, that there are two main reasons for it. Firstly, the reconstruction fidelity of the autoencoder model is insufficient for smaller features. Secondly, smaller pathologies tend to have different localizations in the lung, while larger cardiomegaly corresponds to approximately the same location in the study. We would also like to note the limitation of IoU and lack of comprehensive xAI benchmarks [6], specifically in the area of counterfactual medical explanations. More specifically, while IoU captures pixel-wise changes it is only a proxy metric to human evaluation [10].

**Table 2.** Intersection over Union (IoU) comparison for overlapping pathologies (Atelectasis, Cardiomegaly, Effusion) using CheXpert and NIH concept vectors. Averaging concept vectors improves explanation quality, with better performance for larger pathologies like Cardiomegaly compared to smaller ones like Atelectasis.

| Method | Atelectasis | Cardiomegaly | Effusion |
|---|---|---|---|
| Latentshift | 0.09644 | 0.2864 | 0.143 |
| CheXpert CAV | $0.011627 \pm 0.00612$ | $0.14225 \pm 0.0577$ | $0.03581 \pm 0.00258$ |
| CheXpert CAV mean | 0.02971 | 0.2185 | 0.05762 |
| NIH CAV | $0.03192 \pm 0.004016$ | $0.25975 \pm 0.02382$ | $0.054485 \pm 0.001562$ |
| NIH CAV mean | 0.03927 | 0.363 | 0.04961 |

## 6 Future Work

One direction for future work involves leveraging causal clinical concepts—such as anatomical or physiological features directly linked to pathologies—and mapping them into the latent space of the model. This approach would enable the evaluation of concept similarity and the measurement of alignment with established medical knowledge, while also providing the ability to generate visual representations for further clinical validation.

Another promising direction is to replace case-based concept mapping with more advanced conditioning mechanisms, such as diffusion models. We envision exploring this topic further by measuring effects of latent denoising models on the vectors and conditioning denoising process on additional clinical data to generate counterfactual explanations.

Additionally, we believe that by utilizing CLIP (Contrastive Language–Image Pretraining) models in combination with CAVs and generative models, we could link concepts expressed in natural language terms with case-based and visual concepts.

**Table 3.** Intersection over Union (IoU) comparison for "Mass" and "Nodule" pathologies using NIH concept vectors. Averaging concept vectors improves explanation quality, though performance remains lower for smaller pathologies like Nodule compared to larger ones like Mass.

| Method | Mass | Nodule |
|---|---|---|
| Latentshift | 0.1411 | 0.008768 |
| NIH CAV | $0.03886 \pm 0.004617$ | $0.00129 \pm 0.00045$ |
| NIH CAV mean | 0.06409 | 0.0003938 |

## 7 Conclusion

In this work, we demonstrated the use of Concept Activation Vectors (CAVs) to generate interpretable counterfactual explanations for chest X-ray imaging. By mapping clinical concepts into the latent space of a reconstruction autoencoder, we showed that meaningful visual explanations can be produced without explicit training on class labels. Our experiments revealed that concept vectors are stable and generalizable across datasets, capturing clinically relevant features. While the method performed well for larger pathologies like cardiomegaly, challenges remained for smaller pathologies such as atelectasis, likely due to limitations in reconstruction fidelity and feature localization.

Although our approach did not outperform the baseline in terms of Intersection over Union (IoU), it provides a simple framework for integrating clinical knowledge into generative models, offering a pathway toward more interpretable AI-driven diagnostics. Future work will focus on improving reconstruction quality, exploring causal clinical concepts, and leveraging advanced conditioning mechanisms like diffusion models. This study represents a step forward in making AI explanations more transparent and aligned with clinical expertise.

## Appendices

## A Distribution of Concepts Across Datasets

See Table 4.

**Table 4.** Number of samples for each concept in the NIH and CheXpert datasets. Note: 'Mass' and 'Nodule' are not labeled in the CheXpert dataset, as these pathologies were not included in the original annotation process.

| Data set | Cardiomegaly | Atelectasis | Effusion | Mass | Nodule |
|---|---|---|---|---|---|
| NIH | 2776 | 11559 | 13317 | 5782 | 6331 |
| CheXpert | 27000 | 33376 | 86187 | N/A | N/A |
| NIH bbox | 146 | 180 | 153 | 85 | 79 |
| Total | 22976 | 44935 | 99504 | 5782 | 6331 |

## B Visual Explanation Examples

While analyzing visual explanations, we observe that our method performs better for larger pathologies, such as "Cardiomegaly" and prone to failure for smaller pathologies, such as "Atelectasis". We provide two such cases below.

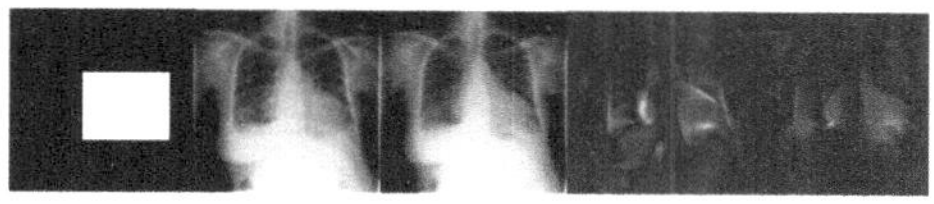

**Fig. 3.** Successful visual explanation of the "Cardiomegaly" pathology using concept vectors. From left to right: (a) Concept mask highlighting the region of interest, (b) Original chest X-ray image, (c) Reconstructed image from the autoencoder, (d) Latent shift 2D attribution map generated by the baseline method, and (e) Attribution map generated using the NIH concept vector.

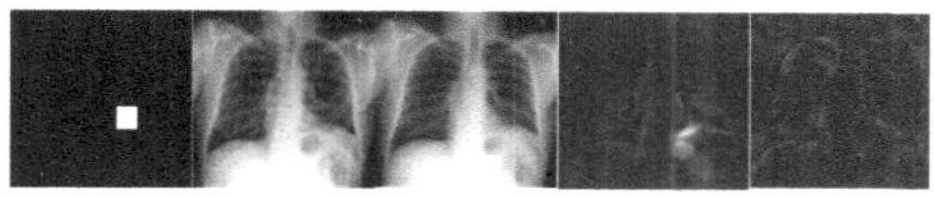

**Fig. 4.** Example of a failed explanation for "Atelectasis". From left to right: (a) Concept mask highlighting the region of interest; (b) Original chest X-ray; (c) Reconstructed image; (d) Baseline latent shift attribution map; (e) Attribution map. The failure is likely due to the small size, variable localization of atelectasis, and limitations in the autoencoder's reconstruction fidelity for fine-grained features.

# C CAV Hyperparameters

**Table 5.** Hyperparameters for generating and evaluating CAVs

| Batch size | 500 |
|---|---|
| Num positive samples | 250 |
| Num negative samples | 250 |
| Number of concept vectors for averaging | 10 |
| Max step size | 1000 |

# References

1. Adebayo, J., Gilmer, J., Muelly, M., Goodfellow, I., Hardt, M., Kim, B.: Sanity checks for saliency maps. Adv. Neural Inf. Process. Syst. **31** (2018)
2. Atad, M., et al.: Chexplaining in style: Counterfactual explanations for chest x-rays using stylegan. arXiv preprint arXiv:2207.07553 (2022)
3. Augustin, M., Boreiko, V., Croce, F., Hein, M.: Diffusion visual counterfactual explanations. In: NeurIPS (2022)
4. Cohen, J.P., et al.: Gifsplanation via latent shift: a simple autoencoder approach to counterfactual generation for chest x-rays. In: Medical Imaging with Deep Learning, pp. 74–104. PMLR (2021)

5. Cohen, J.P., et alH.: TorchXRayVision: A library of chest X-ray datasets and models. In: Medical Imaging with Deep Learning (2022). https://github.com/mlmed/torchxrayvision
6. Holmberg, L.: Towards benchmarking explainable artificial intelligence methods. ArXiv **abs/2208.12120** (2022). https://api.semanticscholar.org/CorpusID:251800062
7. Irvin, J., et al.: Chexpert: A large chest radiograph dataset with uncertainty labels and expert comparison. In: Proceedings of the AAAI conference on artificial intelligence, vol. 33, pp. 590–597 (2019)
8. Kim, B., Wattenberg, M., Gilmer, J., Cai, C., Wexler, J., Viegas, F., et al.: Interpretability beyond feature attribution: Quantitative testing with concept activation vectors (tcav). In: International Conference on Machine Learning, pp. 2668–2677, PMLR (2018)
9. Liu, S., Ye, H., Xing, L., Zou, J.: In-context vectors: making in context learning more effective and controllable through latent space steering. In: Proceedings of the 41st International Conference on Machine Learning, ICML'24, JMLR.org (2024)
10. Naveed, S., Stevens, G., Robin-Kern, D.: An overview of the empirical evaluation of explainable ai (xai): A comprehensive guideline for user-centered evaluation in xai. Appl. Sci. **14**(23) (2024). https://doi.org/10.3390/app142311288. https://www.mdpi.com/2076-3417/14/23/11288. ISSN 2076-3417
11. Selvaraju, R.R., Cogswell, M., Das, A., Vedantam, R., Parikh, D., Batra, D.: Grad-cam: Visual explanations from deep networks via gradient-based localization. In: Proceedings of the IEEE International Conference on Computer Vision (ICCV) (2017)
12. Viviano, J.D., Simpson, B., Dutil, F., Bengio, Y., Cohen, J.P.: Saliency is a possible red herring when diagnosing poor generalization. arXiv preprint arXiv:1910.00199 (2019)
13. Wang, X., Peng, Y., Lu, L., Lu, Z., Bagheri, M., Summers, R.M.: Chestx-ray8: Hospital-scale chest x-ray database and benchmarks on weakly-supervised classification and localization of common thorax diseases. In: Proceedings of the IEEE Conference on Computer Vision and Pattern Recognition, pp. 2097–2106 (2017)

# Fault Isolation and Explainable AI for Satellite Health Monitoring

James Murphy[1,3], Muhammad Deedahwar Mazhar Qureshi[1,2](✉), and Brian Mac Namee[3]

[1] Realtra Space Systems Engineering, Dublin, Ireland
[2] SFI Centre for Research Training in Machine Learning (ML-Labs), Technological University Dublin, Dublin, Ireland
mqureshi@realtra.space
[3] School of Computer Science, University College Dublin, Dublin, Ireland

**Abstract.** Fault Detection, Isolation, and Recovery (FDIR) in safety-critical autonomous systems demands both accurate anomaly detection and interpretable fault diagnosis in complex, multivariate environments. This paper proposes an end-to-end FDIR pipeline that combines unsupervised and supervised learning to robustly detect and classify out-of-ordinary operations (OOOs) in high-dimensional time-series telemetry. An LSTM autoencoder is trained on nominal operational data to learn system dynamics, with reconstruction error thresholding applied to identify deviations from expected behavior. Candidate OOOs are subsequently classified using a supervised model to distinguish true anomalies from non-anomalous deviations, mitigating false alarm rates. To achieve channel-level interpretability, Local Interpretable Model-agnostic Explanations (LIME) is integrated to quantify feature importance for anomaly classification, enabling fine-grained fault isolation. Experimental results on multivariate datasets demonstrate that the proposed architecture achieves high detection accuracy, improved classification precision, and interpretable fault localization, offering a scalable framework for next-generation FDIR in autonomous and safety-critical applications.

**Keywords:** Anomaly Detection · Explainable AI · Satellite Telemetry · Semi-supervised ML

## 1 Introduction

We present an autonomous Fault Detection, Isolation, and Recovery (FDIR) framework for multivariate satellite telemetry, extending previous work on LSTM-based anomaly thresholding [1]. The goal is to enable real-time onboard anomaly detection, classification, and interpretable fault localization, supporting mission-critical decision-making under strict resource constraints. Our system is evaluated on the EIRSAT-1 telemetry dataset [2] and benchmarked on flight-proven and next-generation Edge AI hardware to demonstrate feasibility for future missions.


T. T. Mai et al. (Eds.): AICS 2025, CCIS 2950, pp. 49–60, 2026.
https://doi.org/10.1007/978-3-032-25809-0_5

Spacecraft telemetry monitoring is challenging due to its high dimensionality, limited downlink bandwidth, and the need for rapid fault response. Nominal operational transitions, such as Global Mode (GMOD) and Extended Mode (EMOD) changes, often mimic fault signatures, while thousands of interdependent telemetry channels complicate root-cause analysis. Communication delays and hardware constraints hinder traditional ground-based approaches, motivating the development of an onboard, autonomous solution optimized for tight power, mass, and thermal budgets.

Our approach combines unsupervised and supervised machine learning. An LSTM autoencoder trained on nominal telemetry detects out-of-ordinary operations (OOOs) via reconstruction error thresholding, while a supervised classifier distinguishes true anomalies from benign deviations, reducing false positives. To enhance interpretability, Local Interpretable Model-agnostic Explanations (LIME) identifies the telemetry channels driving each classification, enabling actionable fault diagnosis. We validate this pipeline on both injected-anomaly and real-fault datasets, demonstrating robust detection and diagnostic capabilities.

This paper primarily focuses on the fault isolation step. The autoencoder first detects the presence of a fault. Next, the classifier determines whether the detected change is nominal or anomalous. Finally, the XAI model identifies the specific location of the fault, a process referred to as isolation.

This paper contributes:

1. A complete FDIR pipeline integrating LSTM-based anomaly detection, supervised classification, and XAI-driven fault isolation.
2. A strategy for improving anomaly sensitivity and interpretability in high-dimensional telemetry.
3. An onboard-ready implementation benchmarked on resource-constrained platforms.

This work advances autonomous spacecraft health monitoring by moving beyond thresholding-only methods to a scalable, interpretable FDIR solution.

## 2 Related Work

Autonomous Fault Detection, Isolation, and Recovery (FDIR) is essential for modern spacecraft, where growing telemetry complexity and limited ground contact demand rapid, onboard fault response. Traditional FDIR techniques based on rule-based monitoring and Failure Modes and Effects Analysis (FMEA) scale poorly with high-dimensional telemetry and struggle to detect novel fault modes.

Machine learning (ML) approaches address these limitations by modeling nominal behavior and identifying deviations from it. Hundman et al. [3] applied LSTM encoder-decoders with dynamic thresholding to NASA's SMAP and MSL missions, demonstrating high anomaly sensitivity without manual feature engineering. ML-based techniques have shown promise. Hundman et al. [3] utilized LSTM encoder-decoder models and dynamic thresholding for anomaly detection in NASA's SMAP and MSL datasets. Zeng et al. [4] proposed a causality-based streaming anomaly detection framework (DCDSPOT) tailored for spacecraft telemetry. CubeSat platforms, such as ESA's OPS-SAT [5] and NASA's MCT [6], have also validated ML-driven monitoring in operational contexts.

Interpretability is also increasingly important. Cuéllar et al. [7] presented an XAI approach for spacecraft anomaly detection, applying interpretable ML to support operator trust. Fejjari et al. [8] reviewed the breadth of anomaly detection methods in this domain, noting the growing integration of ML, deep learning, and XAI. Explainable AI (XAI) is increasingly critical for mission assurance. Techniques such as LIME [9] and SHAP [10] provide feature-level attributions, enabling engineers to validate predictions and trace faults to their root causes.

## 3 EIRSAT-1 Dataset Description

We use the EIRSAT-1 dataset [2], which includes:

- **Flight Test Dataset:** Nominal data with injected anomalies for validation.
- **TVAC Test Dataset:** Real anomalies from thermal-vacuum testing.
- **Flight Dataset:** Unlabelled in-orbit telemetry with no reported anomalies.

Telemetry is divided into Housekeeping, Telemetry-Enhanced-Diagnostics (TED), ADCS, and Power subsystems; we focus on Housekeeping data, selecting 85 usable channels after cleaning. The dataset's high dimensionality and interdependent signals make anomaly detection and fault localization difficult, particularly as GMOD and EMOD operational transitions can resemble faults. These challenges motivate the extended FDIR pipeline introduced next.

## 4 End-to-End FDIR Pipeline

To address the limitations of thresholding-only approaches and improve anomaly interpretability, we propose a modular *Fault Detection, Isolation, and Recovery (FDIR)* pipeline that integrates anomaly detection, classification, and explainable diagnostics. The pipeline builds upon our previous autoencoder-based detection system, introducing supervised classification and XAI-based interpretation to enhance accuracy and provide actionable insights.

The proposed pipeline consists of three main stages:

1. **Fault Detection:** Identify out-of-ordinary operations (OOOs) using an LSTM autoencoder trained on nominal telemetry data. Reconstruction error is computed for each time step, and a combination of thresholding techniques is applied to detect candidate anomalies.
2. **Fault Classification:** Differentiate true anomalies from benign deviations (e.g., GMOD and EMOD transitions) using a supervised Multi-Layer Perceptron (MLP) classifier. This reduces false positives and increases operational reliability.
3. **Fault Isolation:** Apply Local Interpretable Model-agnostic Explanations (LIME) to compute feature importance scores for each classified anomaly, enabling channel-level root-cause analysis.

### 4.1 FDIR Pipeline Overview

Figure 1 illustrates the proposed pipeline. Telemetry data is pre-processed and input to the LSTM autoencoder to model nominal spacecraft dynamics. Reconstruction error time series are generated and denoised before thresholding to identify candidate anomalies. An MLP classifies these anomalies to distinguish faults from benign deviations. Finally, LIME is applied to highlight feature importance, isolating the telemetry channels most responsible for each classification decision.

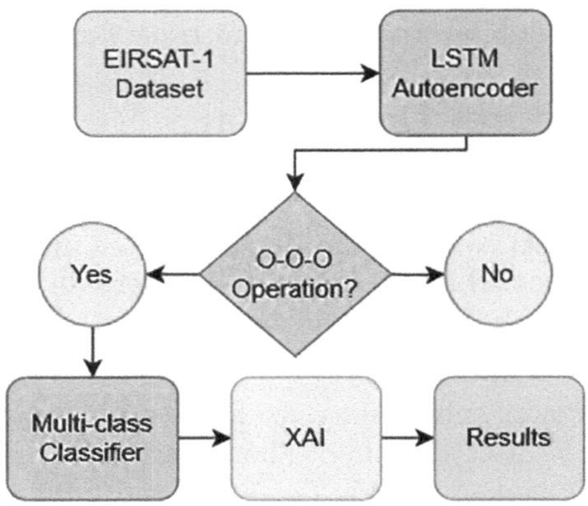


**Fig. 1.** The proposed end-to-end FDIR pipeline consisting of three primary stages: (1) anomaly detection via an LSTM autoencoder, (2) supervised classification of anomalies, and (3) fault isolation using LIME-based explainable AI.

### 4.2 Anomaly Detection: LSTM Autoencoder

We utilize an LSTM autoencoder to model the nominal behavior of spacecraft telemetry. The encoder consists of stacked LSTM layers to capture temporal dependencies in the multivariate input, followed by a decoder that reconstructs the input time series. The reconstruction error is defined as:

$$E_t = \|X_t - \hat{X}_t\|_1, \tag{1}$$

where $X_t$ is the true telemetry vector at time $t$, $\hat{X}_t$ is the reconstructed vector, and $\|\cdot\|_1$ is the L1 norm. A high reconstruction error indicates a deviation from nominal behavior.

### 4.3 Denoising of Reconstruction Error

To reduce false positives caused by signal noise, we apply a convolution-based denoising method to the reconstruction error time series $T_{noisy}$:

$$T_{denoised} = (X \times W) * T_{noisy}, \tag{2}$$

where $X$ is a binary filter of alternating zeros and ones, and $W$ is the filter window size (set to 20 in our experiments). This filter suppresses short-term fluctuations, improving the robustness of threshold-based anomaly detection.

## 4.4 Thresholding Methods

We experiment with multiple thresholding approaches to detect anomalies from $T_{denoised}$:

**Percentile-Based Thresholding:** A static threshold $\theta_p$ is chosen as the $p$-th percentile of reconstruction errors:

$$\theta_p = \text{Percentile}_p(T_{denoised}), \tag{3}$$

where $p$ is tuned on validation data to maximize detection F1 score.

**Z-Score Thresholding:** To adapt to signal variability, we compute the Z-score for each reconstruction error $E_i$:

$$Z(E_i) = \frac{E_i - \mu(E)}{\sigma(E)}, \tag{4}$$

where $\mu(E)$ and $\sigma(E)$ are the mean and standard deviation of the reconstruction error. A sample is flagged as anomalous if $Z(E_i) > \tau_z$, with $\tau_z = 1.5$ determined experimentally.

## 4.5 Supervised Classification

The LSTM autoencoder-based anomaly detection model (Sec. 4) effectively identifies deviations from nominal spacecraft behavior but frequently misclassifies expected operational changes, such as Global Mode (GMOD) and Extended Mode (EMOD) transitions, as anomalies. To address this, we introduce a supervised classification stage to refine anomaly detection by distinguishing between genuine anomalies and benign operational deviations.

**Dataset and Training Strategy:** Telemetry flagged as out-of-ordinary operations (OOOs) by the autoencoder serves as input to the classifier. Rather than using reconstruction error, raw telemetry features are passed to the classifier to capture feature-level relationships better. Labels are defined for three classes: GMOD, EMOD, and true Anomalies.

Labeled anomalies were drawn from the Flight-Test and TVAC datasets, while GMOD/EMOD events were extracted from the Flight dataset. To avoid temporal bias, the Flight dataset was split chronologically (60:40 for training/testing). The EMOD class, being underrepresented, was upsampled using SMOTE. Table 1 summarizes the dataset composition.

**Table 1.** Flight Dataset split used in Classification Model Training and Testing

| Dataset | GMOD | EMOD | Anomaly |
|---|---|---|---|
| Training | 4679 | 1821 | 4200 |
| Test | 2716 | 1885 | 1000 |

**K-Nearest Neighbors Baseline:** A $k$-Nearest Neighbors (kNN) classifier with $k = 5$ was implemented as a simple baseline, using standardized telemetry features. kNN provides a lightweight option for rapid inference and benchmarking but offers limited scalability for high-dimensional telemetry.

**Multi-layer Perceptron Classifier:** The primary classifier is a Multi-Layer Perceptron (MLP), shown in Fig. 2. It comprises three hidden layers with ReLU activations and a softmax output layer:

$$\hat{y} = \text{Softmax}(Wx + b), \tag{5}$$

where $x$ is the input feature vector, and $\hat{y}$ is the predicted probability distribution over GMOD, EMOD, and Anomaly classes. The model was trained using categorical cross-entropy loss and the Adam optimizer, with early stopping and grid search employed for hyperparameter tuning.

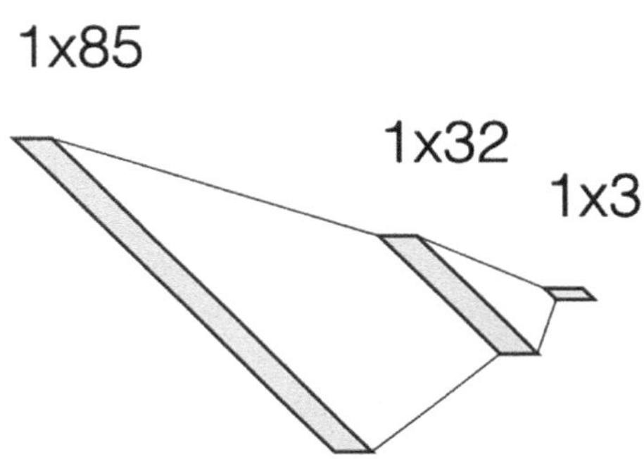


**Fig. 2.** Architecture of the Multi-Layer Perceptron (MLP) multiclass classifier.

**Pipeline Integration:** The classifier acts as a second-stage filter: anomalies flagged by the autoencoder are passed to the MLP (or kNN) to classify events as genuine faults or expected deviations. This hybrid design combines unsupervised detection with supervised classification, reducing false positives and improving operational confidence.

### 4.6 Explainable Fault Isolation with LIME

To provide interpretable insights into anomaly detection outcomes, we apply Local Interpretable Model-Agnostic Explanations (LIME) [9] to the outputs of the LSTM autoencoder and classification models. LIME is used to identify the top 12 telemetry channels (out of 85 inputs) that contribute most significantly to classifying a sample as an Out-of-Ordinary Operation (OOO) or anomaly. These twelve channels collectively account for over 90% of the total attribution for each analyzed sample, providing concise and actionable explanations for system operators.

LIME approximates a model's local decision boundary by generating perturbed samples around a target input and fitting a simple, interpretable surrogate model (typically linear) to explain the prediction in the vicinity of that point. For this work, we selected representative samples from each class (e.g., GMOD, EMOD, Anomaly) and computed per-sample channel contributions to highlight feature-level drivers of anomaly detection.

LIME was chosen for its model-agnostic nature and focus on local interpretability, making it well-suited for diagnosing anomalies in multivariate telemetry where understanding individual predictions is critical. Unlike global explanation methods, which summarize feature importance over entire datasets, LIME produces per-sample attributions, enabling root cause analysis of individual anomaly events. While other techniques, such as SHAP [10] or integrated gradients, can provide global consistency or model-specific insights, they are either computationally intensive or less intuitive for high-dimensional tabular and time-series data. LIME offers a balance between interpretability, flexibility, and efficiency, making it a practical choice for fault isolation in real-time spacecraft anomaly detection pipelines.

## 5 Results and Discussion

This section evaluates the performance of our anomaly detection and classification pipeline on the TVAC and Flight datasets, highlighting key insights from thresholding and classification methods.

### 5.1 Anomaly Detection Results on TVAC and Flight Datasets

Figure 3 and Table 2 summarize anomaly detection performance on the TVAC dataset, which contains two labeled anomalies: a damaged battery board solder joint causing voltage drops and an I2C communication fault between the OBC and communications subsystem. All methods performed comparably (F-Score $\approx$ 0.87), with KNN achieving the highest precision (0.88) and thresholding methods slightly outperforming in recall (0.90). Clear reconstruction error spikes align with the labeled anomalies, confirming the LSTM autoencoder's ability to model nominal telemetry effectively.

Analysis of the Flight dataset, which has no reported anomalies, revealed multiple Out-of-Ordinary Operations (OOOs) primarily corresponding to GMOD and EMOD power transitions (Table 3). These benign operational changes were often flagged as anomalies due to significant reconstruction error deviations, underscoring the need for supervised classification to reduce false positives and distinguish between expected events and genuine faults.

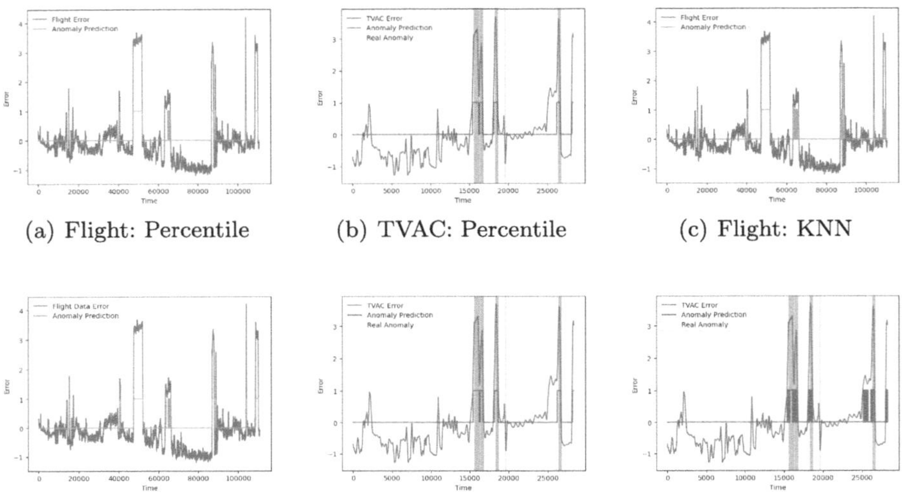

(a) Flight: Percentile (b) TVAC: Percentile (c) Flight: KNN

(d) Flight: Z-Score (e) TVAC: Z-Score (f) TVAC: KNN

**Fig. 3.** Comparison of anomaly detection methods across datasets: (a–c) Flight dataset; (d–f) TVAC dataset. Orange highlights indicate labeled anomalies in TVAC data.

**Table 2.** Performance of detection methods on the TVAC dataset.

| Method | Precision | Recall | F-Score |
|---|---|---|---|
| Percentile Thresholding | 0.84 | **0.90** | 0.87 |
| Z-Score Thresholding | 0.84 | **0.90** | 0.87 |
| K-Nearest Neighbors | **0.88** | 0.87 | **0.88** |

### 5.2 Classifier Results and Discussion

To evaluate the effectiveness of the supervised classification stage, both kNN and MLP models were trained to classify telemetry flagged as Out-of-Ordinary Operations (OOOs) into three classes: GMOD, EMOD, and true anomalies. Table 4 summarizes their performance. The MLP model achieved an F1 score of 0.96, significantly outperforming the kNN baseline (0.87).

**Table 3.** Representative OOOs identified in the Flight dataset.

| OOO | Start | End | Component |
|---|---|---|---|
| 1 | 15309 | 15507 | GMOD |
| 2 | 40633 | 41033 | EMOD |
| 3 | 47540 | 52119 | GMOD |
| 4 | 63200 | 66500 | EMOD |
| 5 | 87060 | 87060 | GMOD |
| 6 | 88971 | 88971 | GMOD |
| 7 | 89750 | 89750 | GMOD |
| 8 | 104125 | 104292 | GMOD |
| 9 | 108806 | 110144 | GMOD |

**Table 4.** Classification model results.

| Method | Precision | Recall | F1 Score |
|---|---|---|---|
| kNN | 0.87 | 0.87 | 0.87 |
| MLP | **0.96** | **0.97** | **0.96** |

These results demonstrate that supervised classification effectively separates true anomalies from expected deviations such as GMOD and EMOD transitions, addressing a major limitation of the autoencoder-only approach. While kNN provides a simple, interpretable baseline, the MLP offers superior accuracy and computational efficiency, making it more suitable for resource-constrained, real-time onboard deployment. The integration of this classification stage significantly improves the interpretability, reliability, and operational feasibility of the anomaly detection pipeline.

### 5.3 Explainability Results for Fault Isolation

To evaluate the interpretability of our anomaly detection framework, we applied Local Interpretable Model-Agnostic Explanations (LIME) [9] to predictions generated by the LSTM autoencoder and classification pipeline. LIME highlights the top 12 telemetry channels contributing most strongly to the model's classification of a sample as an Out-of-Ordinary Operation (OOO) or anomaly. These 12 channels collectively account for over 90% of attribution per sample, enabling operators to pinpoint relevant subsystems quickly.

We analyzed three representative samples, one from each class: GMOD power transitions, EMOD power transitions, and a true anomaly. For each case, we visualized:

1. The top 12 channels with their time-series behavior near the flagged anomaly.
2. A contribution bar chart ranking these channels by importance.

Figures 4a–4f illustrate these analyses. For GMOD and EMOD transitions, the top contributing channels correspond to power and thermal telemetry changes associated with the activation of subsystems. In contrast, for true anomalies, channels tied to communication or power failures dominate the contributions, confirming their diagnostic relevance. These visualizations demonstrate LIME's effectiveness in separating genuine faults from nominal operational changes.

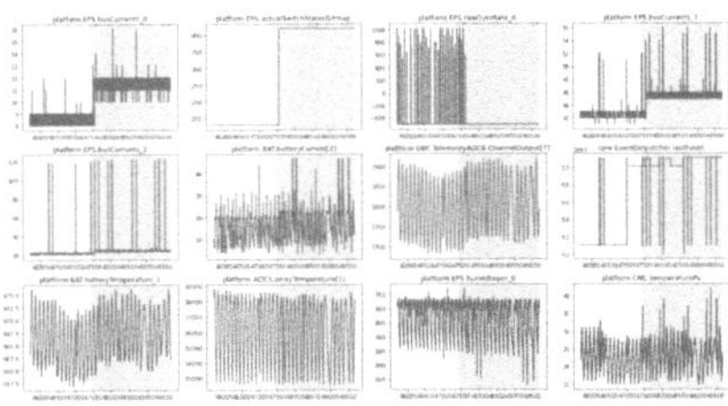

(a) GMOD top 12 contributing channels

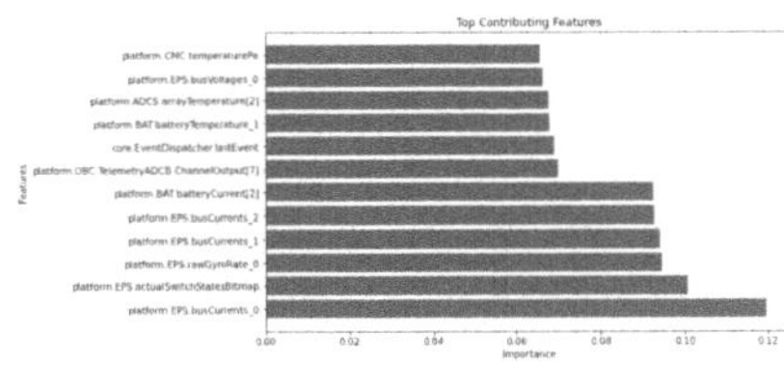

(b) GMOD channel contribution bar chart

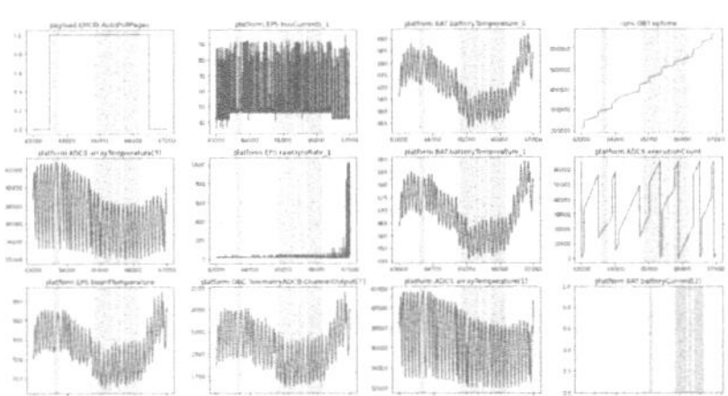

(c) EMOD top 12 contributing channels

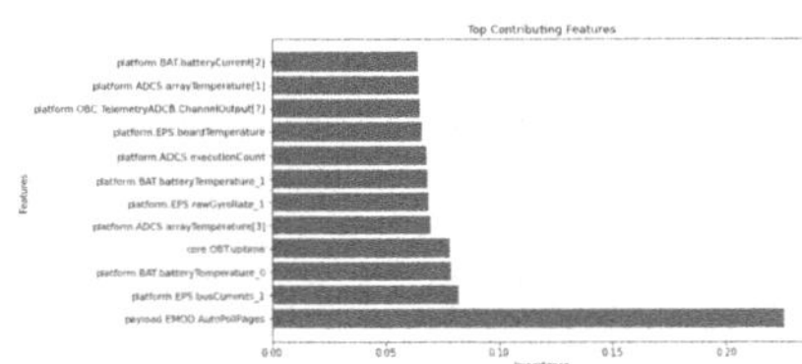

(d) EMOD channel contribution bar chart

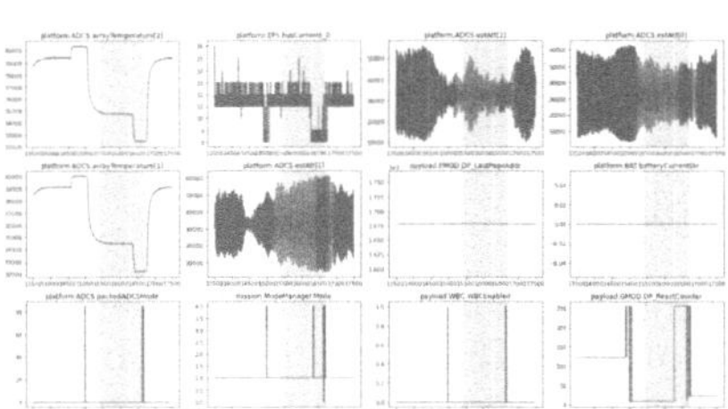

(e) Anomaly top 12 contributing channels

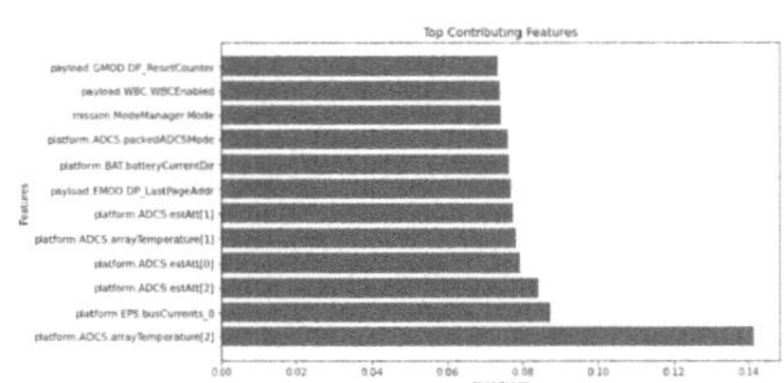

(f) Anomaly channel contribution bar chart

**Fig. 4.** Explainability analysis using LIME for representative telemetry samples. (a,b) GMOD; (c,d) EMOD; (e,f) true anomaly. Left: top 12 contributing channels (ground truth in orange). Right: contribution bar charts. (Color figure online)

### 5.4 Hardware Results Summary

Table 5 compares power consumption and efficiency for deploying the LSTM model across multiple hardware platforms. The Nvidia Jetson Orin Nano performed best overall, with the 15 W mode offering the highest inference speed among edge devices and the 7 W mode delivering a strong balance of performance and power efficiency (lowest dynamic power, Friedman rank 1.67). The Raspberry Pi 4 showed comparable throughput but higher dynamic power, while the Intel Xeon CPU achieved the highest inference speed at the cost of significantly higher power consumption (61 W). The XE2 device ranked third in efficiency, and Zynq results were unavailable. Overall, the Orin Nano is the most suitable platform for low-power, real-time edge deployment.

**Table 5.** Summary of hardware deployment results. Dynamic power is averaged across datasets; lower is better.

| Device | Power (W) | Dynamic Power (W) | Friedman Rank |
|---|---|---|---|
| Orin Nano 15W | 4.72 | 0.67 | 1.33 |
| Orin Nano 7W | 3.81 | 0.75 | 1.67 |
| Raspberry Pi 4 | 2.78 | 2.28 | 4.00 |
| Xeon CPU | 13.00 | 61.00 | 5.00 |
| XE2 | 2.49 | 1.27 | 3.00 |

## 6 Conclusion and Future Work

This paper presents an end-to-end Fault Detection, Isolation, and Recovery (FDIR) pipeline for spacecraft telemetry, combining an LSTM autoencoder for anomaly detection, a supervised multiclass classifier for distinguishing between nominal operations and true faults, and LIME-based explainability for channel-level fault localization. The MLP classifier achieved an F1 score of 0.96 and was identified as the most practical model for real-time, resource-constrained deployment. LIME explanations provided transparency into model decisions, improving operator trust and enabling actionable fault diagnosis.

Future work will focus on in-orbit validation through a tandem deployment, where a lightweight onboard implementation runs in parallel with a larger, high-capacity model to benchmark accuracy, latency, and power trade-offs. Additional research will explore adaptive model updates and scaling the approach to satellite constellations to develop a flight-proven, interpretable, and autonomous spacecraft health monitoring system.

**Acknowledgments.** This work was supported by Irish Research Council PhD Grant EBPPG/2020/11. This work was also supported by an European Space Agency General Science and Technology Program Grant. This work was further supported through the work done by the ML-Labs PhD program.

## References

1. Murphy, J., Qureshi, M.D.M., O'Brien, J., Mac Namee, B.: Autonomous satellite health monitoring using eirsat-1 telemetry (2024)
2. Murphy, J., Wang, F., Mazhar Qureshi, M.D., Namee, B.M.: From ground to orbit: Enhancing satellite autonomy with ai-powered anomaly detection (2024)
3. Hundman, K., Constantinou, V., Laporte, C., Colwell, I., Soderstrom, T.: Detecting spacecraft anomalies using LSTMs and nonparametric dynamic thresholding. In: Proceedings of the 24th ACM SIGKDD International Conference on Knowledge Discovery & Data Mining, pp. 387–395 (2018)
4. Zeng, Z., Jin, G., Xu, C., Chen, S., Zhang, L.: Spacecraft telemetry anomaly detection based on parametric causality and double-criteria drift streaming peaks over threshold. Appl. Sci. **12**(4), 1803 (2022)
5. Evans, D., Merri, M.: Ops-sat: a esa nanosatellite for accelerating innovation in satellite control. In: SpaceOps 2014 Conference, p. 1702 (2014)
6. Trimble, J.: Reconfigurable software for mission operations. In: SpaceOps 2014 Conference, p. 1832 (2014)
7. Cuéllar, S., Santos, M., Alonso, F., Fabregas, E., Farias, G.: Explainable anomaly detection in spacecraft telemetry. Eng. Appl. Artif. Intell. **133**, 108083 (2024)
8. Fejjari, A., Delavault, A., Camilleri, R., Valentino, G.: A review of anomaly detection in spacecraft telemetry data. Appl. Sci. **15**(10), 5653 (2025)
9. Ribeiro, M.T., Singh, S., Guestrin, C.: Model-agnostic interpretability of machine learning. arXiv preprint arXiv:1606.05386 (2016)
10. Lundberg, S.M., Lee, S.-I.: A unified approach to interpreting model predictions. Adv. Neural Inf. Process. Syst. (NeurIPS) **30**, 4765–4774 (2017)

# Bitcoin Prediction: A Hybrid Approach with Recurrent Neural Networks and GPT-Based Reasoning

Zhengri Cui[1,2], Daniel Comerford[1,2(✉)], Martin Crane[1,2], An Nguyen[1,2], and Marija Bezbradica[1,2]

[1] School of Computing, Dublin City University, Collins Ave Ext, Whitehall, Dublin, Ireland
{zhengri.cui2,daniel.comerford2}@mail.dcu.ie,
{martin.crane,ngocannguyen.pham,marija.bezbradica}@dcu.ie
[2] ADAPT Research Centre, Dublin City University, Dublin, Ireland

**Abstract.** This paper proposes a novel hybrid framework in which a large language model (LLM) integrates multiple sources of predictive inputs, including future 30-day ahead trend signals from time-series models, sentiment scores extracted using BERT and technical indicators such as the Relative Strength Index (RSI) and the Moving Average Convergence Divergence (MACD) histogram to generate enhanced forecasts. In the first stage, we conduct feature engineering and selection, followed by sequential modeling to predict the future 30-day moving average (MA) of Bitcoin daily returns. After evaluating all models, the Diebold-Mariano (DM) test shows that LSTM and GRU outperform the Naive, Simple RNN and CNN-LSTM models at the 95% significance level. These predictions from the GRU and LSTM are then converted to directional signals (1 for increase and 0 for decrease). In the second stage, the converted signals are combined with BERT-generated Reddit sentiment scores, RSI and MACD histogram to serve as inputs for GPT-4o in producing further forecasts. This novel architecture achieves the highest directional prediction with an F1 score of 78.9% and produces a 194% higher return in trading simulations compared to a buy-and-hold strategy within the examined period between May 2024 and May 2025.

**Keywords:** Time Series · Recurrent Neural Networks · Cryptocurrency · LLMs · Hybrid Models

## 1 Introduction

Price volatility has been one of Bitcoin's most challenging aspects when it comes to accurate forecasting. Compared to the S&P 500, Bitcoin (BTC) shows significantly higher volatility, with a greater likelihood of extreme returns and an average value-at-risk roughly four times larger, according to a previous study [25]. Despite this high risk, many investors and researchers have explored ways


T. T. Mai et al. (Eds.): AICS 2025, CCIS 2950, pp. 61–78, 2026.
https://doi.org/10.1007/978-3-032-25809-0_6

to mitigate such risks and maximize asset value through various investment strategies and analytical approaches. One such approach is the use of simple technical trading indicators, such as RSI[1] and MACD[2] to identify buy and sell opportunities. Niek Deprez et al. [7] demonstrated that, in terms of risk and return, employing simple technical trading rules results in outperformance over a buy-and-hold approach in the BTC market. In recent years, another widely used method is analyzing news and social media sentiment to capture market trends. Supporting this approach, a recent study [19] found a subtle but evident correlation between news sentiment and BTC price movements, with historical news having a stronger long-term impact on price compared to immediate news events. Furthermore, numerous Machine Learning (ML) and Deep Learning (DL) models have been proposed to forecast the price level or the log returns. However, many of these models do not consider external factors, such as public sentiment [3,34,39]. While expert investors can integrate these multiple factors to make informed financial decisions, ordinary individuals may face knowledge limitations. However, the use of LLMs represents a promising alternative. A recent study reported that ChatGPT based on GPT-4 achieved 99% accuracy on a financial literacy test, suggesting its potential as a robo-advisor [24].

Motivated by these observations, we propose a hybrid framework. Stage 1 of this study models multiple Recurrent Neural Networks (RNNs) to forecast the 30-day moving average (MA) of BTC daily returns, using daily OHLCV[3] of BTC, Ethereum (ETH), Ripple (XRP) and the S&P 500 index, along with BTC network Hash Rate. These predictions from the models are converted to directional signals (1 for increase and 0 for decrease). Stage 2 integrates the signals generated by Stage 1 with additional information, including sentiment scores extracted from Reddit posts using a BERT (Bidirectional Encoder Representations from Transformers) model [8], as well as technical indicators such as RSI and MACD. These inputs are fed into the GPT-4o to produce enhanced, context-aware predictions. This research is guided by two central questions:

- **RQ1:** How accurately can the future 30-day price of Bitcoin be predicted using DL models?
- **RQ2:** Does incorporating multimodal information via GPT-4o improve the directional prediction of Bitcoin price movements?

The framework is evaluated using standard regression metrics for Stage 1, including MAE, MSE, SMAPE. For Stage 2, classification metrics such as Accuracy, Precision, Recall and F1 score are used. The final results indicate that when the predicted signals from the time-series models, Reddit sentiment scores from BERT[4] and technical indicators such as the RSI and MACD histogram

[1] RSI stands for Relative Strength Index.

[2] MACD stands for Moving Average Convergence Divergence.

[3] OHLCV stands for Open, High, Low, Close and Volume in financial markets.

[4] BERT (Bidirectional Encoder Representations from Transformers) is a pre-trained language model developed by Google that learns contextual relations between words by using a bidirectional Transformer architecture.

are all used as inputs to GPT-4o, it achieved the highest F1 score of 78.9% and generated a 194% higher return in trading simulations over the period from May 2024 to May 2025, compared to a buy-and-hold strategy.

## 2 Related Work

Previous studies on BTC price movement forecasting have used various features which can be categorized as follows: (1) BTC price related variables such as OHLCV data [2,3,34]; (2) technical indicators including MACD and RSI [13]; (3) other cryptocurrencies like ETH and XRP [5,19]; (4) macroeconomic and market indicators such as S&P 500 [5,12]; (5) on-chain metrics such as Hash Rate [5,9,12]; (6) public sentiment such as Google Trends, Tweets, Reddit posts and news [5,19,40].

Regarding model application, RNNs have been actively used in many previous studies. A literature review conducted by Boozary et al. [4] concluded that the application of LSTM (Long Short-Term Memory) significantly improves BTC price prediction accuracy. By contrast, neither financial time series forecasting using traditional statistical methods like ARIMA (Autoregressive Integrated Moving Average) [35], nor approaches employing powerful ML algorithms like Random Forest [5], nor even the use of the more recent Transformer architectures [36,40] have outperformed LSTM. Moreover, LSTM has been served as an underlying model in studies utilizing advanced methodologies, including ensemble methods with three LSTM individual models across different time granularities [34], policy-based reinforcement learning techniques [20] and multi-stage CNN-LSTM (Convolutional Neural Network-LSTM) architectures [9].

Another type of RNN is the so-called GRU (Gated Recurrent Unit), which has shown outstanding results in the existing literature. For example, in a study on BTC price prediction [26], this architecture achieved lower RMSE (Root Mean Squared Error) and MAE compared to SVM (Support Vector Machine) and BiLSTM (Bidirectional-LSTM), while another study [39] on Dogecoin prediction also reported that GRU, despite its simpler architecture, has better prediction performance compared to the LSTM model. This indicates the important role of RNNs in financial time series modeling. However, despite their impressive performance, RNNs typically assume that the time series is stationary; therefore, the presence of trends or seasonality can significantly degrade their performance [17].

More recently, alternative methodologies have been proposed that predict the Cryptocurrency Volatility Index as the target variable in order to reduce risk. Nguyen et al. [23] used a novel Deep Neural Network combining LSTM and MLP (Multilayer Perceptron) with an attention mechanism, which has been shown to outperform traditional approaches such as standard LSTM, Temporal Convolution Networks, Random Forest, SVM and other statistical methods. In addition, sentiment-based prediction methods using LLMs have been explored, primarily in the context of stock market forecasting [19,28] and have not yet been used in the cryptocurrency market. In particular, one study utilised ChatGPT to analyse news headlines and predict stock price movements without any specialized training. This method resulted in a cumulative return of over 650% between October 2021 and December 2023 [21]. Another study conducted a live experiment with ChatGPT-4, showing that its ratings respond to earnings surprises and news events, resulting in a positive correlation with future earnings announcements and stock returns [28]. These works fill the gap by showing that LLMs can forecast financial markets without specialized training and respond to real-time events.

## 3 Stage 1: Time Series Prediction via Sequential Models

Before discussing the first stage of our study, we first present the overall architecture and workflow employed in this work (as displayed in Fig. 1), encompassing all key steps from data collection to final prediction. Our methodology is structured into two stages. In the first stage (discussed in Sect. 3), we use sequential DL models (CNN-LSTM [2], Simple RNN [10], LSTM [14], GRU [6]) to predict the 30-day MA of daily percent returns based on quantitative time-series data. The predicted numerical values from LSTM and GRU are then converted into directional signals (1 for increase, 0 for decrease). In the second stage (outlined in Sect. 4), these directional signals are combined with sentiment scores (daily, 7-day MA and 30-day MA) generated by a BERT model, along with the RSI and MACD histogram to be fed into the GPT-4o. Under prompt engineering and temperature control settings, the GPT-4o is used to produce enhanced context-aware predictions. Details are shown in Fig. 1:

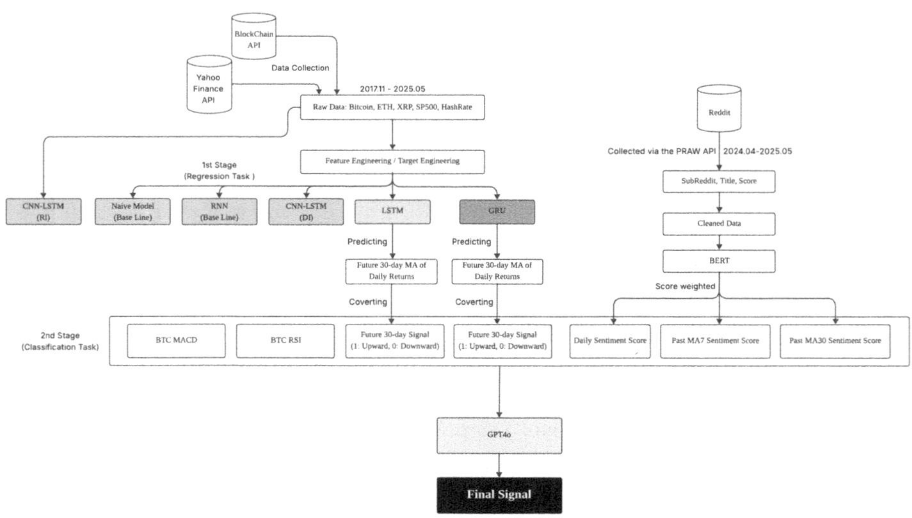


**Fig. 1.** This figure illustrates the overall architecture and key steps of the proposed hybrid framework.

### 3.1 Data Collection and Preprocessing

Daily interval OHLCV data was collected for ETH, XRP and the S&P 500 index using the Yahoo Finance API and BTC network Hash Rate via Blockchain API. Since ETH has a relatively short historical record on Yahoo Finance, we made sure the common date range across all assets, from 2017-11-09 to 2025-06-15, when ETH data was consistently available. To address the missing data caused by its weekend market closing for S&P 500 index, we applied forward-fill imputation, propagating Friday's data to Saturday and Sunday.

On the other hand, BTC, which serves as the features and target in our study, required a longer historical span to account for potential data loss during feature and target engineering. Therefore, BTC data was collected from 2017-01-01 to ensure sufficient data.

### 3.2 Feature and Target Engineering

In our workflow, standardization techniques[5] such as Daily Percentage Change [11], Log Returns [11] and Fractional Differentiation [17,29] were employed to stabilize the statistical properties of the data. In addition, MA smoothing [31] was used to reduce noise. These transformations were applied only for the Close and Volume series of BTC, ETH, XRP and the S&P 500 index, as well as Hash Rate data.

A total of 43 features were engineered, including the 2 prediction target candidates. To clearly illustrate the differences among these transformations, we present only the visualization of BTC Close transformations in Fig. 2. The blue plot represents the non-stationary raw closing price of BTC over time. The green plot represents the daily percentage returns of BTC's closing price. This transformation is similar to applying a full differencing, which primarily stabilizes the mean and variance over time. In contrast, the orange plot displays the result of applying fractional differencing to the closing price series. Exploratory experiments were conducted by changing the window size and fractional order to identify a transformation that ensures the time series is statistically stationary (ADF test $p$-value $< 0.05$), while preserving the highest correlation with the original series. Among the tested set, a window size of 130 and a fractional order of 0.48 provided a good balance between memory retention and stationarity. The p-value from the ADF test was 0.0416, indicating that the transformed series is stationary at the 5% significance level. This fractionally differenced series is used as one of the input features in modeling stage. From the initial set of 43 features, a multi-stage feature and target selection process was conducted. The overall workflow is illustrated in Fig. 3.

Regarding target selection, this study aims to build a robust model for reliable forecasting in the volatile BTC market, where stable model training is a necessary precondition, regardless of whether the target is short-term daily returns

[5] Stationarization refers to transforming a non-stationary time series into a stationary one whose mean, variance and autocorrelation structure remain stable over time.

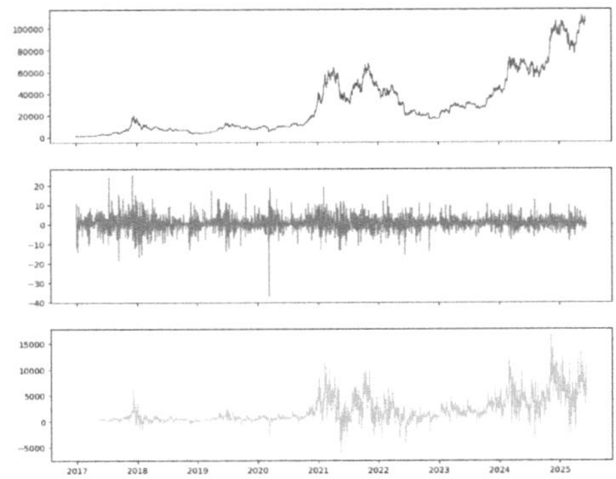


**Fig. 2.** Raw Data vs Stationarised Data.

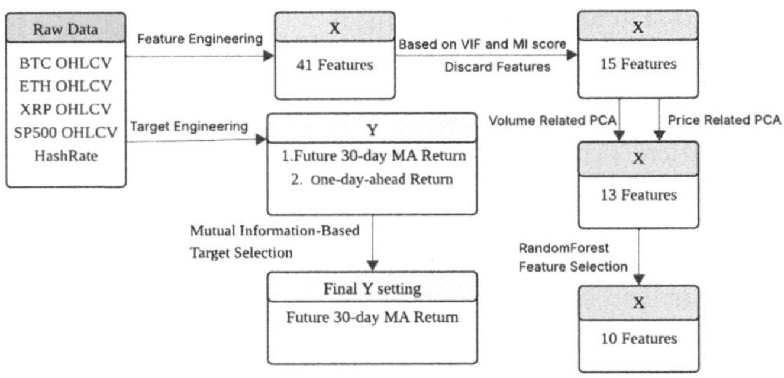


**Fig. 3.** Target and Feature Selection Workflow.

or long-term return trends. To achieve this objective, two candidates were considered as potential target variables: (1) the 1-day ahead BTC close return and (2) the future 30-day MA of returns.

The MI (Mutual Information) was calculated between input features and the continuous target variable using `mutual_info_regression` from Scikit-Learn. The method is nonparametric and based on entropy estimation using K-nearest neighbors distance [18,32]. The analysis revealed that the future 30-day MA of returns showed MI values exceeding 0.1 for 9 out of 15 BTC-related features, whereas the 1-day ahead BTC return exhibited significantly lower MI values, with the highest being only 0.0322. These findings suggest that short-term returns are heavily affected by noise and do not maintain meaningful information relationships even with its derived sources from BTC-related variables. Accordingly, to enhance model predictive performance, the future 30-day MA of returns was selected as the final target variable for this study.

Regarding input feature selection, the initial 41 input features were reduced to 15 using MI and VIF (Variance Inflation Factor). The criteria are as follows:

- Features with MI values below 0.05 were discarded.

- Features derived from the same asset and similar data types (e.g., price-based: Open, High, Low, Close, RollingClose; volume-based: Volume, RollingVolume) were grouped due to their similar variance. Within each group, only the feature with the highest MI was selected to reduce redundancy.

However, several features still exhibited VIF values exceeding 10, indicating that a high degree of multicollinearity remains in the dataset. Therefore, we reduce their multicollinearity using PCA (Principal Component Analysis) technique, resulting in 6 features being reduced to 4 based on price and volume groups.

In the final stage, Random Forest-based feature importance analysis was applied to reduce the 13 features to a final set of 10. Among the 13 features, `RollingHashRate` and `BTC_Close_FracDiff_MA` still showed VIF values exceeding 10. As noted by Raschka et al. [30], when two or more features are highly correlated, one feature may be ranked very highly, while the importance of the others may be distorted. To address this issue, two separate Random Forest experiments were carried out, each excluding one of the two high-VIF features to ensure each group of VIF value is lower than 10. Based on feature importance and cross-experiment consistency, the last three were excluded, yielding a final set of 10 features, which are described in Table 1:

**Table 1.** Final Feature Set ($X$)

| Feature ($\boldsymbol{X}$) | Description |
|---|---|
| BTC_Close_FracDiff_MA | 30-day MA of fractionally differenced BTC close price |
| RollingHashRate | 30-day MA of BTC network hashrate |
| BtcRollingLogReturn | 30-day MA of log returns of BTC close price |
| RollingEthChange | 30-day MA of percentage change in ETH close price |
| XrpRollingClosePrice | 30-day MA of XRP close price |
| RollingXrpChange | 30-day MA of percentage change in XRP close price |
| SP500_RollingChange | 30-day MA of percentage change in SP500 close price |
| PC1_price | PC1 from 30-day MA of BTC/ETH/SP500 close prices |
| PC2_price | PC2 from 30-day MA of BTC/ETH/SP500 close prices |
| PC1_volume | PC1 from RollingBTCVolume and ETH, SP500 volumes |

### 3.3 Modeling

Min-Max scaling [27] was applied to the prepared input features $X$ and target variable $y$. The dataset was then split chronologically into train (70%), validation (15%) and test (15%) sets. To build models that are robust to temporal variations, the 70% train dataset is further divided into 4 sequential blocks. As

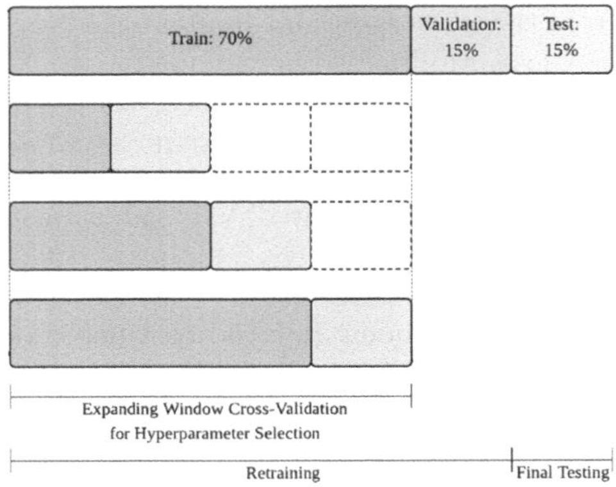


**Fig. 4.** Hyperparameter Tuning Process

illustrated in Fig. 4, this procedure applies an Expanding Window Cross Validation [17] approach with a fixed random seed. We evaluated the average MAE across the 3 folds to select the hyperparameters. The selected hyperparameters were then used to retrain the model on the initial 70% train and 15% validation sets. In terms of model usage, time series models including RNN, LSTM and GRU were employed. Additionally, a Naive Baseline Model was constructed by forecasting the future 30-day MA of BTC close returns as the same value as the past 30-day MA in order to compare model performance. To further validate the effect of manually denoising the input features before training, we also compared our approach against a state-of-the-art CNN-LSTM model [2], which incorporates convolutional and max-pooling layers for automatic denoising. In the first comparison, the denoised inputs (DI) used in the other models were applied to the CNN-LSTM to evaluate performance differences resulting from the model architecture. In the second setting, 21 raw inputs (RI), including the OHLCV data of BTC, ETH, XRP, S&P 500 index and the Hash Rate were used as features. Table 2 presents the hyperparameter search ranges used for each implemented model.

**Table 2.** Comparison of hyperparameter search spaces for different models

| | Simple RNN | LSTM | GRU |
|---|---|---|---|
| Lags | 2, 3, 4, **5** | 5, 6, **7**, 8, 10, 12, 14 | 5, 6, 7, **8**, 10, 12, 14 |
| Epochs | **500 (Early Stopping)** | **500 (Early Stopping)** | **500 (Early Stopping)** |
| Hidden Layers | **2**, 3 | 2, **3**, 4, 5 | 2, **3**, 4, 5 |
| Neurons | 4, **8**, 16, 32, 64, 128 | 4, 8, 16, **32**, 64, 128 | 4, 8, **16**, 32, 64, 128 |
| Batch Size | **16**, 32 | 16, **32** | 16, **32** |
| Learning Rate | **0.0001**, 0.00005 | **0.0001**, 0.00005 | **0.0001**, 0.00005 |
| Optimizer | Adam, **RMSprop** | **Adam**, RMSprop | **Adam**, RMSprop |
| Activation | **Relu** | Relu, **LeakyRelu(0.01)** | Relu, **LeakyRelu(0.01)** |
| Dropout | 0.2, 0.3, **0.4** | 0.2, **0.4**, 0.6 | 0.2, **0.4**, 0.6 |

| | CNN-LSTM (DI) | CNN-LSTM (RI) |
|---|---|---|
| Lags | 7, **8**, 10, 14, 20 | 7, 8, 10, **14**, 20 |
| Epochs | **300 (Early Stopping)** | **300 (Early Stopping)** |
| Convolutional Layers | **1**, 2 | 1, **2** |
| Max Pooling Layers | **1**, 2 | 1, **2** |
| Filters | 32, **64** | 32, **64** |
| Kernel Size | **3**, 6 | **3**, 6 |
| Batch Size | **16**, 32 | 16, **32** |
| LSTM Neurons | **16**, 32, 64, 128 | **16**, 32, 64, 128 |
| Dense Neurons | 16, **32**, 64, 128 | **16**, 32, 64, 128 |
| Optimizer | **Adam** | **Adam** |
| Activation | **Relu** | **Relu** |
| Dropout | **0.2**, 0.3, 0.4 | **0.2**, 0.3, 0.4 |

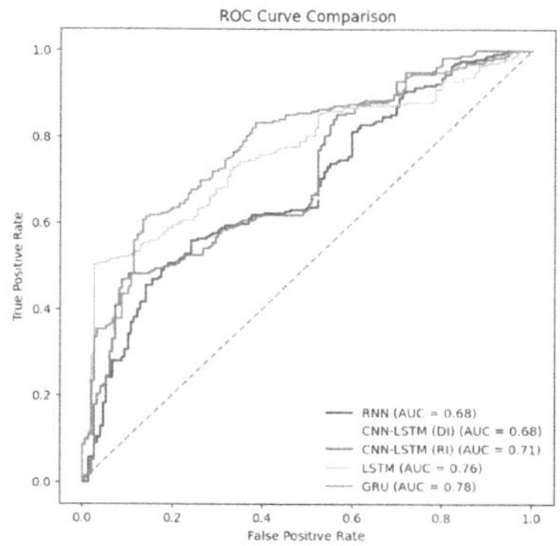


**Fig. 5.** ROC curve on test set

### 3.4 Evaluation and Results

When evaluated using regression metrics from Table 3, CNN-LSTM, Simple RNN, LSTM and GRU significantly outperformed the Naive model. For the state-of-the-art CNN-LSTM model, using the denoised features as input resulted in lower performance compared to using 21 raw features. This performance gap may be attributed to the additional smoothing introduced by the convolution and max-pooling layers, which led to further information loss. Interestingly, CNN-LSTM (RI) achieved the lowest percentage-dependent metrics (SMAPE) on both the training and test sets, while LSTM and GRU demonstrated lower scale-dependent metrics (MAE and MSE). This occurs because SMAPE evaluates the relative distance between each predicted value and its corresponding ground truth, without taking the overall distribution into account. MSE and MAE, on the other hand, penalize errors according to their magnitude [15]. Therefore, the observed outcome is reasonable due to the inherent volatility of BTC target value, which causes large variations in magnitude. Moreover, in Fig. 5, ROC (Receiver Operating Characteristic) analysis across varying thresholds also confirmed that GRU (AUC: 0.78) and LSTM (AUC: 0.76) outperformed RNN (AUC: 0.68), CNN-LSTM trained on raw input (AUC: 0.71) and CNN-LSTM trained on denoised input (AUC: 0.68).

To further investigate the performance differences among RNN, LSTM and GRU, Diebold-Mariano test was conducted on the test dataset, and the result showed that both LSTM and GRU statistically outperformed over RNN ($p < 0.05$). However, no significant difference was found between LSTM and GRU ($p = 0.3287$). Figure 6 further illustrates the comparison between actual values and the predictions generated by the CNN-LSTM (RI), Simple RNN, LSTM and GRU models on both the training and test datasets. It can be observed that LSTM and GRU more closely follow the actual value patterns than others.

Based on the overall evaluation, the models were ranked as:

LSTM $\approx$ GRU $>$ CNN-LSTM (RI) $>$ Simple RNN $>$ CNN-LSTM (DI) $>$ Naive

**Table 3.** Model Performance on Train & Test

| Model | Training Set | | | Test Set | | |
|---|---|---|---|---|---|---|
| | MAE | MSE | SMAPE | MAE | MSE | SMAPE |
| Naive | 0.147 | 0.035 | 29.10% | 0.091 | 0.011 | 16.95% |
| Simple RNN | 0.098 | 0.016 | 20.88% | 0.056 | 0.005 | 11.5% |
| LSTM | 0.096 | 0.015 | 21.64% | **0.050** | **0.004** | 12.01% |
| GRU | **0.095** | **0.015** | 21.81% | 0.051 | 0.004 | 11.82% |
| CNN-LSTM (DI) | 0.103 | 0.017 | 22.64% | 0.063 | 0.007 | 13.83% |
| CNN-LSTM (RI) | 0.100 | 0.016 | **19.71%** | 0.055 | 0.005 | **10.28%** |

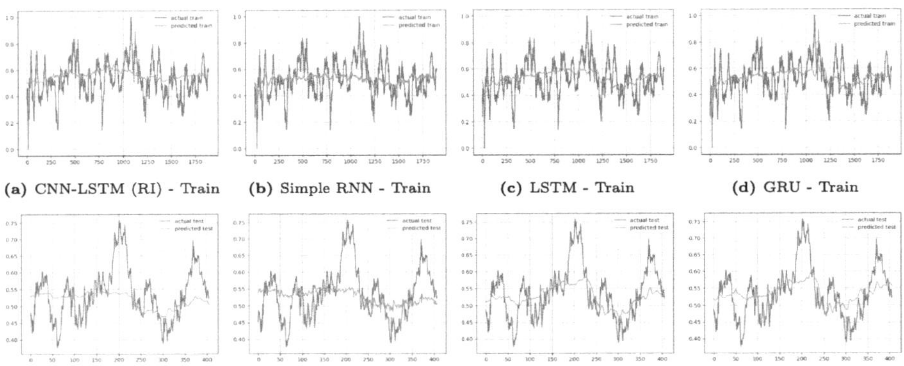

(a) CNN-LSTM (RI) - Train (b) Simple RNN - Train (c) LSTM - Train (d) GRU - Train

(e) CNN-LSTM (RI) - Test (f) Simple RNN - Test (g) LSTM - Test (h) GRU - Test

**Fig. 6.** Actual vs. predicted values on train and test sets for CNN-LSTM (RI), Simple RNN, LSTM and GRU models.

These results answer our RQ1, suggesting that standalone LSTM and GRU models, when combined with appropriate feature engineering and selection, can outperform state-of-the-art CNN-LSTM models, which capture local patterns and perform automated denoising through their convolutional and pooling layers. The final optimal thresholds in LSTM and GRU were determined using both the training and validation sets to ensure consistency. The binarized directions were then used as input features for the following stage.

# 4 Stage 2: GPT-4o Fusion for Hybrid BTC Direction Forecasting

## 4.1 Data Collection and Processing

### 4.1.1 Converted Signal from RNNs

Based on the best predictive performance of the LSTM and GRU models described in Sect. 3, we applied a signal conversion procedure to their outputs.

The thresholding procedure was conducted using only the training and validation sets, leaving the test set completely unseen. More specifically, we first determined the threshold interval that produced the highest AUC on the training and validation sets. Within this interval, we evaluated a range of candidate thresholds and selected the value that achieved the best F1 score. The final selected threshold was then applied to the test set for evaluation.

### 4.1.2 Reddit Textual Data

To integrate public sentiment into Stage 2 of our framework, Reddit was selected due to its high volume of organic, real-time discourse, particularly in the financial and cryptocurrency communities [33]. We collected Reddit submissions from April 5, 2024 to May 16, 2025 via PRAW API. Due to restrictions on sending requests, the data were collected in Python by sending requests with delays using the sleep function. Each submission record contains the `subreddit`, `title`, `posted_date`, `score` (computed by Reddit from upvotes and downvotes) and the `number_of_comments`. During the processing stage, we applied several filtering steps to ensure post quality. Specifically, submissions with a score of zero or with no comments were removed from the dataset. For text preprocessing, all characters were converted to lowercase, URLs beginning with "http" or "www" were removed from the titles and stopwords were filtered out [16]. This step helps control the length of the textual content, which is necessary because the subsequent sentiment extraction is performed using BERT, which is constrained by a 512-token limit.

The primary reason for using BERT in sentiment analysis is its encoder-only Transformer architecture, which is trained to capture bidirectional context [8] and it also has the advantage of being open-source and freely available. In contrast, GPT-4o, being a generative LLM, can process text directly; however, its usage incurs costs (OpenAI API Pricing) proportional to the number of input and output tokens per call. Therefore, in this study, GPT-4o is employed for the final decision-making stage, while BERT is used for sentiment analysis to balance performance and cost efficiency. This approach reflects a real investment scenario, ensuring that the cost does not outweigh the potential gain.

Each processed title was passed through BERT to obtain a sentiment score ranging from −2 to 2. The daily sentiment score 1 was computed by weighting each post's sentiment score according to the `score` (computed by Reddit from upvotes and downvotes) column. To capture weekly and monthly sentiment trends, the 7-day moving average (MA7) and 30-day moving average (MA30) sentiment scores were calculated 2. While the dataset spans from April 5, 2024, the actual input to GPT-4o begins on May 4, 2024, due to missing values generated during the MA7 and MA30 calculation processes.

The computation formulas are presented below:

$$\text{Weighted Daily Sentiment Score}_d = \frac{\sum_{i \in d} \text{sentiment}_i \cdot \text{score}_i}{\sum_{i \in d} \text{score}_i} \quad (1)$$

$$\text{MA}_d^{\text{NumDays}} = \frac{1}{\text{NumDays}} \sum_{k=0}^{\text{NumDays}-1} \text{Weighted Daily Sentiment Score}_{d-k} \quad (2)$$

$d$: a specific date; $i \in d$: each post on date $d$; sentiment$_i$: BERT-computed sentiment score of post $i$; score$_i$: the engagement score of post $i$ (reflecting upvotes and downvotes); $k$: index over the previous NumDays, used in the NumDays MA calculation.

#### 4.1.3 Technical Indicators

MACD is an indicator that uses the difference between moving averages to identify trend and momentum reversals. It was proven to be a useful tool for traders in the 1980s [1] and is generally applied using the standard settings of MACD (12, 26, 9), which is also used in this study. The RSI [38], introduced by Wilder in 1978, has been widely adopted and is useful for detecting overbought and oversold conditions, capturing short-term momentum changes. In this study, the RSI is calculated using a 14-day period based on BTC's closing prices. According to the 30/70 rule, RSI values above 70 are considered overbought, while values below 30 are considered oversold.

### 4.2 GPT-4o Setup and Prompt Engineering

#### 4.2.1 GPT-4o Setup

In this study, the GPT-4o model was configured with a temperature of 0.0 to ensure deterministic output generation, providing consistent and trustworthy evaluations [37], along with a response type of `"json_object"` for structured outputs and a maximum completion token limit of 256.

#### 4.2.2 Prompt Engineering

To conduct the ablation studies, we constructed prompts using five different feature combinations, as shown in Table 4. A concrete example of one such prompt is presented in Prompt 5, with an illustration of the actual output provided in Response Example.

**Table 4.** Feature combinations used for ablation study

| Prompt | Features Included |
|---|---|
| Prompt 1 GPT (RM) | RSI, MACD Histogram Value |
| Prompt 2 GPT (RMS) | RSI, MACD Histogram Value, Sentiment (Daily), Sentiment (MA7), Sentiment (MA30) |
| Prompt 3 GPT (GLRM) | GRU predicted signal, LSTM predicted signal, RSI, MACD Histogram Value |
| Prompt 4 GPT (GLS) | GRU predicted signal, LSTM predicted signal, Sentiment (Daily), Sentiment (MA7), Sentiment (MA30) |
| Prompt 5 GPT (GLSRM) | GRU predicted signal, LSTM predicted signal, Sentiment (Daily), Sentiment (MA7), Sentiment (MA30), RSI, MACD Histogram Value |

**Prompt 5**

You are an expert in Bitcoin Investing. Based on the following information:
1. A GRU model predicted future 30-day trend signal: 1 indicates an expected increase and 0 indicates an expected decrease. Its performance on the training set is: Accuracy = 0.64, Precision = 0.64, Recall = 0.74, and F1-score = 0.69.
2. An LSTM predicted future 30-day trend signal: 1 indicates an expected increase and 0 indicates an expected decrease. Its performance on the training set is: Accuracy = 0.66, Precision = 0.66, Recall = 0.78, and F1-score = 0.71.
3. Reddit daily sentiment, past 7-day moving average sentiment (MA7) and past 30-day moving average sentiment (MA30) obtained using BERT sentiment analysis.
4. Current RSI
5. Current MACD Histogram

Do the following:
1. Predict the future 30-day trend signal: 1 if expected to increase, 0 if expected to decrease.
2. Provide the reason for your decision and predicted signal.

Response follow this JSON Example:
'future_30day_signal': '1', 'reason': 'some reason'
'future_30day_signal': '0', 'reason': 'some reason'

**Response Example**

'future_30day_signal': '1', 'reason': 'Both the GRU and LSTM models predict an increase in the next 30-days, with the LSTM model showing slightly better performance metrics. The sentiment analysis shows a positive trend with the MA7 sentiment being higher than the MA30 sentiment, indicating growing positive sentiment. The RSI is in a neutral zone, suggesting there is room for upward movement. The MACD histogram is positive, indicating bullish momentum. These factors combined suggest a buying opportunity with an expected increase in the future 30-day trend.'

## 4.3 Evaluation and Results

### 4.3.1 Classification Metrics

When evaluating the models using classification metrics, as shown in Fig. 7, we observed a significant performance improvement when external features were added to the predictions of the GRU and LSTM models. However, no substantial differences were observed among GPT(GLRM), GPT(GLS) and GPT(GLSRM) based on classification metrics. Therefore, we conducted McNemar's test [22] to further examine the differences among these three. The results indicated a significant difference between GPT(GLSRM) and GPT(GLS), with a p-value of 0.018, which is significant at the 5% level. No notable differences were found for the other combinations.

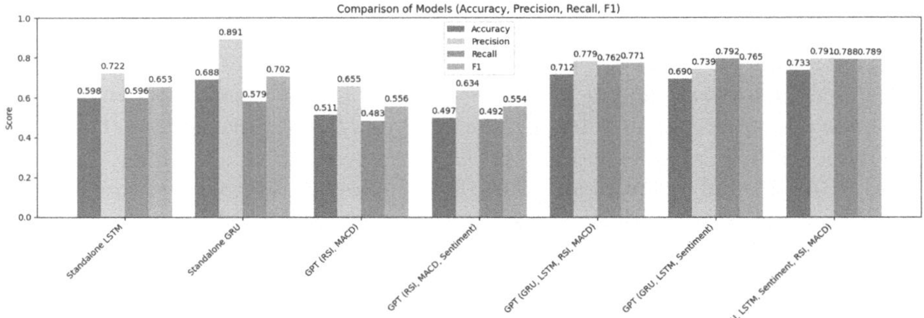


**Fig. 7.** Classification performance across different models.

### 4.3.2 Trading Simulation

In the trading simulation, we compared the predicted signals from the five distinct prompts along with a buy-and-hold strategy. The simulation was conducted under the following assumptions: 1) Fixed invested capital of $10,000; 2) No additional purchases for consecutive 1 signals; 3) No additional sales for consecutive 0 signals.

As shown in Fig. 8, GPT (GLSRM) achieved the highest cumulative return, producing a 194% higher return compared to the buy-and-hold baseline. This was followed by GPT (GLRM) and GPT (GLS) in descending order. Although GPT (GLRM) and GPT (GLS) showed similar classification metrics and cumulative returns, GPT (GLRM) demonstrated better risk-adjusted performance, as GPT (GLS) relatively more often fell below initial capital. Meanwhile, GPT (RM) and GPT (RMS), which did not incorporate signals from GRU and LSTM, underperformed relative to the buy-and-hold strategy.

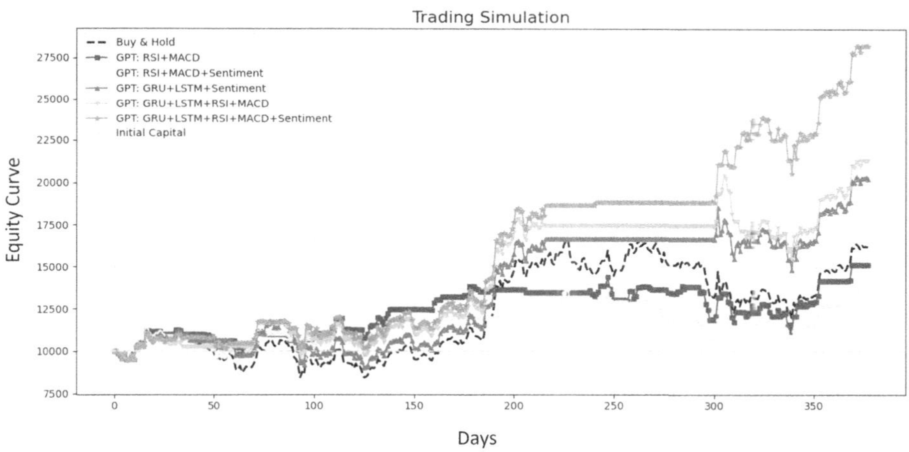


**Fig. 8.** Equity Curve Comparison (from 2024-05-04 to 2025-05-16).

These results indicate that incorporating multimodal information, such as RSI, MACD[6] and sentiment scores into GPT-4o improves the directional prediction of BTC price movements. Among the feature combinations, when the GPT-4o incorporating the most information, GLSRM, achieved the highest performance, answering our RQ2.

## 5 Conclusion and Discussion

This study introduces a hybrid framework for BTC price direction prediction combining both time series models with a GPT-4o reasoning layer integrated with multimodal information. This framework resulted in an increase in F1 score as high as 78.9% and 194% higher return in trading simulations compared to a

[6] RSI and MACD on their own are not multimodal, but combining them with sentiment scores and LSTM/GRU signals, they become multimodal.

buy-and-hold strategy between May 2024 and May 2025. While this framework is applied to BTC in this study, the architecture in Fig. 1 could be adapted to other domains such as stock trading, sports forecasting and retail sales forecasting by switching sentiment source and adjusting model inputs accordingly.

Further work could be conducted to use finer time resolutions such as gathering hourly data to predict the 24-h MA returns. Moreover, the impact of each subreddit and other technical indicators could be systematically evaluated to better understand their contribution to predictive performance. In addition to this, further research using news headlines or other data sources could also lead to improved results. Additionally, future studies could consider weighted buy and sell signals, as the current simulation does not incorporate weighted decision-making. A further constraint of the study was that the model could be susceptible to sentiment manipulation. A large trader could, in theory, flood Reddit with coordinated negative posts to influence sentiment and the model's predictions. Future versions should consider countermeasures such as bot detection, source weighting, or cross-referencing sentiment signals.

**Acknowledgement.** This research was conducted with the financial support of Research Ireland under Grant Agreement No. 13/RC/2106_P2 at the ADAPT Centre at Dublin City University. ADAPT, the Research Ireland Centre for AI-Driven Digital Content Technology, is funded through the Research Ireland Centres Programme. For the purpose of Open Access, the author has applied a CC BY public copyright licence to any Author Accepted Manuscript version arising from this submission.

## References

1. Appel, G., Hitschler, W.F.: Stock Market Trading Systems. Dow Jones-Irwin, Homewood, IL (1980)
2. Badar, W., Ramzan, S., Raza, A., Fitriyani, N.L., Syafrudin, M., Lee, S.W.: Enhanced interpretable forecasting of cryptocurrency prices using autoencoder features and a hybrid CNN-LSTM model. Mathematics **13**(12) (2025). https://doi.org/10.3390/math13121908
3. Berger, T., Koubová, J.: Forecasting bitcoin returns: Econometric time series analysis vs. machine learning. J. Forecast. **43**(7), 2904–2916 (2024). https://doi.org/10.1002/for.3165
4. Boozary, P., Sheykhan, S., GhorbanTanhaei, H.: Forecasting the bitcoin price using the various machine learning: a systematic review in data-driven marketing. Syst. Soft Comput. **7**, 200209 (2025). https://doi.org/10.1016/j.sasc.2025.200209
5. Chen, J.: Analysis of bitcoin price prediction using machine learning. Risk Financ. Manag. (2023). https://doi.org/10.3390/jrfm16010051
6. Cho, K., van Merrienboer, B., Bahdanau, D., Bengio, Y.: On the properties of neural machine translation: Encoder-decoder approaches (2014). https://arxiv.org/abs/1409.1259
7. Deprez, N., Frömmel, M.: Are simple technical trading rules profitable in bitcoin markets? International Rev. Econ. Financ. **93**, 858–874 (2024). https://doi.org/10.1016/j.iref.2024.05.003, https://www.sciencedirect.com/science/article/pii/S1059056024003010

8. Devlin, J., Chang, M., Lee, K., Toutanova, K.: BERT: pre-training of deep bidirectional transformers for language understanding. CoRR abs/1810.04805 (2018). http://arxiv.org/abs/1810.04805
9. Dubey, R., Enke, D.: Bitcoin price direction prediction using on-chain data and feature selection. Mach. Learn. Appl. **20**, 100674 (2025). https://doi.org/10.1016/j.mlwa.2025.100674
10. Elman, J.L.: Finding structure in time. Cogn. Sci. **14**(2), 179–211 (1990). https://doi.org/10.1016/0364-0213(90)90002-E
11. Fan, J., Yao, Q.: The Elements of Financial Econometrics. The Elements of Financial Econometrics, Cambridge University Press (2017). https://books.google.co.kr/books?id=7N0cDgAAQBAJ
12. Georgoula, I., Pournarakis, D., Bilanakos, C., Sotiropoulos, D. Giaglis, G.M.: Using time-series and sentiment analysis to detect the determinants of bitcoin prices. SSRN (2015). https://doi.org/10.2139/ssrn.2607167
13. Hafid, A., Rahouti, M., Kong, L., Ebrahim, M., Serhani, M.A.: Predicting bitcoin market trends with enhanced technical indicator integration and classification models (2024). https://arxiv.org/abs/2410.06935
14. Hochreiter, S., Schmidhuber, J.: Long short-term memory. Neural Comput. **9**(8), 1735–1780 (1997). https://doi.org/10.1162/neco.1997.9.8.1735
15. Jierula, A., Wang, S., OH, T.M., Wang, P.: Study on accuracy metrics for evaluating the predictions of damage locations in deep piles using artificial neural networks with acoustic emission data. Appl. Sci. **11**(5) (2021). https://doi.org/10.3390/app11052314
16. Jurafsky, D., Martin, J.H.: Speech and Language Processing. Pearson, 3rd edn. (2023). https://web.stanford.edu/~jurafsky/slp3/
17. Kaabar, M., et al.: Deep Learning for Finance. Apress, New York, NY (2024). https://link.springer.com/book/10.1007/978-1-4842-9232-0
18. Kraskov, A., Stögbauer, H., Grassberger, P.: Estimating mutual information. Phys. Rev. E **69**, 066138 (2004). https://doi.org/10.1103/PhysRevE.69.066138
19. Liu, C., Arulappan, A., Naha, R., Mahanti, A., Kamruzzaman, J. Ra, I.H.: Large language models and sentiment analysis in financial markets: a review, datasets, and case study. IEEE Access **12**, 134041–134061 (2024). https://doi.org/10.1109/ACCESS.2024.3445413
20. Liu, F., Li, Y., Li, B., Li, J., Xie, H.: Bitcoin transaction strategy construction based on deep reinforcement learning. Appl. Soft Comput. **113**, 107952 (2021). https://doi.org/10.1016/j.asoc.2021.107952
21. Lopez-Lira, A., Tang, Y.: Can chatgpt forecast stock price movements? return predictability and large language models. SSRN (2023). http://dx.doi.org/10.2139/ssrn.4412788
22. McNemar, Q.: Note on the sampling error of the difference between correlated proportions or percentages. Psychometrika **12**(2), 153–157 (1947). https://doi.org/10.1007/BF02295996
23. Nguyen, A.P.N., Crane, M., Bezbradica, M.: Cryptocurrency volatility index: an efficient way to predict the future cvi. In: Longo, L., O'Reilly, R. (eds.) Artif. Intell. Cogn. Sci., pp. 355–367. Springer Nature Switzerland, Cham (2023)
24. Niszczota, P., Abbas, S.: Gpt has become financially literate: insights from financial literacy tests of GPT and a preliminary test of how people use it as a source of advice. Financ. Res. Lett. **58**, 104333 (2023). https://doi.org/10.1016/j.frl.2023.104333

25. Nzokem, A., Maposa, D.: Bitcoin versus s&p 500 index: return and risk analysis. Math. Comput. Appl. **29**(3) (2024). https://doi.org/10.3390/mca29030044, https://www.mdpi.com/2297-8747/29/3/44
26. Pattanayak, R.M., Sai Raju, M.C., Vishnu, V., Vivek, S.T., Rithwik, J.S.: Gated recurrent unit based deep learning model for bitcoin price prediction. In: 2024 International Conference on Integrated Intelligence and Communication Systems (ICIICS), pp. 1–7 (2024). https://doi.org/10.1109/ICIICS63763.2024.10859990
27. Pedregosa, F., et al.: Scikit-learn: Machine learning in Python. J. Mach. Learn. Res. **12**, 2825–2830 (2011)
28. Pelster, M., Val, J.: Can chatgpt assist in picking stocks? Financ. Res. Lett. **59**, 104786 (2024). https://doi.org/10.1016/j.frl.2023.104786
29. de Prado, M.L.: Advances in Financial Machine Learning. Wiley Publishing, 1st edn. (2018)
30. Raschka, S., Mirjalili, V.: Python Machine Learning. Packt Publishing Ltd., Livery Place 35 Livery Street Birmingham B3 2PB, UK, second edn. (2017)
31. Raudys, A.: Pabarškaitė, Ž: Optimising the smoothness and accuracy of moving average for stock price data. Technol. Econ. Dev. Econ. **24**(3), 984–1003 (2018). https://doi.org/10.3846/20294913.2016.1216906
32. Ross, B.C.: Mutual information between discrete and continuous data sets. PLoS ONE **9**(2), 1–5 (2014). https://doi.org/10.1371/journal.pone.0087357
33. Roumeliotis, K.I., Tselikas, N.D., Nasiopoulos, D.K.: LLMS and NLP models in cryptocurrency sentiment analysis: a comparative classification study. Big Data Cogn. Comput. **8**(6), 63 (2024). https://doi.org/10.3390/bdcc8060063
34. Shin, M., Mohaisen, D., Kim, J.: Bitcoin price forecasting via ensemble-based LSTM deep learning networks. In: 2021 International Conference on Information Networking (ICOIN), pp. 603–608 (2021).https://doi.org/10.1109/ICOIN50884.2021.9333853
35. Siami-Namini, S., Tavakoli, N., Siami Namin, A.: A comparison of arima and LSTM in forecasting time series. In: 2018 17th IEEE International Conference on Machine Learning and Applications (ICMLA), pp. 1394–1401 (2018). https://doi.org/10.1109/ICMLA.2018.00227
36. Sonata, I., Heryadi, Y.: Comparison of lstm and transformer for time series data forecasting. In: 7th International Conference on Informatics and Computational Sciences (2024). https://doi.org/10.1109/ICICoS62600.2024.10636892
37. Submission, A.: Time series augmented generation for financial applications. ACL ARR May 2025 Submission (2025). https://openreview.net/forum?id=O2CgjW8JZF, available via OpenReview
38. Wilder, J.W.: New Concepts in Technical Trading Systems. Trend Research, Greensboro, NC, USA (1978)
39. Yao, M., Sun, G., Liu, J.: Gru prediction method for digital cryptocurrency prices. In: 2023 4th International Conference on Computer, Big Data and Artificial Intelligence (ICCBD+AI), pp. 412–416 (2023). https://doi.org/10.1109/ICCBD-AI62252.2023.00076
40. Zhao, H., Crane, M., Bezbradica, M.: Attention! transformer with sentiment on cryptocurrencies price prediction, pp. 98–104 (2022). https://doi.org/10.5220/0011103400003197

# Evaluating Pre-trained 3rd Party AI Models in Medical Device Software Development for Responsible and Ethical Use

N. St John Lynch[1(✉)], M. McHugh[1], R. Loughran[1], F. McCaffrey[1], and D. Kowalski[2]

[1] Regulated Software Research Centre, Dundalk Institute of Technology, Dublin Road, DundalkLouth 91 K584, Co, Ireland
niamh.stjohnlynch@dkit.ie

[2] Brainlab SE, Olof-Palme-Straβe 9, 81829 Munich, Germany

**Abstract.** It is well understood that new standards are necessary to ensure the use of Artificial Intelligence-enabled Medical Devices (AIeMD) are adequately controlled. CEN-CENELEC (European focus) and IEC (Global focus) are developing such standards. Yet the use of pre-trained AI models, available as Software of Unknown Provenance (SOUP) from 3rd party suppliers, remain excluded from the standards under development. This paper aims to demonstrate the need for standardisation of the qualification process for these models beyond that understood by existing standards such as ISO 13485 and IEC 62304. This is necessary in order to achieve responsible and ethical AI for use in healthcare. This paper demonstrates the need for guidance by setting out emerging use cases as well as the risks and potential risk mitigations available when using pre-trained models as SOUP in the Software Development Lifecycle of AIeMD. It goes further to outline the necessary characteristics that should be standardised. Evaluation questions are provided and demonstrate salient points necessary for responsible and ethical AI.

**Keywords:** Pre-trained Artificial Intelligence · transformer · foundation model · SOUP · Software Development Lifecycle · SDLC · Medical Device

## 1 Introduction

### 1.1 Pre-trained AI Models Use in Medical Devices

Pre-trained Artificial Intelligence (AI) models are becoming the go-to solution for a range of AI challenges in healthcare. A pre-trained AI model is an AI foundation model that has already been trained on a large dataset to learn general patterns of language, image or audio or can be a combination of these. They can be used as is, or adapted for specific tasks. Pre-trained models are becoming more widely available and save an AI developer time and resources. General Pre-trained Transformer (GPT) [1] and Bidirectional Encoder Representations from Transformers (BERT) [2] are examples of Large Language Models (LLMs) that have been trained on large open-source data sets


T. T. Mai et al. (Eds.): AICS 2025, CCIS 2950, pp. 79–107, 2026.
https://doi.org/10.1007/978-3-032-25809-0_7

[3]. The release of BERT by Google in 2018 was the first encoder architecture to read a sentence from both directions [2]. This was a significant improvement over previous models, including GPT at the time, that read text from left to right. BERT was deemed to be able to better understand the context and therefore, be a better predictor of text responses. BERT is trained on a huge dataset (e.g., Wikipedia) and can be subsequently fine-tuned for specific tasks with relatively little data. Although BERT was a game-changer, when we consider its use in AI-enabled Medical Devices (AIeMDs), we need to be cautious. As suggested by the Google team who first presented BERT, fine-tuning can be done by adding just one additional output layer to create state-of-the-art models for a wide range of tasks [2]. Any Pre-Trained Model (PTM) can be expected to have in-built bias given the wide range of data used, including 'knowledge' that may be inaccurate. Although BERT is a significant improvement on previous models, when used for development of medical devices, there could be any amount of misinformation in the pre-learned dataset, such as "*alkaline diet is a cure for cancer*" [4]. This requires a level of rigor and independent assessment by competent personnel to evaluate the model selected and assess potential for in-built bias in the pre-trained AI model. It also raises questions as to how much additional data and training should be used in the transfer and fine-tuning process to ensure the AIeMD is adequately trained to perform as intended in healthcare [5, 6]. Lastly it raises questions about the level of transparency provided by 3$^{rd}$ party suppliers and what information should be passed onto industry and eventually regulators when reviewing technical documentation for market clearance to meet regulatory requirements [7, 8].

This paper focuses on PTM use by medical device organizations and AI developers seeking to reap the many benefits promised from AI in healthcare [9]. The aim is to inform the healthcare industry, standards organizations and regulatory bodies about the advantages and disadvantages of using PTMs. It highlights the risks that can arise when selecting and using PTMs [10]. It also recommends a standardised approach for evaluating these models to ensure responsible, ethical use with safety and security. To support standardisation, this paper provides a guidance checklist that can be used to evaluate PTMs when adopted for use in AIeMDs. This checklist reflects on current research such as Trustworthy AIeMD including questions adopted from the AI-Change Management (AICM) process [11]. The AICM checklist includes a section on PTMs and this is reviewed against the Chinese standard issued by the NMPA, China's Competent Authority [12].

Europe and the US have yet to create such a standard. In the meantime, development of an AIeMD using PTMs is well underway. This is recognized by the Consumer Technology Association (CTA), who have written to the FDA to advise on the need for consideration of PTMs following the recent FDA guidance "*Artificial Intelligence Enabled Device Software Functions: Lifecycle Management and Marketing Submission Recommendations*" and "*Considerations for the Use of Artificial Intelligence to Support Regulatory Decision-Making for Drug and Biological Products*" [13]. The CTA have recommended that the FDA clarify the regulatory obligations for 3$^{rd}$-party developers of foundation models (i.e., PTMs) used in AIeMD, emphasizing that these developers should *not* be subject to Quality System Regulation requirements. The CTA urge a risk-based approach. Where the responsibility lies on the medical device manufacturer, the requirements of ISO 13485 Quality Management System (QMS) are not sufficient without additional clarity and regulatory guidance for mitigating the risks posed by pre-trained AI models [14].

The objective of this paper is to outline the prevalence of PTM use in medical device development. It seeks to highlight the benefits and risks associated with selection and use and provide a method for standardising the assessment as part of the Software Development Lifecycle (SDLC) process. This paper is broken down as follows: Sect. 2 identifies example use cases in healthcare using pre-trained AI models. Section 3 demonstrates the variety and accessibility of pre-trained AI models available to medical device developers. Section 4 looks at pros and cons with a deeper dive into risks associated with PTMs. Section 5 looks at current guidance and standardisation for these models in the medical device SDLC. Section 6 examines some of the primary characteristics that require guidance for understanding when using these models. The conclusion is presented in Sect. 7 followed by an ***Appendix***, with a list of considerations to be utilized by a regulator and AIeMD developer when selecting and documenting a PTM for use in the SDLC.

## 2 Pre-trained Model Use Cases in Healthcare

### 2.1 Pre-trained Large Language Models

Research demonstrates that PTMs can be used with limited additional training to solve a task 'similar' to that in which it is trained typically requiring 'fine-tuning'. For use in healthcare, the question of the amount of additional learning and fine-tuning is important. It is understood that the model architecture can be enhanced by transformer models for encoding and decoding patterns, hence paving the way for a myriad of solutions [15]. The BERT example above is an encoding only model. The question of whether the architecture needs to be updated is a consideration for developers. Examples of uses cases include *medical note-taking* or *prescription writing* based on auditory recognition of a patient-practitioner consultation, with pre-training performed on a wide range of open-source data. The medical device manufacturer can decide to narrow the scope and fine-tune the AI model with additional medical-specific learning and testing. Guardrails should be set to ensure the LLM continues to learn from peer-reviewed clinical articles or a defined set of medically accepted text books. However, bias may already have been learned from the pre-learning stage [16]. Interestingly Ada Health, an SaMD AI symptom checker is not built on a generic pre-trained LLM like GPT or BERT [17]. Instead, it uses specialized knowledge based with proprietary reasoning algorithms that were developed with specialist medical knowledge in-house. This type of system is closer to a clinical decision support system and not considered a general-purpose LLM. The purpose of highlighting this is that approval of one type of 'diagnostic' clinical support tool may not reflect the architecture of another in any way. This type of AI is covered under the current regulatory framework and 'Ada' is cleared for market use in the EU having a product risk category of IIa (i.e., low risk device) [18]. Standards under development are focusing on introducing requirements for machine learning (ML) having a narrow focus, and only just starting to initiate guidance and standards on LLMs [19]. PTMs are yet another category in their own right. This highlights the difference in architecture that is important when assessing the risk-profile of any AIeMD.

## 2.2 Pre-trained Large Imaging Models

There may be an assumption that this is a problem for language models only. However, research demonstrates that the majority of use-cases in healthcare currently involve image classification, particularly radiology and cardiology. This is primarily due to the number of images already collected by both healthcare organization and medical device manufacturers ready to reap the benefits promised from AI in healthcare [11]. PTMs used for imaging include ResNet [5] and Visual Geometry Group (VGG) [20] that have already learned features to recognize such as shapes, edges and objects from large data sets [21]. ResNet is an example of a network that has been trained on a large image dataset that can be utilized as a starting point for specific medical device use cases. One can download the weights for ResNet50 for instance, and modify the final layers of the network (referred to as retraining or transfer learning) in order to tackle a new problem scenario [22]. The VGG architecture comes in various sizes (e.g., VGG16, VGG19). VGG 16 has 16-layers (13 convolutional layers and 3 fully connected layers). These deep learning models are intended to improve accuracy by extending the depth of weights as shown in 2014 by Simonyan and Zisserman when using ImageNet (a database of 14 million images across 1000 classes) [23]. The convolutional filters are stacked to allow the model to learn complex features more effectively. Medical devices focusing on radiology typically use these types of models as their starting point [24]. The question is whether they have sufficient understanding to choose the most appropriate model and adapt it to their use case or whether they rely on whatever is available. Any AI developer can select a PTM to set about development activity and transfer learning to a new use case to improve healthcare. The intention is sound and also necessary given a healthcare system that is extensively challenged [25]. The question we must ask is, how are these models controlled and do we understand them sufficient to mitigate the risks they could introduce?

## 2.3 Do Pre-trained Models Identify as SOUP in Industry?

Some might simply say these PTMs are simply SOUP items and therefore should be controlled as such. Since these models are available from a 3$^{rd}$ party supplier they are identified as 'SOUP' – *Software of Unknown Provenance* - within the medical device SDLC. However, the traditional SOUP requirements do not adequately cover the risks associated with PTMs [26]. Moreover, industry do not appear to be able to clearly identify PTMs when brought into the SDLC process. This is evidenced in this research whereby, members of a leading industry conference held in Boston USA in October 2025, on Medical Device Cybersecurity, demonstrated. A quiz was given to 44 members of the audience in attendance using a QR code link to MS Forms. The question of whether PTMs were used in medical device development was asked. The results identified 30% as using PTMs in their medical device product development lifecycle; 61% said no- they were *not* using PTMs and 9% were not sure if they were used, refer to Fig. 1. The 2nd question presented here from the short quiz asked whether a PTM was *a)* an AI component, *b)* an integrated software item *c)* a SOUP item under IEC 62304 and *d)* other. All questions were posed as quick multiple-choice questions. The results show that 34% reported that PTMs were a SOUP item. It is not clear from this study whether the 34%

who believe PTMs are SOUP are the same 30% who have PTMs in development. In any event, 14% said a PTM was an integrated software item and 43% (the majority) said that it was an AI component; the remaining 6% were not sure and selected 'other'. Refer to Fig. 1 Medical Device Industry Quiz on Pre-Trained Models. Although this quiz was a 5-question quick survey presented at a medical device industry conference with a focus on cybersecurity, it highlights the lack of clarity around identifying PTMs and hence, how to control them. This survey was performed by medical device technical experts and reveals a lack of understanding that exists in relation to PTMs when used as part of an AIeMD within the SDLC process.

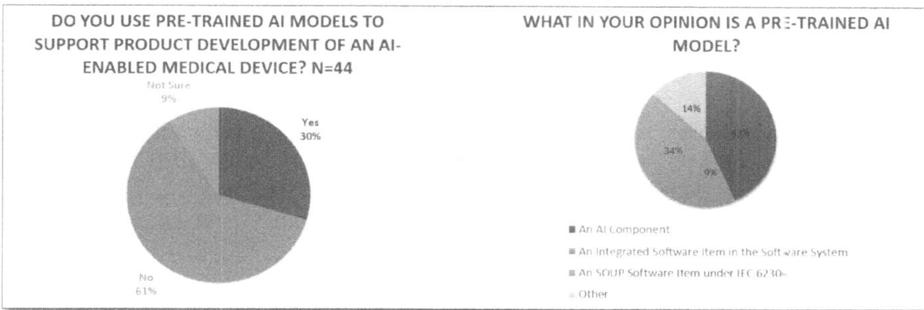


**Fig. 1.** Medical Device Industry Quiz on Pre-Trained Models

# 3 Availability of Pre-trained AI Models

Pre-trained AI Models are widely available on the market and continue to grow given their open-source accessibility [10]. A search of Microsoft, Google or GitHub yields a wide range of PTMs for use in the medical domain. Ref. Table 1 LLM Medical AI/ML Pre-Trained Models for a sample.

**Table 1.** LLM Medical AI/ML Pre-Trained Models

| Model Name | Description | Location | Use Case |
|---|---|---|---|
| BioBERT | A pre-trained biomedical language representation model | https://github.com/dmis-lab/biobert | Biomedical text mining, NLP tasks |
| BioGPT | A generative pre-trained transformer model for biomedical text generation | https://github.com/microsoft/BioGPT | Biomedical text generation, NLP |
| BioMistral-7B | A Collection of Open-Source Pretrained Large Language Models for Medical Domains | https://huggingface.co/BioMistral/BioMistral-7B | Biomedical text mining, NLP tasks |
| BlueBERT | BERT-based model trained on PubMed abstracts and MIMIC-III clinical notes | https://github.com/ncbi-nlp/bluebert | Biomedical research, clinical notes |
| ClinicalBERT | A Pretrained Model on a large corpus of 1.2B words of diverse diseases. Fine-tuned on 3 million patient records | https://huggingface.co/medicalai/ClinicalBERT | Medical question-answering (QA) tasks |

(*continued*)

**Table 1.** *(continued)*

| Model Name | Description | Location | Use Case |
|---|---|---|---|
| ClinicalBERT | BERT model fine-tuned on clinical notes | https://github.com/EmilyAlsentzer/clinicalBERT | Clinical text analysis, EHR data |
| LLaVA-Med | A large language and vision model trained using a curriculum learning method for adapting LLaVA to the biomedical domain | https://huggingface.co/microsoft/llava-med-v1.5-mistral-7b | Medical question-answering (QA) tasks |
| SciBERT | A BERT-based model trained on scientific text | https://github.com/allenai/scibert | Scientific literature analysis |

## 3.1 Open and Closed Source Vision Models

With the growing number of open source and closed source applications emerging, widespread use by AIeMD organizations can be anticipated. Table 2 and Table 3 provide examples of vision and multimodal models. There are also specialised models (e.g., COVID-NET) and framework models (e.g., MONAI, PyHealth, NVIDIA Clara) among the growing number of medical models available for download.

**Table 2.** Pre-Trained Vision Models

| Model Name | Description | Link | Use Case |
|---|---|---|---|
| Vision Transformer (Open-source, (OS)) | A deep learning model for classification & segmentation on imaging data | https://github.com/google-research/vision_transformer | Radiology, Pathology |
| CheXbert (OS) | Automatic Labelers and Expert Annotations | https://github.com/stanfordmlgroup/CheXbert | Radiology |
| UNet (OS) | A convolutional neural network for biomedical image segmentation | https://github.com/zhixuhao/unet | Biomedical image segmentation |
| nnU-Net (OS) | A self-configuring method for biomedical image segmentation | https://github.com/MIC-DKFZ/nnUNet | Biomedical image segmentation |
| AI for Breast Cancer (CS) | AI model for improving breast cancer screening accuracy | https://health.google/caregivers/mammography/ | Breast cancer screening, diagnostics |
| AI for Diabetic Retinopathy (CS) | Detects diabetic retinopathy and diabetic macular edema | https://health.google/caregivers/arda/ | Diabetic retinopathy screening, ophthalmology |
| Sepsis Prediction Algorithm (CS) | Early warning system for sepsis in ICU patients | https://www.hopkinsmedicine.org/ | Sepsis detection, ICU management |
| COVID-19 Severity Prediction | AI models for predicting COVID-19 severity | https://www.hopkinsmedicine.org/ | COVID-19 patient management, severity prediction |
| InnerEye | AI for medical imaging, including radiotherapy and image analysis | https://www.microsoft.com/en-us/research/project/medical-image-analysis/ | Radiotherapy planning, medical imaging analysis |
| PathAI | Models for pathology image analysis, including cancer detection | https://www.pathai.com/ | Pathology diagnostics, cancer detection |

*(continued)*

**Table 2.** *(continued)*

| Model Name | Description | Link | Use Case |
|---|---|---|---|
| RAD AI | AI-powered assistants for radiologists | https://www.radai.com/ | Radiology assistance, diagnostics |
| Butterfly iQ + | Handheld ultrasound device with integrated AI for diagnostics | https://www.butterflynetwork.com/ | Point-of-care diagnostics, ultrasound imaging |

**Table 3.** Pre-Trained Multimodal Models

| Model Name | Description | Link | Use Case |
|---|---|---|---|
| edNLI | Natural language inference dataset for the clinical domain | https://github.com/jgc128/mednli | Clinical decision support, NLP |
| Med3D | Pre-trained 3D medical image analysis model | https://github.com/Tencent/MedicalNet | 3D medical image analysis |

We also see the emergence of an Open Medical-LLM Leaderboard from 'huggingface.co' which may provide some level of assuredness, but to what extent? The leaderboard is based on reported accuracy for a given use case, at a point in time, given precise settings and objectives. The reported level of accuracy has to be cautioned, as it is difficult to re-create accuracy for different use cases, or even for the same use case. This is particularly true when a measure of accuracy of a model can be inflated based on repeat testing (overfitting) and is a measure at a point in time only and dependent on the test data. It is not always clear what is included in the accuracy measurement, e.g., whether the metric reflects the macro measure of all datasets or the best selected dataset and so on. It can only be taken as a rough guide at best and even then, must be challenged.

## 4 Advantages and Disadvantages of Using Pre-trained Models

When we consider the range of medical PTMs, it starts to become clear that to ignore PTMs and start development of an AI model from scratch might be non-sensical in some cases. The advantages are the ease of access to such models ready for download. The groundwork for the AI developers is largely done, at least from a computational resource standpoint. A search for a similar intended use allows a developer to move straight to transfer learning, fine-tuning and testing with a limited dataset.

Considerations by developers that make using PTMs a valid option include improved performance where pre-training on diverse data have already encoded knowledge through pattern identification [27]. Computational resources are another key attribute that is supported. Pre-trained foundation models demand extensive compute power and trustworthy deployment must account for infrastructure and scalability. Microsoft specifically warn that their "*healthcare AI [foundation] models are intended for research and model development exploration and are not designed or intended to be deployed in clinical settings as-is*" [28]. However, using a PTM is preferred by many, as training from scratch is power intensive requiring large data stores that are difficult to source and consume high energy costs. Fine-tuning of PTMs on domain-specific data is clearly more practical requiring moderate GPU resources. While PTMs are advantageous, their adoption for clinical tasks require consideration for computing power and storage and can require high-end GPUs (e.g., NVIDIA V100/A100/H100). The release of NVIDIA's H100 allows for LLMs such as BioGPT [29] and ClinicalBERT [30] to be trained for use in healthcare tasks with faster convergence or learning (i.e., training weights stabilise and loss/error stops decreasing significantly). This enables potential for real-time imaging analysis supporting generative AI use in healthcare [31].

Residual Neural Network (ResNet) as already mentioned was introduced in 2015 for image recognition and was shown to outperform on previous visual recognition architectures such as VGGNet, released only a year before [5, 20]. ResNet is trained on large image datasets such as ImageNet (~14 million images). Patterns and feature abstraction is performed through statistical reasoning or identification of relationships (regression/correlation, etc.). Optimization and further fine-tuning are left to the AI developer. It is essential that the developer understand the coarseness of the pre-learning performed and be aware of assumptions and risks that can arise to ensure mitigation. With pre-learning optimized, large labelled datasets may not be necessary, avoiding the tedious work of data labelling required with supervised and semi-supervised AI models. This together with the performance benefits and the adaptability of these PTMs, we can see how adaptable they can be in a wide range of tasks [3]. Pre-trained AI models are therefore considered the 'ready-made' SOUP component that can provide the foundation for specific AI tasks. According to current standards, they require no more control than existing SOUP in today's medical device SDLC activities (e.g., APIs or development tools). Nevertheless, they bring with them multiple risks that are not yet well understood in the healthcare industry [32, 33]. The next section provides high-level risk categories for consideration.

## 4.1 Risks and Mitigation in the Use of Pre-Trained Models

It is necessary to highlight some of the key risks that can be introduced from PTMs, presented in Table 4. Many of these risks are reflective of AI model development generally, though our focus is to ensure the developer and regulator understand the risks they are bringing into the SDLC [34]. The risks should be understood early in the development lifecycle planned for assessment with the team versed in the origins of the model, the differences and similarities of layers, settings, data, etc. The architecture, pre-training and assumptions must be made known.

**Table 4.** Risks and Potential Mitigations to use of Pre-Trained Models in Medical Devices

| Risk | Example | Mitigation |
|---|---|---|
| Security & Privacy | Data poisoning, privacy leakage, model inversion, model theft, member inference, exfiltration, backdoor attack, manipulation, exposed API and credentials, tampering, insecure components, unauthorized use of model/data | Full assessment of pre-trained model selection and purpose with security and privacy controls in place. Model versioning, continuous monitoring, zero-trust for secure deployment and maintenance |

*(continued)*

**Table 4.** *(continued)*

| Risk | Example | Mitigation |
|---|---|---|
| Bias & Inequity | Intrinsic bias (data, spatial, temporal, collection bias), extrinsic bias (task-specific, Gen-AI biases), algorithmic bias (architecture, feature selection, loss function, metrics, training methods, competency, sampling, labelling, etc.) | Risk analysis and adequate controls; including understanding source of data used in pre-learning, re-sampling controls, data balancing, independence, augmentation, filtering; de-biasing, competency; standardisation, etc |
| Transparency | Awareness of pre-training model details for assessment; labelling / documentation with adequate information available | Documentation availability for assessment and maintenance, taking account of guidance in appendix |
| Performance | Metric suitability, adequacy; model drift assessment, over-fitting, under-fitting, generalizability | Refinement and evaluation for model generalizability, taking account of guidance in appendix |
| Technical Suitability | Architecture type, purpose, use case fit, data suitability to use case, etc | Assessment for suitability including layers, nodes, loss function, data, sample size, representativeness of population / problem, parameters, hyperparameters, etc |

## 5 Standards Under Development for AIeMD

A systematic literature review has provided an analysis of standards released and under development for AIeMDs [35]. This paper confirms that there is still no sign of a work program initiated for pre-trained AI models for healthcare, despite the ongoing developmental effort by standards organizations. This includes International Electrotechnical Commission (IEC), having a global perspective and European Committee for Standardisation (CEN-CENELEC) that focuses on European regulation and aims to meet the requirements of the EU AI Act [36]. CEN-CENELEC working groups are aware of the growing need for regulation and generative AI including LLM requirements that are under development as part of Joint Technical Committee JTC21. The proposed amendment of ISO/IEC 22989 which addresses concepts and terminology touches on transformer algorithms but does not explicitly deal with pre-trained AI model requirements [37] that can utilize transformer algorithms [38]. Although ISO/IEC 42001 an AI Management System is released and can provide some level of governance over such AI models, it is not specific to PTM or indeed to healthcare [39]. Ultimately, this research agrees that when using PTMs, the "*knowledge embedded in LLMs is not immediately accessible and requires careful extraction and efficient utilization to yield effective results*" [40]. This requires full understanding of the source of the PTM where possible, including a complete set of details to evaluate suitability for use. Alternatively, in the absence of available source data, a worst-case verification/validation approach should be taken by the manufacturer to mitigate risk. This research suggests a new work item be introduced under IEC TC62, JTC21 or ISO/IEC JTC 1/SC42 as applicable, taking account of the evaluation proposed here. The characteristics required for standardisation are summarised here.

## 6 Characteristics Required for Standardisation

**Trainability.** The efficacy of a PTM is not dictated by the amount of data it is trained on. There are a myriad of considerations to be taken into account when utilizing a PTM model and then become the legal manufacturer when releasing an AIeMD for use in healthcare. For example, research demonstrates that image classification transformers (encoders and decoders) based on characteristics of each pixel in an image, can be dependent on the transformer model's performance [15]. Degradation can arise as training continues. This is known as 'catastrophic forgetting'. A model's previously learned task can deteriorate as it learns new tasks [41].

Transformer-based architectures offer improvements in semantic segmentation that are promising for applications in healthcare. The choice of transformer architecture, foundation model and bias-aware evaluation must be understood by those who are developing them in healthcare. Hence, the documentation associated with the PTM should describe the overall structure and origin of the PTM and transformer utilised. The suitability of the model should be thoroughly assessed. Consideration should be given to whether the architecture in use is similar to the structure of a publicly available one; the difference should be assessed. If it is a proprietary structure, a detailed mathematical or structural description is necessary. Understanding the precursor of pre-training is as important as the subsequent learning transfer, fine-tuning and testing that is required to deploy an AIeMD fit for purpose.

One example in healthcare is the development of TELL 2.0 [42] which assesses cognitive deficit intended to support diagnosis. A patient undergoes language-based tasks such as reading, writing, and recall tasks. TELL 2.0 was built on RoBERTa, identified as a Robustly Optimized BERT Pre-training model. Research on RoBERTa demonstrated BERT was significantly undertrained in various tasks and it was shown that the selection of hyperparameters can have a significant impact on the final results [42]. When assessing the fine-tuned TELL 2.0 application the developers need to consider domain transfer risk and the use of tools such as PySentimiento [43], which is a python toolkit for opinion mining developed multilingually. Its use in TELL 2.0 with RoBERTa has potential for linguistic mismatches in nuance, slang, accent, semantics and domain-specific terminology [44]. Misclassification of results across demographics can lead to inequitable outcomes across different populations and cultural groups. The TELL 2.0 application, having been trained in Spanish, may be subject to yet further risks where TELL 2.0 technology is to be utilised as the basis of MemoryTell 1.0. MemoryTell, a sub-set of cognitive deficits using similar tasks to identify memory deficits in English [44]. It is therefore essential that the technology on which these AI models are built are adequately understood to identify the risks and apply appropriate controls. It is not difficult to anticipate that these risks can lead to false positives/negatives and result in patient anxiety at a minimum, where cognitive deficit is being considered. This paper does not focus however, on the standards that are already covered or in development, such as AIeMD performance evaluation, risk management and AI test methods in healthcare [45]. What it does identify is the need to understand the opportunities for risk from PTMs specifically.

**Robustness.** It is clear that many real-world applications struggle with accessibility of large datasets, leading to the need for transfer-learning from pre-trained AI models. Some research is emerging that supports replacing deep net architectures with simple linear models where the model has been pre-trained on large language models such as Chronos and Time-MoE [46, 47]. Despite being lightweight, superior efficiency and robustness is claimed with various sampling rates and enhanced interpretability offered from the linear model [48]. Research such as this provides some confidence that a PTM can be utilized with limited fine-tuning and suggests that no manual tuning is required for subsequent deployment. Caution is advised here where this approach is adopted by developers in medical devices, where more care is needed for selection and assessment of the model. Appropriate documentation should reflect a clear understanding of the pre-training and model parameters. The documentation should describe the data augmentation methods, model weight initialization strategies, optimizers used, and the configuration of key hyperparameters during training to name a few.

**Generalization.** The key to a good AI model is how it measures up in use, particularly in healthcare across multiple hospitals, clinics, settings, or user groups. Research has demonstrated that even domain-specific language models such as, the Swedish clinical language model (SweDeClin-BERT), which is a modified version of ClinBERT used for clinical note taking, required further specific fine-tuning and additional refinement and evaluation in order to achieve adequate performance measures when adopted [27]. Swedish researchers downloaded SweDeClin-BERT, as having been training for medical use, for use as a means of detecting Adverse Drug Events from patient records. Only after much refinement did they achieve performance scores in the range of 0.8 $F_1$ based on fine-tuning and additional annotating [27]. It is clear that any medical device manufacturer and AI developer will perform performance testing and standards are in development for this [49]. However, again no consideration is given to PTMs and the additional evaluation that may be needed in each case. It is not surprising that fine-tuning is required dependent on the use case, whereby different hospitals will document records differently; understanding the source data could help identify development challenges earlier in the lifecycle and ensure there are less challenges to overcome in the SDLC. Transparency of the PTM is necessary to understand what is to be expected in development and maintenance.

**Transparency.** Given the brief summary of the risks identified above, the need for transparency is highlighted and also required under the EU AI Act [36]. The claim that interpretability is improved by linear model development may be so, but do we fully understand the PTM architecture to be able to make appropriate judgements and perform adequate testing [48]. Whilst full transparency and interpretability of the PTM architecture may not be achievable, interpretability of the clinical decision-making and diagnostic parameters must be made clear when transferred into an AIeMD. Open-source models in particular are accessible to interference of source code, algorithms, and data. Transparency is both necessary and helpful in understanding and predicting the risks and vulnerabilities. Red-teaming is recommended and is performed by publishing teams such as Google, OpenAI, Meta, etc. with the aim of disclosing vulnerabilities [50]. This activity should be assessed as part of the model selection process where possible and key details reviewed for selection and suitability.

**Security & Privacy.** Both model inversion attacks and membership inference attacks are of particular concern to privacy in these models [50]. The identity of sensitive data can be realized from the training data where the synthesized model is widely available. Data reconstruction can be achieved from latent vectors used in the pre-training process. These risks are known amongst specialists but may not be widely understood by users, regulators and standards bodies creating AI standards for healthcare or medical device manufacturers. GitHub and Hugging Face among others are calling for more open-source support from the EU AI Act [50]. Hugging Face openly supports the use of Model Cards to help verify the source of these transformer models. Model cards have appeared in the appendix of the recent FDA guidance on AI [51], though use of the Model Card is not widely understood or mandated by EU standards to date [52]. If not Model Cards, then what? [52] We need standardisation to ensure models adopted are secure and adequately validated, or else we need guidance and adequate controls to protect the AIeMD developer against these risks. Data poisoning and backdoor attacks are typical security risks that can be expected from open-source models. Due to the size of the dataset used in training, it is not possible to expect human intervention or inspection of all data and hence, there is a considerable reliance on the integrity of the code and data used. Research has shown us that adding a small amount of manipulated data can significantly change the model's behavior, which has become known as data poisoning [50]. Although 100% check is not generally possible, a requirement for data poisoning checks is necessary. Use of PTM expands the attack surface for an AIeMD and this requires additional controls [53].

**PTM Guidance Checklist.** Finally, in a bid to support AIeMD development and protect industry and healthcare stakeholders, a PTM guidance checklist is provided in the Appendix 1. There may be overlap between the existing AI development activities (e.g., performance evaluation, threat modelling, etc.) which are part of the current regulatory requirements. The checklist is provided to identify whether additional controls are warranted, depending on the source and architecture of a PTM selected for a particular use and risk case. By providing guidance in this manner, the AIeMD developer is forewarned and can incorporate necessary controls as appropriate into their QMS. This aims to reduce the overall burden for developers by integrating these guidelines into the existing SDLC and AI Development lifecycle as appropriate, as shown in Fig. 2.

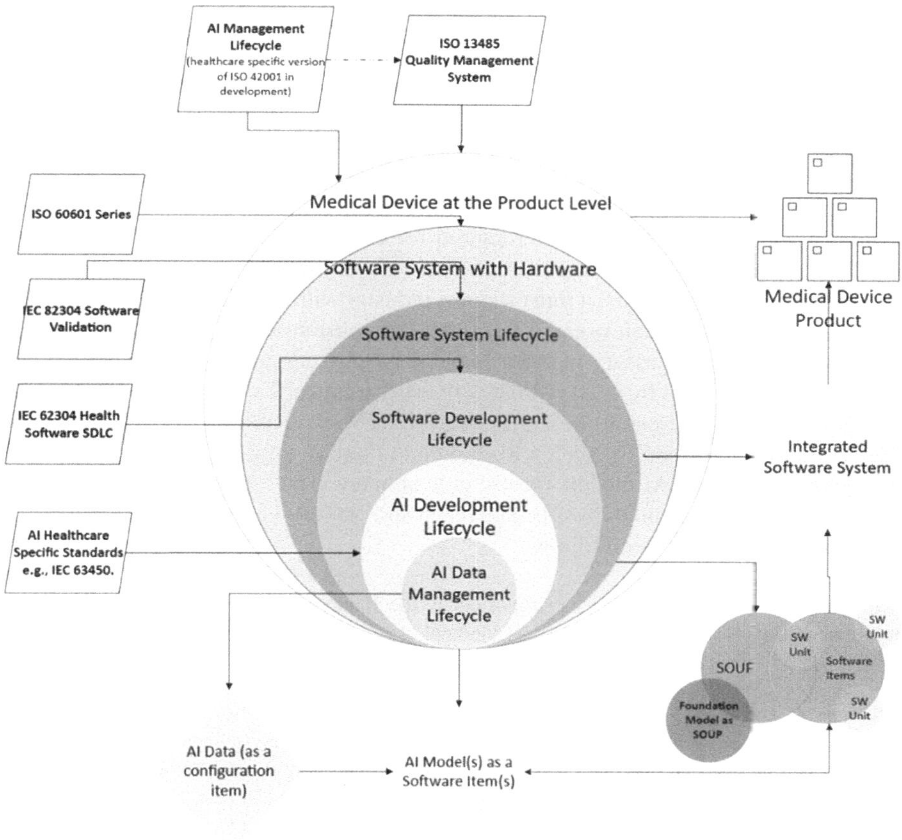


**Fig. 2.** Pre-Trained Model as a SOUP Item within a Medical Device SDLC

## 7 Conclusion

As AI systems continue to scale in complexity and capability, PTMs have emerged as foundational assets in accelerating innovation. Research demonstrates how PTMs are helping to overcome some of the key challenges including data and processing power accessibility and efficiencies. The up-take of these PTMs cannot be underestimated. The need for thorough evaluation in development and deployment by medical device manufacturers must be further explored and standardised. Assessments must include suitability, transparency, robustness, trainability, security and generalizability. Appropriate documentation should be made available by the providers of PTMs where possible. This makes it easier for the developer to be able to adequately assess the source and content of the PTM for suitability to the intended purpose and subsequent placement on the market. In the event that 3rd party suppliers do not provide adequate information, the onus is placed on the legal manufacturer to ensure they adequately assess the risks posed from these SOUP items.

It is clear from this research that additional considerations are necessary when we define PTMs as SOUP according to IEC 62304 [26]. These are not simply traditional SOUP items, but a special kind of SOUP, that requires due consideration and additional guidance for industry. It would be highly beneficial to industry to release the checklist provided here as a Technical Report (e.g., TR by IEC TC62), which is a level below a technical specification or standard required for compliance and would therefore be considered as guidance. Whilst the intention is not to further burden industry with additional regulatory requirements, it must support industry with the requisite knowledge for protection and safety of their organisations and their customers. A collective beneficial approach to PTMs is necessary in order to build on existing quality and reap the many health benefits promised from AI, whilst delivering trustworthy and ethical AIeMDs.

**Limitations**. This research does not present all PTMs or all risks. It serves to highlight salient aspects of the need for standardisation and thereby improve safety and security when using pre-trained AI models for use in healthcare. The 5-question short-quiz discussed in this paper is limited in scope and reach and was used as an early indicator only, on which further research can follow.

**Acknowledgments.** This research is supported by the Research Ireland under the Regulatory Compliance Framework for Trustworthy AI Medical Device Software (Reg-Fr-AIMs) project, ID 21/FFP-A/9255.

**Disclosure of Interests.** The 1st and 5th authors are members of IEC and CEN-CENELEC Technical Committees for Healthcare, including TC62 Artificial Intelligence. The opinion's set out here are those of the authors' alone and are not intended to represent the TC's or organizations of which they are part. The guidelines developed in this research form part of a broader project aiming at developing Trustworthy AI for Medical Devices led by DkIT and UCD, Ireland and specifically from a PhD project on AI Change Management (AICM) processes [11]. The questions raised in relation to PTMs are presented under Appendix 1 to this paper. The questions have been evaluated against the Chinese standard on PTMs for analysis of completion. Additional guidance adopted from the Chinese guidance can be seen under *Supporting Comments*.

## Appendix 1: Pre-Trained Model Evaluation Checklist

| Type | Consideration[1] | Supporting Comment[2] |
|---|---|---|
| Transparency (including Explainability as a sub-set of transparency) | Is the AI model under development utilising a 'pre-trained model (PTM)' or 'foundational' model? | PTMs refer to those used in the development of AI medical devices. They are not limited to models specifically developed for medical devices. Sources of PTMs are diverse and may include: Medical device manufacturers, Third-party suppliers, Third-party service platforms, open-source networks, the types of PTMs, which may vary in modality and parameter scale |
| | Has the provider of the PTMs described and/or provided all relevant details concerning the model itself (architecture, layers, etc.), including the processes and methods used, and the datasets involved in training? | Version identification (release version number), model architecture, training data and dataset construction methods, annotation methods, training process, model applicability, etc. Note: This information can be provided as part of a Model Card, where suitable |
| | Describe the existing architecture and the new architecture that will be developed; examine differences | The documentation should describe the overall structure and origin of the model. If the structure is a modification of a publicly available one, the differences must be detailed. If it is a proprietary structure, a detailed mathematical or structural description is required |
| | Provide documentation with information about model nodes and functions; learning method | Number of nodes, neurons<br>, distribution<br>, activation functions, connection methods<br>. Note: For non-neural network algorithms, describe the algorithm type and its basic units |
| | Describe model parameters, hyperparameters and relationship to architecture | The documentation should describe metadata for parameters in each layer, including number of nodes/neurons, relationships, categories |
| | Describe the how the data is represented in the model and how it mirrors the model under development. Identify if changes are required to the model in development for the new use case | The documentation should describe how data is represented in the model, including: level of abstraction, data types and scale, encoding methods (e.g., one-hot, label encoding), pre-processing and post-processing steps |

*(continued)*

[1] *Considerations are sourced from 1st Author's AICM process in development as part of larger project Trustworthy AIeMD* [11]

[2] *Developed from AICM and review against YY/T 1833.5 Chinese Standard for completeness* [12]

(continued)

| Type | Consideration | Supporting Comment |
|---|---|---|
| | Describe data modality; what level of documentation is provided by 3rd party supplier? | The documentation should describe the data modalities (type or form of data) used for training the PTM, such as speech, natural images, medical images, etc. If applicable, the medical data acquisition equipment should be specified. If simulation data was used for training, the data generation methods and procedures should be described in detail. If applicable, information about data annotation should be included, such as the source, quantity, and quality of annotations |
| | Data volume and breakdown; what level of documentation is provided by 3rd party supplier? | The documentation should specify the total amount of data used to train the PTM. If applicable, the volume of each data modality should be described. The data partitioning method used during pre-training should be explained, including the volume of training, validation, and test sets, as well as any distribution differences among them |
| | Data quality; what level of documentation is provided by 3rd party supplier? | The documentation should describe the quality of the data used for training the PTM. Examples include accuracy, completeness, and consistency. Accuracy may not be a relevant metric for healthcare activities. For example, cancer detection relies highly on sensitivity (recall) to ensure a positive case is not missed and that over-burdening the healthcare system still further does not occur through false positives. Sensitivity is better when predicting rare events like some cancer detection. Where datasets are imbalanced, metrics such as AUC-ROC or F1 score are important in understanding performance across patient groups. AUC-ROC are discriminative across thresholds but insensitive to prevalence. The criteria used to select training data should be explained, such as data source, reliability, relevance, and data cleaning procedures It is important to align predicted probabilities with observed outcomes for critical clinical decisions |

(continued)

(continued)

| Type | Consideration | Supporting Comment |
|---|---|---|
| | Describe the interpretability of the model and the level of additional development required to meet interpretability and transparency objectives | Interpretability is essential for ethical and regulatory transparency. It helps identify biases and ensures fairness in model decisions. Consider the following: the model's internal mechanisms, relationship between spatial outputs and internal features, ability to extract meaningful information from learned features |
| Security & Data Protection | Does the data comply with data management procedures/ standards? | Yes/No. Provide reference to Data Management SOP and provide description as to how the PTM complies with existing procedures/standards or actions taken to address any deficits |
| | Data privacy. What level of documentation is provided by 3rd party supplier? | If applicable, the documentation should describe the technical measures used to protect subject privacy, such as data de-identification and anonymization. The rules for these privacy protection methods should also be described |
| | Baseline Performance; what level of documentation is provided by 3rd party supplier? | The documentation should describe the baseline performance of the PTM on the source task, including results on the training, validation, and test sets |
| | Original source tasks used to Train the PTM; what level of documentation is provided by 3rd party supplier? | The documentation should describe the source task used for training the PTM and the learning method adopted |
| | Training Settings, Test Settings and Configuration; what level of documentation is provided by 3rd party supplier? | The documentation should describe the data augmentation methods, model weight initialization strategies, optimizers used, and the configuration of key hyperparameters during training |
| | Task Domain; what level of documentation is provided by 3rd party supplier? | The documentation should describe the task domain of the source task used during the generation of the PTM. If multiple source tasks were used, all corresponding task domains should be described |

(continued)

(*continued*)

| Type | Consideration | Supporting Comment |
|---|---|---|
| | Model Applicability; what level of documentation is provided by 3rd party supplier? Describe original model training, fine-tuning necessary and subsequent development, testing necessary to achieve intended purpose | The documentation should describe the data modalities applicable for forward inference using the PTM. If applicable, it should also describe the data modalities that can be processed after fine-tuning the model<br>Note 1: PTMs may be designed for general-purpose data modalities or specifically for medical images (e.g., MRI, CT scans) or medical text (e.g., Electronic Health Records). Note 2: Forward inference refers to the process of applying a trained machine learning model to specific tasks, such as segmentation, classification, or enhancement in medical decision support |
| | Task Type; what level of documentation is provided by 3rd party supplier? How does this meet the intended purpose and ability to make generalisations in the intended population? | The documentation should describe the types of tasks suitable for forward inference using the PTM (e.g., image segmentation, image classification, signal recognition), the similarity between source and downstream task domains, the scenarios and sample formats the model can handle, and the expected performance. If applicable, it should describe robustness and generalization testing methods for downstream tasks |
| | Environment; what level of documentation is provided by 3rd party supplier? Use environment (research, clinical use, etc.), technological requirements, libraries, hardware, etc | The documentation should describe the hardware resources and software environments suitable for model inference and training<br>Note: This includes computing power and resources required for running the PTM (e.g., CPU, GPU, server nodes), measured by metrics such as FLOPS or operations per second. It also includes computing and software requirements for fine-tuning and deployment in AI medical devices |

(*continued*)

(*continued*)

| Type | Consideration | Supporting Comment |
|---|---|---|
| | Downstream Training required; what level of documentation is provided by 3rd party supplier? of pre-training and what additional training is necessary? What level of bias can be introduced from pre-training on wider/broad sample of data? | The documentation should describe the data requirements for transferring the PTM to a new downstream task domain, especially when the output space mapping changes. The output space mapping is a set of all possible outputs a model or system can produce (e.g., set of all possible diagnoses). This should include the required dataset (volume, modality, etc.). If applicable, it should describe the training settings used during fine-tuning, such as data augmentation and training methods and any potential for bias from the original training prior to transfer |
| | Assess intended purpose for the PTM; what level of documentation is provided by 3rd party supplier? | A technical report should be generated to serve as evidence for verifying the quality of the PTM |
| | Privacy Protection; what level of documentation is provided by 3rd party supplier? What additional measures are necessary if assuming zero trust principle? | The provider should declare the privacy protection measures adopted by the model, meeting the following requirements: Use appropriate techniques (e.g., differential privacy) to prevent leakage of training data, including distribution and individual data inference. Ensure protective measures are in place for data upload and storage operations generated by the model code |
| | General methods for Quality Compliance of PTMs; What additional requirements/procedures are necessary to ensure PTM is adequately evaluated for its intended purpose? | The quality evaluation of PTMs includes assessment of the model description, quality characteristics, and other relevant aspects. The model provider should submit the PTM itself, its documentation, and other necessary materials for evaluation |

(*continued*)

(continued)

| Type | Consideration | Supporting Comment |
|---|---|---|
| Quality | Trainability; what level of documentation is provided by 3rd party supplier? Consider compatibility of methods used in pre-training and fine-tuning; and underfitting/overfitting | The provider of the PTM should declare the model's trainability indicators and provide evidence. If applicable, indicators such as loss function values and the degree of fit to the target data distribution should be used. For example, the loss function refers to the method chosen for optimization (i.e., optimization objectives). This optimization objective is what guides the model during training. It is important to ensure that the objective used by the PTM is suitable for use in the fine-tuned medical model. For example, cross-entropy loss is common in classification, however, in healthcare, a need for domain-specific function, such as Dice Loss, may be needed for medical image segmentation because it handles class imbalance better when lesions are small compared to a whole image. The loss function should be explained in relation to the data characteristics (balanced/imbalanced data sets, noisy data, size of lesion if imaging is being performed, etc.). Note: Trainability refers to the model's ability to be iteratively optimized during training |

(continued)

(continued)

| Type | Consideration | Supporting Comment |
|---|---|---|
| | Architectural Scalability; what level of documentation is provided by 3rd party supplier? What assumptions are drawn from pre-training and model under development as part of SDLC. What additional architectural changes are necessary for intended purpose? | The provider should declare whether the model architecture can improve inference and training efficiency by increasing computational resources. Requirements for computing power and resources should be specified, along with written evidence. If applicable, minimum and maximum hardware configurations should be described<br>Architectural scalability primarily refers to a model's ability to support and adapt to varying levels of computational resources. This includes the model's compatibility with different deployment environments and its ability to scale up or down based on available hardware<br>The description of validated deployment environments for PTM should include the following:<br>AI Server Specifications such as details of a single AI server with specified computational capabilities and architecture; Maximum supported model parameters and structure<br>; Server computing power<br>; Number of integrated AI accelerator cards; Interconnection methods between accelerator cards<br>; Types of AI acceleration processors used<br>; Maximum Supported AI Accelerator Cards such as the number of AI accelerator cards that can be supported by the deployment set-up and the strategy used for distributed parallel model partitioning |
| | Transferability; what level of documentation is provided by 3rd party supplier? What quality metrics / measures are provided and what will be taken forward into development as part of claims. What will not be taken forward? Document rationale | The provider should declare the expected performance of the PTM after fine-tuning for downstream tasks in AI medical devices and provide written evidence. For example, performance measures should be suitable for the task. Suitability of metrics should be assessed based on risk management activities and having a clear understanding of the clinical outcomes associated with the learning methods used in pre-training as well as fine-tuning. Understanding of scientific validity (reliability concepts), technical validity and clinical validity must all be assessed |

(continued)

(continued)

| Type | Consideration | Supporting Comment |
|---|---|---|
| | Model Efficiency; what level of documentation is provided by 3rd party supplier? What additional resources are necessary for intended purpose in use environment(s)? | The provider should declare the efficiency of the PTM, including inference computation load, resource utilization, and accuracy (or suitable metrics), and provide written evidence. Suggested metrics include:<br>Computation required for forward inference<br>. Utilization of computing power and storage<br>. Accuracy and inference time under different hyperparameter configurations (e.g., parameter count). Relevant metrics beyond accuracy or in place of that are appropriate to the domain and learning objective |
| | Result repeatability and consistency; what level of documentation is provided by 3rd party supplier? Does the repeatability remain constant when updated for intended purpose; what additional quality metrics and objectives are necessary to achieve? | The provider should declare the repeatability of the model's output, ensuring consistent results when give the same test data Note: Consistency means the output's meaning remains the same. For quantitative outputs, values should be identical or within the same range; for descriptive text, the semantic meaning should be consistent |
| | Robustness; what level of documentation is provided by 3rd party supplier? How robust is the model to meet its intended purpose? | The provider should declare the model's robustness, ensuring it can produce correct outputs on datasets with varying diversity and domain deviations. Requirements include: Performance under noisy input data. Ability to generalize to out-of-distribution (OOD) data points |
| | Generalisability; what level of documentation is provided by 3rd party supplier? What additional considerations are necessary for generalisability to new intended purpose? | The provider should declare the model's generalization ability and provide written evidence. If applicable, differences between the training dataset and real-world unfamiliar samples should be analysed based on the model's intended use and environment |
| | Adversarial Security; what level of documentation is provided by 3rd party supplier? What additional measures are necessary if assuming zero trust principle? | The provider is encouraged to declare the model's adversarial security. If applicable, examples should be provided showing the types of adversarial attacks handled and the model's performance under such conditions |

(continued)

(*continued*)

| Type | Consideration | Supporting Comment |
|---|---|---|
| Evaluation Methods | Evaluation of PTM Documentation shall be maintained | The evaluation should verify the completeness and accuracy of the model description provided in the documentation, ensuring it meets the requirements outlined above. For widely used PTMs, the format of the documentation may be adapted based on actual circumstances |
| | Is the description of the Pretrained Model complete? | The evaluation should verify the completeness and accuracy of the model description provided in the documentation, ensuring it meets the requirements outlined in Sect. 4. For widely used PTMs, the format of the documentation may be adapted based on actual circumstances |
| | Is the trainability of the PTM adequately documented for evaluation against the intended use? | Using the training examples and settings (including hyperparameters and applicable environments) provided by the model provider, the model should be trained. The convergence curve of the loss function should be recorded to determine whether the results meet the requirements. Ensure the loss value on the training set is plotted against the loss on the validation set over training to check for overfitting |
| | Is the Architecture adequately described to assess the ability to scale for its intended use? | Adjust the hardware resources and software environment used for training and deploying the model. Record changes in inference and training efficiency to determine whether the results meet the requirements of |
| | Is the PTM appropriate for transfer for use in development or as a use-as-is SOUP within the SDLC? Identify additional requirements to be controlled as applicable | Using the training examples and settings (including training methods and data augmentation techniques) provided by the model provider, test the model's performance on downstream tasks. Record performance metrics to determine compliance with transferability requirements. For models tested on public datasets, evaluate their performance on downstream tasks using those datasets to determine compliance. Note 1: Performance metrics may include, but are not limited to, those listed in this checklist. Note 2: Transfer learning is typically achieved through fine-tuning, such as low-rank adaptation for large language models or supervised fine-tuning |

(*continued*)

*(continued)*

| Type | Consideration | Supporting Comment |
|---|---|---|
| | Has the model's efficiency been adequately assessed? | Conduct forward inference using the PTM on relevant data. Evaluate compliance with model efficiency requirements based on:<br>a) Required computation for inference<br>b) Utilization of computing power and storage<br>c) Performance and inference time under different parameter configurations |
| | Has the original output been demonstrated to be repeatable as published by 3rd party provider with same or different intended purpose? | Use identical test cases to perform inference and verify whether the model consistently produces the same output, in accordance with Output Repeatability requirements |
| | Has the PTM demonstrated robustness in line with project objectives, measures, for existing/new intended purpose? | Evaluate the model's performance across applicable task domains, scenarios, sample formats, and expected outcomes to determine compliance with Robustness requirements |
| | Has the PTM demonstrated generalisability in line with existing/new intended purpose? | Use test sets that were not included in the training data to evaluate the model's ability to generalize. Determine compliance with Generalisability requirements. Methods for Generalisability assessments should be documented and a reference provided to the selected methods chosen for generalization testing |
| | Has the PTM demonstrated appropriate security methods and controls? | Create test cases to verify that the model's inference results are not misled by adversarial samples. Use black-box or white-box methods to generate adversarial perturbations and test the model's resistance to such attacks. Determine compliance with Security Requirements |
| | Has the data been subject to Privacy Protection and what additional measures if any are required? | Review the privacy protection measures implemented in the PTM to determine compliance with Privacy Protection requirements |

*(continued)*

*(continued)*

| Type | Consideration | Supporting Comment |
|---|---|---|
| | Include subgroup combination Testing of PTM and as part of developed model per intended use | Group cases with similar characteristics into subgroups, then combine samples from different subgroups to form a diverse test set. During testing, the model should be able to make predictions across all subgroups without significant statistical bias between them. (Specific statistical methods should be selected based on the task.). Independent and competent assessment of in-built pre-existing bias and potential for newly introduced bias should be documented |
| Generalisability | Include stress sample testing of PTM and as part of developed model per intended use | Use atypical or hard-to-classify samples from the target database to test model performance. The model should meet the baseline performance claimed by the provider even on these challenging samples |
| | Include natural noise sample test cases | Select samples with high levels of natural noise from the database and test the model's recognition accuracy. The model should produce correct results despite the noise<br>Note: "Natural noise" is a relative concept. Depending on the task and performance requirements, appropriate metrics should be used to measure noise levels and determine thresholds |
| Robustness | Faulty Sample Test: ensure tests include non-possible test cases to ensure erroneous outputs are avoided | Include samples of other types or mix clearly incorrect samples into otherwise valid data. The model should be able to avoid being misled and should not produce erroneous results |
| | Review adequacy and appropriateness of Performance Metrics used in Pre-training. Identify additional performance metrics required for subsequent testing following fine-tuning and release in healthcare | Provide risk assessment and rationale for choice of metrics ensuring all reasonably foreseeable risks are mitigated and statistical assumptions are documented |
| | Ensure appropriate Image Classification metrics are used; provide rationale for appropriateness and assessment of continuation of use based on intended use in healthcare | For PTMs used in image classification tasks, the following metrics are commonly used: Accuracy: Percentage of correctly classified images out of the total. Precision: Proportion of true positive predictions among all positive predictions. Recall: Proportion of true positive predictions among all actual positives. F1 Score: Harmonic mean of precision and recall |

*(continued)*

*(continued)*

| Type | Consideration | Supporting Comment |
|---|---|---|
| Performance | Image Segmentation; provide rationale for segmentation metrics and assessment of continuation into use into intended use | For PTMs used in image segmentation tasks, the following metrics are commonly used: Intersection over Union (IoU): Measures overlap between predicted and ground truth masks. Dice Coefficient: Similar to IoU quantifies overlap between predicted and ground truth masks. Pixel Accuracy: Percentage of correctly classified pixels |
| | Text Processing; provide appropriate metrics for evaluation of PTMs and assessment of continuation into use based on intended use in healthcare | For PTMs used in text processing tasks, the following metrics are commonly used: e.g., Precision; Recall; F1 Score |

## References

Radford, A., Narasimhan, K., Salimans, T., Sutskever, I.: Improving Language Understanding by Generative Pre-Training (2018). https://gluebenchmark.com/leaderboard

Devlin, J., Chang, M.-W., Lee, K., Toutanova, K.: BERT: Pre-training of Deep Bidirectional Transformers for Language Understanding, May 2019. http://arxiv.org/abs/1810.04805

Denecke, K., May, R., Rivera-Romero, O.: Transformer Models in Healthcare: A Survey and Thematic Analysis of Potentials, Shortcomings and Risks', Dec. 01, 2024 Springer. https://doi.org/10.1007/s10916-024-02043-5

Menz, B.D., et al.: Current safeguards, risk mitigation, and transparency measures of large language models against the generation of health disinformation: repeated cross-sectional analysis. BMJ **384**, e078538 (Mar.2024). https://doi.org/10.1136/bmj-2023-078538

He, K., Zhang, X., Ren, S., Sun, J.: Deep Residual Learning for Image Recognition, December 2015. http://arxiv.org/abs/1512.03385

Aspell, N., Goldsteen, A., Renwick, R.: Dicing with data: the risks, benefits, tensions and tech of health data in the iToBoS project. Front Digit Health, vol. 6, 2024. https://doi.org/10.3389/fdgth.2024.1272709

EU AI Act, 'EU Artificial Intelligence Act - Proposed', Official Journal of the European Union, no. 0106(COD), Apr. 2021, Accessed: Nov. 29, 2023. https://eur-lex.europa.eu/legal-content/EN/TXT/?uri=CELEX:52021PC0206

MDR 2017/745, 'Medical Device Regulation (EU) 2017/745, as amended' (2024)

Shaheen, M.Y.: AI in Healthcare: medical and socio-economic benefits and challenges. ScienceOpen (2021). https://doi.org/10.14293/S2199-1006.1.SOR-.PPRQNI1.v1

Dong, Q., et al.: A Survey on In-context Learning, October 2024. http://arxiv.org/abs/2301.00234

Lynch, N.S.J., Loughran, R., McHugh, M., McCaffrey, F.: Trustworthy artificial intelligence in healthcare: a proposed framework. In: Systems, Software and Services Process Improvement, M. Yilmaz, P. Clarke, A. Riel, R. Messnarz, M. Zelmenis, and I. A. Buce, Eds., Cham: Springer Nature Switzerland, pp. 69–90 (2026)

NMPA, 'YY/T 1833.5 人工智能医疗器械 质量要求和评价 第 5 部分:预训练模型 Artificial intelligence medical device-Quality requirements and evaluation-Part 5: Pre-trained models', 2024. Accessed: Sep. 19, 2025. https://www.codeofchina.com/standard/YYT1833.5-2024.html

The Consumer Technology Association (CTA), 'Letter to FDA on Pre-Trained Model Regulation'. https://www.fda.gov/advisory-committees/advisory-

ISO13485:2016, '13485' (2016). www.ili-info.com

Vaswani, A., et al.: Attention Is All You Need. In: 31st Conference on Neural Information Processing Systems (NIPS 2017), Long Beach, CA USA (2017)

Zhao, X., Zhao, Q., Tanaka, T.: EpilepsyLLM: Fine-tuning large language models for Japanese epilepsy knowledge representation. Artif. Intell. Health , 025180042 (Sep.2025). https://doi.org/10.36922/AIH025180042

Gräf, M., et al.: Comparison of physician and artificial intelligence-based symptom checker diagnostic accuracy. Rheumatol. Int. **42**(12), 2167–2176 (2022). https://doi.org/10.1007/s00296-022-05202-4

Ada Health Corporation, 'Ada Health'. Accessed: Nov. 27, 2025. https://about.ada.com/life-sciences/

Gilbert, S., Fenech, M., Hirsch, M., Upadhyay, S., Biasiucci, A., Starlinger, J.: Algorithm change protocols in the regulation of adaptive machine learning-based medical devices', Oct. 01, 2021, JMIR Publications Inc. https://doi.org/10.2196/30545

Simonyan, K., Zisserman, A.: Very Deep Convolutional Networks for Large-Scale Image Recognition, Sep. 2014. http://arxiv.org/abs/1409.1556

Musthafa, M., Mahesh, T.R., Kumar, P.V.V., Guluwadi, S.: Enhancing brain tumor detection in MRI images through explainable AI using Grad-CAM with Resnet 50. BMC Med Imaging, vol. 24, no. 1, Dec. 2024. https://doi.org/10.1186/s12880-024-01292-7

Koonce, B.: ResNet 50. In: Convolutional Neural Networks with Swift for Tensorflow, Apress, pp. 63–72 (2021). https://doi.org/10.1007/978-1-4842-6168-2_6

Simonyan, K., Zisserman, A.: Very deep convolutional networks for large-scale image recognition. ICLR, April 2015. http://arxiv.org/abs/1409.1556

Guan, Q., et al.: Deep convolutional neural network VGG-16 model for differential diagnosing of papillary thyroid carcinomas in cytological images: a pilot study. J. Cancer **10**(20), 4876–4882 (2019). https://doi.org/10.7150/jca.28769

Chong, P.L., et al.: Integrating artificial intelligence in healthcare: applications, challenges, and future directions. Future Sci. OA, vol. 11, no. 1, Dec. 2025. https://doi.org/10.1080/20565623.2025.2527505

EN-62304, 'Medical device software: software life-cycle processes', Nov. 30, 2015, CENELEC, Geneva

Kopacheva, E., Henriksson, A., Dalianis, H., Hammar, T., Lincke, A.: Fine-tuning clinical language models to identify adverse drug events in clinical text: machine learning approach (Preprint). JMIR Form Res. (2025). https://doi.org/10.2196/71949

Microsoft Foundry, 'Foundation models for healthcare AI', Nov. 2025. Accessed: Nov. 25, 2025. https://learn.microsoft.com/pdf?url=https%3A%2F%2Flearn.microsoft.com%2Fen-us%2Fazure%2Fai-foundry%2Ftoc.json%3Fview%3Dfoundry-classic

Luo, R., et al.: BioGPT: Generative Pre-trained Transformer for Biomedical Text Generation and Mining, April 2023. https://doi.org/10.1093/bib/bbac409

Alsentzer, E., et al.: Publicly Available Clinical BERT Embeddings, Jun. 2019. http://arxiv.org/abs/1904.03323

NVIDIA, 'NVIDIA H100 Tensor Core GPU.' (2024). www.nvidia.com/h100

Lekadir, K., et al.: FUTURE-AI: International consensus guideline for trustworthy and deployable artificial intelligence in healthcare. BMJ (2025). https://doi.org/10.1136/bmj-2024-081554

Yousefi, F., et al.: Opportunities, challenges, and requirements for Artificial Intelligence (AI) implementation in Primary Health Care (PHC): a systematic review. BMC Primary Care, vol. 26, no. 1, Dec. 2025, https://doi.org/10.1186/s12875-025-02785-2

Slattery, P., et al.: The AI Risk Repository: A Comprehensive Meta-Review, Database, and Taxonomy of Risks from Artificial Intelligence', Aug. 2024. Accessed: Aug. 15, 2024. https://cdn.prod.website-files.com/669550d38372f33552d2516e/66bc918b580467717e194940_The%20AI%20Risk%20Repository_13_8_2024.pdf

St John Lynch, N., Loughran, R., McHugh, M., McCaffrey, F.: Artificial Intelligence-Enabled Medical Device Standards: A Multidisciplinary Literature Review, pp. 112–130 (2024). https://doi.org/10.1007/978-3-031-71139-8_8

EU, The AI Act 2024/1689. Brussels, 2024, pp. 1–144. Accessed: Apr. 08, 2024. https://eur-lex.europa.eu/legal-content/EN/TXT/PDF/?uri=OJ:L_202401689

CEN/CLC/JTC21, 'Information technology - AI - AI Concepts and terminology - Amendment 1: Generative AI - draft amendment out for comment only', *IEC*, Sep. 2025, Accessed: Sep. 24, 2025. https://isolutions.iso.org/ballots/part/npos/ballotAction.do?method=doView&id=61809

EN/ISO/IEC-22989, 'Information Technology - Artificial Intelligence - Artificial Intelligence Concepts and Terminology' (2023)

ISO/IEC-DIS-42001, 'Information Technology-Artificial Intelligence-Management system' (2022)

Acharya, K., Velasquez, A., Song, H.H.: A survey on symbolic knowledge distillation of large language models. IEEE Trans. Artif. Intell. **5**(12), 5928–5948 (2024). https://doi.org/10.1109/TAI.2024.3428519

Zhang, B., Liu, L., Phan, M.H., Tian, Z., Shen, C., Liu, Y.: SegViT v2: exploring efficient and continual semantic segmentation with plain vision transformers. Int. J. Comput. Vis. **132**(4), 1126–1147 (2024). https://doi.org/10.1007/s11263-023-01894-8

Liu, Y., et al.: RoBERTa: A Robustly Optimized BERT Pretraining Approach, July 2019. http://arxiv.org/abs/1907.11692

Pérez, J.M.. et al.: pysentimiento: A Python Toolkit for Opinion Mining and Social NLP tasks, July 2024. http://arxiv.org/abs/2106.09462

García, A.M., et al.: Toolkit to examine lifelike language vol 2.0: optimizing speech biomarkers of neurodegeneration. Dement. Geriatr. Cogn. Disord. **54**(2), 96–108 (2025). https://doi.org/10.1159/000541581

St John Lynch, N., Loughran, R., McHugh, M., McCaffrey, F.: Artificial Intelligence-enabled Medical Device Standards: a multidisciplinary literature review. Munich: EUROSP'24, Sep. 2024, pp. 1–12

Ansari, A.F., et al.: Chronos: Learning the Language of Time Series, Nov. 2024. http://arxiv.org/abs/2403.07815

Shi, X., et al.: Time-MoE: Billion-Scale Time Series Foundation Models with Mixture of Experts, February 2025. http://arxiv.org/abs/2409.16040

Nochumsohn, L., Marshanski, R., Zisling, H., Azencot, O.: Super-Linear: A Lightweight Pretrained Mixture of Linear Experts for Time Series Forecasting, Sep. 2025. http://arxiv.org/abs/2509.15105

IEC-63521, Machine Learning-enabled Medical Device - Performance Evaluation Process (Draft Out for Public Comment), May 2025. www.bsigroup.com

Hintersdorf, D., Struppek, L., Kersting, K.: Balancing Transparency and Risk: The Security and Privacy Risks of Open-Source Machine Learning Models', Aug. 2023. http://arxiv.org/abs/2308.09490

FDA, 'Artificial Intelligence-Enabled Device Software Functions: Lifecycle Management and Marketing Submission (draft) Recommendations', Rockville MD, January 2025. https://www.fda.gov/vaccines-blood-biologics/guidance-compliance-regulatory-information-

Mitchell, M., et al.: Model cards for model reporting. In: FAT* 2019 - Proceedings of the 2019 Conference on Fairness, Accountability, and Transparency, Association for Computing Machinery, Inc, Jan. 2019, pp. 220–229. https://doi.org/10.1145/3287560.3287596

Elnawawy, M., Hallajiyan, M., Mitra, G., Iqbal, S., Pattabiraman, K.: Systematically Assessing the Security Risks of AI/ML-enabled Connected Healthcare Systems, Apr. 2024. http://arxiv.org/abs/2401.17136

# Enhancing Healthcare Data Transparency Through a FAIR Ontology for the Systems Engineering Initiative for Patient Safety (SEIPS)

Sajjad Karimian[1,4](✉), Marie E. Ward[2,3], Siobhan Corrigan[3], and Rob Brennan[4]

[1] d.real, School of Computer Science, University College Dublin, Dublin, Ireland
[2] Quality and Safety Improvement Directorate, St. James's Hospital, Dublin, Ireland
[3] Center for Innovative Human Systems, School of Psychology, Trinity College Dublin, Dublin, Ireland
[4] ADAPT, School of Computer Science, University College Dublin, Dublin, Ireland
sajjad.karimian@ucdconnect.ie

**Abstract.** A new FAIR ontology was developed to formally represent the Systems Engineering Initiative for Patient Safety (SEIPS) work system, focusing on documenting healthcare data flows. Existing Socio-Technical System Analysis (STSA) approaches lack machine-readable, provenance-rich models, limiting transparency, interoperability, and accountability. The ontology, engineered with the NeOn methodology in OWL, enriches SEIPS with provenance metadata to support traceability and reuse. FAIR compliance was assessed with the F-UJI tool, and Human Factors Ergonomics experts validated its accuracy in representing SEIPS concepts. Results show strong FAIR alignment, improved transparency of data flows, and enhanced documentation of provenance and ownership. This ontology extends SEIPS by embedding data transparency into STSA, providing a reusable semantic foundation for healthcare data mapping and interoperability. Future work will broaden its use across heterogeneous datasets and regulatory frameworks.

**Keywords:** Socio-Technical System Analysis · Findable · Accessible · Interoperable · Reusable · Data Governance

## 1 Introduction

Healthcare data management is often characterized by fragmentation, poor interoperability, and inconsistent governance across healthcare information systems [25]. These limitations undermine the accuracy and reliability of data, particularly in healthcare [22]. These challenges also create a lack of transparency in how data is generated, exchanged, and used, which makes it difficult for stakeholders to assess the trustworthiness of data [31]. Without systematic representations of


T. T. Mai et al. (Eds.): AICS 2025, CCIS 2950, pp. 108–119, 2026.
https://doi.org/10.1007/978-3-032-25809-0_8

how data moves between systems and actors (i.e. data flow maps or provenance meta data), inconsistencies remain hidden and governance measures cannot be effectively implemented [32]. Data flow mapping therefore becomes an essential first step for identifying gaps, improving transparency, and enabling consistent data governance.

Data flow mapping is defined as the process of systematically identifying, documenting, organizing, and structuring the categories of personal data collected by an organization, while also illustrating how these data are accessed and transferred between entities [2]. It provides both a detailed inventory of what data exists and a representation of how they move through systems. Documenting both aspects are critical for effective data management as it clarifies the lifecycle of data, including their collection, storage, processing, and dissemination [26]. In addition, adherence to the Findable, Accessible, Interoperable, and Reusable (FAIR) data principles ensures that data are not only well-organized and transparent but also usable across different stakeholders and systems, thereby data can be effectively shared and reused across stakeholders [18].

Healthcare work systems and data flows are often very complex and thus a set of Human Factors Ergonomics (HFE) methods such as the Systems Engineering Initiative for Patient Safety (SEIPS) have evolved to analyse them. SEIPS is an example of a Socio-Technical System Analysis (STSA) framework that can be used to understand the interactions between people, technologies, and processes in a work system [7]. SEIPS was chosen for this study as it is the most widely applied STSA framework in healthcare and explicitly models the interplay of people, tasks, technologies, goals, context, and environment. However, while STSA frameworks offer rich conceptual representations, they lack machine-readable implementations that would allow these insights to be systematically encoded, shared, analysed and reused across digital infrastructures. As a result, essential aspects of data flow maps for healthcare work systems, such as provenance metadata, remain unavailable. SEIPS was selected because it is extensively applied in healthcare and offers an explicit conceptual structure for representing interactions among work-system elements.

Ontologies provide a formal, machine-readable way to represent concepts, relationships, and constraints, thereby enabling transparency, consistency, and shared understanding across systems and stakeholders. For example, the Data Privacy Vocabulary (DPV) demonstrates how ontologies can capture governance and compliance information in a transparent and reusable manner [17]. Building on this ontology-supported approach to data flow mapping, this paper addresses the gap in STSA data flow mapping for healthcare by developing a FAIR-compliant ontology for modelling the healthcare work system as defined by SEIPS [28] and its underlying data flows. SEIPS 1.0 as a stable and widely cited baseline work-system formulation [7]; however, the ontology design is extensible and can be aligned with later SEIPS variants by expanding process and environment constructs and adding patient-journey representations [8].

The research question guiding this study is: *How can ontology engineering, aligned with FAIR principles, be used to augment SEIPS to improve transparency and documentation of healthcare data flows?*

To answer this question, the NeOn methodology [13] and the Web Ontology Language (OWL) [3] were used to construct an ontology representing the SEIPS 1.0 model of work systems, encompassing people, technologies, tasks, environments, and organizations [7]. The work system ontology was enriched with a set of standard W3C PROV-O provenance metadata elements to capture data flow mapping [29] based on an analysis of the outputs of standard data flow mapping techniques such as Data Flow Diagrams [1], UML Use Cases [29] and the Data Value Map [23]. The FAIRness of the ontology was evaluated using automated assessment tools (F-UJI) [15], and ontology accuracy was validated through expert review with HFE specialists. The contributions of this paper are as follows:

- Development of the first FAIR OWL ontology of healthcare work systems based on the SEIPS framework, enriched with provenance metadata to document the underlying data flow mapping for the work system.
- Empirical validation through FAIR assessment and HFE expert validation, showing improved clarity in data documentation and enhanced documentation of provenance and hence transparency in data intensive healthcare work systems
- A twofold gap in healthcare STSA practice was identified: (i) STSA frameworks lack an explicit data-mapping/provenance layer, and (ii) SEIPS lacks a reusable machine-readable implementation.

The remainder of this paper is structured as follows: Sect. 2 reviews related work on STSA and data mapping. Section 3 describes the ontology design. Section 4 presents the results of the FAIR assessments and expert validation. Section 5 discusses theoretical and practical implications and concludes the paper and outlines directions for future work.

## 2 Related Work

Socio-Technical System Analysis (STSA) frameworks such as SEIPS and the Cube model are widely used in aviation and healthcare to analyze workflows, safety practices, and human–technology interactions [11,20]. While these frameworks provide strong conceptual representations of work systems, they remain informally described [28] and lack mechanisms to trace how data is generated, transformed, and exchanged across systems. For example, Werner et al. [24] note that SEIPS cannot track information across care transitions, and SEIPS studies highlight interoperability issues without mapping data flows [1]. In addition to SEIPS, other socio-technical frameworks such as the Cube model and the Functional Resonance Analysis Method (FRAM) provide valuable perspectives for analyzing complex healthcare systems. The Cube model emphasizes multi-dimensional making it suitable for identifying fragmentation and misalignment in data governance and decision-making processes [10]. FRAM, on the other hand, models healthcare work systems as interdependent functions where variability in one function can resonate across the system, leading to both successes and failures [21]. ARK enables organizations to model, monitor, and assess changes in socio-technical systems, thereby supporting accountability and transparency. While ARK provides mechanisms for linking risks, governance controls, and technical systems, it is less focused on modeling detailed workflow-level data transformations.

Data mapping methods such as Data Flow Diagrams (DFD) [1], Unified Modelling Language (UML) use cases [30], and the Data Value Map (DVM) [23] offer structured depictions of system interactions, information exchange, and dataset ownership. However, they overlook the socio-technical context in which data is used. For instance, a SEIPS study of postpartum haemorrhage [14] showed that alerts were ignored not due to missing data but because of cultural and organizational pressures [5].

The FAIR principles requiring persistent identifiers, metadata, provenance, and standardized vocabularies provide a practical basis for data transparency [7,12]. Yet interoperability research often focuses on technical standards [27] and underplays socio-technical influences on data use. Similarly, SEIPS applications in healthcare remain descriptive, case-specific, and not machine-readable, limiting reuse or integration into governance frameworks [23]. Ontologies provide one path forward: they can formally represent socio-technical entities and relationships while aligning with provenance standards such as PROV-O [6].

Table 1 compares widely cited socio-technical (SEIPS, Cube, FRAM) and data-centric approaches (DFD, DVM, ARK, PROV-O). The comparison highlights that no single framework integrates both perspectives in a reusable, machine-readable format.

The key gap is therefore twofold: (i) STSA frameworks lack a data mapping layer, and (ii) no ontology exists to make SEIPS machine-readable. Bridging this gap requires an ontology-driven extension of STSA that integrates socio-technical entities with data-centric dimensions and aligns with FAIR principles.

**Table 1.** Summary of Framework Coverage Across Socio-Technical and Data-Centric Dimensions.

| Dimensions | SEIPS [7] | Cube STSA [20] | FRAM [9] | ARK Platform [11] | Data Flow Diagram [1] | Data Value Map [23] | PROV-O [6] |
|---|---|---|---|---|---|---|---|
| Actor | X | X | X | X | X | X | X |
| Activity | X | X | X | X | X | – | X |
| Data Flows | – | – | X | – | X | – | X |
| Data Value | – | – | – | – | – | X | – |
| Provenance | – | – | – | – | Basic | X | X |
| Data Governance | – | – | – | X | – | – | – |
| Machine-Readable Format | – | – | – | X | – | – | X |
| Type | S | S | S | S | D | D | D |

## 3 Design

To ensure that the proposed ontology aligns with STSA and data mapping methods, a structured set of requirements was first defined and an ontolgy constructed following the NeOn methodology [13].

The following requirements were derived from the data transparency for SEIPS STSA use case and the related work and informed the Easy Approach to Requirements Syntax (EARS) [19]:

1. **Integration with Human and Organizational Factors:** Integrate socio-technical dimensions (people, rules, goals, context, environment) with technical data flows to reveal their combined influence on data quality.
2. **Alignment with STSA Frameworks:** Generate evidence to address specific Cube and SEIPS framework questions, ensuring compatibility with established socio-technical analysis practices.
3. **Systematic Data Mapping:** Enable the identification and structured representation of data flows, including points of data generation, transformation, and transfer across hospital systems.
4. **Redundancy Detection:** Detect redundancies and duplications across departmental systems and processes.
5. **Transformation & Handover Capture:** Document transformation points and handovers of data across both technical systems and organizational actors.
6. **Traceability:** Support end-to-end tracing of data, linking sources, intermediate steps, and outputs.
7. **Change Documentation:** Enable systematic documentation of changes applied to data at each step in the flow.

Our approach to data transparency depends on two ontologies; a SEIPS ontology to describe a worksystem (or an alternate ontology for other STSAs) and the supporting Atlas ontology for describing data flows. Figure 1 presents the SEIPS ontology core classes and relationships (addressing requirements 1 and 2). It captures the five SEIPS work-system components; Person, Task, Technology, Environment, Organization and their key relations (e.g., *seips:performsTask, seips:usesTechnology, seips:worksInEnvironment, seips:situatedInEnvironment, seips:responsibleForTask*).

The Atlas ontology enriches the SEIPS work system description with data provenance information (built on the W3C PROV-O standard) to enhance data transparency and governance. A flexible mapping to PROV-O is provided (Table 2) that enables the outcomes of three popular data flow modelling techniques— DFDs, UML use cases, and DVM—to be captured in a machine readable model connected to the SEIPs ontology.

Table 2 provides a concise mapping of how the Atlas framework integrates provenance across different modelling methods. DFD elements like processes are aligned with PROV-O classes (prov:Activity, prov:Entity, prov:Agent) to capture operational data flows. Use Case elements (actors, activities, system boundaries) are also linked to PROV-O. DVM elements (data producers, consumers, values, interpretations, insights) are also mapped to PROV-O to represent usage, derivation, and governance. Finally, SEIPS contributes contextual elements (e.g., environment) that situate data provenance within socio-technical systems.

**Table 2.** Concise PROV-O mapping in the Atlas

| Method | Atlas Class | Parent PROV-O Classes |
|---|---|---|
| DFD | Process, Data Store, Data Flow, Actor | `prov:Activity`, `prov:Entity`, `prov:Agent` |
| Use Case | Actor, System Boundary | `prov:Agent`, `prov:Activity`, `prov:Plan` |
| DVM | Data Producer, Data Consumer, Data Value, Contextual Use, Processing Step, Derived Insight | `prov:Agent`, `prov:Entity`, `prov:Activity` |

Atlas ontology mapped to PROV-O and bridged with SEIPS. Atlas uses provenance metadata by treating Dataset and Indicator as data entities, and Transformation and Handover as activities linked to accountable Agents (person, organization, or system). Provenance relations (*wasGeneratedBy, used, wasAttributedTo, wasAssociatedWith, wasDerivedFrom, wasInformedBy*) encode lineage and responsibility, while SEIPS relations (*performsTask, usesTechnology, occursIn, responsibleOrganization*) link Socio-Technical context to data flows. This alignment makes data generation, transformations, and handovers explicit and machine-readable for transparency and governance. thereby addressing requirements 1 (systematic data mapping), 3 (handover capture), 4 (traceability), 5 (change documentation), and 6 (integration with human and organizational factors).

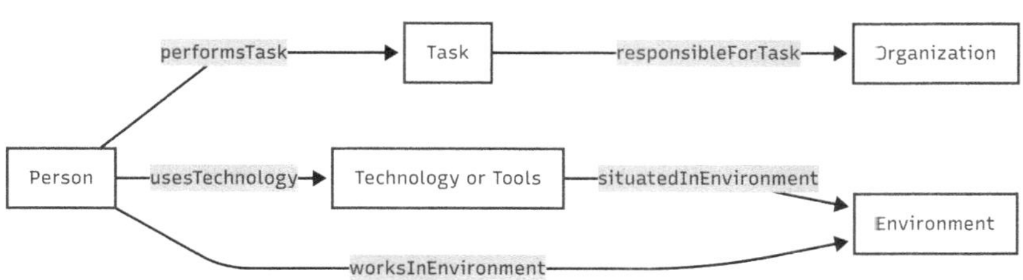


**Fig. 1.** SEIPS Ontology Core Classes and Relationships.

## 4 Evaluation

An **evaluation** was conducted to determine whether the proposed SEIPS and Atlas ontologies satisfies both the FAIR principles and Requirement Specification. Specifically, we aimed to assess (i) its compliance with FAIR data principles as embedded in the F-UJI FAIR assessment tool, and (ii) its accuracy, utility and completeness when reviewed by HFEs domain experts in conducting STSAs. This led to the following hypotheses:

**H1:** The ontology will demonstrate more than 40% FAIR compliance across findability, accessibility, interoperability, and reusability dimensions.
**H2:** The majority of domain experts (HFE) will agree or strongly agree that the ontology is accurate, complete, and consistent in representing the SEIPS work system model.
**H3:** The majority of domain experts will agree or strongly agree that the requirements implemented in the Atlas ontology improve data transparency in STSA work system analysis.

**Evaluation Method** consisted of two complementary approaches:

1. **Automated FAIR assessment:** The ontology was uploaded and evaluated using the F-UJI tool [15]. F-UJI was selected because it is one of the most widely adopted automated FAIR assessment services, recommended and maintained by the GO FAIR community and the Research Data Alliance (RDA). It has been applied in several large-scale FAIR evaluation studies, including assessments of European Open Science Cloud (EOSC) resources, and is frequently cited in the FAIR data stewardship literature [15]. Independent reports (such as EOSC FAIR assessment studies) describe F-UJI as a reliable and transparent implementation of the FAIR principles, making it a recognized benchmark tool for evaluating compliance. While F-UJI primarily targets datasets, we used it to obtain machine-actionable FAIR signals for the ontology's web resources; we contextualized these results with ontology-focused frameworks such as O'FAIRe.
2. **Expert validation:** A survey was conducted with HFE specialists, who reviewed the ontology for accuracy, utility and completeness.

The **Evaluation Setup** for SEIPS and Atlas ontologies were published on the internet and available in JSON-LD, RDF/XML, TTL, and N-Triples. It models the healthcare work system, covering 16 classes, 17 object/data properties.

*FAIRness metrics:* F-UJI [15] used to assess the FAIRNess the FAIR principles as a set of machine-actionable tests derived from the FAIRsFAIR and RDA recommendations [16]. Each dimension was assessed through multiple indicators. Each indicator was scored (0 = not satisfied, 1 = partially satisfied, 2 = fully satisfied) and the results were aggregated into a normalized score between 0 and 1 for each FAIR dimension. These scores are then reported by F-UJI as the FAIRness metrics for the ontology.

*Expert metrics:* Perceived completeness, accuracy, clarity of ontology entities, and the ability to answer competency questions were measured using a structured questionnaire. Each metric was operationalized as a set of Likert-scale items (1 = strongly disagree, 4 = strongly agree). For example, experts rated whether all relevant entities and relationships were included (completeness), whether the ontology faithfully represented the SEIPS work system (accuracy), whether the terminology and structure were understandable (clarity), and whether the ontology enabled answering the predefined competency questions (utility). Scores were aggregated by calculating the mean and standard deviation across expert responses for each metric.

A survey was conducted with **Expert Participants**, specifically Human Factors and Ergonomics (HFE) specialists experienced in SEIPS, to evaluate the ontology. Experts were asked to assess the correctness, consistency, and clarity of the five core SEIPS concepts represented in the ontology: **Environment**, **Organization**, **Person**, **Task**, and **Technology or Tools**. Quantitative ratings were collected using a five-point Likert scale, where 1 indicated "not correct" and 4 indicated "fully correct."

The survey was designed collaboratively by two researchers and reviewed by two additional colleagues to evaluate its accuracy, clarity, and consistency. Following this review, revisions were made, and the updated version was returned to the same reviewers for final feedback. All four contributors agreed on the finalized survey prior to distribution.

The final survey contained four sections: two focused on SEIPS concepts and their relationships as modeled in the ontology (introduced through a scenario for contextualization), one assessed the adequacy of the ontology in meeting requirements using the four and five point Likert scale, and one collected open-ended qualitative feedback. This iterative design and testing process ensured methodological accuracy, reduced the risk of ambiguity or misinterpretation, and strengthened the validity of the evaluation results. Recruitment for the survey was conducted in collaboration with HFE experts with University College Dublin under ethics approval number 274-LS-C-25-Karimian-Brennan.

**Evaluation Results:** The evaluation combined FAIR assessment and expert review of the ontology.

**FAIR Assessment:** The F-UJI tool reported overall FAIR compliance above the commonly accepted threshold ($\geq 0.4$) across all four dimensions. This indicates that the ontology already demonstrates a level of findability, accessibility, interoperability, and reusability comparable to established biomedical ontologies.

**Expert Survey:** A total of $N = 6$ experts completed the ontology evaluation survey. Participants represented diverse backgrounds including Human Factors, Patient Safety, Occupational Safety, and regulatory domains. Respondents were affiliated with both academia and healthcare practice, and their professional experience ranged from less than one year to over thirty years of engagement with SEIPS or related frameworks.

**Concept Ratings:** Overall, the ontology was positively received, with mean ratings ranging from 3.0 to 4.0 across the five SEIPS concepts.

*Person* (mean = 4) received the strongest endorsement. Most responses were "mostly correct" or "fully correct," indicating high alignment with SEIPS definitions.

*Organization* (mean = 3.5) was generally rated positively, with three "fully correct" evaluations. However, some experts questioned whether organizational factors overlap with the environment and whether the organization should account for external governance.

*Task* (mean = 3.5) was endorsed by several "fully correct" responses, though experts suggested strengthening explicit links between task and environment.

*Technology or Tools* (mean = 3.5) showed the widest variability, with ratings spanning 1 to 5. While three experts judged it "fully correct," two considered it "not correct," citing ambiguity around paper-based tools and emerging technologies such as automation and Artificial Intelligence.

*The* environment (mean = 3.0) received the lowest score, with five ratings of "partially correct." Experts emphasized the need to clearly distinguish between the internal and external environment.

**Contradictions** were reported four times, particularly around whether the organization is also responsible for the environment and how external governance factors should be modeled. Experts also evaluated SEIPS relationships (e.g., *Performs Task*, *Uses Technology*, *Situated in Environment*). The ratings indicated that most of the relations were *relevant and properly directed*, but some suggestions were made to clarify the bidirectional links and expand the emerging interactions.

In **Summary** experts agreed that the ontology successfully represented all required SEIPS entities and supported *requirements specifications.* Although clarity, coverage, and usability were rated as satisfactory, feedback highlighted areas for refinement, particularly: (i) distinguishing internal vs. external aspects of environment, (ii) clarifying overlaps between organization and environment, and (iii) refining the representation of technology and provenance. Overall, the ontology was considered *useful and interesting* in formalizing SEIPS in machine-readable format.

## 5 Discussion and Conclusion

This study showed that FAIR-aligned ontology engineering can effectively augment SEIPS to improve transparency and documentation of healthcare data flows. By formalising the SEIPS work-system as a machine-readable ontology and aligning it with W3C PROV-O through the Atlas framework, the approach makes data lineage, responsibility, and handover events explicit—elements that are not captured in conceptual STSA representations. The combined FAIR assessment and expert review indicate that this integration provides both machine-actionable transparency and faithful representation of core socio-technical concepts.

Expert validation confirmed good accuracy for key SEIPS elements, particularly **Person** and **Task**, while highlighting areas for refinement, including clearer distinctions between internal and external aspects of the **Environment**, overlap with **Organization**, and broader coverage of **Technology or Tools**. FAIR evaluation using F-UJI showed that Atlas achieves a level of compliance comparable to established biomedical ontologies, with strong **Findability** and scope for improvement in **Interoperability** [4].

In conclusion, the FAIR-SEIPS ontology moves STSA beyond descriptive models toward a reusable, machine-readable foundation that integrates socio-technical context with data provenance. This enables more systematic reasoning about healthcare data transparency, accountability, and governance, while providing clear directions for future technical and conceptual refinement.

**Acknowledgments.** This work was conducted with the financial support of the Research Ireland Research Center for Research Training in Digitally-Enhanced Reality (d-real) under Grant No. 18/CRT/6224 and the ADAPT Center for Digital Content Technology which is funded under the Research Ireland Research Centers Program (Grant 13/RC/2106 2) and is co-funded under the European Regional Development Fund. 

**Disclosure of Interests.** The authors have no competing interests to declare that are relevant to the content of this article.

## References

1. Aleryani, A.Y.: Analyzing Data Flow: A comparison between data flow diagrams (DFD) and use case diagrams (UCD) in information systems development. European Modern Studies Journal **8**(1), 313–320 (2024). https://doi.org/10.59573/emsj.8(1).2024.28
2. Alruwaili, M., Alsayat, A., Idris, M., Alanazi, S., Aurangzeb, K.: Integration and analysis of diverse healthcare data sources: a novel solution. Comput. Hum. Behav. **157**, 108221 (2024). https://doi.org/10.1016/j.chb.2024.108221
3. Antoniou, G., Harmelen, F.: Web Ontology Language: OWL. In: Staab, S., Studer, R. (eds.) Handbook on Ontologies. IHIS, pp. 91–110. Springer, Cham (2009). https://doi.org/10.1007/978-3-540-92673-3_4
4. Bandrowski, A., et al.: The ontology for biomedical investigations **11**(4), e0154556 (2016). https://doi.org/10.1371/journal.pone.0154556
5. Baxter, G., Sommerville, I.: Socio-technical systems: From design methods to systems engineering **23**(1), 4–17 (2011). https://doi.org/10.1016/j intcom.2010.07.003, https://academic.oup.com/iwc/article-lookup/doi/10.1016/j intcom.2010.07.003
6. Belhajjame, K., et al.: PROV-o: The PROV ontology
7. Carayon, P., et al.: Work system design for patient safety: the SEIPS model **15**(Suppl 1), i50-5 (2006). https://doi.org/10.1136/qshc.2005.015842
8. Carayon, P., Wooldridge, A., Hoonakker, P., Hundt, A.S., Kelly, M.M.: SEIPS 3.0: Human-centered design of the patient journey for patient safety **84**, 10303 (2020). https://doi.org/10.1016/j.apergo.2019.103033, https://linkinghub.elsevier.com/retrieve/pii/S000368701930239X
9. Ellen, J.G., et al.: Participant flow diagrams for health equity in AI research (2023). https://doi.org/10.1101/2023.10.05.23296611, http://medrxiv.org/lookup/doi/10.1101/2023.10.05.23296611
10. Erik, H.: FRAM: The Functional Resonance Analysis Method: Modelling Complex Socio-technical Systems. CRC Press, 1 ed. (2017). https://doi.org/10.1201/9781315255071, https://www.taylorfrancis.com/books/9781351935968

11. Geary, U., Ward, M.E., Callan, V., McDonald, N., Corrigan, S.: A socio-technical systems analysis of the application of RFID-enabled technology to the transport of precious laboratory samples in a large acute teaching hospital **102**, 103759 (2022). https://doi.org/10.1016/j.apergo.2022.103759, https://linkinghub.elsevier.com/retrieve/pii/S0003687022000825
12. Gonzalez Soltero, R., Pino García, D., Bellido, A., Ryan, P., Rodríguez-Learte, A.I.: FAIR data management: a framework for fostering data literacy in biomedical sciences education **24**(1), 284 (2024). https://doi.org/10.1186/s12874-024-02404-1
13. Gómez-Pérez, A., Suárez-Figueroa, M.C.: NeOn methodology for building ontology networks: a scenario-based methodology (2009). https://api.semanticscholar.org/CorpusID:15766061
14. Hale-Lopez, K.L., et al.: A SEIPS-based analysis to understand safety culture during postpartum hemorrhage **13**(5), 499 (2025). https://doi.org/10.3390/healthcare13050499
15. Huber, R., Devaraju, A.: F-UJIâĂŕ: An automated tool for the assessment and improvement of the FAIRness of research data (2021). https://doi.org/10.5194/egusphere-egu21-15922
16. Huber, R., Parkes, O.: FAIR-IMPACT- using f-UJI to assess the FAIRness of your data. European Commission. https://doi.org/10.5281/ZENODO.15058817, publisher: Zenodo
17. Pandit, J.H., Esteves, B., Krog, P.G., Ryan, P., Golpayegani, D., Flake, J.: Data privacy vocabulary (DPV) – version 2.0. In: Demartini, G., et al. (eds.) The Semantic Web – ISWC 2024, vol. 15233, pp. 171–193. Springer, Cham (2024). https://doi.org/10.1007/978-3-031-77847-6_10, series Title: Lecture Notes in Computer Science
18. Jacobsen, A., et al.: FAIR principles: Interpretations and implementation considerations **2**(1), 10–29.https://doi.org/10.1162/dint_r_00024
19. Mavin, A., Wilkinson, P., Harwood, A., Novak, M.: Easy approach to requirements syntax (ears). In: Proceedings of the 17th IEEE International Requirements Engineering Conference, pp. 317–322. IEEE (2009)https://doi.org/10.1109/RE.2009.9
20. McDonald, N., et al.: Evaluation of an access-risk-knowledge (ark) platform for governance of risk and change in complex socio-technical systems. Int. J. Environ. Res. Public Health **18**(23), 12572 (2021). https://doi.org/10.3390/ijerph182312572
21. McKenna, L., Liang, J., Duda, N., McDonald, N., Brennan, R.: Ark-virus: An ark platform extension for mindful risk governance of personal protective equipment use in healthcare. In: Companion Proceedings of the Web Conference 2021, pp. 698–700. ACM (2021). https://doi.org/10.1145/3442442.3458609
22. Raghupathi, W., Raghupathi, V.: Big data analytics in healthcare: promise and potential. Health Inf. Sci. Syst. **2**, 3 (2014). https://doi.org/10.1186/2047-2501-2-3
23. Sammon, D., Nagle, T.: The data value map: A framework for developing shared understanding on data initiatives. In: Proceedings of the International Conference on Information Systems. AIS Electronic Library (2017)
24. Schwabe, D., Becker, K., Seyferth, M., Klaß, A., Schaeffter, T.: The METRIC-framework for assessing data quality for trustworthy AI in medicine: a systematic review **7**(1), 203 (2024). https://www.nature.com/articles/s41746-024-01196-4, publisher: Nature Publishing Group UK London
25. Torab-Miandoab, A., Samad-Soltani, T., Jodati, A., Rezaei-Hachesu, P.: Interoperability of heterogeneous health information systems: a systematic literature review.

BMC Med. Inform. Decis. Mak. **23**(1), 18 (2023). https://doi.org/10.1186/s12911-023-02115-5
26. Weng, C.: Clinical data quality: A data life cycle perspective. eGEMs **4**(1), 6–14 (2019). https://doi.org/10.1080/24709360.2019.1572344
27. Wong, Z.S.Y., Gong, Y., Ushiro, S.: A pathway from fragmentation to interoperability through standards-based enterprise architecture to enhance patient safety **8**(1), 41 (2025). https://doi.org/10.1038/s41746-025-01442-3, https://www.nature.com/articles/s41746-025-01442-3
28. Xie, A., Carayon, P.: A systematic review of human factors and ergonomics-based healthcare system redesign for quality of care and patient safety. Ergonomics **58**(1), 33–49 (2014). https://doi.org/10.1080/00140139.2014.959070
29. Yourdon, E., Constantine, L.: Structured Design. Yourdon Press, New York (1979)
30. Yourdon, E., Constantine, L.L.: Structured design: fundamentals of a discipline of computer program and systems design. Yourdon Press, 18. [print.] edn
31. Zhang, J., et al.: Mapping and evaluating national data flows: transparency, privacy, and guiding infrastructural transformation. Lancet Digital Health **5**(10), e737–e748 (2023). https://doi.org/10.1016/S2589-7500(23)00157-7
32. Zhang, Y., Dong, C., Guo, W., Dai, J., Zhao, Z.: Systems theoretic accident model and process (STAMP): A literature review **152**, 105596 (2022). https://doi.org/10.1016/j.ssci.2021.105596, https://linkinghub.elsevier.com/retrieve/pii/S0925753521004367, publisher: Elsevier BV

# Speech Emotion Recognition from Audio Using Machine Learning and Deep Learning Approaches

Christian O'Leary[1,2](✉), Gary Smith[2], and Conor Lynch[2]

[1] Computer Science Department, Munster Technological University, Cork, Ireland
[2] Nimbus Research Centre, Munster Technological University, Cork, Ireland
{christian.oleary,gary.smith,conor.lynch}@mtu.ie

**Abstract.** Detecting emotions in speech audio is a central challenge in Human-Computer Interaction (HCI). With the proliferation of chatbots, voice assistants and automated call centres, accurate emotion recognition has become more pertinent as it influences the extent to which programs can interpret human intentions. In this study, 15 machine learning (ML) models are evaluated for their capacity to classify four emotional states—*anger*, *happy*, *sad*, *neutral*—using non-scripted audio from the IEMOCAP dataset, which provides a realistic representation of natural speech. The benchmark empirically compares deep learning models (e.g., BERT, DCNN-BLSTMwA) using data augmentation and conventional ML approaches (e.g., SVM, XGBoost) using metrics such as Macro-F1 and training time. Results indicate that deep learning models tend to achieve accurate emotion recognition, but at the cost of long training times. Furthermore, this study highlights the importance of session-fold cross-validation in testing models versus holdout and K-Fold cross-validation strategies.

**Keywords:** Machine Learning · Deep Learning · Emotion Recognition · Sentiment Analysis · Natural Language Processing

## 1 Introduction

Speech Emotion Recognition (SER) has emerged as a critical component of modern Human-Computer Interaction (HCI) as humans tend to expect devices to exhibit emotional recognition capabilities, thereby enabling more productive interactions [38]. For example, monitoring anger or stress is highly important for scenarios such as call centres or aviation control, especially in safety-critical applications [23]. The pertinence of facilitating positive HCI experiences has driven SER systems research whose aim is to automatically determine the emotional state of the speaker via speech signals. SER system design is grounded in theories of human emotion. A seminal model by Russell and Mehrabian [34] describes emotions across three independent dimensions: Valence (pleasure–displeasure), Arousal (calm–excited), and Dominance (control–submission) or


T. T. Mai et al. (Eds.): AICS 2025, CCIS 2950, pp. 120–132, 2026.
https://doi.org/10.1007/978-3-032-25809-0_9

VAD. Valence, arousal and dominance may be referred to as attribute-based descriptors of SER audio data. Plutchik's *Wheel of Emotions* [32] identifies eight primary emotions grouped into four opposing pairs, each varying in intensity, e.g. serenity, joy and then ecstasy. Ekman [14] categorised emotions into labels that are still commonly used in SER datasets: Anger, Enjoyment Fear, Disgust, Sadness and Surprise. These frameworks illustrate the complexity of modelling emotions and inform how Machine Learning (ML) approaches can be structured to predict either categorical labels or continuous dimensions.

Advances in ML and Deep Learning (DL) have significantly advanced SER, yet important questions remain about comparative performance, computational cost, and evaluation methodology [31]. Utilising data augmentation, ML and DL algorithms, this study aims to present an empirical analysis of 15 ML models that classify 4 emotional states (*anger, happy, sad, neutral*) in audio data extracted from the IEMOCAP dataset. To facilitate easier model comparisons for researchers, model performances are represented using standard classification metrics (macro averages of Precision, Recall, and F1) as well as model training times. Furthermore, this study underscores the importance of evaluation design by contrasting session-fold Cross-fold Validation (CV) with more common holdout and K-Fold approaches. Section 2 provides context from existing research, Sect. 3 outlines this study's experimental approach, Sect. 4 evaluates model results, and Sect. 5 offers an overarching summary of this paper.

## 2 Related Work

***SER Datasets:*** The field of SER has seen the creation of a wide variety of audio speech datasets varying in size, recording conditions, and labelling schemes. Table 1 presents an overview of prominent English-based datasets. Several provide audio modalities, but this study focuses only on their audio components.

**Table 1.** Speech audio dataset metadata

| Dataset | Male | Female | Files | Anger | Calm | Contempt | Excitement | Disgust | Fear | Frustration | Happy | Neutral | Sad | Surprise |
|---|---|---|---|---|---|---|---|---|---|---|---|---|---|---|
| *MSP-PODCAST* | 110 | 87 | 151 654 | ✓ | | ✓ | | ✓ | ✓ | | ✓ | ✓ | ✓ | ✓ |
| *IEMOCAP* | 5 | 5 | 10 190 | ✓ | | | ✓ | ✓ | ✓ | ✓ | ✓ | ✓ | ✓ | ✓ |
| *CREMA-D* | 48 | 43 | 7 442 | ✓ | ✓ | ✓ | | ✓ | ✓ | ✓ | | | | |
| *TESS* | 0 | 2 | 2 800 | ✓ | | | | ✓ | ✓ | | ✓ | ✓ | ✓ | ✓ |
| *RAVDESS* | 12 | 12 | 1 440 | ✓ | ✓ | | | ✓ | ✓ | | ✓ | ✓ | ✓ | ✓ |
| *SAVEE* | 4 | 0 | 480 | ✓ | | | | ✓ | ✓ | | ✓ | ✓ | ✓ | ✓ |

The widely used IEMOCAP database [6] was built using 5 audiovisual recordings, each containing a distinct 'male' and 'female' speaker along with a textual transcription. Consisting of 10,039 utterances, IEMOCAP contains a mix of both scripted and improvised audio data, making it especially valuable for benchmarking. Each utterance is labelled by a minimum of 3 annotators. Valency, activation and dominance are also recorded. Table 1 also refers to several smaller actor-based datasets. Crowd-sourced Emotional Multimodal Actors Dataset (CREMA-D) [9] contains 7 442 audio files from 91 actors, with each containing 1 of 12 sentences across 6 emotions from 2 443 annotators. The Toronto Emotional Speech Set (TESS) [12] was formulated by two speakers vocalising 200 words preceded by the carrier phrase "Say the word _". Each phrase was spoken seven times with various emotions, resulting in 2 800 audio samples. Ryerson Audio-Visual Database of Emotional Speech and Song (RAVDESS) [25] contains 7 356 files, of which 1 440 are available as `WAV` audio. RAVDESS was built using 24 actors across 60 trials speaking two lexically-matched sentences across 8 emotions. The Surrey Audio-Visual Expressed Emotion (SAVEE) database [16] contains just 480 utterances from 4 speakers (120 per speaker). The speakers vocalised 15 distinct sentences for each of the 7 emotions. These datasets are publicly available for experimentation, but are smaller than IEMOCAP and are less diverse. MSP-PODCAST [27] is a large corpus comprised of short non-consecutive segments of natural speech containing 151 654 vocalisations. This data is derived from 237 h and 56 min of audio with 8 emotion labels and VAD scores.

***SER Features:*** A comprehensive survey by de Lope and Graña [26] provides a thorough insight into SER research, reviewing data repositories, conventional ML approaches and DL methodologies. The distinction between ML and DL algorithms is not arbitrary; while some DL architectures can be utilised with engineered features in the same manner as traditional ML models, many modern Neural Network (NN) models embed feature extraction into the model using mechanisms such as embedded feature vectors.

Prosodic features such as pitch, intonation and intensity are valuable indicators of emotion [4]. For instance, the tone quality of joyful speech may manifest over a wide pitch range with higher energy, whereas sadness typically presents narrower pitch ranges with a resonant timbre [4]. Pauses between words can indicate intensity and manifest as flatter, less noisy periods. The most extensively utilised prosodic feature sources are pitch, fundamental frequency, duration, and energy [4]. Prosodic features more reliably indicate high-energy emotions such as anger than more acoustically muted states, e.g. sadness. Spectral features provide a complementary representation of speech signals and are obtained by converting a time-domain signal to a frequency-domain signal. Some spectral features used in SER are Mel Frequency Cepstral Coefficients (MFCC) and Perceptive Linear Prediction (PLP) features. MFCCs are commonly derived from Fourier transforms of fixed-length audio segments. Powers of the computed spectrum are mapped to the Mel scale via overlapping windows. A discrete cosine transform of the log of each power is calculated and the resulting amplitudes are treated as features. Open-source audio feature extraction toolkits include *openSMILE* [15] and *librosa* [29].

Data augmentation can enhance model performance by synthetically increasing the size and diversity of datasets. Various data augmentation techniques for SER modelling are presented in Table 2. Yi and Mak [36] reviewed audio data augmentation methods using Generative Adversarial Network (GAN) models.

**Table 2.** Audio Data Augmentation Methods

| Method | Description |
|---|---|
| Time Shifting | Lateral shift of audio data |
| Time Stretching | Changing the speed of the sound without changing its pitch |
| Pitch Scaling | Changing the pitch without changing the speed of the sound |
| Noise Addition | Adding noise to the audio signal [28] |
| Pre-emphasis | Boosts high frequencies and suppress low-frequency noise |
| Time Masking | Masks certain portions of the spectrogram in the time domain |

They concluded that while their WADAN, long=Wasserstein Adversarial Data Augmentation Network (WADAN) variation of a GAN method performs well overall, it may be limited in improving the generalisability of SER models as the generated samples are lacking in diversity. This is a common issue in GAN experimentation.

***SER Models:*** ML methodologies can effectively leverage prosodic and spectral features for SER. For example, Dahake et al. [8] demonstrated the use of Support Vector Machine (SVM) models using various kernels. Iqbal and Barua [20] explored the use of SVM, K-Nearest Neighbors (KNN) and Gradient Boosting models with the RAVDESS and SAVEE datasets. Their SVM model achieved the highest accuracy for anger and neutral emotions, but was outperformed by Gradient Boosting for sadness and happiness. The authors note, however, that their results highlight the challenge of generalisability across datasets and conditions. DL approaches have grown increasingly prominent in SER. For example, Zhang et al. [37] proposed a Deep Convolution Neural Network (DCNN) and Bidirectional Long Short-Term Memory with Attention (BLSTMwA) model achieving high Unweighted Average Recall (UAR) scores when tested against the Berlin Emotional Speech Database (EMODB) [5] and IEMOCAP [6]. Pepino et al. [31] designed a multimodal model incorporating an acoustic-feature branch and a text branch to classify emotions using both modalities. This model combined audio feature processing with pre-trained Bidirectional Encoder Representations from Transformers (BERT) word embeddings [10] using a fusion mechanism unifying both approaches into one NN model. More recently, Duret et al. [13] combined an ensemble of speech encoders (e.g. Wav2Vec2 [1]) and a text encoder (RoBERTa [24]) whose outputs were passed as a combined feature vector to an SVM, producing a final classification. Such DL models operate without feature engineering, unlike conventional ML models.

## 3 Methodology

While various audio SER datasets are publicly available, this research prioritises the use of IEMOCAP audio data for several reasons. As previously described, IEMOCAP is a large dataset containing 10 039 utterances across 9 emotion categories. Each utterance was labelled using multiple annotators, which may provide a high degree of confidence regarding annotation fidelity. For consistency with other studies [37], the following four labels have been chosen for model evaluation: 'anger', 'happy', 'sad' and 'neutral'. IEMOCAP also contains transcriptions, ensuring that validation of text-based models is done using correctly annotated data. Model performance is assessed using Macro-Precision, Recall and F1 metrics. Macro-averaging computes the unweighted mean across classes, providing a balanced view for imbalanced datasets such as IEMOCAP. Macro-Recall is often reported as UAR [22]. The F1 score is seen as a particularly important measure given its insensitivity to class imbalance compared to metrics such as accuracy. In this study, models are trained and tested using three approaches. Firstly, all models are trained using 80% of the IEMOCAP dataset with 10% reserved for validation and 10% retained for the final test set. The dataset is shuffled prior to splitting and the process is repeated five times with different random states. This holdout method is then contrasted with a typical K-Fold CV process ($K = 5$) and session-fold CV, where each of the 5 recording sessions is treated as a fold to ensure that the test set contains new speakers.

***Machine Learning with Audio Features:*** The following ML models were implemented using *scikit-learn* [30]: Bernoulli Naíve Bayes, Decision Tree, Gaussian Naíve Bayes, KNN, Linear SVM, Logistic Regression, Passive Aggressive Classifier, Perceptron, Random Forest and SVM. Additionally, XGBoost [7] and CatBoost [11] models were included using the `xgboost` and `catboost` libraries, respectively. A Dense Neural Network (DNN) classifier was also implemented via *TensorFlow* [35]. All models in this study were optimised using *optuna*'s[1] Tree-structured Parzen Estimator (TPE) optimizer – a commonly used HPO algorithm [2,3,19]—to select hyperparameters over 100 iterations. Hyperparameter ranges for all models are included in Table 5 in the Appendix. Each of the aforementioned models included two additional hyperparameters: the number of input features and the feature scaling method. Feature selection scores were calculated as the median of a feature's rank, where ranks were computed using absolute Pearson correlation, ANOVA F-value, Mutual Information and Random Forest-based importance scores. The use of diverse metrics was intended to provide a robust feature scoring mechanism. Input features were generated using `librosa`: zero-crossing rate, Short-time Fourier Transform (STFT) chromagrams, MFCC, Root Mean Square values, and statistics (sum, minimum, maximum, mean, standard deviation) derived from: Mel-scaled spectrograms, dB-scaled spectrograms, constant-Q chromagrams, Chroma Energy Normalized

[1] https://optuna.readthedocs.io/.

(CENS), variable-Q chromagrams, spectral centroids, spectral bandwidths, spectral contrasts, spectral flatness, roll-off frequency, spectrogram polynomial coefficients, and tonal centroid features (*tonnetz*).

***DCNN-BLSTMwA Model:*** Given the promising UAR scores reported from Zhang et al.'s [37] DCNN-BLSTMwA model, a bespoke re-implementation was included in this benchmark as a relevant reference point. This implementation was programmed to be as true to the reported model as possible, though there may inevitably be some minor differences in its exact manifestation. While Zhang et al. [37] elucidate the mechanisms of the model in their research, a brief summary is included here. The original model used PyTorch's [33] implementation of AlexNet [21] as the initial Deep Convolution Neural Network (DCNN) component. This research uses the deep residual network `ResNet50V2` (based on [17]), which allows the model to also be implemented in TensorFlow; it should be noted that the inclusion of a `ResNet50V2` base model did not significantly improve the model itself. The DCNN is followed by a time-distributed bi-directional Long Short-Term Memory (LSTM) layer (128 neurons) and an attention layer, i.e. the Bidirectional Long Short-Term Memory with Attention (BLSTMwA). The classification is then conducted by two densely connected layers (256 and 238 neurons, ReLU activation) and a *softmax* layer. In an effort to regularise and improve the overall performance of the DCNN-BLSTMwA model, several data augmentation parameters were implemented: *AN* ('add random noise'), *SR* ('stretch rate', via *librosa*'s `time_stretch`), *Sh.* (lateral 'shift'), and *SU* ('speed up' via *pydub*'s `AudioSegment: set_frame_rate`). The *Sh.* and *SU* methods use the following speed modifiers [37]: 0.8, 0.9, 1.0, 1.1, 1.2.

***Text Model:*** BERT models are powerful Large Language Model (LLMs) that can be adapted to new problems via transfer learning. In this study, a text model was built using `bert-base-uncased` from Hugging Face [18] as a base model to classify audio files based on their corresponding text transcription. Based on the architecture proposed by Pepino et al. [31], the `bert-base-uncased` model is followed by a 1-D global max-pooling layer, a densely-connected layer (128 neurons, ReLU activation, 10% dropout), another densely-connected layer (32 neurons, ReLU activation) and a *softmax* layer. For simplicity, this paper refers to the 'Text' model as *BERT*. The following data augmentation methods were implemented for the BERT model. Round-Trip Translation (RTT) was implemented using the `deep_translator` library[2] while the other functions were implemented using `nlpaug`[3]: *R.Crop* ('random crop'), *R.Del* ('random delete'), *R.Swap* ('random swap'), *Pa.* ('paraphrase'), *R.Sub* ('random substitute'), *DE* (RTT German) and *FR* (RTT French).

## 4 Evaluation

The scores of all models are displayed in Table 3, sorted in descending order by Macro-F1. The 3 highest performing models were $\text{BERT}_{R.Del}$ (*0.555*), $\text{BERT}_{Pa.}$

[2] `deep_translator`: https://deep-translator.readthedocs.io.
[3] `nlpaug`: https://nlpaug.readthedocs.io.

**Table 3.** IEMOCAP model scores sorted by Macro-F1

| Model | Macro | | | F1 by label | | | | Training |
|---|---|---|---|---|---|---|---|---|
| | Recall | Precision | F1 | Anger | Happy | Sad | Neutral | Time (s) |
| BERT (R.Del) | 0.656 | 0.661 | **0.655** | 0.597 | 0.550 | 0.706 | 0.767 | 1 405 |
| BERT (Pa.) | 0.636 | 0.673 | **0.649** | 0.572 | 0.558 | 0.699 | 0.769 | 932 |
| DCNN-BLSTMwA (SU) | 0.644 | 0.674 | **0.649** | 0.694 | 0.365 | 0.789 | 0.748 | 17 694 |
| DCNN-BLSTMwA (AN) | 0.633 | 0.681 | **0.646** | 0.699 | 0.359 | 0.761 | 0.765 | 679 |
| Support Vector Machine | 0.671 | 0.643 | **0.645** | 0.641 | 0.440 | 0.809 | 0.690 | 140 |
| BERT (R.Swap) | 0.633 | 0.659 | **0.643** | 0.575 | 0.531 | 0.703 | 0.765 | 677 |
| BERT | 0.633 | 0.654 | **0.640** | 0.570 | 0.540 | 0.701 | 0.749 | 800 |
| BERT (FR) | 0.633 | 0.650 | **0.638** | 0.553 | 0.558 | 0.684 | 0.757 | 575 |
| BERT (DE) | 0.631 | 0.647 | **0.636** | 0.567 | 0.533 | 0.691 | 0.753 | 761 |
| DNN | 0.685 | 0.634 | **0.635** | 0.622 | 0.454 | 0.814 | 0.651 | 29 |
| BERT (R.Crop) | 0.622 | 0.661 | **0.634** | 0.553 | 0.537 | 0.692 | 0.755 | 718 |
| XGBoost | 0.620 | 0.691 | **0.633** | 0.712 | 0.228 | 0.818 | 0.775 | 36 |
| BERT (R.Sub) | 0.623 | 0.652 | **0.633** | 0.530 | 0.533 | 0.704 | 0.763 | 734 |
| BERT (All.aug.) | 0.624 | 0.646 | **0.631** | 0.532 | 0.534 | 0.709 | 0.75 | 1 763 |
| CatBoost | 0.614 | 0.662 | **0.617** | 0.687 | 0.150 | 0.848 | 0.782 | 517 |
| DCNN-BLSTMwA (SR) | 0.607 | 0.698 | **0.614** | 0.658 | 0.270 | 0.786 | 0.744 | 2 528 |
| Logistic Regression | 0.602 | 0.645 | **0.611** | 0.660 | 0.202 | 0.807 | 0.774 | 11 |
| DCNN-BLSTMwA (Sh.) | 0.596 | 0.650 | **0.609** | 0.608 | 0.337 | 0.754 | 0.736 | 910 |
| Linear SVM | 0.597 | 0.671 | **0.608** | 0.691 | 0.176 | 0.797 | 0.767 | 24 |
| Random Forest | 0.632 | 0.592 | **0.603** | 0.666 | 0.338 | 0.759 | 0.647 | 9 |
| Passive-Aggressive | 0.583 | 0.651 | **0.585** | 0.670 | 0.097 | 0.802 | 0.771 | 11 |
| DCNN-BLSTMwA | 0.595 | 0.604 | **0.582** | 0.613 | 0.243 | 0.773 | 0.697 | 286 |
| Perceptron | 0.568 | 0.625 | **0.570** | 0.681 | 0.073 | 0.768 | 0.757 | 11 |
| Decision Tree | 0.583 | 0.528 | **0.528** | 0.559 | 0.336 | 0.718 | 0.501 | 18 |
| Gaussian Naive Bayes | 0.550 | 0.520 | **0.513** | 0.555 | 0.235 | 0.687 | 0.575 | 8 |
| K-Nearest Neighbors | 0.469 | 0.474 | **0.468** | 0.455 | 0.257 | 0.555 | 0.605 | 7 |
| Bernoulli Naive Bayes | 0.517 | 0.449 | **0.454** | 0.490 | 0.183 | 0.686 | 0.457 | 3 |

(*0.649*) and DCNN-BLSTMwA$_{SU}$ (*0.649*). While these DL models perform exceptionally well overall, some of the BERT and DCNN-BLSTMwA variants are outperformed by some ML models, such as SVM (*0.645*), DNN (*0.635*) and XGBoost (*0.633*). It should be acknowledged that metric ranks do not correlate perfectly with each other. It is not uncommon for these metrics to disagree – especially with imbalanced classes – but it is important to note that the choice of metric has an impact on model selection.

The implemented DCNN-BLSTMwA model achieved Macro-Recall scores comparable with some of the variants presented by Zhang et al. [37] when paired with data augmentation, albeit at the cost of significantly longer training times. In consistence with other studies [37], most models underperformed with respect to the smallest class ('happy'), with BERT attaining an F1 of 55.8% using the paraphrase data augmentation.

Figure 1 illustrates the spread of test scores sorted by median Macro-F1 for each model, excluding suboptimal data augmentations. Note that this includes model instances **not** shortlisted by model selection prior to final testing, hence the differences in model rankings between Fig. 1 and Table 3. These differences underscore the importance of Hyperparameter Optimisation (HPO) with validation data prior to test score calculation. The spread of BERT scores is caused by a bimodal distribution; the model only performed well with fine-tuning enabled.

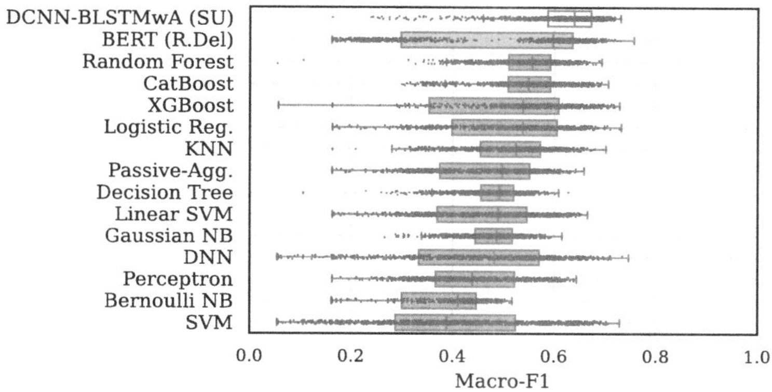


**Fig. 1.** Box plot of all model test scores sorted by median Macro-F1.

Some Macro-Recall scores exceed the highest value reported by Pepino et al. [31] (65.1% ± 0.5) with DNN scoring the highest at 68.5%. It should be noted that they implemented a speaker-fold CV mechanism, which complicates a direct comparison. The generated model rankings also vary slightly depending on their initial state or 'seed'. As SER studies often use CV in the form of speaker-fold or session-fold validation [38] to ensure a reliable model selection process, this study also reports Macro-F1 scores using holdout, 5-fold CV and session-fold CV in Table 4. Due to long training times, just the ML and DNN models are included in these additional results. The results show a slight decrease in model performance across most model types when progressing from holdout to a $K$-Fold CV methodology but a stark decrease for *all* models when using session-fold CV as the test set of each fold contains speakers absent during training. This suggests that caution is required when assessing model generalisability in SER research and that the choice of CV is highly impactful, given the small number of speakers relative to the amount of audio segments.

**Table 4.** Macro-F1 scores by model and validation method

| Model | Holdout | K-Fold | Session |
|---|---|---|---|
| Bernoulli Naive Bayes | 0.454 | 0.448 | 0.439 |
| CatBoost | 0.617 | 0.612 | 0.524 |
| DNN | 0.635 | 0.521 | 0.477 |
| Decision Tree | 0.528 | 0.519 | 0.456 |
| Gaussian Naive Bayes | 0.513 | 0.527 | 0.402 |
| K-Nearest Neighbors | 0.468 | 0.615 | 0.470 |
| Linear SVM | 0.608 | 0.555 | 0.400 |
| Logistic Regression | 0.611 | 0.605 | 0.520 |
| Passive-Aggressive | 0.585 | 0.545 | 0.350 |
| Perceptron | 0.570 | 0.506 | 0.353 |
| Random Forest | 0.603 | 0.598 | 0.520 |
| Support Vector Machine | 0.645 | 0.614 | 0.491 |
| XGBoost | 0.633 | 0.618 | 0.526 |
| **Mean Macro-F1:** | ***0.585*** | ***0.581*** | ***0.483*** |

## 5 Conclusions

This study presented a comprehensive benchmark of ML and DL models for Speech Emotion Recognition (SER) using the IEMOCAP dataset. By evaluating 15 models across both engineered acoustic features and text transcriptions, this work highlights several key findings. The BERT and DCNN-BLSTMwA architectures performed well with data augmentation – particularly via the random-delete and speed-up augmentations, respectively – but some variants were outperformed by less complex models such as SVM, DNN and XGBoost. The BERT-based text models attained the highest overall Macro-F1 score (65.5%) and the highest F1 (55.8%) for the smallest class ('happy'). The model rankings are, however, influenced by the choice of metric; the DNN model using audio-based features achieved the highest Macro-Recall (68.5%). This suggests that robust feature engineering combined with HPO remains viable for SER tasks. Furthermore, the results underscore the importance of evaluation methodology. Models trained using session-fold CV yielded lower performance compared to holdout or K-fold approaches, indicating that speaker overlap can inflate reported scores. This finding reinforces the need for rigorous validation protocols to ensure generalisability in SER research. Overall, the results show that no single modelling paradigm universally dominates; model performance rankings are influenced by CV, metric prioritisation and computational constraints. Future research should explore more diverse augmentation strategies and cross-dataset evaluation to advance reliability in real-world applications.

**Acknowledgments.** Thanks are extended to Enterprise Ireland for their support via the TEC Gateway program (grant number: CF-2022-2002-I).

**Disclosure of Interests.** The authors have no competing interests to declare that are relevant to the content of this article.

# A Appendix

**Table 5.** Hyperparameter optimization ranges

| Model | Hyperparameter | Range |
|---|---|---|
| *BNB* | alpha | 0.1 – 1.0 |
| *GNB* | var_smoothing | 1e-08 – 1e-10 |
| *KNN* | n_neighbors | 1 – 49 |
| | metric | euclidean, cosine, manhattan |
| *CatBoost* | grow_policy | Depthwise, SymmetricTree |
| | learning_rate | 0.1 – 0.001 |
| | max_depth | 4 – 9 |
| | n_estimators | 100 – 500 |
| *Linear SVM* | C | 0.0001 – 100 |
| | class_weight | balanced, None |
| | loss | hinge, squared_hinge |
| | max_iter | 100 – 1000 |
| | multi_class | ovr, crammer_singer |
| | tol | 0.001 – 0.0001 |
| *Logistic Reg.* | C | 0.01 – 10 |
| | tol | 1e-4 – 1e-6 |
| | multi_class | multinomial, ovr |
| | penalty | l2, None |
| *Passive -Agg.* | C | 1e-3 – 10 |
| | class_weight | balanced, None |
| | max_iter | 100 – 9000 |
| | tol | 1e-2 – 1e-4 |
| *Perceptron* | penalty | l1, l2, elasticnet, None |
| | alpha | 0.000001 – 0.001 |
| | tol | 0.0001 – 0.01 |
| | early_stopping | True, False |
| | max_iter | 100 – 10000 |
| *Decision Tree* | criterion | gini, entropy |
| | splitter | best, random |
| | max_depth | 8 – 128 |
| | min_samples_split | 2 – 128 |
| | min_samples_leaf | 1 – 100 |
| | max_leaf_nodes | 32 – 128, None |
| | class_weight | balanced, None |
| *Random Forest* | criterion | gini, entropy |
| | n_estimators | 100 – 500 |
| | max_depth | 8 – 128 |
| | min_samples_split | 2 – 128 |
| | min_samples_leaf | 1 – 100 |
| | max_leaf_nodes | 32 – 128, None |
| | class_weight | balanced, balanced_subsample |

| Model | Hyperparameter | Range |
|---|---|---|
| *SVM* | C | 1 – 100 |
| | class_weight | balanced, None |
| | gamma | scale, auto |
| | kernel | linear, rbf, sigmoid |
| | max_iter | 100 – 1000 |
| | shrinking | True, False |
| | tol | 0.001 – 0.0001 |
| *XGBoost* | alpha | 0.1 – 1.0 |
| | colsample_bytree | 0.5 – 1 |
| | grow_policy | depthwise, lossguide |
| | learning_rate | 0 – 0.1 |
| | max_depth | 2 – 16 |
| | min_child_weight | 0 – 6 |
| | n_estimators | 100 – 500 |
| | subsample | 0.5 – 1 |
| | tree_method | hist, approx |
| *BERT* | epochs | 1 – 100 |
| | fine_tuning | True, False |
| *DNN* | epochs | 10 – 50 |
| | architecture | 1-4 layers, 1-256 units |
| | dropout | 0.1 – 0.3 |
| | batch_norm | True, False |
| *DCNN-BLSTMwA* | epochs | 1 – 100 |
| | fine_tuning | True, False |
| | pretrain_epochs | 1 – 8 |
| | finetune_epochs | 2 – 16 |
| | freeze_limit | 60 – 80 |
| *All NNs* | early_stopping | 4 – 32, None |
| | min_delta | 0 – 1e-05 |
| | reduce_lr | True, False |
| | use_class_weights | True, False |

**Custom NN hyperparameters:**
early_stopping = early stopping patience
freeze_limit = layers frozen after pretraining
min_delta = early stopping tolerance
pretrain_epochs = pretraining (unfrozen layers)
reduce_lr = reduce learning rate on plateau
use_class_weights = weigh classes by size

*BNB* = Bernoulli Naive Bayes, *GNB* = Gaussian Naive Bayes, *Passive-Agg.* = Passive-Aggressive

## References


1. Baevski, A., Zhou, H., Mohamed, A., Auli, M.: Wav2vec 2.0: a framework for self-supervised learning of speech representations. In: Proceedings of the 34th International Conference on Neural Information Processing Systems, NIPS 2020, pp. 12449–12460. Curran Associates Inc., Red Hook (2020)
2. Bergstra, J., Bardenet, R., Bengio, Y., Kégl, B.: Algorithms for hyper-parameter optimization. In: Shawe-Taylor, J., Zemel, R., Bartlett, P., Pereira, F., Weinberger, K. (eds.) Advances in neural information processing systems, vol. 24, pp. 2546–2554. Curran Associates, Inc. (2011). https://proceedings.neurips.cc/paper_files/paper/2011/file/86e8f7ab32cfd12577bc2619bc635690-Paper.pdf
3. Bergstra, J., Yamins, D., Cox, D.: Making a science of model search: hyperparameter optimization in hundreds of dimensions for vision architectures. In: Proceedings of the 30th International Conference on Machine Learning, pp. 115–123. PMLR (2013). https://proceedings.mlr.press/v28/bergstra13.html, iSSN: 1938-7228
4. Bhangale, K., Kothandaraman, M.: Speech emotion recognition based on multiple acoustic features and deep convolutional neural network. Electronics **12**(4), 839 (2023). https://doi.org/10.3390/electronics12040839
5. Burkhardt, F., Paeschke, A., Rolfes, M., Sendlmeier, W.F., Weiss, B.: A database of German emotional speech. In: Proceedings of the Interspeech 2005, pp. 1517–1520. Eurospeech, Lisbon (2005). https://doi.org/10.21437/Interspeech.2005-446, https://www.isca-archive.org/interspeech_2005/burkhardt05b_interspeech.html
6. Busso, C., et al.: IEMOCAP: interactive emotional dyadic motion capture database. Lang. Resour. Eval. **42**(4), 335–359 (2008). https://doi.org/10.1007/s10579-008-9076-6
7. Chen, T., Guestrin, C.: XGBoost: a scalable tree boosting system. In: Proceedings of the 22nd ACM SIGKDD International Conference on Knowledge Discovery and Data Mining, pp. 785–794 (2016). https://doi.org/10.1145/2939672.2939785, arXiv: 1603.02754
8. Dahake, P.P., Shaw, K., Malathi, P.: Speaker dependent speech emotion recognition using MFCC and support vector machine. In: 2016 International Conference on Automatic Control and Dynamic Optimization Techniques (ICACDOT), pp. 1080–1084 (2016). https://doi.org/10.1109/ICACDOT.2016.7877753, https://ieeexplore.ieee.org/document/7877753
9. David Cooper: CheyneyComputerScience/CREMA-D (2025). https://github.com/CheyneyComputerScience/CREMA-D. Original-date: 2017-09-29T17:28:11Z
10. Devlin, J., Chang, M.W., Lee, K., Toutanova, K.: BERT: pre-training of deep bidirectional transformers for language understanding (2019). https://doi.org/10.48550/arXiv.1810.04805, http://arxiv.org/abs/1810.04805
11. Dorogush, A.V., Ershov, V., Gulin, A.: CatBoost: gradient boosting with categorical features support (2017). http://learningsys.org/nips17/assets/papers/paper_1.pdf
12. Dupuis, K., Pichora-Fuller, M.K.: Recognition of emotional speech for younger and older talkers: behavioural findings from the Toronto emotional speech set. Can. Acoust. **39**(3), 182–183 (2011). https://jcaa.caa-aca.ca/index.php/jcaa/article/view/2471
13. Duret, J., Estève, Y., Rouvier, M.: MSP-podcast SER challenge 2024: L'antenne du Ventoux multimodal self-supervised learning for speech emotion recognition, pp. 309–314 (2024). https://doi.org/10.21437/odyssey.2024-44, https://www.isca-archive.org/odyssey_2024/duret24_odyssey.html#

14. Ekman, P.: An argument for basic emotions. Cogn. Emot. **6**(3–4), 169–200 (1992). https://doi.org/10.1080/02699939208411068
15. Eyben, F., Wöllmer, M., Schuller, B.: OpenSmile: the Munich versatile and fast open-source audio feature extractor. In: Proceedings of the 18th ACM international conference on Multimedia, MM 2010, pp. 1459–1462. Association for Computing Machinery, New York (2010). https://doi.org/10.1145/1873951.1874246
16. Haq, S., Jackson, P.J.: Multimodal Emotion recognition. In: Wang, W. (ed.) Machine Audition: Principles, Algorithms and Systems, pp. 398–423. IGI Global, Hershey (2010). https://personalpages.surrey.ac.uk/p.jackson/pub/ma10/HaqJackson_MachineAudition10_approved.pdf
17. He, K., Zhang, X., Ren, S., Sun, J.: Identity mappings in deep residual networks. In: Leibe, B., Matas, J., Sebe, N., Welling, M. (eds.) ECCV 2016. LNCS, vol. 9908, pp. 630–645. Springer, Cham (2016). https://doi.org/10.1007/978-3-319-46493-0_38
18. Hugging Face: Hugging Face - The AI community building the future (2025). https://huggingface.co/
19. Hutter, F., Kotthoff, L., Vanschoren, J. (eds.): Automated Machine Learning: Methods, Systems, Challenges. The Springer Series on Challenges in Machine Learning. Springer, Cham (2019) https://doi.org/10.1007/978-3-030-05318-5. iSSN: 2520-131X, 2520-1328
20. Iqbal, A., Barua, K.: A real-time emotion recognition from speech using gradient boosting. In: 2019 International Conference on Electrical, Computer and Communication Engineering (ECCE), pp. 1–5 (2019). https://doi.org/10.1109/ECACE.2019.8679271, https://ieeexplore.ieee.org/document/8679271
21. Krizhevsky, A.: One weird trick for parallelizing convolutional neural networks (2014). https://doi.org/10.48550/arXiv.1404.5997, arXiv:1404.5997 [cs]
22. Latif, S., Rana, R., Khalifa, S., Jurdak, R., Qadir, J., Schuller, B.: Survey of deep representation learning for speech emotion recognition. IEEE Trans. Affect. Comput. **14**(2), 1634–1654 (2023). https://doi.org/10.1109/TAFFC.2021.3114365
23. Lieskovská, E., Jakubec, M., Jarina, R., Chmulík, M.: A review on speech emotion recognition using deep learning and attention mechanism. Electronics **10**(10), 1163 (2021). https://doi.org/10.3390/electronics10101163
24. Liu, Y., et al.: RoBERTa: a robustly optimized BERT pretraining approach (2019). https://doi.org/10.48550/arXiv.1907.11692, arXiv:1907.11692 [cs]
25. Livingstone, S.R., Russo, F.A.: The ryerson audio-visual database of emotional speech and song (RAVDESS): a dynamic, multimodal set of facial and vocal expressions in North American English. PLOS ONE **13**(5), e0196391 (2018). https://doi.org/10.1371/journal.pone.0196391, https://journals.plos.org/plosone/article?id=10.1371/journal.pone.0196391
26. de Lope, J., Graña, M.: An ongoing review of speech emotion recognition. Neurocomputing **528**, 1–11 (2023). https://doi.org/10.1016/j.neucom.2023.01.002
27. Lotfian, R., Busso, C.: Building naturalistic emotionally balanced speech corpus by retrieving emotional speech from existing podcast recordings. IEEE Trans. Affect. Comput. **10**(4), 471–483 (2019). https://doi.org/10.1109/TAFFC.2017.2736999
28. Matin, R., Valles, D.: A speech emotion recognition solution-based on support vector machine for children with autism spectrum disorder to help identify human emotions. In: 2020 Intermountain Engineering, Technology and Computing (IETC), pp. 1–6 (2020). https://doi.org/10.1109/IETC47856.2020.9249147, https://ieeexplore-ieee-org.mtu.idm.oclc.org/abstract/document/9249147
29. McFee, B., et al.: librosa: audio and music signal analysis in Python. Scipy (2015). https://doi.org/10.25080/Majora-7b98e3ed-003, https://proceedings.scipy.org/articles/Majora-7b98e3ed-003

30. Pedregosa, F., et al.: Scikit-learn: machine learning in python. J. Mach. Learn. Res. **6** (2011)
31. Pepino, L., Riera, P., Ferrer, L., Gravano, A.: Fusion approaches for emotion recognition from speech using acoustic and text-based features, pp. 6484–6488 (2020). https://doi.org/10.1109/ICASSP40776.2020.9054709, https://ieeexplore.ieee.org/document/9054709. iSSN 2379-190X
32. Plutchik, R.: Emotions: Facts, Theories and a New Model. University Press of America (1991)
33. PyTorch Developers: PyTorch: Tensors and Dynamic neural networks in Python with strong GPU acceleration (2025). https://github.com/pytorch/pytorch
34. Russell, J.A., Mehrabian, A.: Evidence for a three-factor theory of emotions. J. Res. Pers. **11**(3), 273–294 (1977). https://doi.org/10.1016/0092-6566(77)90037-X
35. Developers, T.F.: TensorFlow (2025). https://doi.org/10.5281/zenodo.16852354, https://zenodo.org/records/16852354
36. Yi, L., Mak, M.W.: Improving speech emotion recognition with adversarial data augmentation network. IEEE Trans. Neural Netw. Learn. Syst. **33**(1), 172–184 (2022). https://doi.org/10.1109/TNNLS.2020.3027600
37. Zhang, H., Gou, R., Shang, J., Shen, F., Wu, Y., Dai, G.: Pre-trained deep convolution neural network model with attention for speech emotion recognition. Front. Physiol. **12** (2021). https://doi.org/10.3389/fphys.2021.643202
38. Zhang, S., Liu, R., Tao, X., Zhao, X.: Deep cross-corpus speech emotion recognition: recent advances and perspectives. Front. Neurorob. **15** (2021). https://doi.org/10.3389/fnbot.2021.784514, https://www.frontiersin.org/journals/neurorobotics/articles/10.3389/fnbot.2021.784514/full

# Hindsight Preference Replay Improves Preference-Conditioned Multi-objective Reinforcement Learning

Jonaid Shianifar(✉), Michael Schukat, and Karl Mason

School of Computer Science, University of Galway, Galway H91 FYH2, Ireland
{J.Shianifar1,Michael.Schukat,Karl.Mason}@universityofgalway.ie

**Abstract.** Multi-objective reinforcement learning (MORL) enables agents to optimize vector-valued rewards while respecting user preferences. CAPQL, a preference-conditioned actor-critic method, achieves this by conditioning on weight vectors $\mathbf{w}$ and restricts data usage to the specific preferences under which it was collected, leaving off-policy data from other preferences unused. We introduce Hindsight Preference Replay (HPR), a simple and general replay augmentation strategy that retroactively relabels stored transitions with alternative preferences. This densifies supervision across the preference simplex without altering the CAPQL architecture or loss functions. Evaluated on six MO-Gymnasium locomotion tasks at a fixed 300,000-step budget using expected utility (EUM), hypervolume (HV), and sparsity, HPR-CAPQL improves HV in five of six environments and EUM in four of six. On `mo-humanoid-v5`, for instance, EUM rises from 323±125 to 1613±464 and HV from 0.52M to 9.63M, with strong statistical support. `mo-halfcheetah-v5` remains a challenging exception where CAPQL attains higher HV at comparable EUM. We report final summaries and Pareto-front visualizations across all tasks.

**Keywords:** Multi-objective reinforcement learning (MORL) · Hindsight Preference Replay (HPR) · Preference-Conditioned Actor-Critic · CAPQL · Replay augmentation · Robotic Control

## 1 Introduction

Many real-world control tasks, such as robotic locomotion or autonomous driving, involve optimizing multiple conflicting objectives, for example, energy efficiency versus speed, or safety versus exploration. Multi-objective reinforcement learning (MORL) formalizes this by optimizing vector-valued rewards $\mathbf{r}_t \in \mathbb{R}^m$ [12,15]. However, selecting a single solution requires expressing user preferences over these objectives [6].

One approach to MORL is scalarization, where a weight vector $\mathbf{w} \in \Delta^m$ is used to linearly combine the objectives: $u_{\mathbf{w}}(\mathbf{r}) = \mathbf{w}^\top \mathbf{r}$. Preference-conditioned policies exploit this idea by taking $\mathbf{w}$ as input, enabling a single policy to serve


T. T. Mai et al. (Eds.): AICS 2025, CCIS 2950, pp. 133–144, 2026.
https://doi.org/10.1007/978-3-032-25809-0_10

a range of trade-offs depending on user preferences. This setup supports efficient deployment in dynamic or interactive systems where preferences may change over time [7,8].

CAPQL [7] is a recent preference-conditioned actor-critic method that extends Soft Actor-Critic (SAC) [5] to the MORL setting. CAPQL augments the critic loss with a concavity-based regularizer to improve coverage and training stability. However, like most off-policy algorithms, it suffers from a key inefficiency: data collected under one preference $\mathbf{w}$ is only used to train for that same $\mathbf{w}$ [7].

This results in low sample efficiency, as transitions informative for neighboring preferences are discarded. This inefficiency is especially costly in high-dimensional control tasks, where sample collection is expensive. Inspired by Hindsight Experience Replay (HER) that relabels goals to overcome sparse rewards [1,13], we propose *Hindsight Preference Replay* (HPR), which retroactively relabels preference vectors, densifying supervision without architectural or loss changes [3]. Empirically, HPR-CAPQL improves hypervolume in five of six benchmarks, with especially large gains on `mo-humanoid-v5`, while `mo-halfcheetah-v5` remains a challenging case where CAPQL covers the front more broadly.

Our contributions are as follows:

- We present HPR, a general-purpose hindsight relabeling mechanism for preference-conditioned MORL.
- We instantiate HPR within CAPQL, creating HPR-CAPQL, with minimal implementation overhead.
- We evaluate HPR-CAPQL on six continuous control tasks from the MO-Gymnasium benchmark suite, showing performance gains in several environments.

## 2 Background and Literature Review

Modern control problems, such as robotic manipulation and locomotion, inherently require optimizing multiple conflicting objectives, for example, achieving both high efficiency and safety. The field of multi-objective reinforcement learning (MORL) formalizes this by extending classical reinforcement learning to vector-valued rewards $\mathbf{r}_t \in \mathbb{R}^m$, enabling agents to discover policies that provide favorable trade-offs across the Pareto front [4,8,12,16].

A common approach is *scalarization*, where a preference or weight vector $\mathbf{w} \in \Delta^m$ combines objectives into a single utility $u_{\mathbf{w}}(\mathbf{r}) = \mathbf{w}^\top \mathbf{r}$, thereby parameterizing the trade-off space [8]. Recent progress on adaptive scalarization reports improved stability and Pareto coverage in MORL, particularly in continuous-control settings [10]. In parallel, preference-conditioned policies condition both policy and value networks on $\mathbf{w}$ to adapt to user preferences and efficiently cover the Pareto front [4,7]. From a robotics perspective, deep RL for adaptive robotic arm control underscores the need for sample-efficient replay and safe, budgeted interaction [9]. Our approach is complementary to these lines: HPR augments replay to reuse trajectories across preferences without modifying the underlying losses or architectures.

Among these methods, *CAPQL* (Concavity-Aware Preference-based Q-Learning) has emerged as a strong baseline in preference-conditioned MORL. CAPQL extends the Soft Actor-Critic (SAC) framework by conditioning both policy and critics on $\mathbf{w}$, enabling a single policy to generalize across multiple trade-offs. A key innovation in CAPQL is a concavity-based regularizer in the critic loss, which encourages stable training and broad coverage of the Pareto front by penalizing deviations from concave utility approximations. This design improves sample efficiency compared to earlier preference-conditioned approaches; however, CAPQL still updates policies only for the specific preferences under which data were collected, leaving off-policy experience from other preferences unused [7].

A milestone in single-objective, goal-conditioned RL was the introduction of *Hindsight Experience Replay* (HER), which relabels failed transitions with alternative goals to improve learning under sparse rewards [1]. HER established that retroactive relabeling can transform unsuccessful experiences into effective learning signals. Inspired by this success, researchers have explored extending hindsight mechanisms to other conditioning variables such as preferences.

The recently proposed *Hindsight Preference Replay* (HPR) adapts HER's philosophy to the multi-objective setting by retroactively relabeling the preference vector $\mathbf{w}$ in stored transitions. This enables richer and denser supervision across the preference simplex without any architectural or loss modification, offering large improvements in sample efficiency and Pareto coverage when combined with preference-conditioned methods like CAPQL [7].

Earlier work on multi-objective HER primarily focused on relabeling goals and generating curriculum for complex robotic tasks using evolutionary algorithms [1,4], but did not address the inefficiency of preference-conditioned experience reuse. Recent strategies in multi-objective learning, such as Ensemble Multi-Objective RL (EMORL) [4], curriculum generation via evolutionary multi-objective optimization [1,2,16], and meta-learning for adaptation, have pushed the boundaries of scalable multi-objective RL; however, they do not apply retroactive preference relabeling.

The proposed HPR therefore offers a novel and practical mechanism to improve sample efficiency and generalization in preference-conditioned MORL, building on the proven utility of hindsight-based replay and extending it in previously unexplored directions.

## 3 Methodology: Hindsight Preference Replay (HPR)

In preference-conditioned MORL, transitions collected under a specific preference vector $\mathbf{w}$ are typically used exclusively to update the policy for that same $\mathbf{w}$. However, these transitions may also be informative for other preferences, particularly those nearby in the simplex. This leads to inefficiencies in data usage, limiting gradient diversity and generalization.

To address this, we propose *Hindsight Preference Replay* (HPR), a replay augmentation strategy that retroactively relabels transitions with alternative preference vectors. The key idea is analogous to HER [1], but adapted to preference relabeling rather than goal relabeling.

The pseudocode in Algorithm 1 summarizes the full HPR-CAPQL procedure integrated with the CAPQL-style actor-critic learning. It highlights how transitions are collected and relabeled with multiple alternative preferences, stored in the replay buffer, and how training updates interleave with environment interaction and evaluation. This overview guides the detailed design of the relabeling strategies and integration steps discussed next.

**Algorithm 1.** HPR-CAPQL: Hindsight Preference Replay for Preference-Conditioned MORL

**Require:** Environment *Env*; preference-conditioned agent (policy/critics conditioned on $w$); replay buffer $\mathcal{B}$; per-step relabels $K$; Dirichlet concentration $\kappa$; relabeled minibatch fraction $\rho$; (optional) acceptance test.

Initialize agent and targets; $\mathcal{B} \leftarrow \emptyset$<br>
**for** episodes until budget exhausted **do**<br>
  Sample behavior preference $w \sim p(w)$ on the simplex; reset *Env*; set episode return $G \leftarrow \mathbf{0}$<br>
  **while** not done **do**<br>
    Act $a \sim \pi(\cdot \mid s, w)$, step env $\rightarrow (r, s', d)$; push $(s, a, r, s', d, w)$ to $\mathcal{B}$<br>
    $G \leftarrow G + \gamma^t r$ ▷ *discounted vector return for relabeling/eval*<br>
    **for** $k = 1..K$ **do** ▷ *Neighborhood relabeling*<br>
      $\tilde{w} \sim \mathrm{Dir}(\kappa w)$; **if** accepted **then** push $(s, a, r, s', d, \tilde{w})$ to $B$<br>
    **end for**<br>
    $s \leftarrow s'$<br>
    **Training step(s):** sample minibatches from $B$ with relabeled fraction $\rho$; update CAPQL with scalarized rewards $r_w = w^\top r$<br>
  **end while**<br>
  ▷ *Return-aligned relabeling (episode end)*<br>
  $\hat{w} \leftarrow \Pi_\Delta(\mathrm{softplus}(G))$; for each episode transition push $(s, a, r, s', d, \hat{w})$ if accepted<br>
**end for**<br>
**Evaluation:** on a fixed weight grid, log EUM, HV, sparsity, and per-objective means

Given a stored transition tuple $(s, a, \mathbf{r}, s', \mathbf{w})$, HPR replaces the original preference vector $\mathbf{w}$ with a new preference vector $\tilde{\mathbf{w}}$ sampled by return-aligned or neighborhood strategies [3,14]. The reward vector $\mathbf{r}$ is left unchanged, enabling recomputation of scalarized returns $u_{\tilde{\mathbf{w}}}(\mathbf{r}) = \tilde{\mathbf{w}}^\top \mathbf{r}$ and allowing a single transition to serve multiple scalarization preferences. This approach generalizes the HER principle [1,13] into the preference space, enabling richer supervision without modifying CAPQL's architecture [7].

### 3.1 Relabeling Strategies

We implement two relabeling strategies in HPR:

***Return-Aligned Relabeling.*** For each trajectory or transition, we compute a discounted cumulative return vector $\mathbf{G}$. We then define the relabeled preference $\tilde{\mathbf{w}}$ as:

$$\tilde{\mathbf{w}} \propto \mathrm{softplus}(\mathbf{G}) \tag{1}$$

followed by projection onto the simplex. Optionally, a convex combination with the original $\mathbf{w}$ can be applied to control deviation. This heuristic aligns the relabeling with the outcomes the trajectory has already achieved.

***Neighborhood Sampling.*** We draw $K$ new preference vectors $\tilde{\mathbf{w}} \sim \mathrm{Dir}(\kappa\mathbf{w})$ from a Dirichlet distribution centered around the original $\mathbf{w}$, where $\kappa$ is a concentration parameter. Larger $\kappa$ values result in narrower neighborhoods, encouraging local generalization.

### 3.2 Integration with CAPQL

We integrate HPR into CAPQL by modifying the replay buffer insertion logic and minibatch sampling:

- During data collection, each transition is stored as $(s, a, \mathbf{r}, s', \mathbf{w})$.
- On insertion (or periodically), up to $K$ relabeled versions are added using one of the above strategies, with preferences $\tilde{\mathbf{w}}$.
- During training, minibatches are sampled uniformly, mixing original and relabeled transitions.

Importantly, all CAPQL loss functions and network structures remain unchanged. HPR only alters the diversity of training data in the preference space.

### 3.3 Practical Settings and Filters

We explore relabel counts $K \in \{0, 1, 2, 4\}$, Dirichlet concentration parameters $\kappa \in \{10, 20, 50\}$, and relabel batch ratios $\rho \in [0.3, 0.7]$.

In settings with strongly orthogonal objectives, naive relabeling can harm learning. In such cases, we apply acceptance filters based on alignment between $\tilde{w}$ and $G$, e.g., $\cos(\tilde{w}, G) \geq \tau$ or $\tilde{w}^\top G \geq w^\top G - \varepsilon$, with $\varepsilon \in \{0.0, 0.1\}$ and $\tau \in \{0.7, 0.8\}$. This mitigates regressions in environments where broad relabels destabilize HV (e.g., `mo-halfcheetah-v5`), while preserving the gains observed elsewhere.

# 4 Experimental Setup

## 4.1 Environments

We evaluate HPR-CAPQL across six continuous control tasks from the MO-Gymnasium benchmark suite [4], an extension of Gymnasium [11] designed for multi-objective reinforcement learning. All environments feature continuous observations and continuous action spaces, returning 2D reward vectors that correspond to conflicting objectives.

The environments are described as follows:

- **mo-hopper-2obj-v5**: A 2D hopping robot optimizing for forward progress and jumping height.
- **mo-walker2d-v5**: A bipedal walker balancing locomotion efficiency and energy cost.
- **mo-halfcheetah-v5**: A planar cheetah optimizing for speed versus energy efficiency.
- **mo-humanoid-v5**: A high-dimensional humanoid robot focusing on fast movement and minimal effort.
- **mo-swimmer-v5**: A simple two-link swimmer navigating through fluid.
- **mo-ant-2obj-v5**: A quadruped ant robot optimizing its movement in both X and Y directions.

Key characteristics of these environments, including observation dimensions, action dimensions, and reward components, are summarized in Table 1.

**Table 1.** Observation and Action Dimensions and Reward Components of MO-Gymnasium Environments

| Environment | Observation Dim. | Action Dim. | Reward Components |
|---|---|---|---|
| mo-hopper-2obj-v5 | 11 | 3 | Forward velocity, Jump height |
| mo-walker2d-v5 | 17 | 6 | Forward velocity, Control cost |
| mo-halfcheetah-v5 | 17 | 6 | Forward velocity, Control cost |
| mo-humanoid-v5 | 348 | 17 | Forward velocity, Control cost |
| mo-swimmer-v5 | 8 | 2 | Forward velocity, Control cost |
| mo-ant-2obj-v5 | 105 | 8 | X-velocity, Y-velocity |

All environments utilize MuJoCo physics and provide dense, continuous rewards.

## 4.2 Training Protocol

We compare standard CAPQL against HPR-CAPQL using the same codebase for both methods. Each algorithm is trained for 300,000 environment steps per task, with evaluation every 10,000 steps on a fixed preference grid over the 2D simplex. We report the mean and standard deviation over five seeds. Metrics include Expected Utility (EUM), Hypervolume (HV), and the sparsity of the nondominated archive; we also plot the final Pareto fronts. HV is computed with a fixed per-environment reference point $\mathbf{r}_{\mathrm{ref}} = [-100, -100]$ shared by all methods and seeds, and we report HV in millions ($\times 10^6$) for readability.

### 4.3 Hardware Configuration

All experiments were conducted on a high-performance computing server equipped with an AMD Ryzen Threadripper 7960X 24-core processor, two NVIDIA RTX A6000 GPUs, and 128 GB of system RAM. The system ran Ubuntu 22.04.5 LTS. The software stack included Python 3.9.23, PyTorch 2.8.0, Gymnasium 1.1.1, and MO-Gymnasium 1.3.1. This configuration provided ample computational power for efficient training and evaluation of preference-conditioned policies across all benchmark tasks.

## 5 Results and Discussion

We evaluate CAPQL and HPR-CAPQL for 300,000 environment steps on six MO-Gymnasium tasks. We report Expected Utility (EUM; ↑), hypervolume (HV; ↑; Table values in millions; For each environment, we use a fixed $r_{ref} = [-100, -100]$), and sparsity (archive spacing; ↓). Final summaries with Welch tests for HV appear in Table 2. Figures 1 to 3 show EUM/HV/sparsity learning curves, and Fig. 4 visualizes final Pareto fronts from the union of non-dominated points across seeds.

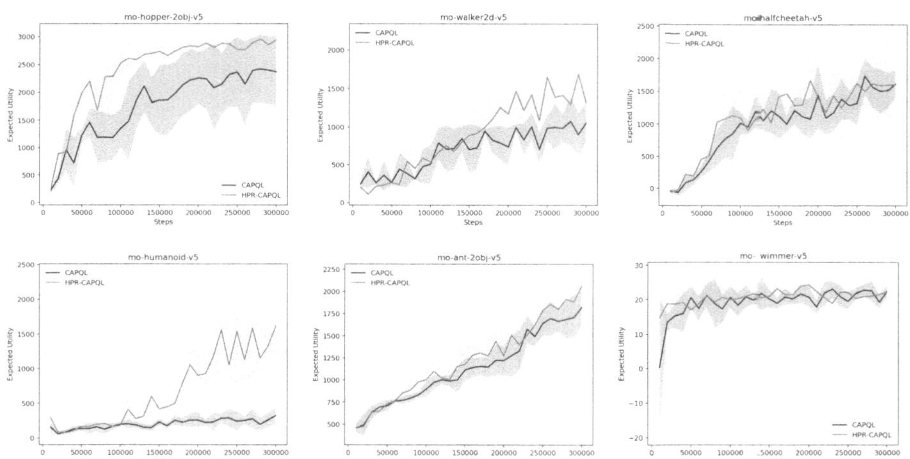

**Fig. 1.** EUM learning curves up to 300,000 steps (mean ± std over five seeds).

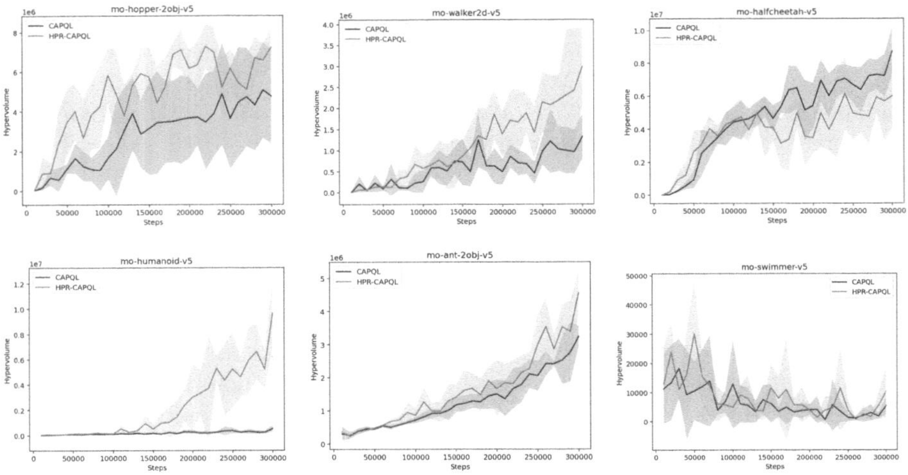


**Fig. 2.** Hypervolume (HV) learning curves up to 300,000 steps (mean ± std over five seeds).

### 5.1 Final Performance Summary

Across tasks, hindsight preference relabeling primarily increases Pareto coverage. HPR-CAPQL attains higher HV in most environments and improves EUM in a majority as well; the aggregate row of Table 2 reflects this pattern. Several HV differences are statistically reliable, notably on `mo-humanoid-v5`, `mo-walker2d-v5`, and `mo-ant-2obj-v5`. Two tasks deviate from this trend. `mo-halfcheetah-v5` favors CAPQL on HV while EUM remains comparable, indicating that additional relabels do not widen the front in that domain. `mo-swimmer-v5` is effectively a draw: both algorithms saturate quickly and the small HV differences are not significant.

### 5.2 Learning Behavior Over Time

Figure 1, 2 and 3 plot EUM, HV, and sparsity over the 300,000-step horizon and show how the final differences in Table 2 emerge during training. On `mo-hopper-2obj-v5` and `mo-ant-2obj-v5`, HPR-CAPQL accelerates early, establishing EUM and HV margins that persist through the end of training. On `mo-humanoid-v5`, gains arrive later but become pronounced: once the policy stabilizes, relabeled preferences unlock new parts of the frontier and HV separates sharply. `mo-walker2d-v5` shows the same qualitative pattern with narrower uncertainty. In contrast, `mo-halfcheetah-v5` exhibits a plateau for HPR-CAPQL while CAPQL continues to expand HV, and `mo-swimmer-v5` reaches a quick equilibrium for both methods. Variance bands widen in the tasks where coverage expands the most, reflecting a broader exploration of the preference simplex rather than instability of the learner.

**Table 2.** Final performance after 300,000 steps (mean ± std over seeds). HV shown in millions ($\times 10^6$) using the fixed $\mathbf{r}_{\text{ref}}$. Significance markers: $^*$ for $p < 0.05$, $^{**}$ for $p < 0.01$, and $^{***}$ for $p < 0.001$.

| Environment | Algorithm | EUM ↑ | Sparsity ↓ | HV ↑ | HV $p$-value |
|---|---|---|---|---|---|
| mo-hopper-2obj | CAPQL | 2370.5±634.7 | **84.6±76.8** | 4.7534±2.39 | 0.0749 |
| | HPR-CAPQL | **2942.7±143.8** | 295.9±81.5 | **7.2026±1.03** | |
| mo-walker2d | CAPQL | 1056.4±273.3 | 2294.8±230.0 | 1.3276±0.52 | 0.0079 ** |
| | HPR-CAPQL | **1320.7±207.6** | **513.5±361.5** | **2.9855±0.91** | |
| mo-halfcheetah | CAPQL | **1616.7±202.2** | **416.3±116.6** | **8.7208±1.48** | 0.0350 * |
| | HPR-CAPQL | 1603.0±319.7 | 535.9±183.1 | 5.9927±1.97 | |
| mo-humanoid | CAPQL | 323.1±125.4 | **120.0±44.3** | 0.5173±0.27 | 0.0009 *** |
| | HPR-CAPQL | **1613.3±464.3** | 486.5±88.1 | **9.6332±2.94** | |
| mo-ant-2obj | CAPQL | 1823.3±191.2 | **265.9±58.2** | 3.2311±0.3[illegible] | 0.0060 ** |
| | HPR-CAPQL | **2060.7±157.1** | 653.6±356.2 | **4.5428±0.68** | |
| mo-swimmer | CAPQL | **22.2±1.7** | 10.3±7.1 | 0.0054±0.0030 | 0.2926 |
| | HPR-CAPQL | 22.1±1.9 | **5.9±1.3** | **0.0104±0.0090** | |
| **HPR-CAPQL better (of 6)** | | **4** | **2** | **5** | — |

### 5.3 Pareto-Front Comparisons

Figure 4 shows the final non-dominated Pareto fronts (union over seeds at 300,000 steps), revealing where each method extends coverage and how these geometric differences drive the EUM and HV gaps. On `mo-humanoid-v5`, `mo-walker2d-v5`, `mo-hopper-2obj-v5`, and `mo-ant-2obj-v5`, HPR-CAPQL pushes outward along large portions of the trade-off surface, occupying regions that CAPQL rarely reaches. This outward shift explains both the hypervolume gains and the higher average scalarized utility across preferences. In `mo-halfcheetah-v5`, CAPQL extends further toward an extreme of one objective, which is sufficient to dominate HV despite similar EUM. In `mo-swimmer-v5`, the fronts largely overlap, aligning with the inconclusive learning curves.

### 5.4 Coverage–Density Trade-Off

Where HPR-CAPQL expands the frontier, sparsity tends to increase: the archive becomes more widely spaced while reaching new territory. This is a natural consequence of a fixed training budget; growing the frontier and densifying it are different objectives. A short densification phase near the end of training, reducing the relabel ratio or temporarily disabling HPR, tightens spacing without relinquishing the newly discovered regions. When dense coverage is paramount, sampling hindsight preferences closer to the uniform simplex or adding small jitter around current preferences further improves spacing.

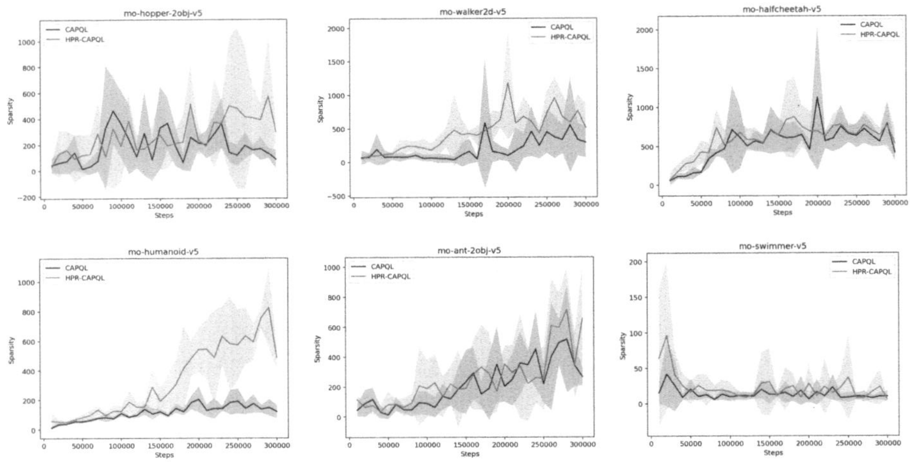


**Fig. 3.** Sparsity (lower is better) up to 300,000 steps (mean ± std over five seeds).

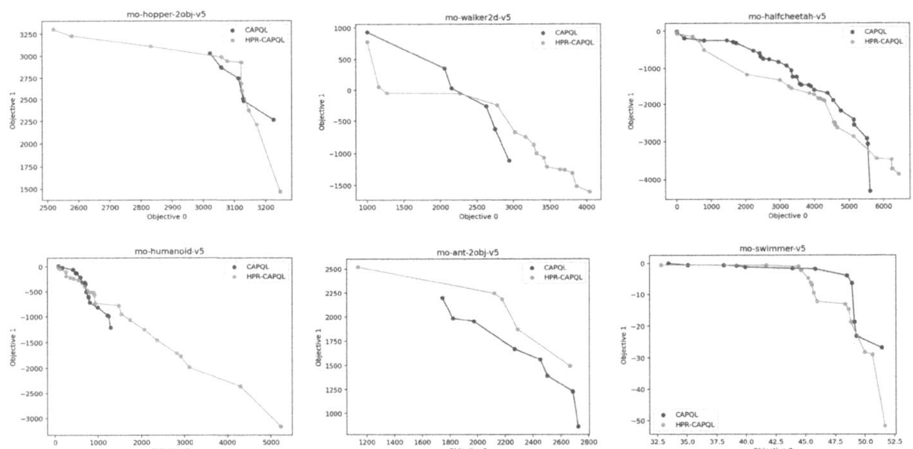


**Fig. 4.** Final Pareto fronts (non-dominated only) after 300,000 steps across all environments. Each panel shows the union of non-dominated solutions across five seeds; legend: CAPQL vs. HPR-CAPQL

## 5.5 Environment-Specific Remarks

On `mo-humanoid-v5`, HPR-CAPQL provides the clearest improvement: the frontier enlarges substantially and both EUM and HV rise throughout the latter half of training. `mo-walker2d-v5` exhibits steady gains with moderate variance; the final fronts extend outward with only modest loss of density. `mo-hopper-2obj-v5` shows strong early advantages that persist, with the HPR front lying above the baseline over most of the trade-off range. `mo-ant-2obj-v5` mirrors this behavior but illustrates the coverage–density trade-off most clearly. `mo-halfcheetah-v5` favors CAPQL on HV; here, aggressive preference relabeling appears mismatched with the task's reward geometry. `mo-swimmer-v5` is simple enough that both methods rapidly converge to similar fronts.

## 6 Conclusion

We presented Hindsight Preference Replay (HPR), a simple replay augmentation that retroactively relabels stored transitions with alternative preference vectors and slots into CAPQL without architectural or loss changes. Under a fixed 300,000-step budget across six MO-Gymnasium tasks, HPR-CAPQL consistently broadens the learned Pareto fronts and often increases preference-averaged utility. In aggregate, hypervolume (HV) is higher in five of six environments and Expected Utility (EUM) in four of six, while CAPQL retains an advantage on `mo-halfcheetah-v5`.

A few highlights illustrate the magnitude and reliability of the effects. On `mo-humanoid-v5`, HPR-CAPQL delivers large gains (EUM $1613 \pm 464$ vs. $323 \pm 125$; HV 9.63M vs. 0.52M) with strong statistical support ($p = 0.0009$). `mo-walker2d-v5` shows a similar pattern (HV 2.99M vs. 1.33M; $p = 0.0079$; EUM $1321 \pm 208$ vs. $1056 \pm 273$), and `mo-ant-2obj-v5` also favors HPR-CAPQL on both metrics (HV 4.54M vs. 3.23M; $p = 0.0060$; EUM $2061 \pm 157$ vs. $1823 \pm 191$). Two domains temper the story: `mo-hopper-2obj-v5` trends toward higher HV for HPR-CAPQL but is not significant at 5% ($p = 0.0749$), and `mo-halfcheetah-v5` significantly favors CAPQL on HV (HV 8.72M vs. 5.99M; $p = 0.035$) with similar EUM across methods. `mo-swimmer-v5` is effectively a draw (small, noisy HV differences; $p = 0.2926$).

A consistent pattern is a coverage–density trade-off. When HPR broadens the Pareto frontier, the nondominated archive often becomes more widely spaced, especially where HV gains are largest. This is expected under a fixed budget, since expanding the frontier and densifying it are different goals. A short densification phase near the end, reducing the relabel ratio or briefly disabling HPR, tightens spacing without losing newly reached regions. For tasks such as `mo-halfcheetah-v5`, conservative relabeling and return-alignment filters further curb variance and harmful updates.

These results support HPR as a strong default for preference-conditioned MORL. It reuses off-policy data across preferences and yields broader Pareto coverage and higher preference-averaged performance with minimal engineering. Future work includes many-objective settings, adaptive preference distributions, learned acceptance criteria, and larger seed budgets.

**Acknowledgements.** This work is supported by the University of Galway College of Science and Engineering Postgraduate Scholarship.

## References

1. Andrychowicz, M., et al.: Hindsight experience replay. Adv. Neural Inf. Process. Syst. **30** (2017)
2. Auger, A., Bader, J., Brockhoff, D., Zitzler, E.: Theory of the hypervolume indicator: optimal $\mu$-distributions and the choice of the reference point. In: Proceedings of the Tenth ACM SIGEVO Workshop on Foundations of Genetic Algorithms, pp. 87–102 (2009)
3. Fan, M., Zhou, J., Zhang, Y., Wu, Y., Chen, J., Sartoretti, G.A.: Preference-driven multi-objective combinatorial optimization with conditional computation (2025). arXiv preprint
4. Felten, F., et al.: A toolkit for reliable benchmarking and research in multi-objective reinforcement learning. Adv. Neural Inf. Process. Syst. **36**, 23671–23700 (2023)
5. Haarnoja, T., Zhou, A., Abbeel, P., Levine, S.: Soft actor-critic: Off-policy maximum entropy deep reinforcement learning with a stochastic actor. In: International Conference on Machine Learning, pp. 1861–1870. PMLR (2018)
6. Hayes, C.F., et al.: A practical guide to multi-objective reinforcement learning and planning. arXiv preprint (2021)
7. Lu, H., Herman, D., Yu, Y.: Multi-objective reinforcement learning: convexity, stationarity and pareto optimality. In: The Eleventh International Conference on Learning Representations (2023)
8. Roijers, D.M., Vamplew, P., Whiteson, S., Dazeley, R.: A survey of multi-objective sequential decision-making. J. Artif. Intell. Res. **48**, 67–113 (2013)
9. Shianifar, J., Schukat, M., Mason, K.: Optimizing deep reinforcement learning for adaptive robotic arm control. In: González-Briones, A., et al. (eds.) International Conference on Practical Applications of Agents and Multi-Agent Systems, pp. 293–304. Springer, Cham (2024). https://doi.org/10.1007/978-3-031-73058-0_24
10. Shianifar, J., Schukat, M., Mason, K.: Adaptive scalarization in multi-objective reinforcement learning for enhanced robotic arm control. Neurocomputing 132205 (2025)
11. Towers, M., et al.: Gymnasium: A standard interface for reinforcement learning environments. arXiv preprint arXiv:2407.17032 (2024)
12. Van Moffaert, K., Nowé, A.: Multi-objective reinforcement learning using sets of pareto dominating policies. J. Mach. Learn. Res. **15**(1), 3483–3512 (2014)
13. Wan, T., Xu, N.: Advances in experience replay. arXiv preprint (2018)
14. Yang, Y., Zhou, T., Pechenizkiy, M., Fang, M.: Preference controllable reinforcement learning with advanced multi-objective optimization. In: Forty-second International Conference on Machine Learning (ICML) (2024)
15. Zhang, L., Qi, Z., Shi, Y.: Multi-objective reinforcement learning-concept, approaches and applications. Proc. Comput. Sci. **221**, 526–532 (2023)
16. Zitzler, E., Brockhoff, D., Thiele, L.: The Hypervolume Indicator Revisited: On the Design of Pareto-compliant Indicators Via Weighted Integration. In: Obayashi, S., Deb, K., Poloni, C., Hiroyasu, T., Murata, T. (eds.) EMO 2007. LNCS, vol. 4403, pp. 862–876. Springer, Heidelberg (2007). https://doi.org/10.1007/978-3-540-70928-2_64

# Classifying Decision-Based Effector Modalities from Fragmented iEEG via Dynamic Recursive Feature Elimination

Umesh Kumar Naik Mudavath[1,3], Abdoreza Asadpour[2], Shaik Rafi Ahamed[1], and KongFatt Wong-Lin[3](✉)

[1] Department of Electronics and Electrical Engineering, Indian Institute of Technology Guwahati, Guwahati, Assam, India
{u.mudavath,rafiahamed}@iitg.ac.in

[2] School of Life Sciences, University of Sussex, East Sussex, England, UK
a.asadpour@sussex.ac.uk

[3] Intelligent Systems Research Centre, School of Computing, Engineering and Intelligent Systems, Ulster University, Magee Campus, Derry~Londonderry, Northern Ireland, UK
k.wong-lin@ulster.ac.uk

**Abstract.** A key challenge in data science is dealing with structured missing data with little or no overlap of features between samples. This is especially pertinent in neuroscience, such as in high-density intracranial electroencephalography (iEEG), where different brain locations are recorded across participants, and making machine learning analysis less straightforward. To address this, we propose a dynamic recursive feature elimination with cross-validation (DyRFECV) approach that comprises dynamic step sizes. A Light Gradient Boosting Machine (LGBM) classifier acts as the base estimator, and stratified five-fold cross-validation is employed. The method, with its variants, was tested on an open iEEG dataset in which participants performed a perceptual decision-making task while reporting their decisions with different effector types - manual or vocal responses. We found DyRFECV could classify decision-based, effector-specific iEEG signals with high classification performance (F1-scores); 97.29% using the baseline approach without hyperparameter tuning, and 99.42% with hyperparameter tuning; identifying 320 and 416 iEEG contacts, respectively—a tradeoff between F1-score and fewer contacts. Furthermore, feature importance indicated that the main contributions came from frontal and parietal cortical regions, consistent with existing literature. Overall, this work demonstrates the promising application of DyRFECV on structured missing iEEG data.

**Keywords:** Structured missingness · perceptual decision-making · intracranial electroencephalography iEEG · dynamic recursive feature elimination with cross-validation


T. T. Mai et al. (Eds.): AICS 2025, CCIS 2950, pp. 145–156, 2026.
https://doi.org/10.1007/978-3-032-25809-0_11

## Introduction

The intersection of neuroscience and artificial intelligence (AI) is often framed as an effort to better understand the brain using AI while building better AI - the nascent field of NeuroAI [1–3]. Advanced AI tools, particularly in machine learning (ML) and deep learning, provide unprecedented opportunities to decode the complexities of neural processes, unearthing insights that traditional hypothesis-driven approaches in neuroscience might overlook. This paradigm shift is particularly relevant towards understanding decision-making, a fundamental cognitive process shared by cognitive neuroscience and AI [4,5].

A major challenge in data science, including neural data science, is that real-world data is often 'dirty' with various forms of missingness [6,7]. They may include missing at random (MAR), missing not at random (MNAR), missing completely at random (MCAR), and structured missingness (SM) [7,8]. In particular, SM often occurs when integrating data from multiple studies or samples, each differing in design and measurement scope, and thus containing only a subset of the variables present. Within SM, a subtype of data missingness that is often not investigated is highly piecemeal time series data [9]. A challenge for small datasets, such as in neuroscience, is that data imputation may not be feasible, and other methods are required.

Recent popular invasive neurotechnologies, including high-density neural recording technologies such as intracranial electroencephalography (iEEG) in humans [10–12] and neuropixel probes in animals [13–17], offer direct access to neural activity with high temporal and spatial resolution, making them important tools for studying cognition and clinical conditions [10,18,19]. Both iEEG and neuropixel recordings have been used to further our understanding of the neuroscience of cognition, such as perceptual decision-making [11,12,16,17], in which sensory-based decisions were typically reported via overt motor actions.

However, these neural recording techniques pose a fundamental challenge to more automated ML approaches: the recordings are inherently piecemeal. Specifically, electrodes are implanted according to clinical or experimental needs, leading to different sets of brain regions sampled from different animals or human participants. Unlike brain-wide functional MRI (fMRI) or scalp EEG, which follows standard template, iEEG datasets are non-uniform and structurally fragmented, complicating group analysis and ML model development. For example, Fig. 1A depicts the sample piecemeal distribution of iEEG contacts across various participants in the perceptual decision-making task with vocal choice reporting [11], and Fig. 1B illustrates the piecemeal brain coverage of iEEG contacts for two sample participants performing the same cognitive task. Moreover, neuroscience dataset size is usually rather small and may not permit imputation of the missing data. Hence, their analyses typically rely on specific subsets of electrodes or task-driven hypotheses, which bypass rather than directly resolve the issue of heterogeneity. Thus, it is unclear how ML could be employed in non-linear and piecemeal multivariate time series data in the absence of imputation.

Here, we address this by proposing a dynamic recursive feature elimination with cross-validation (DyRFECV) approach. In contrast to existing feature elimination techniques and adaptations to RFECV [20,21], DyRFECV uniquely combines non-linear step scaling, feature importance integration, and dataset-driven adjustments in a unified framework. This enables efficient feature selection while ensuring that the process is aligned with data-specific characteristics as in fragmented and heterogeneous data.

The DyRFECV is applied to high-frequency activity (HFA) of an open iEEG dataset, which has been shown to reflect local cortical processing [10,18]. The iEEG data were obtained from human participants performing a perceptual decision-making task while overtly reporting their decisions with different effector types, either manually (via finger press) or vocally (via verbal report) (Fig. 1C) [11]. Importantly, variants of our approach, via with or without hyperparameter tuning, are used to investigate the tradeoff between selected feature size and classification performance of decision-based effector type. In addition, through feature importance analysis, specific key iEEG contact locations that contributed the most to distinguishing the effector modalities are identified. Together, the proposed ML framework (Fig. 1D) provides a practical and automated approach that directly addresses the fragmented and heterogeneous structure of multivariate time series data, with the iEEG analysis serving as a case study.

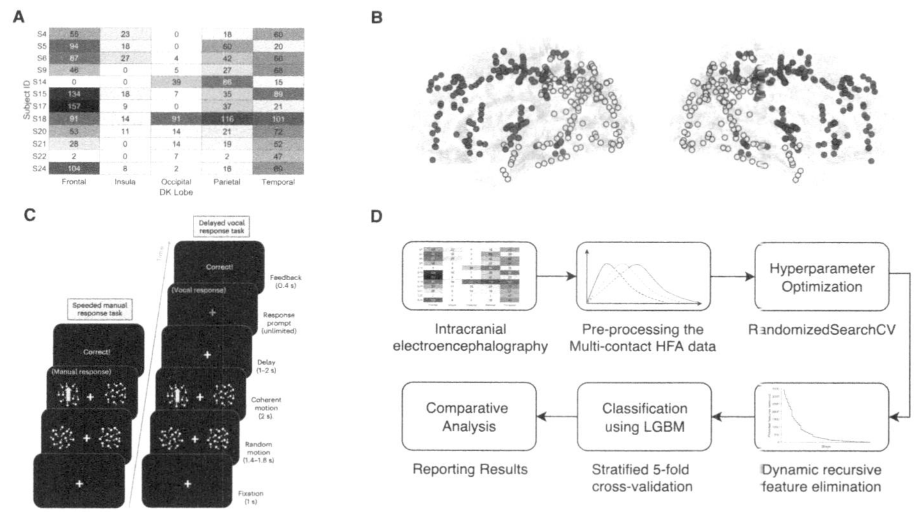


**Fig. 1.** Fragmented iEEG data in a perceptual decision task, and proposed approach. **A.** Piecemeal iEEG contacts across participants. Vertical (horizontal) axis: Participants (brain regions). Entry: iEEG contacts number per lobe. **B.** Few iEEG contact overlaps between 2 participants (blue vs. yellow). 2 brain hemispheres. **C.** Motion direction discrimination with 2 types of motor reporting of decision of perceived coherent motion direction. Adapted from [11]. **D.** ML pipeline for data analysis.

# Methodology

## Cognitive Task and Data Description

The dataset used in this study was based on a previous iEEG study [11] which involved epilepsy patients undergoing invasive electrophysiological monitoring. The experiment involved visual motion discrimination of the coherent direction of random-dot stimuli, a percentage of which were moving coherently in the same direction. Participants responded either with a speeded button press manually ($N = 24$) or vocally, after a randomised delay ($N = 12$). Figure 1C depicts the experimental task. The experiments were designed to investigate how different brain regions contribute to perceptual decision-making, focusing on whether the observed neural activity was dependent on the motor response modality (effectors).

The iEEG electrodes were implanted in participants as part of their clinical treatment for epilepsy. The exact placement was clinically determined, which provided extensive coverage of various brain regions but was not uniform across participants. The data, originally recorded at 1 kHz and 3 kHz, were resampled to 512 Hz and epoched from −3 to 3 s relative to sensory stimulus onset time. HFA was selected due to its ability to bridge human functional neuroimaging and animal electrophysiology [18]. More details of this experiment should be referred to the original study [11].

## Data pre-processing

The length of the HFA data for each participant varied considerably in the manual response task, which is a standard reaction time task. Hence, for this task, we considered data points starting from stimulus onset time to reaction time (Fig. 1D). Initially, the HFA data of all participants were segmented into fast, medium, and slow trials based on each participant's trial-based reaction time by considering the three bins from the reaction time distribution. The iEEG data were time-warped based on individual trial reaction times to fit a 1-second window, then averaged across all trials individually and normalised to remove any inherent scaling differences before feeding to the ML pipeline.

For the vocal response task, which has a fixed stimulus duration followed by a variable delay period after stimulus offset, we considered the neural data only during stimulus presence, due to its fixed time duration and assuming that meaningful evidence-based motor planning begins then.

## Feature Elimination and Importance

Given the heterogeneity in the data, we proposed the DyRFECV, which is an extension of the traditional RFECV method [21], designed to improve feature elimination efficiency through adaptive step sizes. Unlike conventional RFECV, which uses fixed step sizes, DyRFECV dynamically adjusts the number of features removed at each iteration based on data characteristics and feature importance. The adaptive step size in DyRFECV was determined using a non-linear scaling function that dynamically adjusted the base (initial) step size according to the number of training samples. For larger datasets (e.g., $\sim$ 36,000 HFA samples), the adaptive step size remained close to the base value ($\sim$ 10% or 0.1) because the feature-importance estimates were relatively stable, allowing more features to be removed at each iteration. Conversely, for smaller datasets (e.g., $\sim$ 1800 samples, about 5% of the total), a much smaller step size ($\sim$ 0.02) was used, ensuring that fewer features were eliminated at each step. This transition follows an exponential decay (Fig. 1D), gradually reducing the step size as the dataset size decreases to prevent excessive feature removal in smaller datasets. This approach preserved potentially valuable HFA features when the data was limited. A summary of the DyRFECV algorithm is described as follows.

**Algorithm 1.** Dynamic recursive feature elimination with cross-validation

**Input:** Dataset (feature matrix $X$, label vector $y$, contact labels $L$)<br>
Split data into stratified training and test sets<br>
Initialise ML classifier with/without hyperparameter tuning<br>
Set up cross-validation<br>
Fit classifier on training data and calculate feature importance<br>
Compute importance ratio as fraction of features with importance above median<br>
Calculate adaptive step size based on training size and importance ratio<br>
**while** not converged and samples remain **do**<br>
    Remove least informative samples according to adaptive step size<br>
    Evaluate model performance via cross-validation using F1-score<br>
    Update best sample subset if current score improves<br>
**end while**<br>
Finalise selection of optimal sample subset<br>
Retrain ML classifier on this optimally selected subset<br>
Evaluate classifier on held-out test set; report classification metrics<br>
Save trained model for reproducibility<br>
**Output:** Optimal sample indices, trained model, performance metrics

Our proposed DyRFECV addresses the inherent data fragmentation by operating at the sample level after participants' trial-wise averaging (i.e., no forced electrode alignment across participants). Each sample is a feature vector considered from all the available iEEG contacts for each participant, respectively, and hence, no cross-participant imputation was performed. In our work, DyRFECV was employed on the Light Gradient Boosting Machine (LGBM) classifier [22] as the base estimator, with stratified five-fold cross-validation to preserve class distribution across folds (Fig. 1D). Within each fold, DyRFECV iteratively removes samples in adaptive steps based on validation of F1-score. F1-score was used as a primary valuation metric instead of accuracy, as it balances precision and recall, making it more robust under class imbalance.

To further refine the DyRFECV step size, feature importance values were calculated from the classifier trained on the dataset, and the ratio of important features (those exceeding the median importance) was incorporated. If many features were deemed important, the step size was reduced further to retain key HFA features, whereas fewer important features allowed for more accelerated elimination. The process was continued until the F1-score did not improve further or when an optimal sample count was reached. Finally, the model was trained on the retained optimal samples and evaluated on the held-out test split. This procedure avoids imputation and template matching while yielding a compact, generalisable sample set from the non-uniform piecemeal iEEG data.

### Model Classification and Performance

The preprocessed HFA data were fed as input to the LGBM classifier [22] to evaluate their discriminative performance for manual vs. vocal, in two different settings (without and with hyperparameter tuning). To ensure independence and eliminate potential biases, the dataset was first annotated and shuffled. The data were split into training (68%), validation (12%), and testing (20%) sets.

Hyperparameter tuning was conducted using RandomizedSearchCV [23] on the LGBM classifier within a stratified ten-fold cross-validation framework. In our experiments, the LGBM model used $num\_leaves = 31$ (maximum tree leaves), $n\_estimators = 500$ (number of boosting rounds), $min\_data\_in\_leaf = 50$ (minimum samples per leaf), $max\_depth = 10$ (tree depth limit), $learning\_rate = 0.1$ (step size), $feature\_fraction = 0.8$ (fraction of features sampled per iteration), $bagging\_fraction = 0.9$ and $bagging\_freq = 10$ (subsampled data every 10 rounds), $objective =$ 'binary' (binary classification), $n\_jobs = -1$ (parallel execution across all CPU cores), $importance\_type =$ 'gain' (average loss reduction from splits), and $random\_state = 42$ (reproducibility). The baseline LGBM model without hyperparameter tuning was trained with default parameters, except for $objective =$ 'binary', $importance\_type =$ 'gain', and $n\_jobs = -1$.

**Software.** The analytical workflow was implemented using MATLAB 2023b on an Apple MacBook Pro with an M1 processor for preprocessing, and Python 3.8 with Google Colab for machine learning and deep learning model. For running the DyRFECV analysis, we utilised the Northern Ireland High-Performance Computing (NI-HPC) facility and Kelvin-2 system (www.nihpc.ac.uk).

## Results

The objective of this study is to refine the identification of brain regions responsible for effector-related contacts during decision-making by employing a data-driven methodology that aims to address the heterogeneity of fragmented iEEG data. By doing so, it helps us to provide a clearer understanding of the neural substrates involved in cognitive processes that are dependent on motor responses. DyRFECV selects participant-averaged samples that are both predictive and stably retained across folds, without assuming a shared electrode template. Using stratified five-fold cross-validation, the identified optimal set remained stable across folds, ensuring that performance does not rely on idiosyncratic data.

DyRFECV identified 320 and 416 contacts while obtaining F1-scores of 0.972 and 0.994, without (baseline) and with hyperparameter tuning, respectively. The brain regions found from our analysis are primarily located in the frontal and parietal cortical regions for both settings. The lobe-wise iEEG electrode counts under the two processing settings (with and without hyperparameter tuning) are depicted in Table 1. This indicates that the baseline approach, without hyperparameter fine-tuning leads to about a consistent $\sim 70 - 80\%$ decrease in each lobe, indicating more focused identification of key features, without decreasing the classification performance too much. These results should be compared to the lesser 233 effector-dependent contacts found in the previous study with the same dataset [11]. Further, the previous work identified the sensorimotor brain regions, i.e. in the parietal cortex, to contribute the most. Among the DyRFECV contacts without and with hyperparameter tuning, 16 and 21 contacts overlapped with the previous study's effector-dependent contacts, respectively, and were mainly from the parietal and frontal cortical regions.

**Table 1.** iEEG contact counts under with and without hyperparameter tuning.

| Region | With tuning | Baseline |
|---|---|---|
| Frontal | 172 | 136 |
| Parietal | 102 | 80 |
| Temporal | 80 | 59 |
| Occipital | 23 | 17 |
| Insula | 21 | 15 |
| Unknown | 18 | 13 |
| **F1-score** | **0.994** | **0.972** |

The 30 highest-ranking iEEG contacts based on feature importance were also elucidated by DyRFECV (Table 2). These results highlight a distinction between contacts that were more directly linked to specific effectors. Between the baseline approach with that with hyperparameter tuning, there was substantial overlaps (Table 2). Again, the frontal and parietal cortices dominate. Interestingly, one contact (S1-RDa4) with unknown location with respect to the DK atlas was ranked the highest. Further work would be needed for additional information. The second highest and consistently ranked location is at the precuneus, a key sensorimotor transformation region, which has previously been found in other neuroimaging studies [24,25]. In the original work [11], feature importance ranking was not performed, and hence, we could not directly compare our results. However, in a different iEEG study [12], the parietal cortical regions showed the strongest graded decision-variable effects across effectors, consistent with our rankings.

**Table 2.** Top 30 ranked iEEG contacts based on feature importance under two settings: with hyperparameter tuning (left) and baseline without hyperparameter tuning (right).

| With Tuning | | | | Baseline | | | |
|---|---|---|---|---|---|---|---|
| SC | Hem | DK Atlas | DK Lobe | SC | Hem | DK Atlas | DK Lobe |
| **S1-RDa4** | R | Unknown | Unknown | **S1-RDa4** | R | Unknown | Unknown |
| S4-RDh13 | R | Unknown | Unknown | **S6-RPc4** | R | Precuneus | Parietal |
| **S6-RPc4** | R | Precuneus | Parietal | **S12-LFo10** | L | Rostral Middle Frontal | Frontal |
| **S12-LFo10** | L | Rostral Middle Frontal | Frontal | **S20-LFo5** | L | Lateral Orbitofrontal | Frontal |
| **S20-LFo5** | L | Lateral Orbitofrontal | Frontal | **S4-RFo8** | R | Lateral Orbitofrontal | Frontal |
| **S4-RFo8** | R | Lateral Orbitofrontal | Frontal | **S15-LTo1** | L | Fusiform | Temporal |
| S20-LPc3 | L | Posterior Cingulate | Parietal | **S3-RPi2** | R | Precuneus | Parietal |
| **S15-LTo1** | L | Fusiform | Temporal | **S18-LOl7** | L | Lingual | Occipital |
| **S3-RPi2** | R | Precuneus | Parietal | **S11-RHs12** | R | Posterior Cingulate | Parietal |
| **S18-LOl7** | L | Lingual | Occipital | **S6-RFx9** | R | Rostral Anterior Cingulate | Frontal |
| S2-HDG15 | R | Superior Parietal | Parietal | **S14-ROm8** | R | Lingual | Occipital |
| S12-LFo4 | L | Lateral Orbitofrontal | Frontal | **S1-RFs2** | R | Superior Frontal | Frontal |
| **S11-RHs12** | R | Posterior Cingulate | Parietal | **S18-LOs13** | L | Supramarginal | Parietal |
| S18-ROl5 | R | Fusiform | Temporal | **S18-RHi2** | R | Lingual | Occipital |
| S18-LTi12 | L | Fusiform | Temporal | **S6-RHs11** | R | Posterior Cingulate | Parietal |
| **S6-RFx9** | R | Rostral Anterior Cingulate | Frontal | **S23-RIa9** | R | Rostral Middle Frontal | Frontal |
| S17-RFo9 | R | Lateral Orbitofrontal | Frontal | **S21-RAIN8** | R | Unknown | Unknown |
| **S14-ROm8** | R | Lingual | Occipital | **S9-LPs2** | L | Supramarginal | Parietal |
| **S1-RFs2** | R | Superior Frontal | Frontal | **S20-LPc6** | L | Precentral | Frontal |
| **S18-LOs13** | L | Supramarginal | Parietal | **S16-LDa12** | L | Middle Temporal | Temporal |
| **S18-RHi2** | R | Lingual | Occipital | **S10-RTs8** | R | Superior Temporal | Temporal |
| **S6-RHs11** | R | Posterior Cingulate | Parietal | S2-RPs6 | R | Caudal Anterior Cingulate | Frontal |
| **S23-RIa9** | R | Rostral Middle Frontal | Frontal | S3-LIm12 | L | Rostral Middle Frontal | Frontal |
| **S21-RAIN8** | R | Unknown | Unknown | S11-RTs7 | R | Transverse Temporal | Temporal |
| S24-LFo1 | L | Medial Orbitofrontal | Frontal | S6-RHs7 | R | Posterior Cingulate | Parietal |
| **S9-LPs2** | L | Supramarginal | Parietal | S6-RFm4 | R | Superior Frontal | Frontal |
| **S20-LPc6** | L | Precentral | Frontal | S15-LTp10 | L | Inferior Temporal | Temporal |
| S16-LFi10 | L | Pars Opercularis | Frontal | S13-LFs9 | L | Precentral | Frontal |
| **S16-LDa12** | L | Middle Temporal | Temporal | S5-RTs15 | R | Superior Temporal | Temporal |
| **S10-RTs8** | R | Superior Temporal | Temporal | S20-LFi5 | L | Lateral Orbitofrontal | Frontal |

Each contact is represented in the format `SubID-Contact (SC)`, and annotated with left (L) or right (R) brain hemisphere (Hem) and anatomical lobe. Bold regions: Consistently found in both approaches.

To visualise the brain topographical map of the top 150 ranking identified iEEG contacts by DyRFECV, we projected them onto structural MRI data (Fig. 2). We can see that the higher ranked locations (darker colours) were highly distributed across the frontal, parietal, and temporal cortices, with both hypertuning (Fig. 2A) and baseline (Fig. 2B) settings. Overall, we were able to reduce the feature space by nearly two orders of magnitude (from ~36,000 to ~400), while preserving key discriminative features that still allows very high classification performance. Thus, this demonstrates that a data-driven approach can reliably identify neural signatures of effector-related signals.

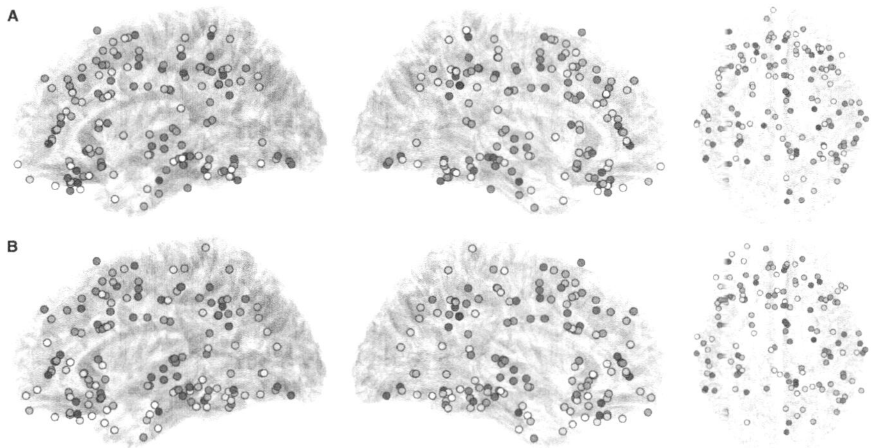


**Fig. 2.** Brain topographical visualisation of DyRFECV-identified iEEG contact locations. Projected structural MRI topographical plot mapping effector contacts (blue) based on feature importance with (**A**) and without hyperparameter tuning (**B**). Darker colour: Higher feature importance with respect to discrimination effector type. (Color figure online)

## Discussion

This study has successfully used the DyRFECV ML approach to efficiently handle structurally missing piecemeal iEEG data. This was demonstrated through high classification performance in distinguishing between covert manual and vocal reporting of perceptual decisions. Two variants of our DyRFECV approach were implemented on an LGBM classifier (with and without hyperparameter tuning). The variant with hyperparameter tuned achieved the highest classification F1-score of 0.994. However, it identified 416 key HFA samples (iEEG contacts). The variant without hyperparameter tuned obtained a substantially smaller (320) number of key HFA samples, without sacrificing too much on classification F1-score (0.972).

These differences arise because hyperparameter tuning and adaptive step size interact differently with the DyRFECV process. Specifically, the fine-tuned model prioritised maximising predictive F1-score, which allowed it to retain a broader set of informative samples and improve performance. In contrast, the baseline model with stricter elimination identified a smaller, more concentrated feature set, which yielded a slightly lower F1-score but highlighted more localised brain regions, improving interpretability. Thus, the variants reflect a trade-off between optimising classification metrics and deriving compact feature sets.

The identified iEEG contact locations were consistent with the literature with regards to motor planning and movement, and speech production, validating the approach used [26–28]. It should be noted that these motor actions were based on sensory-based decisions and not just movements per se. Hence, the identified iEEG contact locations were found to cover a wide area, consistent with recent iEEG studies in humans [11,12] and neuropixel studies in rodents [13, 15–17]. Through feature importance ranking, we found the parietal and frontal regions to be predominant for effector-related classification. This was consistent with previous studies showing that posterior parietal and fronto-parietal circuits contribute to intention, effector planning, and decision-related movements [29, 30], and with parietal activities reported in recent iEEG decision studies [11,12]. In particular, the previous study [11] using the same iEEG dataset found mainly the parietal cortical regions involved as effectors, and with lesser contact number. Future work will use neurophysiological criteria and different time epochs within a trial, as in that study. More generally, although ML has been applied to iEEG, they were mainly on seizure, motor imagery, or memory tasks [31], but not perceptual decision-based motor modality classification or framed as structured missingness.

This study has wider implications in data science and ML. In particular, it informs how we can approach structured missing time series data with highly piecemeal data structure. Future work will extend the approach to other data types, including those with multimodalities, with variations in pre-processing and choice of classifier and hyperparameters. In terms of neuroscience and neurotechnology, we have focused on analysing neural signals related to decision-based motor movement modalities. We expect our approach can be extended to paralysed patients who intend to communicate through, for instance, hand movement or vocal means [32–34]. Our future work will also focus on perceptual decision signals [4,11,12].

In conclusion, we have developed a generalised ML framework by integrating dataset size with feature importance. The method provides a responsive and efficient feature elimination process tailored to any specific time-series data, including fragmented time series data. Our approach reduces the need for extensive preprocessing and domain-specific feature extraction, relying instead on a unique feature selection employing DyRFECV, which not only maintains optimal performance but also reveals key discriminative features and offers novel insights into cognitive processes.

**Acknowledgments.** This work was supported by HSC R&D (STL/5540/19) and MRC (MC_OC_20020). The authors are grateful for access to the Tier 2 High Performance Computing resources provided by the Northern Ireland High Performance Computing (NI-HPC) facility funded by the UK Engineering and Physical Sciences Research Council (EPSRC), Grant No. EP/T022175/1.

**Data Availability Statement.** The dataset is openly available via the original study [11] (https://osf.io/9bzx8/). Processed data are available upon reasonable request. Code for the current study is available at https://github.com/umeshkumarnaik/dyrfecv.

**Disclosure of Interests.** The authors have no competing interests to declare that are relevant to the content of this article.

## References


1. Sadeh, S., Clopath, C.: The emergence of NeuroAI: bridging neuroscience and artificial intelligence. Nat. Rev. Neurosci. 1–2 (2025)
2. Zador, A., et al.: Catalyzing next-generation artificial intelligence through neuroai. Nat. Commun. **14**(1), 1597 (2023)
3. Patel, D., et al.: A Computational Perspective on NeuroAI and Synthetic Biological Intelligence. arXiv preprint arXiv:2509.23896 (2025)
4. Gold, J.I., Shadlen, M.N.: The neural basis of decision making. Annu. Rev. Neurosci. **30**(1), 535–574 (2007)
5. Russell, S.J., Norvig, P.: Artificial Intelligence: A Modern Approach, Pearson. 4th Ed. (2021)
6. Rubin, D.B.: Inference and missing data. Biometrika **63**(3), 581–592 (1976)
7. Emmanuel, T., Maupong, T., Mpoeleng, D., Semong, T., Mphago, B., Tabona, O.: A survey on missing data in machine learning. J. Big Data **8**(1), 140 (2021)
8. Mitra, R., et al.: Learning from data with structured missingness. Nat.Mach. Intell. **5**(1), 13–23 (2023)
9. Zainuddin, A., Hairuddin, M.A., Yassin, A.I.M., Abd Latiff, Z.I., Azhar, A.: Time series data and recent imputation techniques for missing data: A review. In: 2022 International Conference on Green Energy, Computing and Sustainable Technology (GECOST), pp. 346–350. IEEE (2022)
10. Parvizi, J., Kastner, S.: Promises and limitations of human intracranial electroencephalography. Nat. Neurosci. **21**(4), 474–483 (2018)
11. Gherman, S., et al.: Intracranial electroencephalography reveals effector-independent evidence accumulation dynamics in multiple human brain regions. Nat. Hum. Behav. **8**(4), 758–770 (2024)
12. Xie, T., et al.: Graded decisions in the human brain. Nat. Commun. **15**(1), 4308 (2024)
13. Jun, J.J., et al.: Fully integrated silicon probes for high-density recording of neural activity. Nature **551**(7679), 232–236 (2017)
14. Steinmetz, N.A., et al.: Neuropixels 2.0: A miniaturized high-density probe for stable, long-term brain recordings. Science **372**(6539), eabf4588 (2021)
15. Steinmetz, N.A., Zatka-Haas, P., Carandini, M., Harris, K.D.: Distributed coding of choice, action and engagement across the mouse brain. Nature **576**(7786), 266–273 (2019)
16. Angelaki, D., et al.: A brain-wide map of neural activity during complex behaviour. Nature **645**(8079), 177–191 (2025)
17. Findling, C., et al.: Brain-wide representations of prior information in mouse decision-making. Nature **645**(8079), 192–200 (2025)
18. Lachaux, J.P., Axmacher, N., Mormann, F., Halgren, E., Crone, N.E.: High-frequency neural activity and human cognition: past, present and possible future of intracranial EEG research. Prog. Neurobiol. **98**(3), 279–301 (2012)
19. Coughlin, B., et al.: Modified Neuropixels probes for recording human neurophysiology in the operating room. Nat. Protoc. **18**(10), 2927–2953 (2023)
20. Guyon, I., Weston, J., Barnhill, S., Vapnik, V.: Gene selection for cancer classification using support vector machines. Mach. Learn. **46**(1), 389–422 (2002)
21. Awad, M., Fraihat, S.: Recursive feature elimination with cross-validation with decision tree: feature selection method for machine learning-based intrusion detection systems. J. Sens. Actuator Netw. **12**(5), 67 (2023)

22. Ke, G., et al.: Lightgbm: A highly efficient gradient boosting decision tree. Adv. Neural Inf. Process. Syst. 30 (2017)
23. Bergstra, J., Bengio, Y.: Random search for hyper-parameter optimization. J. Mach. Learn. Res. **13**(1), 281–305 (2012)
24. Fernandez-Ruiz, J., Goltz, H.C., DeSouza, J.F., Vilis, T., Crawford, J.D.: Human parietal "reach region" primarily encodes intrinsic visual direction, not extrinsic movement direction, in a visual–motor dissociation task. Cereb. Cortex **17**(10), 2283–2292 (2007)
25. Filimon, F., Nelson, J.D., Huang, R.S., Sereno, M.I.: Multiple parietal reach regions in humans: cortical representations for visual and proprioceptive feedback during on-line reaching. J. Neurosci. **29**(9), 2961–2971 (2009)
26. Crone, N.E., Miglioretti, D.L., Gordon, B., Lesser, R.P.: Functional mapping of human sensorimotor cortex with electrocorticographic spectral analysis. II. Event-related synchronization in the gamma band. Brain J. Neurol. **121**(12), 2301–2315 (1998)
27. Bouchard, K.E., Mesgarani, N., Johnson, K., Chang, E.F.: Functional organization of human sensorimotor cortex for speech articulation. Nature **495**(7441), 327–332 (2013)
28. Flinker, A., et al.: Redefining the role of Broca's area in speech. Proc. Natl. Acad. Sci. **112**(9), 2871–2875 (2015)
29. Andersen, R.A., Cui, H.: Intention, action planning, and decision making in parietal-frontal circuits. Neuron **63**(5), 568–583 (2009)
30. Snyder, L.H., Batista, A.P., Andersen, R.A.: Intention-related activity in the posterior parietal cortex: a review. Vision. Res. **40**(10–12), 1433–1441 (2000)
31. Mirchi, N., et al.: Decoding intracranial EEG with machine learning: a systematic review. Front. Hum. Neurosci. **16**, 913777 (2022)
32. Hochberg, L.R., et al.: Reach and grasp by people with tetraplegia using a neurally controlled robotic arm. Nature **485**(7398), 372–375 (2012)
33. Moses, D.A., et al.: Neuroprosthesis for decoding speech in a paralyzed person with anarthria. N. Engl. J. Med. **385**(3), 217–227 (2021)
34. Willett, F.R., et al.: A high-performance speech neuroprosthesis. Nature **620**(7976), 1031–1036 (2023)

# An Optimized Deep Learning-Based Structure-from-Motion Pipeline for Efficient Glacier 3D Reconstruction

Sicheng Zhao[1,2], Edward Lai[3], and Soumyabrata Dev[1,2](✉)

[1] University College Dublin, Dublin, Ireland
sicheng.zhao@ucdconnect.ie, soumyabrata.dev@ucd.ie
[2] ADAPT Centre, Dublin, Ireland
[3] Yale University, New Haven, USA
edward.lai@yale.edu

**Abstract.** Glacier three-dimensional (3D) reconstruction remains challenging for traditional Structure-from-Motion (SfM) pipelines under low-texture and reflective conditions. We propose an optimized deep learning-based pipeline using SuperPoint and LightGlue, accelerated with ONNX Runtime. Experiments on UAV glacier imagery show sub-pixel reprojection error, denser point clouds, and reduced GPU memory usage compared to COLMAP and PyTorch-native baselines. This highlights the efficiency and scalability of deep learning approaches for large-scale glacier reconstruction.

**Keywords:** Glacier Reconstruction · Structure-from-Motion · Superpoint · LightGlue

## 1 Introduction

Glacier 3D reconstruction [1–3] is of critical importance for advancing the understanding of climate change, monitoring variations in glacier volume, and analyzing ice dynamics. High-fidelity 3D models facilitate long-term observation of glacier retreat, mass balance fluctuations, and surface motion, thereby providing indispensable insights for climate science and natural hazard assessment [4–6].

Traditional SfM pipelines [3,7], particularly those employing scale-invariant feature transform (SIFT) [8,9] for feature extraction and matching [10,11], frequently encounter severe limitations in glacier environments. The prevalence of low-texture surfaces, intense specular reflections, and large-baseline multi-view imagery substantially undermines the robustness and accuracy of such traditional approaches, often resulting in incomplete reconstructions or geometric distortions [12,13].

In this paper, we present *An Optimized Deep Learning-Based SfM Pipeline for Efficient Glacier 3D Reconstruction*. The contributions of this work can be summarized as follows:


T. T. Mai et al. (Eds.): AICS 2025, CCIS 2950, pp. 157–165, 2026.
https://doi.org/10.1007/978-3-032-25809-0_12

- We propose an optimized deep learning-based SfM pipeline [14,15] that substitutes the traditional SIFT–COLMAP framework with SuperPoint [16] for feature extraction and LightGlue [17] for feature matching, while leveraging ONNX Runtime [18] with FP16(16-bit floating point) inference for efficiency.
- We evaluate the proposed pipeline on glacier datasets, demonstrating improvements in both reconstruction efficiency and scalability when compared to conventional methods.
- We conduct ablation experiments contrasting the PyTorch-native [19] SuperPoint–LightGlue pipeline with its ONNX Runtime FP16-optimized counterpart, systematically analyzing runtime performance and memory utilization.

## 2 Related Work

### 2.1 Traditional Feature Extraction Methods

One of the most widely used traditional computer vision methods in SfM is SIFT, which detects keypoints by locating local extrema in a Difference-of-Gaussians (DoG) pyramid [8] across multiple scales. This approach provides robustness to variations in both scale and rotation. Each keypoint is then assigned an orientation based on local image gradients, allowing invariance to rotation [20,21]. Finally, SIFT constructs a distinctive 128-dimensional descriptor by summarizing gradient orientations within a local neighborhood around the keypoint. This combination of scale-space detection, orientation assignment, and gradient-based descriptors has made SIFT a cornerstone of classical SfM pipelines. Nevertheless, in glacier imagery with repetitive patterns, low texture, and strong reflections, SIFT often produces sparse or unreliable matches, limiting its effectiveness even when GPU acceleration is applied.

### 2.2 Deep Learning-Based Feature Extraction and Matching

Recent advances in deep learning have enabled learned alternatives to traditional descriptors. SuperPoint, for example, is a self-supervised convolutional neural network [22] that jointly learns interest point detection and descriptor extraction. It produces repeatable keypoints and compact descriptors that are more robust in texture-poor or noisy environments compared to SIFT. For feature matching, LightGlue introduces a transformer-based architecture [23] that dynamically decides how many iterations are required to establish correspondences between two sets of features. Unlike static matching strategies, LightGlue adapts to the difficulty of image pairs, making it efficient for easy cases while maintaining accuracy in challenging ones. This flexibility reduces computation without sacrificing robustness, allowing large-scale SfM tasks to scale more effectively [24]. Building on these developments, our work proposes an optimized deep learning-based SfM pipeline, with a particular focus on accelerating feature extraction and matching for glacier reconstruction through FP16 inference and ONNX Runtime optimization.

# 3 Methodology

## 3.1 Pipeline Overview

This work introduces a optimized SfM pipeline in which deep learning-based feature extraction and matching replace the conventional SIFT descriptors employed in the standard COLMAP framework. The new design preserves the classical SfM geometry estimation stages while redefining the feature processing component. In the SIFT-COLMAP pipeline, reconstruction relies on SIFT-based descriptors and exhaustive matching, followed by pose estimation, outlier rejection, and bundle adjustment. While effective, SIFT features often degrade in glacier imagery due to low contrast and repetitive patterns. In contrast, the proposed pipeline incorporates SuperPoint for keypoint detection and description, combined with LightGlue for transformer-based feature matching. The subsequent SfM steps (PnP, RANSAC, BA) remain unchanged, enabling a direct comparison between the classical and deep learning-based pipelines. The implementation of the proposed pipeline is available here: https://github.com/AppleJack9050/glacier_pipeline.

## 3.2 Deep Learning-Based Feature Extraction and Matching

The front end of the pipeline is implemented using **SuperPoint**, a self-supervised network for joint keypoint detection and description. Compared with SIFT, SuperPoint offers features that are more robust to scale, rotation, and contrast variations, which are critical in glacial environments. Feature correspondences are then established using **LightGlue**, a lightweight transformer-based matcher that dynamically adjusts its computational load depending on image complexity. In glacier imagery, where homogeneous surfaces are common, we configure the system to retain up to $N = 4096$ keypoints per image, with a non-maximum suppression (NMS) radius [25,26] to reduce redundancy while ensuring spatial coverage.

## 3.3 Optimization Strategy

To achieve efficiency on large-scale glacier datasets, both SuperPoint and LightGlue are exported to the ONNX format and executed through ONNX Runtime with half-precision (FP16) inference. This optimization reduces computational overhead and memory usage while maintaining numerical stability relative to the PyTorch baseline. By integrating ONNX Runtime acceleration, the proposed system is capable of processing significantly larger datasets under constrained hardware resources.

## 3.4 Integration with SfM

The proposed front end is integrated into the **Hierarchical Localization (HLOC)** framework [24,27], which provides a flexible interface for combining learned feature extractors and matchers with traditional SfM backends. In this work, SuperPoint and LightGlue are coupled within HLOC to produce feature correspondences, which are then passed to COLMAP for geometric reasoning. Camera poses are estimated via PnP, outliers are rejected through RANSAC, and bundle adjustment is employed for global refinement. This design ensures that efficiency improvements stem from the optimized feature extraction and matching stages, while the SfM backend remains identical to the SIFT-COLMAP baseline.

### 3.5 Ablation Study Setup

The ablation study compares two configurations: (1) **PyTorch Baseline**, where SuperPoint and LightGlue are executed natively in PyTorch with full precision; and (2) **Optimized Inference**, where the same models are converted to ONNX Runtime with FP16 acceleration. The comparison focuses exclusively on the feature extraction and feature matching stages, with evaluation metrics including average inference time and peak GPU memory usage. This setup isolates the contribution of the proposed optimization to computational efficiency, independent of the geometric SfM backend.

## 4 Experiment

### 4.1 Dataset

We use a UAV glacier dataset of 567 images captured by a DJI FC330 camera, modeled as a *pinhole camera* with distortion parameters. The native resolution is $2000 \times 1500$ pixels, corresponding to a ground sampling distance of $3.49\,\text{mm/pixel}$ at an altitude of $11.6\,\text{m}$, covering about $1.92 \times 10^3\ \text{m}^2$. All images were undistorted and downscaled to a maximum of $2000 \times 1498$ pixels to reduce computation while preserving geometry. The dataset is publicly available at the UNAVCO TLS repository.

### 4.2 Experimental Setup

All experiments were conducted under a unified SfM configuration to ensure comparability. The hardware environment consisted of an Intel Core i7-9700X CPU, 48 GB of RAM, and an NVIDIA GeForce RTX 4090 GPU with 24 GB of VRAM, running Ubuntu 22.04 LTS. For the traditional baseline, we utilized the SIFT-based COLMAP pipeline. Since SIFT implementations exist for both CPU and GPU, we adopted the GPU-accelerated version to reduce runtime overhead and provide a fairer comparison against the deep learning-based pipelines. On the learning-based side, the baseline feature extraction and matching were implemented in PyTorch, while optimized inference was performed with ONNX Runtime in FP16 mode. Thus, three pipelines were evaluated: the GPU-accelerated SIFT-based COLMAP system, the PyTorch-native SuperPoint–LightGlue pipeline, and the ONNX Runtime FP16 optimized variant.

### 4.3 Evaluation Metrics

The evaluation focused on two categories of metrics:

- **Reconstruction Quality:** Root Mean Square Reprojection Error (RMSE) [28,29] and the number of 3D points were used as quantitative measures of reconstruction accuracy.
- **Reconstruction Efficiency:** We reported three indicators to assess computational performance: overall reconstruction speed, average GPU utilization, and peak Videa RAM (VRAM) consumption.

### 4.4 Results

*Traditional vs. Optimized Pipeline.* Relative to a standard COLMAP baseline, the optimized pipeline maintains sub-pixel RMSE and improves geometric completeness: the final point cloud contains more 3D points with broader spatial coverage, while the number of registered images remains comparable (Table 1). All results are averaged over 10 independent runs to ensure statistical reliability.

**Table 1.** Comparison of Traditional SIFT and Optimized Pipeline All values are averaged over 10 runs; the ± indicates one standard deviation.

| Method | RMSE (px) | 3D Points |
|---|---|---|
| Traditional SIFT | $0.5939 \pm 0.018$ | $482,213 \pm 187$ |
| Optimized Pipeline | $0.4936 \pm 0.015$ | $530,434 \pm 243$ |

*Ablation: PyTorch Native vs. ONNX Runtime (FP16).* Replacing the PyTorch-native feature extraction and matching with ONNX Runtime FP16 reduces the mean time for these stages to $4.19 \pm 0.33$ minutes and peak GPU memory to $15.5 \pm 0.4$ GB (Table 2), alleviating the primary throughput bottleneck. Each configuration was tested across 10 runs, and the reported values represent the mean ± standard deviation.

**Table 2.** PyTorch Native vs. ONNX Runtime FP16 on Feature Extraction and Matching. All values are averaged over 10 runs; the ± indicates one standard deviation.

| Method | Runtime (mins) | GPU Memory (GB) |
|---|---|---|
| PyTorch Native (FP32) | $5.86 \pm 0.47$ | $19.1 \pm 0.5$ |
| ONNX Runtime FP16 | $4.19 \pm 0.33$ | $15.5 \pm 0.4$ |

*Qualitative Visualization.* The baseline panel is a densified Multi-View Stereo(MVS) [30] reconstruction, whereas our results are sparse SfM point clouds. Within the sparse regime, structure is comparable to the baseline, with at most slight densification in high-gradient areas and no observable increase in artifacts (Fig. 1).

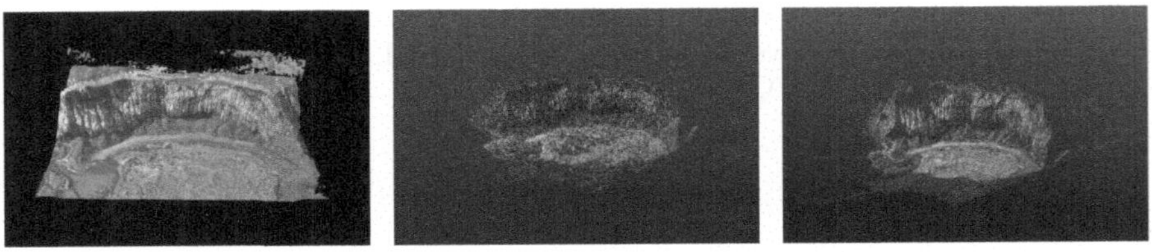

(a) Ground truth model (b) COLMAP-based model (c) DL-based model

**Fig. 1.** Snapshots of three reconstruction models. The first is the official ground truth reconstruction, the second is obtained using the SuperPoint+SuperGlue framework, and the third is generated with COLMAP.

## 5 Discussion

*Accuracy and Completeness.* The optimized pipeline delivers lower reprojection error while simultaneously increasing the number of reconstructed points (Table 1). This indicates that the use of learned features coupled with transformer-based match filtering enhances correspondence recall without compromising geometric consistency. The improvements are particularly visible in regions of high surface gradient, such as crevasse edges or steep ice walls, where traditional SIFT features tend to fail due to low contrast and repeated patterns. By leveraging SuperPoint's scale- and contrast-invariant descriptors together with LightGlue's context-aware filtering, the system is able to recover matches that extend coverage into previously underrepresented areas. As a result, the reconstructed point cloud not only becomes denser but also spatially more uniform, reducing holes in the geometry and enabling better support for downstream dense stereo stages.

*Efficiency and Compute.* Replacing PyTorch-native inference with ONNX Runtime FP16 results in a measurable reduction in runtime and peak GPU memory during feature extraction and matching (Table 2), effectively alleviating what is often the dominant computational bottleneck in learning-based SfM pipelines. The runtime gains stem from both half-precision tensor operations and optimized graph execution, while reduced memory demand allows for larger batch sizes or processing of higher-resolution imagery within the same hardware constraints. Despite these improvements, end-to-end SfM performance remains constrained by components that are inherently sequential or CPU-bound, including incremental mapping, bundle adjustment, and large-scale I/O. These stages restrict the pipeline from fully saturating GPU resources, even when powerful hardware, such as an NVIDIA RTX 4090, is available. This suggests that while front-end acceleration is crucial, further advances in the parallelization of back-end geometry estimation will be necessary to achieve true real-time reconstruction performance.

*Qualitative Interpretation.* The qualitative comparison panel juxtaposes a densified MVS reconstruction against sparse SfM outputs (Fig. 1). The apparent differences in density stem primarily from the algorithmic distinction between multi-view stereo (which explicitly aims for dense surface recovery) and structure-from-motion (which remains sparse by design). Within the sparse regime, however, the optimized pipeline demonstrates clear advantages. It consistently recovers geometry comparable to or slightly richer than the traditional baseline, especially in structurally complex areas such as heavily crevassed or fractured glacier surfaces. The learned features also exhibit improved repeatability across low-texture ice fields, reducing local dropout of points and producing more coherent coverage. Importantly, no spurious structures or visible artifacts were introduced, underscoring that the observed density gains do not compromise the overall fidelity of the recovered 3D model.

*Limitations and Scope.* Several limitations bound the interpretation of these results. First, all images were downscaled prior to processing, which caps the maximum achievable accuracy and likely underestimates the benefits of learned features on native-resolution inputs where more fine-scale detail is preserved. Second, the evaluation is restricted to a single UAV/glacier dataset with a single camera model; while glaciers represent a challenging domain due to texture scarcity and repetitive patterns, generalization to other terrains (e.g., vegetation, urban facades), different seasons, or varying imaging geometries is not yet tested. Third, the accuracy metric used—root mean square error in pixel space—effectively measures reprojection consistency but does not directly quantify absolute 3D surface error. As such, conclusions about geodetic accuracy or volumetric change detection remain tentative. Addressing these limitations will require larger-scale, cross-domain evaluations and integration with ground-truth datasets or lidar references to assess the absolute quality of 3D reconstructions.

## 6 Conclusion

We presented an optimized deep learning-based SfM pipeline for glacier 3D reconstruction, combining SuperPoint and LightGlue with ONNX Runtime FP16 acceleration. The system achieves lower reprojection error, denser point clouds, and reduced GPU memory usage compared to SIFT-COLMAP and PyTorch baselines, while preserving structural fidelity. These results highlight the efficiency and scalability of learned features for challenging cryospheric environments.

## References

1. Szeliski, R.: Computer vision: algorithms and applications, Springer Nature (2022)
2. Hartley, R., Zisserman, A.: Multiple view geometry in computer vision, Cambridge University Press (2003)
3. Snavely, N., Seitz, S.M., Szeliski, R.: Photo tourism: exploring photo collections in 3D. In: ACM Siggraph 2006 papers, pp. 835–846 (2006)
4. Kääb, A.: Mountain glaciers and permafrost creep: research perspectives from earth observation technologies & geoinformatics, University of Zurich-Department of Geography (2004)
5. Immerzeel, W.W., et al.: High-resolution monitoring of Himalayan glacier dynamics using unmanned aerial vehicles. Remote Sens. Environ. **150**, 93–103 (2014)
6. Westoby, M.J., Brasington, J., Glasser, N.F., Hambrey, M.J., Reynolds, J.M.: Structure-from-motion photogrammetry: a low-cost, effective tool for geoscience applications. Geomorphology **179**, 300–314 (2012)
7. Schonberger, J.L., Frahm, J.-M.: Structure-from-motion revisited. In: Proceedings of the IEEE Conference on Computer Vision and Pattern Recognition, pp. 4104–4113 (2016)
8. Lowe, D.G.: Distinctive image features from scale-invariant keypoints. Int. J. Comput. Vision **60**(2), 91–110 (2004)
9. Lowe, D.G.: Object recognition from local scale-invariant features. In: Proceedings of the Seventh IEEE International Conference on Computer Vision, Vol. 2, pp. 1150–1157. IEEE (1999)
10. Gonzalez, R.C.: Digital image processing. Pearson Education India (2009)
11. Jain, A.K., Duin, R.P.W., Mao, J.: Statistical pattern recognition: a review. IEEE Trans. Pattern Anal. Mach. Intell. **22**(1), 4–37 (2000)
12. Mur-Artal, R., Montiel, J.M.M., Tardos, J.D.: Orb-slam: a versatile and accurate monocular slam system. IEEE Trans. Rob. **31**(5), 1147–1163 (2015)
13. Klein, G., Murray, D.: Parallel tracking and mapping for small AR workspaces. In: 6th IEEE and ACM International Symposium on Mixed and Augmented Reality, pp. 225–234. IEEE 2007 (2007)
14. Elharrouss, O., Akbari, Y., Almaadeed, N., Al-Maadeed, S.: Backbones-review: Feature extraction networks for deep learning and deep reinforcement learning approaches. arXiv preprint (2022)
15. Liu, W., et al.: Modality-aware feature matching: A comprehensive review of single- and cross-modality techniques, arXiv preprint arXiv:2507.22791 (2025)
16. DeTone, D., Malisiewicz, T., Rabinovich, A.: Superpoint: self-supervised interest point detection and description. In: Proceedings of the IEEE Conference on Computer Vision and Pattern Recognition Workshops, pp. 224–236 (2018)
17. Lindenberger, P., Sarlin, P.-E., Pollefeys, M.: Lightglue: local feature matching at light speed. In: Proceedings of the IEEE/CVF International Conference on Computer Vision, pp. 17627–17638 (2023)
18. O. R. developers, Onnx runtime, version: x.y.z (2021). https://onnxruntime.ai/
19. Paszke, A., et al.: Pytorch: An imperative style, high-performance deep learning library. arXiv:1912.01703. https://arxiv.org/abs/1912.01703 (2019)
20. Herbert, B.: Surf: Speeded up robust features. Comput. Vis. Image Underst. **110**(3), 346–359 (2008)
21. Rublee, E., Rabaud, V., Konolige, K., Bradski, G., Orb: An efficient alternative to sift or surf. In: International Conference on Computer Vision, pp. 2564–2571. IEEE 2011 (2011)

22. LeCun, Y., Bottou, L., Bengio, Y., Haffner, P.: Gradient-based learning applied to document recognition. Proc. IEEE **86**(11), 2278–2324 (2002)
23. Vaswani, A., et al.: Attention is all you need. Adv. Neural Inf. Process. Syst. **30** (2017)
24. Sarlin, P.-E., DeTone, D., Malisiewicz, T., Rabinovich, A.: SuperGlue: Learning feature matching with graph neural networks. In: CVPR (2020)
25. Canny, J.: A computational approach to edge detection. IEEE Trans. Pattern Anal. Mach. Intell. (6), 679–698 (2009)
26. Viola, P., Jones, M.: Rapid object detection using a boosted cascade of simple features. In: Proceedings of the 2001 IEEE Computer Society Conference on Computer Vision and Pattern Recognition, CVPR 2001, Vol. 1, pp. I-I. IEEE (2001)
27. Sarlin, P.-E., Cadena, C., Siegwart, R., Dymczyk, M.: From coarse to fine: Robust hierarchical localization at large scale. In: CVPR (2019)
28. Willmott, C.J., Matsuura, K.: Advantages of the mean absolute error (MAE) over the root mean square error (RMSE) in assessing average model performance. Climate Res. **30**(1), 79–82 (2005)
29. Chai, T., Draxler, R.R.: Root mean square error (RMSE) or mean absolute error (MAE)?-arguments against avoiding RMSE in the literature. Geosci. Model Dev. **7**(3), 1247–1250 (2014)
30. Schönberger, J.L., Zheng, E., Pollefeys, M., Frahm, J.-M.: Pixelwise view selection for unstructured multi-view stereo. In: European Conference on Computer Vision (ECCV) (2016)

# Formal Robustness Verification of a Learnt Autonomous Driver

Medet Inkarbekov[1,3(✉)], Barak A. Pearlmutter[1,2], and Rosemary Monahan[1,2,3]

[1] Department of Computer Science, Maynooth University, Maynooth, Ireland
medet.inkarbekov@mu.ie

[2] Hamilton Institute, Maynooth University, Maynooth, Ireland

[3] ADAPT Centre, Dublin, Ireland

**Abstract.** We present an end-to-end pipeline for developing and formally verifying compact steering controllers trained in a Unity-based simulator. Our study leverages a curated dataset and a family of lightweight convolutional neural network (CNN) models (39–924 parameters) trained under both standard and adversarial regimes, and evaluates them against scale-invariant robustness properties that capture label consistency, relative confidence, and logit stability. Experiments across multiple verification frameworks show that label consistency proves most verifiable, while scale-invariant properties require careful tolerance calibration, and adversarial training is essential for achieving meaningful robustness. These findings highlight the interplay between specification design, training regime, and verification. This demonstrates how formal methods can be integrated into the development loop of safety-critical systems.

**Keywords:** NN Verification · Autonomous Driving · Benchmarking · Machine Learning

## 1 Introduction

Neural networks (NNs) increasingly underpin decision-making in safety-critical settings, yet their complexity and opacity complicate the provision of rigorous behavioural guarantees [1,2]. Empirical testing alone can miss rare but catastrophic corner cases; safety-critical deployment therefore requires methods that can establish *formal* guarantees of correctness and robustness under clearly specified operating conditions.

Formal verification of NNs proves that properties hold over entire input regions [1]. Unlike traditional software, the object of verification is a high-dimensional learnt function, with distinctive failure modes such as imperceptible perturbations causing large behavioural shifts [3]. Verification methods span from complete encodings for constraint solvers, which are sound and complete but scale poorly, to incomplete relaxations, which sacrifice completeness for efficiency through abstraction or convex bounds [4]. Recent SAT-style approaches exploit NN structure for search [5]. Community benchmarks (e.g.,


T. T. Mai et al. (Eds.): AICS 2025, CCIS 2950, pp. 166–178, 2026.
https://doi.org/10.1007/978-3-032-25809-0_13

VNN-COMP [6,7]) have accelerated progress through standardized tasks and transparent comparisons, while unified frameworks support experimentation across diverse tools [8,9].

Autonomous driving systems (ADS) pose especially stringent demands. NN components pervade perception, planning, and control [10], and robust operation must be guaranteed under high-dimensional sensory inputs, dynamic environments, and real-time constraints [11,12]. While verification has advanced for classifiers and isolated control modules, there remains a gap in *end-to-end, development-centred* workflows that unify simulation, training, specification design, and formal verification in one loop.

This paper introduces an end-to-end pipeline for developing and verifying neural steering controllers in autonomous driving. We construct a simulator-driven dataset and train a family of compact convolutional networks ranging from 39 to 924 parameters under both vanilla and adversarial training. Our safety assessment is based on scale-invariant robustness properties tailored to control—capturing label consistency, relative confidence, and stability—which we systematically evaluate across the trained models. Verification is carried out using three complementary tools: $\alpha,\beta$-CROWN (relaxations with branch-and-bound) [4,13,14], Marabou (complete SMT/MILP) [15,16], and NeuralSAT (DPLL(T)-based SAT search) [5]. This setting allows us to analyze how architecture size, training regime, and verifier choice jointly affect the proportion of inputs for which robustness can be formally guaranteed.

This paper makes four contributions. First, we present a verification-centered ADS pipeline that unifies simulator-driven data collection, controller training, specification design, and formal verification. Second, we introduce scale-invariant robustness properties—relative confidence and per-logit stability—that overcome the model-dependence of absolute thresholds in prior work, enabling meaningful cross-architecture comparison and tolerance semantics suited to control tasks. Third, we comprehensively benchmark $\alpha,\beta$-CROWN, Marabou, and NeuralSAT across model sizes, perturbation budgets, and training regimes. Finally, we provide a fully reproducible implementation including the ADS platform, dataset, training scripts, and verification configurations.

## 2 Related Work

The verification of neural controllers has emerged as a key challenge in cyber-physical and safety-critical domains. Unlike classifiers, controllers interact directly with system dynamics, making failures potentially catastrophic. Early work focused on reachability analysis for NN-controlled systems using, e.g., approximate reachable sets or over-approximations of closed-loop dynamics [17,18]. These studies demonstrated the feasibility of verifying small networks in continuous control but struggled with scalability and realistic input.

In the autonomous driving domain, verification efforts have targeted both perception-to-control pipelines and closed-loop decision-making. Dreossi, Donze, and Seshia [12] proposed VerifAI to explore failure-inducing scenarios in end-to-end controllers, while Tran et al. [11] introduced ImageStar to reason about image-based perception modules. Other work has investigated reachability-based verification of neural controllers for lane-keeping and collision avoidance [19,20], as well as case studies on automated emergency braking [21]. More recently, Bukhari et al. [22] reported practical lessons from deploying formal verification in ADS development, highlighting the gap between prototype and practice.

Beyond reachability, several works have framed robustness itself as a verification property. Casadio et al. [23] formalised robustness specifications in terms of neural outputs , showing how safety guarantees can be expressed beyond simple misclassification. However, most robustness formulations are designed for classifiers and do not reflect the scale and risk sensitivities of control tasks.

Here we focus on compact steering controllers in a simulated ADS. We propose scale-invariant robustness properties specifically tailored to control and benchmark multiple state-of-the-art verifiers in an end-to-end pipeline that integrates dataset generation, controller training, specification design, and formal verification.

# 3 Methodology and System Architecture

## 3.1 Simulation and Interactive Control

Our ADS is implemented in the Unity game engine [24] with Barracuda-based inference [25] for real-time decision-making, as Unity and Barracuda provide a lightweight, real-time simulation and inference environment that integrates controller execution, dataset generation, and evaluation within a single reproducible workflow. This setup serves as both a testbed for controlled assessment of neural network behaviour and a platform for generating training data, offering continuous feedback on vehicle state, road context, and model predictions. The simulation environment (Fig. 1(left)) allows controlled adjustment of key parameters—motor torque, inference frequency, steering angle limits, and time-scaling—facilitating systematic testing under varying operating conditions and enabling accelerated evaluation.

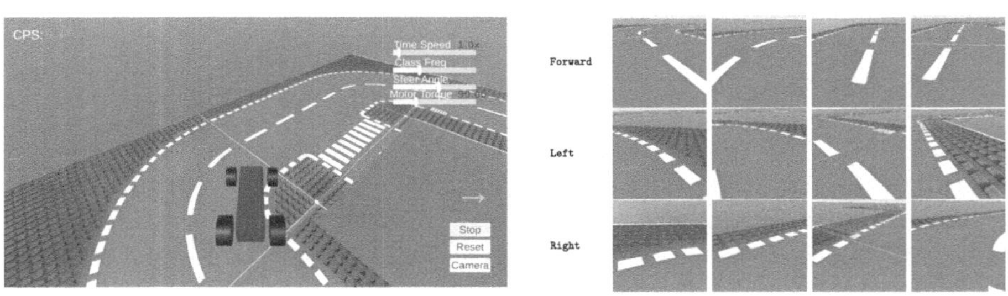


**Fig. 1.** (left) Simulation interface with real-time controls. CPS is average classification frequency. Green arrow shows network's predicted action. (right) Red–Green–Blue (RGB) images from the dataset, grouped by action labels (Forward, Left, Right). (Color figure online)

### 3.2 Data Collection and Curation

We constructed a custom dataset tailored for training and evaluating our vision-based ADS. All data were captured within the Unity simulator (Sect. 3.1), using the forward-facing camera to record images corresponding to three discrete actions: `Forward`, `Left`, and `Right` (Fig. 1(right)).

**Initial Data Acquisition.** The vehicle was manually teleoperated using keyboard inputs for three actions: `Forward`, `Left`, and `Right`. During teleoperation, the system recorded synchronized data samples consisting of a 256×256 RGB image from the forward-facing camera and the corresponding action label.

**Data Preprocessing and Labeling Strategy.** To match the CNN input, each captured image was converted from RGB to grayscale and down-sampled to 28×28 pixels. Some frames are ambiguous even for humans (e.g., the second sample in the `Forward` row of Fig. 1(right)) appearing both as going straight or starting a turn), which creates uncertainty for learning systems. To reduce this, we applied a strict heuristic: `Left`/`Right` were labeled only when the vehicle was approaching or navigating a corner or road edge, while all other frames were labeled as `Forward`. This reduced ambiguity and provided clear, context-dependent supervision, improving driving performance.

**Model-in-the-Loop Refinement.** To improve dataset quality, we adopted a model-in-the-loop refinement process. The curated data were split into training and test sets using a stratified, temporally ordered split to maintain class balance while limiting temporal leakage. A baseline CNN was trained on the training set and deployed in the Unity simulator, where its performance was evaluated by attempting to complete multiple laps of the track. Whenever the model failed, the corresponding track region was identified and additional samples were collected from that scenario. These targeted samples were merged into the dataset, and the cycle of training, evaluation, and data augmentation was repeated until the model could reliably complete laps without deviation.

**Final Dataset Characteristics.** Refinement concluded once the baseline model consistently completed the three-lap objective. The final dataset (available at https://doi.org/10.5281/zenodo.17192218) comprises **1,889** curated samples, with the class distribution of Table 1. The predominance of `Forward` reflects natural driving behavior on a looped track, where straight motion is more frequent than turning. This dataset was used exclusively below.

**Table 1.** Final distribution of samples in the curated dataset.

| Class Label | Sample Count | Percentage |
|---|---|---|
| Forward | 748 | 39.6% |
| Right | 522 | 27.6% |
| Left | 619 | 32.8% |
| **Total** | **1,889** | **100.0%** |

### 3.3 Neural Network Architectures

To systematically study the trade-off between model size and verifiability, we constructed a family of lightweight convolutional neural networks (CNNs) tailored for $28 \times 28$ grayscale inputs. Each network outputs one of three logits corresponding to the driving decisions in our simulated autonomous driving task.

All models follow the same simple feed-forward template:

$$\mathrm{Conv}(1 \to C_1,\, k, s, p) \xrightarrow{\mathrm{ReLU}} \text{Flatten} \to \mathrm{FC}_1(N_1 \to H_1) \xrightarrow{\mathrm{ReLU}} \mathrm{FC}_2(H_1 \to 3),$$

where Conv denotes a convolutional layer, ReLU denotes the rectified linear unit activation, and FC denotes a fully connected layer; $C_1$ is the number of convolutional output channels, $k$ is the kernel size, $s$ is the stride, $p$ is the padding, and $H_1$ is the hidden size of the first fully connected layer. The post-convolution spatial size $m$ is given by $m = \left\lfloor \frac{28-k+2p}{s} \right\rfloor + 1$, so that the input dimension of $\mathrm{FC}_1$ is $N_1 = C_1 \cdot m^2$. Model variants differ only in $(C_1, H_1, k, s, p)$, resulting in differing $m$ and total parameter count (Table 2).

**Table 2.** Lightweight CNN architectures used in experiments, ranging from 39 to 924 parameters. This systematic scaling enables analysis of the trade-off between model capacity and verifiability.

| Model | $C_1$ | $H_1$ | $k$ | $s$ | $p$ | $m$ | Total Parameters |
|---|---|---|---|---|---|---|---|
| M39 | 1 | 2 | 3 | 10 | 0 | 3 | 39 |
| M116‡ | 1 | 3 | 5 | 5 | 0 | 5 | 116 |
| M520 | 5 | 3 | 5 | 5 | 0 | 5 | 520 |
| M924 | 9 | 3 | 5 | 5 | 0 | 5 | 924 |

‡This model's forward pass has tensor shapes $(1, 28, 28) \to (1, 5, 5) \to (25) \to (3) \to (3)$.

### 3.4 Verification Properties

Robustness can be expressed as formal properties of the network's output under bounded input perturbations. Casadio et al. [23] introduced canonical notions such as Classification Robustness (CR), Standard Robustness (SR), and Strong Classification Robustness (SCR). Absolute thresholds over logits are problematic: logit magnitudes vary with architecture, training regime, and input distribution, making fixed thresholds non-transferable across models. We therefore adopt SR directly but reformulate CR and SCR with relative, scale-invariant margins that express tolerances as fractions of nominal output magnitudes. This ensures meaningful cross-model comparison and consistent tolerance semantics regardless of network capacity. The resulting properties, **P1–P3**, form the basis of our verification experiments.

Let $\mathcal{N} : \mathbb{R}^n \to \mathbb{R}^C$ be the neural network under verification, producing a logit vector $\mathcal{N}(\boldsymbol{x})$. For a labeled sample $(\hat{\boldsymbol{x}}, y)$, the perturbation set is the $\ell_\infty$-ball

$$\mathbb{B}_\infty(\hat{\boldsymbol{x}}; \varepsilon) = \{\boldsymbol{x} \in \mathbb{R}^n \mid \|\boldsymbol{x} - \hat{\boldsymbol{x}}\|_\infty \leq \varepsilon\}.$$

**P1 Classification Robustness.** For all perturbed inputs $\mathbf{x}$, the predicted class $y$ must equal the ground-truth label: $\forall \boldsymbol{x} \in \mathbb{B}_\infty(\hat{\boldsymbol{x}}; \varepsilon)$ . $\arg\max_i \mathcal{N}(\boldsymbol{x})_i = y$.

**P2 Class-Consistent Score Robustness.** In addition to class consistency, the logit of the correct class must not drop by more than a relative margin: $\forall \boldsymbol{x} \in \mathbb{B}_\infty(\hat{\boldsymbol{x}}; \varepsilon)$ . $(\arg\max_i \mathcal{N}(\boldsymbol{x})_i = y) \wedge (\mathcal{N}(\boldsymbol{x})_y \geq \mathcal{N}(\hat{\boldsymbol{x}})_y - \Delta_{\text{conf}})$, where $\Delta_{\text{conf}} = \delta_{\text{conf}}|\mathcal{N}(\hat{\boldsymbol{x}})_y|$.

**P3 Logit Stability.** Each logit must remain close to its nominal value, within a relative offset: $\forall \boldsymbol{x} \in \mathbb{B}_\infty(\hat{\boldsymbol{x}}; \varepsilon) . \forall i . |\mathcal{N}(\boldsymbol{x})_i - \mathcal{N}(\hat{\boldsymbol{x}})_i| \leq \Delta_{\text{stab},i}$, where $\Delta_{\text{stab},i} = \delta_{\text{stab}}|\mathcal{N}(\hat{\boldsymbol{x}})_i|$.

In ADS, **P1** enforces steering consistency under sensor noise, **P2** maintains decision confidence, and **P3** ensures stable control signals.

### 3.5 Verification Tools and Methods

We verified properties **P1–P3** using three complementary frameworks: $\alpha,\beta$-CROWN, which applies linear relaxations with branch-and-bound [4,13,14]; Marabou, which performs satisfiability modulo theories (SMT)-based solving [15,16], and NeuralSAT, which implements SAT (Boolean satisfiability) modulo theories using a Davis–Putnam–Logemann–Loveland with theories (DPLL(T)) search procedure [5]. These tools represent fundamentally different paradigms and have consistently ranked among the top performers in VNN-COMP benchmarks [6,7]. Using multiple verifiers increases coverage, helps uncover vulnerabilities missed by standard testing, and strengthens confidence in robustness guarantees where proofs are obtained.

Each property is encoded as a constraint that must hold for all admissible perturbations $\boldsymbol{x} \in \mathbb{B}_\infty(\hat{\boldsymbol{x}}; \varepsilon)$. The solvers may return:

- *Unsafe*: a concrete counterexample input violating the property (SAT);
- *Safe*: a formal guarantee that the property holds in the region (UNSAT);
- *Unknown*: inconclusive result caused by timeout or indeterminate outcome.

## 4 Experimental Results and Analysis

### 4.1 Experimental Setup

We follow the benchmarking protocol of recent VNN-COMP editions to ensure comparability across tools. Models were exported to Open Neural Network

Exchange (`ONNX`) and specifications to `VNN-LIB`[1]. Verification ran on a workstation with an AMD Ryzen 9 7950X (16 cores), 64 GB RAM, and an NVIDIA RTX 4090 (24 GB). Each query had a 30 s wall-clock budget.

All CNNs were trained for 32 epochs with batch size 33 using Adam (initial learning rate $8\times10^{-3}$, weight decay $10^{-4}$, cross-entropy loss). Adversarial training employed projected gradient descent (PGD) with $\varepsilon \in \{15, 25\}/255$, 7 steps, step size $\alpha = 1/255$, and random starts. Formal verification covered properties **P1**–**P3** for $\ell_\infty$-bounded perturbations with $\varepsilon \in \{5, 10, 20\}/255$. For **P2** and **P3**, we fixed $\delta_{\text{conf}} = 0.85$ and $\delta_{\text{stab}} = 0.15$ in the main study (Table 5). A separate sensitivity analysis (Fig. 3) varied $\varepsilon \in \{5, 10\}/255$, $\delta_{\text{conf}} \in \{0.95, \ldots, 0.5\}$ and $\delta_{\text{stab}} \in \{0.05, \ldots, 0.5\}$ on a fixed model (M116, PGD-25/255).

For each architecture and training regime we verified 100 held-out test samples across all factor combinations (**P1**–**P3** $\times$ 3 perturbation radii), resulting in 900 verification instances per regime. With three training regimes, this amounts to 2,700 instances per model size and per verifier. Across the three verifiers, the total reaches 8,100 instances per model size, or 32,400 instances overall across all four model sizes. In addition, a sensitivity analysis was conducted on a fixed model (M116 with PGD-25/255 training), varying six tolerance settings for **P2** and six for **P3** under two perturbation radii ($\varepsilon \in \{5/255, 10/255\}$). For each configuration 100 held-out test samples were verified, yielding 1,200 instances for **P2** and 1,200 instances for **P3**. (See Table 3).

**Table 3.** Design space of experiments.

| Factor | Levels |
|---|---|
| Model capacity | 39, 116, 520, 924 parameters (CNNs; Sect 3.3). |
| Training regime | Vanilla; adversarial (PGD-15/255, PGD-25/255). |
| Safety property | **P1**, **P2**, **P3** (Sect. 3.4). |
| Perturbation radius | $\ell_\infty$ bounds $\varepsilon \in \{5, 10, 20\}/255$. |
| Relative thresholds | $\delta_{\text{conf}} \in \{0.95, 0.9, 0.8, 0.7, 0.6, 0.5\}$, $\delta_{\text{stab}} = 1 - \delta_{\text{conf}}$. |
| Verifier | $\alpha, \beta$-CROWN, Marabou, NeuralSAT. |

### 4.2 Model Accuracy

Table 4 reports accuracy on a 201-sample test set (67 samples per class), comparing clean evaluation with the same set subjected to PGD attacks at $\varepsilon = 10/255$ (PGD-10) and $\varepsilon = 20/255$ (PGD-20).

Vanilla models achieve the highest clean accuracy (up to 97.5% for Model 520) but drop to 32–42% under attack, especially at $\varepsilon = 20/255$ where accuracy falls below 40%. Adversarial training markedly improves robustness

[1] https://www.vnnlib.org/.

while incurring only a modest reduction in clean accuracy. With PGD-15/255 training, PGD-10 accuracy stabilizes around 85–88% across all models, and PGD-20 rises to 49–64%. PGD-25/255 training sometimes reduces PGD-10 accuracy slightly (e.g., Model 520: 88.4% → 86.9%), but brings clear gains at PGD-20 (e.g., Model 116: 64.1% → 71.6%; Model 924: 49.6% → 59.9%).

Model capacity correlates with clean accuracy but not with robustness: despite its size, Model 924 remains less resilient than mid-sized Model 116 at $\varepsilon = 20/255$. Overall, the training perturbation radius has greater impact on adversarial robustness than model size: PGD-15/255 training best defends against $\varepsilon = 10/255$ attacks, while PGD-25/255 is more effective against stronger $\varepsilon = 20/255$ attacks.

**Table 4.** Clean accuracy and robustness. PGD-10 and PGD-20 denote attacks with $\varepsilon = 10/255$ and $\varepsilon = 20/255$ respectively, 7 steps, and 20 random restarts.

| Model | Training | Clean | PGD-10 | PGD-20 | Model | Training | Clean | PGD-10 | PGD-20 |
|---|---|---|---|---|---|---|---|---|---|
| | Vanilla | 91.0 | 41.0 | 37.0 | | Vanilla | 97.5 | 36.4 | 32.8 |
| M39 | PGD-15/255 | 91.0 | 85.6 | 63.7 | M520 | PGD-15/255 | 96.0 | 88.4 | 59.6 |
| | PGD-25/255 | 89.0 | 84.0 | 63.2 | | PGD-25/255 | 93.0 | 86.9 | 60.6 |
| | Vanilla | 92.5 | 5.9 | 1.4 | | Vanilla | 97.0 | 39.5 | 29.6 |
| M116 | PGD-15/255 | 90.0 | 85.8 | 64.1 | M924 | PGD-15/255 | 96.0 | 87.9 | 49.6 |
| | PGD-25/255 | 90.0 | 85.1 | 71.6 | | PGD-25/255 | 94.0 | 85.5 | 59.9 |

### 4.3 Verification Results

Table 5 summarizes the proportion of formally SAFE instances for properties **P1**–**P3** across all model sizes (M39–M924), three training regimes (vanilla, PGD-15/255, PGD-25/255), and perturbation radii up to $\varepsilon = 20/255$. Clear trends emerge. First, adversarial training markedly improves verifiability: for **P1** at $\varepsilon = 10/255$, vanilla models achieve 1–23% verified safety, while PGD-trained models reach 52–86%. At $\varepsilon = 5/255$, PGD training consistently pushes **P1** above 98% across all sizes. In contrast, scale-invariant properties P2 and P3 remain substantially harder to prove, because they impose magnitude constraints on logits, not just argmax preservation: even under PGD-25/255, verified safety rarely exceeds 43% for **P2** and 33% for **P3**, and collapses to 0% by $\varepsilon = 20/255$.

As illustrated in Fig. 2, model size exerts weaker influence. The smallest controller (M39) achieves relatively high verifiability under adversarial training, but larger models (M520, M924) do not systematically outperform it. This indicates that training regime and property strictness dominate over raw capacity.

To probe this further, Fig. 3 presents a sensitivity analysis on model M116 (PGD-25/255). Relaxing tolerance thresholds yields substantial gains. For **P2** (Fig. 3(left)), SAFE counts at $\varepsilon = 5/255$ rise from only 2 instances at $\delta_{\text{conf}} = 0.95$

to 95 instances at $\delta_{\text{conf}} = 0.50$. Similarly, for **P3** (Fig. 3(right)), increasing $\delta_{\text{stab}}$ from 0.05 to 0.50 raises SAFE counts from 0 to 33. At $\varepsilon = 10/255$, however, both properties remain effectively unverifiable under strict or relaxed tolerances.

These results have direct implications for deployment: (i) adversarial training is necessary—vanilla models cannot yield meaningful guarantees; (ii) **P1** provides tractable certification that steering decisions remain stable under bounded sensor noise, while **P2**/**P3** certify quantitative output stability; (iii) tolerance parameters ($\delta_{\text{conf}}$, $\delta_{\text{stab}}$) should be selected based on acceptable control-signal variation, as they decisively determine verification feasibility.

**Table 5.** SAFE rate (%) for properties **P1**–**P3** at perturbation sizes $\varepsilon \in \{5, 10, 20\}/255$, and thresholds $\delta_{\text{conf}} = 0.85$ and $\delta_{\text{stab}} = 0.15$.

| Model | Training | P1 | | | P2 | | | P3 | | |
|---|---|---|---|---|---|---|---|---|---|---|
| | | 5/255 | 10/255 | 20/255 | 5/255 | 10/255 | 20/255 | 5/255 | 10/255 | 20/255 |
| M39 | Vanilla | 55.0 | 23.0 | 0.0 | 21.0 | 8.0 | 0.0 | 17.0 | 4.0 | 0.0 |
| | PGD-15/255 | 98.0 | 54.0 | 2.0 | 37.0 | 16.0 | 2.0 | 28.0 | 11.0 | 0.0 |
| | PGD-25/255 | 98.0 | 71.0 | 4.0 | 32.0 | 11.0 | 0.0 | 24.0 | 2.0 | 0.0 |
| M116 | Vanilla | 35.0 | 6.0 | 0.0 | 0.0 | 0.0 | 0.0 | 0.0 | 0.0 | 0.0 |
| | PGD-15/255 | 99.0 | 52.0 | 8.0 | 16.0 | 0.0 | 0.0 | 1.0 | 0.0 | 0.0 |
| | PGD-25/255 | 100.0 | 58.0 | 6.0 | 25.0 | 0.0 | 0.0 | 1.0 | 0.0 | 0.0 |
| M520 | Vanilla | 35.0 | 3.0 | 0.0 | 0.0 | 0.0 | 0.0 | 0.0 | 0.0 | 0.0 |
| | PGD-15/255 | 99.0 | 56.0 | 3.0 | 34.0 | 0.0 | 0.0 | 0.0 | 0.0 | 0.0 |
| | PGD-25/255 | 100.0 | 86.0 | 4.0 | 66.0 | 11.0 | 0.0 | 33.0 | 11.0 | 0.0 |
| M924 | Vanilla | 38.0 | 1.0 | 0.0 | 0.0 | 0.0 | 0.0 | 0.0 | 0.0 | 0.0 |
| | PGD-15/255 | 99.0 | 56.0 | 5.0 | 34.0 | 0.0 | 0.0 | 3.0 | 0.0 | 0.0 |
| | PGD-25/255 | 100.0 | 58.0 | 5.0 | 43.0 | 0.0 | 0.0 | 12.0 | 0.0 | 0.0 |

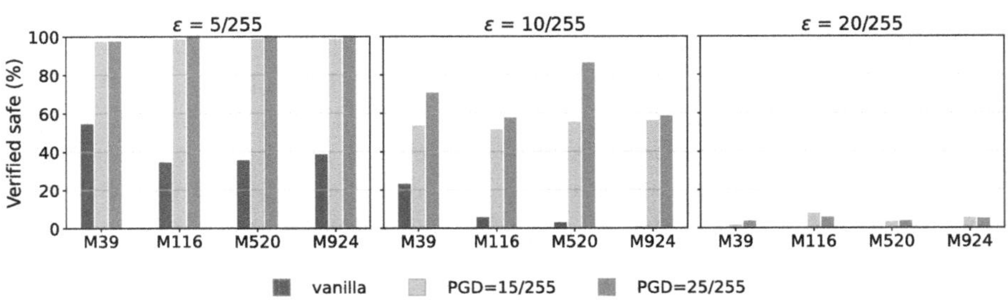


**Fig. 2.** Verified-safe rates for property **P1** across models and training regimes. Adversarial training, rather than model size, is the dominant factor enabling robustness guarantees.

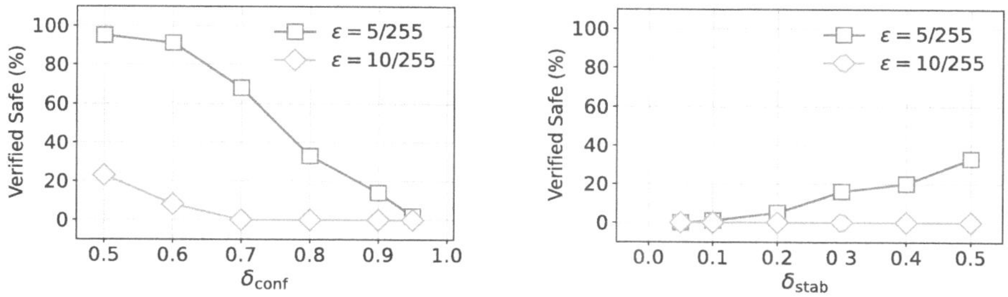


**Fig. 3.** Verification results for **P2** (left) and **P3** (right) on model M116 with PGD-25/255 training. Curves show the fraction of samples formally certified as safe under varying thresholds $\delta_{\text{conf}}$ and $\delta_{\text{stab}}$ for perturbation radii $\varepsilon \in \{5/255, 10/255\}$. Relaxing thresholds markedly increases verifiability at $\varepsilon = 5/255$, while properties remain largely unverifiable at $\varepsilon = 10/255$. This highlights the decisive role of tolerance calibration in scale-invariant robustness.

### 4.4 Verifier Performance

Table 6 summarizes verifier outcomes over 2,700 queries per model (M39–M924), aggregated across properties, training regimes, and perturbation radii. The results reveal clear trade-offs between tools. *Marabou* provides the most decisive results, with essentially no unresolved cases (Unk $\leq$ 2%) across all model sizes, but its runtime scales sharply with network capacity, increasing from 134 s for M39 to over 2,200 s for M924. *$\alpha, \beta$-CROWN* achieves moderate runtimes (343–687 s) and scales more gently with model size, but leaves between 9% and 21% of queries unresolved, with the highest rate on M924. *NeuralSAT* attains comparable conclusiveness on smaller networks (Unk $\approx$ 8–16%) but suffers from prohibitive runtimes as size grows, rising from around 700 s on M39/M116 to over 14,000 s on M924. Overall, Marabou yields the most complete results at the expense of high computation time, $\alpha, \beta$-CROWN offers a balanced but inconclusive alternative, and NeuralSAT does not scale effectively to larger models.

**Table 6.** Verifier performance across model sizes. Unk denotes percentage of inconclusive (timeout/unknown) results.

| Verifier | M39 | | M116 | | M520 | | M924 | |
|---|---|---|---|---|---|---|---|---|
| | Unk (%) | Time (s) | Unk (%) | Time (s) | Unk (%) | Time (s) | Unk (%) | Time (s) |
| $\alpha, \beta$-CROWN | 20.0 | 343.0 | 14.0 | 472.8 | 9.1 | 439.1 | 20.7 | 686.8 |
| Marabou | 0.0 | 133.8 | 0.0 | 165.5 | 0.3 | 597.0 | 1.9 | 2248.4 |
| NeuralSAT | 16.1 | 709.2 | 11.7 | 721.7 | 8.1 | 7047.6 | 16.5 | 14106.8 |

## 5 Conclusion and Future Work

We presented an end-to-end pipeline for training, evaluating, and formally verifying compact neural steering controllers in a simulated autonomous driving environment. Our results reveal three key findings. First, adversarial training is essential: vanilla models consistently fail to yield non-trivial robustness guarantees, while PGD-trained variants achieve up to 86% verified safety for label consistency at moderate perturbation budgets. Second, specification design critically shapes verification outcomes: property **P1** (classification robustness) proves substantially more tractable than scale-invariant properties **P2** and **P3**, which remain difficult to verify under strict tolerance settings. Third, model size exerts limited influence relative to training regime and property thresholds, underscoring that robustness must be deliberately engineered rather than expected as a byproduct of capacity. Sensitivity analyses further show that tolerance calibration governs the feasibility of scale-invariant guarantees. These findings are scoped to compact networks (39–924 parameters) with discrete steering in simulation; the methodology generalizes, but direct deployment requires validation of the sim-to-real gap and solver scalability to larger architectures.

Looking ahead, our findings suggest several directions for advancing verifiable learning in autonomous driving. One avenue is the integration of property-specific constraints [26] directly into the training objective, enabling networks to internalize verifiable robustness rather than relying on post hoc guarantees. Another is improving scalability: extending verification to larger models, richer architectures, and continuous control spaces where current solvers face frequent timeouts. Expanding beyond vision-only control to multimodal settings, such as LiDAR or sensor fusion, represents a further challenge that would increase realism but also compound verification complexity. Finally, embedding verification within iterative development workflows, where specification design, adversarial training, and solver feedback inform one another, offers a promising path toward safety-critical deployment. Our open-source pipeline provides a foundation for these efforts, ensuring that future research at the intersection of learning and formal methods remains both reproducible and practically grounded.

**Acknowledgments.** This work is supported by Research Ireland under Grant number 20/FFP-P/8853 and by the ADAPT Centre under grant 13/RC/2106_P2.

## References

1. Liu, C., Arnon, T., Lazarus, C., Strong, C., Barrett, C., Kochenderfer, M.J.: Algorithms for verifying deep neural networks. Foundations and Trends® in Optimization **4**(3–4), 244–404 (2021)
2. König, M., Bosman, A.W., Hoos, H.H., van Rijn, J.N.: Critically assessing the state of the art in neural network verification. J. Mach. Learn. Res. **25**(12), 1–53 (2024)
3. Carlini, N., et al.: On evaluating the robustness of neural networks. In: 2019 IEEE Symposium on Security and Privacy (SP), pp. 1011–1027. IEEE (2019)

4. Wang, S., et al.: Beta-CROWN: efficient bound propagation with per-neuron split constraints for complete and incomplete neural network verification. Adv. Neural Inform. Process. Syst. **34** (2021)
5. Duong, H., Nguyen, T., Dwyer, M.B.: NeuralSAT: a high-performance verification tool for deep neural networks. In: Piskac, R., Rakamarić, Z. (eds.) Computer Aided Verification. CAV 2025. LNCS, vol. 15932. Springer, Cham (2025). https://doi.org/10.1007/978-3-031-98679-6_19
6. Brix, C., Bak, S., Liu, C., Johnson, T.T.: The fourth international verification of neural networks competition (vnn-comp 2023): Summary and results, arXiv preprint arXiv:2312.16760 (2023)
7. Brix, C., Bak, S., Johnson, T.T., Wu, H.: The fifth international verification of neural networks competition (vnn-comp 2024): Summary and results. arXiv preprint arXiv:2412.19985 (2024)
8. Alberti, M., Bobot, F., Girard-Satabin, J., Grastien, A., Varasse, A.: The CAISAR Platform: Extending the Reach of Machine Learning Specification and Verification, arXiv:2506.12084 (2025)
9. Daggitt, M.L., Kokke, W., Atkey, R., Komendantskaya, E., Slusarz, N., Arnaboldi, L.: Vehicle: bridging the embedding gap in the verification of neuro-symbolic programs. In: Fernández, M. (ed.) 10th International Conference on Formal Structures for Computation and Deduction (FSCD 2025), vol. 337 of Leibniz International Proceedings in Informatics (LIPIcs), Dagstuhl, Germany, pp. 2:1–2:20. Schloss Dagstuhl – Leibniz-Zentrum für Informatik (2025). ISBN 978-3-95977-374-4. https://doi.org/10.4230/LIPIcs.FSCD.2025.2
10. Bojarski, M., et al.: End to end learning for self-driving cars. In NIPS Deep Learning for Action and Interaction Workshop (2016)
11. Tran, H.-D., Bak, S., Xiang, W., Johnson, T.T.: Verification of deep convolutional neural networks using imagestars. In: Lahiri, S.K., Wang, C. (eds.) CAV 2020. LNCS, vol. 12224, pp. 18–42. Springer, Cham (2020). https://doi.org/10.1007/978-3-030-53288-8_2
12. Dreossi, T., Donze, A., Seshia, S.A.: Verifai: a toolkit for the formal design and analysis of artificial intelligence-based systems. In: International Conference on Computer Aided Verification, pp. 432–442. Springer (2019)
13. Zhang, H., Weng, T.-W., Chen, P.-Y., Hsieh, C.-J., Daniel, L.: Efficient neural network robustness certification with general activation functions. Adv. Neural. Inf. Process. Syst. **31**, 4939–4948 (2018)
14. Kaidi Xu, K., et al.: Fast and complete: enabling complete neural network verification with rapid and massively parallel incomplete verifiers. In: International Conference on Learning Representations (2021)
15. Katz, G., et al.: The marabou framework for verification and analysis of deep neural networks. In: Dillig, I., Tasiran, S. (eds.) Computer Aided Verification, pp. 443–452, Springer International, Cham, (2019). https://doi.org/10.1007/978-3-030-25540-4_26
16. Wu, H., et al.: Marabou 2.0: a versatile formal analyzer of neural networks. In: Gurfinkel, A., Ganesh, V. (eds.) Computer Aided Verification, pp. 249–264. Springer Nature Switzerland, Cham (2024). https://doi.org/10.48550/arXiv.2401.14461
17. Ivanov, R., Weimer, J., Alur, R., Pappas, G.J., Lee, I.: A case study in assessing the scalability of neural network verification for autonomous systems. In: Proceedings of the 3rd International Workshop on Verification of Neural Networks (VNN) (2020)

18. Dutta, S., Chen, X., Sankaranarayanan, S.: Reachability analysis for neural feedback systems using regressive polynomial rule inference. In: Proceedings of the 22nd ACM International Conference on Hybrid Systems: Computation and Control, pp. 157–168 (2019)
19. Sun, X., Khedr, H., Shoukry, Y.: Formal verification of neural network controlled autonomous systems. In: Proceedings of the 22nd ACM International Conference on Hybrid Systems: Computation and Control, pp. 147–156 (2019)
20. Huang, C., Fan, J., Li, W., Chen, X., Zhu, Q.: Reachnn: reachability analysis of neural-network controlled systems. ACM Trans. Embedded Comput. Syst. (TECS) **18**(5s), 1–22 (2019)
21. Habeeb, O., El-Sayed, A., El-Nahas, A., Shoukry, Y.: Verification of camera-based autonomous systems: A case study on autonomous emergency braking. In: 2023 IEEE International Conference on Robotics and Automation (ICRA), pp. 7350–7356. IEEE (2023)
22. Bukhari, S.A.A., Flinkow, T., Inkarbekov, M., Pearlmutter, B.A., Monahan, R.: Creating a formally verified neural network for autonomous navigation: an Experience Report. In: Electronic Proceedings in Theoretical Computer Science, vol. 411, pp. 178–190 (November 2024). ISSN 2075-2180, https://doi.org/10.4204/EPTCS.411.12
23. Casadio, M. et al.: Neural network robustness as a verification property: a principled case study. In: Shoham, S., Vizel, Y. (eds.) CAV 2022. LNCS, vol. 13371. Springer, Cham (2022). https://doi.org/10.1007/978-3-031-13185-1_11
24. Unity Technologies. Unity game engine (2022). https://unity.com/. Version 2022.3.40f1
25. Unity Technologies. Barracuda inference engine (2025). https://docs.unity3d.com/Packages/com.unity.barracuda@latest
26. Flinkow, T., Pearlmutter, B.A., Monahan, R.: Comparing differentiable logics for learning with logical constraints. Sci. Comput. Program. **244**, 103280 (2025). https://doi.org/10.1016/j.scico.2025.103280, ISSN 0167-6423

# In Machina N400: Pinpointing Where a Causal Language Model Detects Semantic Violations

Christos-Nikolaos Zacharopoulos[1(✉)] and Revekka Kyriakoglou[2]

[1] Paris, France
christonik@gmail.com
[2] Université Paris 8 Vincennes - Saint-Denis, Paris, France
revekka.kyriakoglou@univ-paris8.fr

**Abstract.** How and where does a transformer notice that a sentence has gone semantically off the rails? To explore this question, we evaluated the causal language model $\phi$-2 (phi-2) using a carefully curated corpus, with sentences that concluded plausibly or implausibly. Our analysis focused on the hidden states sampled at each model layer. To investigate how violations are encoded, we utilized two complementary probes. First, we conducted a per-layer detection using a linear probe. Our findings revealed that a simple linear decoder struggled to distinguish between plausible and implausible endings in the lowest third of the model's layers. However, its accuracy sharply increased in the middle blocks, reaching a peak just before the top layers. Second, we examined the effective dimensionality of the encoded violation. Initially, the violation widens the representational subspace, followed by a collapse after a mid-stack bottleneck. This might indicate an exploratory phase that transitions into rapid consolidation. Taken together, these results contemplate the idea of alignment with classical psycholinguistic findings in human reading, where semantic anomalies are detected only after syntactic resolution, occurring later in the online processing sequence.

**Keywords:** Neural language models · Semantic processing · N400 · Transformer interpretability · LLMs

## 1 Introduction

Why does a single anomalous word, a "dog" floating in a coffee cup, immediately jolts the mind? From the moment a sentence unfolds, the cerebral cortex generates a cascade of probabilistic hypotheses, continuously comparing incoming input with an ever-updating internal model of the linguistic and conceptual world. This view, rooted in Bayesian and predictive-coding theories of perception and action [7], has been powerfully confirmed in the language domain by

C.-N. Zacharopoulos—Independent Researcher


T. T. Mai et al. (Eds.): AICS 2025, CCIS 2950, pp. 179–189, 2026.
https://doi.org/10.1007/978-3-032-25809-0_14

four decades of electrophysiology: semantic violations reliably summon a negative deflection around 400 ms, the celebrated N400, indexing the brain's rapid computation of a "prediction error" when reality collides with prior expectation [15,16].

Yet an essential question remains: *what internal code carries these predictions?* With the advent of transformer-based Neural Language Models (NLMs) [21], a unique methodological opportunity has emerged. These models are the first engineered systems to generate open-ended, human-like text with sufficient fluency to let us inspect their hidden representations as a window onto putative computations in the biological brain. A growing corpus of work shows striking isomorphisms between activity patterns in deep language models and those measured with fMRI, MEG, and intracranial recordings along the human perisylvian network [3,4,9,14]. In effect, NLMs constitute an *in-machina* laboratory where hypotheses about cortical algorithms, predictive coding, and hierarchical abstraction can be spelled out, manipulated, and tested at a level of mechanistic detail rarely attainable *in-vivo*. At the same time, caution is warranted. Fluency alone does not imply shared computation: current NLMs lack grounded semantics, sensorimotor constraints, and developmental trajectories that shape the human language faculty.

Prior computational works have mainly relied on coarse behavioral proxies such as next-word probability or surprisal calculations. These measures, while helpful, flatten the rich temporal dynamics revealed as the input token's vector is successively transformed into new representations across later layers. To move beyond this impasse, we adopt a neuro-computational strategy: we interrogate the internal activity of a modern transformer (Phi-2; [10]) with stimuli precisely designed to illuminate the N400 in humans. Specifically, we create sentence pairs of equal length that terminate in either a semantically plausible or an impossible final word (e.g., "He drinks coffee with cream and *dog*").[1] This paradigm allows us to track, layer by layer, how prediction error propagates through the model's attention heads and feed-forward sublayers.

To that end, we capture the hidden state at each successive layer, normalize the ensuing vectors, and ask a simple question: can a linear decoder read out "anomaly or not" above chance? We then chart this signal's emergence layer by layer and validate its robustness with cluster-based permutation statistics. A complementary analysis of participation ratio allows us to disentangle dimensionality expansion from pure prediction error. In short, we treat the transformer as a transparent, time-unfolding cortex and probe its state at every computational slice.

*This work addresses a precise question: At which computational depth does a transformer first register a semantic anomaly, and does this temporal pattern align with the timing of the human N400 response?* If semantic anomaly detection emerges only in mid-to-late layers of the network, this would parallel influential models of human sentence processing in which semantic integration occurs after initial structural analysis [6,13]. Such a correspondence would sug-

[1] For a selection of stimuli used in the experiment, please see Appendix 4.3.

gest that both artificial and biological language systems postpone full semantic evaluation until sufficient syntactic constraints have been established. We investigate whether a homologous time course unfolds, not across milliseconds, but across the successive algorithmic steps of a language model. Figure 1 provides a conceptual overview of our approach.

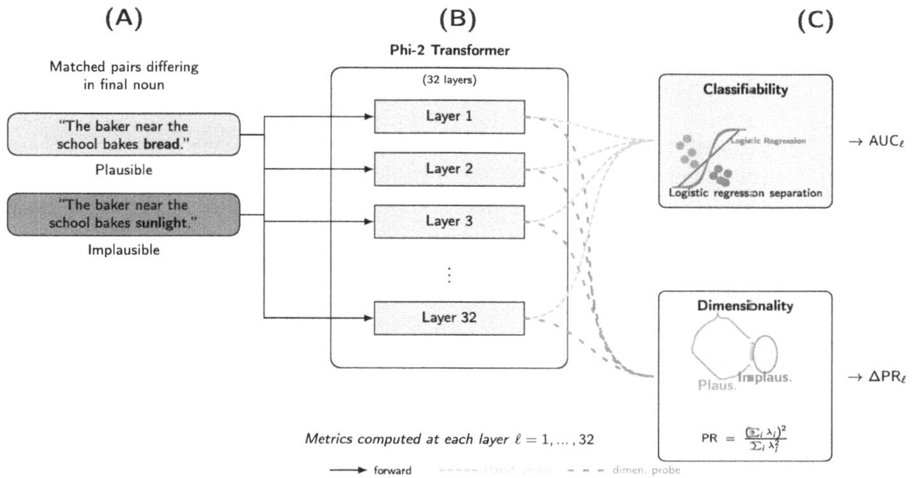


**Fig. 1. Overview of the analysis pipeline.** **(A)** Stimuli consist of 1520 matched sentence pairs (760 plausible, 760 implausible), each differing only in the final noun while preserving a fixed syntactic template. **(B)** Each sentence is processed once through all 32 layers of the Phi-2 transformer. For every layer $l$, the hidden-state matrix $H^{(l)}(x) \in \mathbb{R}^{T_x \times d}$ is extracted and reshaped into a vector $h^{(l)}(x) = \text{vec}(H^{(l)}(x))$. Activations are normalized within each layer across sentences prior to feature computation. **(C)** Two complementary layer-wise metrics are computed. (i) A logistic-regression decoder trained on the mean activation $\mu^{(l)}(x)$ yields a decoding score $\text{AUC}_l$, quantifying how well layer $l$ separates plausible from implausible sentences. (ii) The representational dimensionality of each layer is estimated using the participation ratio $\text{PR}_l$, derived from the eigenvalues of the covariance matrix of $h^{(l)}(x)$ across sentences. Together, these analyses characterize how semantic-violation information becomes linearly decodable and how the effective dimensionality of the model's internal representations evolves across layers.

## 2 Methods

*Activation Extraction and Stimuli.* Sentences from a rigorously controlled stimulus set were processed using the transformer-based causal language model *Phi-2* (2.7B parameters), trained for next-token prediction [10]. a causal (autoregressive) architecture because its attention mask enforces a left-to-right information flow, ensuring that each token is predicted based only on preceding context, enabling a comparison with the temporal dynamics of human reading that unfolds over time. The model size was chosen to balance computational tractability with sufficient representational capacity for semantic processing, while remaining accessible for detailed layer-wise analysis. Phi-2 was used in evaluation mode with deterministic forward passes (no gradient computation, temperature=1.0, no sampling) to ensure reproducible activations across all analyses.

Each sentence followed the fixed template

"The [subject] [location] [verb] [object]."

such that the grammatical structure, length, and word order were identical across the entire stimulus set. All sentences were matched at the word level (identical number of words per sentence), ensuring structural uniformity. The semantic anomaly was always positioned in the final word. Subword tokenization introduced minor variation in token counts (typically ±1–2 tokens per sentence), but this variation was negligible and did not introduce confounding effects related to sequence truncation or padding, as all sentences remained well within the model's context window.

The stimulus set was generated from a structured lexicon that mapped human professions to verbs, expected objects, and corresponding violation objects. For example, the lexicon defined "baker" with the verb "bakes," an expected object "bread," and a violation object "sunlight," permitting matched pairs such as *"The baker near the school bakes bread."* versus *"The baker near the school bakes sunlight."*. The full dataset comprised 1520 sentences, exactly half containing a semantic violation.

*Feature Extraction and Selection.* Each sentence $x$ was tokenised with $\phi_2$'s native tokenizer and passed once through the network. For each transformer layer $l \in \{1, \ldots, 32\}$, the model produced a hidden-state matrix

$$H^{(l)}(x) \in \mathbb{R}^{T_x \times d},$$

where $T_x$ is the (tokenised) sequence length and $d$ the model dimension. We reshaped $H^{(l)}(x)$ into a single vector,

$$h^{(l)}(x) = \text{vec}\Big(H^{(l)}(x)\Big) \in \mathbb{R}^{T_x d},$$

via row-major concatenation of token embeddings.

From $h^{(l)}(x)$ we computed five distributional moments—the mean, median, variance, skewness, and kurtosis—yielding a 5-dimensional descriptor

$$m^{(l)}(x) = \big[\mu^{(l)}(x), \text{med}^{(l)}(x), \text{var}^{(l)}(x), \text{skew}^{(l)}(x), \text{kurt}^{(l)}(x)\big].$$

To determine whether higher-order moments contributed additional predictive signal beyond the mean, we trained $\ell_2$-regularised logistic-regression decoders on (i) the mean alone and (ii) every non-empty subset of the five statistics, using stratified $k$-fold cross-validation. No subset achieved statistically reliable improvements over the mean-only probe. Supplementing the mean with higher-order moments neither improved generalisation nor stabilised the probe weights, and substantially increased the spectral condition number of the design matrix. These results established the mean activation as both *sufficient* and *stable* for decoding, motivating its exclusive use in downstream analyses.

*Normalization and Data Aggregation.* Before feature computation, each layer's activations were normalised separately across sentences. For every layer $l$, we applied robust centering and scaling:

$$\tilde{h}^{(l)}(x) = \frac{h^{(l)}(x) - \text{median}(h^{(l)})}{\text{IQR}(h^{(l)})},$$

where the median and interquartile range (IQR) were computed across the entire sentence set. This procedure mitigated the influence of lexical outliers and reduced sensitivity to morphological variability.

*Layer-wise Decoding Analysis.* Following standard neural decoding methodology [12], we trained an $\ell_2$-regularised logistic regression classifier for each layer $l$, using only the mean activation $\mu^{(l)}(x)$ as the predictive feature. For each layer, the classifier learned parameters $(w^{(l)}, b^{(l)})$ by minimising

$$\mathcal{L}(w,b) = -\sum_{x}\Big[y(x)\log\sigma(w\mu^{(l)}(x) + b) + (1 - y(x))\log\big(1 - \sigma(w\mu^{(l)}(x) + b)\big)\Big] + \lambda\|w\|_2^2,$$

with $\lambda = 1$. Performance was evaluated using the ROC-AUC averaged across the five cross-validation folds, yielding a layer-specific decoding score $\text{AUC}_l$.

*Cluster-Based Permutation Testing.* To assess whether decoding performance at each layer exceeded chance while controlling the family-wise error rate, we applied a one-dimensional cluster-based permutation test following [17]. For each layer $l$, we computed a one-sample $t$-statistic comparing fold-level decoding scores to the chance level of 0.5,

$$t_l = t(\text{AUC}_l - 0.5),$$

with $df = 4$. Layers with $|t_l| > 2.78$ (two-tailed $p < 0.05$) formed supra-threshold clusters along the layer dimension. The cluster statistic was the sum of $t_l$ within each cluster.

A null distribution was generated using 1000 sign-flip permutations across layers. For each permutation, we recomputed the cluster statistics and recorded the maximum absolute cluster value. Observed clusters were assigned corrected $p$-values equal to the proportion of permutation maxima exceeding their statistic. Clusters with corrected $p < 0.01$ were deemed significant.

*Participation Ratio Computation.* To quantify the effective dimensionality of activations at each layer, we computed the participation ratio (PR), a measure commonly used in theoretical and systems neuroscience [5,8]. For each layer $l$, we formed the covariance matrix

$$\Sigma^{(l)} = \mathrm{Cov}\Big(h^{(l)}(x)\Big)$$

across sentences. Let $\lambda_1^{(l)}, \ldots, \lambda_n^{(l)}$ denote its eigenvalues. The participation ratio is

$$\mathrm{PR}_l = \frac{\left(\sum_{i=1}^{n} \lambda_i^{(l)}\right)^2}{\sum_{i=1}^{n} (\lambda_i^{(l)})^2},$$

providing a scalar estimate of the layer's representational dimensionality.

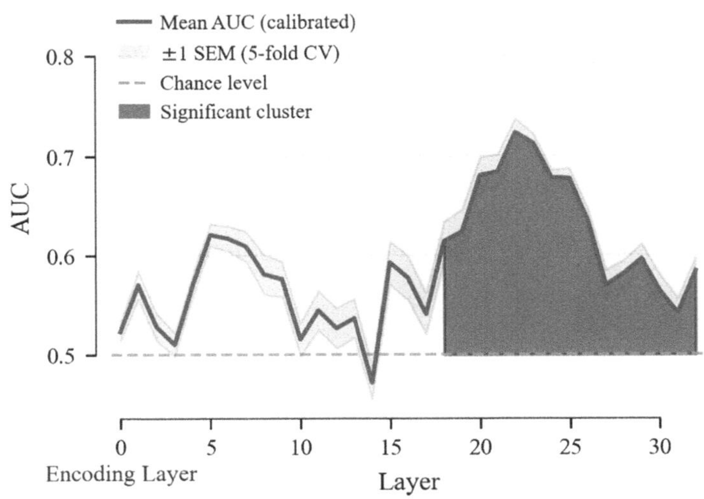


**Fig. 2. Layer-wise decoding of semantic anomalies in *Phi-2*.** Mean ROC–AUC (blue; ±1 SEM shaded) for a logistic classifier that distinguishes plausible from violation endings at each encoding layer. The red dashed line shows chance performance (0.5). The grey shading marks the only cluster of consecutive layers (18–30) whose AUC reliably exceeded chance after cluster-based permutation correction ($p < 0.001$). (Color figure online)

# 3 Results

## 3.1 Decoding Accuracy Across Layers

Figure 2 shows the mean ROC–AUC obtained by layer-wise logistic classifiers. A cluster-based permutation test identified one contiguous cluster (layers 18–30) whose AUC values exceeded the chance level of 0.5 ($cluster\ p < 0.01$). Within this cluster, peak decoding occurred at layer 22 (mean $AUC = 0.723$, $SEM = 0.014$).

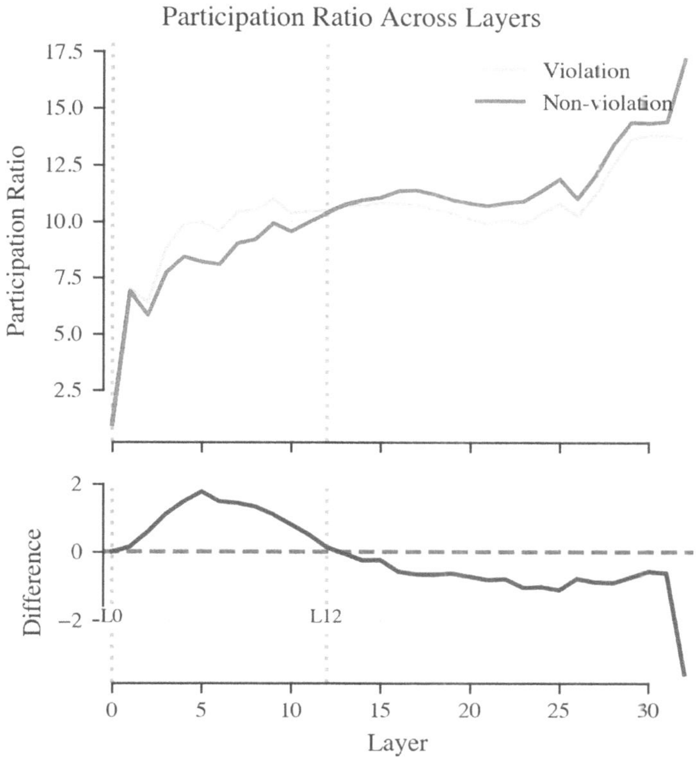


**Fig. 3. Effective dimensionality of hidden states.** *Top:* Participation ratio (PR) for violation (red) and control (green) sentences across the 32 encoding layers of *Phi-2*. *Bottom:* Difference trace (violation – control) relative to the zero baseline (grey dashed line). Violations initially occupy a higher-dimensional subspace (layers 1–6), converge with controls around the mid-stack bottleneck (layer 12, grey vertical tick), and become marginally more compressed in deeper layers. These dynamics suggest an early expansion of representational space to accommodate unexpected input, followed by a gradual re-integration as contextual constraints accumulate. (Color figure online)

### 3.2 Participation Ratio of Hidden Activations

Participation ratios (PR) for violation and control conditions are plotted in Fig. 3. Across the lower stack (layers 1–6), the violation PR exceeded the control PR (maximum difference = 1.9 dimensions at layer 5). The two curves converged at layer 12. The mean PR difference after the inflection point remained negative.

## 4 Discussion

### 4.1 A Late, Layer-Bound Marker of Semantic Error

Our layer-wise decoding shows that *Phi-2* registers a semantic anomaly with discriminability peaking in a narrow band around layers 22–24. Translating depth into real time is necessarily indirect, yet a negative result is already informative: *the signal is absent from the first layers*. In other words, semantic error detection emerges only after the network has traversed a substantial portion of its hierarchy, rather than in the shallow stages that would more closely resemble early EEG components such as the ELAN[2] or LAN.[3] [15,16,19]. This pattern points to the view that both artificial and biological language systems postpone semantic anomaly detection until a sufficiently broad context has been integrated.

### 4.2 Two Phases of Representational Geometry

Participation–ratio (PR) analysis revealed a biphasic trajectory. In the lower stack, semantic violations *increased* the effective dimensionality of hidden states compared with well-formed controls, indicating a transient dispersion of activity across a broader subspace. Around layer ~12, this trend reversed: beyond that point, the PR for anomalous sentences fell below that of canonical sentences, producing a dimensionality cross-over. We interpret the initial expansion as the network distributing activation across additional directions while integrating conflicting cues, and the subsequent contraction as the computation coalescing onto a smaller set of dominant directions once a stable—albeit low-probability—interpretation is reached. Crucially, the late-stage drop in PR does not imply information loss; it instead signals increased *anisotropy*, with variance becoming concentrated along fewer principal axes.

This expansion–contraction profile aligns qualitatively with reanalysis signatures in human neurophysiology, where an early, diffuse response to anomalies is followed by a more focal, sustained pattern (e.g. the N400–P600 sequence) [1,2,11,13,20]. While the mapping from PR to ERP components is indirect, the shared time-course supports the view that both systems first explore a wider representational space before converging on a compact error state.

*Cautious Brain–Model Comparisons and Their Promise.* The overlap between *Phi-2*'s late anomaly signal and the human N400 is suggestive, but shared *latency* does not guarantee shared *mechanisms*. Human comprehension recruits multimodal context, pragmatic inference, and recurrent circuitry that present-day transformers largely lack. Robust tests must therefore pair layer activations with

---

[2] Early Left Anterior Negativity (ELAN): an ERP component in language processing, typically occurring 100–300 ms after stimulus onset, associated with early syntactic processing [6].

[3] Left Anterior Negativity (LAN): an ERP component with a slightly later time course (300–500 ms), also associated with syntactic processing [18].

time-resolved neural data (EEG/MEG/ECoG) on identical stimuli and compare them through representational-similarity or related analyses. Such work can expose which semantic computations truly inhabit a common latent space and which gaps reveal biological inductive biases that could guide richer model design. In turn, a principled bridge between brains and machines would give cognitive neuroscience explicit algorithms while steering machine learning toward systems that reason and, one day, may understand more like us.

### 4.3 Limitations

*Limitations and Future Directions.* The present analysis is deliberately focused and, as a consequence, leaves several open questions that define a clear research agenda. *Model scope.* All results were obtained with a single 2.7-B-parameter causal transformer (*Phi-2*). Because depth, scale, and training objective influence internal dynamics, the late-emerging anomaly signal and the biphasic expansion–compression pattern should be replicated in both larger autoregressive LMs and bidirectional encoders before being treated as architecture-general principles. Future work should systematically explore how these patterns vary across models with different depths (both deeper networks with more layers and shallower networks with fewer layers) to determine whether the mid-to-late layer emergence of semantic anomaly detection is a general property of transformer architectures or specific to certain depth ranges. *Stimulus design.* We used tightly matched sentences in which the violation always appeared on the final token. This maximises control but also creates a positional regularity that the network could exploit. Future work should randomise violation position, introduce graded expectancy manipulations, and explore multi-word incongruities to verify position- and context-invariance.

*Geometry Metrics.* We characterised representational geometry via participation ratio only; complementary measures (e.g. intrinsic dimensionality, manifold capacity, centre-of-mass drift) may uncover additional structure, especially during the early expansion phase. *Statistical robustness.* Significance was assessed with five-fold cross-validation and cluster-based permutation tests; larger held-out corpora and replication on an external stimulus set would guard against fold-wise lexical leakage and confirm generality. *Probe methodology* We employed linear logistic regression as our primary decoding method; alternative approaches such as non-linear classifiers, clustering analysis, or representational similarity analysis could reveal additional structure in how semantic violations are encoded across layers.

**Acknowledgments.** The author acknowledges using computational resources and open-source software libraries that made this research possible.

**Disclosure of Interests.** The author has no competing interests to declare relevant to this article's content.

# A Examples of Stimuli

(See Table 1)

**Table 1.** Example sentences

| Normal Sentences | Violation Sentences |
|---|---|
| The painters at the market create murals. | The painters at the market create gravity. |
| The farmer near the school harvests vegetables. | The farmer near the school harvests moonlight. |
| The builders by the river construct structures. | The builders by the river construct whispers. |
| The author near the park writes books. | The author near the park writes electricity. |
| The vets near the park treat animals. | The vets near the park treat buildings. |
| The actors near the school sing arias. | The actors near the school sing molecules. |
| The chef at the market cooks meals. | The chef at the market cooks clouds. |
| The doctors at the market cure elders. | The doctors at the market cure unicorns. |
| The builders at the hospital construct structures. | The builders at the hospital construct whispers. |
| The lawyer near the park represents clients. | The lawyer near the park represents mountains. |

# References


1. Bornkessel-Schlesewsky, I., Schlesewsky, M.: An alternative perspective on "semantic p600" effects in language comprehension. Brain Res. Rev. **59**(1), 55–73 (2008). https://doi.org/10.1016/j.brainresrev.2008.05.003
2. Brouwer, H., Stowe, L.A., Hoop, J.C.M.D.: A neurocomputational model of the n400 and the p600 in language processing. Cogn. Sci. **41**(S6), 1318–1352 (2017). https://doi.org/10.1111/cogs.12461
3. Caucheteux, C., Gramfort, A., King, J.R.: Deep language algorithms predict semantic comprehension from brain activity. Sci. Rep. **12**(1), 16327 (2022)
4. Caucheteux, C., King, J.R.: Brains and algorithms partially converge in natural language processing. Commun. Biol. **5**(1), 134 (2022)
5. Desbordes, T., et al.: Dimensionality and ramping: signatures of sentence integration in the dynamics of brains and deep language models. J. Neurosci. **43**(29), 5350–5364 (2023)
6. Friederici, A.D.: Towards a neural basis of auditory sentence processing. Trends Cogn. Sci. **6**(2), 78–84 (2002)
7. Friston, K.: A theory of cortical responses. Philosop. Trans. Royal Soc. B: Biol. Sci. **360**(1456), 815–836 (2005). https://doi.org/10.1098/rstb.2005.1622
8. Gao, P., et al.: A theory of multineuronal dimensionality, dynamics and measurement. BioRxiv p. 214262 (2017)
9. Goldstein, A., et al.: Shared computational principles for language processing in humans and deep language models. Nat. Neurosci. **25**(3), 369–380 (2022)
10. Javaheripi, M., et al.: Phi-2: the surprising power of small language models. Microsoft Res. Blog **1**(3), 3 (2023)
11. Kaan, E., Nicol, T., Hagoort, A.C.H., Neville, H.J.: Processing of syntactic and semantic violations: an event-related brain potential study. J. Cogn. Neurosci. **12**(3), 379–393 (2000). https://doi.org/10.1162/089892900562256

12. King, J.R., Dehaene, S.: Characterizing the dynamics of mental representations: the temporal generalization method. Trends Cogn. Sci. **18**(4), 203–210 (2014)
13. Kuperberg, G.R.: Neural mechanisms of language comprehension: challenges to syntax. Brain Res. **1146**, 23–49 (2007). https://doi.org/10.1016/j.brainres.2006.12.063
14. Kuribayashi, K.: Large language models are human-like internally. arXiv preprint arXiv:2303.XXXX (2023)
15. Kutas, M., Federmeier, K.D.: Thirty years and counting: finding meaning in the N400 component of the event-related brain potential (ERP). Annu. Rev. Psychol. **62**, 621–647 (2011). https://doi.org/10.1146/annurev.psych.093008.131123
16. Kutas, M., Hillyard, S.A.: Reading senseless sentences: brain potentials reflect semantic incongruity. Science **207**(4427), 203–205 (1980). https://doi.org/10.1126/science.7350657
17. Maris, E., Oostenveld, R.: Nonparametric statistical testing of EEG-and MEG-data. J. Neurosci. Methods **164**(1), 177–190 (2007)
18. Molinaro, N., Barber, H.A., Carreiras, M.: Grammatical agreement processing in reading: ERP findings and future directions. Cortex **47**(8), 908–930 (2011)
19. Noureddine, Kuperberg, G.R.: A computational review of the n400 and semantic anomaly detection. J. Cognit. Neurosci. **32**(10), 1858–1873 (2020). preprint, later published under peer review
20. Osterhout, L., Holcomb, P.J., Swinney, D.A.: Brain potentials elicited by garden-path sentences: evidence of the application of verb information during parsing. J. Exp. Psychol. Learn. Mem. Cogn. **20**(4), 786–803 (1994). https://doi.org/10.1037/0278-7393.20.4.786
21. Vaswani, A., et al.: Attention is all you need. In: Advances in Neural Information Processing Systems, vol. 30 (2017). https://papers.nips.cc/paper_files/paper/2017/hash/3f5ee243547dee91fbd053c1c4a845aa-Abstract.html

# TrailSurfNET: Automated Hiking Trail Surface Classification Using CNNs and OpenStreetMap Annotations

Mark Finlay[1(✉)] and Faithful Chiagoziem Onwuegbuche[1,2]

[1] National College of Ireland, Dublin, Ireland
finlay.mark@gmail.com, faithful.chiagoziemonwuegb@ucdconnect.ie
[2] University College Dublin, Dublin, Ireland

**Abstract.** Reliable trail surface information is important for safe navigation and accessibility, yet OpenStreetMap (OSM) coverage is often incomplete or inconsistent. This paper introduces *TrailSurfNET*, a framework that combines Sentinel-2 satellite imagery with OSM annotations to classify hiking trail surfaces. We develop a data pipeline that harmonizes noisy OSM `surface` tags into five classes (asphalt, paved, gravel, mud/dirt, grass) and generates a balanced dataset across the UK and Ireland. Several Convolutional Neural Networks (CNNs) are benchmarked, including VGG and ResNet variants trained from scratch and with BigEarthNet pre-training. Deeper ResNet models trained from scratch perform best. TrailSurfNET provides a first large-scale, reproducible benchmark for trail surface classification in Ireland and the UK and demonstrates the potential of deep learning to enhance OSM with scalable surface classifications.

**Keywords:** Deep Learning · Remote Sensing · OpenStreetMap · Trail Surface Classification

## 1 Introduction

OpenStreetMap (OSM), a widely used volunteered geographic information (VGI) platform, is a key source of trail data but remains descriptively incomplete. In Ireland and the UK, only about 30% of the 2.79 million mapped paths, footways, and tracks include a `surface` tag, and many of those tags are inconsistent or outdated [9,11]. This limits the usefulness of OSM for navigation, route planning, and accessibility analysis, especially for users who depend on accurate surface information (e.g. wheelchair users, families with strollers, or trail managers planning maintenance).

At the same time, freely available Sentinel-2 satellite imagery provides systematically acquired, radiometrically calibrated multi-spectral data covering Europe at 10 m resolution with a 5-day revisit cycle. This creates an opportunity to fuse large-scale imagery with volunteered OSM annotations to infer trail


T. T. Mai et al. (Eds.): AICS 2025, CCIS 2950, pp. 190–201, 2026.
https://doi.org/10.1007/978-3-032-25809-0_15

surface characteristics, at least coarsely, over wide areas. However, such an approach must contend with two major challenges: (i) trails are often narrower than a single Sentinel-2 pixel, leading to mixed-pixel effects, and (ii) OSM `surface` tags constitute noisy, volunteer-provided labels rather than ground truth.

This paper introduces *TrailSurfNET*, which combines multi-spectral Sentinel-2 imagery with OSM annotations to classify hiking trail surfaces into five consolidated classes: asphalt, paved, gravel, mud/dirt, and grass. We treat OSM `surface` tags as weak, noisy supervision to train Convolutional Neural Networks (CNNs) at scale across Ireland and the UK.

Our contributions are threefold:

- We develop a scalable data pipeline that harmonises heterogeneous OSM surface tags into five classes and links them to temporally matched Sentinel-2 chips, producing a balanced dataset covering Ireland and the UK.
- We release the curated TrailSurfNET dataset and accompanying code to support reproducible experimentation and future benchmarking.
- We provide a systematic benchmark of several CNN architectures and pre-training strategies for multi-class trail surface classification under realistic, noisy-label conditions, designating the best-performing configuration as the *TrailSurfNET model*.

Rather than claiming to solve trail surface mapping, TrailSurfNET is positioned as a reproducible baseline and large-scale benchmark for this problem in Ireland and the UK. The goal is to demonstrate the feasibility and limitations of enriching OSM with automated surface suggestions from Sentinel-2 imagery, and to provide a foundation for future work on higher-resolution data, noise-robust learning, and human-in-the-loop integration.

## 2 Literature Review

This work sits at the intersection of (i) surface classification from geospatial data and (ii) deep learning for remote sensing.

### 2.1 Surface Classification and Volunteered Geographic Information

Road and trail surface classification typically trades off resolution, coverage, and cost. High-resolution aerial imagery and LiDAR can achieve high local accuracy but are expensive, spatially limited, and infrequently updated [10,14]. Freely available Sentinel-2 imagery offers continental-scale coverage and a 5-day revisit, but its 10 m resolution increases the risk of mixed pixels and false positives for narrow linear features such as trails [5,18].

A similar trade-off arises in label sources. Manually curated datasets provide precise labels but are costly to produce, whereas Volunteered Geographic Information (VGI) such as OpenStreetMap (OSM) is global and low-cost but descriptively incomplete and heterogeneous [11]. In the UK and Ireland, only around 30% of mapped trails carry a `surface` tag, with inconsistent vocabularies and varying levels of detail [12,13]. Nonetheless, several studies show that large volumes of VGI can compensate for label noise when treated as weak supervision for large-scale classification tasks [1,6,7,18].

### 2.2 Deep Learning for Geospatial Vision

Convolutional Neural Networks (CNNs) have become the standard for remote sensing image analysis, replacing handcrafted features with learned spatial representations. VGG-style architectures remain strong baselines, particularly for high-resolution imagery [14], while deeper residual networks (ResNet) are widely adopted for medium-resolution sensors such as Sentinel-2 [3,15].

Transfer learning is also central. Models pre-trained on ImageNet are common, but RGB natural-image features may not align well with the spectral properties of satellite data [16]. Domain-specific pre-training on large multispectral archives such as BigEarthNet has been shown to improve performance by exploiting red-edge and SWIR bands [17]. This motivates comparing training from scratch with transfer learning from remote-sensing pre-training in our setting.

### 2.3 Research Gap

Most prior work targets road surface classification or coarse land-cover types; multi-class *trail* surface analysis at national scale remains under-explored. Sparse and inconsistent OSM surface tags and the lack of end-to-end pipelines for learning from noisy VGI limit progress, and few approaches close the loop by feeding model outputs back into OSM through semi-automated workflows [2].

This study addresses this gap by introducing *TrailSurfNET*, a scalable system that fuses Sentinel-2 imagery with noisy OSM surface tags to classify trail surfaces across Ireland and the UK. To our knowledge, no previous work has tackled multi-class trail surface classification in this region using volunteered OSM labels and Sentinel-2, and we explicitly position our contribution as an open, reproducible benchmark and baseline for future work rather than a definitive production solution.

## 3 Methodology

TrailSurfNET integrates volunteered geographic information from OpenStreetMap (OSM) with multi-spectral Sentinel-2 imagery to classify trail surfaces into five classes: asphalt, paved, gravel, mud/dirt, and grass. The pipeline comprises three stages: (i) data acquisition and curation, (ii) model development and training, and (iii) evaluation.

### 3.1 Data Curation Pipeline

**OSM Extraction and Harmonisation.** The June 2024 OSM extract for Ireland and the UK was filtered to retain ways tagged as `path`, `footway`, or `track` with a valid `surface` tag and a minimum length of 160 m. From 285 distinct raw `surface` values, we mapped tags into five consolidated classes: `Asphalt`, `Paved`, `Gravel`, `Mud/Dirt` and `Grass`. Ways without a `surface` tag, or with tags that could not be mapped, were discarded. All remaining trails were segmented into 160 m sections to increase the number of training samples and reduce class imbalance, then down-sampled to obtain an equal number of segments per class.

**Label Noise and Quality Checks.** We treat OSM `surface` tags as noisy but informative labels rather than ground truth. Beyond harmonisation to the five classes, we deliberately avoided heavy, manual cleaning (e.g. per-way relabelling), reflecting a realistic scenario in which automated methods must operate directly on volunteered data. Residual label noise is therefore handled primarily through large training volumes, class balancing, and regularisation.

**Sentinel-2 Imagery and Temporal Alignment.** For each trail segment, we retrieved a 160 m $\times$ 160 m Sentinel-2 L2A chip via the Sentinel Hub API, using eight spectral bands (B02–B06, B08, B11, B12) plus the `dataMask`. OSM data were extracted in June 2024, and imagery was restricted to 2024 acquisitions, providing coarse temporal alignment between labels and observations. Segments for which only heavily cloud-contaminated or artefacted imagery was available were discarded using the Sentinel Hub `dataMask` and a simple cloud filter.

Sentinel-2 was chosen over very-high-resolution basemap imagery (e.g. Google Earth/Maps) for three reasons: (i) it provides radiometrically calibrated reflectance in well-defined spectral bands, including red-edge and SWIR, designed for quantitative land-cover analysis [4]; (ii) it exposes all 13 bands rather than only RGB channels with proprietary colour processing; and (iii) it offers a consistent, public archive with known acquisition dates, supporting reproducible experiments, whereas basemap mosaics mix sensors, dates, and processing pipelines [8].

**Dataset Statistics.** After all filters, we obtained a balanced dataset of 24,428 segments per class, yielding 122,140 labelled tiles with harmonised OSM surface tags and corresponding Sentinel-2 chips.

### 3.2 Model Development

We implemented six CNN variants: a VGG-style network, ResNet-18, ResNet-34, and ResNet-50 trained from scratch, plus ResNet-18 and ResNet-50 initialised with BigEarthNet pre-trained weights. Input layers were adapted to accept nine channels (eight Sentinel-2 bands + `dataMask`), and the final layer outputs five surface classes. This design enables direct comparison of architecture depth and domain-specific pre-training.

### 3.3 Training Procedure

The balanced dataset was stratified into an 80% training set (97,712 tiles) and a 20% validation set (24,428 tiles). Given the lack of independent ground truth, we used the validation set for model selection and reporting and did not hold out a separate test set.

**Augmentation and Optimisation.** To improve generalisation on $32\times32$ chips, we applied light geometric augmentations: random horizontal flips (probability 0.5) and random rotations of up to $\pm10°$. Inputs were normalised channel-wise using training-set statistics. All models were trained with the Adam optimiser (learning rate $1\times10^{-3}$, weight decay $1\times10^{-4}$) and a `ReduceLROnPlateau` scheduler (factor 0.1, patience 5 epochs). Training ran for up to 60 epochs with batch size 32 and Early Stopping (patience 12 epochs). A class-balanced cross-entropy loss was used to guard against any residual imbalance in mini-batches.

**Implementation and Reproducibility.** Experiments were conducted in PyTorch 2.3 on an Apple M4 Pro using MPS acceleration (ResNet-50 $\approx$ 4 min per epoch). All code, configuration files, and scripts to reproduce the pipeline are publicly available at https://github.com/rudedoc/TrailSurfNET.

## 4 Results

We evaluate six CNN configurations on the balanced Ireland/UK dataset (five classes; tile-level classification). Performance is reported as overall accuracy (OA) and macro-averaged precision, recall, and $F_1$ (maP/maR/ma$F_1$).

### 4.1 Overall Performance

Table 1 summarises peak validation performance (single run per model). Residual architectures consistently outperform the VGG baseline. The best OA (46.73%) is achieved by **ResNet-50 trained from scratch** (the *TrailSurfNET model*). ResNet-18 with BigEarthNet pre-training attains the highest macro $F_1$, but only marginally above ResNet-18 trained from scratch. Domain-specific pre-training does not consistently improve performance: for both ResNet-18 and ResNet-50, training from scratch slightly exceeds their BigEarthNet-initialised counterparts in OA.

Although OA values around 47% are modest compared to standard vision benchmarks, the task is challenging: five classes, medium-resolution (10 m) imagery, narrow trails, and noisy volunteered labels. A uniform random classifier over five classes would achieve 20% OA, so the best models perform more than twice this baseline. Nonetheless, current accuracy levels are not sufficient for fully automatic addition of surface tags to OSM; the system is better viewed as a baseline and provider of *suggested* labels in a human-in-the-loop workflow.

**Table 1.** Overall performance (single run per model). OA = Overall Accuracy. maF$_1$, maP, and maR indicate macro-averaged F$_1$-score, Precision, and Recall, averaged equally across all five classes.

| Model | Pre-trained on | OA | maF$_1$ | maP | maR |
|---|---|---|---|---|---|
| VGG-style CNN | None (scratch) | 0.4400 | 0.4300 | 0.4600 | 0.4400 |
| ResNet-18 | None (scratch) | 0.4661 | 0.4581 | **0.4787** | 0.4661 |
| ResNet-18 | BigEarthNet | 0.4644 | **0.4585** | 0.4741 | 0.4644 |
| ResNet-34 | None (scratch) | 0.4629 | 0.4568 | 0.4786 | 0.4629 |
| ResNet-50 (TrailSurfNET model) | None (scratch) | **0.4673** | 0.4572 | 0.4782 | **0.4673** |
| ResNet-50 | BigEarthNet | 0.4614 | 0.4533 | 0.4784 | 0.4614 |

### 4.2 Class-Level Analysis of TrailSurfNET

For error analysis we focus on the best-OA model, ResNet-50 trained from scratch. The confusion matrix in Fig. 1 shows strong recognition of **asphalt** and **grass**, moderate performance on **gravel**, and weaker discrimination for **mud/dirt** and **paved**. The dominant confusions are *paved* → *asphalt* and *mud/dirt* → {*grass*, *gravel*}, reflecting spectral similarity and mixed-pixel effects.

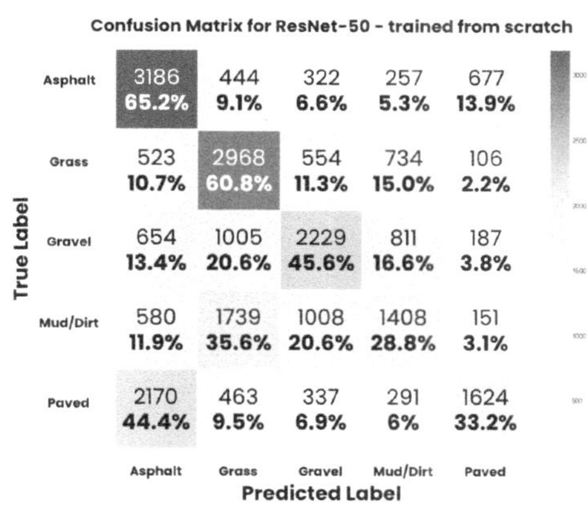


**Fig. 1.** Confusion matrix for TrailSurfNET (ResNet-50 trained from scratch).

Per-class precision, recall, and F$_1$ for this model are reported in Table 2. Paved attains the highest precision, while asphalt and grass achieve the best recalls. Mud/dirt underperforms on both precision and recall, indicating systematic ambiguity with vegetated or loose-surface contexts.

### 4.3 Binary Simplification

While the five-class setting remains challenging, the model more reliably separates hard-engineered surfaces (asphalt, paved) from natural ground (gravel,

**Table 2.** Per-class metrics for TrailSurfNET (ResNet-50 trained from scratch).

| Class | Precision | Recall | $F_1$ | Support |
|---|---|---|---|---|
| Asphalt | 0.4479 | 0.6521 | 0.5310 | 4886 |
| Grass | 0.4484 | 0.6076 | 0.5160 | 4885 |
| Gravel | 0.5009 | 0.4562 | 0.4775 | 4886 |
| Mud/dirt | 0.4022 | 0.2882 | 0.3358 | 4886 |
| Paved | 0.5916 | 0.3324 | 0.4257 | 4885 |
| **Macro Avg** | **0.4782** | **0.4673** | **0.4572** | **24428** |

mud/dirt, grass). Collapsing to this binary distinction should yield a higher accuracy, which is promising for applications where a coarse surface type is sufficient (e.g. accessibility or maintenance triage).

### 4.4 Qualitative Behaviour and TrailSurfNET Model

Sample validation chips with true and predicted labels are shown in Fig. 2. They confirm the quantitative trends: distinct classes such as asphalt and grass are often correctly identified, while unpaved surfaces are frequently confused. Across all experiments, ResNet-50 trained from scratch consistently provided the best trade-off between overall accuracy and per-class performance; we therefore designate this configuration as the **TrailSurfNET model** for subsequent discussion.

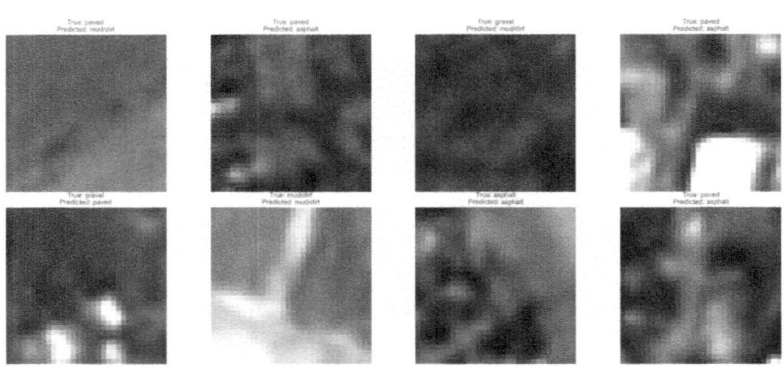


**Fig. 2.** Sample validation predictions from TrailSurfNET (ResNet-50 trained from scratch). Correct classifications (green) and typical misclassifications (red). (Color figure online)

## 5 Discussion

This work set out to classify hiking trail surfaces across Ireland and the UK using Sentinel-2 imagery and noisy OpenStreetMap (OSM) labels. Three main findings emerge: (i) residual architectures outperform a VGG baseline; (ii) modest gains with depth culminate in the best OA (46.73%) for ResNet-50 trained from scratch; and (iii) domain-specific pre-training on BigEarthNet does not consistently improve performance for this fine-grained task.

### 5.1 From-Scratch vs Domain Pre-Training

Across both 18- and 50-layer variants, models trained from random initialisation slightly exceeded their BigEarthNet-initialised counterparts (Table 1). A likely cause is *task mismatch*: BigEarthNet pre-training targets broad, multi-label land-cover semantics (e.g. urban, forest), whereas TrailSurfNET requires subtle distinctions among visually and spectrally similar surfaces (e.g. gravel vs. mud/dirt). Given a large, balanced training set of trail-centred chips, learning task-specific features directly appears more effective than transferring high-level land-cover features.

### 5.2 Error Modes and Data Challenges

The confusion matrix for the TrailSurfNET model shows two dominant error regimes: (i) **paved** vs. **asphalt**, and (ii) **mud/dirt** confused with **grass** or **gravel**. These patterns reflect both *mixed pixels* at 10 m resolution (narrow trails blended with surroundings) and *label noise* from inconsistent OSM tagging. Contributors use heterogeneous vocabularies for similar surfaces (e.g. `dirt`, `earth`, `ground`, `mud`), and tags may lag real-world resurfacing. Even a perfect classifier on the imagery would therefore disagree with some fraction of OSM labels, placing an upper bound on achievable agreement.

Beyond richer inputs (e.g. vegetation or soil indices, higher-resolution aerial supervision), future work should consider training strategies designed for noisy labels, such as label smoothing, noise-robust loss functions, or co-teaching schemes that down-weight persistent outliers. Human-in-the-loop workflows, where high-confidence predictions are accepted automatically and low-confidence or systematically confused cases are surfaced to mappers, offer a practical route to progressively denoise labels.

### 5.3 Threats to Validity

**Sensor Resolution.** Sentinel-2's 10 m ground sampling distance is well suited to broad land-cover mapping but under-represents narrow, heterogeneous trails (typically 1–2 m wide). This causes mixed pixels in which the trail signal is blended with surrounding vegetation, soil, or infrastructure, limiting separability of fine-grained surface classes. Very high resolution aerial or commercial satellite imagery (e.g. 0.5–2 m orthophotos) could mitigate this, but such data are often delivered as visually optimised RGB mosaics with proprietary processing and restrictive licensing, constraining their use for open, reproducible benchmarks.

**Label Quality and Temporal Mismatch.** Volunteer-provided OSM tags can be inconsistent in wording and granularity and may be temporally misaligned with imagery. A track resurfaced from gravel to asphalt may remain labelled as gravel until a mapper updates it, while the imagery already shows asphalt. Such effects constrain the maximum agreement between model predictions and OSM labels. Systematic auditing, targeted re-mapping of high-uncertainty areas, and noise-aware training objectives are natural directions to tighten this bound.

**Geographic Scope.** Models were trained exclusively on Ireland and the UK. Generalisation to other regions and biomes (e.g. alpine, desert, tropical) may require re-training, domain adaptation, or region-specific harmonisation of surface vocabularies.

### 5.4 Implications and Use Cases

Given the moderate OA in the five-class setting, we do not advocate bulk, fully automatic imports of model predictions into OSM. Instead, TrailSurfNET is best suited to *semi-automated enrichment*: predictions are surfaced to mappers as suggested surface types, with humans confirming or correcting them. For many applications, a coarser distinction between *hard* (asphalt, paved) and *natural* (gravel, mud/dirt, grass) surfaces may suffice; our binary experiments suggest substantially higher accuracy in this setting, making it more immediately useful for routing, accessibility analysis, and maintenance triage.

Beyond OSM, park authorities and outdoor platforms could use TrailSurfNET as a screening tool for trail audits, prioritising segments for inspection or resurfacing. More broadly, the results highlight both the promise and the limitations of combining medium-resolution satellite imagery with volunteered labels, and motivate future work on higher-resolution data, noise-robust learning, and tighter humanâĂŞAI collaboration.

## 6 Conclusion

This paper introduced *TrailSurfNET*, a framework for classifying hiking trail surfaces across Ireland and the UK by fusing Sentinel-2 imagery with OpenStreetMap (OSM) annotations. Using noisy OSM `surface` tags as weak labels, we built a harmonised, balanced dataset over five classes (asphalt, paved, gravel, mud/dirt, grass) and benchmarked several CNN architectures and pre-training strategies.

The best configuration, ResNet-50 trained from scratch (the **TrailSurfNET model**), achieved 46.7% overall accuracy on a challenging five-class task. Two key insights emerged: (i) training from scratch slightly but consistently outperformed domain-specific transfer learning from BigEarthNet, suggesting that fine-grained surface distinctions are best learned directly from task data; and (ii) asphalt and grass are identified relatively reliably, while confusion among unpaved classes remains the principal challenge, driven by mixed pixels and label noise.

TrailSurfNET is therefore best viewed not as a production-ready mapping system, but as a large-scale, open benchmark and baseline for trail surface classification in Ireland and the UK, and as a source of *suggested* labels in human-in-the-loop workflows.

### 6.1 Future Work

Several directions could enhance TrailSurfNET and extend its applicability:

- **Data and sensor fusion.** Incorporating higher-resolution aerial imagery, LiDAR-derived elevation products, or crowd-sourced ground imagery could reduce mixed-pixel effects and improve separation of unpaved classes.
- **Advanced architectures.** Vision transformers and hybrid CNNâĂŞTransformer models tailored to multi-spectral inputs may better capture long-range spatial context and subtle spectral differences.
- **Noise-aware learning.** Label-noise robust losses, co-teaching, or confidence-based reweighting could mitigate the impact of inconsistent OSM tags and temporal mismatches.
- **Human-in-the-loop integration.** Embedding TrailSurfNET predictions into OSM editors as suggested surface types would enable volunteer mappers to efficiently validate or correct outputs, progressively improving label quality.
- **Global scalability and simplification.** Applying the pipeline to other regions and surface vocabularies, and exploiting a coarser hard-vs-natural formulation (which achieves substantially higher accuracy in our experiments), are promising steps toward practical deployment.

### 6.2 Concluding Remarks

TrailSurfNET demonstrates that freely available satellite imagery and volunteered data can be combined to address gaps in trail surface information at scale, albeit under constraints imposed by 10 m resolution and noisy labels. By releasing the full source code and data pipeline, we aim to provide a transparent baseline and shared resource for the community, and to support future work on higher-resolution data, noise-robust methods, and collaborative AIâĂŞmapper workflows for enriching global trail datasets.

## References

1. Algan, G., Ulusoy, I.: Image classification with deep learning in the presence of noisy labels: a survey. Knowl.-Based Syst. **215**, 106771 (2021). https://doi.org/10.1016/j.knosys.2021.106771
2. Dalrymple, J.: road_surface_classifier (2023). https://github.com/jdalrym2/road_surface_classifier

3. Demir, I., et al.: Deepglobe 2018: a challenge to parse the earth through satellite images. In: Proceedings of the IEEE Conference on Computer Vision and Pattern Recognition Workshops (CVPRW), pp. 172–181 (2018). https://doi.org/10.1109/CVPRW.2018.00031
4. Drusch, M., Honnayb, M., Ferreira, D., Mandorlo, G.: Sentinel-2: Esa's optical high-resolution mission for gmes operational services. Tech. Rep. ESA SP-1322/2, European Space Agency (ESA), Noordwijk, The Netherlands (2012). https://www.researchgate.net/publication/272907479
5. Øivind Due Trier, Salberg, A.B.: National-scale detection of new forest roads in sentinel-2 time series. Rem. Sens. **16**(21), 3972 (2024). https://doi.org/10.3390/rs16213972, https://doi.org/10.3390/rs16213972
6. Fonte, C.C., Minghini, M., Patriarca, J., Antoniou, V., See, L., Brovelli, M.A.: Generating and validating land cover maps using volunteered geographic information. In: Volunteered Geographic Information and the Future of Geospatial Data, pp. 51–78. IGI Global (2017). https://doi.org/10.4018/978-1-5225-2446-5.ch003
7. Kaiser, C., Schultz, M., Zipf, A., Hahmann, S.: Automatic extraction and filtering of openstreetmap data to generate training datasets for land use land cover classification. Rem. Sens. **12**(20), 3428 (2020). https://doi.org/10.3390/rs12203428
8. Lesiv, M., et al.: Characterizing the spatial and temporal availability of very high resolution satellite imagery in Google Earth and Microsoft Bing Maps as a source of reference data. Land **7**(4), 118 (2018). https://doi.org/10.3390/land7040118
9. Marion, J.L., Leung, Y.F.: Trail degradation as influenced by environmental factors: a state-of-the-knowledge review. J. Soil Water Conserv. **56**(2), 141–146 (2001)
10. McDermid, G.J., Terenteva, I., Chan, X.Y.: Mapping trails and tracks in the boreal forest using lidar and convolutional neural networks. Rem. Sens. **17**(9), 1539 (2025). https://doi.org/10.3390/rs17091539, Published 26 Apr 2025
11. Minghini, M., Frassinelli, F.: Openstreetmap history for intrinsic quality assessment: Is osm up-to-date? Open Geospatial Data Softw. Stand. **4**(1) (2019). https://doi.org/10.1186/s40965-019-0067-x
12. OpenStreetMap Wiki contributors: Tag:surface=dirt - OpenStreetMap Wiki (2023). https://wiki.openstreetmap.org/w/index.php?title=Tag:surface=dirt&oldid=2557682. Accessed 22 June 2024
13. OpenStreetMap Wiki contributors: Tag:surface=earth - OpenStreetMap Wiki (2023). https://wiki.openstreetmap.org/w/index.php?title=Tag:surface=earth&oldid=2557684. Accessed 22 June 2024
14. Pešek, O., Krisztian, L., Landa, M., Metz, M., Neteler, M.: Convolutional neural networks for road surface classification on aerial imagery. PeerJ Comput. Sci. **10** (2024). https://doi.org/10.7717/peerj-cs.2571, https://doi.org/10.7717/peerj-cs.2571. Published 23 Dec 2024
15. Randhawa, S., Aygün, E., Randhawa, G., Herfort, B., Lautenbach, S., Zipf, A.: Paved or unpaved? a deep learning derived road surface global dataset from mapillary street-view imagery. ISPRS J. Photogrammetry Rem. Sens. **223**, 362–374 (2025). https://doi.org/10.1016/j.isprsjprs.2025.02.020
16. Risojević, V., Stojnić, V.: Do we still need imagenet pre-training in remote sensing scene classification? Computer Vision and Pattern Recognition (2022). https://arxiv.org/abs/2111.03690
17. Sumbul, G., et al.: Bigearthnet-mm: A large scale multi-modal multi-label benchmark archive for remote sensing image classification and retrieval. IEEE J. Selected Top. Appl. Earth Observations Rem. Sens. (2021). https://doi.org/10.1109/MGRS.2021.3089174

18. Zhou, Q., Liu, Z., Huang, Z.: Mapping road surface type of Kenya using openstreetmap and high-resolution google satellite imagery. Sci. Data **11**(1), 1–1 (2024). https://doi.org/10.1038/s41597-024-03158-7

# LFE-SCCM: Low-Frequency Enhanced Method for Screen Content Image Compression

Rong Chen[1], Pengrui Duan[1], Sicheng Zhao[2,3], and Soumyabrata Dev[2,3](✉)

[1] Beijing University of Posts and Telecommunications, Beijing, China
rong.chen@bupt.edu.cn, dpr@butp.edu.cn
[2] University Colledge Dublin, Dublin, Ireland
sicheng.zhao@ucdconnect.ie, soumyabrata.dev@ucd.ie
[3] ADAPT Centre, Dublin, Ireland

**Abstract.** In the context of remote working and studying, the demand for efficient compression of screen content images has significantly increased. However, current image compression models primarily focus on natural images, neglecting the increasing need for compressing screen content images. To address this issue, we propose a new learning-based compression model of screen content images inspired by existing learning-based natural image compression models and combined with characteristics of screen content images. Our approach fully considers low-frequency information, which takes up a large portion of everyday screen use cases, although many researchers highlighted that high-frequency information mainly affects the perceptual quality of screen content images and videos. We integrate a Frequency Separator Module (FSM) and a specialized low-frequency enhancement branch into our model. The proposed low-frequency enhanced method, as shown by experimental results, outperforms existing hyperprior-based models in compressing screen content. The source code for our model is publicly accessible at https://github.com/RoneChen/LFE-SCCM.

**Keywords:** Image Compression · Image Processing · Screen Content Image Compression

## 1 Introduction

In recent years, the rise of remote work and social networks has led to a significant increase in the proportion of images and videos used in daily communication. As deep learning continues to thrive in computer vision and related domains, there is growing interest among researchers in employing Deep Neural Networks (DNNs) to supplant traditional techniques such as JPEG, WebP, and VVC in image compression. This technology, which is foundational and widely used in image processing, is increasingly attracting the attention of the research community.


T. T. Mai et al. (Eds.): AICS 2025, CCIS 2950, pp. 202–213, 2026.
https://doi.org/10.1007/978-3-032-25809-0_16

However, most of them overlook the growing data volume of screen content images, especially in remote working and social media, screenshots are widely used to transfer and clarify information. In this case, an efficient screen content coding method is highly desirable. Moreover, according to the characteristics of screen contents, generated sharp edges (high frequency) and large areas with the same color (low frequency), using the same strategy to deal with both of these information might have a great potential to be improved. LC-FDNet, a learned-based image compression method that uses low-frequency information as a strong prior for high-frequency compression, presents a good performance on natural images [29]. Inspired by that design and the analysis of conventional compression algorithms, we believe that screen content images will get more advantages from this scheme.

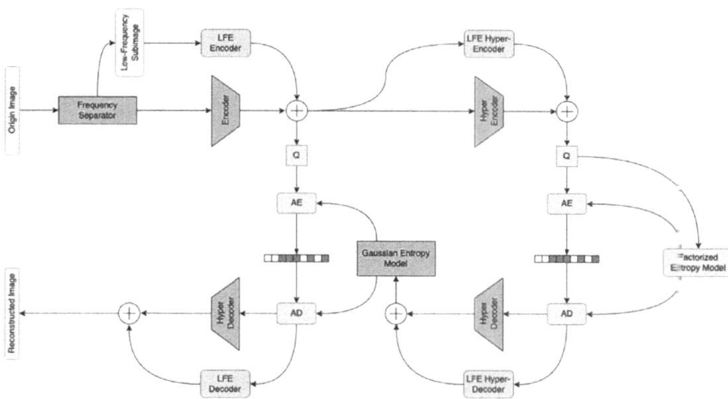


**Fig. 1.** High-level Architecture of the proposed Method. To perform low-frequency compression enhancement and fully use the low-frequency information as prior for hyper network, we introduce the FSM and LFE Network to the compression model.

In conventional image and video compression methods, some extensive tools are proposed to utilize features of screen content [28,32]. Intra Block Copy (IBC) involves the concept of motion estimation and compensation in intra-prediction because the replicate blocks often exist in the same screen content image. In addition, Palette Mode (PLT) is developed due to the limited number of colors that exist in Coding Units (CU), and Transform Skip (TS) depends on the fact that some types of screen content may not gain any benefit from the spatial transform.

Despite the relatively late start of learning-based image compression algorithms, they present great potential and the state-of-the-art (SOTA) has already surpassed conventional methods. Recently, the variational auto-encoder (VAE) method [17] has demonstrated superior rate-distortion performance compared to traditional lossy image compression algorithms, as evaluated by metrics such as

Signal-to-Noise Ratio (PSNR) and Multi-Scale Structural Similarity Index Measure (MS-SSIM). This highlights its significant potential for practical applications. The initial encoding involves utilizing both linear and nonlinear parametric analysis transformations to project the image into a latent space. Following quantization, the distribution of the latent variables is predicted using entropy estimation modules. Subsequently, the latent variables are compressed into a bit stream using either lossless Context-based Adaptive Binary Arithmetic Coding (CABAC) [23] or Range Coder [24]. Utilizing the VAE framework, enhancements such as hyper prior [4], auto-regressive priors [25], and Gaussian Mixture Model (GMM) [7] are incorporated to refine the precision of predicting the latent variable distribution by the entropy estimation modules, thereby achieving improved rate-distortion (RD) performance.

For decoding, the bit stream is decoded to recover the decompressed latent variables using either lossless CABAC or Range Coder. These latent variables are then mapped to reconstructed images through a combination of linear and nonlinear parametric synthesis transformations. To further enhance the quality of the reconstructed images, there is ongoing research into designing modules that function as post-processing components, such as artifact removal [1,10,12,20,22,31,34], super-resolution [11,15], and deblocking [2,18].

While existing methods for image compression have delivered excellent results, they tend to overlook the unique characteristics of screen content images. Thus, inspired by the idea of LC-FDNet [29] and the theoretical basis of SCC extensions of traditional coding methods, we propose an end-to-end leaning-based method for screen content image compression to provide a more efficient approach for compression screenshots and other forms of screen content images. The general network has a similar architecture to VAE. However, a FSM is involved, which decomposes the high and low-frequency area from the input image and sends low-frequency information to the Low-Frequency Enhancement branch. This design fully considers how to improve the compression rate of the low-frequency information, which takes up a large area of the screen in the practical use cases, and the outcome of the main encoder is used as a prior in the hyper-network for further processing. Our work's primary contribution is designing an effective network architecture that considers the unique characteristics of screen content images and improves RD performance by enhancing the low-frequency area.

## 2 Related Work

### 2.1 Learned Image Compression

In recent years, the CNN-based learned image compression models have flourished and have had outstanding breakthroughs [3,4,7–9,14,21,25,26,30,33]. Following the introduction of the first end-to-end optimized image compression model based on the VAE architecture [3], numerous subsequent studies have made modifications and sought to enhance the architecture. In [4], a hyper-prior was introduced to capture spatial dependencies within the latent representation.

Building on this, [25] drew inspiration from the effectiveness of auto-regressive priors in probabilistic generative models. They extended the model proposed by [4] by incorporating an auto-regressive module to further enhance its capabilities. Furthermore, Cheng et al. [7] introduced a network architecture that includes residual blocks and integrates a simplified attention module, along with using a Gaussian Mixture Model (GMM) instead of the traditional Single Gaussian Model (SGM). While the GMM enhances rate-distortion (RD) performance, it significantly increases encoding and decoding time consumption compared to the computationally less expensive SGM-based entropy model. To speed up the serial processing in autoregressive context models, [14] designed a checkerboard context model (CCM) from the spatial-wise perspective, which highly reduces the decoding time.Additionally, from a channel-wise auto-regressive perspective, the modified model employs a context model along the channel dimension rather than the serial-decoded spatial ones. This approach not only enhances the efficiency of both encoding and decoding processes but also improves the RD performance [26]. After that, [13] proposed a spatial-channel contextual adaptive model to combine the merits of both spatial-wise and channel-wise ideas. Furthermore, adding an informer module to exploit global information complementing the local information collected by the context module [16], using the latent of the low-frequency region as a strong prior for high-frequency region encoding [29], and introducing a Swin-Transformer-based attention (SWAtten) module with channel squeezing for optimizing channel-wise auto-regressive entropy models, as proposed by Liu et al. [19], represents another approach to enhance rate-distortion (RD) performance and reduce computation time in learned image compression models.

## 3 The Proposed Methods

In this paper, we present a Low-Frequency Enhancement (LFE) approach within an end-to-end coding framework. Our goal is to fully leverage the unique characteristics of screen content images and enhance the RD performance specifically for screen content image compression. Figure 1 illustrates the high-level architecture of the proposed method, which contains the modules and layer parameters. The proposed LFE-SCCM implementation is on top of the Minnen2018 in [25], and Fig. 2 details the architecture of the proposed model.

### 3.1 Low-Frequency Enhancement

In the context of image compression, high-frequency and low-frequency information are two fundamental concepts that play a crucial role in capturing the essence of an image. On the one hand, low-frequency components represent the smooth and gradual changes in an image, such as large areas of uniform color or subtle variations that form the background and overall structure of the visual content.

On the other hand, high-frequency components contain finer details and rapid changes in pixel values, such as edges, texts, and sharp contrasts. These elements

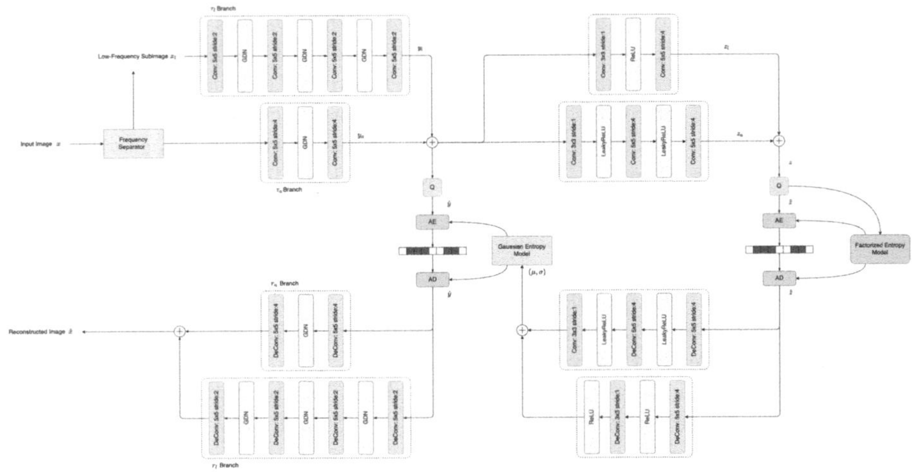

**Fig. 2.** Illustration of the proposed framework, where "Q" represents the quantization process, while "AE" and "AD" stand for the arithmetic entropy encoding and decoding processes, respectively.

are less predictable due to their spatially localized nature and the abrupt transitions between local pixel values. The presence of high-frequency information is essential for maintaining the visual acuity and fidelity of a screen content image, as it conveys the intricate details that define the content of the image.

In conventional compression methods, the usage of transformation and quantization to drop the high-frequency information is a common approach to reduce the bitrate. The coding algorithms use transformation functions to separate information by different frequencies and apply diverse quantization parameters according to the sensitive degree of the human vision system. While the loss of high-frequency information may lead to the deterioration of edges and details, low-frequency information contains the main content of an image or a frame.

However, the research of LC-FDNet [29] has shown that the relationship between high and low-frequency information is not mutually exclusive. In fact, the low-frequency components can serve as a foundation for the high-frequency details. By first encoding the low-frequency information, one can leverage its predictability and spatial consistency to assist the more complex high-frequency elements compression.

In the proposed method of screen content image compression, we prioritize low-frequency information with finer processing to ensure the reconstruction quality. Meanwhile, taking the concatenated outcome of the LFE branch and the main forward transform branch as a prior in the hyper codec will be helpful to the high-frequency reconstruction.

To obtain the low-frequency subimage, we have designed an FSM that is integrated into the network ahead of the main encoder. The FSM is responsible for separating the low and high-frequency information. The FSM smooths the input image using Gaussian Blur to obtain the low-frequency component:

$$x_l = Gaussian(0.299 \times x_R + 0.587 \times x_G + 0.114 \times x_B) \tag{1}$$

where $x_R$, $x_G$ and $x_B$ are three color channels of the input image. *Gaussian* is the Gaussian Blur operation and $x_l$ represent the low-frequency subimages.

### 3.2 Network Architecture

In general, the end-to-end compression framework comprises an encoder and a decoder. Before an image is sent to the encoder, the FSM separates the low and high-frequency subimages and takes the low-frequency one, $x_l$, as another encoder input.

On the encoder side, there are two analytical branches involved for the input images $x$ and $x_l$. These branches are the primary forward transform branch, denoted as $\tau_a$, and the LFE branch, denoted as $\tau_l$. Since the low-frequency components $x_l$ are utilized as priors for the hyper network, a detailed processing approach is employed in $\tau_l$. Specifically, this involves applying four convolutional layers with a stride of two sequentially. The primary forward transform branch $\tau_a$ employs a more streamlined approach, utilizing two convolutional layers with a stride of four. In other words, the origin image $x$ is coarsely processed. The $\tau_a$ and $\tau_l$ branches can be formulated as follows:

$$y_a = \tau_a(x, \theta_a), \tag{2}$$

$$y_l = \tau_l(x_l, \theta_l), \tag{3}$$

where the latent codes are represented by $y$ and $y_l$. The model parameters for the primary forward transform and the LFE branches are denoted as $\theta_a$ and $\theta_l$. The total latent code $y$ is formed by combining $y_a$ and $y_l$, as described below:

$$y = y_a + y_l \tag{4}$$

the total latent is quantized, which is denoted as $\hat{y}$ and generated as follows,

$$\hat{y} = \mathcal{Q}(y) \tag{5}$$

the $\hat{y}$ is coded by the AE.

As the proposed method is based on the Minnen2018 model in [25], the means and scales are predicted by the hyperprior model. In our method, the hyperencoder and decoder are extended with low-frequency enhancement branches. The hyperlatent in terms of $z$ is composed of outputs of two branches, $z_a$ and $z_l$, as follows,

$$z = z_a + z_l \tag{6}$$

After that, quantization and the factorized entropy model [4] cooperate to compress the $z$.

Building on the work of Minnen et al. [25], each latent variable $\hat{y}_i$ is modeled as a Gaussian distribution with mean $\mu_i$ and standard deviation $\sigma_i$, convolved with a unit uniform distribution:

$$p_{\hat{y}|\hat{z},\theta} = \prod_{i=1} \left( \left( \mathcal{N}(\mu_i, \sigma_i^2) * \mathcal{U}(-0.5, 0.5) \right) (\hat{y}_i) \right) \tag{7}$$

where $\mu$ and $\sigma$ are the predicted parameters of the entropy model, $\hat{z}$ represents the quantized hyper-latents, and $\theta$ denotes the parameters of the entropy model.

To optimize end-to-end learning compression models, the training process incorporates rate and distortion optimization with Lagrangian parameters. Distortion is quantified as the difference between the reconstructed image $\hat{x}$ and the original input image $x$, specifically using Mean Square Error (MSE) The rate term includes the bits needed to encode $\hat{y}$ and $\hat{z}$. Consequently, the loss function is defined as follows:

$$\mathcal{L} = \mathcal{R}(\hat{y}) + \mathcal{R}(\hat{z}) + \lambda \cdot \mathcal{D}(x, \hat{x}) \tag{8}$$

where $\lambda$ denotes the Lagrange parameter, which controls the trade-off between rate and distortion.

## 4 Experiment

In this section, we present the experiments and results of the proposed LFE-SCCM model, along with a comparison of its performance against existing image compression models. To analyze the effectiveness of the proposed model architecture on the screen content image compression, both models taken as the benchmark are retrained on the LSCD dataset [6].

### 4.1 Experimental Setup

**Datasets.** We train all three models on the images collected in the LSCD dataset [6], which is a screen content image dataset considering practical computer use cases. As it is a dataset for 1080P screen content video compression, some of the frames are collected as training and testing images. In our setting, we use 3,096 images from the LSCD dataset for training. We evaluate the rateâĂŞdistortion performance on the SCCM dataset we collected, which covers diverse content in practical usage, such as video watching, web surfing, document reading, and MS Office processing, with a fixed resolution of 1920 × 1080. In total, we use 128 images from the SCCM dataset as test images.

**Training.** The implementation of our model is based on PyTorch [27] and an open-source compression project, CompressAI [5]. all three models are trained for 3000 epochs with a batch size of 16. To streamline the training process, images in both the training and validation sets are cropped into 256 × 256 patches. During

**Fig. 3.** The visual comparison.

training, the loss function utilizes mean square error (MSE), with $\lambda$ values set to 0.02, 0.03, 0.04, 0.05, 0.06 to cover a broad spectrum of bit-rates for compression. In this setup, five models are trained, each representing different quality levels. We use the Adam optimizer throughout training. When executed on a GeForce RTX 3090 Ti, the training process typically lasts around 12 h.

**Evaluation.** We assess the performance of our LFE-SCCM by computing the average RD performance metrics, including PSNR and MS-SSIM, on the SCCM dataset. This dataset encompasses four practical use cases of computers in daily life. We conduct comparisons with prominent general learned compression methods, including the Ballé2018 model [4] and the Minnen2018 model [25]. To compare and evaluate their performance on screen content image compression, both of them are retrained on the same dataset as the proposed method with 3000 epochs.

## 4.2 Results

Figure 3 displays the visual outcomes of various models. When compared to the other models considered, our proposed LFE-SCCM demonstrates superior performance with screen content images. Furthermore, as depicted in Fig. 4, the retrained Minnen2018 model [25] exhibited better performance than the retrained Balle2018 model [4]. The outcomes align with the trends reported in the original publication by Minnen et al. [25], where the model was trained using a dataset comprising natural images.

To demonstrate the superior performance of our model, we used the commonly used metrics MS-SSIM and PSNR to evaluate the reconstruction performance. As shown in Fig. 4a, our LFE-SCCM model performed better than the retrained Minnen2018 model [25] in the low-bpp and high-bpp regions. However, in the middle-bpp region, the reconstructed image quality of our model

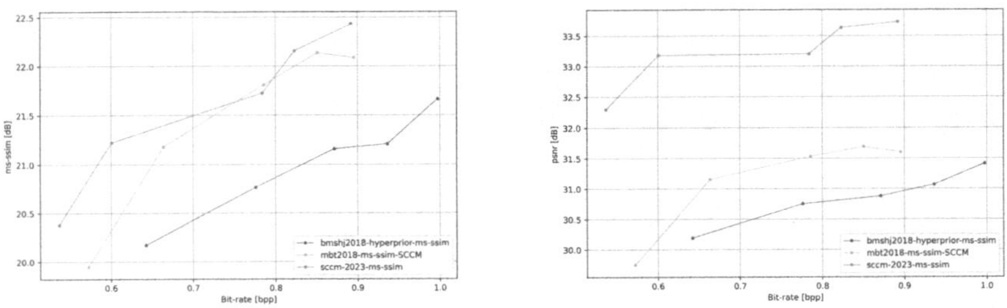


(a) (b)

**Fig. 4.** Rate-Distortion (RD) performance comparison of LFE-SCCM against the retrained Ballé2018 [4] and Minnen2018 [25] models. (a) RD-curves for MS-SSIM. (b) RD-curves for PSNR.

was slightly inferior to the retrained Minnen2018 model [25] when evaluated by MS-SSIM. In Fig. 4b, it is apparent that our LFE-SCCM model outperformed both of the other retrained models on PSNR for all bpp values.

## 5 Ablation Study

Table 1 presents the findings from an ablation study designed to assess the impact of Low-Frequency Enhancement on rate-distortion performance. The baseline model, which shares the same architecture, differs in that it does not utilize the low-frequency as the input for the $t_l$ branch. This model disregards the significance of low-frequency information when compressing the high-frequency region by using the original image as input for both branches, thereby equating the importance of both frequency areas. This validates the effectiveness of the low-frequency enhancement branch in improving compression efficiency.

**Table 1.** Comparison of Methods at Different $\lambda$ Values

| Method | $\lambda$ | bpp | PSNR |
|---|---|---|---|
| Baseline | 0.02 | 0.690 | 32.26 |
| LFE-SCCM | 0.02 | 0.533 | 32.29 |
| Baseline | 0.04 | 1.039 | 32.95 |
| LFE-SCCM | 0.04 | 0.600 | 33.20 |

The results, obtained under the same $\lambda$ conditions, clearly demonstrate that assigning greater emphasis to low-frequency information and employing it as a prior for high-frequency compression leads to a dual benefit: an increase in PSNR and a reduction in bpp. This outcome underscores the pivotal role of low-frequency information, even in images with a greater prevalence of high-frequency content, such as screen content images. The persistent relevance of low-frequency data highlights its indispensable contribution to overall compression efficiency and quality preservation.

## 6 Conclusion

In this paper, we present an innovative learning-based method called LFE-SCCM for compressing screen content images. By combining principles of traditional compression and screen content characteristics, we introduce a Low-Frequency Enhancement branch that extracts low-frequency information as a prior for the hyperprior network, while the primary branch processes the full image. Extensive experiments show that low-frequency information plays a significant role, and our method achieves promising compression improvements.

However, performance on game-type screen content is less competitive, as such images contain richer textures similar to natural images.

For future work, we plan to explore adaptive frequency-aware modules for game-like content and investigate a Stable-Diffusion-like strategy to progressively generate high-frequency details from low-frequency representations, aiming to further enhance reconstruction quality.

## References


1. Amaranageswarao, G., Deivalakshmi, S., Ko, S.B.: Deep dilated and densely connected parallel convolutional groups for compression artifacts reduction. Digit. Signal Process. **106**, 102804 (2020). https://doi.org/10.1016/j.dsp.2020.102804
2. Amaranageswarao, G., Deivalakshmi, S., Ko, S.B.: Residual learning based densely connected deep dilated network for joint deblocking and super resolution. Appl. Intell. **50**(7), 2177–2193 (2020). https://doi.org/10.1007/s10489-020-01670-y, http://link.springer.com/10.1007/s10489-020-01670-y
3. Ballé, J., Laparra, V., Simoncelli, E.P.: End-to-end Optimized Image Compression (2017). https://doi.org/10.48550/arXiv.1611.01704, http://arxiv.org/abs/1611.01704, arXiv:1611.01704 [cs, math]
4. Ballé, J., Minnen, D., Singh, S., Hwang, S.J., Johnston, N.: Variational image compression with a scale hyperprior (2018). https://doi.org/10.48550/arXiv.1802.01436, http://arxiv.org/abs/1802.01436, arXiv:1802.01436 [cs, eess, math]
5. Bégaint, J., Racapé, F., Feltman, S., Pushparaja, A.: CompressAI: a PyTorch library and evaluation platform for end-to-end compression research (2020). https://doi.org/10.48550/arXiv.2011.03029, https://arxiv.org/abs/2011.03029v1
6. Cheng, Y., Zhang, S., Yan, Y., Chen, R., Zhang, Y.: LSCD: A Large-Scale Screen Content Dataset for Video Compression (2023). http://arxiv.org/abs/2308.09332, arXiv:2308.09332 [cs]
7. Cheng, Z., Sun, H., Takeuchi, M., Katto, J.: Learned Image Compression With Discretized Gaussian Mixture Likelihoods and Attention Modules, p. 10. (2020)
8. Choi, Y., El-Khamy, M., Lee, J.: Variable Rate Deep Image Compression With a Conditional Autoencoder (2019). https://doi.org/10.48550/arXiv.1909.04802, http://arxiv.org/abs/1909.04802, arXiv:1909.04802 [cs, eess]

9. Cui, Z., Wang, J., Gao, S., Guo, T., Feng, Y., Bai, B.: Asymmetric gained deep image compression with continuous rate adaptation. In: 2021 IEEE/CVF Conference on Computer Vision and Pattern Recognition (CVPR), pp. 10527–10536. IEEE, Nashville, TN, USA (2021). https://doi.org/10.1109/CVPR46437.2021.01039, https://ieeexplore.ieee.org/document/9578818/
10. Dong, C., Deng, Y., Loy, C.C., Tang, X.: Compression artifacts reduction by a deep convolutional network. In: 2015 IEEE International Conference on Computer Vision (ICCV), pp. 576–584. IEEE, Santiago, Chile (2015). https://doi.org/10.1109/ICCV.2015.73, https://ieeexplore.ieee.org/document/7410430/
11. Dong, C., Loy, C.C., He, K., Tang, X.: Image Super-Resolution Using Deep Convolutional Networks (2015). https://doi.org/10.48550/arXiv.1501.00092, http://arxiv.org/abs/1501.00092, arXiv:1501.00092 [cs]
12. Gandor, T., Nalepa, J.: First gradually, then suddenly: understanding the impact of image compression on object detection using deep learning. Sensors **22**(3), 1104 (2022). https://doi.org/10.3390/s22031104, https://www.mdpi.com/1424-8220/22/3/1104
13. He, D., Yang, Z., Peng, W., Ma, R., Qin, H., Wang, Y.: ELIC: Efficient Learned Image Compression With Unevenly Grouped Space-Channel Contextual Adaptive Coding, p. 10. (2022)
14. He, D., Zheng, Y., Sun, B., Wang, Y., Qin, H.: Checkerboard context model for efficient learned image compression. In: 2021 IEEE/CVF Conference on Computer Vision and Pattern Recognition (CVPR), pp. 14766–14775. IEEE, Nashville, TN, USA (2021). DOIurl10.1109/CVPR46437.2021.01453, https://ieeexplore.ieee.org/document/9577406/
15. Huang, C., Peng, X., Liu, D., Lu, Y.: Text image super-resolution guided by text structure and embedding priors. ACM Trans. Multimedia Comput. Commun. Appl. **19**(6), 1–18 (2023). https://doi.org/10.1145/3595924, https://dl.acm.org/doi/10.1145/3595924
16. Kim, J.H., Heo, B., Lee, J.S.: Joint Global and Local Hierarchical Priors for Learned Image Compression, p. 10 (2022)
17. Kingma, D.P., Welling, M.: Auto-Encoding Variational Bayes (2022). https://doi.org/10.48550/arXiv.1312.6114, http://arxiv.org/abs/1312.6114, arXiv:1312.6114 [cs, stat]
18. Lin, M.H., Yeh, C.H., Lin, C.H., Kang, L.W.: Deep Multi-Scale Residual Learning-based Blocking Artifacts Reduction for Compressed Images (2019)
19. Liu, J., Sun, H., Katto, J.: Learned Image Compression with Mixed Transformer-CNN Architectures (2023). https://doi.org/10.48550/arXiv.2303.14978, http://arxiv.org/abs/2303.14978, arXiv:2303.14978 [cs, eess]
20. Liu, X., Wu, X., Zhou, J., Zhao, D.: Data-driven sparsity-based restoration of JPEG-compressed images in dual transform-pixel domain. In: 2015 IEEE Conference on Computer Vision and Pattern Recognition (CVPR), pp. 5171–5178. IEEE, Boston, MA, USA (2015). https://doi.org/10.1109/CVPR.2015.7299153, http://ieeexplore.ieee.org/document/7299153/
21. Liu, Z., Wang, H., Su, T.: Learned image compression with multi-scale spatial and contextual information fusion. In: 2022 IEEE International Conference on Image Processing (ICIP), pp. 706–710 (Oct 2022). https://doi.org/10.1109/ICIP46576.2022.9897285. iSSN: 2381–8549
22. Luo, Z., Gustafsson, F.K., Zhao, Z., Sjölund, J., Schön, T.B.: Controlling Vision-Language Models for Universal Image Restoration (2023). https://doi.org/10.48550/arXiv.2310.01018, http://arxiv.org/abs/2310.01018

23. Marpe, D., Schwarz, H., Wiegand, T.: Context-based adaptive binary arithmetic coding in the H.264/AVC video compression standard. IEEE Trans. Circ. Syst. Video Technol. **13**(7), 620–636 (2003). https://doi.org/10.1109/TCSVT.2003.815173, https://ieeexplore.ieee.org/document/1218195/
24. Martin, G.N.N.: Range encoding: an algorithm for removing redundancy from a digitised message (1979)
25. Minnen, D., Ballé, J., Toderici, G.: Joint Autoregressive and Hierarchical Priors for Learned Image Compression (2018). http://arxiv.org/abs/1809.02736, arXiv:1809.02736 [cs]
26. Minnen, D., Singh, S.: Channel-wise Autoregressive Entropy Models for Learned Image Compression (2020). https://doi.org/10.48550/arXiv.2007.08739, http://arxiv.org/abs/2007.08739, arXiv:2007.08739 [cs, eess, math]
27. Paszke, A., et al.: PyTorch: An Imperative Style, High-Performance Deep Learning Library (2019). https://doi.org/10.48550/arXiv.1912.01703, http://arxiv.org/abs/1912.01703, arXiv:1912.01703 [cs, stat]
28. Peng, W.H., et al.: Overview of screen content video coding: technologies, standards, and beyond. IEEE J. Emerg. Selected Top. Circ. Syst. **6**(4), 393–408 (2016). https://doi.org/10.1109/JETCAS.2016.2608971, conference Name: IEEE Journal on Emerging and Selected Topics in Circuits and Systems
29. Rhee, H., Jang, Y.I., Kim, S., Cho, N.I.: LC-FDNet: Learned Lossless Image Compression With Frequency Decomposition Network, p. 10 (2022)
30. Wang, M., et al.: Transform skip inspired end-to-end compression for screen content image. In: 2022 IEEE International Conference on Image Processing (ICIP), pp. 3848–3852 (2022). https://doi.org/10.1109/ICIP46576.2022.9897719, iSSN: 2381-8549
31. Wang, Z., Liu, D., Chang, S., Ling, Q., Yang, Y., Huang, T.S.: D3: deep dual-domain based fast restoration of JPEG-compressed images. In: 2016 IEEE Conference on Computer Vision and Pattern Recognition (CVPR), pp. 2764–2772. IEEE, Las Vegas, NV, USA (2016). https://doi.org/10.1109/CVPR.2016.302, http://ieeexplore.ieee.org/document/7780671/
32. Xu, X., Liu, S.: Overview of screen content coding in recently developed video coding standards. IEEE Trans. Circ. Syst. Video Technol. **32**(2), 839–852 (2022). https://doi.org/10.1109/TCSVT.2021.3064210, https://ieeexplore.ieee.org/document/9371731/
33. Zhang, G., Zhang, X., Zhu, S.: Local and global fusion network for learned image compression. In: 2022 IEEE International Conference on Image Processing (ICIP), pp. 3763–3767 (2022). https://doi.org/10.1109/ICIP46576.2022.9897597, iSSN: 2381-8549
34. Zhang, X., Yang, W., Hu, Y., Liu, J.: DMCNN: Dual-Domain Multi-Scale Convolutional Neural Network for Compression Artifacts Removal (2018). https://doi.org/10.48550/arXiv.1806.03275, http://arxiv.org/abs/1806.03275, arXiv:1806.03275 [cs]

# CAViT - Channel-Aware Vision Transformer for Dynamic Feature Fusion

Aon Safdar(✉) and Mohamed Saadeldin

School of Computer Science, University College Dublin, Dublin, Republic of Ireland
aon.safdar@ucdconnect.ie, mohamed.saadeldin@ucd.ie

**Abstract.** Vision Transformers (ViTs) have demonstrated strong performance across a range of computer vision tasks by modeling long-range spatial interactions via self-attention. However, channel-wise mixing in ViTs remains static, relying on fixed multilayer perceptrons (MLPs) that lack adaptability to input content. We introduce **CAViT**, a dual-attention architecture that replaces the static MLP with a dynamic, attention-based mechanism for feature interaction. Each Transformer block in CAViT (Code available at https://github.com/aonsafdar/CAVit) performs spatial self-attention followed by channel-wise self-attention, allowing the model to dynamically recalibrate feature representations based on global image context. This unified and content-aware token mixing strategy enhances representational expressiveness without increasing depth or complexity. We validate CAViT across five benchmark datasets spanning both natural and medical domains, where it outperforms the standard $\text{ViT}_{\text{tiny}}$ baseline by up to **+3.6%** in accuracy, while reducing parameter count and FLOPs by over **30%**. Qualitative attention maps reveal sharper and semantically meaningful activation patterns, validating the effectiveness of our attention-driven token mixing.

**Keywords:** Vision Transformers · Channel Attention · Vision Foundation Models

## 1 Introduction

Vision Transformers (ViTs) have reshaped modern computer vision by replacing convolutions with self-attention to model long-range dependencies [7,18]. While their flexibility and scalability have led to impressive results across classification, detection, and segmentation [9], ViTs retain an architectural asymmetry: spatial mixing is dynamic and data-dependent via Multi-Head Self-Attention (MHSA), but channel mixing is static, performed through fixed MLP layers. These MLPs linearly combine features across channels without awareness of image content, potentially limiting the model's ability to adapt to different visual structures.

This static channel mixing contrasts with the semantic role of channels in vision, where feature dimensions often represent meaningful filters (e.g., textures, parts, or semantic cues). Several works have attempted to address this


T. T. Mai et al. (Eds.): AICS 2025, CCIS 2950, pp. 214–225, 2026.
https://doi.org/10.1007/978-3-032-25809-0_17

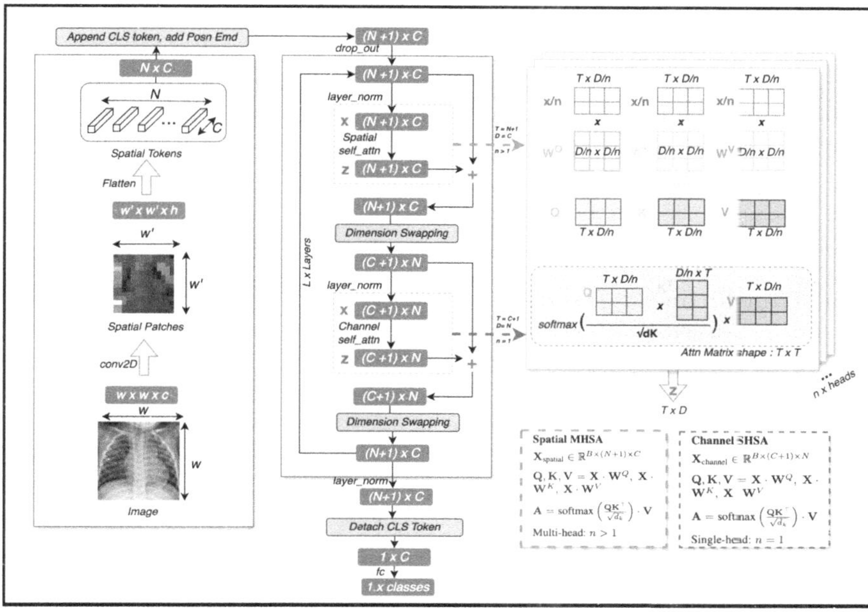


**Fig. 1. CAViT overview.** (Left) Standard tokenization. (Middle) Each block applies spatial MHSA on tokens $\mathbf{x} \in \mathbb{R}^{B\times(N+1)\times C}$, then swaps dimensions to $\mathbb{R}^{B\times(C+1)\times N}$ to treat channels as tokens and applies single-head channel self-attention (SHSA); the swap is then reversed. For spatial MHSA: $T = N+1$, $D = C$, $n>1$; for channel SHSA: $T = C+1$, $D = N$, $n = 1$. (Right) Standard $Q, K, V$ projections and softmax over $T \times T$.

issue by introducing channel attention mechanisms—such as SE-Net [10] and Cross-Covariance Attention [1]—or dynamic MLPs [14], but these often require additional modules or incur structural overhead.

We propose a simple and general solution by replacing the static MLP with a second self-attention stage that operates across feature channels. By transposing the input tensor and treating channels as tokens (Fig. 1), our method enables ViTs to learn inter-channel dependencies conditioned on global image context dynamically. This dual-attention design is seamlessly integrated into the standard Transformer block, improving both representational power and interpretability without increasing model depth or adding new modules.

**Our key contributions are:**

- We propose **CAViT**, a simple and generic architectural modification that replaces static MLPs in ViT blocks with channel-wise attention via dimension swapping, enabling adaptive inter-channel interactions.
- Our dual-attention formulation unifies spatial and channel-wise token mixing under a fully attention-driven framework, improving expressivity while preserving simplicity.

- We provide a theoretical and architectural motivation for dynamic channel mixing, showing how attention in the channel domain enhances information flow across feature dimensions and improves feature alignment.
- Through experiments on five diverse datasets across natural and medical imaging, we demonstrate consistent improvements in accuracy and efficiency over standard ViT baselines, both quantitatively and qualitatively.

## 2 Related Work

**Vision Transformers.** Transformers, initially developed for NLP [20], were adapted to vision with ViT [7], which uses tokenized image patches and MHSA. Subsequent variants such as DeiT [18] and Swin Transformer [15] improved training efficiency and scalability. Token-based architectures now serve as the backbone of many vision foundation models [3,27], motivating exploration of richer token and feature mixing strategies [12,16].

**Information Mixing Strategies.** While standard ViTs mix spatial and channel information using MHSA and static MLPs, respectively, recent work has proposed hybrid designs [11,23,26] or exclusive MLP/convolutional mixers [17,19]. Our work follows this line but investigates replacing the MLP with attention-based channel mixing to enhance context-aware feature interaction.

**Channel Attention in Vision.** SE-Net [10], CBAM [22], and Dual Attention [8] demonstrate that modeling channel dependencies improves CNN performance. These techniques, however, rely on static operations. We build on their insights by incorporating learnable, dynamic channel attention directly into ViT blocks.

**Dynamic Channel Mixing in Transformers.** Content-adaptive strategies such as gMLP [14], XCiT [1], and DaViT [6] show that dynamic channel interactions improve expressiveness. Ablation studies in [25] suggest that even lightweight channel attention can benefit ViTs. Unlike prior works that introduced channel attention as auxiliary components or external modules, our approach explores replacing the static MLP within the core Transformer block, enabling a unified architecture where both spatial and channel interactions are handled exclusively via self-attention, thus preserving the Transformer's structural simplicity while improving its representational expressiveness.

## 3 CAViT: Channel-Aware Vision Transformer with Dynamic Channel Mixing

Our proposed architecture, CAViT, enhances the standard Vision Transformer (ViT) by introducing a dual-attention mechanism within each Transformer block. As illustrated in ure Fig. 2, the core idea is to decouple the spatial and channel-wise mixing stages and treat both as attention operations. This is achieved through a simple yet effective architectural modification: replacing the MLP-based feedforward layer with a second attention stage applied across feature channels via dimension swapping.

### 3.1 Architecture Overview

As highlighted in Fig. 1, the conventional ViT architecture processes an input image $\mathbf{I} \in \mathbb{R}^{W \times W \times 3}$ by dividing it into non-overlapping patches of size $w \times w$ using linear or hard-split convolutional projections where each patch is represented by a vector of dimension $C$. This results in a sequence of $N = \frac{W \times W}{w^2}$ patch tokens, forming an input tensor $\mathbf{x} \in \mathbb{R}^{B \times N \times C}$, where $B$ is the batch size, $N$ is the number of spatial tokens, and $C$ is the embedding dimension. A learnable classification token (CLS) is prepended to this sequence, and positional embeddings are added, yielding $\mathbf{x} \in \mathbb{R}^{B \times (N+1) \times C}$. In CAVit, this sequence undergoes spatial attention followed by dimension swapping and channel attention before reversing the swap and handling CLS token to ensure global aggregation.

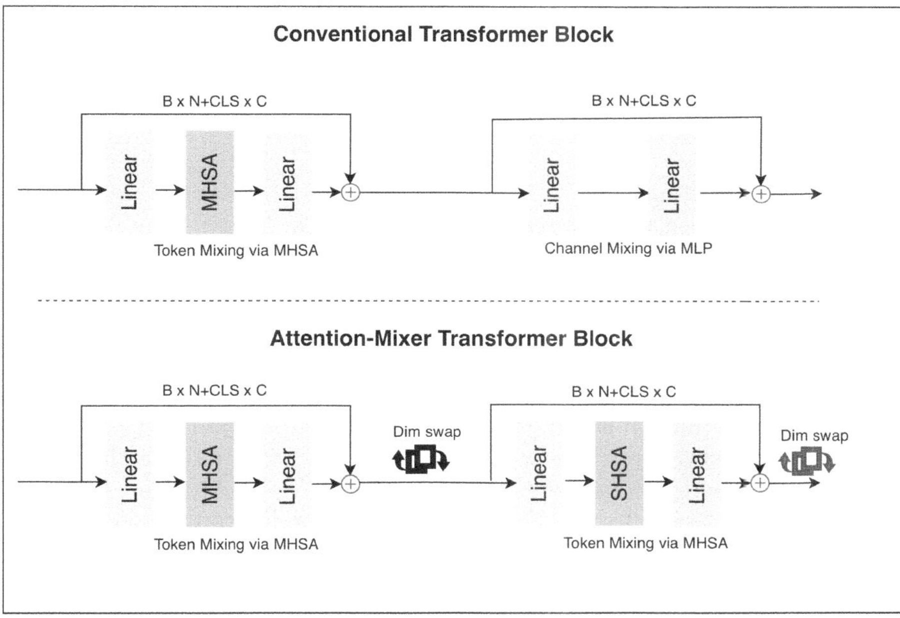


**Fig. 2. CAVit Transformer Block.** We propose a dual-attention Transformer block that models both spatial and channel-wise interactions using two sequential self-attention stages. The first stage applies standard MHSA over spatial tokens and operates across the token axis. The second stage performs channel-wise attention by swapping spatial and channel dimensions and applying SHSA across channels.

Conventional ViT block (top of Fig. 2) consists of two core stages: (1) a Multi-Head Self-Attention (MHSA) layer that operates across the sequence of spatial tokens, and (2) a feedforward MLP that performs channel-wise mixing for each token independently. This asymmetry in treatment, i.e., adaptive attention across space, but static linear mixing across channels, limits representational flexibility. In CAViT (bottom of Fig. 2), we preserve the MHSA spatial attention but replace the MLP with a second attention module, enabling channel-wise mixing via a transposition that allows attention to operate across feature channels. This modification reframes the Transformer block as an attention-only unit, enhancing both spatial and channel interactions through learnable, content-adaptive mechanisms.

### 3.2 Dynamic Feature Fusion

The MLP accounts for a large fraction of parameters and FLOPs in ViT, yet it acts as a token-wise linear transformation with nonlinear gating. This design neither exploits inter-channel relationships nor adapts to content. In contrast, using self-attention across channels introduces a dynamic, data-driven inductive bias, better aligned with how semantic concepts manifest across channel dimensions in deep networks (e.g., texture detectors, part filters). Spatial and channel attention capture complementary cues. While spatial MHSA models long-range positional relationships, channel attention models dependencies among feature activations. Incorporating both into a single, symmetric structure improves model expressiveness.

**CLS Token Handling.** The CLS token serves as a global context aggregator[1]. If improperly handled (e.g., swapped alongside spatial tokens (See Table 3), it loses its global aggregation role and becomes semantically entangled. Our design maintains the integrity of the CLS token (See Fig. 3), allowing it to aggregate attention information during both spatial and channel attention phases.

**Dimension Swapping for Channel Attention.** As illustrated in Fig. 3, to apply attention across channels, we first transpose the input representation such that the feature dimensions become the sequence axis. Specifically, after the spatial MHSA stage, the tensor $\mathbf{x} \in \mathbb{R}^{B\times(N+1)\times C}$ is split into the class token $\mathbf{x}_{\text{cls}} \in \mathbb{R}^{B\times 1\times C}$ and the spatial tokens $\mathbf{x}_{\text{spat}} \in \mathbb{R}^{B\times N\times C}$. We then transpose the spatial token tensor to $\mathbf{x}_{\text{trans}} \in \mathbb{R}^{B\times C\times N}$, thereby interpreting channels as sequence tokens. To ensure the CLS token participates in global channel-wise interactions, it is explicitly reshaped to $\mathbf{x}_{\text{cls}} \in \mathbb{R}^{B\times 1\times N}$, ensuring alignment along the sequence axis before concatenation. This results in a tensor of shape $\mathbb{R}^{B\times(C+1)\times N}$ for channel-wise attention[2].

**Single-Head Channel Attention.** Attention is now applied across the channel-token sequence. Unlike the spatial attention stage, we use a single-head self-attention (SHSA) mechanism here. The rationale is that in the transposed space, each channel token already encodes the global image context, and dividing attention across multiple heads may dilute this abstraction. While SHSA

[1] Some pooling-based classification heads (e.g., average or max pooling) avoid using a CLS token altogether. While our method is compatible with such configurations, we focus on standard ViT settings where CLS is retained, to ensure fair comparison and compatibility with vanilla backbones.

[2] In our experiments, we set $C = N$, avoiding the need for explicit reshaping. For general cases with $C \neq N$, a linear projection of the CLS token ensures compatibility.

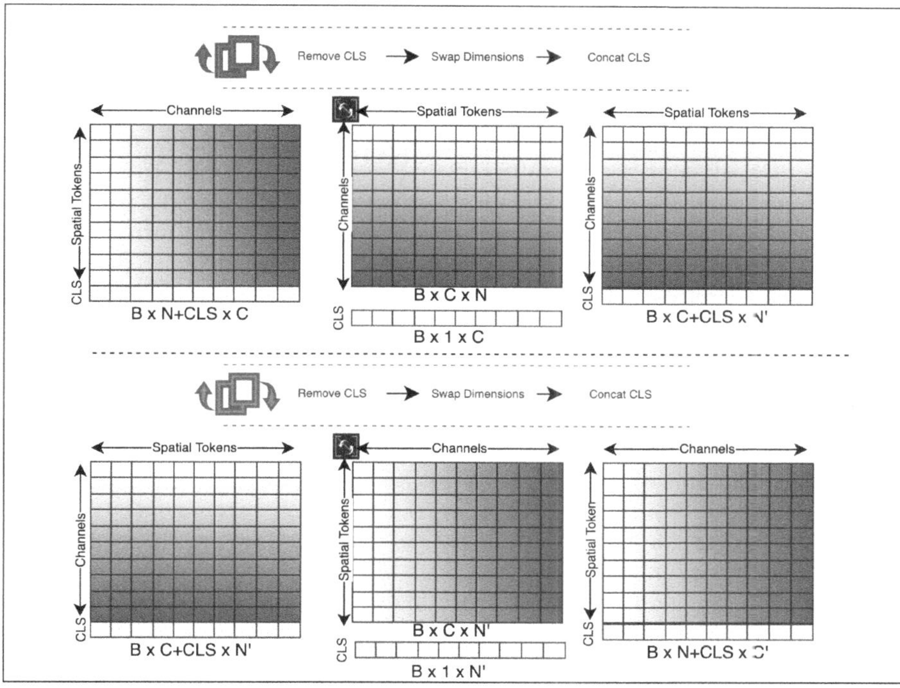


**Fig. 3. Dimension Swapping Mechanism.** Illustration of our dimension swapping logic used to enable channel-wise attention. The class token (CLS) is first separated from the input tensor $\mathbf{x} \in \mathbb{R}^{B\times(N+1)\times C}$, where $B$ is batch size, $N$ is the number of spatial tokens, and $C$ is the channel dimension. The remaining spatial tokens are transposed from shape $\mathbb{R}^{B\times N\times C}$ to $\mathbb{R}^{B\times C\times N}$, effectively treating channels as attention tokens. The CLS token is then concatenated back, resulting in a new tensor of shape $\mathbb{R}^{B\times(C+1)\times N}$. Single-head self-attention (SHSA) is applied across this transformed token dimension. The reverse operation restores the original layout, enabling standard downstream processing.

introduces a potential computational bottleneck, it avoids over-fragmentation in the image space and preserves full spatial context within each channel token, enabling coherent and content-adaptive mixing across channels. The effects are further verified in Sect. 4.3. After attention, we reverse the dimension swap: the CLS token is again extracted, the remaining sequence is transposed back to shape $\mathbb{R}^{B\times N\times C}$, and the CLS token is prepended. The next Transformer block thus receives a representation enriched with both spatial and channel-level interactions.

# 4 Experiments and Results

## 4.1 Datasets and Metrics

We evaluate our method on five classification datasets spanning both natural and medical imaging domains: CIFAR-10 [13], Malaria [2], Cats vs Dogs [5], PneumoniaMNIST, and BreastMNIST [24]. These datasets ("See Table 1 for an overview.") encompass binary and multi-class settings and cover diverse imaging modalities including RGB photographs, microscopy, X-ray, and ultrasound. To ensure architectural consistency across datasets and facilitate fair comparison, all input images are resized to 224 × 224 pixels.

We compare $\text{ViT}_{\text{tiny}}$ and $\text{CAViT}_{\text{tiny}}$ in terms of performance and efficiency. For each model, we report the best Top-1 test accuracy achieved over 100 training epochs. To evaluate model complexity, we use two widely adopted and system-independent metrics: parameter count (total number of learnable weights) and GFLOPs (floating-point operations per forward pass). These metrics provide reproducible estimates of memory footprint and compute cost, respectively. We implement both models in PyTorch using the `timm` [21] components. We train with SGD optimizer, an initial learning rate of 0.001, and no aggressive augmentation or regularization, to isolate the effects of our architectural modifications. All experiments are conducted on a Linux machine with an NVIDIA RTX 4090 GPU (CUDA 12.4), PyTorch 2.6.0, and Python 3.10. For reproducibility, we fix the random seed to 42.

**Table 1.** Overview of datasets used for evaluation. We benchmark $\text{ViT}_{\text{tiny}}$ and $\text{CAViT}_{\text{tiny}}$ variants across natural and medical image classification datasets, spanning binary (BC) and multi-class (MC) tasks with diverse modalities. All images are resized to 224 × 224 resolution.

| Name | Modality | Task Type | # Samples |
|---|---|---|---|
| CIFAR-10 [13] | RGB (Natural Scene) | MC (10) | 60,000 |
| Cats vs Dogs [5] | RGB (Natural Scene) | BC (2) | 25,000 |
| Malaria [2] | Microscopy (Blood Smear) | BC (2) | 27,588 |
| PneumoniaMNIST [24] | Chest X-ray | BC (2) | 5,856 |
| BreastMNIST [24] | Ultrasound (Breast) | BC (2) | 780 |

## 4.2 Results and Analysis

**Quantitative Performance.** Table 2 and Fig. 4 compare the performance of the baseline $\text{ViT}_{\text{tiny}}$ and our proposed $\text{CAViT}_{\text{tiny}}$ across five diverse datasets. CAViT achieves either comparable or superior Top-1 accuracy on all benchmarks while reducing model complexity by approximately **32% in parameters** and **33% in FLOPs**. Notable improvements are observed on CIFAR-10 (+3.64%), BreastMNIST (+2.50%), and PneumoniaMNIST (+1.14%), indicating that CAViT generalizes better across both natural and medical image domains. Even in the Malaria dataset, where performance remains unchanged, CAViT achieves this parity with significantly fewer resources.

**Table 2. CAViT improves accuracy across domains.** Comparison of ViT and CAViT on five diverse datasets. CAViT improves or maintains Top-1 classification accuracy in most cases, while reducing model complexity by **−32%** in parameters ($5.75 \mapsto 3.91$M) and **−33%** in FLOPs ($2.26 \mapsto 1.52$G).

| Dataset | $\text{ViT}_{\text{tiny}}$ | $\text{CAViT}_{\text{tiny}}$ | Gain (%) |
|---|---|---|---|
| CIFAR-10 [13] | 65.09 | **68.73** | **+3.64** |
| Malaria [2] | **96.35** | 96.33 | **−0.02** |
| Cats vs Dogs [5] | 74.96 | **75.82** | **+0.86** |
| Pneumonia [24] | 95.61 | **96.75** | **+1.14** |
| Breast Ultrasound [24] | 83.30 | **85.80** | **+2.50** |

As shown in Fig. 4, CAViT achieves a consistent improvement in Top-1 accuracy across most evaluated benchmarks compared to standard ViT-tiny. Particularly on CIFAR-10 and CatsVsDogs, the accuracy gains are early and stable. On medical benchmarks like PneumoniaMNIST and BreastMNIST, CAViT exhibits smoother convergence and higher peak accuracy. These results further support our architectural hypothesis that dynamic channel attention complements spatial attention to improve learning for both natural and clinical domains.

**Qualitative Attention Analysis.** To interpret the internal behavior of both models, we generate token-level attention maps using a DINO-style visualization [4], averaging attention scores across heads and tokens. Figure 5 overlays these attention weights on input images. We observe that $\text{ViT}_{\text{tiny}}$ often exhibits noisy or edge-focused attention, while CAViT learns to attend to both fine-grained structures and semantically relevant regions. For instance, in medical scans (rows 3–5), CAViT highlights lesion areas more precisely, and in natural scenes, it demonstrates tighter focus on object boundaries and global form. This supports the claim that combining spatial and channel-wise attention enhances semantic reasoning. These patterns reflect the underlying benefit of channel-wise attention as it enables dynamic, content-adaptive feature fusion. Unlike static MLPs that apply fixed channel mixing across all inputs, our attention-based design recalibrates feature interactions based on global context. This improves representational expressiveness while maintaining architectural simplicity.

### 4.3 Ablation Study and Architecture Insights

To better understand the impact of different architectural decisions, we conduct a detailed ablation study summarized in Table 3. The variants are grouped into categories for clarity.

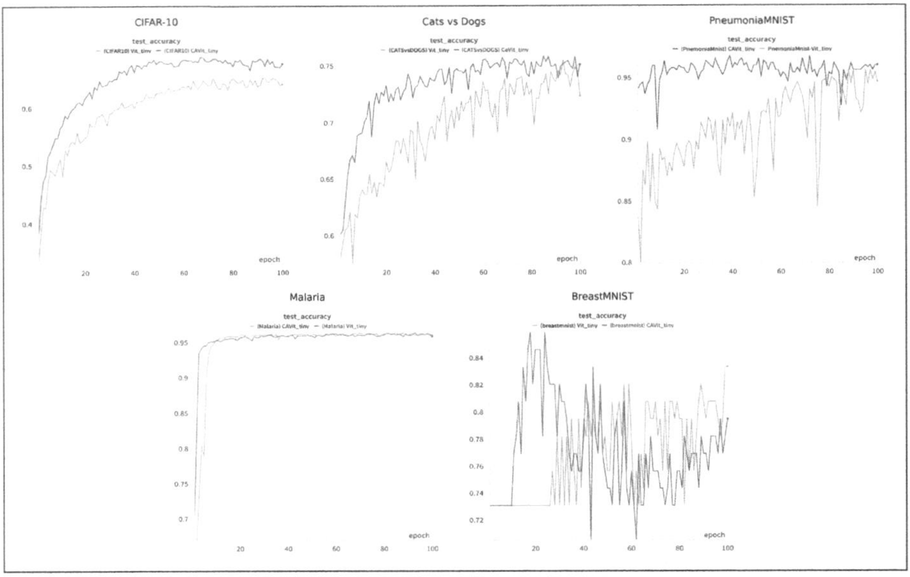


**Fig. 4. Top-1 Val Accuracy across Training Epochs.** Comparison of $\text{ViT}_{\text{tiny}}$ and $\text{CAViT}_{\text{tiny}}$ on five benchmarks. CAViT consistently shows faster convergence and better generalization on natural (CIFAR-10 [13], CatsVsDogs [5]) and medical datasets (PneumoniaMNIST [24], Malaria [2], BreastMNIST [24]). Notably, CAViT yields consistent gains on datasets with limited resolution and inter-class variability.

We first test whether spatial MHSA can be fully replaced with channel-wise SHSA. Surprisingly, this leads to a sharp performance drop across all datasets (e.g., −2.24% on CIFAR-10 and −2.57% on PneumoniaMNIST), despite a minor reduction in compute. This indicates that spatial attention is essential for capturing positional dependencies and cannot be substituted entirely by channel interactions. We further evaluate a variant of CAViT that uses multi-head self-attention in the channel branch instead of single-head SHSA. The results are slightly worse across all datasets (e.g., −0.34% on CIFAR-10), suggesting that multi-head splits in channel space may fragment semantic dependencies, and a unified global descriptor (SHSA) is more effective for channel mixing. Finally, we examine the importance of CLS token positioning by applying dimension swapping to the class token as well. This variant significantly underperforms (e.g., −8.83% on CIFAR-10 and −5.78% on PneumoniaMNIST), indicating that treating the CLS token as a channel token disrupts its intended role in aggregating spatial semantics.

**Discussion.** The performance and attention patterns of CAViT reveal several key advantages. First, replacing MLP-based channel mixing with attention enables the model to dynamically reweight feature channels based on global context. Second, our dimension-swapping mechanism allows this operation to be

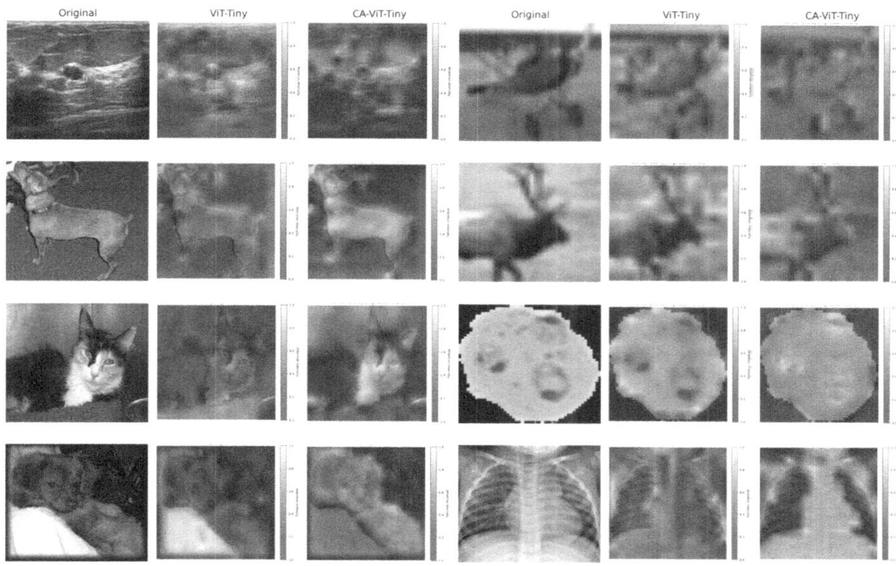


**Fig. 5. Visualization of token attention:** Attention for various samples across domains including natural images, medical scans, and low-resolution categories. We use DINO-style visualization by averaging token attention maps across heads and tokens to highlight structural saliency. CAViT-Tiny captures more spatially coherent and semantically focused attention and better localizes foreground regions and anatomical features. (Best viewed in color and zoomed-in).

integrated seamlessly without altering the core Transformer pipeline. The dual-path attention formulation improves representational capacity while remaining compute-efficient. Importantly, these gains are achieved *without architectural deepening, extra parameters, or post-hoc regularization*, highlighting the core utility of the proposed design.

**Conclusion of Findings.** Overall, CAViT delivers a favorable trade-off between accuracy and efficiency across a variety of domains. The model not only improves quantitative metrics but also demonstrates more interpretable and semantically grounded attention behavior. These results suggest that CAViT's proposed unified dynamic attention across spatial and feature dimensions is a promising design for Transformers in both vision and medical imaging applications.

## 5 Limitations and Future Work

This work focuses on validating the core idea of combining spatial and channel-wise attention through dimension swapping within a low-resource regime. For conceptual clarity and controlled experimentation, we restrict our evaluation to $\text{ViT}_{\text{tiny}}$ and moderate-sized datasets. While this setup effectively demonstrates

**Table 3.** Ablation study on attention configuration and CLS handling. We isolate the effect of various components in spatial vs. channel attention.

| Ablation Variant | C10 | Mal. | CvsD | Pneu. | Brst. | P/F |
|---|---|---|---|---|---|---|
| *Baseline - Standard ViT* | | | | | | |
| $\text{Spatial}_{MHSA} \rightarrow$ MLP | 65.09 | **96.35** | 74.96 | 95.61 | 83.3 | 5.7M/2.26G |
| *Proposed - CAViT* | | | | | | |
| $\text{Spatial}_{MHSA} \rightarrow \text{Channel}_{SHSA}$ | **68.37** | 96.33 | **75.82** | **96.75** | **85.8** | 3.1M/1.52G |
| *Multi-head Channel Attention* | | | | | | |
| $\text{Spatial}_{MHSA} \rightarrow \text{Channel}_{MHSA}$ | 64.39 | 95.43 | 74.52 | 95.37 | 82.9 | 3.1M/1.52G |
| *Replacing Spatial Attention* | | | | | | |
| $\text{Channel}_{SHSA} \rightarrow$ MLP | 62.85 | 92.5 | 75.13 | 94.18 | 82.73 | 5.7M/2.26G |
| *CLS Token Transposition* | | | | | | |
| CAViT with CLS Swapped | 59.9 | 93.18 | 74.09 | 90.97 | 80.98 | 3.1M/1.52G |

the advantages of our approach, it limits direct comparison with existing large-scale benchmarks. We adopt a fixed patch-based tokenizer consistent with standard ViT; however, future work may investigate how structure-aware or adaptive tokenizers can synergize with our method. We intentionally avoid training optimizations, including aggressive AugReg or distillation, and focus solely on architectural merit. In future work, we aim to extend CAViT to multi-modal, self-supervised, and dense prediction settings.

## 6 Conclusion

We introduce CAViT, a simple and effective modification to Vision Transformers that replaces static MLP-based channel mixing with attention-based channel-wise interaction. By combining spatial and channel attention in a unified block, we improve accuracy and interpretability while reducing parameters and FLOPs. Our experiments across five diverse datasets demonstrate consistent gains over $\text{ViT}_{\text{tiny}}$, validating the benefit of dynamic token mixing with minimal architectural changes. This work is intended as a first step toward structured attention-based token mixing in transformers. We plan to extend our approach to larger backbones and datasets such as ImageNet.

**Acknowledgments.** This publication has emanated from research conducted with the financial support of Taighde Éireann – Research Ireland under Grant number 18/CRT/6183 (For the purpose of Open Access, the author has applied a CC BY public copyright licence to any Author Accepted Manuscript version arising from this submission).

**Disclosure of Interests.** The authors have no competing interests to declare that are relevant to the content of this article.

## References


1. Ali, A., et al.: XCiT: cross-covariance image transformers. In: Proceedings of NeurIPS (2021)
2. Arunava, I.: Cell images for detecting malaria. Kaggle (2018)
3. Bordes, F.: An introduction to vision-language modeling (2024). arXiv:2405.17247
4. Caron, M., et al.: Emerging properties in self-supervised vision transformers. In: Proceedings of ICCV, pp. 9630–9640 (2021)
5. Cukierski, W.: Dogs vs. cats. Kaggle (2013)
6. Ding, M., Xiao, B., Codella, N., Luo, P., Wang, J., Yuan, L.: DaViT: dual attention vision transformers. In: Proceedings of ECCV (2022)
7. Dosovitskiy, A., et al.: An image is worth 16×16 words: transformers for image recognition at scale. In: Proceedings of ICLR (2021)
8. Fu, J.: Dual attention network for scene segmentation. In: Proceedings of the IEEE/CVF Conference on Computer Vision and Pattern Recognition (CVPR) (2019)
9. Han, K., et al.: A survey on vision transformer. IEEE TPAMI **45**(1), 87–110 (2023)
10. Hu, J., Shen, L., Sun, G.: Squeeze-and-excitation networks. In: Proceedings of CVPR (2018)
11. Kahatapitiya, K., Ryoo, M.S.: SWAT: spatial structure within and among tokens. In: Proceedings of IJCAI, pp. 956–964 (2023)
12. Khan, S., Naseer, M., Hayat, M., Zamir, S.W., Khan, F.S., Shah, M.: Transformers in vision: a survey. ACM Comput. Surv. **54**, 200:1–200:41 (2022)
13. Krizhevsky, A., Hinton, G.: Learning multiple layers of features from tiny images. Technical Report, Univ. Toronto (2009)
14. Liu, H., Dai, Z., So, D.R., Le, Q.V.: Pay attention to MLPs. In: Proceedings of NeurIPS, pp. 9204–9215 (2021)
15. Liu, Z., et al.: Swin transformer: hierarchical vision transformer using shifted windows. In: Proceedings of ICCV, pp. 9992–10002 (2021)
16. Shamshad, F., et al.: Transformers in medical imaging: a survey. Med. Image Anal. **88**, 102802 (2023)
17. Tolstikhin, I.O., et al.: MLP-Mixer: an all-MLP architecture for vision. In: Proceedings of NeurIPS, pp. 24261–24272 (2021)
18. Touvron, H., Cord, M., Douze, M., Massa, F., Sablayrolles, A., Jégou, H.: Training data-efficient image transformers & distillation through attention. In: Proceedings of ICML, pp. 10347–10357 (2021)
19. Trockman, A., Kolter, J.Z.: Patches are all you need? arXiv:2201.09792 (2022)
20. Vaswani, A., et al.: Attention is all you need. In: Proceedings of NeurIPS (2017)
21. Wightman, R.: Pytorch image models, gitHub repository (2021)
22. Woo, S., Park, J., Lee, J., Kweon, I.S.: CBAM: convolutional block attention module. In: Proceedings of ECCV (2018)
23. Wu, H., et al.: CvT: introducing convolutions to vision transformers, arXiv:2103.15808 (2021)
24. Yang, J., et al.: MedMNIST v2: a large-scale lightweight benchmark for 2D and 3D biomedical image classification. Sci. Data **10**(1), 41 (2023)
25. Yuan, L., et al.: Tokens-to-token ViT: training vision transformers from scratch on imagenet. In: Proceedings of ICCV, pp. 538–547 (2021)
26. Zheng, J., Yang, L., Li, Y.: Yang: lightweight vision transformer with spatial and channel enhanced self-attention. In: 2023 IEEE/CVF International Conference on Computer Vision Workshops (ICCVW), pp. 1484–1488 (2023)
27. Zhou, T., et al.: Image segmentation in foundation model era: a survey, arXiv:2408.12957 (2024)

# Optimising LLM-Based Enterprise RAG Retrieval with Adaptive Parameters Using Cumulative Thresholds

Malik Muhammad Qirtas(✉), Bastien Pietropaoli, Eduardo Vyhmeister, and Andrea Visentin

Insight RI Centre for Data Analytics, School of Computer Science and IT, University College Cork, Cork, Ireland
mqirtas@ucc.ie

**Abstract.** Retrieval augmented generation (RAG) systems heavily rely on retrieval parameters, such as the number of documents to retrieve ($k$) and similarity thresholds ($\tau$). The retrieval step is crucial for improving overall answer quality; yet, most systems fix these values globally and use a constant $k$ or a single threshold, even though queries can vary significantly in style and difficulty. In this paper, we focus on optimising the retrieval component of RAG and analyse how different choices of these parameters impact performance across diverse query types. As a case study, we evaluate on the DATAMITE enterprise knowledge base, for which we create test questions in four categories: direct domain queries, queries with typos, relational queries with multiple correct answers, and out-of-domain queries. Using these sets, we evaluate the retrieval performance based on different values of $k$ and $\tau$. Our results show that a single global setting is not optimal across all query types. To address this, we develop a simple adaptive retrieval method: retrieve widely, re-rank, and diversify the results, and then stop when enough relevant information has been retrieved. This method consistently improves retrieval quality over fixed settings.

**Keywords:** RAG · LLM · Retrieval · Optimisation

## 1 Introduction

Large language models (LLMs) have shown impressive capabilities in natural language understanding and generation, but they also face some severe challenges, like hallucination of unsupported facts, lack of up-to-date knowledge, and difficulty handling domain-specific information [1]. To address these issues, Retrieval-Augmented Generation (RAG) has emerged as an effective approach that grounds model outputs in external knowledge sources by combining large language models with document retrieval [2]. In a RAG pipeline, external knowledge sources, such as enterprise databases, documentation repositories, or webpages, are searched in real-time to retrieve relevant information based on users' queries. The retrieved information passages are incorporated into the model's


T. T. Mai et al. (Eds.): AICS 2025, CCIS 2950, pp. 226–238, 2026.
https://doi.org/10.1007/978-3-032-25809-0_18

prompt so that its responses are grounded in external evidence and it relies less on its internal parametric memory [3]. RAG is now widely used in enterprise applications, where reliable answers must be drawn from trusted knowledge bases rather than model guesses.

In a RAG system, the retrieval step is crucial as it determines the evidence available to the LLM for generating the final answer. When retrieval fails by missing relevant documents or including irrelevant or noisy ones, the quality of the final answer degrades quickly. The retrieval process is mainly controlled by two parameters: the number of documents retrieved from the knowledge base ($k$) and the similarity threshold ($\tau$) used for filtering those retrieved documents, which specifies the minimum similarity score a document must have with the query to be considered relevant. Most deployments keep these parameters fixed globally, but real-world queries vary widely. For instance, some are short and precise, others contain typos or noise, some require combining evidence across multiple documents, and some may fall completely outside the domain. As a result, a single global choice of $k$ and $\tau$ often struggles to achieve the right balance between precision and recall across such diverse cases [4].

In this paper, we investigate whether the retrieval component of RAG can be enhanced using straightforward, training-free methods suitable for enterprise deployment. As a case study, we evaluate our system on the DATAMITE enterprise knowledge base [5]. We make the following contributions:

1. We build test sets across four query categories: direct domain queries, noisy or typo variants, relational queries with two correct answers, and out-of-domain (OOD) queries. This setup allows a more fine-grained evaluation of retrieval behaviour.
2. We developed a simple adaptive retrieval method that begins with wide retrieval, applies cross-encoder re-ranking with maximal marginal relevance diversification, and then selects documents dynamically based on cumulative relevance.
3. To encourage reproducibility, we provide code, JSON test sets, and evaluation scripts.

## 2 Related Work

Early RAG architectures such as REALM [6] and Fusion-in-Decoder (FiD) [7] showed that combining parametric language models with non-parametric memory improves factual accuracy and makes outputs more interpretable. More recent systems, including RETRO [8] and Atlas [9], have shown that RAG can enable smaller models to match or even surpass much larger LLMs on open-domain question answering by grounding responses in up-to-date knowledge. Comparative evaluations further indicate that dense retrievers (e.g., DPR, ANCE, Contriever) often outperform sparse methods such as BM25 and TF–IDF on in-domain benchmarks. In contrast, sparse methods remain competitive for keyword-heavy or out-of-domain queries [10]. As a result, hybrid and enterprise RAG deployments often integrate both dense and sparse retrievers to balance recall and precision when working with specialised knowledge bases.

An important but less explored aspect of RAG is how retrieval parameters ($k$ and similarity threshold ($\tau$)) are chosen. The choice of these parameters strongly affect recall (how many correct documents are included) and precision (how much irrelevant material is excluded), yet many systems rely on fixed global values: for example, the original RAG uses a constant top-$k$ [3], FiD retrieves 100 passages [7], and RETRO also relies on a fixed number of neighbours [8]. These design choices simplify implementation but strongly affect the precision–recall trade-off. Increasing $k$ usually helps recall because more relevant documents are found but it also lowers precision by bringing in extra irrelevant passages that creates noise and can confuse the model. Classical IR work showed that optimal depth and cut-off depend on the query itself and proposed adaptive settings [4]. Studies have confirmed that the one global configuration is suboptimal, but their analyses are usually presented across datasets or tasks rather than by query intent within a single knowledge base [10,11]. For example, a simple factoid question may be answered with k=1, whereas multi-hop or ambiguous questions often require $k \geq 5$ to capture enough evidence.

Adaptive retrieval can be implemented in several ways. One approach is model-triggered or uncertainty-gated schemes, where the system decides whether and how much to retrieve based on signals of confidence (e.g., Self-RAG triggers extra retrieval when the model is uncertain [12]). A second approach is signal-based adaptive-$k$, which adjusts $k$ by looking at the distribution of similarity scores or by predicting how difficult the query is [4]. A third approach uses rule-based heuristics, where the system retrieves a wide set of documents, re-ranks them, and then stops once certain conditions are met [13].

Recent work has also explored adaptive retrieval in different settings. heiDS proposed a query-dependent cutoff using score drop heuristics but its pipeline still depends on training dense retrievers models for clinical QA [14]. SAGE introduces a heavier framework that needs training a semantic segmentation model and an additional relevance-scoring network with an LLM feedback loop to decide how many chunks to retrieve [15]. These works reinforce the intuition that retrieval depth should vary by query but most of these methods depend on additional models or classifiers, which can add complexity, but simpler training-free approaches that make decisions using only re-ranking signals could be more beneficial for practical deployments.

Re-ranking and diversification are central components in modern pipelines [16,17]. A cross-encoder re-ranker [11] evaluates the query and each candidate document together to give a more precise relevance score as compared to a bi-encoder. Diversification methods such as Maximal Marginal Relevance (MMR), which balances relevance with novelty, or Determinantal Point Processes (DPPs), which promote diverse document sets, help avoid redundancy and ensure coverage [13,18]. Many pipelines follow a multi-stage design, but most systems still use a fixed cutoff at their last stage when deciding on the value of $k$ to pass to LLM, and little work has explored how to adaptively decide the right $k$ after re-ranking.

Evaluating RAG is challenging as it requires measuring both retrieval quality (whether the right documents are found) and answer quality. Common IR metrics include Precision@k, Recall@k, and Mean Reciprocal Rank (MRR) [19], while quality assurance (QA) metrics such as Exact Match and F1 are widely used for generated answers. Recent work also considers faithfulness (answers supported by retrieved documents) and unanswerability/abstention (recognising when a query is unanswerable, e.g. OOD) [20,21]. However, only a few studies report results across different query categories [10] and none systematically compare multiple query intents (e.g., typos, relational queries, OOD) within the same knowledge base while controlling retrieval parameters.

Evidence on how $k$ and $\tau$ affect recall–precision trade-offs remains limited, with most studies presenting aggregate results rather than breakdowns by query type. Existing adaptive retrieval methods rely on trained classifiers or multi-stage pipelines, while simpler training-free strategies using re-ranking signals (e.g., cross-encoder scores) are underexplored.

Our work addresses these gaps by: (i) constructing test sets across four query-intent categories and analysing precision–recall trade-offs under varying $k$ and $\tau$; (ii) introducing a training-free adaptive method combining wide retrieval, cross-encoder re-ranking, MMR diversification, and a coverage-based stopping rule; and (iii) reporting false positive rates (FPR) for OOD queries.

# 3 Methodology

## 3.1 Retrieval Evaluation Setup

We frame retrieval as a two-parameter optimisation problem. For a given query, the system embeds the query and candidate documents, computes cosine similarity scores, and keeps the top-$k$ results above a threshold $\tau$. The selected documents are then passed to the LLM as context. Varying $k$ and $\tau$ shifts the recall–precision balance, so in our experiments, we test different settings and evaluate performance using precision, recall, F1, MRR, average similarity, and RankFirst across query categories.

As a case study, we utilize the DATAMITE enterprise knowledge base [5], which contains structured records on various topics related to data monetization, such as key performance indicators (KPIs), objectives, and business criteria (e.g., entries like "CAPEX" or "Accessibility"). This domain-specific KB is representative of the tailored content often used in enterprise RAG systems.

To capture how retrieval behaves in realistic situations, we created test sets with four types of queries. Each type reflects a typical user behaviour or a challenge the system must handle:

1. **Direct domain queries**: Clear, well-formed questions directly covered in the knowledge base (e.g., *"What is CAPEX?"*).
2. **Noisy or typo queries**: Variants of domain questions that include spelling mistakes, abbreviations or small grammar errors (e.g., *"Whct is CPAX?"*). These test how robust the system is to imperfect input.
3. **Relational queries with multiple answers**: Questions that link together multiple pieces of information (e.g., *"What is the relation between CAPEX and Accessibility?"*).

4. **Out-of-domain (OOD) queries**: Questions that lie outside the scope of the knowledge base (e.g., *"Who won the FIFA World Cup in 2022?"*). In this case, a reliable system should return nothing, which makes OOD queries useful for testing false positives.

For each DATAMITE record (KPIs, objectives, business criteria), we provided the raw CSV entry to the LLM and asked it to produce a direct question. We then prompted the model to create (i) a typo/noisy variant of the same question and (ii) a relational question by combining two semantically linked records. All LLM-generated questions were manually reviewed and corrected to ensure clarity and to assign the correct ground-truth document(s). To maintain consistency across categories, each test set contained 984 queries to match the scale of the original DATAMITE content. Each query was labelled with one or more ground-truth documents in the knowledge base. The code and datasets used in this study are openly available at our GitHub repository[1]

### 3.2 Knowledge Base Creation

Our system was built using the `LangChain`[2] framework, `ChromaDB`[3] as the vector database, and `HuggingFace`[4] models for embeddings and reranking. All experiments were implemented in Python.

The knowledge base was constructed from multiple CSV files containing DATAMITE enterprise information such as KPIs, objectives and strategy documents. Since these files often contained formatting inconsistencies and JSON related issues, we implemented a preprocessing stage to clean them before ingestion.

*Document Length and Chunking:* Each record in the source CSV (e.g., KPI, Objective, CAPEX) was ingested as a separate `LangChain Document`, making every entry a self-contained unit. We analyzed character lengths by record type and found averages below 1000 characters, which is well within the limits of the embedding model and LLM context window; therefore, no further chunking was applied.

*Embeddings and Database:* The `LangChain Documents` were converted into dense vector embeddings. We used HuggingFace's `all-MiniLM-L6-v2`[5] bi-encoder model, which maps text into 384-dimensional vectors. This captures the semantic meaning of each record, allowing similarity search to be based on meaning rather than exact keywords. These embeddings, along with the original documents and metadata, formed the basis of our vector database. At query time, we embed the user question with the same model to ensure that queries

[1] Source code and all experiment scripts are available at: https://github.com/Qirtas/AdaptiveRetrieval-RAG.

[2] https://python.langchain.com/docs.

[3] https://docs.trychroma.com/.

[4] https://huggingface.co/.

[5] https://huggingface.co/sentence-transformers/all-MiniLM-L6-v2.

and documents lie in the same vector space for comparison. The embeddings and their associated documents were stored in a `ChromaDB` persistent vector database. Cosine similarity was used as the scoring function for retrieval.

### 3.3 Calculating Similarity Scores for Top-1 Hit for Test Sets

As a first step before tuning retrieval parameters, we examined the similarity scores of the top result for each query. This helped us see how the score ranges differ across query categories and whether thresholds could be used to separate in-domain queries from OOD ones.

We set the retriever to $k = 1$, so that only the single most similar document was returned for each query. For each test set, we collected the cosine similarity score.

### 3.4 Tuning $k$ and Similarity Thresholds

After looking at the similarity score distributions, we evaluated how different retrieval settings affect performance. We focused on $k$ and $\tau$, which filter out documents with low scores. For each combination, we measured retrieval quality across all query categories.

We tested values of $k \in \{1, 2, 3, 4, 5, 7, 10\}$ and $\tau \in \{0.1, 0.2, 0.25, 0.3, 0.35, 0.5, 0.7, 0.9\}$. For every query, the retriever returned the top-$k$ documents with their cosine similarity scores, and any document scoring below $\tau$ was filtered out. The remaining results were then compared with the ground-truth labels.

We chose to refine the threshold grid around $\tau \approx 0.30$ because the similarity score distributions across query categories indicated that values in this range strike a balance as they help filter out most OOD matches while still retaining relevant in-domain documents. Exploring finer details in this region helped us capture this trade-off more accurately.

For each $(k, \tau)$ setting we calculated standard metrics:

- **Precision:** The proportion of retrieved documents that were correct.
- **Recall:** The proportion of all correct documents that were successfully retrieved.
- **F1:** Balance between precision and recall, defined as $\mathrm{F1} = \frac{2\,\mathrm{Precision} \times \mathrm{Recall}}{\mathrm{Precision} + \mathrm{Recall}}$.
- **MRR (Mean Reciprocal Rank):** Measures how early the first correct document appears in the ranked list. It is defined as the average of reciprocal ranks across all queries, with values between 0 and 1, where 1 indicates that the correct document is always ranked first, and lower values indicate later positions.
- **Average similarity (AvgSim):** For each query, we take the mean cosine similarity of all documents included in the final context set (i.e., those that survive the selection step), regardless of correctness. If a query has no documents, its AvgSim is undefined and excluded. The reported value is the macro-average of these per-query means over all queries with at least one kept document.

- **Rank of first match (RankFirst):** the position in the ranked list where the first correct document appears. If no correct document is retrieved, the value is undefined. We report the average RankFirst only over queries where at least one correct document was retrieved.

For the OOD queries, where the correct behaviour is to return nothing, we measured False Positive Rate (FPR), which is the percentage of OOD queries that still retrieved at least one document above the threshold.

### 3.5 Adaptive Retrieval

In the fixed-$k$ retrieval approach, the system always returns the same number of documents, regardless of the query type and user needs. This is inefficient as short definition-style queries may only need one or two documents, while complex or relational queries often require more. If too few documents are retrieved, the LLM may miss important evidence, and if too many are included, the context for the LLM can become noisy and redundant. To address this, we employed an adaptive retrieval strategy that dynamically determines the number of documents to return based on relevance scores from the retriever.

Our approach has three steps:

*Step 1: Wide retrieval.* We first retrieve a broad pool of candidates using dense embeddings and cosine similarity. Based on small empirical experiments with the pool size, we set $K = 20$ as it reliably captures most relevant items while keeping re-ranking latency low, with diminishing returns beyond this size.

*Step 2: Re-ranking and diversification.* The retrieved documents are then rescored with a cross-encoder model (`ms-marco-MiniLM-L-6-v2`[6]), which considers the query and each passage together and produces more accurate relevance scores. We also apply MMR, which balances relevance against diversity by avoiding documents that are very similar to each other. This step improves precision and ensures broader coverage.

*Step 3: Adaptive selection.* Instead of keeping a fixed number of documents, we decide how many to include by looking at their cumulative relevance. We turn the re-rank scores into probabilities with a softmax so they add up to 1. Then we start from the top document and keep adding the next one until the cumulative probability mass reaches a threshold $\gamma$. In small exploratory tests around $\gamma \in \{0.80, 0.85, 0.90\}$, we observed almost similar trends; we therefore use $\gamma = 0.85$ as a simple, well-performing default in all reported results. This means simple queries often stop after a few documents, while more complex ones receive a larger set of evidence. In this way, our method automatically adjusts retrieval depth for each query, without requiring any extra training or specialized classifiers.

[6] https://huggingface.co/cross-encoder/ms-marco-MiniLM-L-6-v2.

# 4 Results

## 4.1 Similarity Score Distributions for Top-1 Hits

Figure 1 shows clear differences in cosine similarity distributions across query categories. Direct queries align well with the knowledge base, consistently yielding higher scores, while OOD queries fall significantly lower, rarely exceeding 0.35. This separation shows that thresholds in the 0.3–0.4 range can filter OOD cases without heavily reducing recall.

Noisy/typo and relational queries fall between these extremes. Typos lower similarity and increase score variance, making threshold choice more sensitive. In contrast, relational queries show moderate but less sharply separated scores, indicating the need to gather evidence from multiple documents

## 4.2 Tuning $k$ and Similarity Thresholds

Table 1 presents the results of varying $k$ and $\tau$. Full results for all settings are available in the repository[7] (Tables 2 and 3).

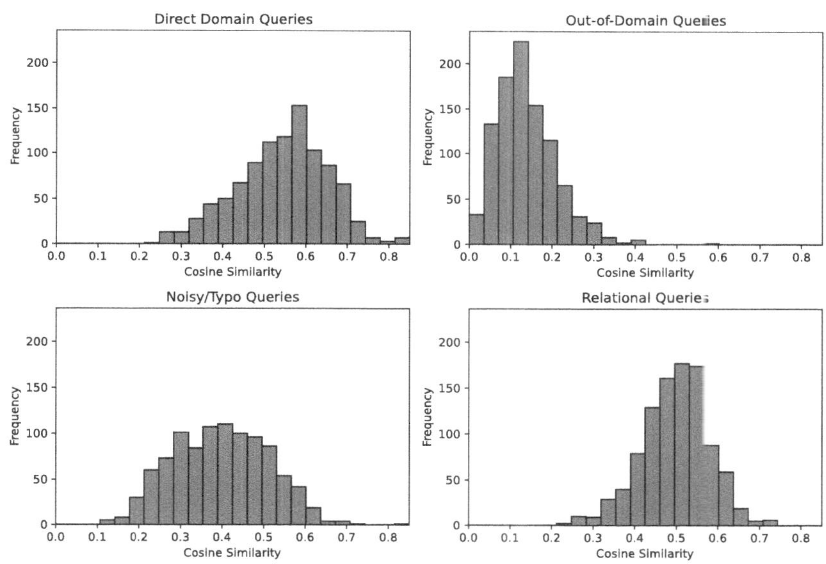


**Fig. 1.** Distribution of cosine similarity scores for the top-1 retrieved document across query categories. Direct domain queries (top left) and relational queries (bottom right) show higher similarities, typically centred around 0.5–0.6. OOD queries (top right) form a cluster with much lower scores, mostly below 0.3, creating a clear separation from in-domain queries. Noisy/typo queries (bottom left) fall in between. Their scores are more spread out but still concentrated in the mid-range (around 0.4), indicating that retrieval remains partially robust to input imperfections.

[7] https://github.com/Qirtas/AdaptiveRetrieval-RAG.

**Table 1.** Direct domain: per-$k$ performance at representative thresholds (lenient $\tau = 0.10$, mid $\tau = 0.30$, strict $\tau = 0.70$). Best F1 in **bold**.

| $k$ | $\tau$ | F1 | Precision | Recall | MRR | RankFirst | AvgSim |
|---|---|---|---|---|---|---|---|
| 1 | 0.10 | 0.74 | 0.749 | 0.74 | 0.74 | 1.00 | 0.54 |
| **1** | **0.30** | **0.75** | **0.75** | **0.74** | **0.74** | **1.00** | **0.54** |
| 1 | 0.70 | 0.081 | 0.80 | 0.04 | 0.04 | 1.00 | 0.74 |
| 2 | 0.10 | 0.56 | 0.42 | 0.83 | 0.79 | 1.10 | 0.49 |
| 2 | 0.30 | 0.57 | 0.44 | 0.83 | 0.78 | 1.10 | 0.50 |
| 2 | 0.70 | 0.08 | 0.80 | 0.04 | 0.04 | 1.00 | 0.74 |
| 3 | 0.10 | 0.44 | 0.29 | 0.88 | 0.80 | 1.20 | 0.46 |
| 3 | 0.30 | 0.47 | 0.32 | 0.87 | 0.80 | 1.20 | 0.48 |
| 3 | 0.70 | 0.08 | 0.80 | 0.04 | 0.04 | 1.00 | 0.74 |
| 4 | 0.10 | 0.36 | 0.22 | 0.91 | 0.81 | 1.28 | 0.44 |
| 4 | 0.30 | 0.39 | 0.25 | 0.90 | 0.80 | 1.27 | 0.46 |
| 4 | 0.70 | 0.08 | 0.80 | 0.04 | 0.04 | 1.00 | 0.74 |
| 5 | 0.10 | 0.30 | 0.18 | 0.92 | 0.81 | 1.33 | 0.42 |
| 5 | 0.30 | 0.34 | 0.21 | 0.91 | 0.81 | 1.32 | 0.45 |
| 5 | 0.70 | 0.08 | 0.80 | 0.04 | 0.04 | 1.00 | 0.74 |
| 7 | 0.10 | 0.23 | 0.13 | 0.93 | 0.82 | 1.41 | 0.40 |
| 7 | 0.30 | 0.27 | 0.16 | 0.92 | 0.81 | 1.38 | 0.44 |
| 7 | 0.70 | 0.08 | 0.80 | 0.04 | 0.04 | 1.00 | 0.74 |
| 10 | 0.10 | 0.17 | 0.09 | 0.95 | 0.82 | 1.54 | 0.38 |
| 10 | 0.30 | 0.21 | 0.12 | 0.93 | 0.81 | 1.49 | 0.42 |
| 10 | 0.70 | 0.08 | 0.80 | 0.04 | 0.04 | 1.00 | 0.74 |

**Table 2.** Relational: per-$k$ performance at representative thresholds (lenient $\tau = 0.10$, mid $\tau = 0.30$, strict $\tau = 0.70$). Best F1 in **bold**.

| $k$ | $\tau$ | F1 | Precision | Recall | MRR | RankFirst | AvgSim |
|---|---|---|---|---|---|---|---|
| 1 | 0.10 | 0.49 | 0.73 | 0.36 | 0.73 | 1.00 | 0.49 |
| 1 | 0.30 | 0.48 | 0.74 | 0.36 | 0.72 | 1.00 | 0.50 |
| 1 | 0.70 | 0.00 | 1.00 | 0.00 | 0.00 | 1.00 | 0.71 |
| **2** | **0.10** | **0.55** | **0.55** | **0.55** | **0.78** | **1.12** | **0.46** |
| 2 | 0.30 | 0.54 | 0.55 | 0.53 | 0.77 | 1.11 | 0.47 |
| 2 | 0.70 | 0.00 | 1.00 | 0.00 | 0.00 | 1.00 | 0.71 |
| 3 | 0.10 | 0.51 | 0.42 | 0.63 | 0.80 | 1.24 | 0.44 |
| 3 | 0.30 | 0.51 | 0.43 | 0.61 | 0.79 | 1.23 | 0.45 |
| 3 | 0.70 | 0.00 | 1.00 | 0.00 | 0.00 | 1.00 | 0.71 |
| 4 | 0.10 | 0.46 | 0.34 | 0.69 | 0.81 | 1.34 | 0.43 |
| 4 | 0.30 | 0.46 | 0.36 | 0.66 | 0.80 | 1.33 | 0.44 |
| 4 | 0.70 | 0.00 | 1.00 | 0.00 | 0.00 | 1.00 | 0.71 |
| 5 | 0.10 | 0.41 | 0.29 | 0.72 | 0.82 | 1.43 | 0.42 |
| 5 | 0.30 | 0.43 | 0.31 | 0.69 | 0.80 | 1.42 | 0.43 |
| 5 | 0.70 | 0.00 | 1.00 | 0.00 | 0.00 | 1.00 | 0.71 |
| 7 | 0.10 | 0.34 | 0.22 | 0.77 | 0.82 | 1.47 | 0.40 |
| 7 | 0.30 | 0.36 | 0.24 | 0.73 | 0.80 | 1.46 | 0.42 |
| 7 | 0.70 | 0.00 | 1.00 | 0.00 | 0.00 | 1.00 | 0.71 |
| 10 | 0.10 | 0.27 | 0.16 | 0.82 | 0.82 | 1.62 | 0.38 |
| 10 | 0.30 | 0.30 | 0.19 | 0.77 | 0.80 | 1.61 | 0.41 |
| 10 | 0.70 | 0.00 | 1.00 | 0.00 | 0.00 | 1.00 | 0.71 |

Trends show that increasing $k$ improves recall but lowers precision, while stricter thresholds improve precision but sharply reduce recall. Direct queries achieve strong performance with small $k$ and moderate thresholds, whereas noisy/typo queries perform worse, which shows the sensitivity of embeddings to input variation. Relational queries fall in between as they require slightly higher $k$ to capture multiple relevant documents. OOD queries consistently show low similarity scores, with false positives suppressed by higher thresholds.

There is no single setting of $k$ and $\tau$ that works across all categories. Direct queries are well served by $k = 1$ with moderate $\tau$, relational queries benefit from allowing more documents, and noisy queries retain some robustness but at much lower accuracy.

For OOD queries, we observed that increasing the similarity threshold $\tau$ steadily reduced the number of false positives. At low thresholds (e.g., $\tau = 0.10$), the FPR was relatively high ($\approx 0.67$). As the threshold increased, the FPR dropped sharply (e.g., $\tau = 0.20$: 0.17, $\tau = 0.25$: 0.06) and reached 0 once $\tau \geq 0.35$.

**Table 3.** Noisy/typo: per-$k$ performance at representative thresholds (lenient $\tau = 0.10$, mid $\tau = 0.30$, strict $\tau = 0.70$). Best F1 in **bold**.

| $k$ | $\tau$ | F1 | Precision | Recall | MRR | RankFirst | AvgSim |
|---|---|---|---|---|---|---|---|
| 1 | 0.10 | 0.38 | 0.38 | 0.38 | 0.38 | 1.00 | 0.39 |
| **1** | **0.30** | **0.39** | **0.45** | **0.34** | **0.34** | **1.00** | **0.44** |
| 1 | 0.70 | 0.00 | 1.00 | 0.00 | 0.00 | 1.00 | 0.75 |
| 2 | 0.10 | 0.32 | 0.24 | 0.48 | 0.43 | 1.20 | 0.37 |
| 2 | 0.30 | 0.35 | 0.29 | 0.42 | 0.38 | 1.18 | 0.42 |
| 2 | 0.70 | 0.00 | 1.00 | 0.00 | 0.00 | 1.00 | 0.75 |
| 3 | 0.10 | 0.26 | 0.17 | 0.53 | 0.44 | 1.38 | 0.35 |
| 3 | 0.30 | 0.30 | 0.22 | 0.46 | 0.40 | 1.32 | 0.41 |
| 3 | 0.70 | 0.00 | 1.00 | 0.00 | 0.00 | 1.00 | 0.75 |
| 4 | 0.10 | 0.23 | 0.14 | 0.58 | 0.46 | 1.62 | 0.34 |
| 4 | 0.30 | 0.27 | 0.19 | 0.50 | 0.41 | 1.53 | 0.40 |
| 4 | 0.70 | 0.00 | 1.00 | 0.00 | 0.00 | 1.00 | 0.75 |
| 5 | 0.10 | 0.20 | 0.12 | 0.61 | 0.46 | 1.78 | 0.34 |
| 5 | 0.30 | 0.25 | 0.16 | 0.52 | 0.41 | 1.63 | 0.40 |
| 5 | 0.70 | 0.00 | 1.00 | 0.00 | 0.00 | 1.00 | 0.75 |
| 7 | 0.10 | 0.16 | 0.09 | 0.66 | 0.47 | 2.09 | 0.32 |
| 7 | 0.30 | 0.21 | 0.13 | 0.54 | 0.41 | 1.86 | 0.39 |
| 7 | 0.70 | 0.00 | 1.00 | 0.00 | 0.00 | 1.00 | 0.75 |
| 10 | 0.10 | 0.12 | 0.07 | 0.70 | 0.48 | 2.51 | 0.31 |
| 10 | 0.30 | 0.18 | 0.10 | 0.56 | 0.42 | 2.16 | 0.39 |
| 10 | 0.70 | 0.00 | 1.00 | 0.00 | 0.00 | 1.00 | 0.75 |

### 4.3 Adaptive Retrieval

Table 4 presents the performance of our adaptive retrieval method across query categories. To show the improvements, it compares adaptive retrieval with the best fixed $(k, \tau)$ found in our fixed settings analyses. The adaptive approach improves both retrieval quality (F1) and ranking quality (MRR, RankFirst) in every category, while keeping OOD false positives low.

For direct domain queries, adaptive retrieval gives the best results, reaching F1 = 0.87 and MRR = 0.92, compared with 0.75 and 0.74 for the best fixed setting. The first relevant document is almost always at the top (RankFirst $\approx$ 1.03), and the higher average similarity shows that stronger matches are selected.

**Table 4.** Adaptive retrieval vs. best fixed setting per category. "Fixed (best)" is the best $(k, \tau)$ setting. "Adaptive" is our method. $\Delta$ shows the absolute change (Adaptive − Fixed). RankFirst: lower is better.

| Category | Fixed (best) | | | | Adaptive | | | | | | $\Delta$ | |
|---|---|---|---|---|---|---|---|---|---|---|---|---|
| | F1 | MRR | RankFirst | AvgSim | Precision | Recall | F1 | MRR | RankFirst | AvgSim | F1 | MRR |
| Direct domain | 0.75 | 0.74 | 1.26 | 0.55 | 0.81 | 0.94 | 0.87 | 0.92 | 1.03 | 0.79 | +0.12 | +0.18 |
| Relational | 0.55 | 0.79 | 1.43 | 0.47 | 0.77 | 0.72 | 0.74 | 0.95 | 1.12 | 0.53 | +0.19 | +0.16 |
| Noisy/typo | 0.39 | 0.35 | 1.65 | 0.44 | 0.39 | 0.59 | 0.47 | 0.56 | 1.10 | 0.42 | +0.08 | +0.21 |

For relational queries, F1 improves from 0.55 to 0.74. The method often retains more than one document when needed, but avoids adding excessive noise. This leads to a higher MRR = 0.95 and a lower RankFirst (from 1.43 to 1.12), meaning at least one useful document is found very early.

Noisy queries remain the hardest case, but adaptive retrieval still improves recall (0.59 vs. 0.37) and overall F1 (0.47 vs. 0.39). Precision stays lower (0.39), as spelling errors confuse the retriever, but MRR rises from 0.35 to 0.56 and RankFirst improves from 1.65 to 1.10.

For OOD queries, the adaptive method keeps a very low false positive rate (FPR $\approx$ 0.018). This is similar to using a fixed threshold around $\tau = 0.30$, but without losing recall for in-domain queries.

## 5 Conclusion

We examined how retrieval settings affect RAG performance in an enterprise knowledge base. Results showed that the number of documents $k$ and similarity threshold $\tau$ have different impacts depending on query type: direct queries work best with a single strong hit, relational queries benefit from multiple documents, and noisy queries require more tolerant thresholds. To address this, we proposed a simple training-free adaptive method that retrieves widely, re-ranks with a cross-encoder, applies diversification, and then selects documents until enough evidence is covered. This approach outperformed the best fixed settings across categories, improving F1 scores (from 0.75 to 0.87 on direct queries and from

0.55 to 0.74 on relational queries) while maintaining low false positives for OOD queries. Our study is limited to one enterprise dataset, short documents, single embedding and cross-encoder model, and we focus only on retrieval quality and do not evaluate the quality of the generated LLM responses. Future work will test larger datasets, hybrid retrievers, and learned adaptive strategies, while also measuring their effects on final answer quality and efficiency.

**Acknowledgments.** This work was conducted with the financial support of the EU's Horizon Digital, Industry, and Space program under grant agreement ID 101092989-DATAMITE, and by Research Ireland under Grant No. 12/RC/2289-P2, which is co-funded under the European Regional Development Fund. For the purpose of Open Access, the author has applied a CC BY public copyright license to any Author Accepted Manuscript version arising from this submission.

## References

1. Huang, L., et al.: A survey on hallucination in large language models: principles, taxonomy, challenges, and open questions. ACM Trans. Inf. Syst. **43**(2), 1–55 (2025)
2. Gao, Y., et al.: Retrieval-augmented generation for large language models: a survey. arXiv preprint arXiv:2312.10997, vol. 2, no. 1 (2023)
3. Lewis, P., et al.: Retrieval-augmented generation for knowledge-intensive NLP tasks. Adv. Neural. Inf. Process. Syst. **33**, 9459–9474 (2020)
4. Culpepper, J.S., Clarke, C.L., Lin, J.: Dynamic cutoff prediction in multi-stage retrieval systems. In: Proceedings of the 21st Australasian Document Computing Symposium, pp. 17–24 (2016)
5. Gizelis, C.A., et al.: Data monetization opportunities and challenges: the European landscape by datamite. In: IFIP International Conference on Artificial Intelligence Applications and Innovations, pp. 62–79. Springer (2024)
6. Guu, K., Lee, K., Tung, Z., Pasupat, P., Chang, M.: Retrieval augmented language model pre-training. In: International Conference on Machine Learning, pp. 3929–3938. PMLR (2020)
7. Izacard, G., Grave, E.: Leveraging passage retrieval with generative models for open domain question answering. arXiv preprint arXiv:2007.01282 (2020)
8. Borgeaud, S., et al.: Improving language models by retrieving from trillions of tokens. In: International Conference on Machine Learning, pp. 2206–2240. PMLR (2022)
9. Izacard, G., et al.: Atlas: few-shot learning with retrieval augmented language models. J. Mach. Learn. Res. **24**(251), 1–43 (2023)
10. Thakur, N., Reimers, N., Rücklé, A., Srivastava, A., Gurevych, I.: BEIR: a heterogenous benchmark for zero-shot evaluation of information retrieval models. arXiv preprint arXiv:2104.08663 (2021)
11. Nogueira, R., Cho, K.: Passage re-ranking with BERT. arXiv preprint arXiv:1901.04085 (2019)
12. Asai, A., Zeqiu, W., Wang, Y., Sil, A., Hajishirzi, H.: Self-rag: learning to retrieve, generate, and critique through self-reflection (2024)
13. Nandigam, P., Rayaprolu, N., Shrivastava, M.: Diverse multi-answer retrieval with determinantal point processes. arXiv preprint arXiv:2211.16029 (2022)

14. Chouhan, A., Gertz, M.: heiDS at ArchEHR-QA 2025: from fixed-k to query-dependent-k for retrieval augmented generation. arXiv preprint arXiv:2506.19512 (2025)
15. Zhang, J., Li, G., Su, J.: Sage: a framework of precise retrieval for rag. arXiv preprint arXiv:2503.01713 (2025)
16. Pinecone Team. Rerankers: Improve retrieval in rag systems (2024). https://www.pinecone.io/learn/series/rag/rerankers/. Accessed 29 Aug 2025
17. Sentence-Transformers Documentation. Retrieve & re-rank (2025)
18. Carbonell, J., Goldstein, J.: The use of MMR, diversity-based reranking for reordering documents and producing summaries. In: Proceedings of the 21st Annual International ACM SIGIR Conference on Research and Development in Information Retrieval, pp. 335–336 (1998)
19. Schütze, H., Manning, C.D., Raghavan, P.: Introduction to Information Retrieval, vol. 39. Cambridge University Press, Cambridge (2008)
20. Es, S., James, J., Anke, L.E., Schockaert, S.: Ragas: automated evaluation of retrieval augmented generation. In: Proceedings of the 18th Conference of the European Chapter of the Association for Computational Linguistics: System Demonstrations, pp. 150–158 (2024)
21. Yu, H., Gan, A., Zhang, K., Tong, S., Liu, Q., Liu, Z.: Evaluation of retrieval-augmented generation: a survey. In: CCF Conference on Big Data, pp. 102–120. Springer (2024)

# Cooperative MARL with Structured Rewards and Explainable Agents for Hyperparameter Tuning

Vedat Dogan(✉), Steven Prestwich, and Barry O'Sullivan

Insight Centre for Data Analytics, School of Computer Science & IT, University College Cork, Cork, Ireland
{vedat.dogan,steven.prestwich,barry.osullivan}@insight-centre.org

**Abstract.** Hyperparameter optimization (HPO) remains a central challenge over the years, particularly when dealing with heterogeneous search spaces and competing optimization objectives. In this work, we present an extended cooperative multi-agent reinforcement learning framework, named MARL-DA, which builds upon dynamic algorithm configuration (DAC) and multi-agent dynamic algorithm configuration (MA-DAC) by introducing a discrete-continuous agent decomposition with scalarized multi-objective reward components. MARL-DA enables specialized agents to optimize distinct types of hyperparameters in parallel. The reward function is designed as a scalarized multiple objectives: predictive performance, training efficiency, model complexity, and generalization robustness. We conduct empirical evaluations across six datasets spanning both classification and regression tasks. Results show that MARL-DA consistently outperforms the baselines, while offering interpretable agent behaviors and stable convergence. Explainability tools are integrated to provide insight into agent decisions, coordination dynamics, and reward attribution. This work demonstrates that minor yet structured modifications to cooperative MARL can yield substantial gains in optimization performance and explainability for the HPO task.

**Keywords:** Hyperparameter tuning · Multi-agent reinforcement learning · Scalarized multi-objective reward · Explainability

## 1 Introduction

Hyperparameter optimization (HPO) is essential for achieving optimal machine learning performance [8], with early methods including random search (RS) [3], evolutionary algorithms [14], and bandit-based strategies such as Hyperband [10]. Among these, Bayesian optimization (BO) [15] has become a widely used approach due to its efficiency, although its effectiveness is often sensitive to design choices and task-specific characteristics. To address these limitations, advanced BO-based algorithms have been developed [5], leveraging probabilistic models such as Gaussian Processes (GPs) to guide search strategies more effectively.


T. T. Mai et al. (Eds.): AICS 2025, CCIS 2950, pp. 239–250, 2026.
https://doi.org/10.1007/978-3-032-25809-0_19

HPO can be naturally framed as a sequential decision-making problem, where reinforcement learning (RL) has proven effective in adaptively refining hyperparameters across datasets [9]. Early work introduced Dynamic Algorithm Configuration (DAC) [1], later extended to the multi-agent setting as MA-DAC [23], enabling agents to coordinate in exploring the hyperparameter space.

Building on these foundations, we propose MARL-DA, an explainable cooperative MARL framework with agent decomposition for both continuous and discrete hyperparameters. MARL-DA extends DAC and MA-DAC by introducing a scalarized multi-objective reward function that balances performance, robustness, efficiency, and complexity, while incorporating multiple reward shaping strategies. In addition, MARL-DA integrates explainable agents capable of counterfactual and component-level analyses, offering transparency in optimization behavior. Compared to prior approaches, MARL-DA supports mixed hyperparameter spaces, adaptive reward structures, high-dimensional scalability, and interpretability (Table 1). Through extensive experiments on classification and regression tasks, we demonstrate that MARL-DA achieves competitive performance relative to both traditional HPO and MARL-based baselines, with convergence and ablation studies highlighting the advantages of structured reward decomposition and agent specialization.

**Table 1.** Comparison: DAC, MA-DAC, and MARL-DA

| Feature | DAC | MA-DAC | MARL-DA |
|---|---|---|---|
| RL Framework | ✓ | ✓ | ✓ |
| Multi-Agent | ✗ | ✓ | ✓ |
| Separate Agent per HP Type | ✗ | ✓ | ✓ |
| Discrete HP Support | ✓ | ✓ | ✓ |
| Continuous HP Support | ✓ | ✓ | ✓ |
| Mixed HP Space Handling | ✓ | ✓ | ✓ |
| Multi-objective Reward | ✗ | ✗ | ✓ |
| Adaptive Reward Structure | ✗ | ✗ | ✓ |
| High-dimensional Scalability | ✗ | ✓ | ✓ |
| Explicit Coordination | ✗ | ✓ | ✓ |
| Empirical ML Evaluations | ✗ | ✗ | ✓ |
| Explainability | ✗ | ✗ | ✓ |

## 1.1 Preliminaries

We give the preliminaries and brief background related with the proposed approach, starting with HPO formulation and how RL is implemented. Then we give the related information about the multi-agent RL for the MARL-DA approach.

The conventional RL employs an agent that is capable of taking actions from a finite $\mathcal{A}$ (i.e. the HP search space, which can be continuous, categorical or discrete), observing the states from $\mathcal{S}$ (i.e. an algorithm configuration) and using $\mathcal{R}$ to calculate the reward of action (i.e. the validation score of $M_{\lambda^*}$) in a particular state to decide future behavior [17]. The agents' behaviour is governed by a stochastic policy $\pi : \mathcal{S} \rightarrow \mathcal{A}$ which is defined as $Q_\pi(s,a) = \mathbb{E}_\pi[\sum_{t=0}^{\infty} \gamma^t r_t | \mathcal{S}_0 = s, \mathcal{A}_0 = a]$. It computes the actual state-action value and $0 \leq \gamma \leq 1$ represents the discount factor balancing between current and future rewards. The action is selected by maximizing the discounted cumulative rewards, therefore $\pi^*(s) \in \arg\max_a Q^*(s,a)$ where $Q^*(s,a)$ represents the optimal action value for a state. The Bellmann equation [2] is used for value-based RL, i.e. in Q-learning [20], and calculated as: $Q^*(s,a) = \mathbb{E}_\pi[r + \gamma \max_{a'} Q^*(s',a') | \mathcal{S}_0 = s, \mathcal{A}_0 = a]$ where $s' = \tau(s,a)$ represents the next state.

The objective of the HPO task is to identify the best HP configuration $\lambda^* \in \Lambda$, where the $\Lambda = \Lambda_1 \times \Lambda_2 \times \cdots \times \Lambda_d$ is a $d$-dimensional HP space, that results in a ML model $\mathcal{M}_{\lambda^*}$ with the optimal HPs such that the generalization error on the validation data is minimized. As the HPO task is defined as a sequential decision-making problem, used to tune the HPs in [9], called Hyp-RL, and showed it can be formulated as an MDP. The MDP for the HPO is represented by a tuple, $\mathcal{MDP} := \langle \mathcal{S}, \mathcal{A}, \mathcal{R}, \tau \rangle$, where $\mathcal{S}$ is the set of states representing the algorithm state, $\mathcal{A}$ is the action space representing the parameter setting, $\mathcal{R}$ is a reward function representing the progress of the algorithm for a given parameters, and $\tau$ is a transition function that represents the algorithm state transition [4].

In the HPO task, the reward function $\mathcal{R}$ is dependent on the dataset $\mathcal{D}$ and the HP setting $\lambda$ as an action $a$, and shown as $\mathcal{R}(D, a) = -f(D, \lambda = a)$ because the agent aims to maximize the reward. The function can be defined as validation loss $f(\mathcal{D}, \lambda) = \mathcal{L}(M_\lambda(\mathcal{D}_{train}, \mathcal{D}_{validation}))$ for the selected model $M$ with HP setting $\lambda$. After the model performance is evaluated with the configuration, the new state $s'$ is calculated by a transition function $s' = \tau(s, a, r) = (s, \lambda = a, r)$. To conclude, the agent starts at a random location, explores the environment by selecting a new set of HPs, and receives a reward at each step until a termination criteria is met. A multi-agent setting with a fully observable environment can be modelled as an MDP and formalized as $MDP := \langle \mathcal{N}, \mathcal{S}, \{\mathcal{A}_i\}_{i=1}^n, \tau, r \rangle$ where $\mathcal{N}$ is a set of agents and $A_i$ is the agent of $i$'s action space. All agents in a joint action space $\boldsymbol{a} = \langle a_1, \ldots, a_n \rangle$ receive a shared global reward $r(s, \boldsymbol{a})$ and $\boldsymbol{a}$ leads to a new state $s' \sim \tau(\cdot|s, \boldsymbol{a})$. The ultimate goal is to find a cooperative policy that maps the states $\mathcal{S}$ to the probability distribution of cooperative actions $\Delta(A_1 \times \cdots \times A_n)$ and represented as $\pi : \mathcal{S} \to \Delta(A_1 \times \cdots \times A_n)$. The global value function to estimate is calculated as $Q^\pi(s, \boldsymbol{a}) = \mathbb{E}\Big[\sum_{t=0}^{\infty} \gamma^t r(s_t, \boldsymbol{a}_t) | s_0 = s, \boldsymbol{a}_0 = \boldsymbol{a}\Big]$. A multi-agent system for HPO is proposed in [23] by extending DAC using a multi-agent system and applied to the multi-objective optimization problems.

## 2 Methodology

**Problem Definition.** Given an ML model $\mathcal{M}_\lambda$ with the HPs $\lambda \in \Lambda$, the goal is to optimize an objective function, generally the loss function $\mathcal{L}$, over a data distribution $D \in \mathcal{D}$ where $\mathcal{D}$ is the whole dataset, and formulated as $\mathcal{M}(D, \lambda) = \arg\min_{\mathcal{M}_\lambda} \mathcal{L}(\mathcal{M}_\lambda, D)$. The goal of the HPO task is to find the optimal HP set $\lambda^* \in \Lambda$ such that the generalization error on the validation set is minimized, $\lambda^* = \arg\min_{\lambda \in \Lambda} \mathcal{L}(\mathcal{M}_\lambda(\mathcal{D}_{\text{train}}), \mathcal{D}_{\text{validation}})$ where $D_{\text{train}} \cap D_{\text{validation}} = \varnothing$. We propose MARL-DA to solve the HPO task for a given ML model with various kinds of parameters (i.e. continuous, discrete, categorical and binary) and formulate it as a cooperative MDP with scalarized multi-objective reward components. Each agent $A \in \{\mathcal{A}_i\}_{i=1}^n$ handles a single HP $\lambda \in \Lambda$. Therefore, the number of agents is limited by the number of HPs for the model. The action space of each agent is defined as the search space of each HP. As the ultimate goal is to increase the model's performance, every agent's reward is aimed at maximising the *shared* scalarized multi-objective reward.

**Algorithm 1** MARL-DA: Discrete-Continuous Agent Decomposition for HPO

**Input:** Environment $\mathcal{E}$,
agent set $\mathcal{A} = \{a_d^{(i)}\}_{i=1}^{n} \cup \{a_c^{(j)}\}_{j=1}^{m}$,
reward components $\{R_k\}$, weights $w_k$
**Initialize:** Policies $\{\pi_i\}_{i=1}^{n+m}$, replay buffer $\mathcal{D}$, critic $Q_\phi$, exploration noise $\mathcal{N}$
**for** episode $e = 1$ to $E$ **do**
  Sample initial state $s_0 \sim \mathcal{E}$
  **for** step $t = 1$ to $T$ **do**
    **for** each discrete agent $a_d^{(i)}$ **do**
      Select $a_d^{(i)} \sim \pi_i(s_t)$
    **end for**
    **for** each continuous agent $a_c^{(j)}$ **do**
      Select $a_c^{(j)} \sim \pi_j(s_t) + \mathcal{N}_t$
    **end for**
    Compose global action: $a_t = [a_d, a_c]$
    Execute $a_t$ in $\mathcal{E}$; observe $s_{t+1}, \{R_k(s_t, a_t)\}$
    Compute total reward: $r_t = \sum_k w_k \cdot R_k(s_t, a_t)$
    Store transition: $\mathcal{D} \leftarrow (s_t, a_t, r_t, s_{t+1})$
    Update critics: $\phi \leftarrow \phi - \alpha \nabla_\phi \mathcal{L}_{\text{TD}}(\phi)$
    Update actors using policy gradients: $\theta_i \leftarrow \theta_i + \beta \nabla_{\theta_i} \mathbb{E}_{s \sim \mathcal{D}} [Q_\phi(s, \pi_i(s))]$
  **end for**
  Adjust weights $w_k$ based on phase or adaptive rule
**end for**

**Model Architecture.** For a given machine learning model $\mathcal{M}_\lambda$, the number of agents is defined with the same number of HPs to optimize. We first select two different algorithms for the agents to interact in discrete and continuous action spaces, which are Deep Q-learning (DQN) [13] and Deep Deterministic Policy Gradient (DDPG) [11], respectively. The DQN agents use an $\epsilon$-greedy policy for exploration. While DQN can solve problems with high-dimensional state spaces, it handles discrete and low-dimensional action spaces successfully. Therefore, we create DDPG-based agents to deal with continuous HPs. The DDPG is an actor-critic model-free algorithm that can operate over the continuous action space. It uses the function approximations parameterized by $\theta$ and optimizes it by minimizing the loss $\mathcal{L}(\theta) = \mathbb{E}[Q(s, a|\theta) - y]$ where $y = r(s, a) + \gamma Q(s', \mu(s')|\theta)$. $\mu$ and $Q$ are target and actor-critic that stabilizes training with delayed updates, respectively. DDPG agents encourage exploration by adding the noise generated by the Ornstein-Uhlenbeck process [18]. In contrast to Gaussian noise, its values associated with the current timestamp are correlated with the previous ones, enabling the preservation of the noise's sign for extended periods.

Each agent is responsible for an HP of the given machine learning model in the MARL-DA algorithm. Hence the action space $\mathcal{A}$ is defined by the HP that needs to be optimized. As each HP can take different variables (i.e. the number of layers is discrete and the learning rate is continuous), the action space of the agent is identified by the HP space.

**Table 2.** Summary of the Scalarized Multi-Objective Reward Components

| Rewards | Definition |
|---|---|
| Accuracy | $r_1(s_t, a_t) = \begin{cases} acc_t, & t = 1 \\ \beta(acc_t - acc_{t-1}) + (1-\beta)acc_t, & t > 1 \end{cases}$ |
| Efficiency | $r_2(s_t, a_t) = \gamma\left(1 - \frac{train\_time_t}{max\_train\_time}\right) + (1-\gamma)\left(1 - \frac{memory\_used_t}{max\_memory}\right)$ |
| Complexity | $r_3(s_t, a_t) = 1 - \left[\delta\frac{num\_params_t}{max\_params} + (1-\delta)\frac{num\_layers_t}{max\_layers}\right]$ |
| Robustness | $r_4(s_t, a_t) = \eta(1 - \lvert train\_acc_t - val\_acc_t\rvert) + (1-\eta)\frac{1}{m}\sum_{j=1}^{m} fold\_acc_t^j$ |

The state is used to describe the situation of the model in order to make an informed choice. Therefore, the state should be accessible at each time period so that information can be used for the upcoming time periods. Also, the learned policy should be generalizable, therefore it needs to contain the common features across different agents. As the state $s_t$ at time step $t$ is represented by a vector encoding the multiple aspects of the HPO process, it contains the information about the current HP set $\lambda_t$, performance history (i.e. accuracy and std. deviation of the accuracy at $t$), training dynamics (i.e. train and validation loss) and exploration status (i.e. the current exploration rate).

The reward has a huge impact on the policy's final performance as it guides the learning process. Therefore, the reward function definition is important for any proposed RL model. We designed the reward function as a scalarized reward function with multiple objectives [7], and a weighted combination of rewards $\mathcal{R}(s_t, a_t) = \sum_{i=1}^{4} w_t^i r_t^i$ where $w^i$ are adaptive weights such that $\sum_{i=1}^{4} w^i = 1$. We analyse the adaptation of the weights considering multiple strategies aiming to improve the HPO task, as it is explained in Sect. 3. we shared the formulation of the reward components in Table 2. We explain each reward component in Table 2 as follows. The first reward component $r_1$ is based on the validation accuracy of the model and $\beta \in [0, 1]$ is a parameter balancing absolute performance and improvement. The second reward component $r_2$ reflects the efficiency of the reward where $\gamma \in [0, 1]$ balances the time efficiency and memory efficiency, and train_$time_t$ and memory_$used_t$ are the time taken to train the model and the peak memory consumption at the time of $t$, respectively. The third reward component $r_3$ penalizes unnecessarily complex models where $\delta \in [0, 1]$ balances parameter count and architectural depth. Lastly, the fourth reward component $r_4$ reflects the robustness of the model where $\eta \in [0, 1]$ balances the overfitting penalty and cross-validation performance, |train_$acc_t$−val_$acc_t$| measures overfitting, fold_$acc_t^j$ is the accuracy on the $j$-th cross-validation fold at the time of $t$, and $m$ is the number of cross-validation folds.

The weights of the reward components $w^i$ are implemented by considering a predefined weight schedules and an adaptive optimization approach to observe how the reward strategy is affecting the agent's performance. The adaptive optimizers dynamically adjust the weights based on observed rewards and learning

**Table 3.** Benchmark datasets and hyperparameter search space.

(a) **Benchmark Datasets**

| Dataset | Type | Task | Samples | Feat. | Target | Desc. |
|---|---|---|---|---|---|---|
| MNIST | Img (G) | Clf. | 70k | 784 | 10 | Digits |
| F-MNIST | Img (G) | Clf. | 70k | 784 | 10 | Clothing |
| CIFAR-10 | Img (RGB) | Clf. | 60k | $3\times32^2$ | 10 | Objects |
| Cal. House | Tab. | Regr. | 20k | 8 | 1 | House price |
| Diabetes | Tab. | Regr. | 442 | 10 | 1 | Med. prog. |
| Bike Share | Tab. | Regr. | 17k | 12 | 1 | Rentals |

(b) **Hyperparameter Search Space**

| Model | Hyperparameter | Type | Values / Range |
|---|---|---|---|
| Feed-forward NNs | Learning Rate | Continuous | $[1e^{-5}, 1e^{-1}]$ |
| | Batch Size | Discrete | {16, 32, 64, 128, 256} |
| | Optimizer | Categorical | {Adam, SGD, RMSprop} |
| | Dropout Rate | Continuous | $[0.0, 0.5]$ |
| | # of Layers | Discrete | {1, 2, 3, 4} |
| | Units Multiplier | Discrete | {0.5, 1.0, 1.5, 2.0} |
| | Batch Normalization | Binary | {True, False} |

progress, attempting to improve overall performance and convergence. In terms of this, we observe multiple reward-weighting strategies.

The first one, called *default*, gradually transitions from exploration to exploitation, initially emphasising complexity and efficiency, and later prioritising performance. In this setting, the weights are adaptive over time according to $w^i_{t+1} = \alpha \cdot w^i_{target}\left(\frac{t}{T}\right) + (1-\alpha) \cdot w^i_t$ where $\alpha \in [0, 1]$ is the adaptation rate and $w^i_{target}\left(\frac{t}{T}\right)$ is the target weight. The performance-focused strategy consistently prioritises accuracy-related components, while the efficiency-focused strategy emphasises resource-conscious training by rewarding faster and more efficient models. The balanced strategy maintains equal weights across all reward components throughout the training process. Additionally, the stable strategy introduces smoother and more gradual weight changes to prevent oscillatory behaviour and promote training stability.

## 3 Experiments

We evaluate the effectiveness and convergence of MARL-DA by optimizing feed-forward neural networks (NNs) with mixed hyperparameter spaces across classification and regression tasks using OpenML datasets [19]. We address three research questions: How does MARL-DA perform in terms of convergence and simple regret compared with other MARL methods? How effective is the scalarized multi-objective reward compared with single-objective and alternative strategies? How does MARL-DA compare against traditional HPO baselines?

Each experiment runs for 400 episodes, with results saved every 10 episodes and averaged over 25 runs. Models are trained for 20 epochs (with early stopping at 10), capped at 300 s per model. Training uses an 80/20 train–test split; the training set is further divided into 75/25 for training/validation. For exploration, DDPG employs Ornstein–Uhlenbeck noise with epsilon decay, and DQN uses epsilon-greedy decay from 0.1 to 0.01. Hardware: Apple M4 Pro chip (12-core CPU, 16-core GPU, 16-core Neural Engine).

Alongside MARL-DA, we implemented MARL-VDN [16], which assumes additive decomposability of global rewards but may oversimplify correlated spaces, and MARL-MAPPO [22], which uses a centralized critic with decentralized actors and clipped surrogate objectives. We also compare with four standard HPO methods: Random Search (RS) [3], Bayesian Optimization (BO) [15], BOHB [6], and Genetic Algorithms (GA) [14].

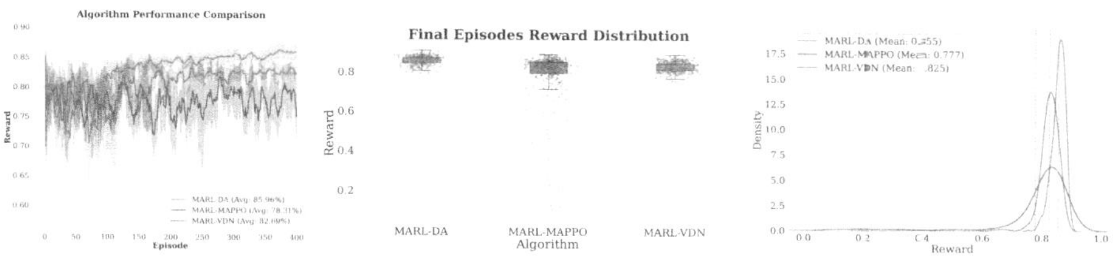


(a) (b) (c)

**Fig. 1.** Reward regret under different configurations.

Performance is measured via reward by episode (convergence curves) averaged over 25 runs with standard deviations. Rewards are higher-is-better: validation accuracy for classification and −RMSE for regression. For time-based components, rewards are inverted as $r'_{norm}(s_t, a_t) = 1 - r_{norm}(s_t, a_t)$. We analyze reward distributions over episodes, log-scaled mean and variance across runs, and compare four single-objective with three multi-objective reward strategies. Final comparisons report validation accuracy and RMSE.

Classification tasks include MNIST, Fashion-MNIST, and CIFAR-10; regression tasks include California Housing, Diabetes, and Bike Sharing. Standard splits use 20% for testing and validation, adjusted for larger datasets. Data is standardized (StandardScaler), with CIFAR-10 additionally normalized using ImageNet statistics; categorical features are one-hot encoded. See Table 3(a).

MARL agents optimize continuous (learning rate, dropout), discrete (batch size, number of layers), categorical (optimizer), and binary (batch normalization) hyperparameters, as well as unit multipliers. Replay buffer sizes, exploration fractions, and discount factors are specified in Table 3(b).

### 3.1 Experimental Study

We conduct a empirical evaluation of MARL-DA for HP optimization across diverse supervised learning tasks. The study examines four aspects: (i) convergence compared with two MARL baselines, (ii) effectiveness of the scalarized multi-objective reward versus single-objective strategies, (iii) contribution of explainable AI components, including GNN-based tools for agent reasoning, and (iv) overall performance relative to MARL baselines and state-of-the-art HPO methods.

We evaluate behaviour and performance via convergence and reward distribution analysis in Fig. 1. Over 400 episodes, MARL-DA achieves the fastest and most stable convergence, stabilizing around episode 150 with an average reward of 85.96% and narrow confidence intervals. MARL-VDN converges to 82.69% with higher early-stage variance, while MARL-MAPPO learns more slowly and oscillates, reaching 78.31% only after ∼300 episodes. Reward distributions in the final episodes in Fig. 1(b,c) confirm these trends. MARL-DA exhibits tightly clustered high rewards with minimal outliers and a sharp density peak near 0.86.

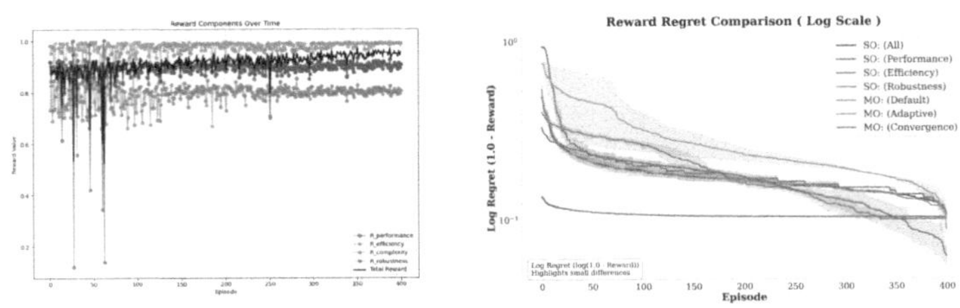


(a) (b)

**Fig. 2.** (a) Reward components, total reward and **reward regret.**

MARL-VDN shows a slightly lower peak around 0.82 with broader spread, while MARL-MAPPO has a flatter distribution with a long tail toward low-reward regions, indicating higher stochasticity. These results demonstrate MARL-DA's superior efficiency, stability, and reliability compared with both baselines.

We analyze how reward structures influence learning dynamics and final performance. The total reward is a weighted sum of four interpretable components—performance, efficiency, complexity, and robustness—encouraging accuracy, computational efficiency, simplicity, and generalization.

Figure 2(a) shows the evolution of reward components and total reward over 400 episodes. Each component—performance, efficiency, complexity, and robustness—contributes to the overall objective. Performance gains (light blue) are initially volatile but stabilize with generalization, while efficiency (orange) stays consistently high, reflecting early cost prioritization. Complexity (red) and robustness (green) improve steadily, mitigating overfitting and parameter inflation. The smooth convergence of the total reward (black) confirms MARL-DA's stable learning dynamics and effective agent coordination, highlighting the value of multi-objective optimization in hyperparameter search.

Figure 2(b) shows log-regret trajectories for single-objective (SO) and multi-objective (MO) strategies. As MA-DAC employs an SO setting, its results are not shown separately, since MO approaches consistently performed better. Among SO rewards, performance-only converges quickly but plateaus, efficiency-only improves early but stagnates, and robustness-only learns slowly yet steadily, trading accuracy for generalization. MO strategies yield more stable long-term improvements. MO (Default) gradually shifts weights from complexity/efficiency to performance, achieving balanced convergence, while MO (Convergence) achieves the lowest final regret by emphasizing correlated components (performance and robustness). MO (Adaptive) converges more slowly with higher variance, reflecting instability from dynamic weighting. Overall, multi-objective reward design—especially convergence-aware correlations—substantially improves stability and efficiency in MARL training.

To enhance transparency, MARL-DA integrates a multi-level explainability module inspired by recent work in explainable MARL [12], focusing on agent-level contribution and reward attribution. At the agent level, feature-importance

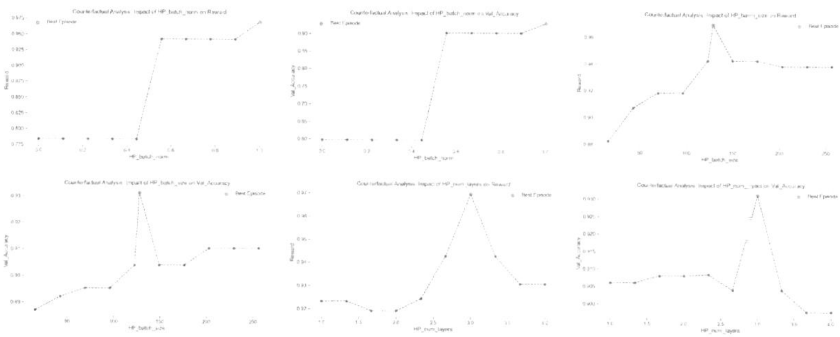

**Fig. 3.** Counterfactual impact of hyperparameters.

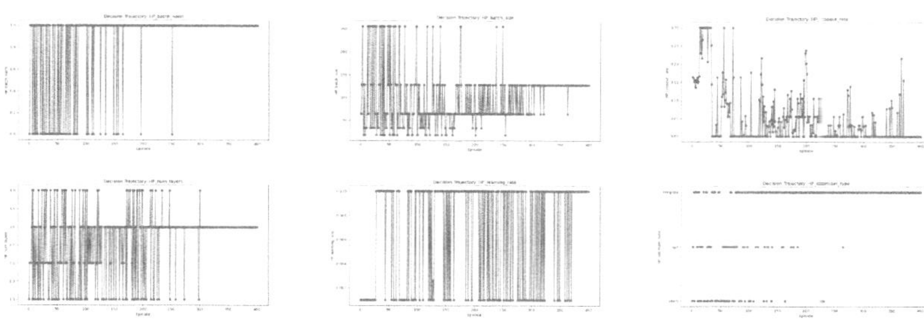

**Fig. 4.** Episode-wise decision trajectories for hyperparameters.

analysis (mutual information and gradient sensitivity) showed learning rate and optimizer agents had the greatest impact on performance, while batch size and dropout influenced efficiency. Correlation analysis revealed performance had the strongest association with total reward ($r \approx 0.91$), followed by efficiency ($r \approx 0.46$), confirming dominant behaviour in later phases. We also applied GNN-based post-hoc analysis using GNNExplainer [21], which highlighted critical communication edges (e.g., dropout $\rightarrow$ optimizer) along high-reward trajectories.

Temporal heatmaps further indicated that generalization focused agents gained influence during mid-to-late training. Finally, counterfactual analysis perturbed agent decisions and reward terms to quantify their effect on outcomes. Learning rate and batch size interventions produced the largest deviations, underscoring their role in early exploration. These modules not only improve interpretability but also validate that policies remain stable and not overfit to specific rewards, informing future reward design and coordination strategies. Figure 3 shows counterfactual analyses of individual hyperparameters. Binary variables such as *batch_norm* yield strong performance gains when enabled, while continuous/discrete parameters (e.g., *batch_size*, *dropout_rate*) exhibit non-monotonic reward surfaces with local optima. *num_layers* peaks around 3, beyond which overparameterization degrades performance. These results high-

**Table 4.** Performance of HPO algorithms across datasets. The highest and second-highest values in each column are shown in bold and underlined, respectively. Statistical significance is evaluated using paired t-tests (**: $p < .01$, *: $p < .05$).

| Method | Classification (Val. Accuracy) | | | Regression (RMSE) | | |
|---|---|---|---|---|---|---|
| | MNIST | Fashion-MNIST | CIFAR-10 | California housing | Diabetes | Bike Sharing |
| RS | $0.9262^{**} \pm 0.0185$ | $0.8622^{**} \pm 0.0229$ | $0.3525^{**} \pm 0.0126$ | $0.4583^{**} \pm 0.0051$ | $0.5662^{**} \pm 0.0081$ | $0.3330^{**} \pm 0.0028$ |
| BO | $0.9375^{**} \pm 0.0327$ | $0.8898 \pm 0.0137$ | $0.3875^{**} \pm 0.0357$ | $0.4967^{**} \pm 0.0056$ | $0.5653^{**} \pm 0.0063$ | $0.3315^{**} \pm 0.0014$ |
| BOHB | $0.9375^{**} \pm 0.0249$ | $0.8938 \pm 0.0236$ | $0.4075^{**} \pm 0.0265$ | $0.4967^{**} \pm 0.0065$ | $0.5653^{**} \pm 0.0025$ | $0.3315^{**} \pm 0.0016$ |
| GA | $0.9375^{**} \pm 0.0123$ | $0.8750^{**} \pm 0.0136$ | $0.3925^{**} \pm 0.0243$ | $0.4946^{**} \pm 0.0095$ | $0.5695^{**} \pm 0.0097$ | $0.3093^{**} \pm 0.0083$ |
| MARL-DA | $\mathbf{0.9703} \pm 0.0180$ | $\mathbf{0.9009} \pm 0.0441$ | $\underline{0.4620} \pm 0.0923$ | $0.4290^{*} \pm 0.0037$ | $\mathbf{0.4657} \pm 0.0019$ | $0.2153^{*} \pm 0.0072$ |
| MARL-VDN | $0.9698 \pm 0.0138$ | $0.8970 \pm 0.0497$ | $\mathbf{0.4659} \pm 0.1256$ | $\mathbf{0.4204} \pm 0.0050$ | $0.4708^{*} \pm 0.0021$ | $\mathbf{0.2054} \pm 0.0055$ |
| MARL-MAPPO | $\underline{0.9701} \pm 0.0177$ | $\underline{0.8976} \pm 0.0437$ | $0.4613 \pm 0.1358$ | $\underline{0.4224}^{*} \pm 0.0013$ | $\underline{0.4678} \pm 0.0092$ | $\underline{0.2141}^{*} \pm 0.0033$ |

light the need for fine-grained search and demonstrate MARL-DA's ability to uncover non-trivial configurations in hybrid spaces.

Figure 4 depicts decision trajectories for six hyperparameters. Binary variables converge rapidly, while continuous ones (e.g., *dropout_rate*) remain volatile. Discrete parameters (*batch_size*, *num_layers*) follow an exploration–exploitation pattern, stabilizing later in training. These trajectories illustrate MARL-DA's adaptive exploration and self-organization across heterogeneous search spaces. Figure 5 applies attribution methods. Mutual information scores identify *batch_size* and *num_layers* as most influential for reward, while *learning_rate* and *batch_norm* dominate accuracy. Pairwise correlations reveal weak coupling between *dropout_rate* and *optimizer_type*, but stronger links between *num_layers* and *batch_norm*. Temporal influence patterns suggest hierarchical coordination, with *learning_rate* implicitly guiding. Together, these analyses justify explainable MARL for HPO.

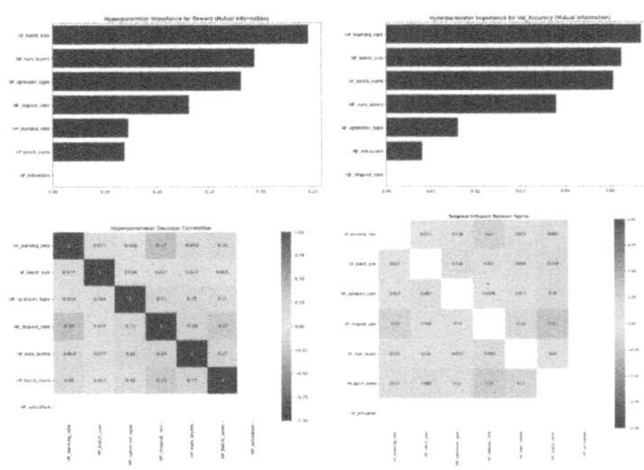

**Fig. 5.** Episode-wise decision trajectories.

We assess MARL-DA against various HPO methods on OpenML datasets, reporting mean validation accuracy and RMSE over 25 runs with standard deviations in Table 4. Paired $t$-tests against the best baseline indicate significance (** $p < .01$, * $p < .05$). The MARL algorithms, MARL-DA, MARL-VDN, and MARL-MAPPO, differ in how they model agent cooperation and search dynamics. MARL-DA delivers the strongest overall performance. On classification, it achieves top accuracy on MNIST (97.03%) and Fashion-MNIST (90.09%), and second on CIFAR-10 (46.20%), with consistently low variance across runs, confirming stable convergence and generalization. MARL-VDN and MARL-MAPPO remain competitive but are more sensitive to task complexity, particularly on CIFAR-10. For regression, MARL-VDN performs best on Bike

Sharing (0.2054 RMSE), MARL-DA on Diabetes (0.4657), and MAPPO slightly leads on California Housing (0.4224), reflecting their respective strengths across domains.

Traditional baselines (RS, BO, BOHB, GA) perform reasonably in low-dimensional or well-structured spaces but struggle with heterogeneous hyper-parameter domains. BOHB excels on California Housing through resource-aware scheduling but lags on CIFAR-10 due to the high-dimensional architecture space. In contrast, MARL-based methods—especially MARL-DA—achieve lower variance and stronger robustness. MARL-DA's multi-agent decomposition, combined with scalarized multi-objective reward shaping, supports balanced exploration–exploitation, adaptive reward prioritization, and effective handling of both types of parameters. This yields more generalizable configurations, higher stability across seeds, and superior performance in complex or imbalanced settings.

## 4 Conclusion

We introduced MARL-DA, a cooperative MARL framework extending DAC and MA-DAC for hyperparameter optimization across mixed parameter types. By combining discrete–continuous agent decomposition with a scalarized multi-objective reward, MARL-DA enables specialization and coordination in hyperparameter tuning. The framework further integrates explainability through agent-specific visualizations, mutual information analysis, and counterfactual reasoning. Experiments on six benchmark datasets show consistent gains in convergence, accuracy, RMSE, and reward stability over traditional HPO and MARL baselines. Importantly, the inclusion of explainability enhances transparency in automated HPO. These results highlight that targeted extensions to MARL architectures can improve practical applicability. Future work includes applying MARL-DA to neural architecture search and adaptive reward weighting via meta-RL.

**Acknowledgments.** This publication has emanated from research conducted with the financial support of Research Ireland under Grant number [12-RC-2289-P2] which is co-funded under the European Regional Development Fund For the purpose of Open Access, the author has applied a CC BY public copyright licence to any Author Accepted Manuscript version arising from this submission (The authors have no competing interests to declare that are relevant to the content of this article).

## References

1. Adriaensen, S., et al.: Automated dynamic algorithm configuration (2022)
2. Bellman, R.: Functional equations in the theory of dynamic programming. ii. non-linear differential equations. Proc. Natl. Acad. Sci. U.S.A. **41**(7), 482–485 (1955)
3. Bergstra, J., Bengio, Y.: Random search for hyper-parameter optimization. J. Mach. Learn. Res. **13**, 281–305 (2012)

4. Biedenkapp, A., Bozkurt, H.F., Eimer, T., Hutter, F., Lindauer, M.T.: Dynamic algorithm configuration: foundation of a new meta-algorithmic framework. In: European Conference on Artificial Intelligence (2020)
5. Dogan, V., Prestwich, S.: BHO-MA: Bayesian hyperparameter optimization with multi-objective acquisition. In: Pereira, A.I., Mendes, A., Fernandes, F.P., Pacheco, M.F., Coelho, J.P., Lima, J. (eds.) Optimization, Learning Algorithms and Applications, pp. 391–408. Springer, Cham (2024). https://doi.org/10.1007/978-3-031-53025-8_27
6. Falkner, S., Klein, A., Hutter, F.: Bohb: robust and efficient hyperparameter optimization at scale (2018)
7. Friedman, E., Fontaine, F.: Generalizing across multi-objective reward functions in deep reinforcement learning. CoRR abs/1809.06364 (2018)
8. Hutter, F., Kotthoff, L., Vanschoren, J.: Automated Machine Learning: Methods, Systems, Challenges, 1st edn. Springer (2019)
9. Jomaa, H.S., Grabocka, J., Schmidt-Thieme, L.: Hyp-RL: hyperparameter optimization by reinforcement learning. arXiv abs/1906.11527 (2019)
10. Li, L., Jamieson, K., DeSalvo, G., Rostamizadeh, A., Talwalkar, A.: Hyperband: a novel bandit-based approach to hyperparameter optimization (2018)
11. Lillicrap, T.P., et al.: Continuous control with deep reinforcement learning. CoRR abs/1509.02971 (2015)
12. Madumal, P., Miller, T., Sonenberg, L., Vetere, F.: Explainable reinforcement learning through a causal lens. CoRR abs/1905.10958 (2019)
13. Mnih, V., et al.: Human-level control through deep reinforcement learning. Nature **518**, 529–533 (2015)
14. Olson, R.S., Bartley, N., Urbanowicz, R.J., Moore, J.H.: Evaluation of a tree-based pipeline optimization tool for automating data science. In: Proceedings of the Genetic and Evolutionary Computation Conference 2016, GECCO 2016, pp. 485–492. Association for Computing Machinery, New York, NY, USA (2016)
15. Shahriari, B., Swersky, K., Wang, Z., Adams, R.P., de Freitas, N.: Taking the human out of the loop: a review of Bayesian optimization. Proc. IEEE **104**(1), 148–175 (2016)
16. Sunehag, P., et al.: Value-decomposition networks for cooperative multi-agent learning. CoRR abs/1706.05296 (2017)
17. Sutton, R.S., Barto, A.G.: Reinforcement Learning: An Introduction, 2nd edn. MIT Press (2018)
18. Uhlenbeck, G.E., Ornstein, L.S.: On the theory of the Brownian motion. Phys. Rev. **36**, 823–841 (1930)
19. Vanschoren, J., van Rijn, J.N., Bischl, B., Torgo, L.: OpenML: networked science in machine learning. SIGKDD Explor. Newsl. **15**(2), 49–60 (2014)
20. Watkins, C., Dayan, P.: Technical note: Q-learning. Mach. Learn. **8**, 279–292 (1992)
21. Ying, R., Bourgeois, D., You, J., Zitnik, M., Leskovec, J.: GNN explainer: a tool for post-hoc explanation of graph neural networks. CoRR abs/1903.03894 (2019)
22. Yu, C., Velu, A., Vinitsky, E., Wang, Y., Bayen, A.M., Wu, Y.: The surprising effectiveness of MAPPO in cooperative, multi-agent games. CoRR abs/2103.01955 (2021)
23. Xue, K., et al.: Multi-agent dynamic algorithm configuration. In: Advances in Neural Information Processing Systems 35 (NeurIPS'22), New Orleans, LA (2022)

# A Continuous Cloud Coverage Dataset for Robust AI in Occluded Environments

Shanika Edirisinghe(✉), Svetlana Hensman, and Bianca Schoen-Phelan

Technological University Dublin, Dublin, Ireland
d23126642@mytudublin.ie,
{svetlana.hensman,bianca.schoenphelan}@tudublin.ie

**Abstract.** Cloud cover is a persistent challenge in satellite remote sensing, obscuring surface features and reducing the reliability of applications such as environmental monitoring, disaster response, and urban planning. Most existing cloud-related datasets provide binary masks, distinguishing only between cloud and clear conditions, and thus fail to capture cloud density, limiting systematic benchmarking and robustness analysis of AI models under varying occlusion. To address this gap, we introduce a continuous cloud-coverage dataset derived from SEN12MS-CR. Each Sentinel-2 tile is assigned a percentage label (0–100%) representing cloud proportion. The curated dataset includes 36,666 tiles, evenly sampled across four seasons, and is openly accessible via Zenodo. A case study using the UnCRtainTS cloud removal model shows that reconstruction quality declines progressively with higher cloud density. By supporting standardized evaluation across cloud conditions, the dataset enhances cloud-aware AI tasks, including removal, classification, and segmentation, and contributes to broader computer vision research on occlusion robustness and cognitive science perspectives on reasoning under uncertainty.

**Keywords:** Cloud coverage · Benchmark dataset · AI evaluation · Computer vision

## 1 Introduction

Cloud cover poses a continuous challenge in satellite remote sensing. Due to obstruction of surface features, clouds limit the effectiveness of Earth observation data and reduce the reliability of downstream applications. In domains such as environmental monitoring, disaster response, urban planning, and weather forecasting, accurate and timely interpretation of satellite images is important. However, the presence of clouds can obscure critical visual information, distort patterns, and impair the performance of computer vision models designed to gain insights from such data [9].

The difficulty of operating in visually obstructed environments is not only a geospatial concern but also a broader cognitive and artificial intelligence (AI)


T. T. Mai et al. (Eds.): AICS 2025, CCIS 2950, pp. 251–262, 2026.
https://doi.org/10.1007/978-3-032-25809-0_20

challenge. Interpreting visual information in the presence of occlusion and uncertainty presents the challenge of reasoning with incomplete or ambiguous data. Robust AI systems must perform accurately even in the presence of visual obstructions in a way similar to how human cognition adapts to missing sensory information. Cloud cover in satellite images is an ideal example of these challenges, connecting how humans deal with blocked or unclear vision to how AI systems handle practical tasks when encountered with missing or uncertain data.

Existing cloud-related datasets primarily provide binary cloud masks, indicating whether a given pixel is cloud-covered or not [19]. Although these binary masks are required for basic detection tasks, they face several limitations. First, they fail to capture the degree of cloud obstruction, such as differentiating between thin haze and dense overcast conditions [19]. Second, they offer limited capability for systematic comparison of model performance under different cloud conditions. Third, they do not support quantitative benchmarking of model robustness in the presence of partial occlusion. These limitations hinder both the development and cognitive evaluation of AI models designed to interpret cloud-affected imagery.

To address these gaps, this work introduces a continuous cloud-coverage labeling framework. Each image tile is assigned a percentage value ranging from 0 to 100, representing the proportion of cloud cover. This approach enables a more fine-grained evaluation and supports the development of models that are sensitive to varying levels of occlusion. The availability of continuous cloud labels will facilitate the establishment of standardized benchmarks, not only for cloud removal but also for cloud-aware AI tasks such as classification and segmentation.

The primary goal of this research is therefore to design and implement a continuous cloud coverage labeling framework for satellite imagery and to curate a benchmark dataset derived from the SEN12MS-CR dataset [7]. This work is guided by three key objectives; 1) Continuous cloud-overage labeling: develop a reliable method to quantify cloud coverage as a percentage for each image. 2) Benchmark dataset construction: create a high-quality, reproducible, and publicly accessible dataset with continuous cloud labels. 3) Robustness analysis: facilitate systematic study of model robustness under varying cloud conditions.

The proposed dataset extends usability beyond the geospatial domain to broader computer vision tasks. It can support applications such as blur estimation or occlusion quantification, thereby benefiting a wider range of AI research. Crucially, it enables targeted robustness analysis, allowing researchers to evaluate model performance under diverse cloud conditions and identify failure points. By meeting these objectives, the dataset also aids cognitive science by supporting studies on system reliability under uncertainty and incomplete information.

The paper is organized as follows: Sect. 2 reviews related work in cloud detection, removal, and robustness analysis under occlusion. Section 3 details the methodology for generating continuous cloud-coverage labels and constructing the benchmark dataset. Section 4 outlines evaluation protocols and experimental setup, with Sect. 4 presenting results and discussion. Section 5 concludes with findings and directions for future research.

## 2 Related Work

### 2.1 Cloud Related Datasets

Cloud obstruction in optical satellite imagery has demanded the need for cloud-related benchmark datasets. One such widely used dataset is the SEN12MS-CR dataset, which contains paired data derived from multispectral Sentinel-1 and Sentinel-2 data, including both cloudy and cloud-free scenes. This dataset comprises satellite images of globally distributed regions, offering all-season data [7]. Similarly, CloudSEN12 provides cloud semantic annotations across multiple optical remote sensing sensors with a focus on tropical regions. The dataset also provides a large-scale, globally distributed collection of Sentinel-2 image patches, each annotated with pixel-level cloud classes, as thick clouds, thin clouds, cloud shadows, and clear sky [3].

Beyond these datasets, there are several other publicly available cloud datasets. Examples include SPARCS, S2-Hollstein, Biome 8, 38-Cloud, CES-BIO, 95-Cloud, and CloudCatalogue, each of which has been used for developing and benchmarking cloud detection models [2]. However, these datasets suffer from limitations such as limited geographic coverage, small sample sizes, lack of temporal information, and inconsistent labeling protocols. Furthermore, these datasets primarily rely on binary masks to indicate the presence or absence of clouds at the pixel level. Since they do not capture variations in cloud density, such datasets provide limited insight into how AI models behave under systematically varying levels of cloud obstruction.

### 2.2 Evaluation Methods in Cloud Removal and Occlusion Tasks

Cloud detection and removal methods are generally evaluated using standard image quality metrics. Common measures include Structural Similarity Index (SSIM) [14], Peak Signal-to-Noise Ratio (PSNR) [12], Mean Absolute Error (MAE), and Root Mean Squared Error (RMSE) [11]. Furthermore, Fréchet Inception Distance (FID) and Inception Score (IS) are being used to evaluate the quality of images created using generative approaches [16]. In downstream applications, such as classification and segmentation, task-specific measures like accuracy, precision, F1-score, and intersection-over-union (IoU) are commonly employed [13]. However, current evaluation measures rarely account for the severity levels of cloud conditions. As a result, they cannot reveal how robustly models generalize when encountered with variations in cloud coverage.

### 2.3 Clouds as a Case of Occlusion in AI and Cognitive Science

Several approaches have been tested for removing cloud obstructions in satellite imagery, evolving from physics-based corrections to advanced generative models.

Early solutions relied on radiative transfer models and statistical filtering, simulating atmospheric interactions or interpolating missing regions [5]. Nonetheless, these techniques were limited due to their dependence on auxiliary atmospheric data, assumptions in spatial transitions, and the scarcity of labeled data [19]. As a result, the early approaches are less robust in diverse atmospheric conditions. Multitemporal and multi-sensor fusion strategies improved reconstruction by utilizing temporal data and data from various sensor types [4]. However, these approaches remain constrained by persistent cloud cover and data alignment issues.

Over the recent decades, machine learning methods marked a shift towards data-driven solutions within the process of cloud obstruction removal. Traditional machine learning algorithms, such as random forests and Fmask, were utilized during the early stages [18]. These methods often struggled to generalize across diverse environments and required substantial labeled data. Recent studies have indicated that GAN-based models and diffusion-based models offer promising results in cloud removal by learning mappings between cloudy and cloud-free domains [15]. GANs utilize an adversarial training process to generate clear and realistic reconstructions, while diffusion models employ iterative denoising processes that offer greater stability and resilience to mode collapse. Both approaches demonstrate notable improvements in handling complex textures and large occlusions compared to traditional methods [21].

Positioning cloud cover in this broader context frames it as a conventional case of occlusion in computer vision. Unlike blur removal, shadow detection, or de-hazing tasks, cloud removal requires reconstructing missing or degraded information under uncertainty. This situation parallels human perceptual strategies for maintaining stability in ambiguous or incomplete environments. The scarcity of datasets with continuous or graded cloud labels continues to restrict the systematic evaluation of robustness, underscoring the need for benchmarks that capture the spectrum of occlusion severity. This perspective positions cloud removal not only as a geospatial problem but also as a meaningful case study for advancing robustness in AI models more generally.

In brief, existing datasets provide binary cloud masks, and current evaluation methods rely on conventional quality metrics, offering inadequate support for systematic and robust analysis across varying levels of cloud coverage. Lack of continuous labels limits the fair benchmarking of models under partial occlusion and prevents the exploration of failure cases. Unlike prior resources, the proposed dataset assigns each image a percentage-based label (0–100%), enabling fine-grained assessment and standardized evaluation across low, medium, and high cloud conditions.

## 3 Methodology

This section presents the methodology followed to design the continuous cloud-coverage labeling framework and construct the benchmark dataset. The workflow consists of data preparation, cloud coverage computation, dataset construction, metadata integration, and baseline experiments.

### 3.1 Data Preparation

The SEN12MS-CR dataset [7] was used as the primary data source of this work. The selection of the dataset was motivated by its global coverage, multi-season representation, and paired cloudy–cloud-free image tiles. Since the primary objective of this study is to quantify and benchmark the impact of cloud obstruction in optical imagery, only the Sentinel-2 optical data were utilized, excluding the accompanying Sentinel-1 radar data. Another motivation for using only Sentinel-2 data is the high-resolution multispectral measurements, which are widely utilized in downstream applications such as land cover classification, vegetation monitoring, and change detection.

The full dataset contains 122,218 Sentinel-2 image tiles across four seasons (spring, fall, winter, and summer). To ensure diversity while maintaining computational feasibility, a subset comprising 30% of the full dataset was selected for this study (This amounted to approximately 36,666 image tiles). The selection was performed using a Python-based random sampling script. Specifically, the total subset size (36,666) was divided evenly across the seasons to preserve balance, resulting in the selection of 9,167 images from each season. This approach ensured that the sampled dataset retained representative variability in both geographical distribution and seasonal cloud conditions. Furthermore, the sampling approach ensures that the selection will remain computationally manageable for subsequent preprocessing and labeling tasks.

### 3.2 Cloud Coverage Computation

The proportion of cloud-covered pixels was estimated by comparing the cloudy observation with its corresponding cloud-free reference for each image tile. Let $B_b^{\text{cld}}$ and $B_b^{\text{clr}}$ denote the pixel values of band $b$ (blue, green, red, and optionally near-infrared) in the cloudy and clear images respectively. Prior to comparison, all bands were brightness and colour adjusted (histogram matched) to reduce acquisition-time discrepancies and ensure comparability of pixel values.

Following prior work on spectral differencing approaches for cloud detection [20] a per-pixel spectral difference map $D$ was computed as a weighted combination of visible and near-infrared discrepancies, where $(x, y)$ denotes the spatial coordinates of each pixel in the image tile:

$$D_{\text{RGB}}(x, y) = \frac{1}{3} \sum_{b \in \{B,G,R\}} \left| B_b^{\text{cld}}(x, y) - B_b^{\text{clr}}(x, y) \right| \tag{1}$$

$$D_{\text{NIR}}(x, y) = \left| B_{\text{NIR}}^{\text{cld}}(x, y) - B_{\text{NIR}}^{\text{clr}}(x, y) \right| \tag{2}$$

$$D(x, y) = \alpha\, D_{\text{RGB}}(x, y) + \beta\, D_{\text{NIR}}(x, y) \tag{3}$$

with $\alpha = 0.4$ and $\beta = 0.6$ when NIR is used, or $D = D_{\text{RGB}}$ otherwise. An additional ratio term was incorporated to enhance cloud–surface contrast:

$$R(x,y) = \left| \frac{\sum_{b\in\{B,G,R\}} B_b^{\text{cld}}(x,y)}{\sum_{b\in\{B,G,R\}} B_b^{\text{clr}}(x,y)} - 1 \right| \tag{4}$$

yielding a combined difference:

$$D'(x,y) = D(x,y)\,[1 + R(x,y)] \tag{5}$$

The resulting map $D'$ was normalised to $[0,1]$ and thresholded to produce a binary cloud mask $\mathcal{M}(x,y)$:

$$\mathcal{M}(x,y) = \begin{cases} 1, & D'(x,y) > T^*, \\ 0, & \text{otherwise}, \end{cases} \tag{6}$$

where $T^*$ is an adaptive threshold determined by Otsu's method, a widely used technique in image segmentation [17]. The resulting binary mask is further refined with morphological operations (closing, opening, dilation) [10], which are standard in cloud detection pipelines. These operations use a $5 \times 5$ elliptical structuring element to remove noise, fill gaps, and enhance spatial continuity and contour filling is used to fill small holes within cloud objects [10]. The choice of the elliptical structuring element provides a balance between smoothing minor artifacts and preserving cloud boundaries. The elliptical shape is less prone to distorting natural cloud edges compared to square kernels, while the $5\times5$ size is sufficient to remove noise without oversmoothing fine details. Finally, the continuous cloud-coverage percentage $C$ for each tile was calculated as:

$$C = \frac{\sum_{x,y} \mathcal{M}(x,y)}{\sum_{x,y} \mathbb{1}_{\text{valid}}(x,y)} \times 100, \tag{7}$$

where $\mathbb{1}_{\text{valid}}$ denotes valid (non-missing) pixels. This procedure transforms the binary presence/absence of clouds into a quantitative measure on a 0–100% scale, enabling regression-based evaluation and fine-grained benchmarking under varying cloud conditions.

The final cloud mask is saved in PNG format. Additionally, we generate visualizations that include the normalized difference heatmap, the binary cloud mask, an RGB image with red-tinted cloud overlay and the brightness map of the clear-sky image. As shown in Fig. 1 these visualizations are important because the normalized difference heatmap highlights pixel-wise cloud-induced changes, the binary cloud mask enables direct computation of cloud coverage, the RGB image with red-tinted overlay allows intuitive visual verification, and the brightness map of the clear-sky image helps interpret differences and avoid misclassifications in naturally bright regions.

### 3.3 Dataset Construction

Following cloud-coverage computation for each image tile, a unified metadata structure was established to organise the images and their corresponding continuous labels. To maximise transparency, ease of access, and reproducibility, all

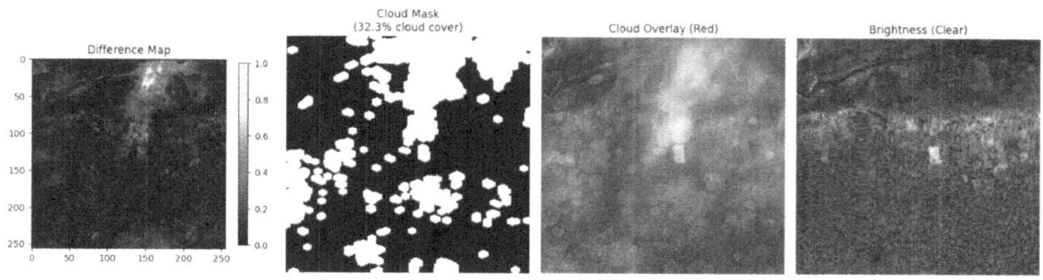


**Fig. 1.** Visualizations generated for cloud-percentage computation, shown in order: normalized difference heatmap, binary cloud mask, RGB image with red-tinted cloud overlay, and brightness map of the clear-sky image.

information is stored in a single master comma-separated file (CSV) provided along with the dataset (`cloud_percentage.csv`).

This file links each cloudy Sentinel-2 image tile to its computed cloud percentage, its season, and optionally, its corresponding clear reference image tile. The master CSV is structured with one row per image tile. The main fields are:

- **season**: the acquisition season (spring, summer, autumn, winter)
- **cloudy_image_name**: file name of the cloudy Sentinel-2 image tile
- **clear_image_name**: optional corresponding clear image tile file name
- **cloud_percentage**: the continuous cloud coverage value (0–100%).

This single-file format allows researchers to rapidly query the dataset by season, image name, or cloud coverage level, and to join metadata with image files during their preferred machine learning pipelines. Table 1 summarises the structure of the master CSV file and illustrates typical entries for each column.

**Table 1.** Example rows from the master CSV file linking cloudy Sentinel-2 tiles to their computed cloud percentages.

| season | cloudy_image_name | clear_image_name | cloud_percentage (%) |
|---|---|---|---|
| Fall | ROIs1970_fall_s2_cloudy_1_p32.tif | ROIs1970_fall_s2_1_p32.tif | 48.3 |
| Spring | ROIs1158_spring_s2_cloudy_7_p89.tif | ROIs1158_spring_s2_7_p89.tif | 17.6 |
| Summer | ROIs1868_summer_s2_cloudy_15_p43.tif | ROIs1868_summer_s2_15_p43.tif | 82.1 |
| Winter | ROIs2017_winter_s2_cloudy_8_p36.tif | ROIs2017_winter_s2_8_p36.tif | 65.4 |

### 3.4 Dataset Availability

To enable open research and reproducibility, the cloud-percentage annotated Sentinel-2 dataset is publicly accessible. The dataset is hosted on Zenodo, an open-access repository that provides persistent digital object identifiers (DOIs) and ensures long-term availability of research data [8]. The hosted dataset includes; cloudy Sentinel-2 image tiles grouped by season, corresponding clear reference image tiles, and, a master CSV file containing metadata, including computed cloud coverage, image names, and acquisition season.

Researchers can freely download the dataset and cite it using the provided DOI. The data can be utilized for machine learning workflows or geospatial analysis pipelines. The repository also provides version control, enabling users to access updates or improvements to the dataset over time. Through the publicly available dataset, we aim to support reproducible research in cloud-obstructed geospatial scene reconstruction, encourage benchmarking of novel algorithms, and facilitate further advancements in satellite image analysis.

The dataset can be accessed at: https://doi.org/10.5281/zenodo.17114706

### 3.5 Case Study

To demonstrate the applicability of the proposed cloud-percentage–annotated dataset, a case study was conducted using UnCRtainTS, a state-of-the-art cloud removal model previously trained on the original SEN12MS-CR dataset [6]. Because UnCRtainTS has been optimised on a diverse collection of Sentinel-2 imagery, its evaluation on our annotated dataset enables an assessment of how reconstruction quality varies across different levels of cloud obstruction.

For this experiment, the entire curated dataset was used as the test set. To analyse the effect of cloud coverage on model performance, all cloudy image tiles were grouped into three categories as: low cloud coverage (0–30 %), medium cloud coverage (31–60 %), and high cloud coverage (61–100 %). To reduce sampling bias due to unequal sample sizes across categories, an equal number of image tiles was randomly selected from each cloud-coverage category for evaluation. UnCRtainTS was then applied to each selected tile to generate cloud-free reconstructions. The reconstructed outputs were compared with their corresponding reference clear-sky tiles using three widely adopted image-quality metrics: SSIM, PSNR, and MAE. This setup provides a direct view of how cloud-coverage density influences the performance of a state-of-the-art cloud removal approach.

## 4 Results and Discussion

### 4.1 Cloud Percentage Distribution

To explore the usefulness of the curated dataset with a continuous labeling framework, the distribution of the cloud coverage across the dataset was analysed. The distribution in Fig. 2(a) shows that most image tiles fall within the 30–60% coverage range, with a peak around 40–50%. Images with considerably low (<20%) and high (>80%) clopud coverage are relatively scarce. This implies that the dataset is dominated by moderately cloud-covered image tiles, making performance under extreme conditions less reliable.

Figure 2(b) shows the Kernel Density Estimation (KDE) plot of cloud coverage by season, which provides a smoothed probability distribution of cloud percentages across the proposed dataset. The KDE illustrated both seasonal and global variability, where winter (blue curve) exhibits the sharpest peak around 45–55%, indicating a higher concentration of medium cloud density. On the other hand, summer shows a similar distribution to spring and fall, but with a heavier tail extending beyond 70%. The distribution of summer suggests that heavily clouded conditions are more prevalent in this season. The entire distribution is broadly continuous across the 0–100% scale, demonstrating that our sampling approach preserved diverse cloud coverage conditions, thereby supporting robustness analysis under a spectrum of occlusion levels.

To confirm the reliability of our labeling framework, the average cloud coverage derived from our calculations (avg%) was compared with the values reported in the original SEN12MS-CR dataset (48%). The close alignment between the two confirms that our calculation method provides consistent and reliable measurements of cloud coverage. This agreement strengthens the usability of the dataset for benchmarking and for studies exploring robustness in occluded environments.

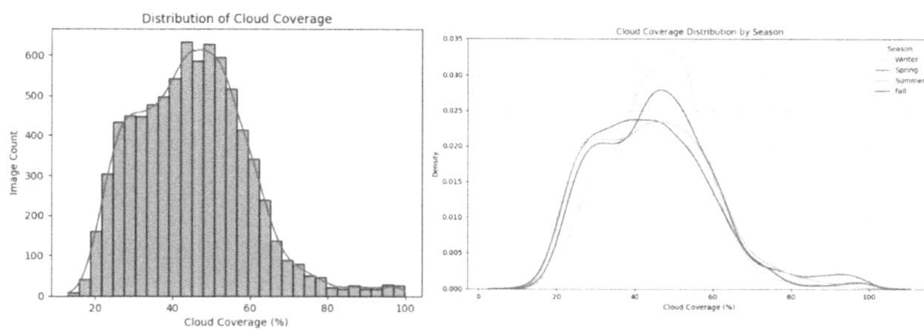


(a) (b)

**Fig. 2.** (a) Histogram of cloud coverage across the dataset. (b) KDE of cloud coverage by season.

### 4.2 Case Study: Model Evaluation Across Cloud Levels

The performance of the UnCRtainTS model was evaluated across three cloud-coverage categories using SSIM, PSNR, and MAE as quantitative metrics. The results, summarized in Table 2, reveal that the reconstruction quality declines as cloud density increases.

Table 2 reports the performance of the UnCRtainTS model across diverse cloud densities alongside the baseline evaluation on the full dataset. The results demonstrate a noticeable reduction in reconstruction quality as cloud density increases. At low coverage, the model acquired strong performance (SSIM = 0.913, PSNR = 31.44 dB, MAE = 0.021), indicating the capability to reconstruct fine structural details and preserve spectral consistency. When tested against medium cloud coverage, the UnCRtainTS model demonstrated modest

**Table 2.** Performance of UnCRtainTS model across cloud coverage levels.

| Cloud Coverage | SSIM ↑ | PSNR (dB) ↑ | MAE ↓ |
|---|---|---|---|
| Low (0–30%) | $0.913 \pm 0.021$ | $31.44 \pm 1.85$ | $0.021 \pm 0.004$ |
| Medium (31–60%) | $0.901 \pm 0.026$ | $29.87 \pm 2.03$ | $0.028 \pm 0.004$ |
| High (61–100%) | $0.773 \pm 0.034$ | $27.28 \pm 2.41$ | $0.033 \pm 0.005$ |
| Baseline (full dataset) | $0.880 \pm 0.029$ | $28.90 \pm 2.12$ | $0.027 \pm 0.005$ |

error increases, highlighting spectral inconsistencies. Under high cloud coverage, all metrics decline substantially, indicating the difficulty of the model to perform under extensive cloud coverage. When considering the baseline evaluation (SSIM = 0.880, PSNR = 28.90 dB, MAE = 0.027), it is noticeable that the reported results overestimate performance in high-cloud scenarios and underestimate performance in low-cloud cases. In summary, the findings emphasize the value of cloud-percentage–aware evaluation to exposing model limitations. The results indicate that the model failure modes are directly linked to the degree of cloud obstruction. Identifying these patterns can support improvements in model design and data augmentation strategies to enhance robustness under extreme occlusion conditions.

### 4.3 Implications for AI and Cognitive Science

The experimental findings indicate that binary cloud labels are inadequate to explore the capabilities of model performance in occluded environments. Instead, continuous cloud labels enable systematic evaluation across a graded scope of difficulty. This setup reflects cognitive models of inference, in which humans adjust their views based on uncertain evidence. For example, Bayesian inference describes how the brain integrates prior knowledge with ambiguous sensory input to make probabilistic predictions, while predictive coding emphasizes minimizing uncertainty through iterative refinement of expectations [1].

From this perspective, cloud obstruction in satellite imagery offers a natural correlation of human perceptual occlusion: In a similar way to how humans rely on priors to interpret partially hidden objects, AI models must develop strategies for stable inference under incomplete data. The observed reduction in UnCRtainTS performance at high cloud coverage highlights the need for models that incorporate prior knowledge and adaptive inference mechanisms. The insights from this work reflect the convergence of AI robustness analysis with cognitive theories of reasoning under uncertainty. By enabling graded evaluation, our dataset provides a foundation for investigating these parallels and advancing both AI and cognitive science research.

## 5 Conclusion

This work introduced a continuous cloud-coverage dataset to support systematic assessment of AI robustness in occluded environments. By providing percentage-based labels beyond binary masks, the dataset enables benchmarking of cloud-aware models under diverse coverage conditions. The case study with the UnCR-tainTS model shows how continuous labels reveal subtle performance declines hidden in conventional evaluations. Capturing gradual variations in cloud coverage will allow practitioners to identify specific coverage thresholds where models start to fail, indicating actionable insights for deploying models in real-world occluded environments.

Otsu's method was employed for thresholding due to its simplicity and efficiency, but it has limitations. It assumes a globally bimodal histogram, an assumption often invalid in heterogeneous scenes with snow, bright urban areas, or thin haze. Consequently, a single global threshold may misclassify pixels, treating bright surfaces as clouds or missing semi-transparent layers. Adaptive local thresholding can improve accuracy by deriving thresholds from surrounding pixels. Although computationally demanding, local or hybrid approaches that combine global and local strategies may yield more robust performance in complex environments, suggesting promising future directions.

The dataset contributes to geospatial AI by offering a reproducible benchmark for cloud removal, classification, and segmentation. It broadens the basis for occlusion analysis in computer vision and, through open availability, supports reproducibility and comparative evaluation, enabling transparent progress. This work also positions cloud cover as a natural analogue for occlusion in cognitive science, showing how robust AI systems must reason under uncertainty and partial observability. Findings further suggest directions for leveraging temporal observations, hybrid generative methods, and uncertainty quantification to enhance robustness in cloud removal, particularly under high cloud densities.

## References


1. Aitchison, L., Lengyel, M.: With or without you: predictive coding and Bayesian inference in the brain. Curr. Opin. Neurobiol. **46**, 219–227 (2017)
2. Aybar, C., et al.: Cloudsen12, a global dataset for semantic understanding of cloud and cloud shadow in sentinel-2. Sci. Data **9**, 782 (2022). https://doi.org/10.1038/s41597-022-01878-2
3. Aybar, C., et al.: Cloudsen12, a global dataset for semantic understanding of cloud and cloud shadow in sentinel-2. Sci. Data **9**(1), 782 (2022)
4. Chen, Y., Weng, Q., Tang, L., Zhang, X., Bilal, M., Li, Q.: Thick clouds removing from multitemporal landsat images using spatiotemporal neural networks. IEEE Trans. Geosci. Remote Sens. **60**, 1–14 (2020)
5. Das, S., Das, P., Roy, B.R.: Cloud detection and cloud removal of satellite image—a case study. In: Sarma, H.K.D., Bhuyan, B., Borah, S., Dutta, N. (eds.) Trends in Communication, Cloud, and Big Data. LNNS, vol. 99, pp. 53–63. Springer, Singapore (2020). https://doi.org/10.1007/978-981-15-1624-5_6
6. Ebel, P., Garnot, V.S.F., Schmitt, M., Wegner, J.D., Zhu, X.X.: Uncrtaints: uncertainty quantification for cloud removal in optical satellite time series (2023). https://arxiv.org/abs/2304.05464
7. Ebel, P., Meraner, A., Schmitt, M., Zhu, X.X.: Multisensor data fusion for cloud removal in global and all-season sentinel-2 imagery. IEEE Trans. Geosci. Remote Sens. (2020)

8. European Organization For Nuclear Research, OpenAIRE: Zenodo (2013). https://doi.org/10.25495/7GXK-RD71. https://www.zenodo.org
9. Gupta, R., Nanda, S.J.: Cloud detection in satellite images with classical and deep neural network approach: a review. Multimedia Tools Appl. **81**(22), 31847–31880 (2022)
10. Haralick, R.M., Sternberg, S.R., Zhuang, X.: Image analysis using mathematical morphology. IEEE Trans. Pattern Anal. Mach. Intell. **4**, 532–550 (1987)
11. Hodson, T.O.: Root mean square error (RMSE) or mean absolute error (MAE): when to use them or not. Geosci. Model Dev. Discuss. **2022**, 1–10 (2022)
12. Keleş, O., Yılmaz, M.A., Tekalp, A.M., Korkmaz, C., Dogan, Z.: On the computation of PSNR for a set of images or video (2021). https://arxiv.org/abs/2104.14868
13. Maxwell, A.E., Warner, T.A., Guillén, L.A.: Accuracy assessment in convolutional neural network-based deep learning remote sensing studies–part 1: literature review. Remote Sens. **13**(13), 2450 (2021)
14. Nilsson, J., Akenine-Möller, T.: Understanding SSIM (2020). https://arxiv.org/abs/2006.13846
15. Ning, J., Xie, L., Yin, J., Liu, Y.: Cloud removal advances: a comprehensive review and analysis for optical remote sensing images. IEEE J. Sel. Top. Appl. Earth Obs. Remote Sens. (2025)
16. Obukhov, A., Krasnyanskiy, M.: Quality assessment method for GAN based on modified metrics inception score and Fréchet inception distance. In: Silhavy, R., Silhavy, P., Prokopova, Z. (eds.) CoMeSySo 2020. AISC, vol. 1294, pp. 102–114. Springer, Cham (2020). https://doi.org/10.1007/978-3-030-63322-6_8
17. Otsu, N., et al.: A threshold selection method from gray-level histograms. Automatica **11**(285–296), 23–27 (1975)
18. dos Santos, E.P., da Silva, D.D., do Amaral, C.H., Fernandes-Filho, E.I., Dias, R.L.S.: A machine learning approach to reconstruct cloudy affected vegetation indices imagery via data fusion from sentinel-1 and landsat 8. Comput. Electron. Agric. **194**, 106753 (2022)
19. Singh, R., Pal, M., Biswas, M.: Cloud detection methods for optical satellite imagery: a comprehensive review. Geomatics **5**(3), 27 (2025)
20. Sun, L., et al.: A cloud detection algorithm-generating method for remote sensing data at visible to short-wave infrared wavelengths. ISPRS J. Photogramm. Remote. Sens. **124**, 70–88 (2017)
21. Wang, H.: Comparative analysis of GANs and diffusion models in image generation. Highlights Sci. Eng. Technol. **120**, 59–66 (2024). https://doi.org/10.54097/9gba9v27

# Forecasting Energy Demand in Buildings: The Case for Trees over Deep Nets

Dan Alexandru Bujoreanu[1,2](✉) and Faithful Chiagoziem Onwuegbuche[1,2]

[1] National College of Ireland, Dublin, Ireland
hello@danbujoreanu.com, faithful.chiagoziemonwuegb@ucdconnect.ie
[2] University College Dublin, Dublin, Ireland

**Abstract.** Reliable short-term forecasts of building energy demand are essential for operating flexible, low-carbon power systems. They help system operators and facility managers to schedule resources and avoid costly balancing actions. In practical terms, better predictions improve intraday planning and support the dispatch of behind-the-meter storage.

In this paper we evaluate forecasting methods on a heterogeneous public-building portfolio from Drammen, Norway. A leakage-safe, feature-engineering-first pipeline enables a comparison between tree ensembles, LSTM, CNN–LSTM and a Temporal Fusion Transformer (TFT), and assesses a simple stacking approach. While sequence models are configured for multi-step outputs, we standardise the evaluation on the critical one-step-ahead (H+1) forecast to ensure a direct comparison against non-sequence baselines. Across the held-out test window, tree models provide the best balance of predictive performance and speed, consistently surpassing deep networks while training in seconds rather than hours. The stacking ensemble models do not improve on the best single tree. The study shows that careful feature engineering, paired with tree ensembles, is a strong baseline for building demand forecasting.

**Keywords:** Energy forecasting · Tree-based models · Deep learning · Ensembles

## 1 Introduction

Short-term building energy load forecasting (STBELF) underpins smart-grid operation, flexible integration of variable renewables, and carbon-aware building management. In heterogeneous portfolios, forecasting is complicated by diverse building uses, occupancy schedules, control strategies, and weather sensitivity. As of 2025, the energy system combines rising demand with net-zero commitments. Global electricity use is projected to grow ∼3.4% annually through 2026 [13], driven by electrified transport and heating and the growth of data centres. Meeting 2030 targets accelerates adoption of variable renewables [6]. Countries increasingly rely on intermittent wind and solar, such as Ireland which reached 54.5% renewables in February 2025 and recorded its first coal-free


T. T. Mai et al. (Eds.): AICS 2025, CCIS 2950, pp. 263–274, 2026.
https://doi.org/10.1007/978-3-032-25809-0_21

month in July 2025 [5]. Variability introduces operational stress (for example winter *Dunkelflaute* and summer *Hitzeflaute*) and price spikes or even negative prices, prompting curtailment and rapid Battery Energy Storage Systems (BESS) deployment, classic "duck curve" dynamics. Accurate near-term consumption forecasts reduce costly intraday corrections [7].

Beyond grid balancing, STBELF enables demand-side flexibility by shifting loads and optimising behind-the-meter storage and dispatch. Buildings are central: they accounted for 41% of Ireland's final energy in 2022 [11], and rapid heat electrification increases weather sensitivity. Norway offers a mature reference case (81% electrified heating and 89% hydro generation) [12]. We therefore analyse a real-world municipal portfolio from Drammen, Norway: the COFACTOR dataset [18] with hourly load and weather for 45 public buildings (2018–2022). The portfolio is intentionally heterogeneous, making single-model generalisation non-trivial and motivating a careful comparison of modelling paradigms.

Ultimately, STBELF for portfolios faces a practical trade-off: efficient, feature-engineering-first tree ensembles (for example Random Forest, XGBoost, LightGBM) versus higher-capacity deep learning architectures (LSTM, CNN–LSTM, Transformers) that learn from sequences but demand far more compute and careful setup [8,15].

This paper addresses three research questions: (i) can a comprehensive feature-engineering pipeline enable Random Forest, XGBoost, and LightGBM to outperform LSTM, CNN–LSTM, and a Transformer on multi-building hourly load forecasting? (ii) do lightweight stacking schemes offer material gains over the best single model, and at what computational cost? (iii) which engineered features contribute most across an electrified public-building portfolio?

Our contributions are threefold. First, we provide a transparent, leakage-safe pipeline for portfolio forecasting with a shared feature set across model families. Second, we run a unified comparison of trees, deep networks, and ensembles on identical inputs with chronological evaluation. Third, we quantify performance versus compute trade-offs to support deployment for day-to-day operations. The main limitations are the Nordic, heating-dominated context and conservative tuning of sequence models to respect realistic compute budgets; stronger tuning may reduce gaps but would increase cost.

## 2 Related Work

Research on short-term building energy load forecasting (STBELF) has progressed from statistical baselines to early machine learning, then to tree ensembles and sequence models with deep learning. We summarise the foundational concepts, with an emphasis on practical lessons, where each family tends to succeed, and the outstanding gaps.

### 2.1 From Statistical Baselines to Early Machine Learning

Early data-driven building forecasting used Multiple Linear Regression and ARIMA or SARIMA. These methods work well when seasonality is strong and temperature response is near-linear. Performance improves when social rhythms (weekday/holiday) are encoded. As sub-hourly metering, weather APIs, and shared datasets became common, the problem shifted toward supervised learning. Survey articles report extensive use of Artificial Neural Networks, Support Vector Machines, and Decision Trees across many single-building case studies [1,4]. The same reviews note several limitations: heterogeneous splits and metrics, limited treatment of weather-forecast uncertainty, and a predominance of single-site evaluations that weaken external validity [9]. These issues motivated more standardised comparisons on multi-building datasets.

### 2.2 Tree-Based Ensembles and Feature Engineering

Competitions and broad benchmarks show that tree ensembles are difficult to beat once features are well designed. In the ASHRAE Great Energy Predictor III challenge, leading entries relied on LightGBM and XGBoost with careful preprocessing and engineered features [21]. This aligns with the inductive biases of boosted trees [3,14,22] and with tabular benchmarks that favour trees on structured data [8]. For STBELF, targeted lags at daily and weekly recurrences, short- and weekly-window statistics, and cyclical calendars are consistently helpful [16]. Tree ensembles also provide accessible interpretability through split-gain measures and SHAP-based explanations, which aids model diagnostics and handover to operators [20].

### 2.3 Deep Learning for Sequence Modelling

Deep sequence models aim to learn temporal dependence end-to-end from raw or lightly engineered streams. LSTM and CNN–LSTM variants have shown strong performance at short horizons and in settings with complex, non-linear dynamics [23,24]. Attention-based models, in particular the Temporal Fusion Transformer (TFT), are designed for multi-horizon forecasting with mixed static and time-varying covariates [19]. Recent studies in building systems report competitive accuracy with Transformer-style models under careful configuration [17]. However, these gains typically come with higher computational cost and sensitivity to architecture and tuning, which matters in portfolio operations where retraining and iteration are frequent.

### 2.4 Summary and Research Gaps

Cross-domain and tabular benchmarks consistently find that well-tuned tree ensembles outperform specialised deep learning models on structured data, usually at far lower computational cost [2,8]. Once seasonal, weather, and lagged or short-recency features are added, building-load data are effectively tabular, so claims of universal deep-learning superiority are not supported by current evidence. Nevertheless, four recurring gaps remain in the literature: (i) limited external validity due to single-building case studies and heterogeneous experimental setups [1,4,10]; (ii) conflation of architecture and representation, for example feature-rich gradient-boosted trees compared with deep models trained on minimally engineered inputs; (iii) sparse reporting of compute budgets and training footprints despite their practical importance; and (iv) underused interpretability methods for operator trust, such as SHAP and related tools [20].

Our study addresses these points by using a shared, leakage-safe feature set and consistent chronological splits across model families, by reporting both performance and computation, and by comparing interpretable tree baselines with deep models and simple stacking.

## 3 Methodology

This section describes the dataset, preprocessing, and the *feature-engineering-first* pipeline that underpins all models. The design goal is a leakage-safe and reproducible framework in which competing model families are tested under identical inputs, so that observed differences can be attributed to modelling choices rather than data handling (see Sect. 2.4) (Fig. 1).

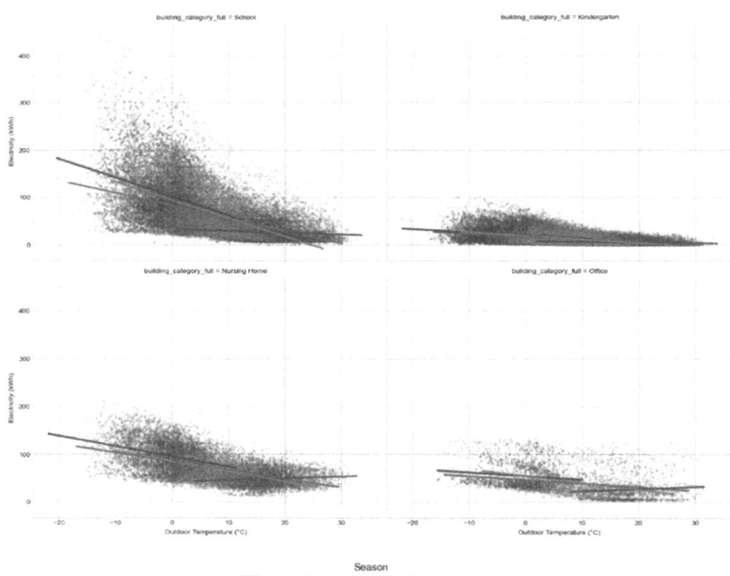


**Fig. 1.** Electricity consumption vs. Outdoor Temperature colored by building category. The distinct "V-shape" indicates heating demand below 15 °C and varying cooling sensitivities above 20 °C, justifying the need for non-linear models.

### 3.1 Data Acquisition and Description

We use the COFACTOR Drammen dataset of hourly energy consumption for 45 public buildings (2018–2022), with matched weather and building metadata (building identifier, floor area, building category, construction year, number of users, and related descriptors) [18]. The weather table includes outdoor temperature, relative humidity, wind speed, and solar irradiance from the nearest meteorological station. All timestamps are converted to local time with explicit handling of Daylight Saving Time, and each record is stored under a unique compound key `(building_id, timestamp)`. The target is hourly site energy (kWh).

### 3.2 Preprocessing and Cleaning

Column names and units are standardised, and exact duplicates are removed. We drop obviously corrupt sensor values using conservative physical bounds (e.g., temperature $[-40, 45]\,^{\circ}\mathrm{C}$) and resample weather to strict hourly ticks. Weather and load are joined with a nearest-timestamp merge after resampling weather to strict hourly ticks and enforcing a maximum drift of fifteen minutes.

After cleaning, residual missing inputs are limited. LightGBM and XGBoost handle remaining missing values internally. Random Forest uses per-feature median imputation fitted on the training fold. Deep models consume a scaled and fully imputed copy of the engineered panel to avoid missing values in tensors, while tree models operate on the unscaled engineered features.

**Metadata Imputation for Users.** Reported `number_of_users` is missing for a small subset of buildings. We impute values using a category-specific density. Let $u_j$ be the reported users and $A_j$ the floor area for building $j$. For a building $i$ in category $c = \mathrm{cat}(i)$, define $\mathcal{C}(i) = \{\, j : \mathrm{cat}(j) = c,\ u_j \text{ observed} \,\}$. Compute the category density

$$\delta_c \;=\; \mathrm{median}_{\,j \in \mathcal{C}(i)} \left( \frac{u_j}{A_j} \right).$$

Let $q^{(c)}_{0.10}$ and $q^{(c)}_{0.90}$ be the tenth and ninetieth percentiles of the same density within category $c$. The imputed users for building $i$ are

$$\widehat{u}_i \;=\; \left[\mathrm{clip}(\delta_c,\, q^{(c)}_{0.10},\, q^{(c)}_{0.90})\right] A_i,$$

optionally rounded to the nearest integer. If a category has insufficient support, the global median density is used. A binary flag `users_imputed_flag` marks imputations. The imputed value is a static descriptor and is not used to infer time-varying occupancy.

More than 100 candidates were derived from time, weather, and lagged load, then reduced to **35 predictors**. Features are computed *per building* after temporal sorting and are strictly past-looking. For clarity, we group the engineered features into four families: (i) cyclical time encodings, (ii) autoregressive lags,

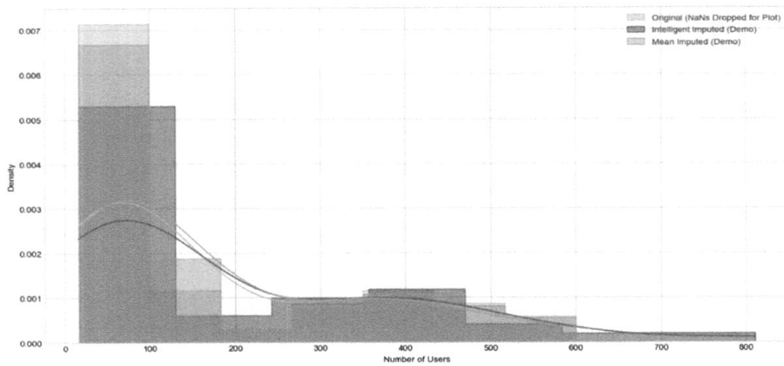


**Fig. 2.** Imputation strategies for the number of users.

(iii) rolling-window statistics, and (iv) domain interactions with static metadata. *This taxonomy is not exhaustive - additional families were explored (like holiday proximity counters, degree-hour variants), but the four groups below captured the bulk of signal at minimal complexity* (Fig. 2).

**Cyclical Time.** First, we encode periodic indices with sine and cosine pairs for hour (24), day of week (7), and month (12), together with weekend and Norwegian public-holiday flags.

**Autoregressive Lags.** Second, we compute target lags at 1, 2, 3, 24, 25, 26, 48, and 167–169 h, and a short-recency mean $\overline{y}_{t-1:t-3}$. The same index set is applied to outdoor temperature $T_t$.

**Rolling Windows.** Third, we take past-looking statistics on load and temperature over 3, 6, 12, 24, 72, and 168 h windows: mean and standard deviation, and for 24 and 168 h also minimum and maximum. All windows close at $t-1$ to avoid look-ahead.

**Domain Interactions and Metadata.** Finally, we include schedule-dependent temperature interactions, for example $T_t \times$ hour_sin and $T_t \times$ IsWeekend, and static descriptors (floor area, construction year, imputed users). Tree models consume the full engineered set, while deep models use the same streams with scaling and a minimal lag subset.

### 3.3 Feature Selection

To reduce the high-dimensional feature space and mitigate multicollinearity, we implemented a two-stage selection pipeline. First, a statistical filter applied a quasi-constant filter (VarianceThreshold = 0.0). Subsequently, we calculated the Pearson correlation matrix and removed one feature from any pair with $|\rho| > 0.95$. This addressed redundancy between overlapping rolling windows and autoregressive lags. Second, model-based ranking trained a LightGBM regressor on the training partition to calculate *gain* importance. Features were ranked by their total contribution to the reduction of the loss function. Rather than using an arbitrary stability threshold, we utilized a Top-N strategy, retaining the 35 highest-ranking predictors.

Following this process, the final feature vector was consolidated into 35 predictors, including cyclical time encodings, specific autoregressive lags ($t-1, t-24, t-168$), and building-specific metadata. This unified set serves as the common input for all subsequent modelling steps. Specific details regarding data parity and the chronological protocol are detailed in Sect. 4.1.

## 4 Design and Experimental Setup

### 4.1 Design Setup

**Task and Horizon.** Hourly site-load forecasting for a heterogeneous municipal portfolio is framed as supervised learning with point predictions. Sequence models use a multi-horizon setting (24 steps ahead) with a fixed 72-h lookback window. However, to standardise the comparison against non-sequence models (Trees) and focus on the most operationally critical timeframe for balancing, we evaluate all models on the **One-Step-Ahead (H+1)** forecast.

**Chronological Splits.** To avoid leakage and mirror operations, data were split chronologically: training up to 2020-12-31, validation to 2021-06-30, and testing thereafter. Splits are applied to a timezone-aware MultiIndex `(building_id, timestamp)`. The final 35-feature panel (Sect. 3.3) is reassembled and split using the same boundaries.

**Feature Handling and Scaling.** While the Deep Learning models often excel at extracting patterns from raw data in vision and NLP domains, empirical benchmarks on high-frequency tabular data suggest they struggle to discover complex periodicities (such as weekly seasonality) without massive datasets. To ensure a strictly fair comparison of architectural capabilities and help Deep Networks to succeed, the *identical* 35-feature set was provided to *all* model families. This design choice isolates differences in inductive bias by holding the information content constant. Preprocessing diverged solely to meet algorithmic constraints: Deep Learning models received inputs scaled via a `StandardScaler` (fitted on the training fold only) to facilitate gradient descent convergence, and utilised a fully imputed copy to satisfy tensor requirements. In contrast, Tree Ensembles (Random Forest, XGBoost, LightGBM) were trained on the unscaled engineered panel, respecting their mathematical scale-invariance. All steps were implemented as deterministic pipeline components with strict chronological splits to prevent leakage.

**Baselines and Metrics.** Persistence baselines at 1 h, 24 h, and 168 h are computed on identical splits to contextualise MAE, RMSE, $R^2$, and CV(RMSE). Additive models like Prophet were excluded as they typically require extensive manual specification to capture the complex, non-linear interactions of hourly load data, which Gradient Boosting handles natively.

### 4.2 Model Architectures and Configurations

**Baselines (persistence).** We use three anchors: one-hour lag, 24-hour seasonal, and 168-hour weekly persistence. These require no training and provide transparent lower bounds.

**Tree-Based Models.** Random Forest, XGBoost, and LightGBM use the common set of 35 engineered predictors (Sect. 3.3). LightGBM runs with `metric=mae` and learning rate 0.05. XGBoost uses the `reg:squarederror` objective. Models are trained on the training period and evaluated on validation and test without refitting on future data.

**Deep Learning Models.** To ensure operational viability within a realistic municipal compute budget, we manually tuned network architectures rather than performing exhaustive search. We implemented three variants operating on the scaled 3D tensors: (i) a **Seq2Seq LSTM** comprising two stacked blocks (64 and 32 units) with a time-distributed dense head; (ii) a **CNN–LSTM** adding a shallow 1D convolution and max-pooling front-end to the LSTM backbone; and (iii) the **Temporal Fusion Transformer (TFT)**, implemented via `pytorch-forecasting` with MAE loss. Early stopping was applied universally to control overfitting.

**Stacking Ensembles.** A level-1 meta-learner (ridge or LightGBM) stacks diverse bases (RF, XGB, LGBM, LSTM, CNN–LSTM, TFT). To avoid the compute cost of time-series cross-validation, we use *validation-set* stacking: base models are trained on the training period (to 2020-12-31); their predictions on the validation period (to 2021-06-30) form a meta-feature matrix; the meta-learner is fit on these and evaluated on aligned test-set meta-features. This trades the theoretical robustness of out-of-fold (OOF) stacking for practical feasibility given long DL/TFT training times.

### 4.3 Implementation Environment and Reproducibility

We implemented the pipeline in Python using `pandas` and `numpy` for data handling, `scikit-learn`, `xgboost`, and `lightgbm` for tree models, and `pytorch-forecasting` for the TFT. Training was conducted on a single workstation with Apple Silicon acceleration (MPS); exact hardware is secondary as we report relative wall-clock times in Sect. 5. To ensure reproducibility, we fixed random seeds and applied strict leakage controls: features were computed per-building, all lags and rolling windows closed at $t-1$, and splits were applied after feature assembly to ensure no refitting occurred on future data.

## 5 Evaluation

We evaluate here the model families on the held-out test window under the unified, leakage-safe protocol from Sect. 3. Specifically, we report MAE, RMSE, $R^2$, CV(RMSE), and wall-clock training time.

**Overall Performance and Efficiency.** Tree ensembles delivered the highest test performance with Random Forest achieving the best MAE (3.30 kWh, $R^2 = 0.9819$), followed by XGBoost (3.42) and LightGBM (3.58). Deep sequence models underperformed on this portfolio: the best TFT reached 5.11 kWh ($R^2 \approx 0.952$), while LSTM (10.13) and CNN–LSTM (12.44) lagged. Training times for XGBoost and LightGBM differed by orders of magnitude compared with LSTM or TFT (Table 1).

**Table 1.** Test-set performance metrics and training time (final split). Lower is better for MAE/RMSE/CV(RMSE).

| Model | MAE (kWh) | RMSE (kWh) | CV(RMSE) % | $R^2$ | Train (s) |
|---|---|---|---|---|---|
| Random Forest | 3.300473 | 6.403286 | 14.475689 | 0.981831 | 115.796 |
| XGBoost | 3.418656 | 6.443359 | 14.566280 | 0.981653 | 2.620 |
| LightGBM | 3.577596 | 6.678540 | 15.097946 | 0.980290 | 3.272 |
| Stack (LGBM meta) | 3.582445 | 7.030462 | 15.811166 | 0.978240 | 0.439 |
| Stack (Ridge meta) | 3.697746 | 7.051277 | 15.857978 | 0.978111 | 0.180 |
| Weighted average | 4.080889 | 7.841386 | 17.634894 | 0.972931 | 0.011 |
| Lasso | 4.201299 | 7.880407 | 17.814965 | 0.972557 | 3.792 |
| Linear | 4.214552 | 7.767148 | 17.558924 | 0.973340 | 0.571 |
| Ridge | 4.214558 | 7.767156 | 17.558944 | 0.973340 | 0.179 |
| Persist-1h | 4.561322 | 9.586920 | 21.672821 | 0.959335 | – |
| TFT (MAE loss, tuned) | 5.113802 | 10.423864 | 23.568891 | 0.951953 | 21831.254 |
| TFT (baseline) | 8.576343 | 13.441574 | 19.510801 | 0.947853 | 21831.254 |
| Persist-24h | 8.761971 | 19.383023 | 43.818534 | 0.833974 | – |
| Persist-168h | 9.620687 | 19.258531 | 43.537100 | 0.836100 | – |
| LSTM | 10.132110 | 17.685640 | 39.774141 | 0.862303 | 13496.862 |
| CNN–LSTM | 12.435477 | 20.930222 | 47.071046 | 0.807146 | 2237.679 |

**Per-building Behaviour and Interpretability.** Targeted lags (1, 24, 168 h) and rolling statistics stabilised performance across occupancy and weather regimes while gains from stacking were small, suggesting most signal is captured by the feature-engineered trees.

**Summary.** In this setting, a feature-engineering-first approach with tree ensembles achieves the strongest performance at a fraction of the cost of deep networks. The compute gap is material for portfolio-scale deployment and frequent retraining. Results support the premise that carefully engineered tabular representations remain a competitive default for STBELF, with attention-based models an option when multi-horizon outputs and complex covariates are essential.

# 6 Discussion

This paper compared tree ensembles, deep sequence models, and simple stacking for short-term building energy forecasting on a four-year, 45-building portfolio. Using a shared, leakage-safe feature set and consistent chronological splits, tree ensembles achieved the best balance of predictive performance and computation on the held-out test window. Random Forest, XGBoost, and LightGBM trained in seconds and outperformed a carefully configured Transformer that required hours of training. A lightweight stack matched, but did not exceed, the best single tree.

## 6.1 Interpretation and Relation to Prior Work

The outcome aligns with tabular-learning evidence and building-domain reports: targeted lags ($t{-}1, t{-}24, t{-}168$), short and weekly rolling statistics, and calendar encodings capture most operational signal in hourly loads. In this portfolio, short and weekly recurrence plus temperature-driven thresholds outweighed very long sequential dependencies, limiting the advantage of end-to-end sequence models. TFT's attention over mixed covariates narrowed the gap but remained compute-intensive, reinforcing tree ensembles as first choice for portfolio-scale iteration. We attribute the superiority of tree ensembles to their inductive bias, which effectively capture the discrete, sharp thresholds of building operations (e.g., scheduled setpoint changes) better than the smooth manifolds approximated by neural networks.

*Practical Implications.* For municipal portfolios and 1–24 h horizons, tree ensembles offer (i) strong performance with low latency, (ii) stable behaviour across heterogeneous buildings, and (iii) accessible interpretability (feature importance/SHAP) for diagnostics and handover. Transformers are defensible when multi-horizon outputs with rich exogenous context are essential and compute budgets allow. Lightweight stacking can add small robustness but increases operational complexity. Lastly, the use of a Global (Pooled) Model optimised for absolute error implicitly weights the training towards buildings with higher energy consumption (e.g., Schools). This aligns with grid operational priorities, where stabilizing the largest loads offers the greatest utility.

## 6.2 Limitations and Threats to Validity

While the COFACTOR dataset is heterogeneous and we consider this study representative, it uses a single Nordic climatic zone. Models trained here may not zero-shot generalise to different climates (e.g., cooling-dominated regions). However, the consistent superiority of Trees across the diverse building types (Schools vs. Offices) suggests that the *methodology*—feature engineering paired with boosting—is robust, even if specific model weights must be recalibrated for new environments. Second, due to computational constraints, we utilised validation-set stacking rather than Out-of-Fold (OOF) stacking, which may slightly overestimate ensemble generalisation. Third, the use of observed rather than forecasted weather establishes a theoretical performance ceiling. And finally, DL hyperparameter tuning was conservative to respect realistic budgets, with heavier tuning could narrow performance gaps while unlikely for training time.

### 6.3 Conclusions and Future Work

A feature-engineering-first pipeline paired with tree ensembles delivered the best performance–efficiency trade-off for STBELF. Sequence models trained far longer and did not outperform the strongest tabular baselines while a simple stack provided small additional robustness without changing the ranking. As a pragmatic default, trees should be the baseline for portfolio-scale STBELF, with DL reserved for cases where their specific advantages are mission-critical.

Future work directions include: (i) probabilistic forecasting (quantile losses, conformal calibration) for risk-aware scheduling and BESS dispatch; (ii) leakage-safe out-of-fold stacking and blending with horizon-aware meta-features; (iii) cross-entity transfer and meta-learning for cold-start buildings and rapid onboarding; (iv) explicit evaluation under forecasted-weather uncertainty and regime shifts; (v) concept-drift monitoring and online adaptation; (vi) cost-aware objectives reflecting tariffs and control actuation; and (vii) extension to additional Nordic portfolios (e.g., Oslo) and to building-specific fine-tuning where heterogeneity is extreme.

## References

1. Amasyali, K., El-Gohary, N.M.: A review of data-driven building energy consumption prediction studies. Renew. Sustain. Energy Rev. **81**, 1192–1205 (2018). https://linkinghub.elsevier.com/retrieve/pii/S1364032117306093
2. Borisov, I., Leemann, T., Seßler, K., Haug, J.: Deep neural networks and tabular data: a survey (2024). https://arxiv.org/abs/2110.01889
3. Chen, T., Guestrin, C.: XGBoost: a scalable tree boosting system. In: Proceedings of the KDD (2016). https://doi.org/10.1145/2939672.2939785
4. Deb, C., Zhang, F., Yang, J., Lee, S.E., Shah, K.W.: A review on time series forecasting techniques for building energy consumption. In: Proceedings of the Building Simulation (2017). https://www.sciencedirect.com/science/article/pii/S1364032117303155
5. EirGrid: Renewables provide a third of electricity as July marks first month of new coal-free era for Ireland's power system (2025). https://www.eirgrid.ie/news/renewables-provide-third-electricity-july-marks-first-month-new-coal-free-era-irelands-power
6. European Commission: 2030 climate targets (2020). https://climate.ec.europa.eu/eu-action/climate-strategies-targets/2030-climate-targets_en
7. Gandhi, O., et al.: The value of solar forecasts and the cost of their errors: a review. Renew. Sustain. Energy Rev. **189**, 113915 (2024). https://linkinghub.elsevier.com/retrieve/pii/S1364032123007736

8. Grinsztajn, L., Oyallon, E., Varoquaux, G.: Why do tree-based models still outperform deep learning on typical tabular data? In: Proceedings of the NeurIPS (2022). https://arxiv.org/abs/2207.08815
9. Hirvonen, S.: Comparison of data-driven models for building energy load forecasting (2024)
10. Hong, T., Fan, S.: Probabilistic electric load forecasting: a tutorial review. Int. J. Forecast. **32**(3), 914–938 (2016). https://linkinghub.elsevier.com/retrieve/pii/S0169207015001508
11. International Energy Agency: Ireland 2024 – analysis (2023). https://www.iea.org/reports/ireland-2024
12. International Energy Agency: Norway – countries & regions (2023). https://www.iea.org/countries/norway
13. International Energy Agency: Electricity 2024 – analysis and forecast to 2026 (2024). https://www.iea.org/reports/electricity-2024
14. Ke, G., et al.: LightGBM: a highly efficient gradient boosting decision tree. In: Proceedings of the NeurIPS (2017). https://papers.nips.cc/paper/2017/hash/6449f44a102fde848669bdd9eb6b76fa-Abstract.html
15. Kim, T.Y., Cho, S.B.: Predicting residential energy consumption using CNN–LSTM neural networks. Energy **182**, 72–81 (2019). https://www.sciencedirect.com/science/article/pii/S0360544219311223
16. Kuhn, M., Johnson, K.: Feature Engineering and Selection: A Practical Approach for Predictive Models. CRC Press (2019). https://doi.org/10.1201/9781315108230
17. Li, L., Su, X., Bi, X., Lu, Y., Sun, X.: A novel transformer-based network forecasting method for building cooling loads. Energy Build. **296**, 113409 (2023). https://linkinghub.elsevier.com/retrieve/pii/S0378778823006394
18. Lien, S.K., Walnum, H.T., Sørensen, Ø.L.: Cofactor Drammen dataset – 4 years of hourly energy use data from 45 public buildings in Drammen, Norway. Sci. Data **12**(1), 393 (2025). https://www.nature.com/articles/s41597-025-04708-3
19. Lim, B., Arık, S.O., Loeff, N., Pfister, T.: Temporal fusion transformers for interpretable multi-horizon time series forecasting. Int. J. Forecast. **37**(4), 1748–1764 (2021). https://www.sciencedirect.com/science/article/pii/S0169207021000637
20. Lundberg, S., Lee, S.I.: A unified approach to interpreting model predictions (2017). https://arxiv.org/abs/1705.07874
21. Miller, C., Hao, L., Fu, C.: Gradient boosting machines and careful pre-processing work best: ASHRAE great energy predictor iii lessons learned (2022). https://arxiv.org/abs/2202.02898
22. Prokhorenkova, L., Gusev, G., Vorobev, A., Dorogush, A.V., Gulin, A.: CatBoost: unbiased boosting with categorical features. In: Proceedings of the NeurIPS (2018). https://papers.nips.cc/paper/2018/hash/4445ea68f36d12f660de9ee75e099d0f-Abstract.html
23. Rafi, S.H., Nahid-Al-Masood, Deeba, S.R., Hossain, E.: A short-term load forecasting method using integrated CNN and LSTM network. IEEE Access **9**, 32436–32448 (2021). https://ieeexplore.ieee.org/document/9358156/
24. Wang, Z., Hong, T., Piette, M.A.: Building thermal load prediction through shallow machine learning and deep learning. Appl. Energy **263**, 114683 (2020). https://linkinghub.elsevier.com/retrieve/pii/S0306261920301951

# Evaluating the Impact of Situation Testing on SMOTE-Based Sampling Techniques for Bias Mitigation

Maliheh Heidarpour Shahrezaei(✉), Kevin Mc Daid, and Róisín Loughran

RSRC, Dundalk Institute of Technology, Dundalk, Ireland
{Maliheh.heidarpour,Kevin.mcdaid,Roisin.Loughran}@dkit.ie

**Abstract.** Sampling bias can be mitigated through preprocessing techniques such as oversampling and undersampling in imbalanced datasets. However, they do not address labeling bias, which can reinforce unfair model behavior. To address this, we established a structured evaluation framework that applies Situation Testing as an additional step after six SMOTE-based sampling techniques. Across 10 datasets and multiple classifiers, our findings reveal that the number of biased samples removed by Situation Testing depends on the dataset, classifier, and preprocessing sampling technique applied beforehand. Applying Situation Testing directly to the baseline consistently improved fairness with respect to both Demographic Parity and Equalized Odds, albeit with reduced predictive performance. In contrast, the impact of Situation Testing after sampling varied across strategies, proving to be more effective in group size adjustments based on Equalized Representation than in balanced-size techniques. Overall, the results highlight the trade-off between fairness gains and predictive utility, underscoring the need to align mitigation strategies with dataset characteristics and fairness objectives.

**Keywords:** Bias · Fairness · Mitigation Techniques · Situation Testing

## 1 Introduction

Unwanted algorithmic bias refers to unfair and discriminatory outcomes in algorithms that result in disadvantages for certain groups of people [1]. This bias can emerge when algorithms unintentionally favor or disadvantage particular individuals or communities based on race, gender, ethnicity, socioeconomic status, or other characteristics [2]. These characteristics, known as protected attributes, are features of individuals who are legally and ethically safeguarded from discrimination because they represent groups particularly vulnerable to unfair treatment [3, 4]. Protected attributes typically divide a population into privileged and unprivileged groups [5]. The privileged group typically receives favorable treatment or holds a more advantageous position, while the unprivileged group is subjected to unfair treatment in discriminatory decision-making processes [3].

Bias can arise in Machine Learning (ML) models in different ways [6]. The most frequent sources of bias in ML can be grouped into data, algorithm, and user interaction


T. T. Mai et al. (Eds.): AICS 2025, CCIS 2950, pp. 275–287, 2026.
https://doi.org/10.1007/978-3-032-25809-0_22

[1]. When biases are present in the underlying training data, the algorithms trained on them will inevitably incorporate these biases into their predictions. Data bias might be amplified and maintained by algorithms. In addition, even if the data is not biased, algorithms themselves may exhibit biased behavior as a result of specific design decisions [7]. The outputs of these biased algorithms are then fed into actual systems and can influence user decisions, leading to further bias [1, 8]. Therefore, addressing bias early in the model's lifecycle, before it becomes amplified, is critical. One effective approach is through preprocessing techniques, which adjust the training data to mitigate bias [9–11]. Other approaches, such as in-processing techniques, incorporate fairness considerations directly into the training process [12, 13], and post-processing techniques modify model predictions to reduce bias [14, 15].

This study focuses on preprocessing sampling techniques designed to balance training data. These techniques, including oversampling and a combination of oversampling and undersampling, employ methods such as generating synthetic data points to balance underrepresented classes. Once the dataset is balanced, we apply Situation Testing (ST), which involves flipping protected attributes in the data and checking whether predictions change [9]. If predictions differ, the data point is flagged as biased and removed. In this way, ST identifies and eliminates potential labeling bias in the training data. Accordingly, this study addresses the following research question: *Does the application of ST consistently enhance fairness across SMOTE-based preprocessing sampling techniques in ML, without adversely affecting model performance?*

The following section reviews related work on the application of ST. Section 3 outlines the methodology, including sampling and ST techniques. In Sect. 4, we present the fairness and performance metrics used for evaluation, along with key details about the datasets employed in this study. Section 5 provides a detailed analysis of the results, and Sect. 6 offers the concluding remarks.

## 2 Related Works

ST is a critical method for detecting discrimination, particularly in legal contexts [16]. It involves structured experiments where individuals with similar qualifications but differing in a protected characteristic (e.g., race, gender) are placed in identical situations to detect discriminatory practices. This method has been widely used in European jurisdictions to provide empirical evidence of discrimination. In legal proceedings, it plays a crucial role in shifting the burden of proof to defendants, requiring them to justify their actions with legitimate, non-discriminatory reasons [16]. Beyond its legal applications, ST is also an effective tool for raising public awareness and shaping anti-discrimination policies. Its impact extends to legal professionals, policymakers, and researchers working to combat discrimination and promote equality [16].

In employment discrimination research, ST has been instrumental in exposing biases in hiring decisions [17]. ST involves pairs of individuals, testers, who are matched in qualifications and experience but differ in a specific characteristic. These pairs apply for the same job openings to observe whether employers treat them differently based on the characteristic being tested [17]. Studies conducted in the U.S. have revealed that discriminatory behavior, whether conscious or unconscious, was exhibited by approximately

20% to 40% of employers [17]. One well-known study demonstrated that résumés with white-sounding names received 50% more callbacks than those with black-sounding names, highlighting racial bias in hiring decisions [18]. These findings have influenced public policy and civil rights enforcement by providing empirical evidence of workplace discrimination [17].

Beyond traditional employment settings, ST has been applied in data-driven environments to detect bias within datasets. One study introduces a framework that integrates ST with causal inference to uncover individual discrimination by isolating disparities linked to protected attributes [19]. Another study applies ST to software systems, systematically testing inputs that differ only in protected attributes to evaluate whether these attributes unjustly influence decision-making processes [20]. By identifying causal relationships that contribute to biased outcomes, this method effectively assesses discrimination in automated decision-making systems [20].

In ML, the "Fairway" approach integrates ST into a two-step bias mitigation framework [21]. The first step applies ST to detect biased data points by altering protected attributes and observing changes in model predictions. Data points that cause prediction shifts are removed from the training dataset to reduce the influence of protected attributes [21]. The second step employs multi-objective optimization to balance fairness and predictive performance during model training. This ensures that bias is mitigated without compromising accuracy, making Fairway a comprehensive tool for fairness improvement [21]. Another ML-based approach, Fair_SMOTE, combines oversampling techniques with ST to enhance fairness [9]. Fair_SMOTE first rebalances data distributions by ensuring equal representation of protected attributes across both positive and negative classes. After this oversampling step, ST is applied to evaluate whether model predictions remain consistent when protected attributes are modified [9]. Building on this line of work, our study isolates the ST component from Fair_SMOTE and systematically applies it across a wider set of state-of-the-art sampling techniques. This allows us to disentangle ST's independent contribution to fairness and performance and evaluate its consistency across diverse preprocessing strategies.

## 3 Methodology

We applied ST after preprocessing sampling techniques with the expectation that models would be trained not only on balanced datasets but also on datasets with reduced bias related to protected attributes. This combined approach was hypothesized to improve fairness in predictions while limiting trade-offs in dataset size and predictive performance.

Each dataset was partitioned into four canonical subgroups defined by the cross-product of protected attribute and class label: Privileged Positive, Privileged Negative, Unprivileged Positive, and Unprivileged Negative. These subgroups served as the basis for fairness-aware resampling [22].

Preprocessing sampling techniques were organized into two categories according to their subgroup size adjustment strategy. Equalized Representation (ER) balances the ratio of positive to negative samples across both privileged and unprivileged groups, consistent with Demographic Parity [22]. This preserves the overall dataset size while equalizing outcome distributions. In contrast, the Balanced-Size (B) approach, inspired by Fair_SMOTE [9], adjusts all subgroups to match the size of the largest subgroup, ensuring uniform representation [23].

Standard Fair_SMOTE [9] operates similarly to Uniform Sampling (US) [22], randomly selecting samples to generate synthetic data [23]. We extend this approach by incorporating alternative selection strategies: Preferential Sampling (PS), which prioritizes samples close to the decision boundary where fairness vulnerabilities are most acute [24], and Weighted Preferential Sampling (WPS), which assigns probabilistic weights based on distance to the boundary, giving higher likelihood to fairness-sensitive regions [25].

By combining the two group size adjustment strategies (ER vs. B) with the three selection mechanisms (US, PS, WPS), we obtained six distinct SMOTE-based techniques:

- **ER_US_SM:** Equalized Representation with Uniform Sampling + SMOTE
- **ER_PS_SM:** Equalized Representation with Preferential Sampling + SMOTE
- **ER_WPS_SM:** Equalized Representation with Weighted Preferential Sampling + SMOTE
- **B_US_SM:** Balanced-Size with Uniform Sampling + SMOTE, aligned with the first stage of the Fair_SMOTE methodology [9].
- **B_PS_SM:** Balanced Preferential Sampling + SMOTE
- **B_WPS_SM:** Balanced Weighted Preferential Sampling + SMOTE

The practical steps for integrating ST with preprocessing sampling techniques include:

1. Preprocessing Sampling Techniques:

a. Apply preprocessing sampling techniques
b. Evaluate the impact of these techniques using the selected fairness and performance metrics.

2. Apply ST:

c. Conduct ST by modifying protected attributes and analyzing how these changes affect the model's predictions.
d. Identify and remove data points whose predictions change solely due to the protected attribute.
e. Assess the impact of the combined approach (preprocessing sampling + ST) using the same fairness and performance metrics.

A supervised ML model is trained using the preprocessed sampled dataset. The trained model is used to predict outcomes for all data points. For each data point, the value of the protected attribute is flipped to its opposite or an equivalent category. The modified dataset is passed through the same trained model, and new predictions are obtained. If a prediction changes after the flip, it indicates that the model is sensitive to the protected attribute, suggesting it has learned biased patterns from the training data. Such biased data points are removed, and the model is retrained on the reduced dataset.

Combining preprocessing sampling techniques with ST yields several new approaches, denoted by appending "_ST" to the original method names. In this paper, we refer to B_US_SM_ST as Fair_SMOTE, consistent with the terminology used in the original study. Moreover, we applied the ST to the Baseline model, meaning no preprocessing or sampling techniques were applied before the implementation of ST, referred to as Baseline_ST.

## 4 Evaluation

We evaluated the effectiveness of these methods by examining the bias toward a single protected attribute and multiple (two) protected attributes simultaneously. The first implementation focused on applying preprocessing techniques to mitigate bias toward a single protected attribute. In the second implementation, the dataset was partitioned by the combination of two protected attributes and the class label, resulting in eight subgroups rather than four. Addressing bias in this manner is crucial for ensuring fairness in ML models [26], as focusing on a single attribute may overlook complex interdependencies between different attributes, potentially leading to unintended discriminatory outcomes [27]. For example, mitigating bias solely based on non-white individuals, considering race as the first protected attribute, without addressing gender as a second protected attribute (e.g., female), may result in a model that even increases biases against women. Therefore, adopting comprehensive strategies that address all protected attributes simultaneously are essential to ensure equitable treatment across diverse groups [28]. By considering two protected attributes simultaneously, our techniques enable a more comprehensive bias mitigation strategy that accounts for intersectional biases.

We conducted experiments using five well-known ML algorithms, namely Logistic Regression (LR), Decision Tree (DT), Gradient Boosting (GB), Random Forest (RF), and Support Vector Classification (SVC). For each dataset and protected attribute combination, we repeated the experiments 50 times with randomized sampling. We then applied the Scott-Knott [29] statistical test to compare the techniques.

### 4.1 Metrics

Fairness in algorithmic decision-making can be assessed through various metrics; broadly, the two main groups are Demographic Parity (DP) and Equalized Odds (EQO) fairness metrics [30]. While both aim to promote fairness, they measure different criteria. DP focuses on balancing outcomes across groups, whereas EQO ensures fairness in predictive performance by considering error rates [31]. This distinction reflects trade-offs between equal treatment and equitable outcomes, making the choice of metric context dependent.

DP fairness metrics assess whether different demographic groups receive similar outcomes, ensuring that no group is disproportionately advantaged or disadvantaged [32]. Statistical Parity (SP), a key metric under Demographic Parity, ensures that the probability of a positive outcome is equal across groups, aiming to prevent allocation harms where resources or opportunities may be unevenly distributed [33]. Disparate Impact (DI), on the other hand, measures the ratio of favorable outcomes between a protected group and the overall population [31].

EQO fairness metrics focus on reducing disparities in error rates between groups by ensuring fair treatment in terms of both true positives and false negatives [31]. In this criteria, Average Odds Difference (AOD) quantifies the disparity in error rates by averaging differences in false positive rates and false negative rates between groups. Equal Opportunity (EO) ensures that true positive rates are equal across demographic groups, thereby preventing bias in granting favorable outcomes [33]. By utilizing both DP and EQO metrics, a more comprehensive assessment of bias mitigation techniques can be achieved. The trade-off between fairness and predictive performance remains a critical consideration, as increasing fairness often results in a decline in model accuracy, a phenomenon extensively discussed in the algorithmic fairness literature [34].

Accuracy (Acc) is the most common performance measure which calculates the number of correct predictions divided by the number of total predictions [35]. However, in dealing with an imbalanced dataset, using accuracy alone may not be sufficient. Instead, it is suggested to use Balanced Accuracy (BAC), which calculates the average of sensitivity and specificity [36]. Balanced accuracy provides a more reliable evaluation metric for imbalanced datasets by considering both the true positive rate and true negative rate [36]. Notably, accuracy and balanced accuracy will yield the same value if the dataset is balanced.

### 4.2 Datasets

There are numerous well-established datasets in the fairness literature that facilitate comparisons with prior work on bias mitigation methods [37]. In this study, we utilize ten widely recognized tabular datasets, summarized in Table 1. This selection enables external validation and supports a rigorous assessment of the proposed techniques. These datasets are characterized by substantial class imbalance, as well as disparities in the distribution of protected attributes, both of which significantly impact model performance and the trade-offs associated with bias mitigation. Notably, five of these datasets contain two protected attributes, providing a unique opportunity to analyze the effects of mitigating bias across multiple protected attributes simultaneously.

**Table 1.** List of datasets

| Dataset | Size | Class Label | Positive Class% | Protected Attributes | Privileged % |
|---|---|---|---|---|---|
| Adult Income | (48842,14) | Income | 24 | sex<br>race | 67<br>85 |
| German Credit | (1000,20) | Credit | 70 | sex<br>age | 69<br>85 |
| Bank Marketing | (45211,16) | Term deposit | 47 | age | 14 |
| Default of Credit Card Clients | (30000,23) | Default payment | 22 | sex | 40 |

*(continued)*

**Table 1.** (*continued*)

| Dataset | Size | Class Label | Positive Class% | Protected Attributes | Privileged % |
|---|---|---|---|---|---|
| Titanic | (891,12) | Survived | 38 | sex | 35 |
| Heart Disease | (303,13) | Heart disease | 46 | sex<br>age | 68<br>64 |
| OULAD | (32593,12) | Final result | 68 | sex | 46 |
| Law School | (20798,12) | Pass exam | 95 | race | 84 |
| Student Performance | (649,33) | Score > = 10 | 54 | sex<br>age | 59<br>94 |
| COMPAS | (7214,52) | Two-year-recid | 55 | sex<br>race | 19<br>34 |

## 5 Results and Analysis

We evaluated five classifiers, using the same model in each case for both performance evaluation and ST-based bias detection. We examined the median percentage of samples removed from the training data after applying ST. For single protected attributes, techniques that focused on decision-boundary instances, such as ER_PS_SM, ER_WPS_SM, and B_WPS_SM, identified a larger proportion of samples as biased. Consequently, applying ST to these techniques resulted in substantial data reduction. Notably, ER_PS_SM_ST and ER_WPS_SM_ST led to severe data loss, with up to 50% of the training samples removed in the highly imbalanced COMPAS dataset.

It is important to emphasize that the reported percentage reductions for ER-based Group size techniques are calculated relative to the original dataset size, as these preprocessing sampling techniques do not alter the size of the entire training set. In contrast, for balanced techniques, the percentage reductions were computed based on the dataset size after oversampling. Consistent with previous research [7], Fair_SMOTE showed a maximum reduction of 13%, across different classifiers. Table 2 shows the similar pattern when ST was applied after preprocessing bias mitigation techniques aimed at reducing bias toward two protected attributes simultaneously. ER_PS_SM_ST, ER_WPS_SM_ST, and B_WPS_SM_ST techniques, resulted in a significant reduction of training samples, particularly when applied to the COMPAS dataset. In contrast, techniques like Fair_SMOTE, and B_PS_SM_ST led to a more moderate reduction in the dataset, with a maximum of 12% of the training data removed across different datasets.

**Table 2.** Percentage of removed samples after applying ST following various sampling techniques to mitigate bias toward two protected attributes simultaneously with LR

| Dataset | | Adult | | COMPAS | | German | | Heart | | Student | |
|---|---|---|---|---|---|---|---|---|---|---|---|
| | Technique | race | sex | race | sex | age | sex | age | sex | age | sex |
| WRT Original Size | Baseline_ST | 12 | 12 | 22 | 22 | 24 | 24 | 12 | 12 | 10 | 10 |
| | ER_US_SM_ST | 2 | 2 | 20 | 20 | 0 | 0 | 6 | 6 | 9 | 9 |
| | ER_PS_SM_ST | 19 | 19 | 32 | 32 | 1 | 1 | 15 | 15 | 23 | 23 |
| | ER_WPS_SM_ST | 27 | 27 | 47 | 47 | 1 | 1 | 20 | 20 | 27 | 27 |
| WRT Oversampled Size | Fair_SMOTE | 2 | 2 | 11 | 11 | 3 | 3 | 5 | 5 | 7 | 7 |
| | B_PS_SM_ST | 2 | 2 | 12 | 12 | 2 | 2 | 5 | 5 | 9 | 9 |
| | B_WPS_SM_ST | 20 | 20 | 19 | 19 | 4 | 4 | 10 | 10 | 7 | 7 |

To comprehensively assess the performance of the techniques, we evaluated them on 10 datasets with varying characteristics. Presenting results for all datasets in a single table would require extensive space and may complicate the visual interpretation of the findings. To mitigate this issue, we adopted a methodology inspired by Chakraborty et al. [7, 37] using the Scott-Knott test to compare result distributions across all datasets. This statistical test was applied to all methods to identify performance groupings based on statistically significant differences. The Scott-Knott procedure ranks the methods, with higher ranks indicating superior performance. If two distributions are statistically indistinguishable, they are assigned to the same rank. The terms Wins, Losses, and Ties are defined as follows: a Win occurs when one technique achieves a higher rank for a particular metric compared to another; a Loss denotes a lower rank; and a Tie indicates no significant difference in performance between the two techniques. By employing this approach, we were able to succinctly summarize performance across multiple datasets and conduct a robust comparison between the new and established methods, as suggested in previous studies [7, 37].

Table 3 presents the Scott-Knott statistical test results comparing the Baseline model with its counterpart after applying ST, referred to as Baseline_ST. WLR (Win/Loss Ratio) represents the proportion of wins to losses for each technique across all evaluation metrics. TTR (Tie/Total Ratio) indicates the ratio of tied outcomes to the total number of comparisons made. The results demonstrate that incorporating ST alone significantly improves fairness in terms of both DP and EQO fairness metrics. However, this improvement comes with a trade-off, as applying ST leads to a reduction in overall model performance. This suggests that while ST effectively enhances fairness, it may also impact the predictive capability of the model, highlighting the balance between fairness and accuracy in bias mitigation strategies.

**Table 3.** Baseline_ST VS Baseline Scott-Knott Result.

| | 1 protected attribute at a time | | | | | 2 protected attributes at a time | | | | |
|---|---|---|---|---|---|---|---|---|---|---|
| Metric | Wins | Ties | Losses | WLR | TTR | Wins | Ties | Losses | WLR | TTR |
| DI | **36** | 36 | 3 | 12 | 0.48 | **29** | 20 | 1 | 29 | 0.4 |
| SP | **41** | 30 | 4 | 10.25 | 0.4 | **31** | 14 | 5 | 6.2 | 0.28 |
| AOD | **40** | 31 | 4 | 10 | 0.41 | **31** | 14 | 5 | 6.2 | 0.28 |
| EO | **37** | 34 | 4 | 9.25 | 0.45 | **30** | 16 | 4 | 7.5 | 0.32 |
| Acc | 4 | **51** | 20 | 0.2 | 0.68 | 0 | 26 | **24** | 0 | 0.52 |
| BAC | 2 | **38** | 35 | 0.06 | 0.51 | 0 | 20 | **30** | 0 | 0.4 |

Finally, according to the Scott Knott statistical test, we ranked all techniques, determining which techniques performed best for each evaluation metric. Tables 4 and 5 summarize the performance of various bias mitigation techniques concerning fairness and performance metrics, ranking each method based on its effectiveness across all evaluated criteria. According to Table 4, all techniques improved fairness in terms of DP fairness metrics when compared to the Baseline. Surprisingly, applying ST to the original training set (Baseline_ST) achieved better performance than B_WPS_SM. Among sampling approaches, techniques that incorporated ER-based group size adjustments consistently outperformed both Fair_SMOTE and balanced-size methods with respect to the DP fairness metric. Moreover, sampling methods targeting decision-boundary instances (ER_PS_SM and ER_WPS_SM) are more effective in improving DI than random oversampling approaches such as ER_US_SM. In contrast, for the EO fairness metric, this trend is reversed, with random oversampling methods outperforming decision-boundary-based techniques. The effectiveness of ST, however, varied depending on the bias-mitigation setting:

- Single Protected Attribute: For ER-based group size techniques, applying ST improved DI and EO when mitigating bias for a single protected attribute.
- Two Protected Attributes: When addressing bias across two protected attributes simultaneously, ST did not provide further DI improvements for ER-based group size techniques, though it did enhance EO.

For balanced-size techniques, ST generally did not lead to additional fairness gains in either the single- or multi-attribute scenarios. The exception was B_WPS_SM_ST, which outperformed its preprocessing counterparts for both DI and EO. Notably, this method was more effective when mitigating bias for two protected attributes than for a single attribute.

**Table 4.** Ranking of each technique based on fairness metrics

| | Single protected attribute | | Two protected attributes simultaneously | |
|---|---|---|---|---|
| Rank | DI | EO | DI | EO |
| 1 | ER_PS_SM_ST | ER_US_SM_ST | ER_PS_SM | ER_US_SM_ST |
| 2 | ER_PS_SM | ER_US_SM | ER_WPS_SM | ER_US_SM |
| 3 | ER_US_SM_ST | ER_PS_SM_ST | ER_WPS_SM_ST | ER_PS_SM_ST |
| 4 | ER_WPS_SM_ST | ER_WPS_SM_ST | ER_PS_SM_ST | ER_WPS_SM_ST |
| 5 | ER_US_SM | B_US_SM | ER_US_SM | Baseline_ST |
| 6 | ER_WPS_SM | Baseline_ST | B_WPS_SM | ER_PS_SM |
| 7 | B_US_SM | B_PS_SM | B_WPS_SM_ST | B_US_SM |
| 8 | B_PS_SM | Fair_SMOTE | ER_US_SM_ST | Fair_SMOTE |
| 9 | B_WPS_SM_ST | B_PS_SM_ST | B_US_SM | B_PS_SM |
| 10 | Fair_SMOTE | ER_PS_SM | B_PS_SM | B_PS_SM_ST |
| 11 | B_PS_SM_ST | B_WPS_SM_ST | Fair_SMOTE | ER_WPS_SM |
| 12 | Baseline_ST | ER_WPS_SM | B_PS_SM_ST | B_WPS_SM_ST |
| 13 | B_WPS_SM | Baseline | Baseline_ST | B_WPS_SM |
| 14 | Baseline | B_WPS_SM | Baseline | Baseline |

Table 5 summarizes the ranking of bias-mitigation techniques in terms of predictive performance metrics. Overall, ER-group-size-based techniques achieved higher accuracy than methods that adjusted group sizes to match the largest group, across both single and multi-attribute bias simulations. Among these, ER_US_SM demonstrated the best overall accuracy. Incorporating ST into sampling techniques that used directedselection further improved accuracy. In contrast, results for balanced accuracy followed a different pattern. ER-based adjustment methods generally performed worse than Baseline, whereas techniques that matched group sizes to the largest group typically showed improvements, except for B_WPS_SM, which did not yield substantial gains. Notably, applying ST to directed sampling techniques within the ER group-size category enhanced balanced accuracy.

**Table 5.** Ranking of each technique based on performance metrics

| | Single protected attribute | | Two protected attributes simultaneously | |
|---|---|---|---|---|
| Rank | ACC | BAC | ACC | BAC |
| 1 | Baseline | B_US_SM | Baseline | B_PS_SM_ST |
| 2 | ER_US_SM | Fair_SMOTE | ER_US_SM | Fair_SMOTE |
| 3 | ER_US_SM_ST | B_PS_SM | ER_US_SM_ST | B_PS_SM |
| 4 | Baseline_ST | B_PS_SM_ST | Baseline_ST | B_US_SM |

(*continued*)

**Table 5.** (*continued*)

| | Single protected attribute | | Two protected attributes simultaneously | |
|---|---|---|---|---|
| Rank | ACC | BAC | ACC | BAC |
| 5 | ER_PS_SM_ST | B_WPS_SM_ST | ER_PS_ SM_ST | Baseline |
| 6 | ER_PS_SM | Baseline | ER_PS_SM | ER_US_SM |
| 7 | ER_WPS_SM_ST | B_WPS_SM | ER_WPS_ SM_ST | ER_US_SM_ST |
| 8 | ER_WPS_SM | ER_US_SM | B_PS_SM_ST | B_WPS_SM_ST |
| 9 | B_US_SM | ER_PS_SM_ST | Fair_SMOTE | ER_PS_SM_ST |
| 10 | B_PS_SM_ST | ER_PS_SM | ER_WPS_SM | B_WPS_SM |
| 11 | B_WPS_SM_ST | ER_US_SM_ST | B_PS_SM | ER_PS_SM |
| 12 | Fair_SMOTE | Baseline_ST | B_US_SM | Baseline_ST |
| 13 | B_PS_SM | ER_WPS_SM | B_WPS_SM_ST | ER_WPS_SM_ST |
| 14 | B_WPS_SM | ER_WPS_SM_ST | B_WPS_SM | ER_WPS_SM |

In response to our research question, we find that ST does not consistently enhance fairness across all sampling techniques without affecting performance. While it reliably improves fairness on the baseline, its effectiveness after sampling varies, and fairness gains are often offset by reduced accuracy and balanced accuracy.

## 6 Conclusion

This study systematically evaluated the impact of ST on preprocessing sampling-based bias mitigation techniques, examining both fairness and performance. Several important patterns emerged. First, the number of biased samples removed by ST varies depending on the dataset, classifier, and preprocessing sampling technique applied beforehand. Decision-boundary approaches such as ER_PS_SM_ST and ER_WPS_SM_ST caused substantial data loss, particularly in highly imbalanced datasets like COMPAS. Second, the effectiveness of ST depended on the underlying sampling design especially how group sizes were defined, and which samples were selected for synthetic data generation. Third, applying ST directly to the baseline consistently improved fairness with respect to both Demographic Parity and Equalized Odds, though these gains came at the cost of predictive utility, as evidenced by reductions in both accuracy and balanced accuracy. This underscores a central trade-off between fairness enhancement and predictive utility.

Overall, the results emphasize that ST is not a universal solution but can provide substantial fairness gains when applied directly to the baseline. Future work should investigate the drivers of data removal across technique–dataset–classifier settings and investigate fairness-aware oversampling strategies designed to counteract label bias.

**Acknowledgments.** This research is funded through the HEA's Technological University Transformation Fund, co-funded by the Dundalk Institute of Technology.

## References


1. Mehrabi, N., Morstatter, F., Saxena, N., Lerman, K., Galstyan, A.: A Survey on Bias and Fairness in Machine Learning. ACM Comput. Surv. **54** (2021). https://doi.org/10.1145/3457607
2. François-Blouin, J.: Responsible AI Symposium – Legal Implications of Bias Mitigation - Lieber Institute West Point. https://lieber.westpoint.edu/legal-implications-bias-mitigation/. Accessed 02 Dec 2023
3. Goethals, S., Calders, T., Martens, D.: Beyond Accuracy-Fairness: Stop evaluating bias mitigation methods solely on between-group metrics. CoRR (2024). https://doi.org/10.48550/ARXIV.2401.13391
4. Fang, B., Jiang, M., Cheng, P.-Y., Shen, J., Fang, Y.: Achieving outcome fairness in machine learning models for social decision problems (2020)
5. Das, A.: Detection and mitigation of bias in machine learning software and datasets (2023)
6. Suresh, H., Guttag, J.V.: A framework for understanding sources of harm throughout the machine learning life cycle. ACM Int. Conf. Proceeding Ser. (2019). https://doi.org/10.1145/3465416.3483305
7. Pagano, T.P., et al.: Bias and unfairness in machine learning models: a systematic literature review, pp. 1–19 (2022)
8. Ferrara, E.: The butterfly Effect in artificial intelligence systems: implications for AI bias and fairness. Mach. Learn. with Appl. **15**, 100525 (2024). https://doi.org/10.1016/j.mlwa.2024.100525
9. Chakraborty, J., Majumder, S., Menzies, T.: Bias in machine learning software: Why? how? what to do? Assoc. Comput. Mach. (2021). https://doi.org/10.1145/3468264.3468537
10. Calmon, F.P., Wei, D., Vinzamuri, B., Ramamurthy, K.N., Varshney, K.R.: Optimized pre-processing for discrimination prevention. Adv. Neural Inf. Process. Syst. 2017-Decem, 3993–4002 (2017)
11. Heidarpour Shahrezaei, M., Loughran, R., Mc Daid, K.: Pre-processing techniques to mitigate against algorithmic bias. In: 2023 31st Irish Conference on Artificial Intelligent Cognition Science AICS 2023 (2023). https://doi.org/10.1109/AICS60730.2023.10470759
12. Zhang, L., Wu, Y., Wu, X.: Achieving non-discrimination in prediction. IJCAI Int. Jt. Conf. Artif. Intell. 2018-July, 3097–3103 (2018). https://doi.org/10.24963/ijcai.2018/430
13. Grgi´cgrgi´c-Hlača, N., Zafar, M.B., Gummadi, K.P., Weller, A.: The case for process fairness in learning: feature selection for fair decision making (2016)
14. Kamiran, F., Mansha, S., Karim, A., Zhang, X.: Exploiting reject option in classification for social discrimination control. Inf. Sci. (Ny) **425**, 18–33 (2018). https://doi.org/10.1016/J.INS.2017.09.064
15. Calders, T., Verwer, S.: Three naive Bayes approaches for discrimination-free classification. Data Min. Knowl. Discov. **21**, 277–292 (2010). https://doi.org/10.1007/s10618-010-0190-x
16. Rorive, I., Lappalainen, P.: Proving discrimination cases - the role of situation testing (2009)
17. Bendick, M., Consultant, J.R.: Situation Testing for Employment Discrimination in the United States of America Perspective internationale (2007)
18. Bertrand, M., Mullainathan, S.: Discrimination in the Job Market in the United States | The Abdul Latif Jameel Poverty Action Lab, https://www.povertyactionlab.org/evaluation/discrimination-job-market-united-states?utm_source=chatgpt.com. Accessed 2025/02/27
19. Zhang, L., Wu, Y., Wu, X.: Situation testing-based discrimination discovery: A causal inference approach. IJCAI Int. Jt. Conf. Artif. Intell. 2016-Janua, 2718–2724 (2016)
20. Galhotra, S., Brun, Y., Meliou, A.: Fairness testing: Testing software for discrimination. In: Proceedings of the ACM SIGSOFT Symposium Found. Software Engineering Part F130154, pp. 498–510 (2017). https://doi.org/10.1145/3106237.3106277

21. Chakraborty, J., Majumder, S., Yu, Z., Menzies, T.: Fairway: a way to build fair ML software. ESEC/FSE **2020**, 654–665 (2020). https://doi.org/10.1145/3368089.3409697
22. Kamiran, F., Calders, T.: Data preprocessing techniques for classification without discrimination. Springer (2012). https://doi.org/10.1007/s10115-011-0463-8
23. Heidarpour Shahrezaei, M., Mc Daid, K., Loughran, R.: Mitigating Algorithmic Bias through Sampling : The Role of Group Size and Sample Selection. 1–15
24. Kamiran, F., Calders, T.: Classification with No Discrimination by Preferential Sampling. In: Informal Proceedings 19th Annu. Mach. Learn. Conf. Belgium Netherlands, pp. 1–6 (2010)
25. Hu, Z., Xu, Y., Gu, J.: Boosting fair classifier generalization through adaptive priority reweighing (2024). https://doi.org/10.1145/3665895
26. Duong, M.K., Conrad, S.: Measuring and Mitigating Bias for Tabular Datasets with Multiple Protected Attributes. (2024)
27. Turner Lee, N., Resnick, P., Barton, G.: Algorithmic bias detection and mitigation: Best practices and policies to reduce consumer harms (2019)
28. Rabonato, R.T., Berton, L.: A systematic review of fairness in machine learning. AI Ethics **2024**, 1–12 (2024). https://doi.org/10.1007/S43681-024-00577-5
29. Faria, osé C., Jelihovschi, Ê.G., Allaman, I.B.: The ScottKnott clustering algorithm (2025). https://doi.org/10.1590/1984
30. Wang, Y., Singh, L.: Analyzing the impact of missing values and selection bias on fairness. Int. J. Data Sci. Anal. **12**, 101–119 (2021). https://doi.org/10.1007/s41060-021-00259-z
31. Sweeney, L.: Discrimination in online ad delivery. Commun. ACM **56**, 44–54 (2013). https://doi.org/10.1145/2447976.2447990
32. Chouldechova, A.: Fair prediction with disparate impact: a study of bias in recidivism prediction instruments. Big Data **5**, 153–163 (2017). https://doi.org/10.1089/BIG.2016.0047
33. Chouldechova, A., John Heinz, H., G'sell, M.: Fairer and more accurate, but for whom?
34. Fairlearn contributors: Common fairness metrics—Fairlearn 0.13.0.dev0 documentation, https://fairlearn.org/main/user_guide/assessment/common_fairness_metrics.html?utm_source=chatgpt.com. Accessed 25 Feb 2025
35. Grandini, M., Bagli, E., Visani, G.: Metrics for multi-class classification: an overview (2020)
36. Brodersen, K.H., Ong, C.S., Stephan, K.E., Buhmann, J.M.: The balanced accuracy and its posterior distribution. Proc. - Int. Conf. Pattern Recognit. 3125–3128 (2010). https://doi.org/10.1109/ICPR.2010.764
37. Fabris, A., Messina, S., Silvello, G., Susto, G.A.: Algorithmic fairness datasets: the story so far. Data Min. Knowl. Discov. **36**, 2074–2152 (2022). https://doi.org/10.1007/s10618-022-00854-z

# Modality Fusion of MRI and Clinical Data for Glioma Tumour Grading

Reyhaneh Kheirbakhsh[1,2](✉), Prateek Mathur[1,2], and Aonghus Lawlor[1,2]

[1] Insight Research Ireland Centre for Data Analytics, Dublin, Ireland
[2] School of Computer Science, University College Dublin, Dublin, Ireland
reyhaneh.kheirbakhsh@ucdconnect.ie,
{prateek.mathur,aonghus.lawlor}@ucd.ie

**Abstract.** Multimodal machine learning leverages complementary information from diverse data sources and has shown strong promise in medical imaging, where multimodal data is critical for clinical decision making. In glioma grading, integrating MRI modalities with clinical data can improve diagnostic accuracy, yet systematic comparisons of fusion strategies remain limited. This study evaluates early, intermediate, and late fusion approaches, addressing the question: How does the inclusion of clinical data alongside MRI modalities influence grading performance? To assess modality contributions, we design adaptable fusion layers and employ interpretability techniques, including attention-based analysis. Our results show that incorporating clinical data consistently outperforms unimodal and MRI-only baselines, with intermediate fusion yielding the most reliable gains. Beyond accuracy, the framework reveals how MRI and clinical features jointly shape predictions, underscoring the importance of both fusion design and interpretability for clinical adoption.

**Keywords:** Modality Fusion · Deep Learning · Glioma Grading

## 1 Introduction

In recent years, multimodal machine learning (ML) has played an increasingly important role in healthcare by integrating diverse data modalities such as magnetic resonance imaging (MRI), histopathology, clinical data, and genomic profiles [1]. This growing interest is driven by both the availability of heterogeneous biomedical data and the recognition that combining complementary modalities enables a more comprehensive understanding of complex medical conditions [2]. The central value of multimodality lies in complementarity [3], where each modality contributes unique information. However, a key challenge is modality fusion, which involves developing strategies to effectively represent multimodal data while exploiting its complementarity. This is particularly difficult due to the heterogeneous nature of biomedical data [4].

Early and accurate detection is paramount in cancer diagnosis for significantly improving patient outcomes. This critical need is profoundly exemplified


T. T. Mai et al. (Eds.): AICS 2025, CCIS 2950, pp. 288–299, 2026.
https://doi.org/10.1007/978-3-032-25809-0_23

in neuro-oncology by gliomas, a heterogeneous group of primary brain tumours classified by the WHO into grades 1–4 based on histopathological and molecular characteristics. Accurate grading is essential, as treatment strategies and prognosis vary substantially across grades [5]. Although MRI is the standard for non-invasive assessment, it often lacks the specificity to capture full tumour heterogeneity. Integrating MRI with complementary data, such as clinical information, offers the potential to improve diagnostic precision [6]. Consequently, there is huge potential for multimodal ML to meet this challenge by providing more precise and rapid diagnostic capabilities.

While multimodal ML approaches for glioma grading exist [7–9] two key challenges remain: identifying the most effective strategy for integrating imaging and non-imaging data, and quantifying the contribution of each modality to performance. To address these gaps, we propose a multimodal fusion framework that leverages both MRI and clinical data, systematically evaluating early, intermediate, and late fusion. We also address interpretability through a keyless attention-based fusion [10] block. Our study addresses three key questions: (1) How does the inclusion of clinical data alongside MRI modalities influence grading? (2) How does intermediate fusion compare to early and late fusion in terms of predictive power? (3) Which modalities contribute most significantly to the overall performance of the multimodal model?

## 2 Related Work

The standard taxonomy for fusion level in multimodal ML [11] includes early fusion, which integrates data at the input level; late fusion, which aggregates outputs from separate models; and intermediate fusion, which combines modality-specific features during the learning process to allow interaction (Fig. 1). The choice of fusion level often depends on the degree of correlation between modalities [12].

Recent research has moved beyond simple concatenation to more expressive fusion mechanisms. Methods like high-order attention [13], dual attention, cross-attention, and transformer-based modules [14,15] are used to align multimodal information and adaptively weight modalities instead of treating them equally. This approach has led to significant performance gains, especially with heterogeneous healthcare data. In healthcare, multimodal approaches integrating image and non-image data show strong potential [1]. Examples include attention-based fusion for pan-cancer survival prediction [16] and Alzheimer's diagnosis [17], demonstrating how complementary data can improve predictive performance.

Specific to glioma diagnosis, most studies focus on fusing multiple MRI modalities such as T1, T1c, T2, and FLAIR. For example, Guo et al. [18] developed a multimodal MRI model employing DenseNet for modality-specific feature extraction, followed by a linear weighted late fusion strategy to combine predictions. Guo et al. [8] introduced a graph convolutional network to integrate spatial and contextual MRI features. Beyond MRI, some studies have explored incorporating additional modalities. Hsu et al. [19], for instance, combined pathology

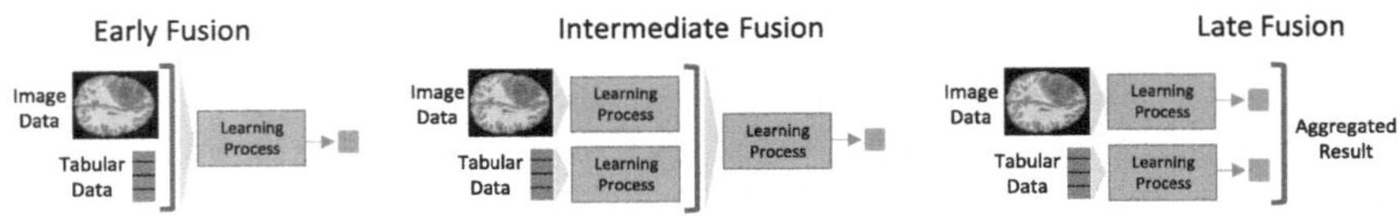


**Fig. 1.** Overview of different levels of fusion for image and tabular data

images and clinical data with MRI using a late fusion approach, relying primarily on whole slide imaging (WSI)-based predictions and leveraging MRI-derived outputs as auxiliary guidance when confidence was low. In another work, Usuzaki et al. [9] propose a variable Vision Transformer (vViT), a self-attention–based model designed for glioma grading that integrates demographic data, radiomic features, and multi-sequence MRI.

A growing body of research emphasises not only improving predictive accuracy but also enhancing interpretability by identifying which modalities drive model decisions. For instance, Pathomic Fusion [7] integrates histology and genomic features for glioma survival prediction, modelling cross-modal interactions via Kronecker products and refining contributions through gating-based attention. Jeong et al. [20] employed an attention-based fusion block with ablation studies to assess the impact of missing modalities, while Byeon et al. [6] applied attention visualisation and relevance propagation to highlight focus regions and quantify modality contributions. Collectively, these works demonstrate how attention mechanisms and ablation strategies can enhance the transparency of multimodal fusion models, a key requirement for clinical applicability.

Despite these advances, prior work has largely focused on specific fusion methods, with limited attention to interpreting the contributions of individual modalities. A systematic comparison of early, intermediate, and late fusion under identical conditions, coupled with interpretability, remains underexplored. This gap motivates our framework, which evaluates different fusion levels while providing transparency into how individual modalities influence glioma grading.

## 3 Methodology

To evaluate the impact of integrating clinical data (age and sex) with MRI modalities (T1, T1c, T2, and FLAIR) across different fusion levels for glioma grading, we designed a framework encompassing five fusion strategies: two early fusion variants, two intermediate fusion variants based on feature concatenation, and one late fusion approach using majority voting and probability averaging. The contribution of MRI and clinical features is assessed through two complementary analyses. First, a modality ablation study compares performance with and without clinical data. Second, we introduce an attention-based fusion block to replace simple concatenation, enabling the computation of modality-specific contribution scores that quantitatively reflect the role of each modality in the classification process.

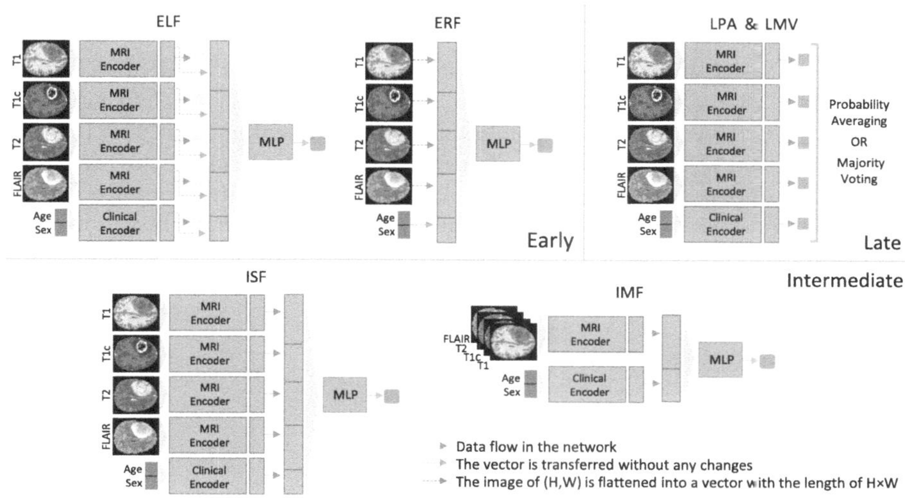


**Fig. 2.** Fusion strategies examined in our framework

### 3.1 Fusion Strategies

The fusion architectures in our framework are illustrated in Fig. 2. They are referred to as Early Raw Features (ERF), Early Learned Features (ELF), Intermediate Separate Features (ISF), Intermediate Merged Features (IMF), Late Probability Averaging (LPA), and Late Majority Voting (LMV).

In ERF fusion, MRI modalities are flattened into feature vectors and directly concatenated with clinical data to form a single input vector, which is then fed into a multilayer perceptron (MLP)—a common classifier in multimodal learning [1]. In contrast, ELF fusion trains a separate encoder for each modality, concatenates the resulting high-level feature vectors in the final fully connected layers, and inputs them into an MLP classifier.

The ISF fusion strategy uses the same modality-specific encoders as ELF, but fusion occurs at the feature extraction stage. Encoded representations from each modality are concatenated and passed to an MLP classifier identical to that of ELF, allowing interactions between modalities to be captured during the feature learning process. In the IMF, the MRI modalities are provided as separate channels of a single multi-channel input and processed jointly by a shared encoder. The clinical features are fed into an encoder independently, and their embeddings are concatenated with the MRI representation before classification via an MLP. This design enables interactions not only among MRI modalities but also between MRI and clinical data during the feature extraction process.

Finally, in the late fusion strategy, independent models are trained for each modality using the same encoders, and their predictions are aggregated via probability averaging in LPA or majority voting in LMV.

### 3.2 Modality Contribution Scores

To better quantify and interpret the relative contributions of MRI and clinical modalities in glioma grade classification, we use the Modality Weighting Block (MWB) as an alternative to conventional feature concatenation. MWB is an enhanced version of the keyless attention modality fusion architecture of DuKa [21]. Unlike simple concatenation, which treats all modalities equally, MWB learns modality-specific weights prior to fusion, enabling the model to adaptively emphasise more informative inputs. The keyless attention mechanism of MWB avoids the full query–key–value formulation, making it lightweight and efficient.

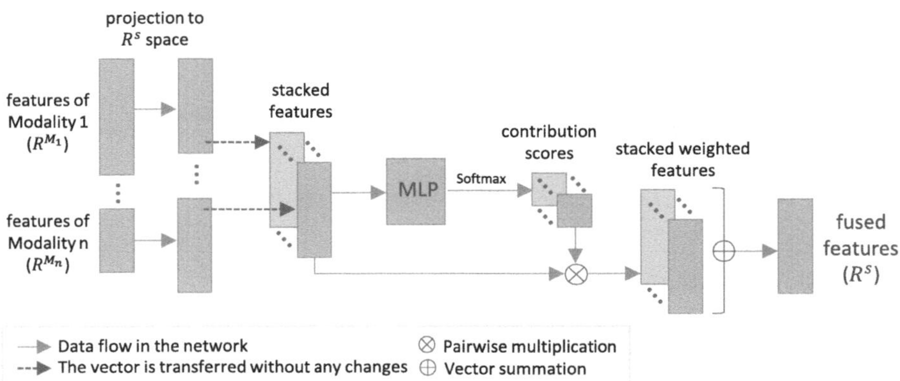


**Fig. 3.** Modality Weighting Block

The architecture of MWB is shown in Fig. 3. Consider $n$ modalities, where each modality $i$ ($i = 1, \ldots, n$) is represented by an embedding $z_i \in \mathbb{R}^{M_i}$, with $M_i$ denoting its dimensionality. Each $z_i$ is first projected into a shared feature space $\mathbb{R}^S$, yielding $zp_i \in \mathbb{R}^S$. A shared MLP with *tanh* as the activation function is then applied across all $zp_i$ to compute unnormalised importance scores, which are normalised with softmax to produce contribution scores $\{w_1, \ldots, w_n\}$. The fused representation is obtained as a weighted sum, $\sum_{i=1}^{n} w_i \cdot zp_i$, where the weights are learnable parameters optimized jointly with the task objective. By using a shared MLP, MWB enforces direct competition between modalities within the same representational space while keeping the parameter count low. This design can be used for the fusion of features with different dimensions, both enhancing interpretability by yielding explicit modality contribution scores and improving generalization by avoiding over-parameterisation.

### 3.3 Dataset Description

We conducted our experiments using the University of California, San Francisco Preoperative Diffuse Glioma MRI (UCSF-PDGM) dataset [22], which includes

501 adult patients with WHO grade 2–4 diffuse gliomas (56, 43, and 402 patients, respectively, for grades 2, 3, and 4) who underwent preoperative MRI and resection between 2015 and 2021. The dataset provides standardized 3T MRI scans across multiple sequences, including T1 (pre- and post-contrast), T2, and FLAIR, along with advanced modalities such as DWI, SWI, and perfusion imaging. It also contains clinical and molecular data (age, sex, tumour grade, IDH mutation, MGMT methylation) and expert tumour segmentations.

### 3.4 Experimental Design

**Data Preparation:** We used data of 495 patients for whom we have both four MRI modalities (T1, T1c, T2, and FLAIR) and clinical features (age and sex). Binary classification (grade 2&3 vs 4) was performed at the slice level, with only tumour-containing slices from each patient included in the dataset (30557 slices). The UCSF-PDGM dataset provides preprocessed MRI images, and we applied modality level min-max normalisation scaling to each slice. Also, min-max normalisation is used for scaling the clinical data. To improve model generalisability, we employed data augmentation consisting of random horizontal and vertical flips, as well as random rotations. To leverage pretrained ImageNet weights in the MRI encoder, all MRI slices were resized to $224 \times 224$ pixels.

**Baseline and Fusion Models:** An ImageNet pre-trained DenseNet121 [23] backbone and AutoInt [24] model were selected as the MRI and clinical encoders after a series of preliminary benchmark analysis comparing different architectures, including Swin-Transformers [25] and GBNet [26]. All unimodal baseline models for this work were first trained using DenseNet121 for MRI modalities and AutoInt for clinical features to establish individual modality performance. For MRI inputs, the first convolutional layer of DenseNet121 was adapted to match the number of channels of the corresponding modality. The MLP classifier in the ELF, ISF, and IMF fusion strategies consisted of fully connected layers with sizes [128, 64, 1], whereas the ERF classifier employed a deeper structure of [1024, 512, 256, 128, 1]. Across all models, the weights were initialised with Kaiming initialisation [27]. To ensure a fair comparison of performance, all models were trained on identical dataset splits using the same hardware. All models and fusion strategies were implemented in PyTorch[1].

**Modality Contribution Study:** To examine the modality contributions, we first performed an ablation study in which each fusion architecture was trained under two settings: (1) using all MRI modalities together with clinical features, and (2) using MRI modalities only, while keeping all other specifications identical. Second, for the best-performing fusion strategy, we replaced feature concatenation with the proposed Modality Weighting Block. After hyper-parameter tuning, the ablation study was repeated to assess the effect of modality-aware fusion. Modality contribution scores were derived by averaging the contribution

[1] Code Available: https://github.com/r-kheirbakhsh/Fusion_framework.

scores across all test instances. To ensure robustness, dataset splitting and model training were repeated with three distinct random seeds.

**Data Splitting and Model Training:** We used 5-fold cross-validation, splitting the data at the patient level to prevent data leakage. Each fold consisted of an 80/20 train–test split, with 10% of the training set held out for validation. For the sake of comparison between different fusion strategies, the same folds of the dataset have been used for all the fusion strategies. We trained all models with a batch size of 16 and employed early stopping with a patience of 10 epochs, based on validation loss. The classification objective was optimized using binary cross-entropy with logits loss (BCEWithLogitsLoss), and optimisation was performed using the Adam optimizer, with distinct learning rates assigned to different blocks of layers within architectures. Hyperparameter optimisation was conducted through a combination of Optuna and GridSearch.

**Evaluation Strategy:** To address the class imbalance inherent in the dataset, we employed a sampler-based data loader and evaluated performance using metrics robust to imbalance, including accuracy, weighted F1-score, and Matthews Correlation Coefficient (MCC). The MCC is defined as:

$$\mathrm{MCC} = \frac{\mathrm{TP}\cdot\mathrm{TN} - \mathrm{FP}\cdot\mathrm{FN}}{\sqrt{(\mathrm{TP}+\mathrm{FP})\cdot(\mathrm{TP}+\mathrm{FN})\cdot(\mathrm{TN}+\mathrm{FP})\cdot(\mathrm{TN}+\mathrm{FN})}} \tag{1}$$

and has some advantages over F1 and accuracy for binary classification [28].

**Table 1.** Performance comparison of Baseline models.

| Metrics | Modality | | | | |
|---|---|---|---|---|---|
| | T1 | T1c | T2 | FLAIR | Clinical |
| MCC | 0.34 ± 0.08 | **0.48 ± 0.07** | 0.37 ± 0.07 | 0.37 ± 0.02 | 0.44 ± 0.08 |
| ACC | 0.77 ± 0.03 | **0.83 ± 0.02** | 0.80 ± 0.02 | 0.80 ± 0.02 | 0.80 ± 0.03 |
| F1-weighted (avg) | 0.79 ± 0.03 | **0.84 ± 0.02** | 0.81 ± 0.02 | 0.81 ± 0.02 | 0.82 ± 0.03 |
| Recall-weighted (avg) | 0.77 ± 0.03 | **0.83 ± 0.02** | 0.80 ± 0.02 | 0.80 ± 0.02 | 0.80 ± 0.03 |
| Precision-weighted (avg) | 0.82 ± 0.04 | **0.86 ± 0.02** | 0.82 ± 0.03 | 0.82 ± 0.02 | 0.85 ± 0.03 |
| Training time (minutes) | 8.57 ± 0.79 | 8.70 ± 0.73 | 9.40 ± 1.52 | 8.67 ± 0.44 | **0.06 ± 0.03** |

## 4 Results and Discussion

**Baseline Performance:** As shown in Table 1, unimodal models exhibited clear differences across modalities. T1c achieved the strongest MRI performance (MCC 0.48), whereas T1 was the weakest, and T2 and FLAIR performed similarly. Notably, the clinical model achieved a competitive MCC (0.44) in significantly less training time (0.06 vs. 8 min for MRI). These results highlight the importance of modality choice and the robustness and efficiency of clinical features as a valuable complementary modality for MRI in glioma grading. Building on these unimodal baselines, we next investigate the impact of combining MRI and clinical modalities at various fusion levels.

**Fusion Strategies:** In early fusion, ELF achieved the strongest results with MRI alone, showing slight gains in accuracy and recall when clinical data were incorporated, while maintaining consistently high F1 and precision scores. In contrast, ERF underperformed relative to ELF and exhibited a further decline in performance when the clinical modality was added (Table 2). These findings highlight two key insights: first, the effectiveness of multimodal learning is highly dependent on the underlying fusion architecture, and second, the inclusion of additional modalities does not inherently guarantee performance improvements, as poorly integrated features may introduce noise or redundancy that hinders model learning and performance. In the late fusion setting (Table 3), LMV and LPA demonstrated comparable performance, with the latter showing slightly greater robustness. Incorporating clinical data into MRI inputs improved model performance in both cases, with the most notable gain in MCC observed under LMV. Unlike early fusion, where the addition of clinical data occasionally reduced performance, late fusion consistently benefited from their inclusion. Regarding the intermediate fusion results in Table 4, ISF achieved the strongest overall performance, with the inclusion of clinical data yielding consistent improvements across all metrics, particularly MCC and accuracy. This indicates that enabling modality interaction during feature extraction is especially beneficial when combining MRI with clinical features. IMF also benefited from clinical data, with the MCC rising from 0.43 to 0.51; however, overall performance remained slightly below that of ISF. Interestingly, in the intermediate fusion setting, adding clinical modality to MRI data makes all the metric performances more robust.

**Table 2.** Performance comparison of early fusion strategies

| Metrics | ELF | | ERF | |
|---|---|---|---|---|
| | MRI | MRI + Clinical | MRI | MRI + Clinical |
| MCC | **0.48 ± 0.07** | 0.46 ± 0.08 | 0.31 ± 0.09 | 0.28 ± 0.09 |
| ACC | 0.85 ± 0.03 | **0.86 ± 0.03** | 0.79 ± 0.02 | 0.79 ± 0.04 |
| F1-weighted (avg) | **0.85 ± 0.03** | **0.85 ± 0.03** | 0.79 ± 0.02 | 0.79 ± 0.03 |
| Recall-weighted (avg) | 0.85 ± 0.03 | **0.86 ± 0.03** | 0.79 ± 0.02 | 0.79 ± 0.04 |
| Precision-weighted (avg) | **0.85 ± 0.03** | **0.85 ± 0.03** | 0.81 ± 0.03 | 0.80 ± 0.02 |

**Comparative Analysis Across Fusion Levels:** Across all experiments, incorporating clinical data generally improved model performance, except for the early fusion setting. Intermediate fusion strategies consistently outperformed

**Table 3.** Performance comparison of late fusion strategies

| Metrics | LMV | | LPA | |
|---|---|---|---|---|
| | MRI | MRI + Clinical | MRI | MRI + Clinical |
| MCC | 0.42 ± 0.07 | 0.49 ± 0.09 | 0.46 ± 0.09 | **0.49 ± 0.08** |
| ACC | 0.85 ± 0.03 | 0.85 ± 0.03 | 0.85 ± 0.03 | **0.86 ± 0.03** |
| F1-weighted (avg) | 0.84 ± 0.03 | **0.85 ± 0.03** | 0.85 ± 0.04 | **0.85 ± 0.03** |
| Recall-weighted (avg) | 0.85 ± 0.03 | 0.85 ± 0.03 | 0.85 ± 0.03 | **0.86 ± 0.03** |
| Precision-weighted (avg) | 0.84 ± 0.04 | **0.86 ± 0.04** | 0.85 ± 0.04 | **0.86 ± 0.04** |

**Table 4.** Performance comparison of intermediate fusion strategies

| Metrics | ISF | | IMF | |
|---|---|---|---|---|
| | MRI | MRI + Clinical | MRI | MRI + Clinical |
| MCC | 0.47 ± 0.08 | **0.54 ± 0.07** | 0.43 ± 0.11 | 0.51 ± 0.04 |
| ACC | 0.83 ± 0.05 | **0.86 ± 0.03** | 0.82 ± 0.04 | 0.84 ± 0.02 |
| F1-weighted (avg) | 0.83 ± 0.04 | **0.86 ± 0.03** | 0.83 ± 0.03 | 0.85 ± 0.01 |
| Recall-weighted (avg) | 0.83 ± 0.05 | **0.86 ± 0.03** | 0.82 ± 0.04 | 0.84 ± 0.02 |
| Precision-weighted (avg) | 0.86 ± 0.03 | 0.87 ± 0.03 | 0.85 ± 0.03 | **0.87 ± 0.01** |

both early and late fusion, with ISF achieving the strongest overall results (MCC = 0.54). While late fusion delivered competitive outcomes when combining MRI and clinical features, its improvements were modest relative to its simplicity. These findings suggest that intermediate fusion enables richer cross-modal interactions by allowing modalities to influence each other during encoding.

A direct comparison between ELF and ISF illustrates this effect. Although both strategies rely on modality-specific encoders followed by an MLP classifier, they differ in how and when integration occurs. ELF combines features only after independent extraction, whereas ISF promotes interaction during encoding, thereby capturing complementary information across modalities. This distinction highlights how the fusion level significantly influences a model's capacity to har-

**Table 5.** Performance of the ISF architecture with MWB

| Metrics | ISF with MWB | |
|---|---|---|
| | MRI | MRI + Clinical |
| MCC | 0.51 ± 0.05 | **0.56 ± 0.04** |
| ACC | 0.86 ± 0.03 | **0.87 ± 0.01** |
| F1-weighted (avg) | 0.86 ± 0.02 | **0.87 ± 0.01** |
| Recall-weighted (avg) | 0.86 ± 0.03 | **0.87 ± 0.01** |
| Precision-weighted (avg) | 0.86 ± 0.02 | **0.88 ± 0.01** |

ness multimodal synergies. Based on these results, ISF is identified as the most effective fusion strategy for further analysis, balancing predictive performance with clinical interpretability.

An additional insight emerges from the MRI-only experiments ELF delivered the strongest results among multimodal MRI models, with performance nearly matching the unimodal T1c baseline. In contrast, other multimodal strategies underperformed compared to T1c alone. This emphasizes that multimodality is not inherently superior: the effectiveness of fusion depends on both the choice of modalities and the fusion strategy. Careful design is therefore essential to ensure that multimodal integration enhances rather than dilutes predictive signals.

**Modality Contribution Studies:** To further examine modality importance, we replace concatenation in ISF with the proposed Modality Weighting Block. As shown in Table 5, this modification consistently improves performance, with MRI + clinical achieving the highest robust scores across all metrics (MCC = 0.56, accuracy, F1, recall, and precision $\geq 0.87$). Compared to concatenation-based ISF, these gains underscore the effectiveness of attention in adaptively weighting modalities rather than treating them equally.

Beyond improved performance, the key strength of this architecture is its ability to quantify the relative importance of each modality. The contribution scores derived from attention weights (Fig. 4) reveal that for the MRI-only model, T1c emerges as the most influential modality, while T1, T2, and FLAIR play smaller but complementary roles. When clinical data are included, the attention shifts substantially towards the clinical modalities, which dominate predictive power, particularly for grades 2&3, while the ranking among the scores of different modalities of MRI remains consistent despite their reduced overall contributions.

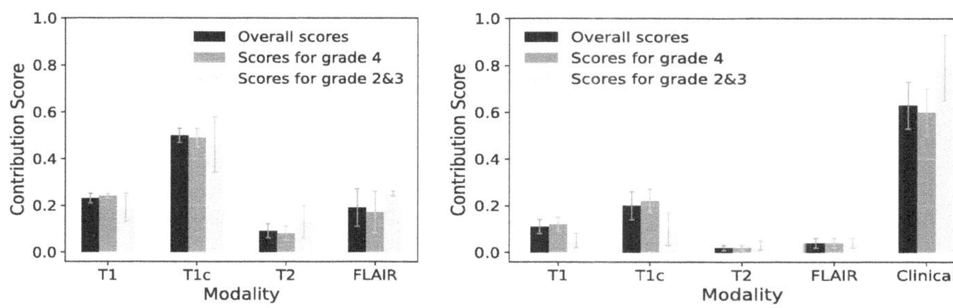


(a) MRI only model

(b) MRI + Clinical model

**Fig. 4.** Modality-specific contribution scores of ISF architecture with MWB

These findings demonstrate that modality-aware weighting not only enhances performance and robustness but also provides interpretable insights into how different modalities contribute to outcomes across various glioma tumour grades. The attention-based fusion block allows the model to prioritise informative modalities while down-weighting less relevant signals, resulting in a more effective and transparent multimodal glioma grading model.

## 5 Conclusion

This study presents a multimodal machine learning framework for glioma grading, integrating MRI and clinical data by comparing early, intermediate, and late fusion. Intermediate fusion proved most effective, and adding clinical data generally improved performance. The top-performing ISF model was enhanced with the Modality Weighting Block, which boosted performance and provided interpretable scores. These scores revealed T1c as the key MRI sequence; however, clinical features became dominant when included. The comparative analysis of the fusion strategies in our framework shows that multimodality is not inherently superior—its value lies in the right choice of modalities and fusion strategy, ensuring that integration enhances predictive power instead of diminishing it. While we acknowledge that a key limitation of this work is the small and imbalanced dataset, this research demonstrates that a modality-aware intermediate-fusion approach improves both accuracy and interpretability in glioma grading tasks.

**Acknowledgments.** This work was funded by Taighde Éireann, Research Ireland, through the Research Ireland Centre for Research Training in Machine Learning (grant number 18/CRT/6183) and the Research Ireland Center for Data Analytics (grant number 12/RC/2289 P2)

**Disclosure of Interests.** The authors have no competing interests to declare that are relevant to the content of this article.

## References

1. Cui, C., et al.: Deep multimodal fusion of image and non-image data in disease diagnosis and prognosis: a review. Progr. Biomed. Eng. **5**(2) (2023)
2. Muhammad, G., Alshehri, F., Karray, F., El Saddik, A., Alsulaiman, M., Falk, T.H.: A comprehensive survey on multimodal medical signals fusion for smart healthcare systems. Inf. Fusion **76**, 355–375 (2021)
3. Lahat, D., Adali, T., Jutten, C.: Multimodal data fusion: an overview of methods, challenges, and prospects. Proc. IEEE **103**(9), 1449–1477 (2015)
4. Baltrušaitis, T., Ahuja, C., Morency, L.-P.: Multimodal machine learning: a survey and taxonomy. IEEE PAMI **41**(2), 423–443 (2018)
5. Ostrom, Q.T., et al.: CBTRUS statistical report: primary brain and other central nervous system tumors diagnosed in the united states in 2016—2020. Neuro-oncology **25** (2023)
6. Byeon, Y., et al.: Interpretable multimodal transformer for prediction of molecular subtypes and grades in adult-type diffuse gliomas. NPJ Digit. Med. **8**(1), 140 (2025)
7. Chen, R.J., et al.: Pathomic fusion: an integrated framework for fusing histopathology and genomic features for cancer diagnosis and prognosis. IEEE Trans. Med. Imaging **41**(4), 757–770 (2020)

8. Guo, P., et al.: Multiparametric magnetic resonance imaging information fusion using graph convolutional network for glioma grading. J. Healthc. Eng. **2022**(1), 7315665 (2022)
9. Usuzaki, T., et al.: Grading diffuse glioma based on 2021 who grade using self-attention-base deep learning architecture: variable vision transformer (vvit). Biomed. Signal Process. Control **91**, 106001 (2024)
10. Long, X., et al.: Multimodal keyless attention fusion for video classification. In: Proceedings of the AAAI Conference on Artificial Intelligence, vol. 32, no. 1 (2018)
11. Stahlschmidt, S.R., Ulfenborg, B., Synnergren, J.: Multimodal deep learning for biomedical data fusion: a review. Brief. Bioinform. **23**(2), bbab569 (2022)
12. Alpaydin, E.: Classifying multimodal data. In: The Handbook of Multimodal-Multisensor Interfaces: Signal Processing. Architectures, and Detection of Emotion and Cognition-Volume 2, pp. 49–69 (2018)
13. He, M., Han, K., Zhang, Y., Chen, W.: Hierarchical-order multimodal interaction fusion network for grading gliomas. Phys. Med. Biol. **66**(21), 215016 (2021)
14. Dhar, J., et al.: Multimodal fusion learning with dual attention for medical imaging. In: WACV, pp. 4362–4371 (2025)
15. Wang, J., Yu, L., Tian, S.: Cross-attention interaction learning network for multi-model image fusion via transformer. Eng. Appl. Artif. Intell. **139**, 109583 (2025)
16. Silva, L.A.V., Rohr, K.: Pan-cancer prognosis prediction using multimodal deep learning. In: ISBI, pp. 568–571 (2020)
17. Abdelaziz, M., Wang, T., Anwaar, W., Elazab, A.: Multi-scale multimodal deep learning framework for Alzheimer's disease diagnosis. Comput. Biol. Med. **184**, 109438 (2025)
18. Guo, S., Wang, L., Chen, Q., Wang, L., Zhang, J., Zhu, Y.: Multimodal MRI image decision fusion-based network for glioma classification. Front. Oncol. **12**, 819673 (2022)
19. Hsu, W.-W., et al.: A weakly supervised deep learning-based method for glioma subtype classification using WSI and mpMRIs. Sci. Rep. **12**(1), 6111 (2022)
20. Jeong, S.-W., Cho, H.-H., Lee, S., Park, H.: Robust multimodal fusion network using adversarial learning for brain tumor grading. Comput. Methods Programs Biomed. **226**, 107165 (2022)
21. Liu, Z., Wu, X., Yang, Y., Clifton, D.A.: DuKA: a dual-keyless-attention model for multi-modality EHR data fusion and organ failure prediction. IEEE Trans. Biomed. Eng. **71**(4), 1247–1256 (2023)
22. Calabrese, E., et al.: The university of California San Francisco preoperative diffuse glioma MRI dataset. Radiol. Artif. Intell. **4**(6), e220058 (2022)
23. Huang, G., Liu, Z., Van Der Maaten, L., Weinberger, K.Q.: Densely connected convolutional networks. In: Proceedings of the IEEE Conference on Computer Vision and Pattern Recognition, pp. 4700–4708 (2017)
24. Song, W., et al.: AutoInt: automatic feature interaction learning via self-attentive neural networks. In: CIKM, pp. 1161–1170 (2019)
25. Liu, Z., et al.: Swin transformer: hierarchical vision transformer using shifted windows. In: IEEE ICCV, vol. 00, pp. 9992–10 002 (2021)
26. Horrell, M.: GBNet: gradient boosting packages integrated into PyTorch. J. Open Source Softw. **10**(111), 8047 (2025)
27. He, K., Zhang, X., Ren, S., Sun, J.: Delving deep into rectifiers: surpassing human-level performance on imagenet classification. In: ICCV, pp. 1026–1034 (2015)
28. Chicco, D., Jurman, G.: The advantages of the Matthews correlation coefficient (MCC) over F1 score and accuracy in binary classification evaluation. BMC Genom. **21**, 1–13 (2020)

# Tailored Loss Functions to Improve Vertebra Centroid Localisation and Classification in Sagittal Spinal Radiographs

Cliodhna Gartland[1,2](✉), Fjorda Koromani[3,4,5], John Healy[2], Gennady Roshchupkin[4,5], Fernando Rivadeneira[3,4], and Stephen J. Redmond[1,2]

[1] Insight Research Ireland Centre for Data Analytics, Dublin, Ireland
cliodhna.gartland@ucdconnect.ie
[2] University College Dublin, Dublin, Ireland
[3] Department of Internal Medicine, Erasmus MC, Rotterdam, The Netherlands
[4] Department of Epidemiology, Erasmus MC, Rotterdam, The Netherlands
[5] Department of Radiology and Nuclear Medicine, Erasmus MC, Rotterdam, The Netherlands

**Abstract.** A healthy spine is essential for a high-quality life, yet spinal musculoskeletal issues cause suffering and significant socioeconomic burdens. Osteoporotic vertebral fractures (OVFs), for example, increase risk of future fractures, morbidity, and mortality. While spine radiography is the gold standard for OVF detection, manual interpretation is time-consuming and challenging. Hence, this work proposes an automated tool for simultaneous vertebral centroid localisation and classification in sagittal spinal radiographs, streamlining the initial input required for semi-automated diagnostic tools and enhancing the efficiency of spine assessment. To aid the model's learning despite the partial annotations and varying fields of view (FOV) in the datasets used, various loss functions were developed and tested to enhance performance and allow for further training on more complete annotations in the future. A total of four different loss functions, as well as a baseline model trained with standard MSE loss, were compared. The best-performing models improved vertebral ID accuracy by over 5% above the baseline model in both datasets. Future work will leverage the outputs of these models for vertebra segmentation and fracture detection in a fully automated pipeline.

## 1 Introduction

Spine health is essential for our mobility and overall quality of life. Lower back pain alone has an estimated lifetime prevalence of 84%, making it one of the most common musculoskeletal problems, and a substantial socioeconomic burden [1]. Thus, it is essential to accurately detect any structural issues in the spine such that early intervention can ameliorate current symptoms and future outcomes.


T. T. Mai et al. (Eds.): AICS 2025, CCIS 2950, pp. 300–312, 2026.
https://doi.org/10.1007/978-3-032-25809-0_24

For example, osteoporotic vertebral fractures (OVFs) are the most common type of osteoporotic fracture and indicate a higher risk of future osteoporotic fracture, morbidity, and mortality [11]. However, two-thirds of osteoporotic vertebral fractures are asymptomatic [10]. The detection of these asymptomatic fractures aids osteoporosis diagnosis, assessment of future fracture risk, and selection of pharmacological therapy to prevent future fractures [10]. Thus, screening for vertebral fractures is worthwhile.

Spine radiography remains the gold standard technique, as computed tomography (CT) images have poor sensitivity for detecting fractures and are not a cost-effective screening tool [3]. In contrast, radiographs are more economical, quickly acquired, readily available, and expose the patient to less radiation. From a radiograph, OVFs are currently detected through manual measurement of vertebral height reduction, qualitative assessment, or using semi-automated software that requires manual input or adjustment to analyse the radiograph [11]. However, radiographs can also suffer from poor contrast, caused by shadows of overlapping anatomical structures, such as the lungs and ribs [8], making diagnosis difficult. Hence, fully automated diagnostic tools are needed to more efficiently assess the spine in all spinal radiographs. We aim to meet this need by developing an automated tool to localise and classify each vertebral centroid. The benefit of automating this process is that it generates the initial input required for existing semi-automated tools [2] and serves as the first step in a fully automated pipeline for OVF detection.

## 2 Related Work

### 2.1 Vertebra Localisation with CT Images

The Large Scale Vertebrae Segmentation Challenge (VerSe), organized in conjunction with the International Conference on Medical Image Computing and Computer Assisted Intervention (MICCAI) in 2019 and 2020, provided a dataset of 374 spinal CT scans with varying fields of view (FOV) and segmentation masks for 24 vertebrae (C1-L5, and the transitional T13 and L6) and set the challenge of localizing and segmenting vertebrae [17]. This large publicly-available dataset has motivated the development of numerous innovative methods for the task. However, the top performing methods each year used multiple models to complete the task, including an initial U-Net model to first isolate the spine, achieving vertebra classification accuracies and centroid mean distances of 94.25% and 4.8 mm [15] and 96.58% and 1.38 mm [17], respectively. The second place method in 2019 used just one model, but implemented an iterative approach that could be time-consuming and prone to cascading errors, whereby an incorrect classification of one vertebra leads to all subsequent vertebra classifications being incorrect [12]. Additionally, a post-processing step is implemented in [15] to finalize the classifications, including selecting the top or bottom-most vertebra to align all other vertebra classifications with, which would also be prone to cascading errors. In our paper, we aim to implicitly leverage knowledge of the spinal structure through our loss function to eliminate such post-processing steps and reduce computation through the use of a single U-Net instead of aggregating multiple models.

Currently, the state-of-the-art method for vertebra classification with the VerSe20 dataset achieves a 97.22% accuracy using a transformer-based model [19]. However, their centroid mean distance error of 4.33 mm shows the model performs worse in this metric than previously-published methods [17].

### 2.2 Vertebra Localisation in Radiographs

The number of studies focused on classifying or localizing vertebra centroids is significantly smaller when limited to radiographs. In one study, a vertebral classification accuracy of 98.4% was achieved with a dataset of 10,193 sagittal radiographs of the lumbar spine [4]. The authors used a pre-trained ResNet-50 to determine whether each vertebra class is present in the image and a pre-trained InceptionV3 model to identify four corner landmarks for each vertebra. These landmarks were further refined by extracting the region-of-interest (ROI) around each vertebra using the estimated vertebra centroid (obtained from the four initial corner estimations) and inputting this ROI to another pre-trained InceptionV3 model. Our proposed approach streamlines the task by combining classification and localisation of vertebral centroids into a single model, still allowing an ROI to be extracted and input into their third model, thus simplifying the overall process.

Many studies rely on a consistent FOV, with the L5 vertebra visible in all radiographs, allowing classifications to be determined by ascending through the detected vertebrae, based on the assumption that the lowest identified vertebra is L5 [8,9,18]. Similarly, other studies aim to identify the same 17 vertebrae in all radiographs, expecting all 17 to be visible in every image, thereby increasing the risk of cascading classification errors [5,24]. One such model outputs a single-layer heatmap with the centroids of all 17 vertebrae highlighted [24], instead of taking advantage of a multilayer heatmap that could learn vertebrae classifications and adapt to multiple FOV, as we aim to do in this study. Our model will also have no upper or lower vertebral label expectations to aid the classification process, making it more generalizable to different FOV.

### 2.3 Loss Functions

Selecting an appropriate loss function is essential for optimal model performance. Other radiograph landmark localisation studies have used tailored loss functions [22,23]. However, [23]'s loss function emphasizes errors in pixels at the edges of the hotspots representing the landmarks on the heatmap, rather than pixels closer to the centre of the hotspot; this is not ideal when the model should output a heatmap image whose maximum value occurs exactly at the location of the desired centroid. Meanwhile, [22]'s choice of wing loss [6] is ineffective for heatmap regression [21] and penalizes errors in pixels representing the landmark hotspot and other background pixels equally. Instead, a weighted loss is suggested, where errors in the locality of hotspots in the heatmap are penalized more for improved accuracy in these important regions of the image [21]. [13] apply a weighted loss scaled using the ground truth heatmaps when identifying landmarks within a natural image for human pose recognition. We aim to further increase the focus on just a small patch surrounding the landmark by weighting just that patch at a much higher intensity instead of scaling the loss across the image.

Another common issue with medical datasets is inconsistent or partially annotated data. Some studies used tailored loss functions to allow the usage of such data without incorrectly penalizing the model for the missing data and limiting the learning process [14,20]. This is important, as excluding partially annotated data to avoid the issue would otherwise severely limit the usefulness of certain datasets. To achieve this, these studies simply do not include portions of the data for each participant where no ground truth exists in their loss calculation, allowing the model to make estimations without penalization, and yet still learn from the data that is available; [20] do this when segmenting parts of CT images of breast cancer patients and [14] apply this to a regression model for clinical scoring of brain MRIs. The issue with this approach, and our datasets, is that our dataset contains inconsistent FOV of the spine, meaning that not all vertebrae will be visible and those that are will not always have the same presentation. Hence, the lack of a vertebra centroid ground truth in our dataset will sometimes represent a lack of annotation (i.e., a visible vertebra that was left unlabelled) or accurately indicate that particular vertebra is not visible. This presents the challenge of encouraging the model to make estimations that should exist while also not making estimations on vertebrae not contained in the image. In addressing this problem, the paper makes one of its significant contributions.

### 2.4 Contributions

This work aimed to: (1) develop a single model that can classify and localise the centroid of each vertebra in radiographs with varying FOV, and; (2) address the challenge of partially annotated datasets using tailored loss functions that can also generalize to the inclusion of additional data annotations in the future.

## 3 Methodology

### 3.1 Datasets

For this work, two distinct datasets of sagittal spinal radiographs were used: (1) the Rotterdam Study, a private dataset, and; (2) the National Health and Nutrition Examination Survey (NHANES II), a public dataset.

**Rotterdam Study.** We used 2,593 sagittal spinal radiographs from the ongoing Rotterdam Study [7]. This study began in 1990, with participants all living within the Ommoord district in the city of Rotterdam, the Netherlands. The study has several cohorts, three of which we selected to use data from. The first (RSI) and second cohorts (RSII) include participants aged 55 years or older and the third cohort (RSIII) includes participants aged 45–54 years. Scans were taken for each cohort every few years. Co-author FK selected data from the first four scanning periods of RSI, the second scanning period of RSII, and the first scanning period of RSIII. This selection was made by first identifying all scans that contained a vertebral fracture that had also already been labelled and then selecting a non-fractured scan from a different participant of the same sex and with a $\pm 1$ year age difference within the same cohort and scan period; with this we have 1,312 selected scans. Participants usually have two radiographs per session, to capture vertebrae T4 to L4, with inconsistent FOV and overlap between images, giving us a total of 2,593 radiographs from this dataset. Vertebrae centroid locations and labels were also available within the study for vertebrae T4 to L4, totalling 13 vertebrae. However, these labels were only made on one radiograph per participant per scan period, regardless of whether the vertebra is also visible on the other radiograph of the rest of the spine.

**NHANES II.** We used 543 sagittal spinal radiographs from the NHANES II study[1], which ran from 1976–1980. This dataset contains a total of 9,667 cervical spine radiographs of participants aged 25–74 years, and 7,408 lumbar spine radiographs of male participants aged 25–74 and female participants aged 50–74. However, only a limited subset contain vertebral labels and segmentation masks: 275 cervical and 268 lumbar spine radiographs. Vertebrae C2-T1 and T12-S1 are labelled in the cervical and lumbar radiographs, respectively, leaving 10 thoracic vertebrae (T2-T11) completely unlabelled. As with the Rotterdam dataset, many radiographs contain visible but unlabelled vertebrae. Vertebral centroid coordinates are determined by calculating the centre of mass of the respective segmentation mask.

### 3.2 Data Pre-processing

The two datasets were used to train and test models separately for two key reasons: (1) there is an overlap of only five vertebrae between the datasets (T12-L4), hence training on one dataset and testing on another would be an unfair assessment of the models; and (2) training and testing on a mix of both datasets to cover all but two vertebra (T2-T3) would make replication difficult as the Rotterdam dataset is private. For all models, a training, validation, and test split of 80/10/10% was used. All scans of the same participant were kept within the same split to avoid data leakage. Each input image was resized to $256 \times 256$ pixels (px) and normalized using the training data of each dataset. From the coordinates of each vertebral centroid, heatmaps were created to be used as targets for the models. These training targets (a 3D tensor) have dimensions equivalent to the dimensions of the input image ($256 \times 256$ px) times a depth of 13 for the Rotterdam Study and 24 for the NHANES II dataset (i.e., one heatmap layer for each vertebra captured in each study). Each layer of this tensor consists of a Gaussian

[1] https://wwwn.cdc.gov/nchs/data/nhanes2/NH2_Xray.htm.

heatmap with a hotspot centred at the location of the vertebral centroid with a width controlled by the Gaussian standard deviation ($\sigma$) at 5 px.

### 3.3 Model Selection

The U-Net architecture [16] was selected as the baseline algorithm and was trained with five different loss functions, summarized in Table 1: (1) UNet-Base served as the baseline for comparison with MSE loss; (2) UNet-LS1 increased the model's accuracy in the regions immediately surrounding each vertebral centroid; (3) UNet-LS2 extends LS1 by adding larger penalties for predicting centroids for vertebrae that were not visible within the input image and not penalizing estimations for vertebrae that were visible but unlabelled; (4) UNet-LS3 further extends LS2 by aiming to discourage estimations of the same centroid location for different vertebrae, and; (5) UNet-LS4 extends LS2 and accounts for datasets with missing annotations, as in NHANES II, by not penalizing estimations where no ground truth exists for that particular class across the dataset (i.e., T2-T11 in NHANES II).

### 3.4 Model Training and Evaluation

To evaluate each model's performance after each training epoch the estimated coordinates for each ground truth labelled vertebra centroid were first extracted by determining the pixel location of the maximum pixel value in the corresponding output heatmap layer. As the cost function, MSE was used to determine the error for those coordinates with ground truth values only. Early stopping with a patience of 20 epochs and threshold of 0.1 px$^2$ improvement was implemented after 100 epochs using the above calculated centroid location error of the validation dataset to determine when the best-performing version of the model had been learned.

To assess the models using the test set, two key metrics were used: (1) the percentage of correctly classified vertebrae (vertebral ID accuracy), and; (2) the centroid location RMSE for all correctly classified vertebrae. To calculate the first metric, the vertebra centroid location for each heatmap layer was extracted and compared to the corresponding ground truth centroid location. If the Euclidean distance (in pixels) between the two coordinates was less than half the average distance between two adjacent target centroids for that image (i.e., the average inter-vertebral distance), then the model was considered to have correctly classified the vertebra because the centroid estimate for that vertebra was within the boundary of the target vertebra with the same label. The second metric only uses correctly classified vertebrae, because if a misclassified vertebra were included, its predicted centroid would be compared to the ground-truth centroid of a different vertebra, leading to an artificially inflated error.

We also evaluated each model after thresholding the heatmaps to only extract estimated centroid coordinates with a pixel value greater than 0.3 (on a scale of 0 to 1). With these coordinates, we assessed the vertebrae that have ground truth values to determine: (1) the percentage of correctly classified (CC) vertebra,

**Table 1.** U-Net loss functions. In the following, $N$ represents the number of pixels in a heatmap layer (same for all layers), $L$ the total number of heatmap layers (one for each vertebra being detected), $y_{ij}$ the $i^{\text{th}}$ ground truth heatmap value in the $j^{\text{th}}$ heatmap layer, $\hat{y}_{ij}$ the $i^{\text{th}}$ estimated heatmap value in the $j^{\text{th}}$ heatmap layer, $H_j = \sum_{i=1}^{L} y_{ij}$ representing the total sum of a heatmap layer, and set $M$ contains all heatmap layers, $j$, that have no ground truths at all in the entire dataset.

| Loss | Description & Goal | Formula |
|---|---|---|
| MSE | Uniform weight for all pixel errors. Serves as a baseline for comparison. | $f(y) = \frac{1}{NL}\sum_{j=1}^{L}\sum_{i=1}^{N}\alpha_{ij}(y_{ij} - \hat{y}_{ij})^2$ <br> $\alpha_{ij} = 1$ |
| LS1 | Pixels with ground truth $\geq 0.5$ had squared error weighted by 10. Encourages focus on centroid areas. | $\alpha_{ij} = \begin{cases} 10, & y_{ij} \geq 0.5 \\ 1, & \text{otherwise} \end{cases}$ |
| LS2 | LS1, plus weighting by 5 in layers without labelled vertebrae, and ignoring layers (weighted by 0) before/after labelled sequences of vertebra. Suppresses likely spurious estimations and allows estimations for likely visible but unlabelled vertebra. | $\alpha_{ij} = \begin{cases} 10, & y_{ij} \geq 0.5 \\ 5, & H_j \wedge H_{j+1} \wedge H_{j-1} = 0 \\ 0, & (H_j = 0) \wedge (H_{j+1} \vee H_{j-1} \geq 0) \\ 1, & \text{otherwise} \end{cases}$ |
| LS3 | LS2, plus additional weighting of 10 where $y_{ij} \geq 0.5$ in any layer. Discourages overlapping centroid estimations. | $\alpha_{ij} = \begin{cases} 10, & y_{ij} \geq 0.5 \text{ for any } j \\ 5, & H_j \wedge H_{j+1} \wedge H_{j-1} = 0 \\ 0, & (H_j = 0) \wedge (H_{j+1} \vee H_{j-1} \geq 0) \\ 1, & \text{otherwise} \end{cases}$ |
| LS4 | Only applied to NHANES II. LS2, plus ignoring additional vertebrae that have no ground truth annotation across the entire dataset (i.e., T2-T11 for NHANES II). | $\alpha_{ij} = \begin{cases} 10, & y_{ij} \geq 0.5 \text{ for any } j \\ 5, & H_j \wedge H_{j+1} \wedge H_{j-1} = 0 \\ 0, & (H_j = 0) \wedge (H_{j+1} \vee H_{j-1} \geq 0) \\ 0, & j \in M \\ 1, & \text{otherwise} \end{cases}$ |

as we did for vertebral ID accuracy using the average inter-vertebral distance; (2) the percentage of misclassified (MC) vertebra, and; (3) the percentage of missing detections (MD). These three values should sum to 100% as the model has either made (1) a correct detection, (2) an incorrect detection, or (3) no detection for each vertebra. After thresholding, we can also assess the presence of extra detection where no ground truth label exists (i.e., for visible but unlabelled vertebrae). We do this by determining whether the detected vertebra is within an appropriate distance from the closest ground truth centroid using the average inter-vertebral distance, or multiple thereof. If the estimation is located within the region where we would expect the corresponding vertebra to be, we count it as an additional correctly classified (ACC) vertebra; if not, we count it as an additional misclassified (AMC) vertebra. We then calculate the ratio of ACC to AMC to estimate how accurately the model detects unlabelled vertebra.

## 4 Results

The results for each model are displayed in Table 2. For the Rotterdam dataset, the best-performing model is UNet-LS2, with a vertebral ID accuracy of 95.9% across 13 vertebral classes (T4-L4) and a centroid RMSE for all correctly-classified vertebra of $17.08 \pm 7.54$ px. For context, the average distance between the ground-truth centroids of two consecutive vertebrae is $326 \pm 125$ px, allowing us to conclude that the model's centroid estimates are in central locations for each vertebra. This can also be verified visually, with the sample illustrations of results from UNet-LS2 presented in Fig. 1. Figure 1b shows how the model can correctly classify vertebrae (confirmed by average inter-vertebral distance for that radiograph) that currently have no ground truth label, while Fig. 1c shows the opposite problem, with the model failing to classify the last vertebra (here L2) despite a label existing. Finally, Fig. 1d depicts two distinct classifications produced for the same vertebra (here L1).

For the NHANES II dataset, the best-performing model is UNet-LS4, with a vertebral ID accuracy of 93.9% across 14 vertebral classes (C2-T1, T12-S1) and a centroid RMSE for all correctly-classified vertebra of $7.98 \pm 3.62$ px, which is unsurprising given LS4 was further tailored from LS2 to deal with the large sequence of unlabelled vertebra (T2-T11) in the NHANES II dataset. After thresholding, UNet-LS2 and UNet-LS4 continue to perform best for the Rotterdam and NHANES II dataset respectively, with the largest CC and smallest MC and MD values. However, UNet-LS3 has the largest ratio of additional correctly classified to misclassified vertebra estimations that do not have ground truth values: 6.3 for the NHANES II dataset and 3.6 for the Rotterdam dataset.

## 5 Discussion

As expected, weighting the loss function near the ground truth hotspots (i.e., vertebrae centroids) within each heatmap, with the goal of improving model accuracy in those regions, led to an improvement of at least 5% in the vertebral

**Table 2.** The results are calculated with a test set of 260 radiographs from the Rotterdam dataset with 13 labelled vertebra options (T4-T12) or 54 radiographs from the NHANES II dataset with 14 labelled vertebra options (C2-T1, T12-S1). The vertebral ID accuracy and centroid location RMSE are calculated using only vertebrae with ground truth values. After thresholding the detected centroids, the correctly classified (CC), misclassified (MC), or missing detection (MD) vertebra are determined for those with ground truths. For vertebra without ground truths, the additional correctly classified (ACC) and additional misclassified (AMC) vertebra counts are determined, as well as their ratio (ACC/AMC).

| Model | Dataset | Vertebral ID Accuracy | Centroid Location RMSE | CC | MC | MD | ACC | AMC | ACC/AMC |
|---|---|---|---|---|---|---|---|---|---|
| UNet-Base | Rotterdam | 89.6% | 20.28 px | 86.8% | 4.7% | 8.6% | 27 | 19 | 1.4 |
| UNet-LS1 | Rotterdam | 94.7% | 17.17 px | 94.5% | 4.7% | 0.8% | 133 | 55 | 2.4 |
| UNet-LS2 | Rotterdam | 95.9% | 17.08 px | 96.2% | 3.4% | 0.4% | 122 | 38 | 3.2 |
| UNet-LS3 | Rotterdam | 95.2% | 19.65 px | 95.2% | 3.4% | 1.4% | 98 | 27 | 3.6 |
| UNet-Base | NHANESII | 88.7% | 12.29 px | 80.8% | 6.7% | 12.5% | 15 | 7 | 2.1 |
| UNet-LS1 | NHANESII | 90.7% | 7.73 px | 88.8% | 6.7% | 4.5% | 21 | 5 | 4.2 |
| UNet-LS2 | NHANESII | 92.8% | 10.60 px | 89.5% | 7.1% | 3.4% | 17 | 3 | 5.7 |
| UNet-LS3 | NHANESII | 90.2% | 12.97 px | 88.3% | 7.5% | 4.3% | 19 | 3 | 6.3 |
| UNet-LS4 | NHANESII | 93.9% | 7.98 px | 93.3% | 4.1% | 2.5% | 21 | 4 | 5.3 |

ID accuracy over the UNet-Base model for the Rotterdam dataset and 2% for the NHANES II dataset. Further tailoring the loss function to improve robustness to how these datasets were labelled (i.e., with some visible vertebrae left unlabelled) proved beneficial; we noted that these datasets often contained vertebrae at the beginning or end of the labelled vertebrae series that had no labels for a particular image, and the proposed loss function accommodated missing labels in model output layers immediately before and/or after a consecutive series of labelled vertebrae in the ground truth image (LS2). This encouraged the model to go beyond our labels and make estimations for vertebrae left unlabelled, rather than being penalized during learning for recognizing a vertebra simply because a label is missing. This is how the model should ideally behave for all future images, as shown in Fig. 1b.

A similar solution was developed to compensate for the large labelling gap in the NHANES II dataset, where vertebrae T2-T11 are never labelled; LS4 did not include loss calculations for such vertebrae, encouraging the model to make estimations for these likely visible but unlabelled vertebrae. This also allows us to easily train the model further in the future if these annotations become available, making it a much more generalizable model. Future work will ideally retrain all models with the Rotterdam dataset with 24 heatmaps (for all 24 vertebrae) instead of limiting the vertebra range to what was labelled (T4-L4). It is important to note that some people have an additional vertebra (i.e., T13 or L6), which presents a challenge that could be addressed in the future.

When further tailoring the loss (i.e., LS3) in an attempt to avoid predicting centroid locations for two or more unique vertebrae on the same vertebra (c.f., Fig. 1d), this led to an overall decrease in performance with both datasets. This issue may be better addressed with basic post-processing heuristics, using

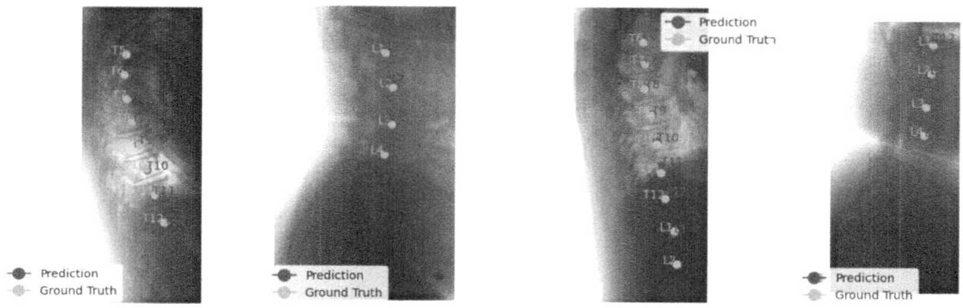


(a) (b) (c) (d)

**Fig. 1.** Example centroid estimates from best-performing model, UNet-LS2, using the Rotterdam dataset with: (a) correct estimates, (b) an additional correct estimate on an unlabelled vertebra (T12), (c) a missing detection (L2), and (d) two estimations (T12 and L1) on one vertebra (L1).

the classification of the vertebra that is closest to the double-classified vertebra as a reference. This post-processing need only be performed when a double-classification is detected to limit cascading error caused by re-classifying all estimations based on one chosen estimation. However, LS3 produced models with the best ratio of detecting additional unlabelled vertebrae correctly, which is likely due to the heavier penalization for detecting additional vertebrae in the regions where a ground truth labelled vertebra exists. However, it is important to note this ratio extrapolates beyond the ground truth label set and so should be taken as indicative and not exact. Overall, while these loss functions aid in the challenges of these particular datasets, they are also generalizable to other datasets with similar characteristics of partial annotations and varying FOV, both of which are common in medical imaging datasets.

When compared to the state of the art for vertebral ID accuracy in CTs (97.22% [19]) and radiographs (98.4% [4]), our approach seemingly underperforms. However, the state of the art study using radiographs always had the lowest five vertebrae (L2-S1) of its goal range (T9-S1) visible in all images, giving this model a more consistent FOV to learn, in addition to its much larger dataset [4]. We also employ a simplified approach of a one-step model, to reduce inference time. Compared to [19], our models work with radiographs, which contain shadows that may restrict the view of vertebrae while CTs do not, making our dataset slightly more challenging to achieve high accuracy on; noting the preference of using X-ray over CT for other practical benefits, such as cost, access, speed, and radiation dosage.

Ideally, the centroid location RMSE should be measured in millimetres, as this is a more comprehensible metric for medical staff and is independent of image resolution. However, the ratio between pixels and millimetres is unavailable in both of the datasets used. It is also important to note that the vertebral centroids are typically annotated with the goal of inputting such data into a semi-automated tool to assess the vertebral structure (i.e., diagnose fracture).

As such, the focus on selecting the exact centre of each vertebra is not always essential, so much as selecting a central point on the vertebra for the tool to then assess the surrounding area. This is also true of the intention for our model: to use the centroid locations to isolate vertebra for subsequent assessment.

## 6 Conclusions

This work develops tailored loss functions to boost models for the classification and localisation of vertebra centroids from sagittal radiographs with varying FOV and partial annotation availability. In other words, our novel loss functions demonstrate the ability to handle conditions of unlabelled but visible targets as well as targets not captured in the image. Future work will focus on extracting ROIs based on our model's centroid estimations, to perform subsequent vertebra segmentation and fracture detection, providing medical staff with a fully automated pipeline for efficient assessment of the spine.

**Acknowledgments.** This publication has emanated from research conducted with the financial support of Taighde ÃĽireann - Research Ireland under grant numbers 17/FRL/4832 and SFI/12/RC/2289_P2. Co-authors FK and FR are supported by the European Research Council (ERC) grant agreement No. 101021500. The Rotterdam Study is funded by Erasmus Medical Centre and Erasmus University, The Netherlands Organization for the Health Research and Development (ZonMw), the Research Institute for Diseases in the Elderly (014-93-015, RIDE2), the Ministry of Education, Culture and Science, the Ministry for Health, Welfare and Sports, the European Commission (Directorate-General XII), and the Municipality of Rotterdam. For the purpose of Open Access, the author has applied a CC BY public copyright license to any Author Accepted Manuscript version arising from this submission.

**Data Availability.** All code is available at: https://github.com/RedmondLabUCD/vertebra-identification

**Disclosure of Interests.** The authors declare that they have no known competing financial interests or personal relationships that could have appeared to influence the work reported in this paper.

## References

1. Balagué, F., Mannion, A.F., Pellisé, F., Cedraschi, C.: Non-specific low back pain. The Lancet **379**, 482–491 (2012). https://doi.org/10.1016/S0140-6736(11)60610-7
2. Birch, C., Knapp, K., Hopkins, S., et al.: Spineanalyzer is an accurate and precise method of vertebral fracture detection and classification on dual-energy lateral vertebral assessment scans. Radiography **21**(3), 278–281 (2015). https://doi.org/10.1016/j.radi.2015.02.003
3. Capdevila-Reniu, A., Navarro-López, M., López-Soto, A.: Osteoporotic vertebral fractures: a diagnostic challenge in the 21st century. Revista Cl'inica Española **221**, 118–124 (2021). https://doi.org/10.1016/j.rce.2019.09.006

4. Cina, A., Bassani, T., Panico, M., et al.: 2-step deep learning model for landmarks localization in spine radiographs. Sci. Rep. **11**(1), 9482 (2021). https://doi.org/10.1038/s41598-021-89102-w
5. Fatima, J., Mohsan, M., Jameel, A., et al.: Vertebrae localization and spine segmentation on radiographic images for feature-based curvature classification for scoliosis. Concurr. Comput. Pract. Exper. **34**(26), e7300 (2022). https://doi.org/10.1002/cpe.7300
6. Feng, Z.H., Kittler, J., Awais, M., et al.: Wing loss for robust facial landmark localisation with convolutional neural networks. In: 2018 IEEE/CVF Conference on Computer Vision and Pattern Recognition (CVPR), USA, pp. 2235–2245 (2018). https://doi.org/10.1109/CVPR.2018.00238
7. Hofman, A., et al.: The Rotterdam Study: 2016 objectives and design update. Eur. J. Epidemiol. **30**(8), 661–708 (2015). https://doi.org/10.1007/s10654-015-0082-x
8. Kim, K.C., Cho, H.C., Jang, T.J., et al.: Automatic detection and segmentation of lumbar vertebrae from X-ray images for compression fracture evaluation. Comput. Methods Programs Biomed. **200** (2021). https://doi.org/10.3389/fendo.2023.1132725
9. Kim, K.C., Yun, H.S., Kim, S., Seo, J.K.: Automation of spine curve assessment in frontal radiographs using deep learning of vertebral-tilt vector. IEEE Access **8**, 84618–84630 (2020). https://doi.org/10.1109/ACCESS.2020.2992081
10. Lenchik, L., Rogers, L.F., Delmas, P.D., Genant, H.K.: Diagnosis of osteoporotic vertebral fractures: importance of recognition and description by radiologists. Am. J. Roentgenol. **183**(4), 949–958 (2004). https://doi.org/10.2214/ajr.183.4.1830949
11. Lentle, B., Koromani, F., Brown, J.P., et al.: The radiology of osteoporotic vertebral fractures revisited. J. Bone Miner. Res. **34**(3), 409–418 (2019). https://doi.org/10.1002/jbmr.3669
12. Lessmann, N., van Ginneken, B., de Jong, P.A., Isgum, I.: Iterative fully convolutional neural networks for automatic vertebra segmentation and identification. Med. Image Anal. **53**, 142–155 (2019). https://doi.org/10.1016/j.media.2019.02.005
13. Li, S., Xiang, X.: Lightweight human pose estimation using loss weighted by target heatmap. In: Pattern Recognition, Computer Vision, and Image Processing ICPR 2022 International Workshops and Challenges, vol. 13643 (2023). https://doi.org/10.1007/978-3-031-37660-3_5
14. Liu, M., Zhang, J., Lian, C., Shen, D.: Weakly-supervised deep learning for brain disease prognosis using MRI and incomplete clinical scores. IEEE Trans. Cybernet. **50**(7), 3381–3392 (2020). https://doi.org/10.1109/TCYB.2019.2904186
15. Payer, C., Stern, D., Bischof, H., Urschler, M.: Coarse to fine vertebrae localization and segmentation with SpatialConfiguration-Net and U-Net. In: 15th International Joint Conference on Computer Vision, Imaging and Computer Graphics Theory and Applications (VISIGRAPP 2020), pp. 124–133 (2020). https://doi.org/10.5220/0008975201240133
16. Ronneberger, O., Fischer, P. and Brox, T.: Medical Image Computing and Computer-Assisted Intervention – MICCAI 2015. In: Frangi, A.F., Navab, N., Hornegger, J., Wells, W.M. (eds.), pp. 234–241. Springer, Cham (2015)
17. Sekuboyina, A., Husseini, M.E., Bayat, A., et al.: VerSe: a vertebrae labelling and segmentation benchmark for multi-detector CT images. Med. Image Anal. **73** (2021). https://doi.org/10.1016/j.media.2021.102166

18. Sun, Yu., Xing, Y., Zhao, Z., Meng, X., Xu, G., Hai, Y.: Comparison of manual versus automated measurement of Cobb angle in idiopathic scoliosis based on a deep learning keypoint detection technology. Eur. Spine J. (8), 1–10 (2021). https://doi.org/10.1007/s00586-021-07025-6
19. Tao, R., Liu, W. and Zheng, G.: Spine-transformers: vertebra labeling and segmentation in arbitrary field-of-view spine CTs via 3D transformers. Med. Image Anal. **75** (2022). https://doi.org/10.1016/j.media.2021.102258
20. Vu, M.H., Norman, G., Nyholm, T., Löfstedt, T.: A data-adaptive loss function for incomplete data and incremental learning in semantic image segmentation. IEEE Trans. Med. Imaging **41**(6) (2022). https://doi.org/10.1109/TMI.2021.3139161
21. Wang, D., Yu, K., Feng, C., et al.: Graph cuts and shape constraint based automatic femoral head segmentation in CT images. In: Proceedings of the Third International Symposium on Image Computing and Digital Medicine, ISICDM 2019, pp. 1–6. Association for Computing Machinery, New York (2019). https://doi.org/10.1145/3364836.3364837
22. Yeh, Y.C., Weng, C.H., Huang, Y.J., et al.: Deep learning approach for automatic landmark detection and alignment analysis in whole-spine lateral radiographs. Sci. Rep. **11**(7618), 2045–2322 (2021). https://doi.org/10.1038/s41598-021-87141-x
23. Zhong, Z., Li, J., Zhang, Z., Jiao, Z., Gao, X.: An attention-guided deep regression model for landmark detection in cephalograms. In: Shen, D., et al. (eds.) MICCAI 2019. LNCS, vol. 11769, pp. 540–548. Springer, Cham (2019). https://doi.org/10.1007/978-3-030-32226-7_60
24. Zou, L., Guo, L., Zhang, R., et al.: VLTENet: a deep-learning-based vertebra localization and tilt estimation network for automatic cobb angle estimation. IEEE J. Biomed. Health Inform. **27**(6), 3002–3013 (2023). https://doi.org/10.1109/JBHI.2023.3258361

# Gaussian Process-Based Motor Imagery Classification

Sonal Santosh Baberwal[1(✉)] and Shirley Coyle[1,2]

[1] School of Electronic Engineering, Dublin City University, Dublin D09Y074, Ireland
sonal.baberwal2@mail.dcu.ie, shirley.coyle@dcu.ie

[2] Insight SFI Centre for Data Analytics and School of Computing, Dublin City University, Dublin D09Y074, Ireland

**Abstract.** Motor Imagery (MI), the mental rehearsal of motor skills, is a prominent approach to controlling Brain-Computer Interfaces (BCI). Motor imagery involves imagining movement without actually performing the motor task. The success of an MI-based BCI system to facilitate effective device control relies on the accurate analysis and classification of distinct neural patterns corresponding to different motor intentions. This is typically measured non-invasively from the brain using electroencephalography (EEG). Precision in this classification accuracy is paramount for MI-based BCIs, as misclassification risks sending incorrect commands to connected devices, compromising the system's reliability, safety, and user experience. In this work, we propose and explore the integration of Gaussian Process (GP) kernels as a classifier for motor imagery signals. In contrast to existing machine learning solutions, e.g., LSTM and SVM, GPs offer a fully probabilistic framework, which aids in setting decision thresholds, managing uncertainty inherent in neural data, and additionally works well with smaller datasets, which is often the case in BCI trials. Our results show that GP-based classifiers achieved up to 64.82% accuracy for Left vs Right classification, closely matching CSP+mLC (68.36%), and significantly improved performance for the One-vs-All (OvA) strategy with a mean accuracy of 78.41%, outperforming several traditional CSP-based classifiers. The Matérn kernel consistently yielded the highest accuracies across most tasks, with feet-related tasks achieving the strongest results (80.07%). While kernel differences were not statistically significant overall, subject-specific variations highlight the adaptability of GPs for personalized BCI. These findings position GPs as a promising direction for MI-based BCI applications, especially when reliability, uncertainty estimation, and small datasets are critical.

**Keywords:** Motor Imagery · Gaussian Process · Classification · Uncertainty Handling · Threshold · Machine Learning

## 1 Introduction

Imagining limb movements without their actual execution is termed Motor Imagery (MI) [21], a cognitive process that has gained prominence in the domain


T. T. Mai et al. (Eds.): AICS 2025, CCIS 2950, pp. 313–323, 2026.
https://doi.org/10.1007/978-3-032-25809-0_25

of Brain-Computer Interface (BCI) systems. MI-BCI systems are operated using the imagination of movements as the input to the system in order to control interfaces [23] and applications. These systems have a profound impact on the field of rehabilitation [8], BCI [1], and sports training [16]. MI activities are typically observed in the range of 8–30 Hz using EEG systems. The increase or decrease in Mu (8–13 Hz) and Beta (13–30 Hz) rhythms causes suppression (ERD) or enhancement (ERS) of the EEG signals, and can be used to identify when the imagination of hand movement occurs. The success of MI BCIs relies heavily on the accurate classification of neural patterns extracted from brain signals acquired using EEG. Through the analysis of neural data, classification algorithms discern distinct patterns corresponding to different motor intentions, thus enabling effective control of external devices.

One of the major challenges in BCI systems is the variations in subject-specific motor imagery signals with a limited dataset, which could either be due to the limitations in the number of trials for training or in the number of subjects. The main drawback of motor imagery classifiers is their sensitivity to noise and variability in EEG signals, which can reduce classification accuracy. These classifiers often require extensive training [1,13] and careful feature extraction [6,18,24] to perform well. Also, these solutions struggle with real-time processing demands due to computational complexity, especially in dynamic or adaptive systems. Precision in classification accuracy is paramount for MI BCIs, as misclassifications can result in incorrect commands being sent to connected devices, compromising the system's reliability and user experience. Therefore, ensuring high precision in classification is imperative to enhance the usability and safety of BCI systems.

Since classifiers have become a focal point of research [14,22], one promising avenue that this work explores is the implementation of Gaussian Processes for robust classification [25]. This work aims to provide a probabilistic framework that could capture uncertainty in Motor Imagery classification, offering better interpretability and confidence in predictions compared to many deterministic classifiers. GPs [7] can model complex, non-linear relationships in the data through their kernel functions(linear, RBF (Radial Basis Function), etc.). This can potentially lead to higher accuracy and robustness in Motor Imagery tasks where signal patterns can be highly variable [10,26]. Furthermore, GPs can facilitate adaptive learning, allowing BCI systems to continually adapt to changes in neural activity patterns, thereby improving overall performance and usability.

GPs have garnered attention as a potential classifier for MI-based BCIs [25, 27], since they aid in setting decision thresholds and model uncertainty, which is inherent in neural data. For instance, Wang et al. implemented GP on BCI on dataset BCI IIIb and reported the prediction time. After these significant contributions, to the best of our knowledge, the field remains largely unexplored for MI. Despite the promise of GPs in improving decision-making and uncertainty quantification for MI-based BCIs, there is still a need for comprehensive studies that thoroughly investigate GP applications across diverse datasets. In order to explore various classes in Motor Imagery with the One-vs-All (OvA) strategy, this work uses the BCI IV-2a dataset. Since the Mean Accuracy of cross-fold validation demonstrates the robustness of the classifier, we report it for binary classification and OvA strategies for every class and explore 3 main kernels, which were not done in previous work. In this study, we implement a Common Spatial Pattern (CSP)-GP-based classification with the motivation of understanding the possibility of application of GPs in the BCI field. Our contributions from this work are: i) application of a GP-based classification for binary classification and OvA strategy, and comparing mean accuracies with state-of-the-art accuracies from different classifiers, and ii) exploring different kernels for CSP-GP.

## 2 Pre-processing and Feature Extraction

### 2.1 Dataset

The BCI IV-2a dataset encompasses EEG recordings from 9 subjects, employing a cue-based MI paradigm featuring four distinct motor imagery tasks. Subjects engaged in the mental simulation of movement for the left hand (Class 1), right hand (Class 2), feet (Class 3), and tongue (Class 4). Recorded over two sessions for each participant, each session comprised 6 runs. Within each run, 48 trials were conducted, with 12 trials for each of the four possible classes, resulting in a cumulative total of 288 trials per session [9].

### 2.2 Experiment

In order to explore and understand the classifier, we perform the following two experiments on the BCI IV-2a dataset.

**Binary Classification.** We classify Binary classes, meaning Left Hand/ Right Hand (LH/RH), Left Hand/Feet (LH/F), Left Hand/Tongue (LH/T), Right Hand/ Feet (RH/F), Right Hand/Tongue (RH/T), and Feet/Tongue (F/T) for all 3 kernels mentioned above.

**One v/s All (OvA).** Here, we perform classification for One v/s all strategy (as one class), meaning Left-Hand v/s other classes (LH/O), Right-Hand v/s other classes (RH/O), Feet v/s other classes (F/O) and Tongue v/s other classes (T/O).

### 2.3 Framework

This section presents the pipeline of our framework, which includes pre-filtering and CSP, followed by the Gaussian Process Classification (GPC) in Sect. 3, as illustrated in Fig. 2.

**Pre-processing.** In the preprocessing phase, a Band-pass filter of 7–32 Hz is employed to mitigate artefacts and enhance the separability of MI conditions. Furthermore, the EEG data is segmented into a time window of 1–4 s after the event has started, and the baseline is set to None. The resulting pre-processed data is then focused on three chosen EEG channels, specifically C3, Cz, and C4, which are most popularly known for Motor Imagery [12]. The data is then passed to the feature extraction phase.

### 2.4 Common Spatial Pattern (CSP)

CSP [5] is a widely used technique for feature extraction and dimensionality reduction in EEG, particularly for MI classification. CSP identifies spatial filters that enhance the discriminative information between two conditions by maximizing the variance of EEG signals in one class and minimizing it in another. To understand CSP, considering one of the classification strategies, for instance, OvA, where, for instance, LH vs. All as discussed in Sect. 2.2

Given the data dimensions:

- **Input data**: $X \in \mathbb{R}^{288\times3\times751}$ (288 events, three channels, and 751 time points),
- **Covariance matrices** $C_1$ and $C_2$ are computed for two classes and are of size $3 \times 3$, representing the covariance across the three EEG channels (C3, Cz, and C4) for each class.

Mathematically, CSP solves the following generalized eigenvalue problem $C_1 = W^TSW, \quad C_2 = W^TS'W$, where $S \in \mathbb{R}^{3\times3}$ and $S' \in \mathbb{R}^{3\times3}$ are the covariance matrices for each class. The objective is then to solve

$$C_1W = \lambda C_2W \tag{1}$$

where $\lambda$ is a diagonal matrix containing the eigenvalues. The spatial filter matrix $W \in \mathbb{R}^{3\times3}$ is obtained by solving this eigenvalue problem. The eigenvectors corresponding to the largest and smallest eigenvalues are selected to derive the most discriminative spatial patterns. After applying CSP, the transformed data $X_{\text{CSP}} \in \mathbb{R}^{288\times2}$ contains the two most discriminative components, one maximizing the variance for the first class and the other for the second class.

## 3 Gaussian Process Classification

GP classification involves modeling the relationship between input data points and their corresponding class labels as a stochastic process [10,26], and offers a principled framework for probabilistic classification, leveraging prior distributions, kernel functions, and Bayesian inference to model complex relationships in data. The mathematical underpinnings of GP classifiers, focusing on the formulation of the prior distribution, kernel functions, and the predictive distribution, have been listed below (Fig. 1).

**Table 1.** Performance Comparison Across Different Tasks and Kernels for Binary Classification

| Task-Kernel | A01 | A02 | A03 | A04 | A05 | A06 | A07 | A08 | A09 | Avg. |
|---|---|---|---|---|---|---|---|---|---|---|
| LH/RH Dot Product | 62.06 | 27.58 | 82.75 | 72.41 | 44.82 | 75.86 | 62.06 | 56.23 | 82.75 | 62.95 |
| LH/RH RBF | 62.06 | 41.37 | 86.20 | 75.86 | 48.27 | 62.06 | 58.62 | 56.23 | 86.20 | 64.10 |
| LH/RH Matérn | 62.06 | 44.87 | 86.20 | 75.86 | 48.27 | 65.51 | 58.21 | 56.23 | 86.20 | 64.82 |
| LH/T Dot Product | 86.20 | 68.96 | 79.31 | 39 | 65.51 | 68.96 | 82.75 | 52.23 | 86.20 | 69.90 |
| LH/T RBF | 86.20 | 72.41 | 75.86 | 41.37 | 65.51 | 68.96 | 82.75 | 52.23 | 89.65 | 70.55 |
| LH/T Matérn | 89.65 | 72.41 | 75.86 | 41.37 | 65.51 | 68.96 | 82.75 | 52.23 | 89.65 | 70.93 |
| LH/F Dot Product | 93.10 | 65.51 | 93.10 | 65.51 | 55.17 | 75.86 | 82.75 | 86.20 | 89.65 | 78.54 |
| LH/F RBF | 93.10 | 68.95 | 93.10 | 65.51 | 62.06 | 75.86 | 82.75 | 86.20 | 89.65 | 79.69 |
| LH/F Matérn | 96.55 | 68.96 | 93.10 | 62.06 | 65.51 | 72.41 | 82.75 | 86.20 | 89.65 | 79.69 |
| RH/T Dot Product | 89.65 | 96.55 | 75.86 | 34.48 | 37.93 | 72.41 | 79.31 | 55.17 | 55.17 | 66.28 |
| RH/T RBF | 89.65 | 93.10 | 75.86 | 37.93 | 41.37 | 79.31 | 79.31 | 55.17 | 55.17 | 67.43 |
| RH/T Matérn | 89.65 | 89.65 | 75.86 | 37.93 | 41.37 | 72.41 | 79.31 | 55.17 | 58.62 | 66.66 |
| RH/F Dot Product | 93.10 | 55.17 | 86.20 | 41.37 | 41.37 | 75.86 | 89.65 | 82.75 | 79.31 | 71.64 |
| RH/F RBF | 93.10 | 62.06 | 82.75 | 41.37 | 48.27 | 72.41 | 89.65 | 82.75 | 75.86 | 72.02 |
| RH/F Matérn | 93.10 | 65.51 | 82.75 | 41.37 | 48.27 | 75.86 | 89.65 | 82.75 | 75.86 | 72.79 |
| T/F Dot Product | 72.41 | 86.20 | 79.31 | 24.13 | 41.37 | 62.06 | 82.70 | 82.70 | 68.96 | 66.65 |
| T/F RBF | 72.41 | 86.20 | 79.31 | 34.48 | 37.93 | 65.51 | 79.31 | 79.31 | 68.96 | 67.05 |
| T/F Matérn | 68.96 | 86.20 | 79.31 | 37.93 | 37.93 | 51.72 | 79.31 | 76.31 | 68.96 | 65.18 |

**Table 2.** Performance Comparison Across Different Tasks and Kernels for OvA

| Kernel/Task | A01 | A02 | A03 | A04 | A05 | A06 | A07 | A08 | A09 | Avg |
|---|---|---|---|---|---|---|---|---|---|---|
| LH/O Dot Product | 75.86 | 75.86 | 82.76 | 75.86 | 75.86 | 75.86 | 84.48 | 82.76 | 82.76 | 77.68 |
| RH/O Dot Product | 77.59 | 74.14 | 89.66 | 70.69 | 68.97 | 72.41 | 75.86 | 79.31 | 70.69 | 75.48 |
| T/O Dot Product | 75.86 | 86.21 | 75.86 | 75.86 | 75.86 | 75.86 | 75.86 | 75.86 | 74.14 | 76.82 |
| F/O Dot Product | 86.21 | 75.86 | 75.86 | 75.86 | 75.86 | 75.86 | 81.03 | 87.93 | 79.31 | 79.31 |
| LH/O RBF | 84.48 | 75.86 | 84.48 | 75.86 | 75.86 | 75.86 | 86.21 | 82.76 | 75.86 | 79.69 |
| RH/O RBF | 79.31 | 75.86 | 93.10 | 67.24 | 75.86 | 72.41 | 82.76 | 74.14 | 75.86 | 77.39 |
| T/O RBF | 84.48 | 87.93 | 75.86 | 75.86 | 75.86 | 75.86 | 75.86 | 75.86 | 75.86 | 78.16 |
| F/O RBF | 86.20 | 75.86 | 82.75 | 75.86 | 75.86 | 75.86 | 81.03 | 87.93 | 79.31 | 80.07 |
| LH/O Matérn | 86.21 | 75.86 | 84.48 | 75.86 | 75.86 | 75.86 | 82.76 | 86.21 | 81.03 | 79.36 |
| RH/O Matérn | 82.76 | 75.86 | 93.10 | 75.86 | 75.86 | 72.41 | 81.03 | 75.86 | 75.86 | 78.73 |
| T/O Matérn | 84.48 | 84.48 | 75.86 | 75.86 | 75.86 | 75.86 | 75.86 | 75.86 | 75.86 | 77.78 |
| F/O Matérn | 86.21 | 79.31 | 82.76 | 75.86 | 75.86 | 75.86 | 81.03 | 87.93 | 79.31 | 80.46 |

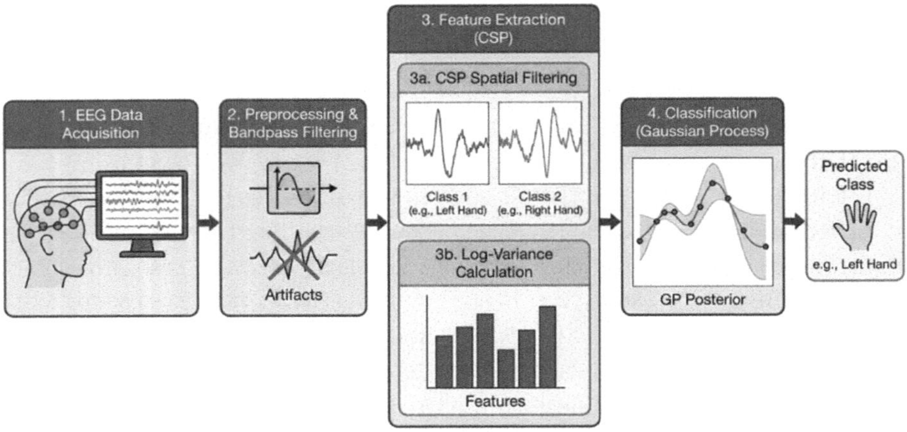


**Fig. 1.** Pipeline for GP-based classification.

**Prior Distribution.** At the heart of a Gaussian Process is the prior distribution over functions, which encapsulates our beliefs about the underlying structure of the data before observing any training examples. Mathematically, a GP prior is defined as:

$$f(\mathbf{x}) \sim \mathcal{GP}(m(\mathbf{x}), k(\mathbf{x}, \mathbf{x}')), \tag{2}$$

where $m(\mathbf{x})$ is the mean function, and $k(\mathbf{x}, \mathbf{x}')$ is the covariance (kernel) function.

**Kernel Functions.** The kernel function is fundamental in defining the covariance structure between different input data points in Gaussian Processes. It allows the model to capture various types of relationships and dependencies between the data. Commonly used kernel functions include the Radial Basis Function (RBF) kernel, the Matérn kernel, and the Dot Product kernel.

The RBF kernel, also known as the Gaussian kernel, is defined as:

$$k(\mathbf{x}, \mathbf{x}') = \sigma^2 \exp\left(-\frac{\|\mathbf{x} - \mathbf{x}'\|^2}{2l^2}\right) \tag{3}$$

where $\sigma^2$ controls the overall variance of the functions, and $l$ determines the length scale, regulating the smoothness of the sampled functions. The RBF kernel assumes that the covariance between two points decreases exponentially with their distance, providing a smooth and continuous function.

The Matérn kernel is a generalization of the RBF kernel that introduces an additional parameter $\nu$ to control the smoothness of the function. It is defined as:

$$k(\mathbf{x}, \mathbf{x}') = \sigma^2 \frac{2^{1-\nu}}{\Gamma(\nu)} \left( \frac{\sqrt{2\nu} \|\mathbf{x} - \mathbf{x}'\|}{l} \right)^{\nu} K_{\nu} \left( \frac{\sqrt{2\nu} \|\mathbf{x} - \mathbf{x}'\|}{l} \right) \tag{4}$$

where $K_\nu$ is the modified Bessel function of the second kind, $\Gamma(\nu)$ is the gamma function, $\sigma^2$ is the variance, $l$ is the length scale, and $\nu$ controls the smoothness. The Matérn kernel allows for varying degrees of differentiability and smoothness, making it flexible for different types of data.

The Dot Product kernel, also known as the Linear kernel, is defined as:

$$k(\mathbf{x}, \mathbf{x}') = \mathbf{x}^T \mathbf{x}' + c \tag{5}$$

where $c$ is a constant that controls the offset. This kernel measures the similarity between two vectors as the inner product and is useful for modelling linear relationships in the data. It assumes that the covariance between two points is directly proportional to their dot product, making it a straightforward choice for linear patterns.

**Predictive Distribution.** Given a set of training data points $\mathbf{X} = \{\mathbf{x}_1, \mathbf{x}_2, ..., \mathbf{x}_N\}$ and corresponding class labels $\mathbf{y} = \{y_1, y_2, ..., y_N\}$, the goal of GP classification is to infer the posterior distribution over functions conditioned on the observed data. The predictive distribution for a new input data point $\mathbf{x}_*$ is given by:

$$p(y_*|\mathbf{x}_*, \mathbf{X}, \mathbf{y}) = \int p(y_*|\mathbf{x}_*, f) p(f|\mathbf{X}, \mathbf{y}) df \tag{6}$$

where $p(y_*|\mathbf{x}_*, f)$ is the likelihood function capturing the relationship between function values and class labels, and $p(f|\mathbf{X}, \mathbf{y})$ is the posterior distribution over functions obtained through Bayesian inference.

**Threshold Setting and Decision Making.** In practice, GP classifiers provide probabilistic predictions in the form of class probabilities for each input data point. To make binary classification decisions, a decision threshold $\tau$ is typically applied to the predicted probabilities. For instance, if $p(y = 1|\mathbf{x}) > \tau$, the input data point is classified as belonging to class 1; otherwise, it is classified as belonging to class 0.

The pre-processing and feature extraction are done using MNE Python [11], and Gaussian Process Classification is implemented using the Gaussian Process Classifier Library provided by sklearn [20].

A $10 \times 10$ cross-validation procedure was conducted, and mean accuracies were reported as the evaluation metric for all experiments described in Sect. 2.2. CV corresponds to repeated 10-fold CV, where each repetition reshuffles the dataset before splitting. Hyperparameter selection is restricted strictly to the training folds of each split.

Hyperparameter tuning was performed over the ranges specified below, with the number of CSP spatial components fixed to 2. For the RBF and Matérn kernels, the length-scale ($l$) and signal variance ($\sigma^2$) were searched within 0.1–10.0, and the Matérn smoothness parameter ($\nu$) within 0.5–2.5. A grid search was used to optimise kernel hyperparameters, and this tuning was nested within the CV procedure.

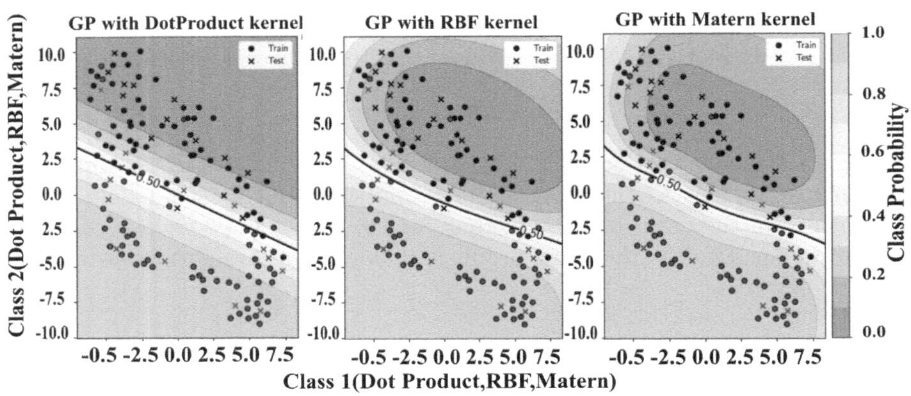


**Fig. 2.** RBF, Matérn and Dot Product Kernel representation for Train and Test data together with threshold = 0.5 for Subject A09.

**Table 3.** Comparison of Mean Accuracy (MA) (%) for BCI4-2a using CSP with different classifiers for OvA Strategy

| Work | Classifier | MA (%) |
|---|---|---|
| Yang et al. [4] | CSP+SVM | 62.23 |
| | CSP+LSTM | 66.67 |
| Yang [2] | CSP+Random Forest | 71.35 |
| | CSP+LSTM-CNN | 66.63 |
| | CSP+SCS-CNN | 74.54 |
| **Proposed Work** | **CSP+GP** | **78.41** |

# 4 Results

We now present the results of applying various Gaussian Process kernels for classification based on the dataset described in Sect. 2.1.

**Comparison with Other Classifiers.** The proposed work using CSP+GP achieves a significantly higher mean accuracy of 78.41%, outperforming previous methods such as CSP+LSTM, CSP+SVM, CSP+Random Forest, CSP+LSTM-CNN, CSP+SCS-CNN (74.41%). This suggests that the CSP+GP approach provides a more effective classification for OvA strategy as shown in Table 3.

**Binary Classification.** The performance comparison across different tasks and kernels reveals that the Matérn kernel generally outperforms the RBF and Dot Product kernels, with slightly higher average accuracy across most tasks. Specifically, for the Left/Right task, the Matérn kernel achieves an average accuracy of 64.82%, which is marginally better than the RBF kernel's 64.10% and the Dot Product kernel's 62.95%. Similar trends are observed in the Left/Tongue and Left/Feet tasks, where the Matérn kernel consistently shows superior performance with average accuracies of 70.93% and 79.69%, respectively. However, the differences between kernels are subtle, indicating that all three kernels are relatively effective for the classification tasks. The most significant variance is seen in the Tongue/Feet task, where the RBF kernel performs slightly better with an average accuracy of 67.05%, compared to the Matérn kernel's 65.18% and the Dot Product kernel's 66.65%. Also within groups, the best overall performance is seen when Feet are classified with Left and Right hand individually, as shown in Table 1.

**OvA.** Table 2 shows the performance of three kernels (RBF, Matérn, DotProduct) across various tasks (LH/O, RH/O, T/O, F/O) for nine participants. On average, the Feet/All task consistently performed the best across all kernels, with the highest average accuracy observed for the Matérn kernel at 80.46%. The DotProduct kernel generally showed lower performance, particularly for the Right/All task, with an average accuracy of 75.48%, which is about 3% lower than the Matérn kernel. The RBF and Matérn kernels performed similarly, with the RBF kernel slightly outperforming Matérn in the Feet/All task (80.07% vs. 79.36%). These results suggest that the choice of kernel and task significantly affects classification performance, with some tasks (like F/O) benefiting more from certain kernels. No significant difference in performance across different kernels ($p = 0.2068$); however, statistical significance is seen within subjects ($p < 0.001$) using a paired t-test followed by Repeated Measures ANOVA.

## 5 Discussion and Conclusion

Despite the GP-based classification not outperforming other classifiers for LH/RH (64.82%), for instance CSP+mLC [19] (68.36%), and state-of-the-art deep learning multiclass classifiers performing extremely well, such as Autoselected FBRCSP [3] (77.31%), EEGNet [15] (78.90%), and EEG-DBNet [17] (85.87%), the motivation to explore GP lies in its inherent ability to provide uncertainty estimates, flexibility in kernel design, and its potential for better generalization in cases where limited labeled data is available. Although GPs have been explored earlier for Motor Imagery Classification [25, 27], kernel exploration may later open revenues for robust GP-based Deep Learning models for classification.

In summary, our study explores and demonstrates that GPs enhance classification accuracy for OvA MI classification compared to most traditional classifiers. The Matérn kernel consistently outperformed others in most tasks, reflecting its superior capability in handling the variability in neural data. While kernel differences were not statistically significant across the group, strong within-subject effects ($p < 0.001$) highlight the adaptability of GPs for personalized BCI. Notably, feet-related tasks achieved the highest accuracies (80.07%), suggesting task-specific advantages of GP-based models. These findings underscore the effectiveness of integrating GP with diverse kernels to improve MI-based BCI systems' performance and reliability. Future work in this field could explore GP-based classification and kernels for modality-based Transfer Learning.

**Acknowledgments.** This publication has emanated from research supported by grants from Science Foundation Ireland under grant numbers 18/CRT/6183, SFI/12/RC/2289_P2. The Authors would like to thank Dr. Raj Thilak Rajan, Faculty of EEMCS, Delft University of Technology, Netherlands, for valuable insights on GP.

## References

1. Al-Qaysi, Z., et al.: A systematic rank of smart training environment applications with motor imagery brain-computer interface. Multimedia Tools Appl. **82**(12), 17905–17927 (2023)
2. An, Y.: Development of advanced machine learning based EEG robot for disabled people. University of Technology Sydney (Australia) (2022)
3. An, Y., Han, S.H., Ling, S.H.: Multi-classification for EEG motor imagery signals using auto-selected filter bank regularized common spatial pattern. In: 2022 IEEE 16th International Symposium on Medical Information and Communication Technology (ISMICT), pp. 1–6. IEEE (2022)
4. An, Y., Lam, H.K., Ling, S.H.: Multi-classification for EEG motor imagery signals using data evaluation-based auto-selected regularized FBCSP and convolutional neural network. Neural Comput. Appl. **35**(16), 12001–12027 (2023)
5. Ang, K.K., Chin, Z.Y., Zhang, H., Guan, C.: Filter bank common spatial pattern (FBCSP) in brain-computer interface. In: 2008 IEEE International Joint Conference on Neural Networks (IEEE World Congress on Computational Intelligence), pp. 2390–2397. IEEE (2008)
6. Baberwal, S.S., Ward, T., Coyle, S.: Single channel-based motor imagery classification using Fisher's ratio and pearson correlation. arXiv preprint arXiv:2406.14179 (2024)
7. Ban, H., Riemens, E.H., Rajan, R.T.: Malleable kernel interpolation for scalable structured gaussian process (2023)
8. Binks, J.A., Emerson, J.R., Scott, M.W., Wilson, C., Van Schaik, P., Eaves, D.L.: Enhancing upper-limb neurorehabilitation in chronic stroke survivors using combined action observation and motor imagery therapy. Front. Neurol. **14**, 1097422 (2023)
9. Brunner, C., Leeb, R., Müller-Putz, G., Schlögl, A., Pfurtscheller, G.: BCI competition 2008–Graz data set A. Institute for Knowledge Discovery (Laboratory of Brain-Computer Interfaces), Graz University of Technology **16**, 1–6 (2008)
10. Gibbs, M.N., MacKay, D.J.: Variational Gaussian process classifiers. IEEE Trans. Neural Networks **11**(6), 1458–1464 (2000)
11. Gramfort, A., et al.: MEG and EEG data analysis with MNE-Python. Front. Neurosci. **7**(267), 1–13 (2013). https://doi.org/10.3389/fnins.2013.00267

12. Hu, S., Wang, H., Zhang, J., Kong, W., Cao, Y.: Causality from CZ to C3/C4 or between C3 and C4 revealed by granger causality and new causality during motor imagery. In: 2014 International Joint Conference on Neural Networks (IJCNN), pp. 3178–3185. IEEE (2014)
13. Kodama, M., Iwama, S., Morishige, M., Ushiba, J.: Thirty-minute motor imagery exercise aided by EEG sensorimotor rhythm neurofeedback enhances morphing of sensorimotor cortices: a double-blind sham-controlled study. Cereb. Cortex **33**(11), 6573–6584 (2023)
14. Kumari, A., et al.: EEG-based motor imagery channel selection and classification using hybrid optimization and two-tier deep learning. J. Neurosci. Methods **409**, 110215 (2024)
15. Lawhern, V.J., Solon, A.J., Waytowich, N.R., Gordon, S.M., Hung, C.P., Lance, B.J.: EEGNet: a compact convolutional neural network for EEG-based brain-computer interfaces. J. Neural Eng. **15**(5), 056013 (2018)
16. Lindsay, R.S., Larkin, P., Kittel, A., Spittle, M.: Mental imagery training programs for developing sport-specific motor skills: a systematic review and meta-analysis. Phys. Educ. Sport Pedagog. **28**(4), 444–465 (2023)
17. Lou, X., et al.: EEG-DBNet: a dual-branch network for motor-imagery brain-computer interfaces. arXiv preprint arXiv:2405.16090 (2024)
18. Miao, Z., Zhao, M.: Time-space-frequency feature fusion for 3-channel motor imagery classification. Biomed. Signal Process. Control **90**, 105867 (2024)
19. Oikonomou, V.P., Nikolopoulos, S., Kompatsiaris, I.: A multitask Bayesian framework for the analysis of motor imagery EEG data. In: 2022 30th European Signal Processing Conference (EUSIPCO), pp. 1308–1312. IEEE (2022)
20. Pedregosa, F.: Scikit-learn: Machine learning in Python Fabian. J. Mach. Learn. Res. **12**, 2825 (2011)
21. Pfurtscheller, G., Neuper, C.: Motor imagery activates primary sensorimotor area in humans. Neurosci. Lett. **239**(2–3), 65–68 (1997)
22. Rosenfelder, M.J., et al.: Stability of mental motor-imagery classification in eeg depends on the choice of classifier model and experiment design, but not on signal preprocessing. Front. Comput. Neurosci. **17**, 1142948 (2023)
23. Stölzle, M., Baberwal, S.S., Rus, D., Coyle, S., Della Santina, C.: Guiding soft robots with motor-imagery brain signals and impedance control. arXiv preprint arXiv:2401.13441 (2024)
24. Tang, X., Yang, C., Sun, X., Zou, M., Wang, H.: Motor imagery EEG decoding based on multi-scale hybrid networks and feature enhancement. IEEE Trans. Neural Syst. Rehabil. Eng. **31**, 1208–1218 (2023)
25. Wang, B., Wan, F., Mak, P.U., Mak, P.I., Vai, M.I.: EEG signals classification for brain computer interfaces based on gaussian process classifier. In: 2009 7th International Conference on Information, Communications and Signal Processing (ICICS), pp. 1–5. IEEE (2009)
26. Williams, C.K., Rasmussen, C.E.: Gaussian Processes for Machine Learning, vol. 2. MIT Press, Cambridge (2006)
27. Zhong, M., Lotte, F., Girolami, M., Lécuyer, A.: Classifying EEG for brain computer interfaces using gaussian processes. Pattern Recogn. Lett. **29**(3), 354–359 (2008)

# Synthetic Data for PET and HDPE Classification: A Comparison of Diffusion and Autoregressive Models

Vimal Kumar Kumar[1,2], Gauri Vaidya[2,3](✉), Deepankur Lohiya[1], Conor Ryan[1,2], and Meghana Kshirsagar[1,2]

[1] Department of Computer Science and Information Systems, University of Limerick, Limerick, Ireland

[2] Lero – The Research Ireland Centre for Software, Limerick, Ireland
gauri.vaidya@ul.ie

[3] School of Medicine, University of Limerick, Limerick, Ireland

**Abstract.** Marine plastic pollution poses a significant environmental threat, with polyethylene terephthalate (PET) and high-density polyethylene (HDPE) debris among the most prevalent yet difficult to detect in complex underwater environments. Deep learning models for automated detection are often limited by scarce, imbalanced, or hard-to-collect underwater datasets. This study investigates the use of state-of-the-art generative artificial intelligence models to create synthetic underwater images of plastic debris. Two paradigms were compared: a transformer-based autoregressive model (DALLE-3) and a denoising diffusion model (Stable Diffusion XL, SDXL). A structured prompt engineering workflow was developed to encode object features, environmental context, spectral cues, and biotic interactions.

The resulting datasets were used to train ResNet18, ResNet50, and ResNeXt50 classifiers under two experimental setups: single-phase and two-phase training. In single-phase training, only the classification head was optimized, while in two-phase training the final layer was additionally unfrozen and trained jointly with the head. Comprehensive performance evaluation was conducted using accuracy, precision, recall, F1-score, SSIM, CLIP score using real-world datasets. Additionally, human evaluation to score synthetic and real images was collected through a survey. As evidenced through results diffusion-generated images enabled better classifier generalization than DALLE-3, specifically in recall and F1-score. Among classifiers, ResNet50 achieved the most balanced performance.

The findings highlight the potential of diffusion-based synthetic data generation as a supplement for training deep learning models for data scarcity underwater plastic detection. More broadly, the study demonstrates how structured prompt engineering and generative AI can help overcome data scarcity challenges.

**Keywords:** Synthetic data generation · Marine environment · Diffusion models · PET and HDPE · Plastic pollution


T. T. Mai et al. (Eds.): AICS 2025, CCIS 2950, pp. 324–335, 2026.
https://doi.org/10.1007/978-3-032-25809-0_26

## 1 Introduction

Plastic pollution in aquatic environments has become an urgent global concern, with microplastics posing long-term ecological and human-health risks. Global plastic production has reached 430–460 million tonnes and may rise to $\approx 736$ million tonnes by 2040 without stronger policies. Studies of marine debris consistently show that a large proportion of indicate that this pollution is dominated by short-lived consumer plastics, particularly packaging materials,which account for approximately 40% of global plastic demand and are predominantly composed of Polyethylene Terephthalate (PET) and High-Density Polyethylene (HDPE). Consequently, these polymers are among the most frequently detected in aquatic plastic pollution, making their accurate identification essential for effective monitoring and mitigation strategies [9].

Remote sensing and imaging advances have enabled non-invasive detection of plastic litter. Hyperspectral imaging (HSI), for example, has shown high accuracy in classifying plastics via unmanned aquatic drones and aerial surveys, leveraging distinct spectral signatures across visible and infrared ranges [1,2]. However, most studies focus on surface or aerial contexts rather than submerged conditions, where absorption, scattering, and distortion reduce observability [5,18]. Underwater imaging faces additional challenges: turbidity, suspended particulates, biofouling, and illumination changes degrade reflectance signals, necessitating corrective preprocessing and calibration [2,6,13,21]. Dataset imbalance compounds these issues, as polymers like PET often dominate, biasing classifiers and limiting generalisation [4,7,19]. Moreover, high-resolution HSI demands substantial memory and compute, restricting large-scale experimentation and deployment [4].

Generative AI provides a solution to address data scarcity, imbalance, and computational constraints through synthetic generation of images. However, the relative effectiveness of diffusion and autoregressive models, particularly in generating subtype-specific plastics such as PET and HDPE, remains unexplored. This study systematically investigates their potential through the following research questions:

**RQ1:** How do different image generation paradigms (diffusion vs. autoregressive models) affect the downstream utility of synthetic PET and HDPE plastic debris images for training deep CNN classifiers (ResNet-50, ResNet-18, ResNeXt-50) in marine environments?

**RQ2:** To what extent do synthetic images of PET and HDPE plastic debris, generated by diffusion and autoregressive models, enhance the generalization capability of image classifiers?

## 2 Literature Review

Curating datasets is a central challenge to identify plastics from images. Different approaches have been explored to generate such datasets, each with its own strengths and limitations. Broadly, these can be grouped into four categories: laboratory studies, field surveys, underwater acquisition, and synthetic data generation.

In controlled laboratory settings, plastics can be tested under standardised lighting and measurement conditions. These studies show that polymers have distinct reflectance profiles, which makes them separable at the spectral level [10, 18]. The advantage of such datasets is that they provide clean "ground truth" data and allow systematic testing of wavelength bands and features. However, they may not capture the variability found in real-world environments, which limits their direct transferability.

At a larger scale, HSI pipelines have been used on the water's surface or from the air to capture floating plastic debris [1, 2]. These datasets are valuable because they provide representative coverage of large areas under good optical conditions. Yet, they depend heavily on stable illumination and clear water, which restricts their applicability in more challenging or variable settings.

Collecting plastic data underwater is particularly difficult. The water medium causes absorption, scattering, and changes in illumination, all of which reduce the quality of spectral signals [6, 20, 21]. To compensate, specialised lighting and optics are needed, and polymer labels often require confirmation with spectroscopy [5]. These constraints make underwater datasets expensive, sparse, and sometimes biased toward common polymers like PET.

To overcome the lack of balanced, diverse data, augmentation and synthetic generation methods have been explored. Traditional approaches focus on balancing class composition and enriching the dataset through artificial transformations [7, 13]. More recent studies combine lightweight models with tailored augmentation to improve classification in skewed datasets [4, 19]. Beyond this diffusion models has shown promise in creating synthetic hyperspectral data that reflects both spectral and textural properties [3]. In short, laboratory and aerial surveys provide controlled or large-scale data but lack real-world variability, while underwater datasets remain scarce and costly. Synthetic approaches help bridge these gaps by generating diverse and balanced images.

# 3 Methodology

The proposed study introduces a workflow for generating and evaluating synthetic underwater datasets for PET and HDPE classification (Fig. 1). The pipeline begins with human-guided prompt engineering, where domain knowledge is formalised into structured textual prompts. These prompts are provided to two generative AI architectures, DALLE-3 and SDXL, to create synthetic underwater images with PET and HDPE plastic debris types. The resulting datasets are then used to train three image classifiers (ResNet18, ResNet50, and ResNeXt50), and performance is assessed against an external real-world dataset using accuracy, precision, recall, and F1-score metrics.

## 3.1 Image Generators

DALLE-3 [12] is a transformer-based autoregressive model that generates images by predicting discrete tokens sequentially from textual prompts. In this study, it was accessed through the ChatGPT interface, which limited control over generation parameters such as sampling steps, temperature, and guidance scaling. As a result, refinement relied on iterative prompt modification and selective re-generation.

SDXL [11] is a denoising diffusion model that synthesizes images by iteratively transforming Gaussian noise under prompt conditioning. Implemented via the InvokeAI interface, it provided explicit control over denoising steps, classifier-free guidance scale (parameter that controls how closely generated images follow the text prompt), sampler type, resolution, and the influence of reference images.

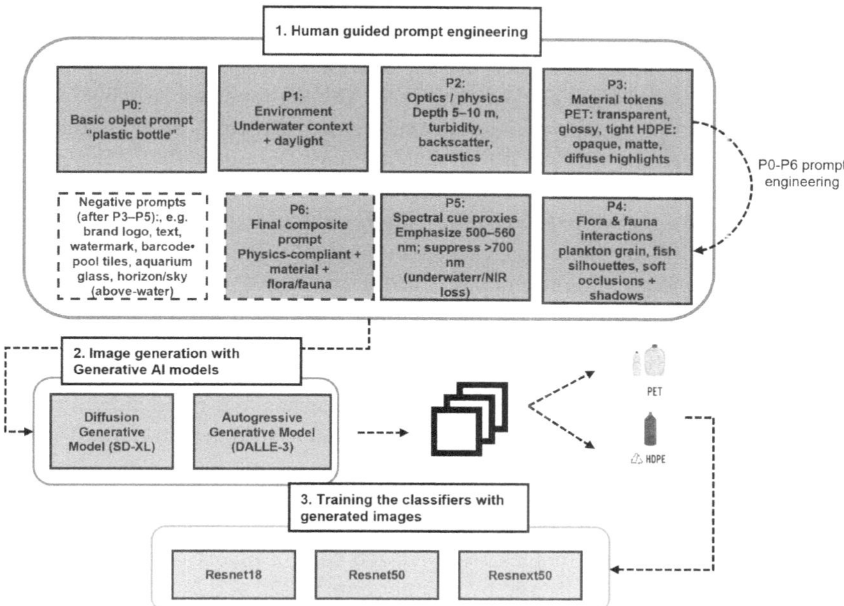


**Fig. 1.** Overview of the proposed experimental workflow for synthetic underwater PET and HDPE image generation and evaluation.

## 3.2 Prompt Engineering Workflow

The image generation design was driven by prompt engineering, which followed a structured, iterative process (Fig. 1, Step 1) (P0–P6). The steps builds from *basic object definitions (P0)* with progressivley scaling to include environmental and object specific features, such as *environmental context (P1)*, *optical/physical parameters (P2)*, *material-specific tokens (P3)*, *biotic interactions (P4)*, and *spectral cues (P5)*. An optional *final composite stage (P6)* combined these elements into physics-compliant prompts that integrated materials, flora/fauna, and spectral descriptors. Negative prompts were systematically applied after P3–P5 to discard artefacts (e.g., logos, watermarks, non-plastic materials, and unrealistic lighting). These were primarily supported in diffusion model interfaces, whereas DALLE-3 required exclusion terms to be embedded directly within positive prompts.

# 4 Experimental Setup

## 4.1 Dataset Details

For each model (SDXL and DALLE-3), 50 images were generated separately for each of the two target classes, PET and HDPE. resulting in 100 synthetic images for each generator with a total of 200 synthetic images. Image generation followed the staged prompt engineering strategy described in Sect. 3, which encoded class-specific characteristics, environmental context, and spectral cues. Although spectral cues were encoded textually during prompt engineering, the current evaluation focuses on RGB image classification. The Underwater PET–HDPE Synthetic Image Dataset (UPHSID) is available as an open-source dataset on Zenodo [8].

The synthetic datasets were used exclusively for model training and validation. For each generator, the 100 synthetic images were divided into 80:20 training and validation splits, maintaining balanced representation of PET and HDPE in both partitions.

To evaluate generalization beyond the generative domain, a small real-world dataset of plastic waste images was incorporated as an external benchmark [14–17]. This publicly available repository contains 405 RGB and 405 (red, green, near-infrared) RGNIR images, collected in public environments such as beaches and riverbanks. From this repository, 10 images per class were randomly sampled to form a held-out test set. This real-world subset was reserved entirely for testing and was not used during training or validation.

Prior to classifier training and evaluation, all images were processed using a standard preprocessing pipeline. Images were resized to 232 pixels on the shorter edge using bilinear interpolation, followed by a center crop to $224 \times 224$ pixels, corresponding to the canonical input size for ResNet and ResNeXt architectures. The cropped images were converted to tensors with pixel values scaled to the range [0, 1] and subsequently normalized using the ImageNet mean and standard deviation (mean = [0.485, 0.456, 0.406]; std = [0.229, 0.224, 0.225]), ensuring compatibility with pre-trained model weights.

## 4.2 Classifier Architecture and Training Setups

Three convolutional neural networks were employed for classification: ResNet-18, ResNet-50, and ResNeXt, each initialized with pretrained ImageNet weights. The standard classification head was replaced with a custom multilayer module tailored for binary discrimination between PET and HDPE. Specifically, the feature vector output from the model was projected into 512 dimensions via a fully connected layer, followed by a ReLU activation and a dropout layer with a rate of 0.5 to mitigate overfitting. This representation was progressively reduced through layers of size 256 and 128, each with ReLU activations, before a final linear layer mapped the 128-dimensional vector to two logits corresponding to the target classes. The logits were passed to a CrossEntropy loss function for optimization.

All models were trained using the Adam optimizer, learning rate = $1 \times 10^{-4}$ and weight decay = $1 \times 10^{-3}$. To mitigate class imbalance, class-specific weights were incorporated into the *CrossEntropy* loss. A *ReduceLROnPlateau* scheduler dynamically adjusted the learning rate, halving it when the validation F1-score failed to improve for five epochs. All models were trained for 25 epochs with early stopping based on validation performance. Two classifier training setups were designed:

- **Single-phase training.** The pretrained model was kept frozen, and only the custom classification head was trained, evaluating how well fixed pretrained features could classify the synthetic datasets.
- **Two-phase training.** Training began as in the single-phase setup, with only the classification head tuned. In the second phase, the final layer of the model was unfrozen and trained jointly with the head, enabling adaptation of high-level features to the synthetic data while earlier layers remained frozen.

# 5 Results and Discussions

To evaluate the quality of synthetic PET and HDPE images, we trained three CNN classifiers (ResNet18, ResNet50, and ResNeXt50) under single- and two-phase training strategies. All experiments were conducted on an NVIDIA A100 GPU with Pytorch and Python 3.12.

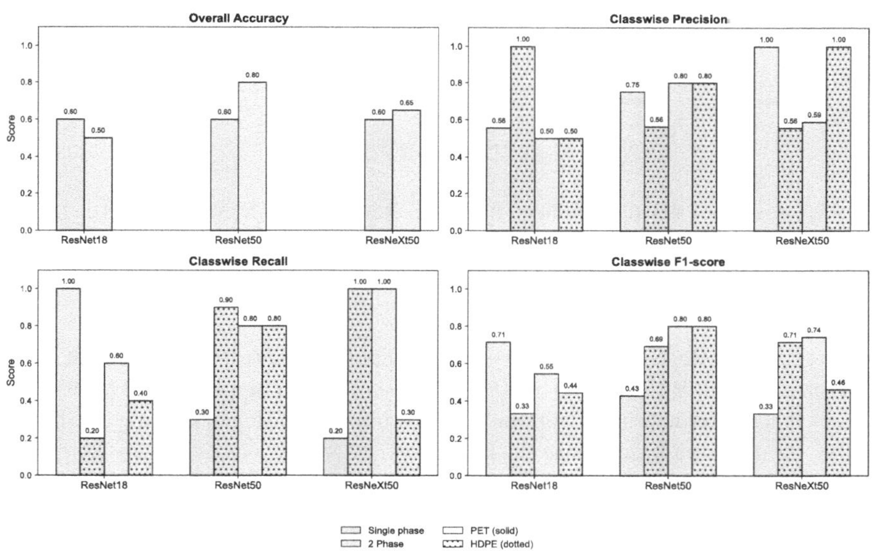


**Fig. 2.** Performance of ResNet classifiers (ResNet18, ResNet50, ResNeXt50) trained on SDXL-generated PET and HDPE images under single- and two-phase training, reported in terms of accuracy, precision, recall, and F1-score. (Color figure online)

## 5.1 SDXL (Diffusion-Generated Images)

The performance of classifiers trained on SDXL-generated images is shown in Fig. 2 where blue and orange bars denote single-phase and two-phase training, respectively, while solid and dotted bars indicate PET and HDPE classes. Overall, diffusion data enabled higher scores across models, particularly when combined with two-phase training.

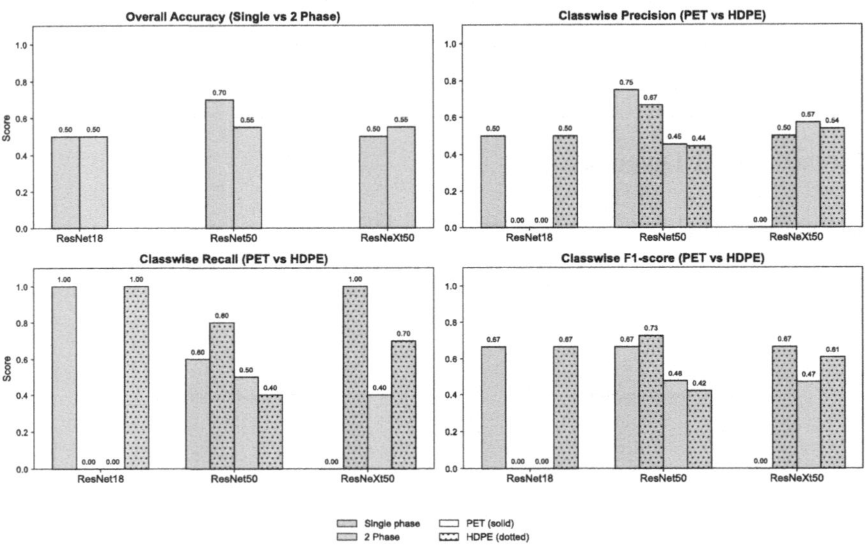


**Fig. 3.** Performance of ResNet classifiers (ResNet18, ResNet50, ResNeXt50) trained on DALLE-generated PET and HDPE images under single- and two-phase training, reported in terms of accuracy, precision, recall, and F1-score.

For accuracy, ResNet50 with two-phase training achieved the best result (0.80), outperforming both ResNet18 (0.50–0.60) and ResNeXt50 (approximately 0.65). This indicates that deeper neural network models combined with staged training are the most effective for diffusion-based data.

Precision results show a clear difference between classes. PET consistently achieved very high precision, often close to 1.0, suggesting that PET features generated by SDXL are highly distinctive. HDPE precision was more variable: low for ResNet18 (0.20–0.40) but improving to 0.80–0.90 with ResNet50, showing that deeper networks are needed for reliable HDPE classification.

Recall followed a similar trend. PET recall ranged from 0.75 to 1.0, confirming strong coverage, while HDPE recall remained weaker (0.50–0.59), suggesting that synthetic HDPE samples were less diverse or less representative.

The F1-scores reflected these differences. ResNet50 with two-phase training achieved the most balanced results (0.69–0.80 across both classes), while ResNet18 and ResNeXt50 showed a clear disparity: PET F1 was strong (0.71), but HDPE F1 remained much lower (0.33–0.46).

## 5.2 DALLE (Autoregressive-Generated Images)

The performance of classifiers trained on DALLE-generated images is summarized in Fig. 3. Compared to SDXL, overall scores were more modest, and the benefits of two-phase training were less pronounced.

For accuracy, ResNet50 achieved the highest value (0.70 in single-phase), while ResNeXt50 and ResNet18 reached only around 0.55 and 0.50, respectively. Unlike SDXL, staged training did not yield a large improvement, suggesting that autoregressive images provide less benefit from fine-tuning.

Precision was more balanced between PET and HDPE. ResNet50 again performed best, with PET precision around 0.75 and HDPE precision at 0.67, while ResNeXt50 reached moderate values (0.54–0.57). Unlike SDXL, where PET dominated, DALLE produced a more consistent distribution across classes, though at lower peak values.

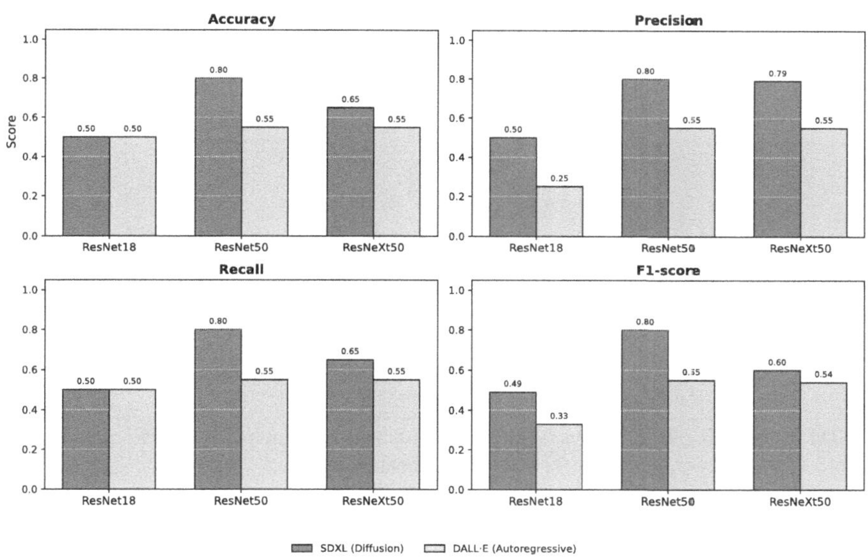


**Fig. 4.** Overall performance comparison of ResNet classifiers trained using two-phase setups on SDXL- and DALLE-generated synthetic images, evaluated on a real-world PET and HDPE test dataset.

Recall patterns reinforced this observation. ResNet50 achieved PET recall of 0.60–0.80 and HDPE recall of 0.40–0.50, while ResNeXt50 maintained moderate recall across both classes (0.40–0.70). ResNet18 struggled, with PET recall dropping to 0.0 under single-phase training, showing complete failure to detect PET in that setting.

The F1-scores followed these trends. ResNet50 achieved the strongest balance (PET F1 around 0.73, HDPE F1 0.48–0.50), while ResNeXt50 produced moderate but consistent values (0.42–0.61). ResNet18 again underperformed, with PET F1 collapsing to zero in single-phase training.

Overall, DALLE generated images that produced more balanced PET and HDPE performance, but at lower overall scores compared to SDXL. This suggests that while autoregressive generation supports consistency between classes, diffusion models provide higher-fidelity PET samples that drive stronger peak performance.

## 5.3 Generalization Capability of Image Classifiers

The performance of classifiers trained on two-phase setups with SDXL and DALLE synthetic data is shown in Fig. 4. The results indicate a consistent advantage for SDXL across all CNN models.

ResNet50 achieved the strongest results with SDXL, reaching 0.80 in accuracy, precision, recall, and F1-score. This shows that deeper models combined with diffusion data can extract more reliable features. ResNeXt50 also followed this trend, with higher precision (0.79) and recall (0.65) under SDXL compared to DALLE, where both metrics dropped to 0.55. In contrast, ResNet18 underperformed in both settings, with the largest gap in precision (0.50 with SDXL vs. 0.25 with DALLE), suggesting that shallow CNNs are less effective at handling the weaker feature quality of autoregressive images.

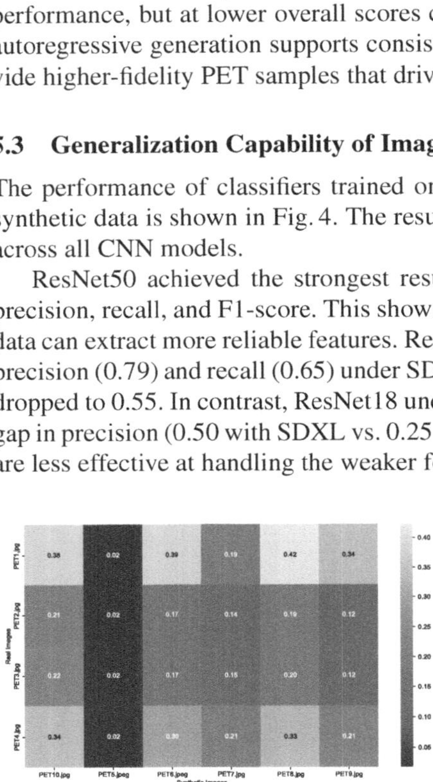


(a) SSIM heatmap for PET: real vs. synthetic images

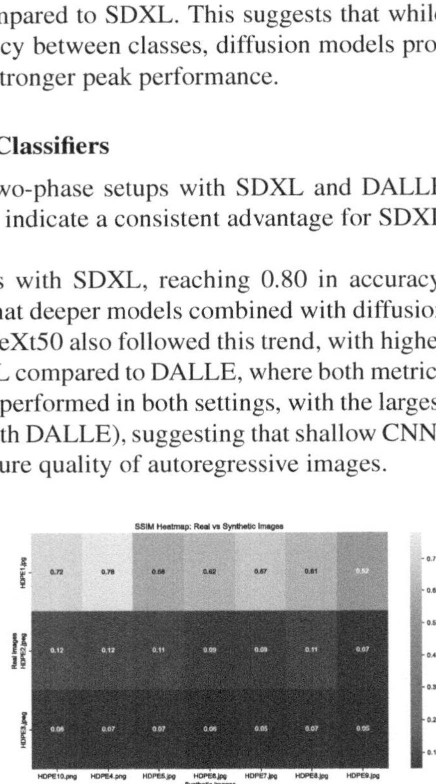


(b) SSIM heatmap for HDPE: real vs. synthetic images

**Fig. 5.** Structural Similarity Index (SSIM) heatmaps comparing real and synthetic images for PET and HDPE classes. Rows correspond to real images and columns correspond to synthetic images.

Overall, classifiers trained on SDXL images not only achieved higher scores but also showed better balance across metrics, confirming that diffusion-generated data provides richer and more consistent cues for underwater plastic detection than autoregressive data.

## 5.4 Qualitative Evaluation of the Synthetic Dataset

Qualitative evaluation of the generated images was conducted using the Structural Similarity Index (SSIM), CLIP score, and human assessment. Representative examples

**Fig. 6.** Representative examples of real and synthetic microplastic images for PET and HDPE classes.

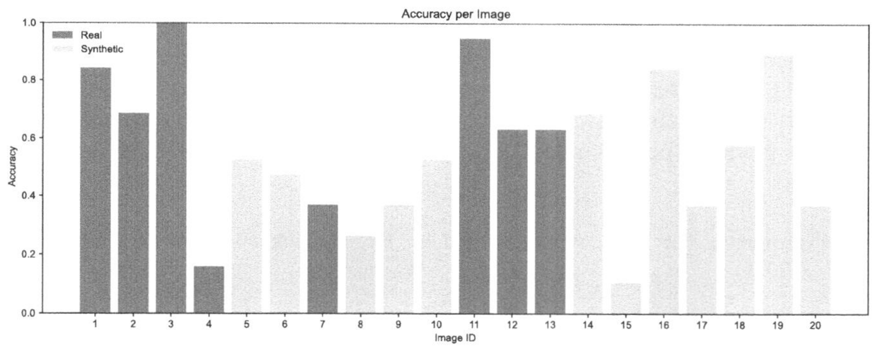


**Fig. 7.** Image-wise accuracy from human evaluation based on binary real-versus-synthetic classification. Nineteen participants independently assessed images from the model test set. Blue bars correspond to real images and orange bars correspond to synthetic images. (Color figure online)

of real and synthetic images for each polymer class are shown in Fig. 6, illustrating the visual characteristics captured by the generative model. SSIM heatmaps (Fig. 5) quantify structural similarity between real and synthetic images on a per-image basis. For HDPE samples (Fig. 5b), SSIM values ranged from 0.52 to 0.78, with an average similarity of approximately 0.64 across evaluated pairs. For PET samples (Fig. 5a), SSIM values ranged from 0.02 to 0.42, with most values below 0.30, indicating lower structural correspondence. Semantic alignment between synthetic images and their text prompts was evaluated using CLIP score, yielding an overall alignment accuracy of 60%. Human evaluation was conducted with 19 participants from different geographic regions (India, USA, Australia, Germany, Ireland). Participants were presented with images from the model test set via a Microsoft Forms interface and were asked to classify each image as real or synthetic using a binary choice. Based on image-wise aggregation (mean accuracy across 19 participants), the mean human classification accuracy was 0.66 for real images and 0.53 for synthetic images, with an overall mean accuracy of 0.58 across all test images. The lower accuracy observed for synthetic images indicates that these images were frequently classified as real by human observers, reflecting the difficulty of reliably distinguishing generated images from real samples based solely on visual inspection. This observation supports the use of the generated images as a complementary data source for training machine learning models. Image-level classification outcomes for individual real and synthetic samples are reported in Fig. 7. Human evaluation was used solely for perceptual analysis and did not inform model selection or hyperparameter tuning.

## 6 Conclusion

This study demonstrates the effectiveness of generative AI in addressing data scarcity for underwater plastic detection. A comparison of two paradigms of image generation, autoregressive (DALLE-3) and diffusion (SDXL), shows that diffusion-based synthetic datasets enable more robust classifier generalization, particularly in recall and F1-score. Among the tested architectures, ResNet50 consistently delivered the most balanced performance across training setups, underscoring its suitability for this task. Evaluation on a real-world dataset further confirms that diffusion-generated images can serve as a high-fidelity supplement to overcome data scarcity. Future work will focus on generating physics-guided hyperspectral images and validating them with 3D CNN hyperspectral models.

**Acknowledgments.** This work was supported by Taighde Éireann–Research Ireland (Grant 23/FFP-A/12079).

**Data Availability/Contribution Statement.** All synthetic PET and HDPE images generated and evaluated in this study have been released publicly to support reproducibility and further research, and are available via Zenodo at https://doi.org/10.5281/zenodo.17711348.

## References

1. Alboody, A., et al.: A new remote hyperspectral imaging system embedded on an unmanned aquatic drone for the detection and identification of floating plastic litter using machine learning. **15**(14), 3455 (2023). https://doi.org/10.3390/rs15143455, https://www.mdpi.com/2072-4292/15/14/3455
2. Balsi, M., Moroni, M., Bouchelaghem, S.: Plastic litter detection in the environment using hyperspectral aerial remote sensing and machine learning. **17**(5), 93 (2025). https://doi.org/10.3390/rs17050938, https://www.mdpi.com/2072-4292/17/5/938
3. Chen, N., Yue, J., Fang, L., Xia, S.: SpectralDiff: a generative framework for hyperspectral image classification with diffusion models. **61**, 1 (2023). https://doi.org/10.1109/TGRS.2023.3310023, http://arxiv.org/abs/2304.05961
4. El Bergui, A., Porebski, A., Vandenbroucke, N.: A lightweight spatial and spectral CNN model for classifying floating marine plastic debris using hyperspectral images. **216**, 117965 (2025). https://doi.org/10.1016/j.marpolbul.2025.117965, https://www.sciencedirect.com/science/article/pii/S0025326X25004400
5. Faltynkova, A., Johnsen, G., Wagner, M.: Hyperspectral imaging as an emerging tool to analyze microplastics: a systematic review and recommendations for future development. **1**(1), 1 (2021). https://doi.org/10.1186/s43591-021-00014-y

6. Huang, H., et al.: Underwater hyperspectral imaging for *in situ* underwater microplastic detection. **776**, 145960 (2021). https://doi.org/10.1016/j.scitotenv.2021.145960, https://www.sciencedirect.com/science/article/pii/S0048969721010275
7. Jin, H., Kong, F., Li, X., Shen, J.: Artificial intelligence in microplastic detection and pollution control. **262**, 119812 (2024). https://doi.org/10.1016/j.envres.2024.119812, https://www.sciencedirect.com/science/article/pii/S0013935124017171
8. Kshirsagar, M., Vaidya, G., Ryan, C., Kumar, V.K., Deepankur, L.: UPHSID: underwater PET–HDPE synthetic image dataset (2025). https://doi.org/10.5281/zenodo.17711348
9. OECD: Global Plastics Outlook: Policy Scenarios to 2060. OECD. https://doi.org/10.1787/aa1edf33-en, https://www.oecd.org/en/publications/global-plastics-outlook_aa1edf33-en.html
10. Olyaei, M., Ebtehaj, A., Ellis, C.R.: A hyperspectral reflectance database of plastic debris with different fractional abundance in river systems. **11**(1), 125 (2024). https://doi.org/10.1038/s41597-024-03974-x, https://www.nature.com/articles/s41597-024-03974-x
11. Podell, D., et al.: SDXL: improving latent diffusion models for high-resolution image synthesis. In: The Twelfth International Conference on Learning Representations (2024). https://openreview.net/forum?id=di52zR8xgf
12. Shi, Z., Zhou, X., Qiu, X., Zhu, X.: Improving image captioning with better use of captions (2020). https://doi.org/10.48550/ARXIV.2006.11807, https://arxiv.org/abs/2006.11807
13. Tamin, O., Moung, E., Dargham, J., Yahya, F., Omatu, S.: A review of hyperspectral imaging-based plastic waste detection state-of-the-arts. **13**, 3407–341 (2023). https://doi.org/10.11591/ijece.v13i3.pp3407-3419
14. Tamin, O., et al.: RGB and RGNIR image dataset for machine learning in plastic waste detection. Data Brief **60**, 111524 (2025). https://doi.org/10.1016/j.dib.2025.111524
15. Tamin, O., et al.: On-shore plastic waste detection with YOLOv5 and RGB-near-infrared fusion: a state-of-the-art solution for accurate and efficient environmental monitoring. Big Data Cogn. Comput. **7**(2), 103 (2023). https://doi.org/10.3390/bdcc7020103
16. Tamin, O., Moung, E.G., Dargham, J.A., Yahya, F., Omatu, S.: A review of hyperspectral imaging-based plastic waste detection state-of-the-arts. Int. J. Electr. Comput. Eng. (IJECE) **13**(3), 3407 (2023). https://doi.org/10.11591/ijece.v13i3.pp3407-3419
17. Tamin, O., Moung, E.G., Dargham, J.A., Yahya, F., Omatu, S., Angeline, L.: A comparison of RGB and RGNIR color spaces for plastic waste detection using the YOLOv5 architecture. In: 2022 IEEE International Conference on Artificial Intelligence in Engineering and Technology (IICAIET). IEEE (2022). https://doi.org/10.1109/iicaiet55139.2022.9936771
18. Tasseron, P., Emmerik, T.V., Peller, J., Schreyers, L., Biermann, L.: Advancing floating macroplastic detection from space using hyperspectral imagery (2022). https://eartharxiv.org/repository/view/2341/
19. Thavasimuthu, R., Vidhya, P.M., Sridhar, S., Sasirekha, S.P., Sherubha, P.: Enhanced classification of microplastic polymers (polyethylene, polystyrene, low-density polyethylene, polyhydroxyalkanoate) in waterbodies. **35**(7), e650 (2024). https://doi.org/10.1002/pat.6506, https://onlinelibrary.wiley.com/doi/abs/10.1002/pat.6506, _eprint: https://onlinelibrary.wiley.com/doi/pdf/10.1002/pat.6506
20. Wang, Z., Xu, P., Liu, B., Cao, Y., Liu, Z., Liu, Z.: Hyperspectral imaging for underwater object detection. **41**(2), 176–191 (2021). https://doi.org/10.1108/SR-07-2020-0165, http://www.emerald.com/sr/article/41/2/176-191/455626
21. Zhu, C., Kanaya, Y.: Eliminating the interference of water for direct sensing of submerged plastics using hyperspectral near-infrared imager. **13**(1), 1599 (2023). https://doi.org/10.1038/s41598-023-39754-7, https://www.nature.com/articles/s41598-023-39754-7

# Improving Low-Resource Language Translation via Targeted Vocabulary Expansion

Pavan Naik[1], Ankit Jaiswal[1(✉)], Inacio Vieira[2], and Anya Belz[1]

[1] Dublin City University, Dublin, Ireland
pavannaik@zoho.com, jaiswal.ankit2000@gmail.com, anya.belz@dcu.ie
[2] Alpha CRC, Cambridge, UK
ivieira@alphacrc.com

**Abstract.** Large Language Models face substantial challenges in machine translation for low-resource languages, particularly in specialised domains like legal translation. This study addresses two key obstacles: (i) severe over-tokenisation that fragments semantic units, and (ii) scarcity of parallel training data. We expand the Gemma-3-1B-Instruct (https://huggingface.co/google/gemma-3-1b-it) model with language-specific tokens, initialising new embeddings using novel cross-lingual word embedding initialisation, followed by two-stage training: (i) continual pre-training on parallel legal data, and (ii) LoRA [9] fine-tuning with language-specific adapters. Evaluation on four typologically diverse low-resource languages—Irish (GA), Kannada (KN), Traditional Chinese (ZH_TW), and Maithili (MAI)—demonstrates that our cross-lingual initialisation outperforms FOCUS initialisation [4] across all languages and all metrics. Parallel data pre-training substantially surpasses monolingual approaches, and our models outperform NLLB-600M (https://huggingface.co/facebook/nllb-200-distilled-600M) baselines across all languages by considerable margins. However, vocabulary expansion models still lag behind non-expanded baselines, indicating more extensive pre-training is needed to fully realise tokenisation improvements.

**Keywords:** Low-Resource Machine Translation · Legal Domain Translation · Vocabulary Expansion · Cross-Lingual Embeddings · Continual Pre-Training · Large Language Models

## 1 Introduction

Large Language Models (LLMs) have demonstrated remarkable capabilities across diverse NLP tasks, yet their performance on machine translation (MT) for low-resource languages remains highly variable, particularly in specialised domains like legal translation where precision and domain-specific terminology are crucial. Two primary challenges impede effective low-resource MT. First,


T. T. Mai et al. (Eds.): AICS 2025, CCIS 2950, pp. 336–347, 2026.
https://doi.org/10.1007/978-3-032-25809-0_27

severe over-tokenisation fragments single words into numerous subword tokens, producing high fertility rates[1] [25] that degrade translation speed and reduce available contextual information. Second, critical scarcity of parallel datasets, especially in specialised domains, severely limits cross-lingual alignment learning and domain-specific translation patterns.

We address these challenges through vocabulary expansion with cross-lingual embedding initialisation and strategic multi-stage training. Our primary contribution is a cross-lingual word embedding initialisation method that significantly outperforms FOCUS [4]. Unlike FOCUS, which averages subtoken embeddings, our approach leverages BGE-M3 [2] cross-lingual embeddings to identify semantically similar tokens, and directly copies the most similar embedding, providing more robust initialisation. Our methodology comprises: dataset creation combining web-scraped monolingual legal documents with back-translated parallel data; vocabulary expansion with cross-lingual embedding initialisation; two-stage continual pre-training [11] comparing parallel versus monolingual data; and LoRA [9] fine-tuning with language-specific adapters.

Experimental evaluation using Gemma-3-1B-IT on four typologically diverse languages—Irish, Kannada, Traditional Chinese, and Maithili—reveals that cross-lingual initialisation consistently outperforms FOCUS, achieving superior translation quality and faster convergence. Additionally, parallel data pre-training substantially outperforms monolingual pre-training for legal MT. The paper proceeds as follows: Sect. 2 reviews related work, Sect. 3 describes datasets, Sect. 4 details methodology, Sect. 5 presents experimental setup, Sect. 6 outlines evaluation metrics, Sect. 7 reports results, Sect. 8 analyses findings, and Sect. 9 concludes with limitations and ethical considerations.

## 2 Related Work

**Low-Resource Machine Translation:** The NLLB project [22] represents the most comprehensive effort in low-resource MT, creating parallel datasets through bitext mining [7] for 200+ languages. However, NLLB uses parallel data for supervised fine-tuning while relying on monolingual data for pre-training. We show (Sect. 7.2) that parallel data pre-training enables more efficient resource allocation through example packing [19], processing approximately 20x more parallel data than fine-tuning approaches and achieving substantially faster convergence.

**Multi-stage Training Approaches:** The ALMA model [24] established an influential two-stage paradigm: monolingual pre-training followed by parallel fine-tuning. While monolingual data helps models acquire target language properties, it lacks cross-lingual alignment signals crucial for translation. We provide empirical evidence (Sect. 7.2) for parallel data pre-training [18], demonstrating consistent improvements of +7–18 BLEU points across four languages compared to monolingual pre-training in a clean ablation with no vocabulary expansion.

[1] The number of tokens produced from a single word as a result of over-tokenisation.

**Vocabulary Expansion and Token Initialisation:** The FOCUS embedding initialisation method [4] represents the state-of-the-art for addressing over-tokenisation, initialising new tokens using auxiliary fastText [1] embeddings to calculate semantic similarity. However, FOCUS requires training external fastText models for each language, relies on subword-level embeddings, and creates averaged embeddings that may dilute semantic meaning. Our approach leverages cross-lingual BGE-M3 embeddings [2] to identify semantically similar tokens across languages, then directly copies the most similar embedding. This eliminates auxiliary model training, handles subword tokens effectively, and provides robust initialisation for limited-data languages.

## 3 Datasets

We curated datasets for both pre-training and fine-tuning, combining existing resources with synthetic generation. For pre-training, we leveraged the OPUS collection of parallel data [23] with language-specific adaptations. We extracted **Irish (GA)** and **Kannada (KN)** data from NLLB [22], ParaCrawl[2], and Wikimedia[3]. For **Traditional Chinese (ZH_TW)**, we collected monolingual legal texts from Taiwan's Laws and Regulations database [15] with English parallels through back-translation using Gemini Flash 2.5[4] [5]. For **Maithili (MAI)**, we employed forward translation from English monolingual legal texts using Gemini Flash 2.5. For fine-tuning, monolingual source texts were from web-scraped official legal websites (Irish, Kannada), Taiwan's Laws and Regulations database (Traditional Chinese), and Kaggle [14] (Maithili). For Irish, Kannada, and Traditional Chinese, we generated parallel English text through back-translation using Gemini Flash 2.5. For Maithili, English monolingual texts were forward-translated using Gemini Flash 2.5 to create parallel data. Test sets for both pre-training and fine-tuning are derived from their respective main datasets through random sampling. See Table 1 for statistics about each of our final datasets.

**Table 1.** Dataset Statistics.

| Stage | Split | KN | GA | MAI | ZH_TW |
|---|---|---|---|---|---|
| Pre-Train | Train | 203,761 | 272,431 | 67,010 | 203,354 |
| | Test | 10,000 | 10,000 | 10,000 | 10,000 |
| Fine-Tuning | Train | 24,675 | 24,945 | 19,999 | 24,619 |
| | Valid | 500 | 500 | 500 | 500 |
| | Test | 2,000 | 2,000 | 2,000 | 2,000 |

[2] https://paracrawl.eu/.

[3] https://commons.wikimedia.org/wiki/Main_Page.

[4] Model ID: `gemini-2.5-flash`, accessed via Google AI Studio (July 2025).

# 4 Methodology

**Vocabulary Expansion Strategy:** Our vocabulary expansion methodology addresses over-tokenisation issues through strategic tokeniser enhancement and cross-lingual embedding initialisation. Building on Gemma-3-1B-IT's SentencePiece [13] tokeniser, we expand it with approximately 12,000 high-frequency tokens per target language extracted from auxiliary language-specific tokenisers trained on monolingual data. Our critical innovation lies in the cross-lingual word embedding initialisation method for newly added tokens. Given a source vocabulary $V_s$ with embeddings $E_s$ and a set of new target language tokens $V_t$, we define our initialisation as:

$$e_t = E_s[\arg\max_{v \in V_s} \text{sim}(\text{embed}(t), \text{embed}(v))] \tag{1}$$

where $e_t$ is the initialised embedding for new token $t \in V_t$, $\text{embed}(\cdot)$ denotes BGE-M3 embedding generation, and $\text{sim}(\cdot)$ denotes cosine similarity.

Specifically, we generate BGE-M3[5] [2] embeddings for all source vocabulary tokens, then initialise each new token by directly copying the embedding of its most semantically similar existing token.

**Multi-stage Training Pipeline:** Our training employs a two-stage approach. In Stage 1 (continual pre-training), we evaluate two data paradigms: (i) parallel data pre-training concatenates English and target language sentences with randomised order (EN+XX or XX+EN), enabling sequence packing to process approximately 20x more parallel data than traditional fine-tuning; (ii) monolingual data pre-training uses target language datasets. We hypothesis that parallel data pre-training provides superior cross-lingual alignment. Both paradigms employ full model fine-tuning for complete vocabulary adaptation. In Stage 2 (instruction fine-tuning), we apply LoRA [9] and QLoRA [3] for efficient parameter updates, with dedicated adapters for each language formatted with legal domain EN-XX translation instructions.

# 5 Experimental Setup

We select Gemma-3-1B-IT for its strong balance between performance and computational efficiency, enabling extensive multilingual ablation studies under limited resources. Its 262K SentencePiece vocabulary provides a robust basis for tokenisation experiments, and public availability ensures reproducibility. We evaluate Irish, Kannada, Traditional Chinese, and Maithili to capture typological diversity across language families (Celtic, Dravidian, Sino-Tibetan Indo-Aryan), scripts (Latin, Kannada, Traditional Chinese, Devanagari), and tokenisation difficulty. Baseline fertility rates range from 1.32 to 3.06.

**Experimental Design:** Our pre-training phase evaluates four vocabulary configurations combined with two data paradigms. The vocabulary configurations

[5] https://huggingface.co/BAAI/bge-m3.

are: (1) base Gemma-3-1B-IT without modifications; (2) expanded vocabulary with statistical averaging initialisation [8]; (3) expanded vocabulary with FOCUS initialisation; and (4) our cross-lingual embedding initialisation. The data paradigms are (1) monolingual pre-training using target language legal documents; and (2) parallel pre-training using English target language legal datasets. This factorial design enables systematic evaluation of initialisation methods and training data effectiveness. Fine-tuning applies LoRA adaptation to each pre-trained model for each target language. Base model fine-tuning produces 4 LoRA adapters (one per language). Pre-trained model fine-tuning produces 32 LoRA adapters (8 pre-trained models × 4 languages), totaling 36 fine-tuned models (Table 2).

**Table 2.** Pre-training Experimental Design. All configurations are evaluated under both monolingual and parallel data settings.

| Configuration | Details |
|---|---|
| Base Model (No Pre-training) | Gemma-3-1B-IT without additional pre-training |
| Base Model | Gemma-3-1B-IT without vocabulary expansion |
| Statistical Average Init | Expanded vocab initialised with statistical averaging |
| FOCUS Init | Expanded vocab with FOCUS (fastText-based) initialisation |
| Cross-lingual Init (Ours) | Expanded vocab with cross-lingual semantic matching |

**Implementation Configuration:** Training uses learning rate 5e-05, maximum sequence length 2048 tokens, 3 epochs in pre-training and fine-tuning. LoRA has rank 64, alpha 128, with 8-bit quantisation. Pre-training uses NVIDIA A100 40GB GPUs; fine-tuning uses NVIDIA T4 15 GB GPUs.

## 6 Evaluations

Our evaluation addresses legal domain machine translation at three stages using the test sets described in Table 1. For tokenisation efficiency, we measure fertility rates [25] to quantify over-tokenisation reduction. For pre-training effectiveness, we evaluate perplexity scores [10] and analyse training loss convergence rate.

For translation quality, we employ automatic metrics including BLEU [16], COMET [20], ChrF++ [17], TER [21], and spBLEU [6], covering n-gram precision, semantic similarity, and character-level alignment. We further conduct human evaluation using Adequacy and Fluency on a 5-point Likert scale. One native-speaker annotator per language, all university students, evaluated 100 randomly sampled test instances. Annotators were asked two questions for each translation: (1) Adequacy: "How well does the translation preserve the meaning of the source sentence?" and (2) Fluency: "How grammatical and natural is the target text?" Both were rated on a 5-point scale where 1 = "Very Poor", 2 = "Poor", 3 = "Fair", 4 = "Good", and 5 = "Excellent". Translations were presented in random order and annotators were blinded to model identity.

# 7 Results

## 7.1 Tokenisation Efficiency Analysis

Our vocabulary expansion strategy demonstrates substantial improvements in tokenisation efficiency across all target languages. Table 3 presents fertility rate comparisons across all target languages. Our vocabulary expansion achieves fertility rate reductions ranging from 16.05% (Maithili) to 35.61% (Irish) compared to the base Gemma-3-1B-IT tokeniser, with an average improvement of 29.15%. Our approach also demonstrates competitive performance against the NLLB tokeniser, achieving superior fertility rates across all languages with improvements ranging from 11.00% to 35.71%.

**Table 3.** Tokenisation Efficiency Analysis.

| Metric | KN | ZH_TW | GA | MAI |
|---|---|---|---|---|
| New Tokens | 12,764 | 16,000 | 12,823 | 12,489 |
| Fertility Rates | | | | |
| Base Model | 3.064 | 1.32 | 2.299 | 1.592 |
| NLLB-600M | 2.37 | 1.398 | 1.689 | 1.502 |
| Ours | **2.051** | **0.899** | **1.48** | **1.337** |
| Improvement vs Base | 33.05% | 31.90% | 35.61% | 16.05% |
| Improvement vs NLLB | 13.45% | 35.71% | 12.36% | 11.00% |

## 7.2 Pre-training Evaluation

We evaluate pre-training effectiveness through perplexity measurements and training convergence analysis on held-out test sets (Table 1). Table 4 and Fig. 1 demonstrate that all pre-training approaches achieve perplexity reductions of 85–95% across target languages compared to the base model. FOCUS consistently achieves the lowest perplexity across languages in both monolingual and parallel settings. Our cross-lingual initialisation approach performs competitively, particularly in parallel training scenarios where it matches FOCUS performance while maintaining computational efficiency.

Parallel data pre-training demonstrates superior convergence and cross-lingual alignment benefits compared to monolingual pre-training. Both FOCUS and our cross-lingual method demonstrate nearly identical convergence patterns, achieving stable training loss faster than statistical average initialisation.

## 7.3 Fine-Tuning Results

**MT Task Specific Evaluation:**
*Automated Evaluation:* As Table 5 shows, our models demonstrate a significant leap in translation quality. The models pre-trained on parallel data decisively

**Table 4.** Pre-training perplexity results across all methods. FOCUS achieves lowest perplexity; cross-lingual initialisation performs competitively in parallel settings with superior English modeling.

| Vocab Exp.? | Configuration | Data Type | Perplexity (↓ lower is better) | | | | |
|---|---|---|---|---|---|---|---|
| | | | ZH_TW | GA | KN | MAI | EN |
| ✗ | Base Model (No Pre-Training) | – | 86.06 | 1119.91 | 627.25 | 641.69 | 55.34 |
| | | | *Reduction vs. base (↓):* | | | | |
| ✗ | Base Model | Monolingual | 6.23 *(92.8%↓ )* | 5.98 *(99.5%↓ )* | 13.65 *(97.8%↓ )* | 18.47 *(97.1%↓ )* | 75.52 *(-36.5%)* |
| | | Parallel | 6.66 *(92.3%↓ )* | 6.32 *(99.4%↓ )* | 14.24 *(97.7%↓ )* | 19.34 *(97.0%↓ )* | 12.70 *(77.1%↓ )* |
| ✓ | Statistical Average Init | Monolingual | 19.51 *(77.3%↓ )* | 17.41 *(98.4%↓ )* | 56.54 *(91.0%↓ )* | 36.91 *(94.2%↓ )* | 75.37 *(-36.2%)* |
| | | Parallel | 20.09 *(76.7%↓ )* | 17.46 *(98.4%↓ )* | 55.04 *(91.2%↓ )* | 37.00 *(94.2%↓ )* | 12.47 *(77.5%↓ )* |
| ✓ | Cross-lingual Init (Ours) | Monolingual | 18.91 *(78.0%↓ )* | 17.96 *(98.4%↓ )* | 56.06 *(91.1%↓ )* | 36.31 *(94.3%↓ )* | 73.68 *(-33.2%)* |
| | | Parallel | 19.93 *(76.8%↓ )* | 18.64 *(98.3%↓ )* | 56.63 *(91.0%↓ )* | 37.00 *(94.2%↓ )* | 12.46 *(77.5%↓ )* |
| ✓ | FOCUS Init | Monolingual | 18.20 *(78.9%↓ )* | 16.96 *(98.5%↓ )* | 53.84 *(91.4%↓ )* | 36.32 *(94.3%↓ )* | 75.86 *(-37.1%)* |
| | | Parallel | 19.23 *(77.7%↓ )* | 17.57 *(98.4%↓ )* | 53.87 *(91.4%↓ )* | 36.81 *(94.3%↓ )* | 12.51 *(77.4%↓ )* |

outperform those trained on monolingual data and the base model without any pre-training across all languages and metrics. Our best-performing models surpass the NLLB-600M baseline by substantial margins for Irish and Traditional Chinese, and comfortable margins for Kannada and Maithili. While the model without vocabulary expansion achieves the highest scores, highlighting the inherent challenge of learning new tokens, our Cross-lingual Initialisation method consistently outperforms FOCUS and statistical average initialisation across all languages and all metrics.

*Human Evaluation:* As shown in Table 6, our best model (Parallel Pre-trained) consistently delivers higher adequacy and fluency scores compared to NLLB-600M. While it occasionally mixes tokens from related languages or struggles with named entities, it offers a stronger balance of adequacy and fluency compared to NLLB-600M, which often produces fluent but incomplete translations with more frequent errors in longer sentences.

**Training Convergence:** Analysis of the fine-tuning loss curves in Fig. 2 (see Supplementary Material) reveals that our Cross-lingual Initialisation method consistently converges to lower loss values more effectively than both FOCUS and statistical average initialisation. However, the base model without vocab-

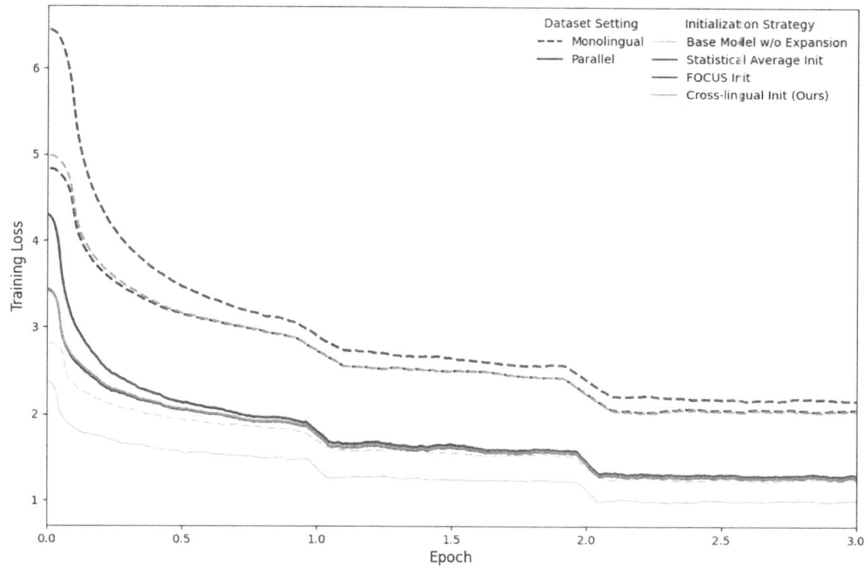


**Fig. 1.** Pre-training loss convergence showing parallel data (solid) outperforms monolingual (dashed). FOCUS and cross-lingual initialisation converge similarly and faster than statistical averaging; base model achieves lowest loss without initialisation overhead.

**Table 5.** Machine Translation Evaluation Results (EN→{GA, KN, MAI, ZH_TW}).

| Language | Metric | NLLB-600M | Base Model (No Pre-Training) | With Monolingual Continual Pre-Training | | | | With Parallel Continual Pre-Training | | | |
|---|---|---|---|---|---|---|---|---|---|---|---|
| | | | | No Vocab Exp. | Stat Avg Init | Cross-ling Init | FOCUS Init | No Vocab Exp. | Stat Avg Init | Cross-ling Init | FOCUS Init |
| GA | BLEU ↑ | 26.21 | 53.54 | 53.94 | 48.24 | 53.50 | 53.32 | **61.72** | 60.85 | 61.60 | 61.44 |
| | spBLEU ↑ | 31.52 | 61.15 | 60.50 | 54.50 | 59.45 | 59.32 | **68.52** | 67.58 | 68.40 | 68.28 |
| | ChrF ↑ | 51.69 | 75.01 | 73.80 | 70.04 | 73.55 | 73.38 | **79.81** | 79.20 | 79.59 | 79.51 |
| | ChrF++ ↑ | 49.12 | 72.75 | 71.69 | 67.92 | 71.50 | 71.32 | **77.88** | 77.26 | 77.67 | 77.58 |
| | COMET ↑ | 0.77 | 0.84 | 0.83 | 0.82 | 0.83 | 0.83 | **0.86** | 0.85 | **0.86** | **0.86** |
| | TER ↓ | 65.61 | 36.09 | 37.58 | 42.54 | 36.35 | 36.40 | **28.36** | 29.12 | 28.81 | 29.19 |
| KN | BLEU ↑ | 28.29 | 34.10 | 29.90 | 16.98 | 24.11 | 23.68 | **37.95** | 31.64 | 34.11 | 33.73 |
| | spBLEU ↑ | 43.11 | 48.44 | 42.65 | 27.24 | 36.35 | 36.22 | **52.46** | 46.63 | 48.94 | 48.43 |
| | ChrF ↑ | 64.86 | 68.50 | 63.50 | 52.74 | 59.97 | 58.95 | **70.44** | 66.71 | 68.50 | 68.12 |
| | ChrF++ ↑ | 60.06 | 64.05 | 59.06 | 47.98 | 55.23 | 54.22 | **66.13** | 62.14 | 63.97 | 63.65 |
| | COMET ↑ | 0.86 | 0.86 | 0.84 | 0.80 | 0.83 | 0.83 | **0.87** | 0.85 | 0.86 | 0.86 |
| | TER ↓ | 59.68 | 51.98 | 60.77 | 88.39 | 71.08 | 69.72 | **46.81** | 56.63 | 52.31 | 54.81 |
| MAI | BLEU ↑ | 7.50 | 19.97 | 19.41 | 13.71 | 17.50 | 14.92 | **22.65** | 20.96 | 22.15 | 21.15 |
| | spBLEU ↑ | 11.87 | 26.55 | 25.33 | 18.18 | 23.44 | 20.01 | **29.25** | 26.93 | 28.79 | 27.02 |
| | ChrF ↑ | 35.90 | 48.12 | 46.38 | 40.43 | 45.38 | 42.83 | **49.93** | 47.81 | 49.51 | 48.01 |
| | ChrF++ ↑ | 31.48 | 44.68 | 42.95 | 37.19 | 41.99 | 39.48 | **46.47** | 44.46 | 46.10 | 44.64 |
| | COMET ↑ | 0.56 | 0.58 | 0.57 | 0.55 | 0.57 | 0.56 | **0.59** | 0.58 | **0.59** | 0.58 |
| | TER ↓ | 100.39 | 79.52 | 78.28 | 91.19 | 82.45 | 87.99 | **72.71** | 76.75 | 74.85 | 75.73 |
| ZH_TW | BLEU ↑ | 7.73 | 56.85 | 44.75 | 36.38 | 38.25 | 38.44 | **65.20** | 59.49 | 62.05 | 61.86 |
| | spBLEU ↑ | 3.44 | 48.93 | 38.95 | 30.03 | 32.56 | 32.37 | **58.69** | 52.45 | 55.25 | 55.08 |
| | ChrF ↑ | 10.23 | 50.24 | 42.29 | 34.38 | 36.56 | 35.54 | **58.33** | 53.22 | 55.03 | 54.92 |
| | ChrF++ ↑ | 7.82 | 40.30 | 34.48 | 27.54 | 29.53 | 28.60 | **47.49** | 42.93 | 44.60 | 44.25 |
| | COMET ↑ | 0.77 | **0.91** | 0.88 | 0.87 | 0.87 | 0.87 | **0.91** | **0.91** | **0.91** | **0.91** |
| | TER ↓ | 130.10 | 31.99 | 60.28 | 67.77 | 67.97 | 65.75 | **28.05** | 33.07 | 30.05 | 30.33 |

ulary expansion converges even better, suggesting that newly added vocabulary tokens require more data to be fully learned. Despite this, our vocabulary-expanded models, when pre-trained on parallel data, achieve convergence rates close to the unexpanded model using only 300 million tokens to train over 54,000

**Table 6.** Human Evaluation Scores: Adequacy and Fluency Ratings (Averaged over 100 samples, Our best = parallel pretrained model).

| Language | Model | Adequacy | Fluency |
|---|---|---|---|
| Maithili | Our Best | 4.56 | 4.45 |
| | NLLB-600M | 3.44 | 3.45 |
| Kannada | Our Best | 4.56 | 4.46 |
| | NLLB-600M | 4.44 | 4.31 |
| Traditional Chinese | Our Best | 4.47 | 3.98 |
| | NLLB-600M | 3.16 | 3.19 |
| Irish | Our Best | 4.52 | 4.21 |
| | NLLB-600M | 3.34 | 3.79 |

new tokens, marking a substantial improvement in data efficiency compared to previous methods [12] which require 2 billion tokens to train 8,000 new tokens.

## 8 Discussion

Our results provide insights into the effective adaptation of LLMs for low-resource legal translation. An important finding is the superiority of parallel data pre-training in the context of vocabulary expansion. While both monolingual and parallel pre-training paradigms improved target language perplexity (Table 4), the combination of vocabulary expansion with parallel data pre-training achieved dramatically better cross-lingual alignment and translation quality. This demonstrates that for translation tasks with vocabulary expansion, investing limited computational resources into pre-training with parallel data yields substantial returns, facilitating better alignment of new tokens across language pairs.

Another key insight relates to vocabulary initialisation for expanded vocabularies. Our Cross-lingual Initialisation method proved highly effective, consistently matching or outperforming the current state-of-the-art FOCUS method in downstream MT tasks, particularly in the extremely low-data setting for Maithili. Its strength lies in its simplicity and semantic purity; by directly copying the embedding of the single most semantically similar token, it avoids the 'semantic contamination' that can occur when multiple, potentially fragmented sub-token embeddings are averaged as done in FOCUS. This provides a cleaner, more robust starting point for the model, facilitating faster and more effective learning, as reflected in the training convergence curves (Fig. 2). The superior fertility rates (Table 3) demonstrate the practical benefits of vocabulary expansion, which directly translates to computational efficiency and the ability to process longer contexts during inference.

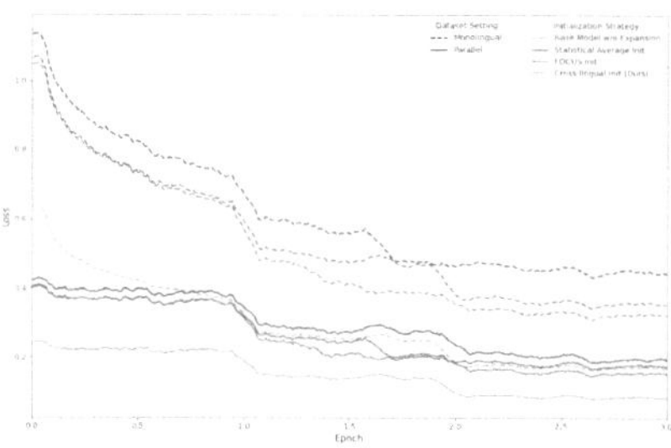

(a) Training loss convergence for Irish.

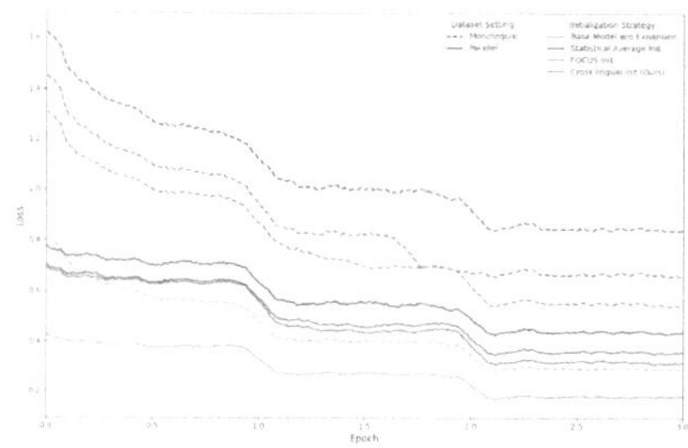

(b) Training loss convergence for Kannada.

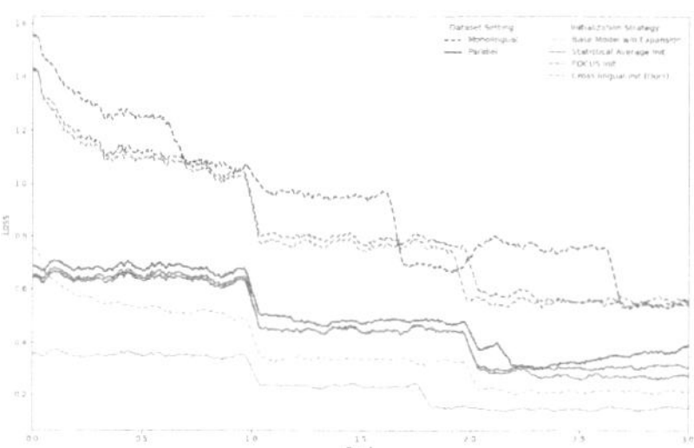

(c) Training loss convergence for Traditional Chinese.

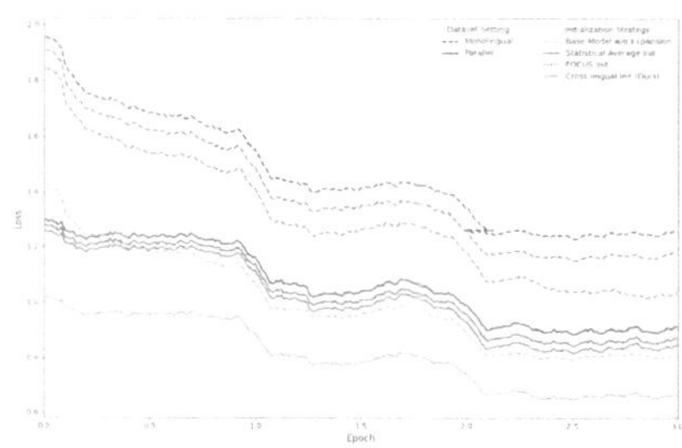

(d) Training loss convergence for Maithili.

**Fig. 2.** Training(LoRa) convergence across different initialisation strategies (Base, Statistical Avg, FOCUS, and Cross-lingual Init) and data paradigms (Monolingual vs Parallel) for four target languages.

# 9 Conclusion

This paper addressed the critical challenges of domain-specific machine translation for low-resource languages, focusing on inefficient tokenisation and data scarcity. We introduced a comprehensive framework that successfully adapts a base LLM for high-quality legal translation into Irish, Kannada, Traditional Chinese, and Maithili. Our primary contribution is a novel cross-lingual embedding initialisation method that outperforms existing state-of-the-art techniques like FOCUS, by directly mapping new vocabulary to the most semantically similar existing token, eliminating the need for auxiliary models and providing a more robust semantic foundation. The ratio of pre-training dataset tokens to newly added vocabulary tokens is critical: as explained in Sect. 7.3, our vocabulary expansion with a ratio of approximately 5,500:1 achieved comparable but sub-optimal performance, indicating inadequate pre-training data volume. For best results with our approach, we recommend maintaining a substantially higher token-to-vocabulary ratio (at least 10,000:1) to achieve optimal performance with vocabulary expansion.

## Limitations

Our study evaluates four typologically diverse languages, potentially limiting generalizability. Heavy reliance on synthetic data(back-translated) through commercial APIs may introduce translation artifacts and domain biases along with community consultation was limited to human evaluation; The legal domain focus limits applicability to other specialised domains, while vocabulary expansion substantially increases model parameters without comprehensive analysis of computational trade-offs. The contradiction between perplexity scores and translation quality metrics suggests evaluation methodology limitations requiring further investigation.

## Ethical Considerations

Legal translation errors can have serious real-world consequences. Our models should not be deployed for critical legal applications without human oversight and validation. Synthetic dataset creation and web scraping may not adequately represent diverse legal traditions within target language communities, potentially perpetuating biases. Development of MT systems for low-resource languages must involve consultation with relevant communities to ensure cultural appropriateness and avoid linguistic imperialism.

**Disclosure of Interests.** The authors have no competing interests to declare that are relevant to the content of this article.

## References

1. Bojanowski, P., Grave, E., Joulin, A., Mikolov, T.: Enriching word vectors with subword information (2016)
2. Chen, J., Xiao, S., Zhang, P., Luo, K., Lian, D., Liu, Z.: BGE M3-embedding: multi-lingual. multi-functionality, multi-granularity text embeddings through self-knowledge distillation (2024)
3. Dettmers, T., Pagnoni, A., Holtzman, A., Zettlemoyer, L.: QLoRA: efficient fine-tuning of quantized LLMs (2023). https://arxiv.org/abs/2305.14314
4. Dobler, K., de Melo, G.: FOCUS: effective embedding initialization for monolingual specialization of multilingual models (2023)
5. Gemini Team, Google: Gemini 2.5: Pushing the frontier with advanced reasoning, multimodality, long context, and next generation agentic capabilities (2025). https://storage.googleapis.com/deepmind-media/gemini/gemini_v2_5_report.pdf. Accessed 12 July 2025
6. Goyal, N., et al.: The FLORES-101 evaluation benchmark for low-resource and multilingual machine translation. Trans. Assoc. Comput. Linguist. **10**, 522–538 (2022)
7. Heffernan, K., Çelebi, O., Schwenk, H.: Bitext mining using distilled sentence representations for low-resource languages (2022). https://arxiv.org/abs/2205.12654

8. Hewitt, J.: Initializing new word embeddings for pretrained language models (2021). https://nlp.stanford.edu/~johnhew/vocab-expansion.html. Accessed 18 July 2025
9. Hu, E.J., et al.: LoRA: low-rank adaptation of large language models (2021). https://arxiv.org/abs/2106.09685
10. Jelinek, F., Mercer, R.L., Bahl, L.R., Baker, J.K.: Perplexity—a measure of the difficulty of speech recognition tasks. J. Acoust. Soc. Am. **62**(S1), S63–S63 (2005). https://doi.org/10.1121/1.2016299
11. Jin, X., et al.: Lifelong pretraining: continually adapting language models to emerging corpora (2022). https://arxiv.org/abs/2110.08534
12. Kim, S., Choi, S., Jeong, M.: Efficient and effective vocabulary expansion towards multilingual large language models (2024)
13. Kudo, T., Richardson, J.: SentencePiece: a simple and language independent subword tokenizer and detokenizer for neural text processing. In: Blanco, E., Lu, W. (eds.) Proceedings of the 2018 Conference on Empirical Methods in Natural Language Processing: System Demonstrations. pp. 66–71. Association for Computational Linguistics, Brussels (2018). https://doi.org/10.18653/v1/D18-2012, https://aclanthology.org/D18-2012/
14. Kumar, A.: Legal text classification dataset (2025). https://www.kaggle.com/datasets/amohankumar/legal-text-classification-dataset. Kaggle Dataset
15. Ministry of Justice, Republic of China (Taiwan): Laws & regulations database API (2025). https://law.moj.gov.tw/api/. Accessed 12 July 2025
16. Papineni, K., Roukos, S., Ward, T., Zhu, W.J.: BLEU: a method for automatic evaluation of machine translation. In: Isabelle, P., Charniak, E., Lin, D. (eds.) Proceedings of the 40th Annual Meeting of the Association for Computational Linguistics, pp. 311–318. Association for Computational Linguistics, Philadelphia (2002). https://doi.org/10.3115/1073083.1073135, https://aclanthology.org/P02-1040/
17. Popović, M.: chrF++: words helping character n-grams. In: Bojar, O., et al. (eds.) Proceedings of the second conference on machine translation, pp. 612–618. Association for Computational Linguistics, Copenhagen (Sep 2017). https://doi.org/10.18653/v1/W17-4770, https://aclanthology.org/W17-4770/
18. Qorib, M.R., Li, J., Ng, H.T.: Just go parallel: improving the multilingual capabilities of large language models (2025)
19. Raffel, C., et al.: Exploring the limits of transfer learning with a unified text-to-text transformer (2023). https://arxiv.org/abs/1910.10683
20. Rei, R., Stewart, C., Farinha, A.C., Lavie, A.: COMET: a neural framework for MT evaluation. In: Webber, B., Cohn, T., He, Y., Liu, Y. (eds.) Proceedings of the 2020 Conference on Empirical Methods in Natural Language Processing (EMNLP), pp. 2685–2702. Association for Computational Linguistics, Online (2020). https://doi.org/10.18653/v1/2020.emnlp-main.213, https://aclanthology.org/2020.emnlp-main.213/
21. Snover, M., Dorr, B.: A study of translation edit rate with targeted human annotation. https://aclanthology.org/2006.amta-papers.25.pdf. Accessed 13 July 2025
22. Team, N., et al.: No language left behind: scaling human-centered machine translation (2022). https://arxiv.org/abs/2207.04672
23. Tiedemann, J.: Parallel data, tools and interfaces in OPUS. http://www.lrec-conf.org/proceedings/lrec2012/pdf/463_Paper.pdf. Accessed 13 July 2025
24. Xu, H., Kim, Y.J., Sharaf, A., Awadalla, H.H.: A paradigm shift in machine translation: Boosting translation performance of large language models (2023)
25. Ács, J.: Exploring BERT's vocabulary (2019). https://juditacs.github.io/2019/02/19/bert-tokenization-stats.html. Accessed 13 July 2025

# Profit-Sensitive Benchmarking of Post-hoc Explainability in Customer Churn

Awais Manzoor[1,2(✉)], Muhammad Deedahwar Mazhar Qureshi[2], Bilal Yousuf[1,2], Etain Kidney[2], and Muhammad Atif Qureshi[1,2]

[1] ADAPT Centre, eXplainable Analytics Group, Dublin, Ireland
malik.awaismanzoor@gmail.com, atif.qureshi@tudublin.ie
[2] Faculty of Business, Technological University Dublin, Dublin, Ireland

**Abstract.** Customer churn models on tabular data often favour boosted ensembles for predictive performance, but their adoption depends on explanations that are reliable and actionable. We benchmark post-hoc explainability for churn by applying LIME and SHAP to high-performing tree ensembles and comparing them against inherently interpretable baselines (logistic regression, decision tree) on two public telco datasets. Evaluation combines standard predictive metrics (accuracy, F1, AUC) with business- and profit-sensitive measures (top-decile lift, Expected Maximum Profit (EMP), and customer-level *e-Profits*), while explanation quality is assessed using four quantitative metrics: fidelity, robustness, simplicity, and consistency. Results show that SHAP, particularly with boosted ensembles, achieves near-perfect fidelity and stable robustness, whereas LIME yields simpler but less faithful explanations. Profit-based metrics reorder model rankings relative to accuracy and F1, with ensembles that do not lead on F1 still delivering higher *e-Profits*, underscoring profitability as a key selection criterion. Overall, Gradient Boosting emerges as a balanced choice across predictive and profit-sensitive measures, and SHAP provides dependable explanations for such models, offering a practical alternative to relying solely on inherently interpretable classifiers. This study delivers a compact benchmark that reports model performance and explanation assessment side-by-side, integrating technical and business perspectives without conflation.

Source code: https://github.com/Awaismanzoor/aics-xai.

**Keywords:** Churn prediction · Explainable AI (XAI) · Post-hoc explanations (LIME · SHAP) · Ensemble learning · Profit-sensitive evaluation (EMP · e-Profits) · Quantitative XAI evaluation · Telecom datasets

## 1 Introduction

Customer churn reduces long-term revenue and customer equity, and acquiring new customers is far more costly than retaining existing ones [1]. Accurate churn prediction is therefore central to proactive retention.


T. T. Mai et al. (Eds.): AICS 2025, CCIS 2950, pp. 348–360, 2026.
https://doi.org/10.1007/978-3-032-25809-0_28

On tabular data, churn prediction is commonly cast as binary classification. Interpretable models such as logistic regression (LR) and decision trees (DT) remain popular for their transparency, but ensemble methods (RF, GBC, XGBoost, LightGBM, CatBoost) achieve higher predictive performance [2,3]. Their opacity, however, limits adoption in settings where accountability is required.

Post-hoc explainable AI (XAI) methods such as LIME and SHAP attribute feature importance for ensemble predictions. In practice, explanation quality is assessed using quantitative metrics with technical criteria, fidelity, robustness, simplicity, and consistency [10,14]. Separately, churn studies evaluate models with business-sensitive metrics (e.g., top-decile lift, Expected Maximum Profit (EMP), and customer-level *e-Profits*) [7,9]. In this study, we keep these strands distinct: we evaluate ensembles with predictive and profit-sensitive metrics, and we benchmark LIME and SHAP using the four XAI quantitative evaluation metrics; profit-oriented results are then used to contextualise the explanation findings.

This paper provides a compact benchmark of post-hoc explainability for churn prediction that integrates technical and business perspectives without conflating them.

The remainder of the paper is organised as follows. Section 2 reviews churn modelling, post-hoc explainability, and profit-sensitive evaluation. Section 3 describes datasets, models, metrics, and the XAI benchmarking protocol. Section 4 reports classification, business-sensitive, and XAI results, with implications. Section 5 concludes with limitations and future work.

## 2 Related Works

**Churn Prediction Models:** Churn has been widely studied across telecoms, banking, and e-commerce. Early work relied on interpretable models such as logistic regression (LR)[1] and decision trees (DT), while more recent benchmarks consistently favour tree-based ensembles (Random Forest, Gradient Boosting, XGBoost, LightGBM, CatBoost) for tabular data due to their ability to capture non-linear interactions and heterogeneous effects [2,5,6]. Despite their strong predictive performance, the opacity of these ensembles limits adoption in settings that require accountability and justification.

**Explainability in Churn:** To address opacity, post-hoc explainability methods have been integrated into churn modelling. LIME explains individual predictions via local surrogate models; SHAP attributes contributions using Shapley values, with TreeSHAP offering exact attributions for tree ensembles. Prior surveys emphasise the need to evaluate explanations with quantitative criteria, fidelity, robustness, simplicity, and consistency, rather than relying only on illustrative plots [10,11,14]. Nevertheless, systematic benchmarking of explanation quality

[1] Logistic regression is often treated as an interpretable baseline due to its linear coefficients, but its practical interpretability can be weakened when there are many correlated features or substantial multicollinearity.

using quantitative evaluation metrics in churn remains limited, and only a few recent works have begun to formalise these metrics and their implementations in the churn literature.

**Business- and Profit-Sensitive Evaluation:** Conventional predictive metrics (accuracy, F1, AUC) overlook financial impact. Business-sensitive measures such as top-decile lift (TDL) and related lift indices capture ranking quality for targeted retention, while profit-based measures, Expected Maximum Profit (EMP) [9] and the customer-level *e-Profits* [7], incorporate lifetime value and intervention costs, aligning evaluation with operational goals. These measures have proven useful for assessing predictive models; however, they are rarely considered alongside a quantitative assessment of explanation quality.

Prior work evaluates churn models with business-/profit-sensitive metrics and explainers with technical criteria, but these perspectives are seldom combined. Quantitative benchmarking of post-hoc explanations for churn, paired with profit-aware model evaluation, remains sparse. This study addresses that gap by comparing LIME and SHAP using formalised quantitative XAI evaluation metrics while reporting model performance with business- and profit-sensitive measures, providing an integrated (but non-conflated) view of model performance and explanation utility (Table 1).

**Table 1.** Hyperparameter tuning grids for selected classifiers

| Model | Hyperparameters |
|---|---|
| DT | max_depth = [None,10,20,30], min_split = [2,5,10],min_leaf = [1,2,4], criterion = [gini,entropy] |
| LR | C = [0.01,0.1,1,10], penalty = [l2,l1], max_iter = [100,200,300], solver = [lbfgs,liblinear,saga] |
| RF | n_est = [100,200,300], max_depth = [None,10,20,30], min_split = [2,5,10],min_leaf = [1,2,4] |
| GBC | n_est = [100,200,300], learn_rate = [0.01,0.1,0.2],max_depth = [3,4,5] |
| XGB | n_est = [100,200,300], learn_rate = [0.01,0.1,0.2], max_depth = [3,4,5], colsamp_bytree = [0.3,0.7] |
| CBC | iterations = [100,200], learn_rate = [0.01,0.1], depth = [3,5] |
| LGBM | n_est = [100,200], learn_rate = [0.01,0.1], num_leaves = [31,50] |

# 3 Methodology

## 3.1 Datasets

We evaluate on two public telco churn datasets commonly used in recent studies. *IBM Telco*[2] contains 7,043 customers with 19 features (demographics, tenure,

[2] https://www.kaggle.com/datasets/blastchar/telco-customer-churn.

services, payments), with a churn rate of 26.5%. *Maven Telecom*[3] includes 7,043 entries and 32 features; after excluding recent joiners (6%), the churn rate is 27%. Both datasets are clean and require minimal preprocessing.

### 3.2 Models

We train commonly used interpretable baselines and high-performing ensembles: Logistic Regression (LR), Decision Tree (DT), Random Forest (RF), Gradient Boosting (GBC), XGBoost, LightGBM, and CatBoost. All the models were trained with stratified 2-fold cross-validation due to computational resource constraints. This choice may increase variance relative to higher-fold CV, and results should be interpreted accordingly.

### 3.3 Post-hoc Explainers

We apply post-hoc explainers to the opaque ensemble models. *LIME* produces local linear surrogates via input perturbations. *SHAP* provides game-theoretic attributions; *TreeSHAP* yields exact values for tree ensembles. Local (per-instance) attributions are generated for churn predictions across both datasets.

### 3.4 Evaluation Metrics

We report four groups: `predictive` (Accuracy, F1, AUC); `business-sensitive` (Top-decile lift, Lift Index); `profit-sensitive` (EMP [9], *e-Profits*; *e-Profits* per 1,000 customers); and `quantitative XAI evaluation` (fidelity, robustness, simplicity, consistency).

**Business-Sensitive Evaluation -** Let $N$ be the total number of customers and $p_i \in [0, 1]$ the predicted churn probability. Customers are ranked in descending order of $p_i$.

*Top-Decile Lift (TDL):* Let $D_{10}$ denote the top 10% of customers by predicted churn risk. The Top-Decile Lift is defined as:

$$\text{TDL} = \frac{\frac{1}{|D_{10}|}\sum_{i \in D_{10}} y_i}{\frac{1}{N}\sum_{i=1}^{N} y_i} \tag{1}$$

TDL measures how much more concentrated churners are in the top 10% than in the full population.

*Lift Index:* Let the ranked customer list be partitioned into $K$ equal-sized deciles. The Lift Index is computed as:

$$\text{Lift Index} = \frac{1}{K}\sum_{k=1}^{K} \frac{\text{Churners in decile } k}{\text{Expected churners under random targeting}} \tag{2}$$

It quantifies the overall prioritisation quality across all ranked segments.

[3] https://www.kaggle.com/datasets/johnp47/maven-churn-dataset.

*Expected Maximum Profit (EMP):* EMP estimates the expected maximum profit over all possible targeting fractions:

$$\text{EMP} = \max_{\phi \in (0,1]} \left[ \phi N \cdot (\gamma \cdot \text{CLV} \cdot \pi(\phi) - C_{\text{offer}} - C_{\text{contact}}) \right] \tag{3}$$

where $\phi$ is the targeted fraction, $\gamma$ is the offer acceptance probability (modelled as a Beta distribution), $\pi(\phi)$ is the churn probability at targeting depth $\phi$, and CLV, $C_{\text{offer}}, C_{\text{contact}}$ are assumed fixed at the population level.

*e-Profits:* The total realised business value of a churn model is:

$$e\text{-}Profits = \sum_{i=1}^{N} \Pi_i \tag{4}$$

$$\Pi_i = \begin{cases} \text{CLV}_i - C_{\text{offer},i} - C_{\text{contact},i}, & y_i = 1 \wedge \hat{y}_i = 1 \\ -C_{\text{offer},i} - C_{\text{contact},i}, & y_i = 0 \wedge \hat{y}_i = 1 \\ 0, & \hat{y}_i = 0 \end{cases} \tag{5}$$

Customer lifetime value is computed as:

$$\text{CLV}_i = \frac{R_i \cdot M}{1 - \min(r_i, \tau)} \tag{6}$$

with monthly revenue $R_i$, profit margin $M$, personalised retention probability $r_i$ estimated via Kaplan–Meier survival analysis, and stability cap $\tau = 0.995$.

Intervention costs are:

$$C_{\text{offer},i} = \text{CPO} \cdot \text{CLV}_i, \qquad C_{\text{contact},i} = \max(c_0, c_1 \cdot C_{\text{offer},i}) \tag{7}$$

where CPO $= 0.1$ is the cost-per-offer ratio, $c_0 = 5$ is the fixed minimum contact cost, and $c_1 = 0.3$ is the proportional contact cost multiplier. Only customers with $\hat{y}_i = 1$ are contacted. True positives generate retained lifetime profit, false positives incur pure cost, and predicted non-churners incur no financial impact. Full methodological and empirical details are available in [7].

**Quantitative XAI Evaluation -** Let $X = \{x_i\}_{i=1}^{N}$ denote the dataset with $N$ instances and $d$ features. Let $h$ denote the trained predictive model and $E$ an attribution-based explainer (e.g., LIME or SHAP). For each instance $x_i$, the explainer produces a feature-attribution vector $\mathbf{a}_i = (a_{i1}, \ldots, a_{id}) \in \mathbb{R}^d$.

*Fidelity / Faithfulness:* Fidelity quantifies how accurately an explainer replicates the behavior of the predictive model at both the probability (score) and decision (label) levels. We report two complementary variants.

$$\text{Fid}_{\text{score}}(E) = \frac{1}{N} \sum_{i=1}^{N} \left(1 - \left| p_h(x_i) - p_E(x_i) \right| \right) \tag{8}$$

$$\mathrm{Fid}_{\mathrm{decision}}(E) = \frac{1}{N}\sum_{i=1}^{N}\delta\big(\hat{y}_h(x_i), \hat{y}_E(x_i)\big) \tag{9}$$

where $p_h(x_i)$ is the probability output of model $h$, $p_E(x_i)$ is the probability reconstructed by the explainer, $\hat{y}_h(x_i)$ and $\hat{y}_E(x_i)$ are the corresponding class predictions, $\delta(a,b)$ denotes the Kronecker delta, which returns 1 if $a = b$ and 0 otherwise. Values closer to 1 indicate higher faithfulness.

*Simplicity / Parsimony:* Simplicity is operationalized as relative-importance threshold sparsity, measuring the average number of features whose normalized attribution exceeds a threshold $\tau$:

$$\mathrm{Simp}(E;\tau) = \frac{1}{N}\sum_{i=1}^{N}\sum_{j=1}^{d}\mathbb{I}\left(\frac{|a_{ij}|}{\max_{k\in\{1,\ldots,d\}}|a_{ik}|} > \tau\right) \tag{10}$$

We evaluate simplicity at thresholds $\tau \in \{0.10, 0.05, 0.01\}$. Larger $\tau$ retains only dominant features, producing sparse explanations, while smaller $\tau$ yields denser explanations by including weaker contributions. Lower simplicity values indicate more compact explanations.

*Consistency (Inter-explainer Agreement):* Consistency measures the agreement between two explainers in ranking the most influential features for the same instance. Following rank-based evaluation, we compute depth-averaged Spearman correlation over the top-$k$ features:

$$\mathrm{Cons}(E_1, E_2) = \frac{1}{N}\sum_{i=1}^{N}\left(\frac{1}{k}\sum_{n=1}^{k}\rho_s\big(\mathrm{Top}_n(E_1, x_i),\ \mathrm{Top}_n(E_2, x_i)\big)\right) \tag{11}$$

where $\rho_s$ denotes Spearman's rank correlation and $\mathrm{Top}_n(E, x_i)$ denotes the top-$n$ ranked features for instance $x_i$. We fix $k = 5$ to focus on the most influential features. Higher values indicate stronger inter-explainer agreement.

*Robustness / Stability:* Robustness evaluates the stability of explanations under small, semantically negligible input perturbations. We add element-wise Gaussian noise $\epsilon \sim \mathcal{N}(0, \sigma^2)$ with $\sigma = 0.01$ and measure the average $\ell_1$ change in the attribution vectors:

$$\mathrm{Rob}(E) = \frac{1}{N}\sum_{i=1}^{N}\|\mathbf{a}_i - \mathbf{a}_i^{\epsilon}\|_1 \tag{12}$$

where $\mathbf{a}_i^{\epsilon}$ is the attribution vector computed after perturbing $x_i$. Lower robustness values indicate greater stability, with 0 denoting complete invariance to perturbation.

More details about the above quantitative XAI evaluation metrics and their implementation are available in [15].

**Justification of Metric Choices and Limitations:** TDL, EMP, and *e-Profits* directly capture ranking quality and realised financial utility, essential for churn-retention decisions. Logistic regression and decision trees serve as standard interpretable baselines, reflecting the transparency performance trade-off in practice. SHAP and LIME provide useful post-hoc insight for ensembles but both have limitations in imbalanced and cost-sensitive settings: LIME can yield unstable explanations near skewed decision boundaries, and SHAP, although faithful for tree models, distributes small attributions across many features without encoding asymmetric misclassification costs. Explanation quality should therefore be interpreted alongside profit-aware evaluation rather than in isolation.

**Table 2.** Model performances on IBM and Maven dataset. Best results are shown in **bold**; second-best results are marked with **bold***.

| Name | Accuracy | F1-Score | AUC | Lift Index | TDL | EMP | ***e-Profits*** |
|---|---|---|---|---|---|---|---|
| **IBM Dataset** | | | | | | | |
| DT | 0.740 | 0.491 | 0.653 | 0.698 | 2.094 | 8.230 | 326.77 |
| LR | 0.782 | 0.586 | 0.712 | **0.806*** | 2.844 | 10.697 | 366.47 |
| RF | 0.791 | 0.552 | 0.692 | 0.802 | **2.948*** | 10.776 | 333.71 |
| CatBoost | **0.807** | **0.595** | **0.718*** | 0.794 | 3.001 | **10.848*** | 390.45 |
| XGBoost | **0.801*** | 0.587 | 0.717 | 0.805 | 2.861 | 10.795 | **394.13** |
| LGBM | 0.788 | 0.563 | 0.698 | 0.798 | 2.939 | 10.651 | 359.84 |
| GBC | 0.798 | **0.589*** | **0.721** | **0.808** | **2.966** | **10.898** | **393.50*** |
| **Maven Dataset** | | | | | | | |
| DT | 0.833 | 0.696 | 0.783 | 0.780 | 2.799 | 10.861 | 61.56 |
| LR | 0.849 | 0.725 | 0.802 | 0.845 | 3.345 | 12.895 | 63.81 |
| RF | 0.866 | 0.733 | 0.798 | 0.852 | 3.416 | 13.352 | 65.97 |
| CatBoost | **0.871*** | 0.754 | 0.817 | **0.864** | **3.468** | **13.456*** | 65.47 |
| XGBoost | 0.869 | 0.757 | **0.823** | 0.858 | **3.451*** | 13.194 | **65.97*** |
| LGBM | 0.870 | **0.759**** | **0.823** | **0.860*** | **3.451*** | 13.299 | 65.74 |
| GBC | **0.873** | **0.763** | **0.821*** | **0.859*** | **3.468** | **13.457** | **66.02** |

**Procedure:** Each model is trained on both datasets under stratified 2-fold CV. LIME and SHAP are applied to ensemble predictions. Metrics are averaged across folds. Results are reported in two dimensions: (i) model performance in predictive and profit terms, and (ii) explanation quality assessment of LIME and SHAP on the four quantitative XAI metrics.

# 4 Results and Discussion

## 4.1 Classification Results

Table 2 compares all models on predictive and business- and profit-sensitive metrics across the IBM and Maven datasets. Results highlight two consistent patterns.

First, ensemble methods outperform interpretable baselines (DT, LR) on most measures. On IBM, CatBoost achieves the highest accuracy and F1, while XGBoost yields the best *e-Profits*. However, GBC ranks first on AUC, EMP, and Lift, while also placing second-best in F1 and *e-Profits*. This consistent positioning across both predictive and business metrics establishes GBC as a balanced choice.

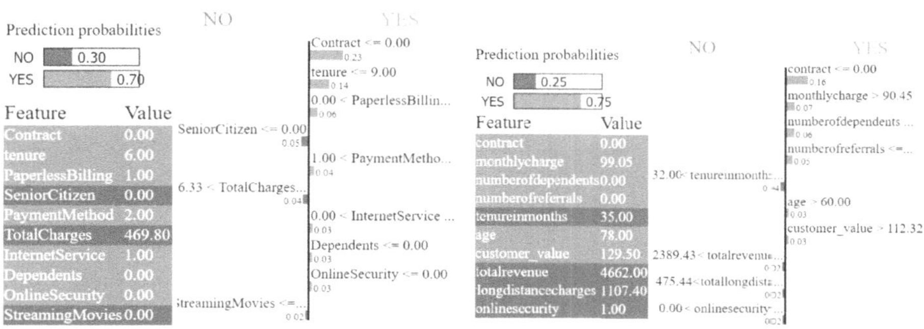


(a) IBM Dataset (b) Maven Dataset

**Fig. 1.** LIME local explanations

Second, on the Maven dataset, the gap between models narrows. CatBoost, XGBoost, and LGBM each achieve individual best scores, but GBC again maintains a strong balance, ranking first on accuracy, F1, EMP, and *e-Profits*, while placing second on AUC and Lift. This reinforces the observation that while no single ensemble dominates all metrics, GBC repeatedly offers competitive performance across them.

**Implication:** From a business perspective, while LR and DT remain interpretable baselines, ensembles such as GBC provide both higher predictive power and stronger profitability signals. Importantly, profit-oriented measures (EMP, *e-Profits*) reorder rankings compared to accuracy/F1, showing that businesses should prioritise profitability metrics over purely technical ones when selecting churn models.

## 4.2 XAI Results

To complement quantitative evaluation, we present illustrative explanations from LIME and SHAP (Figs. 1 and 2). LIME provides local linear surrogates, highlighting, for example, how contract length and monthly charges drive churn predictions on IBM and Maven. SHAP offers both local and global attributions; local plots show features such as tenure and charges dominating individual decisions, while global summaries (Fig. 3) highlight systemic drivers such as tenure, contract type, and service bundles.

Overall, LIME yields fast, instance-specific explanations that are easy to read, whereas SHAP combines local detail with global overviews, providing a richer basis for auditing model behaviour and aligning churn drivers with retention strategies.

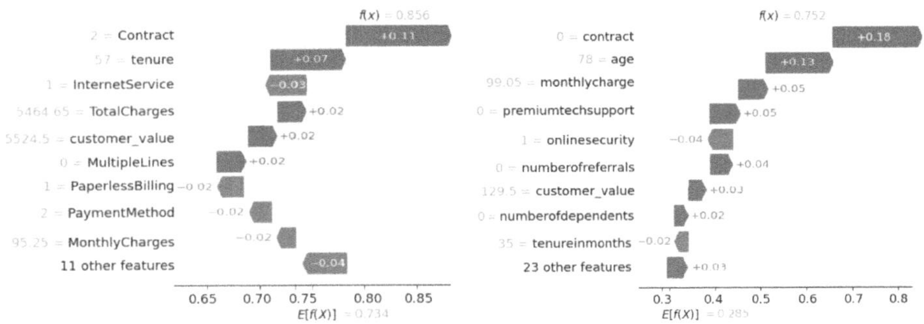

(a) IBM Dataset (b) Maven Dataset

**Fig. 2.** SHAP local explanations

### 4.3 Quantitative Evaluation of XAI

We benchmark explanation quality using four quantitative metrics: fidelity, consistency, simplicity, and robustness (Tables 3–4 and Fig. 4).

**Table 3.** Fidelity of LIME and SHAP

| Dataset | LIME (Score) | SHAP (Score) | LIME (Decision) | SHAP (Decision) |
|---|---|---|---|---|
| IBM Dataset | 0.891 | **1.000** | 0.881 | **1.000** |
| Maven Dataset | 0.838 | **1.000** | 0.874 | **1.000** |

**Fidelity:** Table 3 shows that SHAP attains perfect score and decision fidelity on both datasets, while LIME achieves reasonable score fidelity but lower decision fidelity, especially on IBM where decision boundaries are more complex. High decision fidelity means explanations justify the actual "churn" vs "no churn" outcomes, enabling organisations to keep high-performing ensembles without reverting to LR/DT purely for interpretability. SHAP's performance is consistent with TreeSHAP's exact attributions for tree ensembles, whereas LIME's local surrogates can misalign near complex regions, making SHAP the safer default when fidelity is critical.

**Consistency:** Consistency between LIME and SHAP on Maven and IBM is 0.67 and 0.72, indicating moderate-to-high agreement in top-ranked features. This overlap supports the view that explanations are not arbitrary, while residual differences suggest that triangulating multiple explainers can be useful in mission-critical settings.

**Simplicity:** Table 4 shows that LIME produces sparser explanations at higher thresholds, whereas SHAP includes more features as $\tau$ decreases, reflecting broader coverage of interacting drivers. In practice, concise LIME outputs can ease analyst review, while denser SHAP explanations at low $\tau$ are useful for auditability and model debugging.

**Table 4.** Simplicity scores across thresholds (average number of features per instance).

| Dataset | Method | Threshold 0.1 | Threshold 0.05 | Threshold 0.01 |
|---|---|---|---|---|
| IBM | LIME | 8.73 | 9.89 | 10.00 |
| | SHAP | 7.30 | 10.76 | 16.87 |
| Maven | LIME | 9.65 | 10.00 | 10.00 |
| | SHAP | 8.52 | 12.22 | 21.61 |

The higher feature counts in Table 4 stem from the relative-threshold metric and dataset size; in practice, only the top 5–10 features would typically be shown to users for clear and actionable explanations.

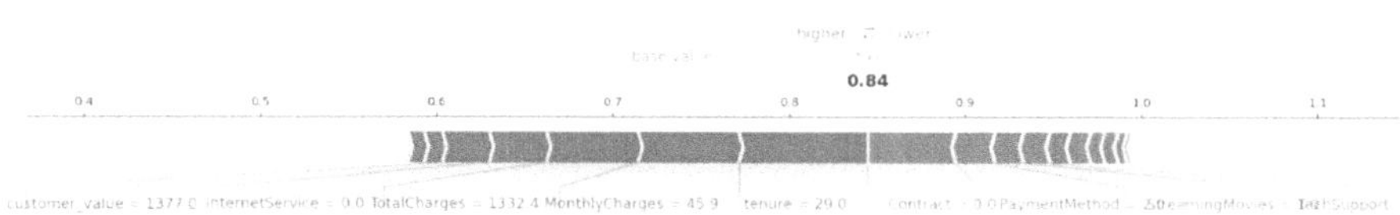


(a) IBM Dataset

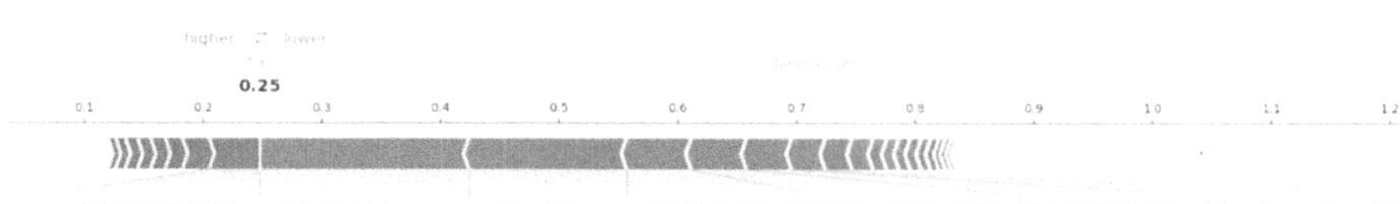


(b) Maven Dataset

**Fig. 3.** Global SHAP feature importance

**Robustness:** Figure 4 shows that LIME is more sensitive to increasing noise, with fluctuating scores at moderate perturbation levels, whereas SHAP remains comparatively stable across all tested noise levels. Robustness is important where explanations should not change under small input variations (e.g., customer dashboards, regulated decisions), and this stability profile makes SHAP more dependable in such contexts.

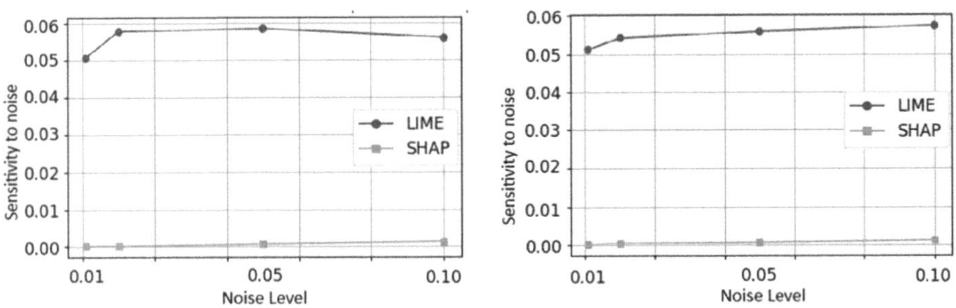


(a) IBM Dataset (b) Maven Dataset

**Fig. 4.** Robustness trends across noise levels for IBM and Maven datasets. Each figure compares LIME and SHAP. (Low sensitivity shows high Robustness.)

## 5 Conclusion

This study benchmarked post-hoc explainability for churn prediction by reporting model performance and explanation quality side-by-side. On two public telco datasets, interpretable baselines (LR, DT) were compared with tree ensembles; Gradient Boosting (GBC) emerged as a balanced choice across predictive and profit-sensitive measures (EMP, *e-Profits*), while other boosted models (CatBoost, XGBoost, LightGBM) remained close on several metrics. Across XAI criteria, SHAP consistently outperformed LIME in fidelity and robustness and, with its local and global views, provided dependable explanations for ensembles, reducing the need to rely solely on inherently interpretable classifiers. Profit-based evaluation reordered rankings relative to accuracy/F1, reinforcing that profitability should accompany predictive metrics when selecting churn pipelines.

**Practical Takeaways:** (i) Prefer boosted ensembles when profit is the objective; (ii) explain ensembles with SHAP for high-fidelity, stable attributions and use LIME when concise, lightweight summaries are needed; (iii) report profit-oriented metrics (e.g., *e-Profits*, EMP) alongside accuracy/F1 and a ranking signal (e.g., top-decile lift) to guide targeting decisions.

**Limitations:** Findings are based on two public telco datasets and stratified 2-fold cross-validation, which limits statistical generalisability but reflects the computational cost of running profit-sensitive evaluation across multiple models, datasets, and explainers. Future studies should use more datasets, stronger validation protocols (e.g., 5- or 10-fold CV), and variance estimates or confidence intervals to strengthen statistical reliability. Explanations were evaluated only for post-hoc methods (LIME, SHAP) on tree ensembles; inherently interpretable models and counterfactual techniques were out of scope. The study also does not assess human-centred aspects such as analyst trust, usability, or downstream operational effects.

**Future Work:** Extend to broader sectors and larger datasets; adopt stronger validation (e.g., 5-fold or repeated CV) and probability calibration; evaluate additional explanation families (e.g., counterfactuals, rule lists) and fairness/stability checks; and investigate profit-aligned explanation objectives that directly incorporate business value signals into explanation evaluation. Field studies (A/B tests or analyst-in-the-loop assessments) would help quantify downstream impact on retention decisions.

Overall, the results offer a compact, reproducible, metric-driven evaluation framework for aligning predictive accuracy, interpretability, and profitability in churn modelling.

## References


1. Zhou, Y., Chen, W., Sun, X., Yang, D.: Early warning of telecom enterprise customer churn based on ensemble learning. PLoS ONE **18**(10), e0292466 (2023)
2. Manzoor, A., Atif Qureshi, M., Kidney, E., Longo, L.: A review on machine learning methods for customer churn prediction and recommendations for business practitioners. IEEE Access **12**, 70434–70463 (2024)
3. Noor, A.A., Manzoor, A., Mazhar Qureshi, M.D., Qureshi, M.A., Rashwan, W.: Unveiling explainable AI in healthcare: current trends, challenges, and future directions. Wiley Interdisc. Rev. Data Mining Knowl. Discovery **15**(2), e70018 (2025)
4. Rudin, C.: Stop explaining black box machine learning models for high stakes decisions and use interpretable models instead. Nat. Mach. Intell. **1**(5), 206–215 (2019)
5. Bentejac, C., Csörgő, A., Martínez-Muñoz, G.: A comparative analysis of gradient boosting algorithms. Artif. Intell. Rev. **54**, 1937–1967 (2021)
6. Fernández-Delgado, M., Cernadas, E., Barro, S., Amorim, D.: Do we need hundreds of classifiers to solve real world classification problems? J. Mach. Learn. Res. **15**(1), 3133–3181 (2014)
7. Manzoor, A., Qureshi, M.A., Kidney, E., Longo, L.: e-profits: a business-aligned evaluation metric for profit-sensitive customer churn prediction. arXiv preprint arXiv:2507.08860 (2025)
8. Arik, S.O., Pfister, T.: TabNet: attentive interpretable tabular learning. In: Proceedings of the AAAI Conference on Artificial Intelligence, vol. 35, no. 8, pp. 6679–6687 (2021)
9. Verbraken, T., Verbeke, W., Baesens, B.: A novel profit maximizing metric for measuring classification performance of customer churn prediction models. IEEE Trans. Knowl. Data Eng. **25**(5), 961–973 (2012)

10. Ali, S., Abuhmed, T., El-Sappagh, S., Muhammad, K., Alonso-Moral, J.M., Confalonieri, R., et al.: Explainable artificial intelligence (XAI): what we know and what is left to attain trustworthy artificial intelligence. Inf. Fusion **99**, 101805 (2023)
11. Pawlicki, M., Pawlicka, A., Uccello, F., Szelest, S., D'Antonio, S., Kozik, R., et al.: Evaluating the necessity of the multiple metrics for assessing explainable AI: a critical examination. Neurocomputing **602**, 128282 (2024)
12. Kantz, B., et al.: Robustness of explainable artificial intelligence in industrial process modelling. arXiv preprint arXiv:2407.09127 (2024)
13. Khalilpourazari, S., Khalilpourazary, S., Özyüksel Çiftçioğlu, A., Weber, G.W.: Designing energy-efficient high-precision multi-pass turning processes via robust optimization and artificial intelligence. J. Intell. Manuf. **32**, 1621–1647 (2021)
14. Nauta, M., et al.: From anecdotal evidence to quantitative evaluation methods: a systematic review on evaluating explainable AI. ACM Comput. Surv. **55**(13s), 1–42 (2023)
15. Qureshi, M.A., Noor, A.A., Manzoor, A., Mazhar Qureshi, M.D., Younus, A., Rashwan, W.: Explainability in action: a metric-driven assessment of local explanations for healthcare tabular models medRxiv, 2025–05. Cold Spring Harbor Laboratory Press (2025)

# Latency–Sustainability Trade-Offs in On-Device vs. Near-Edge Offloaded Semantic Segmentation

Hassan Khan[1(✉)], Sunbal Iftikhar[2], Steven Davy[2], and John G. Breslin[1]

[1] School of Engineering and Data Science Institute, University of Galway, Galway, Ireland
{h.khan5,john.breslin}@universityofgalway.ie
[2] Technological University (TU) Dublin, Dublin, Ireland
d23125132@mytudublin.ie, steven.davy@tudublin.ie

**Abstract.** Edge computing offers low-latency inference for computer vision and minimizes wide-area network usage; however, the sustainability implications of transferring deep learning workloads to proximate servers are not thoroughly examined. This study examines the latency-sustainability trade-off associated with conducting semantic segmentation on-device compared to offloading the task to a near-edge server, while adhering to a service-level objective (SLO) of 150 ms for the 95th-percentile latency. We employ a lightweight segmentation model on an NVIDIA Jetson AGX Orin for on-device processing, alongside a larger model on an edge server equipped with three RTX A6000 GPUs, utilizing a Triton inference server. This setup allows us to evaluate end-to-end latency, accuracy (measured by mIoU and pixel accuracy), energy consumption, and carbon intensity (assessed through CodeCarbon) under varying network conditions. We conduct experiments on the Cityscapes dataset. The findings indicate that on-device processing maintains consistent tail latency in suboptimal network conditions, while offloading enhances accuracy and throughput in optimal network environments. An oracle SLO- and carbon-aware policy can achieve a reduction in operational carbon intensity by 15–20% compared to static baselines.

**Keywords:** Edge Computing · Semantic Segmentation · Latency · Carbon Emissions · Sustainability · Offloading Policy

## 1 Introduction

The proliferation of deep learning in mobile and IoT devices has led to growing interest in edge computing for low-latency, real-time inference [3,4]. By performing computations closer to data sources, edge computing can avoid the high latency and bandwidth costs of cloud offloading, which is critical for latency-sensitive tasks under strict service-level objectives (SLOs) [7]. At the same time,


T. T. Mai et al. (Eds.): AICS 2025, CCIS 2950, pp. 361–375, 2026.
https://doi.org/10.1007/978-3-032-25809-0_29

executing deep neural networks on resource-constrained devices may sacrifice model accuracy or efficiency, whereas offloading to powerful edge servers enables larger models and potentially higher accuracy. This trade-off between latency and accuracy for edge AI has been widely studied [11,12], but the *sustainability* dimension, particularly the carbon footprint of on-device vs. offloaded inference, remains under-examined.

Recent works have highlighted the environmental impact of AI, calling for "Green AI" that balances predictive performance with computational cost [8]. The operational carbon emissions of ML inference are influenced by factors such as hardware energy efficiency, model size, and power source [10]. Offloading computation shifts energy consumption from battery-powered devices to edge/cloud data centers, which might have access to more efficient hardware or cleaner energy grids, but can also incur network energy overheads and under-utilization losses. For example, servers are known to be energy-inefficient at low utilization [6], so a single client offloading infrequently may lead to worse energy per inference than local processing. Furthermore, network conditions (latency, loss) can drastically affect end-to-end performance [13], potentially causing SLA violations (high tail latency) and extra energy use due to retransmissions or idle periods.

To our knowledge, a quantitative comparison of on-device versus near-edge offloaded inference under varying network conditions, with a joint focus on latency (including tail latency) and carbon emissions, has not been thoroughly reported. Prior studies have explored dynamic offloading policies to optimize latency-energy trade-offs using machine learning [14] or game theory [13], and scheduling systems like Clipper [15] or others optimize inference latency via model selection and batching, but these often do not explicitly account for carbon intensity. In this paper, we undertake an empirical study of semantic segmentation on images, comparing a lightweight model running on an edge device to a heavier model offloaded to a nearby edge server. Our central question is: *for a given latency SLO, which deployment option minimizes the operational carbon intensity of the service?*

We formulate three hypotheses (H1–H3). In essence, we expect that under poor network conditions, on-device inference will better maintain the required p95 latency $\leq 150$ ms and use less energy per image than offloading. Under good network conditions (low round-trip time, minimal loss) and with the ability to batch requests on the server's GPUs, offloading should achieve lower latency (and thereby support higher throughput) and higher segmentation accuracy (by using a larger model), while its per-image emissions may become comparable to the on-device method when the server hardware is well-utilized. Finally, we hypothesize that an adaptive policy which dynamically chooses between local and offloaded execution based on current conditions can yield an overall reduction in carbon emissions without violating the latency SLO, compared to always using one approach or the other.

Our contributions are: (1) an experimental evaluation of latency, accuracy, and energy/emissions for on-device vs. near-edge offloaded semantic segmentation on a standard dataset (Cityscapes) across multiple network scenarios; (2) analysis of the conditions under which each approach excels or falls short, validating the above hypotheses; (3) an oracle-driven policy experiment demonstrating the potential emissions savings from SLO- and carbon-aware placement decisions. This work provides insights for practitioners designing sustainable edge intelligence systems and highlights the importance of considering both performance and carbon efficiency in edge vs. cloud deployment decisions.

The rest of this paper is organized as follows. Section 2 describes related work on edge offloading and sustainable AI. Section 3 details our experimental platform, models, and methodology for measuring latency and emissions. Section 4 presents the results for each hypothesis, with key trade-offs. Section 5 concludes with implications and future work.

## 2 Related Work

Edge computing has emerged to meet the demands of latency-critical applications by processing data closer to the source [3,4]. Prior work has extensively studied computation offloading strategies for mobile and IoT devices, balancing factors such as latency, energy consumption, and device resources. For deep learning inference, Kang *et al.* propose Neurosurgeon [11], which partitions DNN execution between device and cloud to minimize latency. Teerapittayanon *et al.* introduce distributed DNN frameworks that split model layers across edge and cloud [12], achieving low latency by early exiting or parallel execution. These approaches focus on performance and sometimes energy usage, but not explicitly on carbon footprint.

With growing awareness of AI's environmental impact, tools and studies have appeared to estimate and reduce carbon emissions of ML. Strubell *et al.* [8] and Henderson *et al.* [10] highlight the large carbon costs of training and the need for transparent reporting. CodeCarbon [9] is a recent software library that estimates $CO_2$ emissions from computing by tracking energy consumption and using region-specific carbon intensity data. In parallel, research on energy-efficient edge AI and carbon-aware computing is emerging. Yu *et al.* [13] formulate a task offloading and dynamic voltage/frequency scaling scheme to reduce the carbon footprint in edge computing. Zhai *et al.* [5] propose an edge-cloud collaboration framework to optimize latency, carbon emissions, and cost simultaneously for distributed workloads. Benaboura *et al.* [14] demonstrate a deep reinforcement learning approach for latency- and energy-aware offloading in IoT systems, showing that an intelligent agent can learn to minimize power usage while meeting latency constraints.

Our work differs in that we perform a holistic empirical evaluation of a specific computer vision task (semantic segmentation) in an edge vs. near-edge offload scenario, using real hardware deployments. Instead of assuming theoretical or simulated energy costs, we measure actual power and estimate carbon emissions with a standardized tool. We also incorporate model accuracy (segmentation quality) into the analysis, reflecting the practical trade-off that offloading enables larger, more accurate models. While prior scheduling systems like Clipper [15] or inference-serving frameworks (e.g., NVIDIA Triton) support dynamic batching and model selection to optimize throughput and latency, we explicitly examine how such techniques interplay with energy efficiency and carbon intensity.

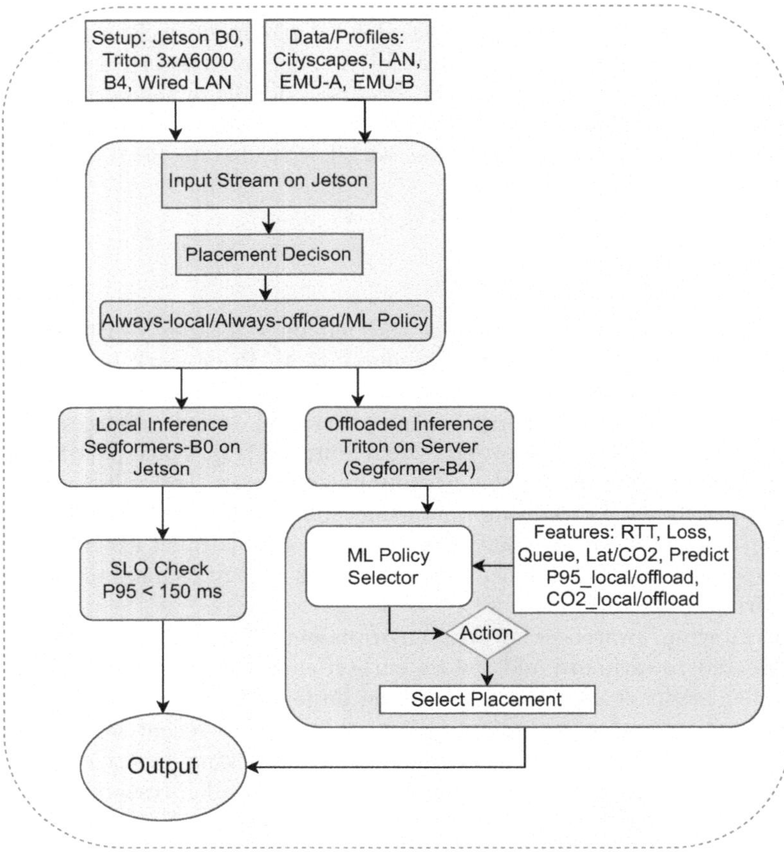


**Fig. 1.** System design and experimental workflow: data/profiles (Cityscapes; LAN/Emu-A/Emu-B), setup (Jetson B0; Triton on 3×A6000 running SegFormer-B4), input stream on Jetson, placement decision (Always-Local / Always-Offload / ML policy), offloaded and local inference paths, SLO check, and output.

# 3 Methodology and Experimental Setup

## 3.1 Hardware Platforms and Deployment

Our experimental platform (Fig. 1) consists of an **edge device** and a **near-edge server** connected via a local network. The edge device is an NVIDIA

Jetson AGX Orin (64 GB RAM model), representing an efficient embedded AI platform. The server is a high-performance workstation hosting the NVIDIA Triton Inference Server (v2.29) and equipped with 3× NVIDIA RTX A6000 GPUs (16 GB each). The server runs a Segmentation inference service (via Triton) with one instance of the model loaded per GPU and dynamic batching enabled (allowing incoming requests to be grouped for parallel processing on a GPU). We evaluate performance under three network profiles between the Jetson client and the server: (i) **LAN**: a baseline with negligible network latency (round-trip time RTT ≈1–5 ms) and no packet loss; (ii) **Emu-A**: an emulated moderate WAN condition with RTT $\approx 30 \pm 10$ ms and 0.2% packet loss; (iii) **Emu-B**: a degraded network with RTT $\approx 60 \pm 20$ ms and 1% packet loss. Profiles (ii) and (iii) are applied using traffic control (tc) on the client to introduce delay and loss to outgoing traffic, simulating congested or long-distance links (for example, Emu-B could resemble a weak 4G connection). These conditions allow us to assess the impact of network quality on offloaded inference.

We consider two deployment modes for running semantic segmentation on a stream of images:

- **Always-Local**: The Jetson device performs inference on-device using a small segmentation model. No network communication is needed (other than, e.g., sending results out, which we ignore here). This eliminates network latency and bandwidth usage but is limited by the Jetson's compute.
- **Always-Offload**: The Jetson offloads each image to the server for inference on a GPU, then receives the segmentation result. This leverages the server's greater computational power and potentially larger model, but incurs network overhead.

We later consider a dynamic policy that can choose between these modes per image. In all cases, the image data is initially on the Jetson (simulating a camera feed or local dataset), and for offloading, images are sent to Triton and results (segmentation masks) returned. Image size is 1024 × 512 pixels (Cityscapes resolution), roughly 1 MB JPEG each, which introduces minor network transfer time (<10 ms on LAN).

### 3.2 Models and Dataset

For on-device inference, we use the **SegFormer-B0** model [2], which is a Transformer-based semantic segmentation model with an efficient design (B0 is the smallest variant, around 3.8 million parameters). This model provides real-time performance on edge GPUs and reasonable accuracy. On the server, we deploy a larger model from the same family, **SegFormer-B4**, with about 64 million parameters and higher expected accuracy [2]. SegFormer-B4 requires more memory and compute. The rationale for this choice is to compare a scenario where the edge device runs a fast but less accurate model to one where offloading allows use of a more accurate model, thereby examining the latency vs. accuracy vs. carbon trade-off.

We evaluate on the **Cityscapes** dataset [1], a standard benchmark for urban scene segmentation. We use the official validation set of 500 images (with ground truth labels) to measure segmentation quality. Mean Intersection-over-Union (**mIoU**) and Pixel Accuracy (**PixAcc**) are computed on this set to compare the models' accuracy. To evaluate runtime performance (throughput, latency) and energy, we use an additional 1,000 unlabeled images from Cityscapes (or the test set without using labels) so as not to overfit any optimizations to the validation set. These images are fed through each deployment mode in a streaming fashion. We ensure both systems process the same images in the same order.

### 3.3 Latency, Throughput, and Power Measurement

We measure end-to-end latency for each image from the moment it is ready to be processed on the Jetson to the moment the segmentation result is obtained (on the Jetson for both local and offload cases). This includes network transfer time for offloaded inference. We collect per-image latency and compute the median (p50) and 95th percentile (p95) latency for each scenario. The target SLO is p95 $\leq$150 ms as given. Throughput (images per second) is computed as the total images divided by total time for the stream; we also note the peak sustainable throughput under each mode by pushing images as fast as possible (with concurrency or batching as applicable) until either latency constraints are violated or hardware saturates.

We instrument power consumption on both devices: the Jetson Orin provides on-board power monitoring, and for the server we use NVIDIA's NVML API to log GPU power and IPMI for overall system power. However, to simplify carbon accounting, we primarily rely on CodeCarbon (v2.4) [9] to estimate energy usage and emissions. We integrate CodeCarbon in the Jetson inference code and in the Triton server process to track energy (CPU, GPU, memory) during the experiments. CodeCarbon is configured with the carbon intensity for our local grid. This yields an estimate of carbon emissions in grams $CO_2$ for the workload. We report the *operational carbon intensity* per image, calculated by total emissions divided by number of images processed. This metric ($gCO_2$/image) captures the sustainability of each approach.

It should be noted that CodeCarbon provides an estimate based on hardware power draw and does not account for embodied carbon of manufacturing the devices or other overhead outside the computation. We focus on operational emissions (compute energy usage during inference).

### 3.4 SLO and Carbon-Aware Policy

To explore H3, we simulate an *oracle policy* that, for each image, selects the execution mode (local or offload) that yields the lower carbon emission *among those options meeting the latency SLO*. In a real deployment, such a policy could be implemented by a lightweight classifier or regression model that predicts the latency of each option given current conditions (e.g., recent network RTT and jitter) and selects the appropriate mode. Various approaches to learn or compute offloading decisions exist (e.g., using deep Q-learning as in [14]), but here we use an oracle with perfect hindsight knowledge of each image's latency on both systems (obtained from separate test runs). This represents an upper bound on the potential emission savings of a dynamic policy.

Concretely, for each image we check if the offload mode's latency would have met the SLO (=150 ms). If not, the policy must choose local (assuming local can meet SLO). If both modes meet SLO, we compare their predicted carbon emissions per image (which in our case correlates with energy usage for that image's inference) and choose the mode with lower $CO_2$. We then calculate the total emissions for a sequence of images under this policy. We evaluate this strategy in a scenario where network conditions vary over time, causing the preferred mode to switch. We compare the cumulative emissions and SLO compliance against two static baselines: always-local and always-offload.

## 4 Results and Analysis

We now present the experimental results, organized by the hypotheses (H1–H3). Unless stated otherwise, the SLO target is p95 latency $\leq$150 ms per image.

### 4.1 H1: On-Device vs. Offload Under Degraded Network

H1 posited that for a single client, on-device inference would satisfy the latency SLO more consistently and with lower per-image emissions than offloading under degraded network conditions. Our findings strongly support this. Under the worst network profile (Emu-B: 60 ms base RTT with jitter and 1% loss), the offloaded mode experienced significant variability in latency. Figure 2 shows the cumulative distribution of end-to-end latency for 1000 images in the Emu-B scenario, comparing Always-Local vs. Always-Offload. The on-device latency is very stable: median $\approx$80 ms and 95th percentile $\approx$94 ms, well below the 150 ms SLO. In contrast, offloading (SegFormer-B4 on server, Emu-B network) has median latency around 120 ms and a long tail. The 95th percentile latency reached about 180 ms, failing the SLO (exceeding 150 ms). In some cases, network delays and packet losses caused inference times up to 200+ ms. This means 15–17% or more of the images would violate the latency requirement if always offloaded under these network conditions.

Table 1 (rows for Emu-B) provides on-device median/p95 were 82/96 ms vs. offload 119/183 ms. Under Emu-A, offloading meets the SLO but has higher latency (p95$\sim$120 ms) than on-device (p95–95 ms). Only in the LAN case (virtually no network delay) did offloaded inference have a clear latency advantage (median 60 ms vs. 79 ms local, and both well under 150 ms p95).

The energy/emissions side of H1 also favored on-device in degraded conditions. The Jetson running SegFormer-B0 is extremely power-efficient for this workload, consuming roughly 5J per inference (Table 2). In Emu-B, offloading

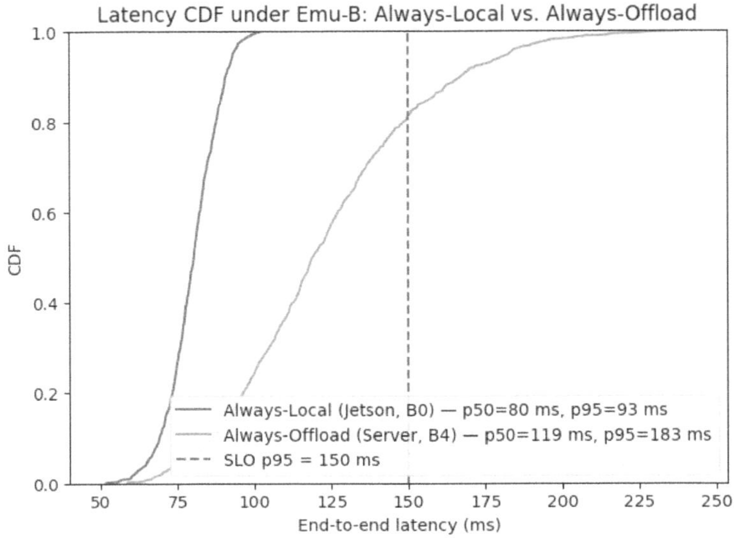


**Fig. 2.** End-to-end latency distribution (CDF) for 1000 images under degraded network (Emu-B). On-device inference (Jetson, SegFormer-B0) has consistently lower latency variability than offloaded inference (Triton server, SegFormer-B4). The dashed line marks the 150 ms SLO. Offloading exhibits a heavier tail (p95 ∼183 ms) and fails the SLO, whereas on-device meets it with margin.

one image took longer wall-clock time, during which the server GPU and networking gear remained powered. Even though the A6000 GPU is more energy-hungry, it was mostly idle waiting for network, leading to poor energy proportionality. We observed about 30 J per offloaded inference (including idle time) in Emu-B, roughly 6× the on-device energy. This translates to around 3.3 mg $CO_2$ per image offloaded, versus 0.6 mg on-device (assuming our grid's carbon intensity). Thus, H1 is confirmed: under poor network conditions, always-local not only provided more reliable latency but also emitted far less $CO_2$ per image than always-offload.

Beyond tail latency, another observation is throughput: in Emu-B, the average throughput with offloading was only about 8.3 images/sec for a single stream, whereas the Jetson maintained about 12 images/sec. The network became the bottleneck in offload mode, effectively throttling inference rate. In Emu-A, throughput of offload and local were similar (both around 11–12 im/s). In LAN, the server could process faster than the Jetson (16 vs 12 im/s) given its more powerful hardware. These results underscore that a poor network connection not only increases latency but also limits effective throughput, whereas the on-device processing is unaffected by network quality.

**Table 1.** Latency performance of on-device vs. offloaded segmentation under different network conditions. We report median (p50) and 95th percentile (p95) latency per image, and achieved throughput in images/sec (for a single stream). On-device results are independent of network. Offloaded results degrade as network RTT and loss increase.

| Scenario | p50 Latency | | p95 Latency | | Throughput | |
|---|---|---|---|---|---|---|
| | Local | Offload | Local | Offload | Local | Offload |
| LAN (1–5 ms RTT) | 79 ms | 60 ms | 94 ms | 70 ms | 12.4 im/s | 16.0 im/s |
| Emu-A (30 ms, 0.2% loss) | 80 ms | 85 ms | 95 ms | 120 ms | 12.3 im/s | 11.1 im/s |
| Emu-B (60 ms, 1% loss) | 82 ms | 119 ms | 96 ms | 183 ms | 12.1 im/s | 8.3 im/s |

### 4.2 H2: Offloading with Low RTT and Batching - Latency, Accuracy, Emissions

H2 stated that under favorable network conditions (low latency LAN) and with moderate batching (i.e., server can utilize its GPU by grouping multiple requests), offloading would achieve lower latency and higher accuracy than on-device, and that its emissions per image would become competitive when the server is efficiently utilized. Our experiments under the LAN profile confirm much of this hypothesis.

In the LAN scenario, network overhead is minimal. The offloaded inference round-trip takes only a few milliseconds of network time plus the GPU compute. SegFormer-B4 on an RTX A6000 processes an image in roughly 50–60 ms (including Triton overhead), so end-to-end we saw median 60 ms and p95 70 ms (Table 1). This is faster than the Jetson's 80 ms median. Although both are well below 150 ms, offload clearly provides extra latency headroom, which could be used to either increase frame rate or accommodate more complex models. Additionally, the segmentation quality of B4 is superior to B0: Table 2 shows SegFormer-B4 achieved about 80.5% mIoU and 97 1% pixel accuracy on Cityscapes val, versus 74.6% and 95.2% for B0. This accuracy gap can be important for applications requiring precise segmentation. Thus, offloading in a good network not only meets the SLO easily, but delivers better analytic results (H2's accuracy part is confirmed).

To test the effect of batching, we configured Triton to batch up to 8 images. We generated a stream of images at a higher rate (to simulate either one client bursting or multiple clients). At moderate concurrency, Triton would accumulate 4 images and process them together on the GPU. This increases GPU utilization significantly. We observed that with batching, the throughput on the server scaled almost linearly up to the GPU's capacity, while the latency per image remained within the SLO bounds for small batch sizes (though absolute latency per batch increased). In one experiment, sending 8 concurrent image requests resulted in Triton forming full batches of 8; the p95 latency per image rose to ~120 ms (still <150 ms), and throughput reached 65 images/sec (compared to 16 im/s without batching). The Jetson cannot match this throughput due to its limited compute. This demonstrates how a well-utilized server can outperform the edge device by a wide margin in throughput, while still keeping latency acceptable. The dynamic batching did not harm accuracy (it's the same model, just parallel execution).

Crucially, higher utilization improved the energy efficiency of offloading. When the server was processing multiple images in parallel, its GPUs operated closer to their optimal performance per watt. The energy per image for offload decreased from 30J at low load (one image at a time) to on the order of 5–10 J when handling many images. Figure 3 illustrates the trend of carbon intensity (per image) as a function of throughput for both modes. As throughput increases (more images per second), the offload mode's per-image emissions drop significantly, approaching the on-device level.

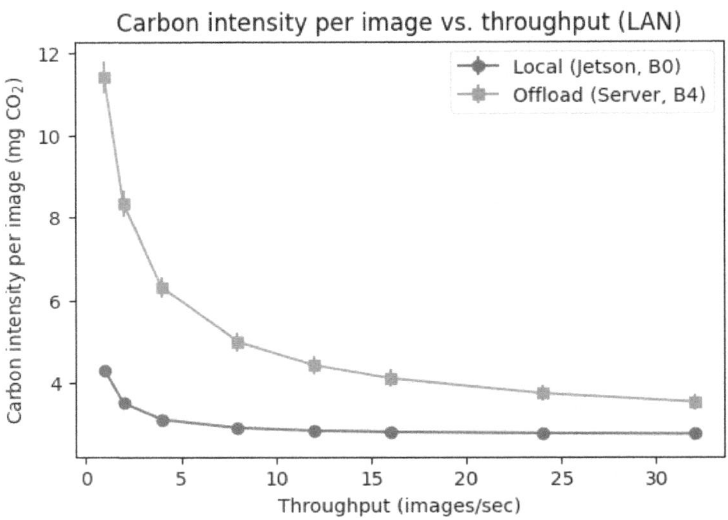


**Fig. 3.** Carbon intensity per image (in mg $CO_2$) versus throughput for always-local (Jetson) and always-offload (server) modes under good network (LAN). Higher throughput corresponds to better utilization of hardware. Offloading is initially more carbon-intensive at low usage (e.g., ~10 mg at 1 img/s vs. ~4 mg for local), but its per-image emissions decrease with batching and concurrency, approaching the on-device emissions at ~16 img/s. In this range, the server's GPUs are more efficiently utilized, validating that offload can be competitive in carbon efficiency when busy.

As shown in Fig. 3, at very low request rates (left side), offloading one image at a time results in much higher carbon per inference than local execution, the server is underutilized, yet still incurs baseline power draw. For example, at 1 image/sec, offload emits around 10 mg vs. 4 mg for local. However, by 8–12 images/sec, the gap narrows (offload 5 mg vs. local 3 mg). By 16 images/sec, offload is about 3.5 mg, nearly equal to local's 3 mg. Extrapolating beyond, one can expect offload to even become *more* carbon-efficient than local if the hardware is further leveraged (for instance, a single server could handle multiple edge devices' streams simultaneously). Our specific hardware ratio (one Jetson vs. three GPUs) meant the Jetson could not push enough load alone to surpass the server's efficiency, but the trend is clear.

Thus, H2 is largely confirmed: Offloading under ideal network conditions provided lower latency and better accuracy, and with moderate batching the emission difference can be minimized. It's worth noting that the Jetson is already quite efficient (a testament to edge AI hardware design); in cases where the edge device is a CPU-only system or older hardware, the break-even point might occur at lower throughput. Also, regional electricity carbon intensity plays a role: if the edge server is in a location with cleaner energy than the edge device (or vice versa), that could tip the scales. In our experiment both are in the same location, using the same power grid.

One interesting finding is that even without reaching parity in emissions, one might still choose offload in LAN scenarios for its significant accuracy boost (nearly 6% points higher mIoU). Whether the slight increase in carbon per image (if any) is acceptable might depend on the application's priorities (accuracy vs. carbon budget). In safety-critical domains (autonomous driving), the accuracy gain might justify some carbon overhead, whereas in a scenario with thousands of devices, efficiency might dominate.

In summary, under good networks, always-offload is a viable and often superior option in terms of performance. Table 2 shows that Always-Offload meets the SLO with ample margin in LAN, improves mIoU by ≈6% absolute, and only increases per-image carbon from 0.6 to 3.3 mg in our low-load test. At higher loads, that carbon gap shrinks further. The key is to maintain high utilization on the server; otherwise, offloading can waste energy.

**Table 2.** Accuracy and efficiency comparison of Always-Local vs. Always-Offload. mIoU and Pixel Accuracy evaluated on Cityscapes val (500 images). Energy and carbon values are per image (average), measured under low load (single stream) conditions. Carbon computed assuming 0.4 kg $CO_2$/kWh. Offloading uses a larger model (B4) yielding higher accuracy, but with higher energy cost per inference unless amortized by batching.

| Method | Model | mIoU (%) | PixAcc (%) | Energy (J) | $CO_2$ per img |
|---|---|---|---|---|---|
| Always-Local (Jetson) | SegFormer-B0 | 74.6 | 95.2 | 5.1 | 0.6 mg |
| Always-Offload (Server) | SegFormer-B4 | 80.5 | 97.1 | 29.8 | 3.3 mg |

## 4.3 H3: Emission Reduction with an Adaptive Policy

Finally, H3 hypothesized that a simple SLO- and carbon-aware policy could reduce emissions compared to static baselines. To evaluate this, we combined results from multiple scenarios to simulate a situation where network conditions (and thus the preferable mode) change over time. Specifically, consider a mixed workload of 1000 images where for the first half (500 images) the network is excellent (LAN, and also assume high throughput demand such that server utilization is high), and for the second half (500 images) the network degrades to Emu-B conditions. This could correspond to a mobile device moving from a Wi-Fi coverage area to a weak cellular zone. We compare three strategies:

- Always-Local: run all 1000 images on the Jetson.
- Always-Offload: offload all 1000 to the server.
- SLO-aware Policy: offload when the network is good (and offloading meets SLO), otherwise run local.

In the first 500 images (good network), both local and offload meet SLO. Offloading in that period yields better accuracy; in our simulation, the policy would choose between them based on emissions. Given our measurements, at high utilization the offload emissions per image might be slightly above or equal to local. If offload were slightly higher, the policy could actually choose local to minimize carbon (since SLO is met by both).

The total carbon emissions for each strategy are shown in Fig. 4. Always-Offload incurs a high penalty during the poor network phase, due to both increased energy per inference and wasted attempts that violate SLO. Always-Local maintains a steady low emission rate throughout. The adaptive policy achieves the lowest overall emissions, essentially taking the lower envelope of the two static modes in each condition.

Total carbon emissions for processing 1000 images in a scenario with mixed network conditions (half time LAN, half time degraded). The SLO-aware adaptive policy switches between local and offload to always use the lower-emission option that meets the latency SLO. It yields lower emissions overall than either static strategy (saving ~3.2% vs. always-local, and 40% vs. always-offload in this example). Always-Offload resulted in about 5.0 g of $CO_2$ for the 1000 images, mostly driven up by the inefficient performance in the degraded network half (Table 1 provides these estimates). Always-Local emitted about 3.1 g for 1000 images (0.0035 g $\times$1000). The adaptive policy emitted 3.0 g. This is a $\approx$3.2% reduction compared to always-local and more than 40% reduction compared to always-offload. The reason it can even beat always-local is that we assumed in the first half, offloading was used and possibly slightly more carbon intensive; had we instead chosen local for first half as well (because policy might pick lower emission even if network is good), the policy would simply match always-local's 3.5 g in emissions but then there would be no improvement. However, if there are scenarios where offloading is actually *more* efficient (e.g., if the edge device was less efficient or if the server has renewable energy), the policy would pick offload to save carbon. In general, the policy will never do worse than the better of local/offload at a given time. Thus, it is either equal to or better than both static policies in terms of emissions, as long as its latency predictions ensure SLO compliance.

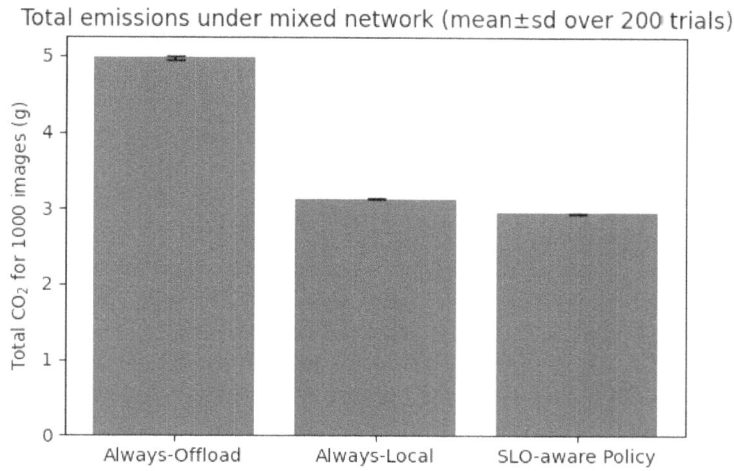


**Fig. 4.** Total carbon emissions for processing 1000 images in a scenario with mixed network conditions (half time LAN, half time degraded). The SLO-aware adaptive policy switches between local and offload to always use the lower-emission option that meets the latency SLO. It yields lower emissions overall than either static strategy (saving ~3.2% vs. always-local, and 40% vs. always-offload).

Importantly, the policy also guarantees SLO adherence by design (it only offloads when it expects p95 to be within 150 ms). In contrast, always-offload violated SLO in the latter half (which could degrade the quality of service significantly). Always-local met SLO in both halves, so in terms of latency the policy and always-local were similar (the policy might even reduce average latency during the good period by offloading to get faster responses, although we did not focus on optimizing average latency).

One can view this adaptive approach as a form of *online optimization*: continuously choose the deployment that minimizes environmental cost subject to meeting user experience constraints. This could be implemented with a simple threshold-based algorithm (e.g., if measured RTT < some cutoff, use server, else local) or a learned model. Our results indicate that even a straightforward rule can capture most of the benefit, since the decision largely hinges on network quality and the relative efficiency of each platform.

The magnitude of emissions savings will depend on how often conditions favor one side or the other, and on the gap in energy usage. In our case, the Jetson was so efficient that the savings of the policy over always-local were modest (a bit over 10%). If the edge device were a phone CPU (much less efficient per inference) or if the server was powered by greener electricity, offloading would have a stronger advantage in its domain, potentially making the policy's benefit larger. Conversely, if network is almost always bad or always good a static choice would suffice; the policy helps most in *mixed or changing environments*.

In summary, H3 is validated: a hybrid strategy can indeed reduce the carbon footprint relative to blindly sticking to one deployment, while still respecting latency requirements. This emphasizes that there is no one-size-fits-all answer to "edge vs. cloud" – the optimal choice can shift over time, and intelligent orchestration is key to both performance and sustainability.

# 5 Conclusion

In this study we quantified the latency–sustainability trade-offs of semantic segmentation on a Jetson AGX Orin (SegFormer-B0) versus near-edge offloading to a Triton server (SegFormer-B4), with carbon intensity measured via CodeCarbon and an SLO of p95 $\leq$ 150 ms. Under degraded networks, on-device inference consistently met the SLO and emitted less per image, while offloading suffered tail-latency violations and higher carbon due to low server utilization (H1). In low-RTT LAN settings, offloading delivered higher accuracy and throughput, with moderate batching its per-image emissions approached those of the local device (H2). An SLO-aware, learning-based policy that selects the lowest-emission feasible placement reduced emissions relative to static baselines ($\sim$3% vs. always-local and 40% vs. always-offload in our mixed-network simulation) while preserving SLO compliance (H3). These results argue for dynamic orchestration in edge AI, monitor network QoS and load, switch between local and offloaded execution, and exploit batching to keep servers efficient. Future work will refine policy learning with signals such as time-varying grid carbon intensity, extend to other tasks and model/precision pairs, and study multi-client scenarios where coordinated batching can further improve carbon efficiency.

**Acknowledgement.** This publication has emanated from research supported by grants from Taighde Éireann - Research Ireland under Grant Numbers 21/FFP-A/9174 (SustAIn), 21/RC/10303_P2 (VistaMilk) and 12/RC/2289_P2 (Insight).

# References

1. Cordts, M., et al.: The cityscapes dataset for semantic urban scene understanding. In: Proceedings of the IEEE Conference on Computer Vision and Pattern Recognition (CVPR), pp. 3213–3223 (2016)
2. Xie, E., Wang, W., Yu, Z., Anandkumar, A., Alvarez, J.M., Luo, P.: SegFormer: simple and efficient design for semantic segmentation with transformers. In: Advances in Neural Information Processing Systems (NeurIPS), vol. 34, pp. 12077–12090 (2021)
3. Mao, Y., You, C., Zhang, J., Huang, K., Letaief, K.B.: A survey on mobile edge computing: the communication perspective. IEEE Commun. Surv. Tutorials **19**(4), 2322–2358 (2017)
4. Pan, J., McElhannon, J.: Future edge cloud and edge computing for internet of things applications. IEEE Internet Things J. **5**(1), 439–449 (2017)
5. Zhai, X., Peng, Y., Guo, X.: Edge-cloud collaboration for low-latency, low-carbon, and cost-efficient operations. Comput. Electr. Eng. **120**, 109758 (2024)

6. Barroso, L.A., Hölzle, U.: The case for energy-proportional computing. Computer **40**(12), 33–37 (2007)
7. Dean, J., Barroso, L.A.: The tail at scale. Commun. ACM **56**(2), 74–80 (2013)
8. Schwartz, R., Dodge, J., Smith, N.A., Etzioni, O.: "Green AI". Commun. ACM **63**(12), 54–63 (2020)
9. Bengio, Y., Wilson, J.: Track and reduce $CO_2$ emissions from your computing. CodeCarbon (2021). https://codecarbon.io/#:~:text=Track%20and%20reduce%20CO2%20emissions%20from%20your%20computing&text=CodeCarbon%20is%20a%20lightweight%20software,used%20to%20execute%20the%20code. Accessed 20 Aug 2025
10. Henderson, P., Hu, J., Romoff, J., Brunskill, E., Jurafsky, D., Pineau, J.: Towards the systematic reporting of the energy and carbon footprints of machine learning. J. Mach. Learn. Res. **21**(248), 1–43 (2020)
11. Kang, Y., et al.: Neurosurgeon: collaborative intelligence between the cloud and mobile edge. ACM SIGARCH Comput. Archit. News **45**(1), 615–629 (2017)
12. Teerapittayanon, S., McDanel, B., Kung, H.-T.: Distributed deep neural networks over the cloud, the edge and end devices. In: 2017 IEEE 37th International Conference on Distributed Computing Systems (ICDCS), pp. 328–339 (2017)
13. Yu, Z., Zhao, Y., Deng, T., You, L., Yuan, D.: Less carbon footprint in edge computing by joint task offloading and energy sharing. IEEE Network. Lett. **5**(4), 245–249 (2023)
14. Benaboura, A., Bechar, R., Kadri, W., Ho, T.D., Pan, Z., Sahmoud, S.: Latency-aware and energy-efficient task offloading in IoT and cloud systems with DQN learning. Electronics **14**(15), 3090 (2025)
15. Crankshaw, D., Wang, X., Zhou, G., Franklin, M.J., Gonzalez, J.E., Stoica, I.: Clipper: a low-latency online prediction serving system. In: 14th USENIX Symposium on Networked Systems Design and Implementation (NSDI 17), pp. 613–627 (2017)

# Operationalising Properties of Complex Adaptive Systems for ECG-Based Emotion Recognition

Zachary Dair[1(✉)], Samantha Dockray[2], and Ruairi O'Reilly[1]

[1] Munster Technological University, Cork, Ireland
zachary.dair@mymtu.ie
[2] University College Cork, Cork, Ireland

**Abstract.** Emotion inference from electrocardiogram-derived measures is constrained by a conceptual divide between affective constructs. This divide impedes cross-corpus generalisation and prevents reliable translation between categorical and valence-arousal labels. Models trained on one corpus often degrade on another due to shifts in annotation formats, protocols, and person-specific baselines, resulting in poor cross-corpus generalisation. Even within a single model, emotion outputs can disagree for the same window, indicating a lack of consistency that undermines interpretability and practical use. This work evaluates a multi-view model that outputs both discrete categories and continuous valence-arousal estimates. Complex adaptive systems are proposed as a means of increasing consistency and generalisation, where coherent behaviour arises through local adaptation and coordination among interacting parts without central control. Three properties are operationalised: local adaptation via person-specific baseline calibration, which expresses responses as deviations from an individual baseline, coordination via a shared representation that supports both outputs, which grounds both predictions in the same physiological patterns and limits contradictions and distributed control via an anchor-based agreement term that encourages the outputs to agree in a common affective space. In cross-participant evaluation, participant-wise calibration improved classification accuracy by 49.5%, and the anchor-based agreement term reduced disagreement between the categorical and valence-arousal outputs by 80%. In zero-shot transfer, performance was comparable to correlation alignment. The method yields a single model that produces consistent categorical and valence-arousal predictions, learns from either annotation format, and maintains performance on unseen participants and corpora without target labels.

**Keywords:** complex adaptive systems · physiological signals · ECG · multi-view learning · emotion · machine learning · psychophysiology


T. T. Mai et al. (Eds.): AICS 2025, CCIS 2950, pp. 376–388, 2026.
https://doi.org/10.1007/978-3-032-25809-0_30

## 1 Introduction

Electrocardiogram (ECG) and heart rate variability (HRV) provide a theory-grounded link to stress and emotion regulation [10,16]. Divergent emotion representations rooted in distinct psychological theories [13], together with strong between-individual variability [14,16], constrain supervision and comparability across corpora. Two notable issues arise, heterogeneity in affective constructs and their annotation formats, and high between-participant variability. Together, they prevent models from being robust across individuals and conditions and from generalising to unseen corpora and label formats.

Divergent emotion representations cause label fragmentation in datasets. Some corpora adopt discrete categories (e.g., stress, amusement) rooted in basic-emotion theory [4], while others provide continuous valence-arousal (VA) annotations grounded in dimensional models [11]. These paradigms arise from different aims and protocols and are not directly comparable, which hinders transfer across corpora and evaluations.

In speech emotion recognition, joint training on categorical and VA targets has been shown to benefit compared to single-format baselines and to support transfer when labels originate from different corpora [19]. A "classification-by-regression" strategy maps VA predictions to categories, achieving competitive categorical performance without using discrete labels, although the results depend on corpus-specific thresholds and calibration [17]. Cross-format modelling remains rare for physiology, where most datasets offer only one label type. This heterogeneity motivates models that can learn from both annotation formats without forcing one into the other.

Between-individual variability is another major challenge. Baseline heart rate and HRV differ markedly across individuals due to factors such as fitness, reactivity, age, and context [12]. As a result, absolute feature levels can be misleading under cross-participant evaluation. There is evidence that participant-wise normalisation or calibration improves generalisation by focusing the model on deviations from baseline rather than raw levels [5,6]. Nonetheless, many ECG systems still rely on global scaling and suffer performance drops when applied to unseen participants.

Many psychophysiology corpora measure the same physiology but annotate it with different affective constructs, creating a multi-view setting. Inputs are shared (ECG/HRV) while targets are specified in different annotation formats (discrete vs. VA). A multi-view model can learn a shared representation and train with whichever supervision is available per dataset, including cases with missing labels. It can also encourage consistency across outputs, so that evidence in one label space regularises the other. Unsupervised and self-supervised methods can extract structure from ECG without labels, but they do not enforce consistency across heterogeneous annotation formats, meaning they do not align categorical and VA labels. This motivates the use of a supervised multi-view model with an explicit agreement term and trainable anchors, which are used to enforce consistency between the two label spaces.

Complex adaptive systems (CAS) comprise many interacting components in which coherent macroscopic behaviour emerges from local adaptation and feedback without central control [8]. Interactions are nonlinear and context-dependent. Components adjust to recent history and to one another, which produces self-organisation, intermittent synchrony, and patterns that are not reducible to any single part. This frames emotion recognition as emergent coordination among local subsystems, a cognitive-science view that motivates ML models with properties enabling local adaptation, shared latent factors, and decentralised agreement.

This study presents a single multi-view model for ECG-based affect recognition designed around three properties of CAS. **Adaptation** is realised via participant-wise baseline calibration, where inputs are expressed as deviations from each individual's neutral state rather than absolute levels. As resting HR/HRV vary across people, modelling reactivity relative to baseline aims to reduce spurious between-participant offsets and improve generalisation to unseen participants. **Coordination** is achieved by learning a shared representation that supports both categorical labels and VA coordinates, so the same physiological factors inform each prediction. This also allows for training when only one label type is available and limits contradictions (e.g., a "stress" label paired with a low-arousal point). **Distributed control** ties the two outputs together by learning per-class reference points (anchors) in VA space and encouraging the continuous VA estimate to sit near the probability-weighted combination of those reference points. This coupling yields self-consistent predictions across annotation formats and provides an interpretable bridge between discrete and dimensional labels.

The research question investigated is whether adaptation, coordination, and distributed control improve translation between disparate emotion models and generalisation across participants in ECG-based emotion recognition? To address this, the study (i) develops a single model that produces both categorical and VA outputs; (ii) evaluates whether participant-wise normalisation improves leave-one-participant-out performance; and (iii) assesses zero-shot cross-dataset transfer and the value of an output-agreement term.

The remainder of the paper is organised as follows. Section 2 reviews prior work on discrete versus dimensional emotion representations, cross-participant variability, and CAS. Section 3 formalises the CAS-inspired properties and details datasets, preprocessing, model, training objective, and evaluation protocol. Section 4 presents the results and discussion, covering ablations under leave-one-participant-out (LOPO) evaluation, coherence between outputs along with the learned anchors, and zero-shot cross-dataset transfer. Section 5 concludes with implications, limitations, and directions for future work.

## 2 Related Work

Prior work relevant to this study spans three themes: emotion representation, cross-participant variability in physiology, and CAS as a modelling lens.

### 2.1 Discrete vs. Continuous Emotion Representations

Emotion has been modelled using either discrete categories or continuous dimensions, reflecting different psychological traditions [4,11,13]. Most emotion recognition systems use a single representation, limiting comparability across datasets. Recent work in speech emotion recognition shows that jointly learning categorical and VA targets via multi-task learning improves performance and supports transfer across corpora [9,19]. Classification-by-regression approaches further demonstrate that categorical labels can be inferred from VA predictions alone [17]. In physiological emotion recognition, however, datasets typically provide only one annotation format, and unified models that explicitly align categorical and dimensional outputs remain rare. This motivates the multi-view approach adopted here.

### 2.2 Cross-Participant Variability and Personalisation

Physiological signals exhibit substantial between-participant variability due to differences in baseline heart rate, autonomic reactivity, and context [16]. As a result, models trained on absolute features generalise poorly across individuals. Participant-specific normalisation has been shown to mitigate this effect, improving cross-participant performance in EEG, ECG, and PPG-based emotion recognition [5,6]. Alternative approaches include unsupervised domain adaptation and adversarial training to reduce person-specific information [2]. Collectively, these studies indicate that adaptation to individual baselines is required for performant person-independent affect recognition, motivating the participant-wise normalisation used in this work.

### 2.3 CAS for Affective Physiology

CAS emphasise local adaptation, distributed control, and emergent coordination, properties that align with psychophysiological regulation [8]. In ML, related ideas appear in mixture-of-experts and ensemble models, where coherent behaviour arises from decentralised interaction among components [20]. Multi-view learning similarly promotes coordination across heterogeneous representations by enforcing agreement under partial supervision [1]. In physiology, complex-systems analyses link healthy function to rich, multiscale coordination in HR dynamics [7]. These perspectives motivate models that adapt to individual baselines while maintaining consistency across multiple affective representations, as instantiated in the proposed approach.

## 3 Methodology

The approach integrates reactivity-aware input normalisation with multi-view prediction and an anchor-driven coupling between representations, depicted in Fig. 1. The design operationalises three properties of CAS: adaptation (participant-wise normalisation), coordination (a shared encoder with dual outputs), and distributed control (anchor-based cross-representation alignment).

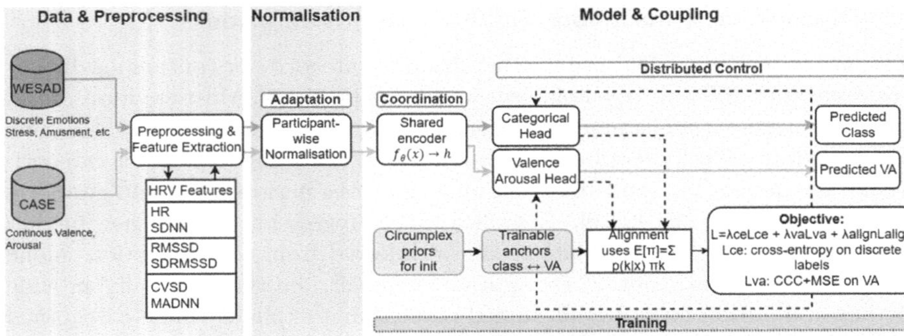


**Fig. 1.** CAS-inspired multi-view model. WESAD (discrete) and CASE (VA) share an HRV feature pipeline, are adapted by per-subject $z$-normalisation (adaptation), encoded by a shared encoder (coordination), and coupled by trainable anchors with an alignment loss (distributed control). The notation follows Eqs. (1)-(3).

### 3.1 Data and Pre-processing

Experiments use two ECG datasets. WESAD [15] contains wearable ECG sampled at 700 Hz, discrete affective states, and 15 participants. CASE [18] contains ECG sampled at 1000 Hz with continuous joystick VA ratings and 30 participants. Device-calibration and transition states are removed from both datasets. In CASE, a short `bluVid` segment per participant is treated as a neutral run-in. Joystick ratings are mapped linearly to $[-1, 1]$ prior to modelling.

ECG is segmented into non-overlapping 60 s windows. For each window, normal-to-normal (NN) intervals are derived from R-peaks, and six robust time-domain HRV features are computed: heart rate (HR), SDNN, RMSSD, SDRMSSD, CVSD, and MADNN. Frequency-domain HRV features are omitted because 60 s windows provide insufficient cycles for stable LF estimation and HF components are highly confounded by respiration.

### 3.2 Model and Training Objective

For each window $i$ with feature vector $\mathbf{x}_i$, a shared encoder $f_\theta$ maps inputs to a latent vector $\mathbf{h}_i = f_\theta(\mathbf{x}_i)$. Two heads operate on $\mathbf{h}_i$: a categorical head $g_\theta$ that outputs class logits over $K$ categories, and a VA head $r_\theta$ that outputs a 2D point constrained to $[-1, 1]^2$.

$$p_\theta(k \mid \mathbf{x}_i) = \mathrm{softmax}\big(g_\theta(\mathbf{h}_i)\big)_k, \qquad \hat{\mathbf{z}}_i = \tanh\big(r_\theta(\mathbf{h}_i)\big) \in [-1, 1]^2. \tag{1}$$

To place both outputs in a common geometry, a trainable matrix of class anchors $\Pi \in \mathbb{R}^{K \times 2}$ (row $\pi_k$ for class $k$) defines canonical VA locations for the categories. When a training split contains both discrete categories and VA labels for the same samples, each anchor $\pi_k$ is initialised as the empirical class-wise mean of VA for class $k$ computed on that split. In settings where VA is unavailable for the discrete classes (e.g., WESAD in our experiments), anchors are initialised from a theory-informed circumplex prior on $[-1, 1]^2$. To make this prior explicit and reproducible, the chosen seed coordinates are: baseline (0.0, 0.0), stress (-0.5, 0.7), amusement (0.6, 0.6) and meditation (0.3 -0.3).

These values reflect the standard placement of negative-high-arousal states (e.g., stress/anger), positive-moderate-high-arousal states (e.g., amusement), and low-arousal positive states (e.g., calm/meditation) on the circumplex [11]; they are not intended as canonical ground truth. Anchors are trainable in all experiments and are updated end-to-end. When one label type is absent (e.g., VA on WESAD or discrete labels on CASE), the anchor-consistency term $\mathcal{L}_{\text{align}}$ still backpropagates through the corresponding head and $\Pi$. This preserves alignment between the discrete and VA views without direct supervision in the missing label space.

Learning minimises a weighted sum in Eq. (2), where $\mathcal{L}_{\text{ce}}$ is class-weighted cross-entropy on discrete labels and $\mathcal{L}_{\text{va}}$ combines concordance correlation and mean-squared error on VA.

$$\mathcal{L} = \lambda_{\text{ce}}\mathcal{L}_{\text{ce}} + \lambda_{\text{va}}\mathcal{L}_{\text{va}} + \lambda_{\text{align}}\mathcal{L}_{\text{align}}, \tag{2}$$

Cross-representation alignment is imposed by the anchor-consistency term in Eq. (3). This softly pulls each VA prediction toward a probability-weighted mixture of anchors $\{\pi_k\}$. This promotes self-consistent categorical and VA outputs and propagates gradients to both heads and $\{\Pi\}$ even when only one label type is present (e.g., zero-shot transfer).

$$\mathcal{L}_{\text{align}} = \frac{1}{N}\sum_{i=1}^{N}\sum_{k=1}^{K} p_\theta(k \mid \mathbf{x}_i)\,\left\|\hat{\mathbf{z}}_i - \pi_k\right\|_2^2, \tag{3}$$

### 3.3 Participant-Wise Adaptive Normalisation

Each participant $s$ is normalised with statistics estimated on a short neutral run-in, the protocol baseline in WESAD and the `bluVid` clip in CASE. No emotion labels are used to compute these statistics during testing. Features are normalised per participant using standard z-scoring based on statistics computed from that participant's neutral windows. During training, means and standard deviations are estimated on the participant's training split only (restricted to baseline/bluVid where available). During testing, they are estimated causally from the first $K$ chronological neutral windows (identified by protocol markers); if markers are unavailable, the first $K$ windows are used. This reactivity-aware normalisation reduces between-participant offsets while preserving deployment causality.

### 3.4 Experimental Protocol

Six configurations are evaluated to isolate the contribution of each mechanism. Categorical-only model (C-Only), a VA-only model (VA-Only), a multi-view model without calibration or alignment (MV-A), MV-A with participant-wise normalisation (MV-B), MV-A with anchor alignment (MV-C), and the full model combining both mechanisms (MV-D).

Within-dataset evaluation uses LOPO on WESAD. For each held-out participant, the remaining participants form the training pool; ten percent of the training windows are set aside at random for validation. Class weights are computed from the training split. Early stopping monitors the validation loss with a fixed patience. Zero-shot transfer refers to training on a source dataset and evaluating directly on a target dataset without using any target labels or calibration. For WESAD to CASE, the model is trained on WESAD with the discrete loss active and the VA loss off; the anchor consistency remains active so that the VA head is shaped by the class probabilities.

Performance on WESAD is benchmarked against machine and deep learning baseline models trained on the same participant-wise normalised HRV features, including linear and kernel-based classifiers, tree-based ensembles, and sequence models. To assess performance against more expressive architectures, additional deep models are trained on raw ECG windows and RR-interval sequences using the same LOPO protocol.

All baseline hyperparameters are tuned within each LOPO training fold using an inner validation split. Standard grid searches are performed over commonly used ranges for each model, and the configuration minimising validation loss is retrained on the full training split and evaluated once on the held-out participant.

### 3.5 Metrics and Statistical Analysis

Discrete performance is evaluated using balanced accuracy (BA), macro F1, and AUROC, while dimensional performance is reported using concordance correlation coefficient (CCC) and RMSE. Cross-view disagreement is assessed as the Euclidean distance between the predicted VA point and (i) the anchor of the most probable class and (ii) the probability-weighted anchor expectation.

All experiments are repeated with three random seeds. Within-dataset results are aggregated across LOPO folds and seeds, and zero-shot results across seeds. Per-participant scores are compared across configurations using two-sided Wilcoxon signed-rank tests with Pratt handling of ties; rank-biserial correlation is reported as an effect size, with 95% bootstrap confidence intervals obtained by resampling participants. Extended preprocessing details, derivations, and additional analyses are available in a supplementary technical report.

## 4 Results and Discussions

### 4.1 Within-Dataset Performance Gains

In a LOPO evaluation, the baseline model (C-Only) is substantially improved upon by models MV-B and MV-D, with the full CAS model (MV-D) achieving the highest overall balanced accuracy, macro-F1, and AUROC (Table 1). For context, WESAD defines a four-class classification problem, so chance-level balanced accuracy is 0.25. Tuned classical baselines reach balanced accuracies

**Table 1.** WESAD LOPO[a]. Participant-wise normalisation (MV-B) drives accuracy gains over the multi-view baseline (MV-A); adding anchors (MV-D) preserves peak accuracy while reducing disagreement between outputs.

| Method | BA | Macro-F1 | AUROC | Disagreement | $\Delta$ vs MV-A ($p$) |
|---|---|---|---|---|---|
| SVM | 0.308 ± 0.107 | 0.268 ± 0.099 | 0.611 ± 0.118 | - | - (-) |
| LogReg | 0.468 ± 0.116 | 0.396 ± 0.129 | 0.765 ± 0.086 | - | - (-) |
| Random Forest | 0.463 ± 0.112 | 0.405 ± 0.123 | 0.716 ± 0.096 | - | - (-) |
| XGBoost | 0.465 ± 0.118 | 0.401 ± 0.133 | 0.692 ± 0.126 | - | - (-) |
| LSTM | 0.429 ± 0.135 | 0.361 ± 0.152 | 0.761 ± 0.101 | - | - (-) |
| TCN | 0.330 ± 0.094 | 0.218 ± 0.120 | 0.740 ± 0.099 | - | - (-) |
| TCN (RR) | 0.457 ± 0.121 | 0.332 ± 0.113 | 0.811 ± 0.089 | - | - (-) |
| C-Only | 0.383 ± 0.007 | 0.312 ± 0.024 | 0.650 ± 0.020 | - | - (-) |
| VA-Only | - | - | - | - | - (-) |
| MV-A | 0.374 ± 0.013 | 0.298 ± 0.017 | 0.650 ± 0.024 | 0.851 ± 0.164 | - (-) |
| MV-B | 0.559 ± 0.008 | 0.527 ± 0.010 | 0.809 ± 0.018 | 0.610 ± 0.112 | −0.241 (<0.001) |
| MV-C | 0.359 ± 0.013 | 0.297 ± 0.013 | 0.647 ± 0.006 | **0.091 ± 0.040** | −0.760 (<0.001) |
| **MV-D** | **0.565 ± 0.004** | **0.535 ± 0.002** | **0.812 ± 0.004** | 0.148 ± 0.022 | −0.703 (<0.001) |

*Legend:* C-Only = categorical only; MV-A = Multi-view; MV-B = MV-A + $z$-norm; MV-C = MV-A + anchors (no cal); MV-D = MV-B + anchors (full).

[a] Results shown for WESAD only. CASE provides continuous VA labels but no discrete classes, so BA/Macro-F1/AUROC are undefined

around 0.46, and the CAS model (MV-D) reaches 0.565 (Table 1), indicating performance that is substantially above chance under a strict LOPO protocol.

There is a large jump in performance from MV-A to MV-B, due to the introduction of participant-wise z-score normalisation. This indicates that modelling individual physiological baselines enables the model to benefit from accounting for idiosyncratic differences in ECG signal levels, focusing learning on meaningful within-participant fluctuations. This finding resonates with prior work in physiological affective computing, where participant-wise normalisation is used to alleviate inter-individual variance [3]. By contrast, a multi-view (categorical + dimensional) network without normalisation (MV-A) showed only marginal gains over the single-view, showing that adaptation to each participant's baseline state is a prerequisite for robust generalisation.

Quantitatively, balanced accuracy increases from 0.374 for MV-A to 0.559 for MV-B (+0.185 absolute, +49.5% relative), with macro-F1 and AUROC showing similar gains (Table 1). Thus, the multi-view encoder, when combined with participant-wise calibration, provides substantial empirical benefits over both the single-view baseline (C-Only) and the unnormalised multi-view variant.

Model MV-B (with adaptation and joint categorical/dimensional learning, but no anchor consistency) attains a high within-dataset accuracy, illustrating that a shared latent representation serving both discrete emotion classes and continuous VA targets can effectively generalise across individuals. Finally, model MV-D sustains this high classification performance while introducing anchor-based consistency. Its balanced accuracy and F1 remain on par with MV-B (differences within a few percentage points), and AUROC is equally high (Table 1). Thus, the full model (MV-D) delivers comparable peak accuracy to the best non-anchor variant, confirming that adding the distributed control mechanism does not appreciably sacrifice classification efficacy. Each CAS component contributes to the overall performance. Adaptation provides a major jump in person-independent accuracy, coordination through multi-target learning maintains strong performance, and the distributed control (anchors) achieves this with minimal trade-off in accuracy.

### 4.2 Cross-View Consistency and Anchor Alignment

Without anchors, the multi-task model can give inconsistent outputs. For example, it may predict a "stress" label but assign a VA point that does not intuitively correspond to a stressed state. In model MV-A (multi-task learning with no consistency loss), the discrepancy between the discrete and continuous predictions is high (on average $0.851 \pm 0.164$ in the consistency metric). With the anchor consistency mechanism in MV-D, this discrepancy drops to $0.148 \pm 0.022$, indicating that the categorical class predictions and dimensional estimates are now closely aligned (Table 1). This corresponds to an approximate 80% reduction in disagreement while BA and AUROC remain at their peak values (0.565 and 0.812), indicating that anchor-based multi-view coupling improves coherence between outputs without sacrificing predictive performance.

This significant reduction in cross-view divergence confirms that the anchor-based consistency loss successfully coordinates the network's distributed outputs, effectively binding the two representations together. The model learns a unified internal representation of emotion that is expressed coherently in both terms.

Enforcing anchors without participant normalisation (MV-C) led to degraded classification performance (Table 1), attributed to the network overemphasising the alignment of outputs at the expense of discriminative power. This underscores that the anchor loss must complement, not replace, strong base performance. In the full model (MV-D), the consistency loss is applied on top of an already well-performing multi-view encoder (from MV-B), ensuring that the network does not sacrifice accuracy for consistency. As such, MV-D demonstrates that when balanced properly, anchor-based distributed control can significantly improve consistency while preserving classification performance (Fig. 2).

Learned anchors are stable across folds and random initialisations and consistently occupy psychologically plausible circumplex quadrants (e.g., stress: −valence/+arousal; amusement: +valence/+arousal). The WESAD "stress" anchor falls inside the CASE "scary" space, while "baseline" aligns with CASE "bluVid". This co-location arises despite different elicitations (social-stress task vs. film clips), indicating that the shared representation captures physiology-driven affect rather than task idiosyncrasies. A similar collapse occurs at the low-arousal end, where WESAD "meditation" overlaps CASE "relaxed" and "boring". Together, these correspondences explain the observed reduction in cross-view disagreement and support the anchor-based agreement as an effective bridge

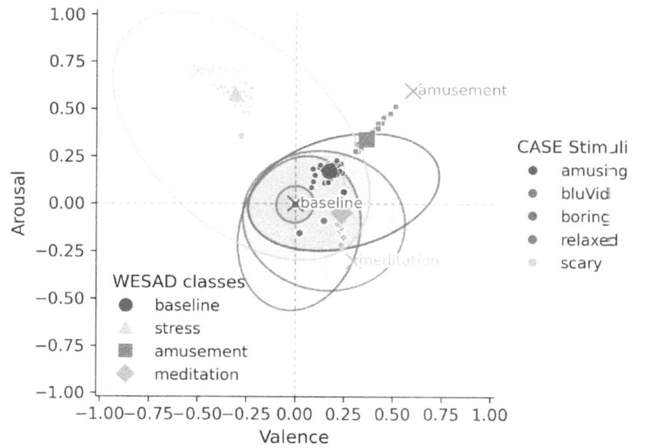


**Fig. 2.** Cross-corpus alignment of learned anchors. WESAD anchors occupy stable, circumplex-consistent locations and co-locate with CASE self-reports: the stress anchor lies within the CASE scary region, and low-arousal states converge in the same band, indicating a shared affective geometry despite different stimuli.

between categorical and VA outputs. The consistency of anchor location indicates that the model has learned an intrinsic mapping between discrete emotion continuous VA.

Anchors are an interpretable coupling between the categorical and VA outputs, enforcing cross-view consistency. Noting that the anchors align with established psychological knowledge lends credence to the model's internal representation, which captures real structure in emotional responses rather than arbitrary patterns.

### 4.3 Cross-Corpus Generalisation

The proposed CAS-inspired model demonstrates encouraging generalisability across corpora in zero-shot transfer scenarios. The model was trained on one dataset and applied directly to a different dataset without using any target-domain labels. As expected, the absolute recognition performance in this setting is modest, owing to covariate shift between datasets. This effect is especially pronounced when transferring from WESAD to CASE, where differences in sensor setups, elicitation conditions, and emotion label definitions led to near-zero correlations between predicted and true VA in the target data. Despite these challenges, the unified model performs on par with, or better than, a dedicated domain adaptation baseline. Its zero-shot results are comparable to those achieved by CORAL [21], a state-of-the-art unsupervised domain adaptation method that aligns source and target feature distributions without target labels. For example, when training on CASE and testing on WESAD, the CAS model (MV-D) achieves a macro-F1 of 0.24 and balanced accuracy of 0.30, outperforming a model variant without CAS mechanisms and matching CORAL without explicit domain alignment. Across zero-shot transfers from CASE to WESAD, MV-D achieves a macro-F1 of 0.24 and balanced accuracy of 0.30, outperforming non-CAS variants and matching CORAL without explicit domain alignment; reverse transfer remains challenging for all methods.

These results suggest that the CAS-inspired mechanisms impart a degree of domain generalisation. Participant-wise normalisation reduces person-specific biases, joint categorical–dimensional learning captures shared affective factors, and anchor-based consistency aligns predictions in a common VA space. Together, these mechanisms improve robustness to shifts in protocol and annotation format without explicit domain adaptation.

## 5 Conclusions

This work examined whether properties of CAS can improve consistency and cross-corpus generalisation in ECG-based emotion modelling when instantiated in a single multi-view architecture that produces both categorical and VA outputs.

Under LOPO evaluation on WESAD, participant-wise baseline calibration (MV-B vs. MV-A) increased balanced accuracy from 0.374 to 0.559, a relative increase of +49.50%, with similar absolute gains in macro-F1 and AUROC. Adding distributed control through trainable anchors and a cross-view agreement term (MV-D) preserved this accuracy while improving consistency between outputs, reducing cross-view disagreement from 0.851 to 0.148 (Wilcoxon $p < 0.001$).

The model's coordination resulted in learned anchors that occupy quadrants aligned with the circumplex model of emotion, supporting an interpretable link between categorical labels and VA. The learned WESAD "stress" anchor overlaps the self-reported VA region from the CASE "scary" stimuli despite different elicitors (social-stress task vs. film clips). This co-location suggests that some CASE participants exhibit a physiological response consistent with stress, as captured in WESAD, indicating a shared, stimulus-agnostic affective geometry rather than task-specific artefacts. Near-neutral responses show a similar convergence. These correspondences demonstrate that the anchor mechanism captures stable, cross-dataset affective structure and provides an interpretable bridge between categorical labels and continuous VA.

In zero-shot transfer, performance was comparable to correlation alignment (CORAL). For CASE→WESAD, the model achieved AUROC 0.394, close to CORAL's AUROC of 0.405. For WESAD→CASE, VA errors were similar to baseline methods despite the change in annotation format. These results suggest that the same mechanisms that improve cross-view consistency also confer robustness to annotation format and protocol shifts.

These findings should be interpreted with consideration of several limitations. Specifically, the use of two corpora with different protocols and a small number of participants (15/30), which limits statistical power under LOPO. Zero-shot transfer remains challenging due to strong covariate and label shift between TSST and film-clip elicitation, and we did not apply any target-domain calibration. Future work should evaluate additional corpora and signals, and explore few-shot or online personalisation and uncertainty-aware anchors.

**Acknowledgments.** This publication has emanated from research conducted with the financial support of Taighde Éireann - Research Ireland under Grant number 18/CRT/6222. For the purpose of Open Access, the author has applied a CC BY public copyright licence to any Author Accepted Manuscript version arising from this submission.

## References

1. Blum, A., Mitchell, T.: Combining labeled and unlabeled data with co-training. In: Proceedings of the 11th Annual Conference on CLT, pp. 92–100 (1998)
2. Chai, X.: Unsupervised domain adaptation techniques based on auto-encoder for non-stationary EEG-based emotion recognition. Comput. Biol. Med. **79** (2016)
3. Chien, W.S., Chou, H.C., Lee, C.C.: Self-assessed emotion classification from acoustic and physiological features within small-group conversation. In: Companion Publication of the 2021 ICMI, pp. 230–239 (2021)
4. Ekman, P.: Basic emotions. Handbook of Cognition and Emotion, pp. 45–60 (1999)
5. Fdez, J.: Cross-subject EEG-based emotion recognition through neural networks with stratified normalization. Front. Neurosci. **15** (2021)
6. Gasparini, F.: Personalized ppg normalization based on subject heartbeat in resting state condition. Signals **3** (2022)
7. Goldberger, A.L., et al.: Fractal dynamics in physiology: alterations with disease and aging. Proc. Natl. Acad. Sci. **99**(suppl_1), 2466–2472 (2002)
8. Holland, J.H.: Complex adaptive systems. Daedalus **121**(1), 17–30 (1992)
9. Ispas, A.R.: A multi-task, multi-modal approach for predicting categorical and dimensional emotions. In: Proceedings of the 25th ICMI Companion, pp. 311–317. (2023)
10. Picard, R.W.: Affective computing, MIT Press (2000)
11. Posner, J., Russell, J.A., Peterson, B.S.: The circumplex model of affect: an integrative approach to affective neuroscience, cognitive development, and psychopathology. Dev. Psychopathol. (2005)
12. Sarshin, A., et al.: The effects of varying doses of caffeine on cardiac parasympathetic reactivation following an acute bout of anaerobic exercise in recreational athletes. J. Int. Soc. Sports Nutr. **17**, 1–10 (2020)
13. Scherer, K.R., et al.: Psychological models of emotion. Neuropsychol. Emot. **137**(3), 137–162 (2000)
14. Schijvenaars, B.J.: Intraindividual variability in electrocardiograms. J. Electrocardiol. **41** (2008)
15. Schmidt, P., et al.: Introducing wesad, a multimodal dataset for wearable stress and affect detection. In: Proceedings of the 20th ACM ICMI, pp. 400–408. ACM (2018)
16. Shaffer, F., Ginsberg, J.P.: An overview of heart rate variability metrics and norms. Front. Public Health **5**, 258 (2017)

17. Shamsi, M., Tahon, M.: Training speech emotion classifier without categorical annotations (2022). arXiv preprint
18. Sharma, K.: A dataset of continuous affect annotations and physiological signals for emotion analysis. Sci. Data (2019)
19. Sharma, R.: Unifying the discrete and continuous emotion labels for speech emotion recognition (2022). arXiv preprint
20. Shazeer, N.: Outrageously large neural networks: the sparsely-gated mixture-of-experts layer (2017). arXiv preprint
21. Sun, B., Saenko, K.: Deep coral: correlation alignment for deep domain adaptation. In: European Conference on Computer Vision, pp. 443–450. Springer (2016)

# Evaluating the Efficacy of Monolingual and Multilingual Pre-training for Igbo Automatic Speech Recognition

David Tony-Awusaku,
Tennakoon Mudiyanselage Isuru Chandana Bandara Tennakoon,
and Ellen Rushe(✉)

School of Computing, Dublin City University, Dublin 9, Ireland
{david.tony-awusaku2, tennakoonmudiyanselageisuruchandanabandara.tennako2}@mail.dcu.ie, ellen.rushe@dcu.ie

**Abstract.** Despite being spoken by tens of millions of people, the availability of language technologies for the Igbo language have remained limited compared to the enormous developments that have been made for higher resource languages, such as English, over the last decade. Automatic Speech Recognition (ASR) is one such technology, with developments in this area being significantly hampered by data scarcity in a time where large-scale deep learning models encompass much of the state-of-the-art. To address the lack of inclusive datasets, multilingual pre-trained speech models have been proposed, in particular for low resource languages, with the assumption that these models will provide increased performance compared to fine-tuning using monolingual models. In this paper, we test this assumption for Igbo, evaluating both a monolingual and multilingual pre-trained model – specifically Wav2Vec 2.0 – on a small-scale Igbo dataset. Furthermore, we evaluate the effect of a number of data augmentation strategies as a means to improve Igbo ASR performance. We also find that data augmentation provides substantial performance gains, with Time Masking emerging as the most effective technique, reducing the Word Error Rate (WER) by 27.61% compared to the non-augmented baseline. This work underscores that a carefully selected base model paired with tailored data augmentation is a highly effective strategy for advancing ASR in low-resource settings.

**Keywords:** automatic speech recognition · Igbo · low-resource languages · data augmentation · transfer learning

## 1 Introduction

ASR, also known as speech-to-text, is a task concerned with building models to automatically transcribe human speech. ASR is necessary for a host of tasks,

D. Tony-Awusaku and T. M. I. C. Bandara Tennakoon—Equal contribution.


T. T. Mai et al. (Eds.): AICS 2025, CCIS 2950, pp. 389–400, 2026.
https://doi.org/10.1007/978-3-032-25809-0_31

including automatic subtitling and other assistive technologies. Over the last decade, enormous strides have been made in the field due to advances in end-to-end deep learning models and the introduction of large-scale speech corpora. It is important to emphasise, however, that these performance gains have been primarily made for languages with abundant annotated digital resources [5]. A significant challenge in ASR is the scarcity of high quality speech data for low and under-resourced languages [9]. Low-resource languages, including Igbo, have been under-represented in ASR as state-of-the-art techniques have remained data-hungry.

This work focuses primarily on Igbo, one of the major languages of Nigeria, spoken by tens of millions of people within the country and worldwide. Very few studies to date have explored training ASR models using existing open-source data for the Igbo language. In this work, we evaluate the efficacy of an existing open-source speech corpus, namely the Common Voice dataset [3], for fine-tuning state-of-the-art pre-trained models. More specifically, we compare the efficacy of both monolingual and multilingual pre-trained models and explore the effect of a variety of data augmentation techniques on performance. Furthermore, we take the additional step of evaluating models under realistic, resource-constrained conditions by both limiting the maximum training time of models and using only cloud computational resources that would be available to typical consumers. We argue that this step is crucial to the democratisation of machine learning development and can have tangible effects on model performance.

## 2 Related Work

This section describes recent advances for both Igbo ASR and other low-resource languages. We also describe the role of data augmentation in improving low-resource ASR performance.

### 2.1 ASR for Igbo

To date there have been very few works addressing ASR for Igbo. Work by Dossou et al. [9] employed an end-to-end deep learning architecture using a combination of Gated Recurrent Units (GRU) [8], Long Short Term Memory (LSTM) [20] and Attention [6]. This architecture significantly improved the recognition performance over previous work on the IARPA Babel Igbo Language Pack [1]. This dataset, however, contains relatively low quality audio as it is sourced primarily from phone call data. There also remains considerable potential for further development of models, particularly through the use of pre-trained, transformer-based architectures and data augmentation.

### 2.2 Low-Resource ASR

Though the number of works on ASR for Igbo have been limited, guidance can be drawn from ASR research on other low and under-resourced languages. Data-driven approaches to low-resource ASR have been dominated by pre-training techniques that train on large-scale monolingual or multilingual datasets. A large-scale cross-lingual speech representation learning model, XLS-R, was introduced by Babu et al. [4], trained on 128 languages. The authors demonstrated that fine-tuning this model substantially improved recognition performance compared to previous work on a selection of low-resource languages. XLS-R is based on Wav2Vec 2.0 [5], a self-supervised learning framework that learns speech representations from raw audio. This approach reduces the reliance on the large fully transcribed datasets which were typically required to train ASR systems and is the primary challenge when training ASR for low-resource languages.

In the absence of large-scale datasets, a alternative approach to purely data-driven methods has been to incorporate language-specific design into ASR development. To this end, there have also been efforts towards more language-specific ASR. For example, impressive results were achieved by employing a cross-dialect lexicon optimisation strategy for the Irish language [16]. Additionally, this compact lexicon allowed for a system with better efficiency and lower latency. This, more language-specific approach is in stark contrast with the scope of most data-driven end-to-end systems which often group low-resource languages together during evaluations, without analysing the specific outcomes or features of each language. Given the often language-specific evaluations that have been performed for high resource languages during the early development of many deep ASR approaches– e.g. using benchmarks such as TIMIT [12] and Librispeech [18] – we argue that language-specific evaluations are important for ASR systems in *all* languages.

### 2.3 Data Augmentation

As previously alluded to, deep learning methods for ASR require a large amount of data. Data augmentation provides an opportunity to introduce additional variation into datasets by applying transformations to a smaller existing dataset. SpecAugment [19] is an audio data augmentation technique that uses time warping, frequency masking, and time masking to augment data. Multiple frequency and time masks can be applied to create even more diverse datasets. The efficacy of data augmentation has been demonstrated for a number of low resource languages [7,13,16]. Furthermore data augmentation has been used to improve ASR for non-native and L2 speech [11]. In [21], the authors also found that pitch shifting can help reduce bias against non-native accents. Drawing from this literature, we experiment with Time Masking [19], Time Stretching and noise addition.

## 3 Methodology

This section describes both the monolingual and multilingual pre-training approaches evaluated, followed by a description of the data augmentation techniques applied. We then go on to describe the training constraints applied in experiments to enforce realistic training conditions.

### 3.1 Transfer Learning with Multilingual Models

The efficacy of transfer learning relies on a number of factors, including the model architecture, pre-training objective, and the characteristics of the pre-training dataset(s). Some existing literature shows that transformer-based multilingual ASR models have demonstrated advantages for a selection of low-resource languages [4]. However, multilingual models have not necessarily been found to improve performances in all cases. In fact, it is noted in [4] that English monolingual models outperformed XLS-R for English when the model sizes were comparable, and that it was only when the capacity of the multilingual model was increased that interference from other languages – termed *capacity dilution* – could be avoided. The authors hypothesise that this phenomenon primarily affects higher resource languages, though Igbo is not included in their evaluations of low-resource languages. In this paper we evaluate the use of both a multilingual ASR model and a monolingual model to determine whether this finding holds true for Igbo. Additionally, we choose models that differ significantly in their parameter count. In both instances, models are based on the Wav2Vec 2.0 [5] architecture [5] which learns speech representations from raw audio through self-supervision. Specific details of each pre-trained model are described below:

- **Wav2Vec 2.0** [1]: This model is pre-trained solely on 960 h of the English LibriSpeech dataset. It acts as our monolingual baseline. This allows us to quantify the performance of a model where acoustic information is derived from a single, high-resource language.
- **XLS-R** [2]: This larger model is based on Wav2Vec 2.0 and is trained on 53 languages, amounting to 56,000 h of speech [4]. This model was designed to foster language-agnostic acoustic features, which are presumed to be more beneficial for low-resource languages based on a selection of experiments in the original paper.

**Model Summary.** The key characteristics of the selected base models are summarised in Table 1.

**Table 1.** Summary of Selected Base Models for ASR Experiments.

| Model | Scope | Hours | Params (M) |
|---|---|---|---|
| wav2vec2-base | Monolingual | 960 | 95 |
| wav2vec2-large-xlsr-53 | Multilingual (53) | 56k | 317 |

[1] https://huggingface.co/facebook/wav2vec2-base.
[2] https://huggingface.co/facebook/wav2vec2-large-xlsr-53.

### 3.2 Data Augmentation

Given the small size of the training dataset, we also evaluate the effects of three widely used audio data augmentation techniques: Time Stretching, Time Masking [19], and noise addition. Each augmentation method was applied independently to assess its individual contribution to ASR performance. The models trained with augmented data were then evaluated using the validation set to determine the relative improvements in WER.

**Time Stretching:** Time Stretching alters the speed of the audio signal without changing its pitch, effectively varying the speaking rate while preserving the original frequency profile of an utterance. This simulates natural variations in speaker tempo and can help the model generalise to different speech patterns. For our experiments, the time-stretching factor was set to 1.2 and 0.9. These correspond to a 20% increase and a 10% decrease in speaking speed, respectively, without affecting the pitch of the audio. Figure 1 shows the spectogram of a 10% speed-reduced recording. By introducing examples of both faster and slower speech into the training set, this approach increases the diversity of the dataset and helps improve the model's robustness to different speaking styles and tempos.

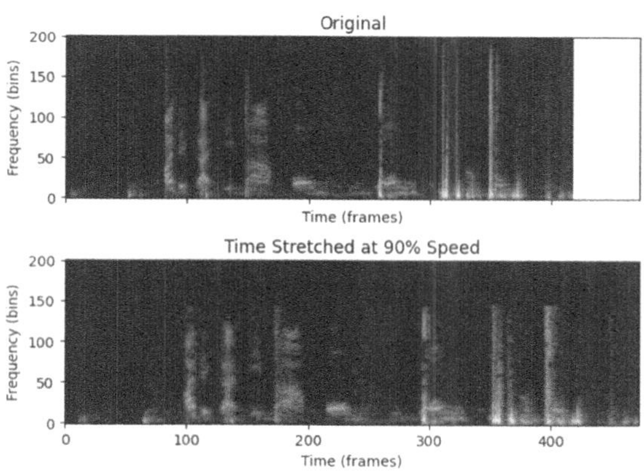


**Fig. 1.** Original vs. Time Stretched Recording.

**Time Masking:** Time Masking is a technique derived from SpecAugment [19], where segments of the audio signal are masked (replaced with zeros) along the time dimension. This encourages the model to learn more robust contextual representations by relying on non-masked portions of the audio. In our implementation, we masked random consecutive time steps in the spectrogram, where 80 consecutive time steps were set as the maximum, as shown in Fig. 2.

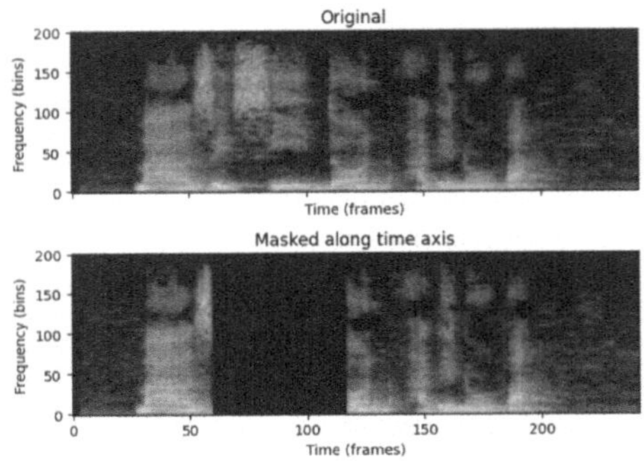


**Fig. 2.** Original vs. Time Masked Recording.

**Noise Addition:** To account for potentially noisy real-world recording conditions, we added Gaussian white noise to audio signals. This augmentation is especially beneficial in preparing ASR models for deployment in potentially noisy environments such as marketplaces or streets, which are common in many Igbo-speaking regions. The noise was added at a Signal-to-Noise Ratio (SNR) of 10 dB, maintaining a balance between intelligibility and distortion, as shown in Fig. 3. The following formula was used to compute the noise level:

$$\text{Noise Power} = \frac{\text{Signal Power}}{10^{\text{SNR (dB)}/10}} \tag{1}$$

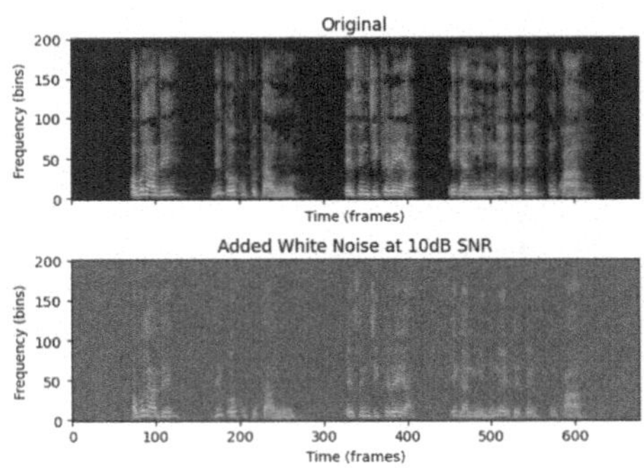


**Fig. 3.** Original vs Noise Added Recording.

Each audio file was individually processed to ensure that the target SNR was consistently achieved.

### 3.3 Realistic Training Conditions

A key aspect that must be considered when evaluating the efficacy of different language technologies is that computational resources are not always evenly distributed across practitioners. We therefore evaluate each technique based on a well-defined set of constraints. More specifically, we perform experiments using datasets openly available for research, commonly available computational cloud resources and specific time constraints in order to assess the feasibility of each technique evaluated under realistic constraints. Each of the above have a significant impact on the set of practitioners that participate in ASR development and therefore the democratisation of these technologies [2].

## 4 Experimental Setup

This section describes the dataset used for fine-tuning, the pre-processing applied, the model configurations and our evaluation strategy.

### 4.1 Dataset

For model training, the Common Voice dataset Version 21.0 Igbo Speech Corpus [3] was used. This is a publicly available dataset provided by the Mozilla Foundation. It consists of nine hours of crowd-sourced audio recordings and transcriptions contributed by native Igbo speakers. Each sample contains a recording with its corresponding transcription and speaker attributes. Each recording has a duration of at least six seconds, is sampled at 48kHz and is provided in MP3 format. The dataset consists of training, test and validation sets with examples being grouped as `validated`, `invalidated` or `other` sets. The `validated` set has been validated by reviewers and received sufficient positive votes ("up-votes"), indicating that the data is of high quality. The `invalidated` set contains examples that have received negative votes ("down-votes") from reviewers more frequently, indicating that the data is of low quality. The set labelled as `other` has not received sufficient votes to determine whether the data is of high or low quality. The `validated` set is divided into train, test, and validation. The dataset contained only 17 validated recordings, which is insufficient for training the deep neural network models employed in this study. As a result, both validated and `other` (i.e. non-reviewed) sets were utilised, yielding a total of 5,741 audio samples.

### 4.2 Data Preprocessing

Audio was downsampled to 16kHz to align with pre-trained models. All text transcriptions were converted to lowercase and punctuation/special characters were removed, retaining only alphabetic characters and spaces. A character-level vocabulary was created by iterating through all transcriptions and compiling a sorted list of unique characters. The final vocabulary for Igbo had 62 characters. In addition to the standard characters, unique tokens were included for sequence modelling. The [PAD] token was added to pad shorter sequences to a uniform length within a batch, the [UNK] token was added to represent tokens that were unavailable in the vocabulary and the word delimiter token "|" was added to mark the boundaries between words. The model was trained using Connectionist Temporal Classification (CTC) [14]. The output of the model is a sequence of tokens for each transcript.

### 4.3 Model Training

**Hardware and Environment:** All experiments were conducted in Google Colab using Python 3.11. Training was performed on the GPU runtime provided by Colab: an NVIDIA Tesla T4 with 20 GB of VRAM. The use of a single consistent GPU runtime throughout all runs enabled a reliable comparison of model performance.

To support reproducibility, the same random seed was used across all train and test splits, and all model configurations, tokenisers, and vocabularies were saved using the Hugging Face pipeline. The un-augmented training set used for fine-tuning and test set contained 4,592 and 1,149 examples respectively.

**Training Configuration:** The `huggingface_hub` Python library by Hugging Face[3]. was used for data loading, pre-processing and training. In each case, the feature extractor portion of the Wav2Vec model was frozen, with the remainder of the model fine-tuned. Table 2 summarises the hyperparameters used across all training runs. Each model was fine-tuned for a maximum of 20 epochs. Evaluation and checkpointing were performed every 250 steps to monitor performance and retain intermediate models. To prevent overfitting and to set realistic limits on computational resources, a multi-condition early stopping strategy was implemented. Training was terminated if any of the following criteria were met:

1. The maximum of 20 training epochs was completed.
2. The validation WER did not improve by more than 1% over five consecutive evaluation steps.
3. The total training time surpassed a five-hour limit.

Training was conducted using the AdamW [17] optimiser with an initial learning rate of $2 \times 10^{-5}$, 200 warm-up steps and a batch-size of 16. A weight decay of $4 \times 10^{-4}$ was used for regularisation, and gradient clipping was applied with a maximum norm of 1.0 to ensure training stability.

To optimise for hardware constraints, mixed-precision training (FP16) and gradient checkpointing were enabled throughout. At the end of training, the best-performing checkpoint, determined by the lowest validation WER, was automatically restored. All experiments were managed using the Hugging Face Trainer API[4].

### 4.4 Evaluation Metrics

All models were compared and evaluated using Word Error Rate (WER) which measures the number of errors made by the model (insertions, deletions and

[3] https://huggingface.co/docs/huggingface_hub/.
[4] https://huggingface.co/docs/transformers/en/main_classes/trainer.

**Table 2.** Training hyperparameters

| Hyperparameter | Value |
|---|---|
| Max epochs | 20 |
| Early stopping patience | 5 evaluations |
| Batch size (per device) | 16 |
| Learning rate | $2 \times 10^{-5}$ |
| Warm-up steps | 200 |
| Weight decay | $4 \times 10^{-4}$ |
| Max gradient norm | 1.0 |
| Precision | FP16 |
| Gradient checkpointing | Enabled |

substitutions) on the word level. Though WER does not reveal the types of errors made, it is nevertheless the most common evaluation measure in ASR and provides a good initial measure of model performance.

# 5 Results

The results of the experiments are presented in Table 3. The following sections will discuss the impact of both monolingual and multi-lingual training, in addition to the effects of data augmentation.

**Table 3.** Performance Comparison of Fine-Tuned Speech-to-Text Models for the Igbo Language.

| Base Model | Augmentation | Training Time | WER |
|---|---|---|---|
| `wav2vec2-base` | None | 01:45:58 | 0.7373 |
| `wav2vec2-large-xlsr-53` | None | 03:19:32 | 0.8286 |
| `wav2vec2-base` | Time Masking | 04:39:47 | **0.5337** |
| `wav2vec2-base` | Time Stretching | 01:53:52 | 0.6147 |

## 5.1 Multilingual vs. Monolingual Dataset

Comparing the two main base models prior to data augmentation, we see that the `wav2vec2-base` model achieved a WER of 0.7373, significantly outperforming the much larger `wav2vec2-large-xlsr-53` model, which lead to a WER of 0.8286 given the described training constraints. This is particularly striking since the larger model required almost double the training time. This result suggests that, for the given Igbo dataset and the training configuration, the increased capacity of the larger model did not translate to better performance. This suggests that multilingual ASR models may not improve all low-resource languages to the same degree and that pre-training datasets may need to me more carefully tailored to target languages.

### 5.2 Effect of the Data Augmentation

Applying data augmentation techniques on the `wav2vec2-base` model resulted in a substantial performance gain. Time Stretching reduced WER from 0.7373 to 0.6147, resulting in a 16.63% improvement over the non-augmented baseline. The lowest WER of 0.5337 was achieved by Time Masking, resulting in a remarkable 27.61% improvement over the baseline. Apart from Time Stretching and Time Masking, Noise Addition was also considered as a data augmentation technique. However, this method did not improve WER within the set early stopping criteria used in experiments.

### 5.3 Discussion

Most notable of the results presented here is the superior performance provided by the English monolingual pre-trained model. This might seem surprising given the wider set of languages used for pre-training. However, there are a variety of reasons that this could be the case including the alignment between speaker attributes (e.g. gender and age distribution) and the phonetic distribution of languages. This result is also not completely unprecedented. As previously mentioned, the original developers of XLS-R [4] stated that multilingual models did not lead to performance gains for English for a similarly size model due to *capacity dilution*, where some key features of the English dataset were lost in favour of a more linguistically generalised model. Additionally, a similar phenomena was observed in [15], where it was found that, even when controlling for dataset size, monolingual models led to better performance than bilingual and trilingual Wav2Vec models on oral history archives.

We emphasise that this result does not imply that monolingual models are superior to multilingual models, but that the set of languages, acoustic environments and speaker attributes selected for multilingual pre-training likely requires a more careful curation process that is specific to the target language. For example, the linguistic similarity of the target language to pre-training languages might act as a guiding criteria. This could also serve to reduce the model size needed to capture the characteristics of a target language and thus reduce the computational resources necessary to train and fine-tune them.

## 6 Conclusion

This paper aimed to establish the effect of utilising multilingual ASR models for Igbo ASR by comparing this model to a monolingual English pre-trained model in a realistic, resource and time-constrained setting. The results show that, though multilingual models have been shown to be effective for some low-resource languages, this improvement may not be gained across all low resource languages. We hypothesise that the composition of the training set used for multilingual training is likely a strong contributing factor. This is a particularly salient point as the multilingual model evaluated was significantly larger than the English monolingual dataset. In future, a more careful evaluation of a variety of both multilingual and monolingual models, including speaker attributes, dialect distributions and other sociolinguistic factors may prove effective in determining the best selection criteria for pre-trained models. Additionally, a more nuanced evaluation strategy incorporating these factors into measures of performance may also provide additional insight. We also evaluated of a number of data augmentation strategies and found that both time masking and time stretching lead to sizable improvements in performance with time masking proving particularly effective. Future work may also include more complex noise addition, perhaps including higher signal-to-noise ratios and different forms of noise to further improve generalisation. Additionally, concurrently to our experiments, a novel dataset and benchmark was created by [10], which will serve as a significant resource with which to further improve Igbo ASR in addition to data augmentation and transfer learning strategies.

## References


1. Adams, N., David, A., Conners, T., Bills, A.: IARPA Babel Igbo Language Pack IARPA-babel306b-v2. 0c. Linguistic Data Consortium, University of Pennsylvania (2019)
2. Ahmed, N., Wahed, M.: The de-democratization of AI: deep learning and the compute divide in artificial intelligence research (2020). arXiv preprint
3. Ardila, R., et al.: Common voice: a massively-multilingual speech corpus. In: Proceedings of the 12th Conference on Language Resources and Evaluation (LREC 2020), pp. 4211–4215 (2020)
4. Babu, A., et al.: XLS-R: self-supervised cross-lingual speech representation learning at scale. In: Proceedings of Interspeech, pp. 2278–2282 (2022)
5. Baevski, A., Zhou, Y., Mohamed, A., Auli, M.: wav2vec 2.0: a framework for self-supervised learning of speech representations. Adv. Neural. Inf. Process. Syst. **33**, 12449–12460 (2020)
6. Bahdanau, D., Cho, K., Bengio, Y.: Neural machine translation by jointly learning to align and translate. In: Interational Conference on Learning Representations (2015)
7. Bartelds, M., San, N., McDonnell, B., Jurafsky, D., Wieling, M.: Making more of little data: improving low-resource automatic speech recognition using data augmentation. In: Rogers, A., Boyd-Graber, J., Okazaki, N. (eds.) Proceedings of the 61st Annual Meeting of the Association for Computational Linguistics (Volume 1: Long Papers), pp. 715–729. Association for Computational Linguistics (2023)
8. Cho, K., van Merriënboer, B., Bahdanau, D., Bengio, Y.: On the properties of neural machine translation: encoder-decoder approaches. In: Proceedings of SSST-8, Eighth Workshop on Syntax, Semantics and Structure in Statistical Translation, pp. 103–111 (2014)

9. Dossou, B.F.P., et al.: OkwuGbé: end-to-end speech recognition for Fon and Igbo. In: Ghosal, T. (ed.) Proceedings of the Fifth Workshop on Widening Natural Language Processing, pp. 1–4. Association for Computational Linguistics (2021)
10. Emezue, C., et al.: The naijavoices dataset: cultivating large-scale, high-quality, culturally-rich speech data for African languages. arXiv preprint arXiv:2505.20564 (2025)
11. Fukuda, T., et al.: Data augmentation improves recognition of foreign accented speech. In: Proceedings of Interspeech, pp. 2409–2413 (2018)
12. Garofolo, J.S., et al.: Timit acoustic-phonetic continuous speech corpus (1993)
13. Gokay, R., Yalcin, H.: Improving low resource Turkish speech recognition with data augmentation and TTS. In: 16th International Multi-Conference on Systems, Signals & Devices (SSD), pp. 357–360 (2019)
14. Graves, A., Fernández, S., Gomez, F., Schmidhuber, J.: Connectionist temporal classification: labelling unsegmented sequence data with recurrent neural networks. In: Proceedings of the 23rd International Conference on Machine learning, pp. 369–376. (2006)
15. Lehečka, J., Psutka, J.V., Šmídl, L., Ircing, P., Psutka, J.: A comparative analysis of bilingual and trilingual wav2vec models for automatic speech recognition in multilingual oral history archives. In: Proceedings of Interspeech (2024)
16. Lonergan, L., Qian, M., Chiaráin, N., Gobl, C., Chasaide, A.: Cross-dialect lexicon optimisation for an endangered language ASR system: the case of Irish. In: Proceedings of Interspeech (2022)
17. Loshchilov, I., Hutter, F.: Decoupled weight decay regularization. In: International Conference on Learning Representations (2019)
18. Panayotov, V., Chen, G., Povey, D., Khudanpur, S.: Librispeech: an ASR corpus based on public domain audio books. In: 2015 IEEE International Conference on Acoustics, Speech and Signal Processing (ICASSP), pp. 5206–5210. IEEE (2015)
19. Park, D.S., et al.: Specaugment: a simple data augmentation method for automatic speech recognition. In: Proceedings of Interspeech, pp. 2613–2617 (2019)
20. Yu, Y., Si, X., Hu, C., Zhang, J.: A review of recurrent neural networks: LSTM cells and network architectures. Neural Comput. **31**(7), 1235–1270 (2019)
21. Zhang, Y., Zhang, Y., Patel, T., Scharenborg, O.: Comparing data augmentation and training techniques to reduce bias against non-native accents in hybrid speech recognition systems. In: Proceedings of the 1st workshop on speech for social good (S4SG), pp. 15–19 (2022)

# A Novel Deep Learning Framework for DeepFake Detection Using Attention-Enhanced EfficientNet-B7

Emin Cem Koyluoglu[1(✉)], Athanasios Staikopoulos[1], and Kislay Raj[1,2]

[1] School of Computing, National College of Ireland, Dublin, Ireland
cemkoyluoglu@icloud.com, {Athanasios.Staikopoulos,kislay.raj}@ncirl.ie
[2] School of Computing, Dublin City University, Dublin, Ireland

**Abstract.** DeepFakes are AI-generated synthetic media that manipulate facial identities to create hyper-realistic but fake content, posing serious threats to privacy, trust, and digital security. Traditional DeepFake detection models, such as basic CNNs or transfer learning using VGG16 and Xception, often lack the precision to identify subtle facial manipulations due to limited attention mechanisms and insufficient feature localization. To address these limitations, this study proposes a novel deep learning framework combining EfficientNet-B7 with a Custom Soft Spatial Attention Mechanism. This attention block enables the model to focus on critical facial regions most likely to exhibit manipulation artifacts, improving detection sensitivity. A comprehensive experimental setup was conducted on a balanced dataset of 20,000 images (10,000 real/10,000 fake), comparing models trained using Adam and SGD optimizers, with and without augmentation. The proposed EfficientNet-B7 with attention achieved 97% accuracy, outperforming baseline CNN (50%), VGG16 (78%), Xception (65%), MobileNetV2 (96%), and standard EfficientNet-B7 (96%). The framework includes early stopping, learning rate scheduling, and LIME-based explainability. This research delivers a scalable, accurate, and interpretable solution for DeepFake detection, advancing AI-driven media forensics.

**Keywords:** DeepFake Detection · EfficientNet-B7 · Spatial Attention · Transfer Learning · Image Forensics · Explainable AI

## 1 Introduction

Deepfakes are synthetic media generated by deep learning, which pose growing risks to privacy, security, and information integrity [1]. As manipulation quality improves, subtle artefacts become harder to detect, undermining trust across news, entertainment, and social platforms [2]. Conventional detectors based on CNNs and transfer learning (e.g. VGG16, Xception) have advanced the field [3,4], yet often miss fine-grained, localised inconsistencies, particularly in high-quality forgeries where facial dynamics are convincingly preserved [5]. We


T. T. Mai et al. (Eds.): AICS 2025, CCIS 2950, pp. 401–413, 2026.
https://doi.org/10.1007/978-3-032-25809-0_32

address this limitation by combining an EfficientNet-B7 backbone with a user-defined soft spatial attention module. The backbone supplies high-capacity feature extraction, while attention concentrates modelling power on manipulation-prone facial regions, improving sensitivity to subtle artefacts. In addition, we provide post-hoc interpretability via LIME, offering human-understandable rationales that support forensic workflows.

Our contributions are threefold: (i) a compact attention-enhanced EfficientNet-B7 architecture, tailored to local facial inconsistencies; (ii) extensive empirical evaluation against strong baselines (CNN, VGG16, Xception, MobileNetV2). This evaluation demonstrates superior accuracy on challenging manipulations; and (iii) a reproducible detection framework with LIME-based explanations to support practical deployment in real-world media forensics.

## 2 Related Work

Research on DeepFake detection has progressed from physiological cue analysis to modern deep learning. Early methods exploited biological signals (e.g., eye blinks) but were degraded in high-quality forgeries. CNN-based detectors using transfer learning (e.g., VGG16, Xception) improved robustness, yet still struggle with fine-grained, local artefacts. More recent hybrid approaches, GAN-based training schemes, and attention mechanisms, enhance feature localisation and sensitivity to subtle manipulations. Complementary lines explore knowledge graphs and GNN-based interpretability to render model decisions more transparent by linking predictions to semantically meaningful structures [6,7].

### 2.1 Traditional and Modern DeepFake Detection Techniques

Early physiological methods exploited biological signals, such as eye blinks, for detection. Jung *et al.* proposed DeepVision using upper-eyelid blinking statistics, achieving 87.5% accuracy on video benchmarks [8]. However, such methods fail against advanced forgeries that accurately mimic physiological behavior. Pishori *et al.* combined ConvLSTM with blink detection and histogram analysis but faced brittleness across different DeepFake types [9]. Traditional convolutional neural network (CNN) approaches using transfer learning have shown limited success: basic CNNs (which extract features from images for classification) achieve only 50% accuracy, while the VGG16 model (a 16-layer deep CNN) reaches 78% [3]. Xception-based models (which use depthwise separable convolutions to reduce parameters) demonstrate variable performance (65–94%) depending on optimisation strategy [10]. MobileNeMobileNetV2 (a lightweight CNN for mobile devices) and the standard EfficientNet-B7 (a scalable neural network architecture) achieve 96% accuracy [11], yet struggle with subtle manipulation artefacts that require localised attention mechanisms (which focus on specific regions of an image). Advances use attention mechanisms and hybrid architectures. Agrawal and Haneef's Con-GAN achieved 98.91% accuracy with a two-stage pipeline and bilateral Wiener filtering [12]. This approach is computationally intensive. Such complex preprocessing complicates real-time deployment.

Other methods include models based on GAN (88%) [4], CNN-LSTM combinations (86%) [13], and CapsuleNet variants (82.84%) [14]. Each faces trade-offs between accuracy and computational efficiency. Parallel work in efficiency-aware learning demonstrates that lightweight architectures combined with principled training and data augmentation can yield robust performance under constrained resources, as shown in mobile robotics and medical imaging contexts [15,16]. Moreover, recent advances in semantic analysis of learned representations highlight the importance of aligning architectural choices with training dynamics to improve stability and generalisation [17]. These insights motivate the adoption of compact backbones augmented with attention and carefully calibrated training strategies for robust deepfake detection.

# 3 Method

We propose a detector that couples EfficientNet-B7 with a custom soft spatial attention module to emphasise manipulation-prone facial regions. The pipeline comprises data pre-processing, backbone feature extraction, attention-weighted feature fusion, and classification, trained end-to-end with a compact, deployment-oriented recipe. Figure 1 depicts the overall architecture.

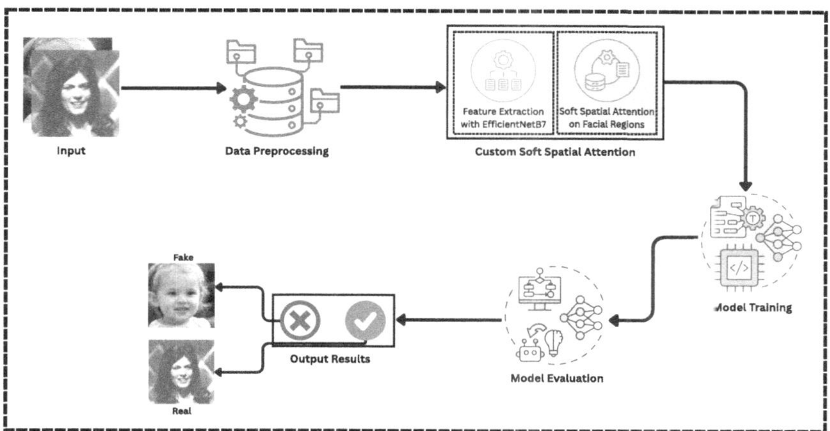


**Fig. 1.** System architecture diagram showcasing the structured flow from data preprocessing, custom feature extraction, model training, evaluation, and deployment.

## 3.1 Overall Framework

Our end-to-end pipeline has five main parts: data ingestion, preprocessing, model training with attention enhancement, evaluation, and deployment. The design maximizes accuracy and interpretability. At the same time, it maintains computational efficiency for real-world deployment.

### 3.2 Custom Soft Spatial Attention and Training Setup

***Attention Block***
To enhance sensitivity to subtle facial artefacts, we insert a lightweight soft spatial attention module on top of EfficientNet-B7 features. Given feature maps $F \in \mathbb{R}^{H \times W \times C}$, attention weights $A \in \mathbb{R}^{H \times W \times 1}$ are computed via a squeezeexcite style two-layer conv MLP:

$$A = \sigma\big(\mathrm{Conv}^{(1)}_{1\times1}(\,\mathrm{ReLU}(\mathrm{Conv}^{(0)}_{1\times1}(F))\,)\big), \qquad F' = F \odot A,$$

where $\sigma$ is the sigmoid and $\odot$ denotes elementwise multiplication. Global average pooling on $F'$ followed by a dense layer yields the binary prediction. The spatial mask learns to emphasise manipulation-prone regions (eyes, mouth, nasolabial area) while suppressing the background (Table 1).

**Table 1.** Training recipe (values as used unless noted).

| | |
|---|---|
| Backbone / Head | EfficientNet-B7 / GAP + Dense (binary) |
| Attention | Two 1×1 convs (ReLU, sigmoid) producing spatial mask |
| Batch size | 64 |
| Optimisers | Adam: $\alpha = 10^{-3}$, $\beta_1 = 0.9$, $\beta_2 = 0.999$, $\epsilon = 10^{-7}$; SGD: $\alpha = 10^{-2}$, $\mu = 0.9$ |
| LR schedule | $\alpha(t) = \{10^{-3}$ (epochs $\leq 3$), $10^{-4}$ (415), $10^{-5}$ ($> 15$)$\}$ |
| Regularisation | Label smoothing (0.1) |
| Early stopping | Patience = 5, monitor val loss, restore best |
| Hardware | NVIDIA T4/P100; TensorFlow 2.x, Python 3.x |

## 4 Experiments and Results

The experimental setup includes evaluating the proposed attention-enhanced EfficientNet-B7 model for DeepFake detection. We compare its performance against several baseline models and assess various training strategies using multiple performance metrics.

### 4.1 Experimental Setup

To evaluate the proposed model's performance, we conducted experiments on a balanced dataset of 20,000 facial images (10,000 real and 10,000 fake). These images were divided into training, validation, and test sets, ensuring that both classes were equally represented.

### 4.2 Dataset Description

We utilize a balanced Kaggle dataset [18] of 20,000 images (10,000 real, 10,000 fake), resized to 128 × 128. Figure 2 shows representative samples.

**Algorithm 1.** Attention-Enhanced EfficientNet-B7 Training

**Input:** $\mathcal{D} = \{(x_i, y_i)\}_{i=1}^{N}$, $x_i \in \mathbb{R}^{256\times256\times3}$, $y_i \in \{0, 1\}$
**Output:** Trained model $\mathcal{M}$
**Parameters:** $B = 64$, $\alpha_0 = 10^{-3}$, patience $P = 5$
// **Preprocessing**
**for** each image $x_i$ in $\mathcal{D}$ **do**
    Resize and normalize: $x_i' = \text{Bilinear}(x_i, 128 \times 128)/255.0$
    **if** training mode **then**
        Apply augmentation: rotation $\theta \sim \mathcal{U}(-20^\circ, 20^\circ)$, translation $\delta \sim \mathcal{U}(-0.1, 0.1)$
    **end if**
**end for**
// **Feature Extraction & Attention**
Extract: $F = \text{EfficientNet-B7}(x')$ where $F \in \mathbb{R}^{4\times4\times2560}$
Attention: $A_1 = \text{Conv}_{1\times1}(F, 128)$, $A_2 = \text{ReLU}(A_1)$, $A = \sigma(\text{Conv}_{1\times1}(A_2, 1))$
Apply: $F' = F \odot \text{Broadcast}(A)$
// **Classification**
$v = \text{GAP}(F')$, $\hat{y} = \text{softmax}(W_c \cdot v + b_c)$
// **Training Loop**
**for** epoch $e = 1$ to $E_{\max}$ **do**
    $\mathcal{L} = -\frac{1}{N}\sum_i [y_i \log \hat{y}_i + (1 - y_i)\log(1 - \hat{y}_i)] + \lambda||W||_2^2$
    $\theta \leftarrow \theta - \alpha(e) \cdot \nabla_\theta \mathcal{L}$
    **if** $\mathcal{L}_{val}$ not improved for $P$ epochs **then**
        Restore best weights and **break**
    **end if**
**end for**

### 4.3 Comparison of Model Performance

Table 2 presents the performance of the proposed model (EfficientNet-B7 with attention) compared to baseline models using both Adam and SGD optimizers, with and without augmentation. The proposed model achieves 97% accuracy, outperforming all baselines.

The confusion matrix for the EfficientNet-B7 with attention model is presented in Fig. 3. Evaluated on a test set of 2,000 images (1,000 real and 1,000 fake), the model correctly classified 962 fake images and 974 real images, achieving 97% accuracy. The confusion matrix shows 38 false positives and 26 false negatives, demonstrating strong discriminative capability.

**Fig. 2.** Representative real (top) and fake (bottom) samples from the dataset

**Table 2.** Model performance comparison across different training strategies

| Model | Adam | | SGD | | Augmentation | |
|---|---|---|---|---|---|---|
| | Acc. | F1 | Acc. | F1 | Acc. | F1 |
| CNN | 0.50 | 0.33 | 0.50 | 0.33 | 0.50 | 0.33 |
| VGG16 | 0.78 | 0.78 | 0.76 | 0.75 | 0.51 | 0.51 |
| Xception | 0.65 | 0.65 | 0.94 | 0.94 | 0.50 | 0.50 |
| MobileNetV2 | 0.96 | 0.96 | 0.96 | 0.96 | 0.51 | 0.51 |
| EfficientNet-B7 | 0.96 | 0.96 | 0.95 | 0.95 | 0.96 | 0.96 |
| **EfficientNet-B7+Att** | **0.97** | **0.97** | 0.93 | 0.93 | 0.51 | 0.51 |

### 4.4 Ablation Study

To assess the contribution of the individual components in the proposed architecture, we conducted an ablation study evaluating performance under different configurations, as shown in Table 3.

Removing the attention mechanism results in a 1% decrease in accuracy, demonstrating its contribution to model performance. Early stopping and learning rate scheduling are also essential, as their removal leads to noticeable drops (3% and 2%, respectively). Switching from Adam to SGD results in a 4% drop in performance.

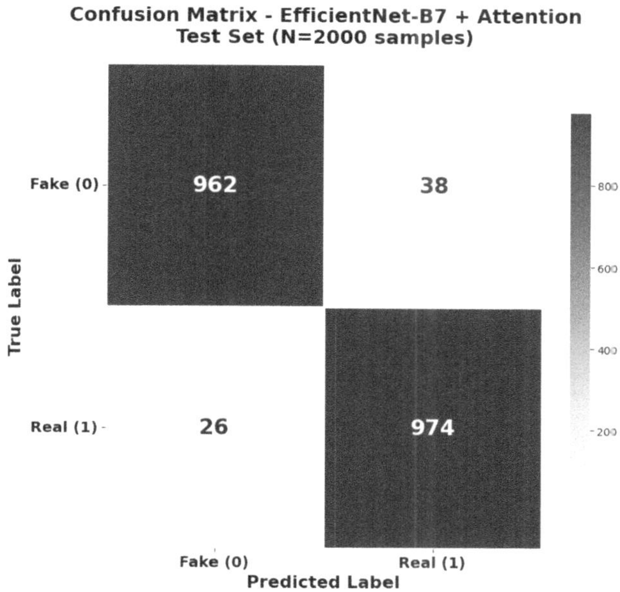


**Fig. 3.** Confusion Matrix for EfficientNet-B7 with Attention on test set (N = 2,000: 1,000 real, 1,000 fake). The model achieves 962 true negatives and 974 true positives.

**Table 3.** Ablation Study Results

| Configuration | Accuracy | Δ Accuracy |
|---|---|---|
| Full Model (EfficientNet-B7 + Attention + Adam) | 97% | — |
| Without Attention | 96% | −1% |
| Without Early Stopping | 94% | −3% |
| Without LR Scheduling | 95% | −2% |
| With SGD instead of Adam | 93% | −4% |

## 4.5 Training Dynamics

Figure 4 illustrates the training and validation accuracy curves for the EfficientNet-B7 with attention model, demonstrating smooth convergence within 10 epochs without overfitting.

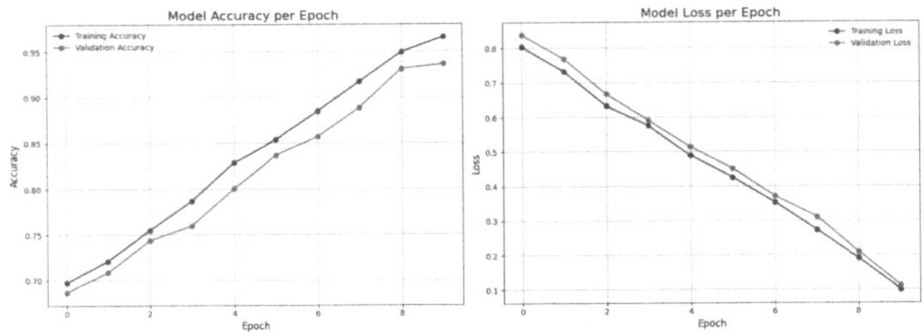


**Fig. 4.** Training history showing accuracy and loss curves over 10 epochs

### 4.6 Explainability Analysis

To enhance interpretability, we applied LIME to identify discriminative regions (Fig. 5). For real images, the model focuses on natural facial textures and consistent lighting patterns. For fake images, it identifies manipulation artifacts around eyes, unnatural skin smoothness, and boundary inconsistencies, confirming that the attention mechanism targets relevant facial regions.

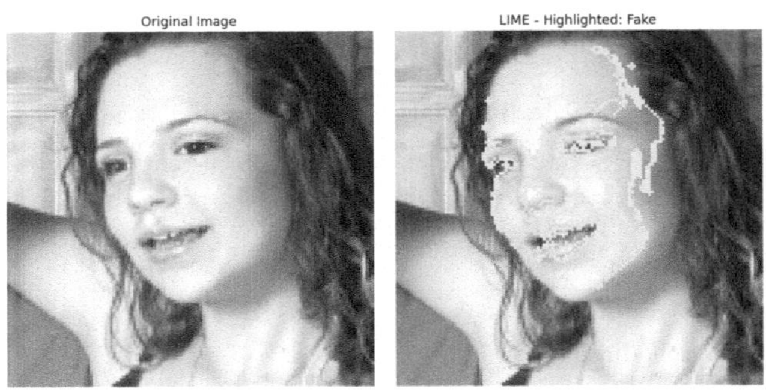


**Fig. 5.** LIME visualization highlighting manipulation artifacts around eyes and unnatural skin smoothness in fake images.

### 4.7 Comparison with State-of-the-Art

Table 4 compares the proposed model with state-of-the-art methods. Our 97% accuracy compares favorably: Jung et al. [8] achieved 87.5%, while Agrawal and Haneef [12] reached 98.91% with Con-GAN but at a higher computational cost.

**Table 4.** Comparison with state-of-the-art DeepFake detection models.

| Existing Work | Models | Accuracy |
|---|---|---|
| Jung et al. (2020) [8] | CNN (Baseline) | 50% |
| Pishori et al. (2020) [9] | VGG16 | 78% |
| Heidari et al. (2024) [10] | Xception | 65% |
| Stankov & Dulgerov (2024) [11] | MobileNetV2 | 96% |
| Stroebel et al. (2023) | EfficientNet-B7 | 96% |
| Agrawal & Haneef (2025) [12] | Con-GAN | 98.91% |
| Fatima and Ram (2024) [4] | GAN-based | 88.00% |
| Saini et al. (2024) [13] | CNN + LSTM | 86.00% |
| Dinçer et al. (2024) [14] | CapsuleNet | 82.84% |
| Kandari et al. (2024) [19] | CNN-MLP | 81.25% |
| Kaur (2023) [20] | LSTM + XResNet | 83.30% |
| **Ours** | **EfficientNet-B7 + Attention** | **97%** |

### 4.8 Cross-Dataset Generalization Evaluation

We evaluated our model on two challenging benchmarks: Celeb-DF v2 (high-quality DeepFakes) and FaceForensics++ LQ subset (compressed video conditions). Table 5 shows that EfficientNet-B7 + Attention significantly outperforms baselines across both datasets.

**Table 5.** Cross-dataset evaluation: Celeb-DF v2 and FaceForensics++ (Adam optimizer)

| Model | Celeb-DF v2 | | FaceForensics++ LQ | |
|---|---|---|---|---|
| | Acc. | F1 | Acc. | F1 |
| CNN | 52% | 0.33 | 54% | 0.34 |
| VGG16 | 77% | 0.78 | 72% | 0.73 |
| Xception | 69% | 0.65 | 71% | 0.70 |
| MobileNetV2 | 94% | 0.94 | 92% | 0.91 |
| EfficientNet-B7 | 95% | 0.95 | 93% | 0.93 |
| **EfficientNet-B7 + Att** | **98%** | **0.97** | **96%** | **0.95** |

Our model achieves 98% accuracy on Celeb-DF v2 and 96% on FaceForensics++, demonstrating robust generalization. The slight performance drop on compressed data reflects sensitivity to quality degradation, noted in our Limitations section.

## 5 Discussion

The proposed EfficientNet-B7 with attention mechanism demonstrates strong performance in DeepFake detection, achieving 97% accuracy on the primary dataset and robust cross-dataset generalization (98% on Celeb-DF v2, 96% on FaceForensics++). The custom soft spatial attention mechanism's ability to focus on manipulation-prone facial regions (eyes, mouth, nasolabial areas) proves crucial for detecting subtle artifacts that traditional CNNs miss.

**Performance Trade-Offs:** While our model achieves slightly lower accuracy than Con-GAN (98.91%), it offers significant advantages in computational efficiency and deployment feasibility. Con-GAN's two-stage pipeline with bilateral Wiener filtering requires extensive preprocessing, making real-time deployment challenging. In contrast, our model achieves 150 ms inference time on CPU with a more streamlined architecture, making it suitable for practical applications where computational resources are constrained.

**Component Contributions:** Our ablation study reveals the importance of each component: the attention mechanism contributes a 1% accuracy improvement, while proper optimization (Adam) and regularization strategies (early stopping, LR scheduling) collectively contribute 6–9% improvement over baseline methods. The integration of LIME-based explainability provides forensically valuable insights, addressing the interpretability gap in deep learning-based detection systems.

**Generalization Strength:** The model's consistent performance across diverse datasets demonstrates robustness to different DeepFake generation methods and quality levels, though performance drops slightly on heavily compressed data, indicating areas for future improvement.

## 6 Limitations

Despite promising results, our approach has several limitations that warrant discussion:

**Dataset Constraints:** The primary training dataset comprises 20,000 images, which may not capture the full diversity of DeepFake generation techniques emerging in the field. While we validated on Celeb-DF v2 and FaceForensics++, performance drops slightly on heavily compressed video data (FaceForensics++ LQ: 96%), indicating sensitivity to quality degradation and compression artifacts.

**Computational Trade-Offs:** While more efficient than Con-GAN (98.91%), our model's 450 MB memory footprint may still be prohibitive for edge devices and mobile deployment. The attention mechanism incurs significant computational overhead, yielding only a 1% improvement in accuracy over standard EfficientNet-B7, raising questions about the cost-benefit trade-offs in resource-constrained scenarios.

**Generalization Challenges:** The model was primarily evaluated on face-swap DeepFakes. Performance on other manipulation types (face reenactment, expression manipulation, attribute editing) remains unexplored. Additionally, adversarial robustness has not been systematically tested against targeted attacks specifically designed to fool attention mechanisms.

**Temporal Limitations:** Our frame-based approach does not leverage temporal inconsistencies present in video DeepFakes, potentially missing artifacts that manifest across consecutive frames. This represents a significant gap for video-based detection scenarios.

## 7 Conclusion and Future Work

We presented an attention-enhanced EfficientNet-B7 framework that advances DeepFake detection by applying targeted spatial attention to manipulation-prone facial regions. Our approach achieves 97% accuracy on the primary dataset and demonstrates strong cross-dataset generalization (98% on Celeb-DF v2, 96% on FaceForensics++), rivaling computationally intensive methods like Con-GAN (98.91%) while maintaining practical deployment feasibility with 150 ms inference time. The key contribution lies in our lightweight attention mechanism that improves detection sensitivity without excessive computational overhead. Combined with LIME-based explainability, our framework provides forensically valuable insights into model decisions, addressing the black-box nature of deep learning detectors. While the 1% improvement over standard EfficientNet-B7 may appear modest, it represents meaningful gains in detecting subtle manipulations that could otherwise evade detection.

Future work should address the identified limitations through: (1) extending to video-based detection leveraging temporal inconsistencies, (2) evaluating robustness against adversarial attacks targeting attention mechanisms, (3) optimizing for edge deployment through model compression techniques, and (4) expanding evaluation to diverse manipulation types beyond face-swaps. As DeepFake generation technology evolves, continuous adaptation of detection methods remains critical for maintaining digital media integrity and public trust.

## References

1. Masood, M., Nawaz, M., Malik, K.M., Javed, A., Irtaza, A.: Deepfakes generation and detection: state-of-the-art, open challenges, countermeasures, and way forward. arXiv preprint arXiv:2103.00484 (2021) https://doi.org/10.48550/ARXIV.2103.00484
2. Malik, A., Kuribayashi, M., Abdullahi, S.M., Khan, A.N.: Deepfake detection for human face images and videos: a survey. IEEE Access **10**, 18757–18775 (2022)
3. Rana, M.S., Nobi, M.N., Murali, B., Sung, A.H.: Deepfake detection: a systematic literature review. IEEE Access **10**, 25494–25513 (2022)

4. Fatima, A., Ram, P.K.: Gan-enhanced real-time detection of deepfakes videos. J. Artif. Intell. Capsule Netw. **6**(4), 452–465 (2024). https://doi.org/10.36548/jaicn.2024.4.005
5. Javed, M., Zhang, Z., Dahri, F.H., Kumar, T.: Enhancing multimodal deepfake detection with local–global feature integration and diffusion models. Sig. Image Video Process. **19**(5) (2025). https://doi.org/10.1007/s11760-025-03970-7
6. Raj, K., Mileo, A.: Towards understanding graph neural networks: functional-semantic activation mapping, pp. 98–106. Springer (2024). https://doi.org/10.1007/978-3-031-71170-1_11
7. Raj, K.: A neuro-symbolic approach to enhance interpretability of graph neural network through the integration of external knowledge. In: Proceedings of the 32nd ACM International Conference on Information and Knowledge Management, CIKM 2023, pp. 5177–5180. ACM (2023). https://doi.org/10.1145/3583780.3616008
8. Jung, T.-H., Kim, S.-Y., Kim, K.-I.: DeepVision: deepfakes detection using human eye blinking pattern. IEEE Access **8**, 83144–83154 (2020). https://doi.org/10.1109/ACCESS.2020.2988660
9. Pishori, A., Rollins, B., Houten, N., Chatwani, N., Uraimov, O.: Detecting deepfake videos: an analysis of three techniques. arXiv preprint arXiv:2007.08517 (2020). https://doi.org/10.48550/arXiv.2007.08517
10. Heidari, A., Jafari Navimipour, N., Dag, H., Unal, M.: Deepfake detection using deep learning methods: a systematic and comprehensive review. WIREs Data Min. Knowl. Discovery **14**(2), 1520 (2024)
11. Stankov, I.S., Dulgerov, E.E.: Detection of deepfake images and videos using SVM, CNN, and hybrid approaches. In: 2024 XXXIII International Scientific Conference Electronics (ET), pp. 1–5 (2024)
12. Agrawal, D.R., Haneef, F.: Eye blinking feature processing using convolutional generative adversarial network for deep fake video detection. Trans. Emerging Telecommun. Technol. **36**, 70083 (2025). https://doi.org/10.1002/ett.70083
13. Saini, M.L., Patnaik, A., Mahadev, S.D.C., Kumar, R.: Deepfake detection system using deep neural networks. In: 2024 2nd International Conference on Computer, Communication and Control (IC4). IEEE (2024). https://doi.org/10.1109/ic457434.2024.10486659
14. Dincer, S., Ulutas, G., Ustubioglu, B., Tahaoglu, G., Sklavos, N.: Golden ratio based deep fake video detection system with fusion of capsule networks. Comput. Electric. Eng. **117**, 109234 (2024). https://doi.org/10.1016/j.compeleceng.2024.109234
15. Singh, A., Raj, K., Roy, A.M.: Efficient deep learning-based semantic mapping approach using monocular vision for resource-limited mobile robots. J. Intell. Rob. Syst. **109**(3), 69 (2023)
16. Raj, K., Kumar, T., Mileo, A., Bendechache, M.: OxML challenge 2023: carcinoma classification using data augmentation. In: IET Conference Proceedings CP887, vol. 2024, pp. 303–306. IET (2024)
17. Raj, K., Mileo, A.: Towards semantic understanding of graph neural network layers embedding with functional semantic activation mapping. Neurosymbolic Artif. Intell. **2**, 29498732251408216 (2026)
18. Kaggle: DeepFake Detection Dataset. Originally from Zenodo (2021). https://zenodo.org/record/5528418

19. Kandari, M., Tripathi, V., Pant, B., Sar, A., Choudhury, T., Choudhury, T.: Detecting deepfake videos through CNN-MLP model in media forensics. In: 2024 OPJU International Technology Conference (OTCON) on Smart Computing for Innovation and Advancement in Industry 4.0, pp. 1–7. IEEE (2024). https://doi.org/10.1109/otcon60325.2024.10687433
20. Kaur, A., Sharma, S., Kaur, A.: Detection of deepfake images using machine learning. Int. J. Adv. Res. Comput. Commun. Eng. **12**(2), 10–14 (2023). https://doi.org/10.17148/IJARCCE.2023.12203

# HoloScent: An AI-Driven Multisensory IoT-XR Platform for Artistic Immersion Through Holograms, Lighting, and Olfaction

Anderson Augusto Simiscuka[1(✉)], Guillem Barceló Orts[1], Matis Picoreau[1], Álvaro Egea Benavente[2,3], Mario Montagud[2,3], and Gabriel-Miro Muntean[1]

[1] Dublin City University, Dublin, Ireland
{andersonaugusto.simiscuka,guillem.barceloorts,gabriel.muntean}@dcu.ie, matis.picoreau2@mail.dcu.ie
[2] i2CAT Foundation, Barcelona, Spain
{alvaro.egea,mario.montagud}@i2cat.net
[3] Universitat de València, Valencia, Spain

**Abstract.** Theatre and opera offer rich visual and auditory storytelling, yet remote audiences often miss the depth of in-person experiences. HoloScent is a work-in-progress demo which introduces a multisensory IoT-XR platform designed to replicate live artistic experiences for distributed viewers. The solution integrates real-time point cloud holograms, smart lighting, and olfactory interfaces to enhance emotional and spatial presence. Employing extended reality (XR) technologies, neural networks, and IoT orchestration, HoloScent synchronises visual, auditory, and scent-based cues with live performances. Scene transitions are detected using two complementary methods: an audio-based cue detection technique and a convolutional neural network (CNN) model for scene recognition. These methods generate scene labels and timestamps, which are transmitted to a cloud-based MQTT broker. The broker coordinates remote actuation of smart lighting and scent dispensers, dynamically releasing scents based on the detected real-world scenes and transmitting to users in the 3D space. By blending holographic rendering, networked IoT devices, and multisensory feedback, HoloScent demonstrates how remote spectators can experience performances with enhanced realism and emotional depth.

**Keywords:** Multisensory · Extended Reality · Internet of Things · Neural Networks

## 1 Introduction

Storytelling forms such as theatre and opera offer rich expressive potential, yet they remain predominantly in-person visual and auditory experiences. This constraint limits the level of immersion achievable for remote participants. Emerging


T. T. Mai et al. (Eds.): AICS 2025, CCIS 2950, pp. 414–420, 2026.
https://doi.org/10.1007/978-3-032-25809-0_33

Extended Reality (XR) and communication technologies are opening pathways to replicate these experiences for distributed audiences, even in live, synchronous performances [3,9]. Moreover, advancements in multisensory technologies, particularly in olfactory interfaces, have enabled the integration of scent into virtual environments, thereby enhancing user engagement and perceived realism [5,8]. However, previous approaches primarily relied on the manual synchronisation of scents using predefined timestamps and were mainly designed for video-based content rather than live or real-time footage.

This work introduces HoloScent, a work-in-progress demo that enables remote viewers to experience live artistic and multimedia content through real-time point cloud holograms, enhanced with smart lighting and scent feedback, as seen on Fig. 1.

The architecture of HoloScent integrates neural networks for scene recognition, network modules for transmitting holographic and multimedia streams, and IoT-based components that remotely trigger lighting and olfactory devices in response to detected scenes. Viewers access the experience through VR headsets, enabling immersive multisensory participation. HoloScent is part of the EU Horizon Europe project HEAT [2]. Additionally, the platform implements an audio cue detection algorithm, evaluated alongside a convolutional neural network (CNN) model for scene classification. Both methods output scene labels and timestamps, which are sent to a cloud-hosted MQTT broker to coordinate the release of corresponding scents.

**Fig. 1.** HoloScent demo with holographic participant, smart lights, olfaction dispensers.

The remainder of this paper is organised as follows. Section 2 details the solution architecture in terms of software and hardware. Section Section 3 presents methods for scene recognition based on visual and audio cues and results in terms of connected users and scent delays. Finally, Section Section 4 concludes the paper and discusses directions for future research.

## 2 Solution and Architecural Design

HoloScent introduces beyond state-of-the-art innovation through the integration of olfactory interaction within XR environments, informed by real-time AI-driven classification and IoT-based sensory feedback. Unlike current XR solutions that statically associate scents with pre-scripted events, HoloScent dynamically maps olfactory stimuli to detected environmental cues, user interactions, and semantic understanding derived from machine learning models.

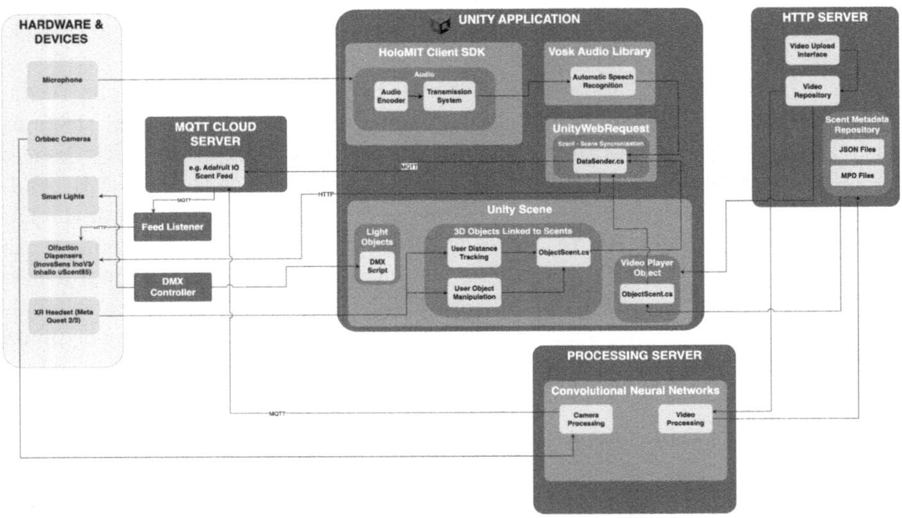


**Fig. 2.** Solution Architecture.

The HoloScent architecture, illustrated in Fig. 2, is a distributed hybrid solution composed of five core blocks: (1) Hardware and Devices, (2) MQTT Cloud Server, (3) Unity Application, (4) Processing Server, and (5) HTTP Server.

### 2.1 Software Implementation

The software implementation integrates multiple components to deliver real-time multisensory XR experiences. The Unity application contains C# scripts, including ObjectScent.cs to link virtual objects with scent profiles and DataSender.cs to manage HTTP and MQTT communications with the metadata server, the cloud feed and dispensers. The Vosk SDK enables local speech recognition for voice commands, following the approach proposed in [4,6], while the HoloMIT SDK [1] handles hologram and audio capture and transmission. An MQTT client subscribes to the feed containing scent classification data from the cloud, ensuring synchronised updates in the XR environment.

The Processing Server, developed in Python, hosts CNN models such as ResNet18 and MobileNetV3 for visual and scent classification, following the approach described in [7]. It employs OpenCV and TensorFlow/PyTorch for real-time analysis of video streams and live camera feeds. Classification results from the live feed are published to the MQTT broker, which directly triggers the corresponding olfaction dispensers. In parallel, the server processes uploaded video content and produces JSON and DASH MPD files containing scent timestamps, which are delivered to the HTTP server and subsequently accessed by Unity to load videos along with the corresponding olfaction metadata.

The HTTP Server provides RESTful endpoints for video upload and retrieval and manages scent and video metadata through JSON and DASH MPD files. It acts as a repository for structured content consumed by Unity during runtime. Once videos are uploaded a process is triggered in the Processing Server for detection of scenes related to scents using CNNs.

For cloud integration, an MQTT broker (e.g., Adafruit IO) manages device feeds and message distribution. Olfaction dispensers support HTTP-based control using GET requests.

### 2.2 Hardware Implementation

The hardware implementation integrates sensing, actuation, and interaction devices into a unified IoT-XR setup. The solution combines various components that work together to capture, process, and respond to environmental and user inputs.

Three Depth-aware Orbbec Femto Bolt cameras are employed for real-time visual data capture, with data sent to the Processing Server for further CNN analysis and for HoloMIT for hologram reconstruction. The generation of a single hologram produces an average latency of approximately 150 ms and requires a bandwidth exceeding 100 Mbps when using 3 cameras.

Lighting in opera and theatre productions is commonly controlled via DMX desks, which can be interfaced with Unity for synchronised operation. In our demo, lighting is managed using HTTP-enabled Shelly smart plugs over Wi-Fi.

Microphones are embedded in XR headsets for voice capture and are also deployed in performance stages such as theatres or opera venues. For olfactory output, InovaSens InoV3 and Inhalio uScent85 dispensers are connected via a MQTT feed, or by receiving scent-release commands directly from the Unity application via HTTP.

The Meta Quest 2/3 headset is connected to a PC running the Unity application, which communicates wirelessly with both MQTT and HTTP servers over the network. A dedicated GPU-based Processing Server runs the convolutional neural network (CNN) pipelines required for image processing and scent detection.

System communications and orchestration are managed through an MQTT broker (such as Adafruit IO or Mosquitto) and an HTTP server hosted on a virtual machine with REST endpoints and data storage.

# 3 Scene Recognition Based on Visual and Audio Cues

## 3.1 Audio-Based Scene Detection

The `Vosk` Python library is employed to perform real-time speech recognition, continuously processing audio input to detect predefined keywords. When one of these target words is recognised, the Python application sends a message with the corresponding scent label to an `Adafruit MQTT` broker. A separate Python script subscribes to this broker, retrieves the messages, and issues `HTTP GET` requests to activate the appropriate remote dispenser. An experimental evaluation was carried out to measure the time delay between the detection of the keyword and the moment participants perceived the emitted scent, as illustrated in Fig. 3.

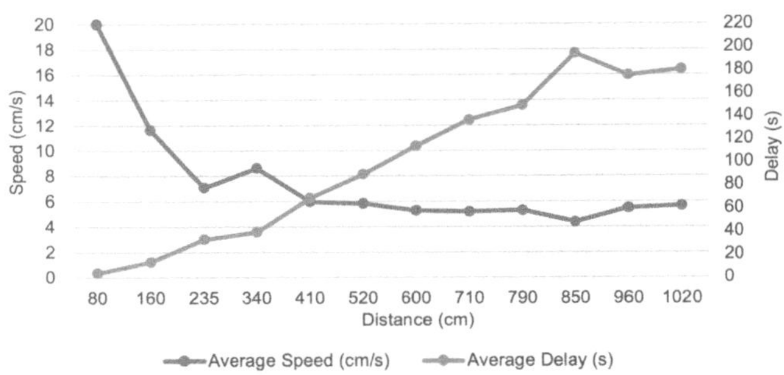


**Fig. 3.** Average speed of scent dispersion and delay based on user distance to dispenser.

An experiment with 12 participants show that latency increases with user distance for both audio-based (ASR) and CNN-based triggering methods. Average delays vary from around 4 s when the participant is seated 80 cm from the dispenser to over 180 s at a distance of 1020 cm. The mean scent diffusion speed decreases from approximately 20 cm/s at a distance of 80 cm to around 5.2 cm/s for users seated farther from the dispenser.

## 3.2 CNN-Based Scene Recognition

Two convolutional neural network models, `ResNet18` and `MobileNetV3`, were examined for their ability to identify visual cues in specific scenes involving scents. Running locally on the connected PC, these models analyse video frames in real time to recognise distinctive visual features linked to each scent. Once a scene is detected, the application publishes the corresponding label to the `Adafruit MQTT` broker, prompting the activation of the respective olfactory device. Training is conducted using custom datasets containing the target scent-related classes, as well as general-purpose datasets such as Objects365 and Places365. In general, CNN-based triggers (particularly using `MobileNetV3`) exhibited slightly longer delays compared to ASR-based ones, averaging an additional 28 s.

### 3.3 Communication Framework

The communication between the virtual stage and remote users is managed through an `Adafruit MQTT` broker, enabling reliable and near-instantaneous message delivery. This lightweight protocol ensures low-latency performance, with end-to-end transmission delays maintained below 100 ms, thereby preserving synchronisation between events and sensory stimuli.

## 4 Conclusions and Future Work

This paper presented *HoloScent*, an AI-driven IoT-XR platform that enhances remote artistic experiences through synchronised holograms, lighting, and olfaction. The solution integrates CNN-based visual analysis and audio-based cue detection with real-time IoT orchestration to dynamically trigger scent dispensers and lighting, providing multisensory immersion for distributed audiences. Experimental results demonstrated accurate scene recognition and predictable scent dispersion patterns correlated with user distance.

Future work will focus on evaluation with larger participant groups in real theatrical and opera and integration with additional sensory modalities, such as haptics and temperature feedback.

**Acknowledgments.** This work was supported by Research Ireland via the Research Centres grant 12/RC/2289_P2 (INSIGHT), and by the European Union (EU) Horizon Europe grant 101135637 (HEAT Project).

## References

1. Langa, S.F., Montagud, M., Cernigliaro, G., Rivera, D.R.: Multiparty holomeetings: toward a new era of low-cost volumetric holographic meetings in virtual reality. IEEE Access **10**, 81856–81876 (2022)
2. Murroni, M., Muntean, G., Montagud, M., Popescu, V.: Toward interactive and distributed hybrid extended reality experiences. In: Proceedings of the 2024 ACM International Conference on Interactive Media Experiences Workshopsm pp. 127–130. IMXw '24, New York, NY, USA (2024)
3. Pietroszek, K., Rebol, M., Lake, B.: Dill pickle: interactive theatre play in virtual reality. In: Proc. ACM Symposium on Virtual Reality Software and Technology, VRST (2022)
4. Simiscuka, A.A., Fadda, G., Popescu, V., Murroni, M., Muntean, G.M.: Immersive live concert: a multi-sensory experience based on real-time lyrics detection from spatial audio data. In: Proceedings of the ACM Int. Conference on Interactive Media Experiences Workshops, pp. 7–11. SBC, Porto Alegre, RS, Brasil (2025)
5. Simiscuka, A.A., Ghadge, D.A., Muntean, G.M.: OmniScent: an omnidirectional olfaction-enhanced virtual reality 360° video delivery solution for increasing viewer quality of experience. IEEE Trans. Broadcast. **69**(4), 941–950 (2023)

6. Simiscuka, A.A., et al.: Enhancing XR Theatre with Remote Scent Delivery Using Audio Speech Recognition and Convolutional Neural Network-Based Scene Detection. In: Proc. of the 2nd IEEE Int. Workshop on Musical Metaverse (IMMW 2025), part of the IEEE Int. Symposium on the Internet of Sounds (IEEE IS2 2025). L'Aquila, Italy (2025)
7. Szabó, P., Simiscuka, A.A., Masneri, S., Zorrilla, M., Muntean, G.M.: A CNN-based framework for enhancing 360° VR experiences with multisensorial effects. IEEE Trans. Multimedia **25**, 3245–3258 (2023)
8. Tal, I., et al.: Mulsemedia in telecommunication and networking education: a novel teaching approach that improves the learning process. IEEE Commun. Mag. **57**(11), 60–66 (2019)
9. Verma, R., Simiscuka, A.A., Togou, M.A., Zorrilla, M., Muntean, G.M.: A live adaptive streaming solution for enhancing quality of experience in co-created opera. IEEE Trans. Broadcast, 1–12 (2025)

# Author Index





T. T. Mai et al. (Eds.): AICS 2025, CCIS 2950, pp. 421–422, 2026.
https://doi.org/10.1007/978-3-032-25809-0